RAF Bomber Command Profiles

103 Squadron

RAF Bomber Command Squadron Profiles

103 Squadron

by Chris Ward

with David Fell

BOMBER COMMAND BOOKS

An imprint of
AVIATION BOOKS

www.aviationbooks.org

This edition first published 2016 by Mention the War Ltd.

This revised edition published 2023 by Aviation Books Ltd., Merthyr Tydfil, UK, CF47 8RY.

Copyright 2016 and 2023 © Chris Ward.

Cover design: Topics - The Creative Partnership www.topicsdesign.co.uk

A CIP catalogue reference for this book is available from the British Library.

ISBN 9781915335241

Unless otherwise credited, all photographs are kindly supplied by David Fell.

Also by Chris Ward from Bomber Command Books:

Casualty of War: Letters Home from Flight Lieutenant Bill Astell DFC

Dambuster Deering: The Life and Death of an Unsung Hero

Dambusters : The Complete WWII History of 617 Squadron
(with Andy Lee and Andreas Wachtel)

Other RAF Bomber Command Profiles:

10 Squadron (with Ian MacMillan)
35 (Madras Presidency) Squadron
44 (Rhodesia) Squadron
49 Squadron
50 Squadron
57 Squadron
75(NZ) Squadron (with Chris Newey)
83 Squadron
101 Squadron
102 (Ceylon) Squadron
103 Squadron (with David Fell)
106 Squadron (with Herman Bijlard)
115 Squadron
138 Squadron (with Piotr Hodyra)
207 Squadron (with Raymond Glynne-Owen)
300 Squadron (with Grzegorz Korcz)
301, 304, 305 Squadrons (with Grzegorz Korcz)
455,458, 462, 464 Squadrons RAF
460 Squadron RAAF
467 Squadron RAAF
514 Squadron (with Simon Hepworth)
619 Squadron

Contents

Introduction

RAF Bomber Command Squadron Profiles first appeared in the late nineties and proved to be very popular with enthusiasts of RAF Bomber Command during the Second World War. They became a useful research tool, particularly for those whose family members had served and were no longer around. The original purpose was to provide a point of reference for all of the gallant men and women who had fought the war, either in the air, or on the ground in a support capacity, and for whom no written history of their unit or station existed. I wanted to provide them with something they could hold up, point to and say, "this was my unit, this is what I did in the war". Many veterans were reticent to talk about their time on bombers, partly because of modesty, but perhaps mostly because the majority of those with whom they came into contact had no notion of what it was to be a "Bomber Boy", to face the prospect of death every time they took to the air, whether during training or on operations. Only those who shared the experience really understood what it was to go to war in bombers, which is why reunions were so important. As they approached the end of their lives, many veterans began to speak openly for the first time about their life in wartime Bomber Command, and most were hurt by the callous treatment they received at the hands of successive governments with regard to the lack of recognition of their contribution to victory. It is sad that this recognition in the form of a national memorial and the granting of a campaign medal came too late for the majority. Now this inspirational, noble generation, the like of which will probably never grace this earth again, has all but departed from us, and the world will be a poorer place as a result.

RAF Bomber Command Squadron Profiles are back. The basic format remains, but, where needed, additional information has been provided. Squadron Profiles do not claim to be comprehensive histories, but rather detailed overviews of the activities of the squadron. There is insufficient space to mention as many names as one would like, but all aircraft losses are accompanied by the name of the pilot. Fundamentally, the narrative section is an account of Bomber Command's war from the perspective of the bomber group under which the individual squadron served, and the deeds of the squadron are interwoven into this story. Information has been drawn from official records, such as group, squadron and station ORBs, and from the many, like myself, amateur enthusiasts, who dedicate much of their time to researching individual units, and become unrivalled authorities on them. I am grateful for their generous contributions, and their names will appear in the appropriate Profiles. The statistics quoted in this series are taken from The Bomber Command War Diaries, that indispensable tome written by Martin Middlebrook and Chris Everitt, and I am indebted to Martin for his kind permission to use them.

Finally, let me apologise in advance for the inevitable errors, for no matter how hard I and other authors try to write "nothing but the truth", there is no such thing as a definitive account of history, and there will always be room for disagreement and debate. Official records are notoriously unreliable tools, and yet we have little choice but to put our faith in them. It is not my intention to misrepresent any person or RAF unit, and I ask my readers to understand the enormity of the task I have undertaken. It is relatively easy to become an authority on single units or even a bomber group, but I chose to write about them all, idiot that I am, which means 128 squadrons serving operationally in Bomber Command at some time between the 3rd of September 1939 and the 8th of May 1945. I am dealing with eight bomber groups, in which some 120,000 airmen served, and I am juggling around 28,000 aircraft serial numbers, code letters and details of provenance and fate. I ask not for your sympathy, it was, after all, my choice, but rather your understanding if you should find something with which you disagree. My thanks to you, my readers, for making the original series of RAF Bomber Command Squadron Profiles so popular, and I hope you receive this new incarnation equally enthusiastically.

This is a vastly upgraded edition of my original 103 Squadron Profile published in 2016 and includes much greater detail of operations and targets. Whenever I have needed additional information on 103 Squadron, I have turned to David Fell as the oracle. He has always been generous in sharing his unparalleled knowledge, and many of the photographs published in my book, 1 Group Bomber Command, Pen & Sword 2014, were provided by David. In the mid eighties David began researching 103 and 576 Squadrons to learn of his uncle, Sgt J Jennings, who lost his life as a member of Canadian F/L Bill Way's crew during an operation to Vire in France on the 6/7th of June 1944. Through his research he was invited to join the RAF Elsham Wolds Association and continued to build a vast resource of information. Although no longer involved with the association, David has continued his research and set up a number of web sites dedicated to the subject. It is a monumental task to break down a squadron Operations Record Book and reduce it to tables of readily accessible information, and many do not appreciate the hundreds of hours of dedication required to do so, and the not inconsiderable costs that can be involved. The fact that people like David exist, enables the rest of us to pick up a book and have all of the facts, figures and information laid out before us without expending any effort. The photographs in this publication have been provided mostly by David with others from Andreas Wachtel, for which I am grateful. My thanks also, as always, to my other gang member/friends, photo editor, Clare Bennett and Steve Smith and Greg Korcz for their additional support. Finally, my appreciation to my publisher, Simon Hepworth of Aviation Books Ltd for his belief in my work and untiring efforts to promote it.

Chris Ward. Skegness. August 2023.

Dedication

This WWII history of 103 Squadron is dedicated to the memory of Sgt Ron Pilcher, who completed 31 sorties as a mid-upper gunner, 29 of them in the crew of F/O Pat Furlong. Their names represent all of those men and women who served with or supported the squadron at Newton and Elsham Wolds, both in the air and on the ground.

F/O "Pat" Furlong pilot
Sgt A F "Ernie" Hall flight engineer
F/Sgt A W H "Alex" Matthews navigator
F/O "Jack" Hamilton RCAF bomb-aimer
Sgt W A "Mac" McGregor wireless operator
Sgt "Ron" Pilcher mid-upper gunner
Sgt "Johnny" Norman rear gunner

103 SQUADRON

Narrative History

1939 Final Quarter

Originally formed on the 1st of September 1917, 103 Squadron moved to France in May 1918 to conduct bombing operations against supply bases and communications behind enemy lines, a role which it would fulfil in almost identical fashion twenty-two years to the month later, when war came once more to Europe. For most of the intervening period, 103 Squadron, like so many others, did not exist after being disbanded in October 1919, and it was not until August 1936 that the squadron was resurrected to once more perform as a light bomber unit. In July 1938 Fairey Battles began to replace the squadron's Hinds, and as the clouds of war gathered in 1939, 1 Group, including 103 Squadron, was earmarked to become the main component of the Advanced Air Striking Force (AASF).

When Germany invaded Poland on the 1st of September, the squadrons of 1 Group were posted to north-eastern France to become part of the AASF, 103 Squadron's sixteen Fairey Battles departing Benson on the 2nd, while the ground crews set off by rail for Southampton and a crossing by sea. The aircraft involved in this transfer were K9264, K9265, K9266, K9268, K9269, K9270, K9271, K9295, K9299, K9372, K9374, K9404, K9409, K9411, K9456 and L4957. The squadron set up camp at Challerange in the Reims area, under the command of W/C Gemmel, and found that no preparations had been put in hand to provide accommodation. Sleeping arrangements were primitive, and aircrew spent the first few nights under their aircraft, grateful that France was enjoying a period of glorious weather. The squadron was initially to form part of 74 Wing with 150 Squadron, which would move to the satellite airfield at Ecury-sur-Coole on the 18th. For the time-being operations were restricted to reconnoitring enemy positions at the front, but most of the activity during this period between September 1939 and April 1940, dubbed by the American press as the "Phoney War", would be spent in training and army co-operation exercises.

The first operational sorties by 103 Squadron were launched on the 17th of September, when S/L Coverdale, F/L Tait and Sgt Perry took off at 08.55 to carry out a reconnaissance of the border between Bouzonville and Lauterbourg from 3,000 feet in K9372, K9871 and L4957 respectively. On the 19th, F/L Tait led a similar operation, which was, likewise, concluded without major incident, although it did draw the first German anti-aircraft fire. Further reconnaissance sorties to the same area were carried out by sections of three aircraft on the afternoons of the 20th, 21st and 22nd, led respectively by F/O Carver, W/C Gemmel and F/O Ingram, before F/L Tait led a six-aircraft element on a high-level photo-reconnaissance flight to Lebach on the morning of the 23rd. P/O Lawman and crew turned back with engine trouble almost immediately, leaving the others to penetrate at 24,500 feet fifteen miles beyond the Franco/German frontier into the coal-rich Saarland region, where the town of Lebach lay an equal distance to the north of the regional capital, Saarbrücken. In the event, ten-tenths cloud thwarted the photographic intentions, and it was discovered that the Vickers K guns would not operate at such lofty altitudes because of the extreme cold. Further reconnaissance flights by three aircraft each were conducted without incident on the 25th and 26th.

On the 27th the squadron personnel moved into the village of Monthois, a mile from the aerodrome, where the billets for both officers and men were a great improvement and an operations room and orderly room could be set up. The squadron aircrew officers, however, remained where they were in Challerange. It was on this day that three 103 Squadron Battles were carrying out a reconnaissance of the front at around 3,000 feet, when they were challenged first by French Curtiss Hawk fighters and then by German BF109s about twenty miles east of Saarbrücken. F/L Wells led the flight down to tree-top height, heading south to the frontier and he and P/O Morgan-Dean made good their escape in K9372 and K9265 respectively, but F/O Vipan's engine began to splutter, possibly because of the sudden loss of altitude. During the engagement with the fighters, Vipan's observer, Sgt Vickers, received a bullet wound to the bladder and he requested to be landed as soon as possible. F/O Vipan selected a field at Rohrbach-les-Bitche and force-landed K9271 with one undercarriage leg extended, causing some damage to the Battle but no further casualties. A BF109 had been seen to crash and burn in a nearby wood, and this was later credited to Vipan's gunner, AC1 Summers, who was subsequently awarded a DFM. The BF109 belonged to JG52, and was flown by Obergefreiter Josef Scherm, who was killed. It is believed that this was the first confirmed RAF kill of WWII. On the following day, W/C Gemmel led a formation of six aircraft on a reconnaissance at 27,000 feet and they returned safely after two-and-a-half hours aloft and S/L Coverdale and two others completed the month's operational activity on the 30th to give a tally of thirty-nine sorties without loss.

The weather broke on the 8th of October, and for a time, heavy, persistent rain threatened to cause flooding of the area surrounding the aerodrome and even the airfield itself. Fortunately, the drainage proved effective and such an eventuality was avoided, but flying was restricted to training whenever the weather allowed. The sad news was received by telephone from AASF HQ that Sgt Vickers had succumbed to his wounds on the 7th. The squadron personnel were kept busy with frequent rugby and soccer matches and a concert party was formed, which hoped to put on a show in early November. It was learned on the 1st of November, that shortly before Sgt Vickers had passed away, he had been awarded the Medaille Militaire on the orders of General Gemelin, a gesture greatly appreciated by the squadron. This was the first French decoration to be bestowed upon a member of the British Expeditionary Force. The squadron was informed on the 9th that it had been allocated the bombing range at Mouronvilliers and it would be put to good use whenever conditions permitted. Every Wednesday during November, the squadron had been entertained by a cinema show put on by the NAAFI, but now, on the 21st, the "Black Swan" Concert Party, produced by F/O Lynn, performed for the Maire de Monthois, some French army officers and two members of the Escadrille Cigognes. Afterwards, the Maire expressed regret that the squadron would shortly be leaving for Plivot, a move that took place smoothly on the 28th. Once settled in, the squadron prepared for what would prove to be a particularly long and bitter winter.

First quarter 1940

The winter of 1939/40 was extremely harsh, and this helped to keep operational flying to a minimum. Aircraft became almost literally frozen to the ground and engines refused to turn, but it was a timely intervention in some ways and an early lesson to those convinced that daylight operations could be undertaken with sustainable losses. There had been a number of costly brushes with enemy fighters involving other Battle squadrons of the AASF during September and October, and these had demonstrated the wisdom of restricting operations to nighttime where possible. There was a change of overall command on the 15th of January, when the AASF officially left Bomber Command. Air Marshal A.S. (Ugly) Barratt was appointed C-in-C British Air Forces in France, and the Battle squadrons were spread among 71, 75 and 76 Wings on the disbandment of 72 and 74 Wings. 103 Squadron was appointed to 75 Wing, where it joined 88 and 218 Squadrons under G/C A.H. Wann.

It was the end of February before winter loosened its grip sufficiently to allow training to continue, but even this was not without risk. In the early hours of the 2nd of March, L5236 crashed at Chandon during an emergency landing, injuring F/O Carver and his crew, and on the 27th P/O Hinton's P2256 crashed in a wood during a low-level night bombing exercise near St-Hilaire-le-Grand, killing all on board. A week earlier, on the night of the 20/21st, F/L Tait, a future commander of the squadron, had carried out the squadron's first leafleting (nickel) sortie, when providing reading matter for the residents of Koblenz. By this time the squadron had changed location again and had been based at Betheniville since the 15th of February. There was also a new commanding officer, W/C Dickens having taken up his post on the 12th of March.

Second quarter 1940

The Phoney War came to an end when German forces began an offensive in Scandinavia on the 9th of April. Airborne troops took Stavanger airfield in Norway, while other elements of the Nazi machine marched unopposed into Denmark. The Command was unable directly to support the ill-fated British and French response at Narvik in the north, lying as it did beyond the safe operating range of the available aircraft, and instead, operations were conducted against the southern airfields of Stavanger and Oslo. It was during this period, on the night of the 13/14th, that 5 Group Hampdens carried out the first mine-laying operation of the war, and this represented the initial tentative steps in a new departure for Bomber Command operations, which would prove to be hugely successful, and by war's end would have sunk or damaged more enemy ships than the Royal Navy. The laying of parachute mines by air was given the code-name "gardening", and the entire enemy-held coastline from the Pyrenees in the south-west to the Baltic port of Königsberg in the north-east, and even the northern Italian coast, was divided into gardens, each with a horticultural or marine biological name. The process of delivery was known as planting, and the mines, themselves, were referred to as vegetables, and it would not be long before the other bomber groups joined in to create a spiders' web of mines in chains across all of the sea-lanes employed by the enemy.

A further month passed before war finally came to the AASF squadrons in France, but when it did so, it was with unimaginable fury. The German advance into the Low Countries began at first light on the 10th, and shortly after midday thirty-two Battles, including a section of four from 103 Squadron, began to take off to attack troop columns advancing through Luxembourg. Murderous light flak accounted for thirteen of them, and three of the casualties were from 103 Squadron. There were no survivors from the crews of P/O Drabble and Sgt Lowne, in K9264 and K9270 respectively, but F/L Wells and crew did at least survive to fall into enemy hands when K9372 was brought down. Ultimately, only F/L Ingram and crew got home to report on the squadron's first real experience of engaging the enemy.

The squadron did not operate on the 11th, but other units were in action, and 88 and 218 Squadrons lost four Battles each. 103 Squadron was pitched into the fray again on the 12th, when three aircraft made a dawn attack on troops and armour and returned without loss. In the afternoon the squadron operated again, first against pontoon bridges across the River Semois led by P/O Fitzgerald, and later to attack troop concentrations also in the Buillon area. Carrying only two men each, L5512 and P2193 were lost, and neither F/O Morgan-Dean nor P/O Morton and their observers survived. P/O Cunningham spotted some tanks before reaching the assigned target area and attacked these before returning safely. It was a black day for the AASF, during which 12 Squadron lost five Battles attacking bridges over the Albert Canal, and XV Squadron seven, which were operating against similar targets over the River Maas. Seven other Battles were either brought down or damaged beyond repair, and thirteen of the home-based Blenheims were lost also in the Maastricht assaults. The problem was that these attacks were launched only after the enemy had been allowed time to establish anti-aircraft defences, and as always, enemy ground forces were well supported by the Luftwaffe. The Fairey Battle, in particular, was obsolete before it entered the war, and both slow and poorly armed, it was easy meat for the marauding BF109s and 110s, and the murderous ground fire took care of the rest.

Most units spent the 13th licking their wounds, but early on the following morning 103 Squadron crews were briefed for the next round of attacks. Shortly after 05.00 on the 14th, F/O Havers led eight aircraft against the pontoon bridges over the River Meuse near Sedan, and, amazingly, all returned to base, although Sgt Perry was badly wounded by ground fire, and was ultimately awarded the DFM for his efforts. He was evacuated to the UK, where he died of his wounds on the 10th of June. In the afternoon elements of the squadron carried out a low-level attack in the face of fierce opposition, and P/O Cunningham's L5516 was hit by flak and blew up in the air. L5190 was also brought down, but despite being injured, F/O Fitzgerald and his observer got back to the squadron next day. Sgt Beardsley's P2191 was the third loss of the operation, but he and his observer also regained the squadron after a walk. The 14th had been a bad day for the Battle squadrons, in which forty-four of the seventy-one aircraft dispatched had been lost, but they would have to endure for another month before the hopelessness of their position forced a withdrawal.

At first light on the 16th the squadron's remaining serviceable Battles were flown out to another new location at Rheges, abandoning K9404 and L5234 at Betheniville. On the 19th, a further assault on troop concentrations resulted in flak damage to some of the six Battles taking part, but all returned to base, and on the 20th a night operation by five aircraft to the Fumay area was also accomplished without loss. 218 Squadron was withdrawn to the UK at this juncture, and 103 Squadron took over its complement of aircraft to bring its own strength up to thirty-one. On the 22nd four aircraft were dispatched to attack armoured fighting vehicles in the Amiens-Abbeville-Arras region, and this was followed on the 26th by an attempt to disrupt a high-level meeting of Luftwaffe officers taking place at the Chateau Roumont. The operation was undertaken by four 103 Squadron crews, with four and two from 142 and 150 Squadrons respectively. F/O Havers led the 103 Squadron section into the attack in driving rain and L5514 failed to return, F/L Leyden alone of his crew surviving in enemy hands, while L5515 was written off on return in an attempt to land with a defective undercarriage. Two days later, New Zealander, F/O Max's Battle suffered engine damage through ground fire during an operation in the Abbeville area in support of the battle raging below. His gunner was wounded in the engagement, but the aircraft remained aloft long enough for him to force-land at Chalons, and he and his crew were able to return to the squadron. These were the early days of a magnificent wartime career, which would eventually see Max in command of 75(NZ) Squadron during the most arduous period of the bombing war, between August 1943 and April 1944.

The final dramas of the disastrous campaign to prevent the fall of France were enacted in June. 103 Squadron moved to Ozouer-le-Doyen on the 4th, and on the afternoon of the 6th, dispatched four aircraft to attack troop positions at Sancourt-Matigny, from which all returned. Day and night sorties were flown on the 7th, and on the 8th N2253 was shot down during an operation against troop columns at Poix, and this time Sgt Beardsley was captured before he had a chance to walk home. P2315 was also shot up during the same operation, but P/O Thorougood, on his first sortie, carried out a successful crash-landing and made it back. S/L Lee and his crew abandoned L5246 on the night of 9/10th, but despite sustaining a broken leg, he also got back. An operation to Vernon on the 10th cost the squadron P/O Thomas and his observer, who were killed in P2328, and K9409 was written off on return. Pontoon bridges at Vesillon provided employment on the 12th, and two further operations were carried out on the 13th. At 06.30 on the 14th the squadron evacuated its sixteen serviceable Battles to Souge, where they joined the remnants of 12 and 226 Squadrons under the command of 76 Wing. That evening four of them were involved in the squadron's final sorties of the campaign, while eight others were placed at one hour's readiness. As a result of these sorties, P/O Hawkins and his observer became PoWs, although Hawkins managed to escape and reach Spain, where he was interned. He did eventually make it back to England and was awarded the Military Cross for his exploits. Sgt Brumby crash-landed following the same operation but did so without injury to himself or his observer. That night, the Luftwaffe paid a visit to Souge and destroyed two more Battles, and returned twice on the following morning as the squadron was preparing to evacuate to England.

At 05.30 on the 15th the anti-aircraft defences were withdrawn from Souge, leaving only Lewis machine guns to protect what remained. Three Battles took off at 10.00 to carry out a final reconnaissance, and they returned safely. At noon orders were received for all aircraft to proceed directly to England, but their departure coincided with a heavy Luftwaffe attack from medium altitude, and some were not able get away in time. W/C Dickens and S/L Tait made a final inspection of the airfield, during which a low-level attack had them scrambling for an open trench, where they narrowly avoided death from strafing and nearby bomb detonations. After the attack they headed for the river adjacent to the airfield but were spotted by an enemy pilot and machine gunned again. One man hid in the river and the other in a tree, and they were able to return to the airfield to ascertain that only one Battle was capable of flying. The engine seemed serviceable, but the main spar was severed, the instruments inoperative and the fuel tanks were holed. W/C Dickens took off with S/L Tait and F/O Max as passengers, and managed to reach Nantes, despite petrol fumes invading the cockpit and a port-wing-low attitude.

Meanwhile, the remainder of the squadron's aircraft had flown directly to Abingdon, although P/O Barratt only just made it across the Channel and had to land at Shoreham. Max flew a reserve aircraft from Nantes, and W/C Dickens and S/L Tait continued on in the wreck, stopping off at Jersey to top up the tanks. The ground party arrived at Brest at 05.00 on the 16th after driving continuously for fifteen hours, and boarded the SS Vienna at 08.00. Twenty-four hours later they arrived at Plymouth, by which time the aircraft and aircrews had already moved into Honington, where the squadron was officially reformed on the 18th. The formation of 1 Group headquarters began at Hucknall, near Nottingham, on the 24th, and 103 Squadron moved to Newton, also in Nottinghamshire, on the 3rd of July, where it was joined by 150 Squadron. Meanwhile, 12 and 142 Squadrons took up residence at Binbrook, and on the 5th 1 Group officially declared itself available for operations in an emergency, although was not yet fully operational.

Third quarter 1940

During much of its time in France, 103 Squadron had not been under the control of Bomber Command. Now that it had returned to the fold, it became one of a very few squadrons to continue operating Battles for the time being at least. Training would occupy the succeeding weeks until the night of the 21/22nd of July, when W/C Dickens led three aircraft in company with three others from 150 Squadron to bomb oil storage tanks at Rotterdam. They took off either side of midnight, but P/O Hayter was back on the ground seventy-five minutes later with an unserviceable gyro. W/C Dickens failed to locate the target in conditions of low cloud and searchlight activity, and he dropped his bombs on an aerodrome believed to be on Goeree Island in the Scheldt estuary. F/L Havers overshot the aiming point but believed his bombs had fallen onto a chemicals factory two miles north of the primary. This was the first bombing operation by Battles under Bomber Command control.

On the following night three aircraft from each squadron were sent to bomb the aerodrome at Schiphol, S/L Tait taking off at 23.05 to be followed into the air at 23.15 and 23.25 respectively by the crews of F/L Blome-Jones and F/O Kelly. S/L Tait and crew dropped four 250 pounders and incendiaries on the primary target and believed that they hit the tarmac, while F/O Kelly and crew failed to observe the impact of theirs. F/O Blome-Jones and crew were thwarted by searchlight dazzle and attacked an aerodrome at Marienbosch near Nijmegen as an alternative, also without observing the outcome. Three Battles each from the four squadrons were sent to bomb the airfield at Evere near Brussels and Hingene near Antwerp on the 25/26th, the crews of F/Os Vipan and Max and P/O Harper representing 103 Squadron and taking off at 00.40 and 01.00, but weather conditions persuaded eight to turn back and just one crew from 150 Squadron attacked the primary target. This concluded operations for the Newton units, which would not operate at all during August. The two Binbrook squadrons moved temporarily to Eastchurch on the 7th for Coastal Command duties, rendering 1 Group effectively ineffective. Two Polish squadrons, 300 and 301, completed their initial training at Bramcote in Warwickshire, and moved into Swinderby during August to bring 1 Group's strength up to six squadrons.

Training continued for the Newton brigade, and L5543 was declared an hour overdue during a training flight late on the 3rd of August. It was 01.20 on the 4th before news came through that it had crashed at Cottesmore in Rutland, after colliding with a tree on its seventh attempt to land. The pilot, Sgt Brams, was killed, his observer mortally injured, and only the wireless operator was able to walk away. It is believed that Sgt Brams had mistaken Cottesmore for Newton and stalled while attempting a climb out. Overhead the Battle of Britain began to gain momentum, and Bomber Command's contribution to the defence of the country came with attacks on industrial targets in the Ruhr and on enemy communications. Gradually, however, with the growing threat of invasion, attention turned to the build-up of barges and other craft being prepared in the Channel ports. August particularly saw an increase in raids on these targets, and as the Battle of Britain reached its crescendo in September, the campaign dominated the Command's efforts.

103 Squadron returned to operations on the evening of the 7th of September, when sending six Battles under S/L Tait, in concert with six others from 150 Squadron to attack barges and shipping in Calais harbour. The 103 Squadron element departed Newton between 19.10 and 19.20 and all reached the target area to encounter poor weather conditions and intense anti-aircraft fire, through which S/L Tait carried out three passes at between 3,000 and 5,000 feet and the other 103 Squadron crews from up to 10,000 feet. Although eleven crews returned with reports of bombing in the target area, none was able to confirm results. The operation was scheduled for a repeat two days later by three aircraft from each of the Newton squadrons, for which 103 Squadron briefed the crew of P/O Harper and those of Midshipman Constable and Sub-Lt De Sanoual-Servier, who were among a number of naval pilots serving with the squadron at the time. They took off from Newton at 19.00 and those returning safely claimed a successful attack, but Sub-Lieutenant De Sanoual-Servier and crew failed to make it back after L5010 had been shot down into the sea by ground fire, and all on board were killed.

The night of the 10/11th saw a further three Battles from each Newton squadron assigned to barge concentrations in Boulogne harbour, and this time the crews of S/L Tait, F/L Havers and Sgt Henderson were on duty and departed Newton between 22.20 and 22.30, each carrying sixteen 40lb bombs. S/L Tait and crew failed to locate the target area in challenging conditions and brought their bombs home, while the Havers and Henderson crews were more successful, and each delivered theirs from 3,000 and 8,000 feet without observing the results. The operation was repeated on the following night again by six aircraft, in which the crews of F/O Crawford and Midshipmen O'Donavan and McDonald represented 103 Squadron and departed Newton between 19.56 and 20.00. They arrived in the target area to find very poor weather conditions, through which the Crawford crew dived down from 11,000 to 6,000 feet to deliver their bombs and watched them burst across the docks. Midshipman O'Donavan and crew hit the embankment and inner harbour with a stick of bombs, but Midshipman McDonald was let down by a faulty bomb release switch and had to return his load to the bomb dump.

The night of the 14/15th was busy for the Command and 157 aircraft were detailed from all groups for operations against oil and railway targets in Belgium and Germany and barge concentrations in the Channel ports. Swinderby joined in the action to launch the very first sorties by Polish squadrons in Bomber Command and three crews each from 103, 150, 300 and 301 Squadrons were briefed for a return to Boulogne. The 103 Squadron crews of P/O Harper and Midshipmen Constable and McDonald took to the air between 19.50 and 20.00, but the McDonald crew turned back early on after L5431 proved to be unable to maintain height. P/O Harper and crew experienced difficulties with navigation and brought their bombs home, leaving the Constable crew to carry out an attack along with the nine from the other participating squadrons, again in very poor weather conditions of low cloud that made it impossible to assess the results.

Twenty-four hours later, on the day that the Battle of Britain reached its zenith, Bomber Command launched 155 aircraft on widespread operations mostly against Channel ports, and among them were six Battles each from Newton and Swinderby, this time 300 Squadron providing all six Polish crews. S/L Tait, F/L Havers and Midshipman O'Donavan and their crews departed Newton between 19.50 and 20.25 and all reached the target area, where S/L Tait delivered sixteen 40lb and two 250lb bombs and Midshipman O'Donavan sixteen 40 pounders, one crew from 700 feet and the other from 10,000 feet, while F/L Havers and crew bombed Le Touquet in error from 10,000 feet. In all, ten aircraft bombed, and this time some explosions were observed in the target area.

According to the 1 Group Operations Record Book (ORB), operations on the night of the 16/17th were cancelled because of the weather, and we must, therefore, conclude, that the entry in the 103 Squadron ORB bearing that date relates to the operations on the night of the 17/18th, when Bomber Command was out in force with a record number of 194 aircraft. Among them was the largest effort yet by the Battle contingent involving three each from 12, 103, 142 and 150 Squadrons and six from 300 Squadron. The 103 Squadron crews of F/O Crawford, P/O Thorougood and Sgt Ralston took off from Newton either side of 22.30 bound for the docks at Boulogne and carried out attacks with 40 and 250 pounders from 1,500 feet without observing the results. At debriefing Sgt Ralston and crew reported that they had also descended to 300 feet and had observed their bombs hit a vessel in the outer harbour. A total of fifteen 1 Group crews reported bombing in conditions of low cloud, and two others were frustrated by the failure to release of their bombs.

The campaign against Boulogne harbour continued on the 18/19th, when the 103 Squadron crews of P/Os Harper and Anderson and Midshipman McDonald departed Newton between 19.40 and 20.14 and arrived at the target to be greeted by a spirited flak response. Midshipman McDonald and crew conducted a high-level run at 10,000 feet, while P/O Anderson and crew favoured a low-level approach at just 400 feet, and all three delivered their sixteen 40 pounders each without observing the outcome through the cloud and searchlight glare. Another busy night of operations on the 20th involved 172 Bomber Command aircraft, most of which were to target barges in the invasion ports. Boulogne was posted as the target yet again for two 1 Group forces to be dispatched hours apart, the first to be over the target between 23.00 and 23.20 and the second between 04.30 and 05.03. The

103 Squadron crews of S/L Tait, P/O Chisholm and Midshipman O'Donavan were assigned to the early shift and departed Newton between 21.20 and 21.30, each loaded with four 250lb delayed-action bombs. They encountered heavy cumulus cloud that forced them down to find clear air, from where P/O Chisholm and crew attacked from 2,500 feet and encountered no opposition. The Tait and O'Donavan crews opted to go in at 300 to 2,000 feet and ran into a forest of twenty to thirty barrage balloons tethered at 1,000 to 1,200 feet in the outer harbour and heavy anti-aircraft fire but came through both unscathed to return home and make their reports.

Calais provided a change of destination for the crews of F/L Havers, F/O Thorougood and Midshipman Constable on the 21st when ninety-two Bomber Command aircraft were abroad to prosecute the anti-invasion campaign. They departed Newton in a five-minute slot from 19.50 and all reached the target to find ideal conditions for a high-level attack. F/L Havers bombed from 10,000 to 11,000 feet and observed his bombs start fires at the back of the town, while Midshipman Constable had to contend with a partially opening bomb door that trapped eight 40 pounders in the bomb bay and forced him to bring them home. There was no entry to provide details of F/O Thorougood's sortie and we must assume that it was completed successfully.

The night of the 23/24th was devoted to a single target, Berlin, wherein eighteen aiming points, predominantly railway yards, electrical power stations and gasworks, were briefed out to 129 crews from all but 1 Group, whose Battles lacked the range and bomb-carrying capacity to take part. 1 Group would not stand idle, however, and briefed eleven crews, nine for Boulogne and two for Calais. The 103 Squadron crews of F/O Crawford, P/O Anderson and Sgt Ralston departed Newton between 02.40 and 02.55 on the 24th bound for Boulogne, each carrying four 250 pounders. All located the target without difficulty in moonlight and while the Anderson and Crawford crews bombed from 8,000 feet, the Ralston crew went in at 500 feet in the face of intense anti-aircraft fire. Fortunately, the flak shells were bursting at least a thousand feet above the bombers and no damage was incurred, but the flashes and searchlight glare created challenging conditions in which to assess the outcome. Meanwhile, the Berlin operation was spread over three hours and some damage was inflicted upon the city at the relatively modest cost of three aircraft.

There was an early morning attack on Boulogne on the 25th, for which the 103 Squadron crews of Sgt Henderson, P/O Harper and Midshipman McDonald departed Newton between 03.00 and 03.10, each carrying four 250lb delayed-action bombs. They located the target without difficulty and carried out their attacks from between 4,000 and 9,000 feet and all were safely back home within four hours. A new target, Ostend, was briefed out to seventeen Battle crews on the morning of the 27th, those of F/L Havers, Sgt Ralston and W/C Dickens representing 103 Squadron and taking off from Newton in that order between 01.00 and 01.25. They located the target, guided by an intense searchlight and flak response, and noted much shipping activity off the coast as they carried out their attacks from between 4,000 and 7,000 feet and observed bomb bursts and fires. Afterwards, Sgt Ralston and crew strafed a searchlight concentration at Dunkerque, before returning to Newton, where they overshot the flare path and came to a halt against the boundary fence. The crew walked away, but such was the damage to L5336, that it had to be sent to Fairey for repair. In all, fifteen crews had attacked the primary target and two others Dunkerque harbour and this proved to be the operational swansong for the Battle in 103 Squadron service.

During the course of September, the squadron took part in twelve operations and dispatched forty-two sorties for the loss of a single Battle and its crew. Not for the only time during the war, the squadron's crews were happy to wave goodbye to an unpopular aircraft type.

Fourth quarter 1940

On the 1st of October 103 and 150 Squadrons were stood down from operations in preparation for the arrival of Wellingtons, and on the 2nd 103 Squadron took delivery of its first two examples, R3275 and T2610. By the 8th, eight examples of the Wellington Mk 1c and a Mk 1a for dual instruction had been taken on charge. Training continued in Battles until the 10th, and by the end of the month all had been disposed of, mostly to maintenance units. By the 24th a further eight Wellingtons had arrived, enabling the training programme to be stepped up through the remainder of October, the whole of November and into December. On the 25th of November, Wing Commander Dickens, the popular commanding officer who had seen the squadron through its trials in France, was posted out to a non-flying post at 33 Empire Flying Training School, it is believed, in Canada, and he was replaced temporarily by the B Flight commander, S/L Tait. Apparently, both men ended up in the River Trent without their trousers after the farewell party at the Unicorn Hotel at Gunthorpe. W/C Littler arrived on posting from 1 Group HQ on the 5th of December to assume command and oversee the transition to operational status.

On the 18th of December 1 Group HQ declared that the Newton and Swinderby squadrons were now ready to resume operations, and that both 103 and 150 squadrons had six Wellingtons and crews immediately available. In the event it would be a further five days before the first six 1 Group Wellington sorties were launched, the crews of S/L Tait, F/O Max and Sgt Elliott representing 103 squadron and departing Newton between 04.45 and 05.05 bound for the docks at Ostend. The Max and Elliott crews carried out a high-level attack with five 500 pounders and two small bomb containers (SBCs) of incendiaries from 10,000 to 11,000 feet, while S/L Tait and crew shallow-dived from 12,000 down to 8,000 feet and all observed the incendiaries to set off fires that remained visible for eight minutes into the return flight.

Five minutes after midnight on Christmas Day a signal was received from one S Claus to the effect that he would be "unable to visit 1 Group Operations having been shot down though uninjured in an 11 Group-defended area. This was the comical culmination of a long-running feud between Bomber Command and the defences located in south-eastern England resulting from the tendency of anti-aircraft batteries to fire at anything that flew within range. Bomber Command had complained and had been asked to route bombers over Orfordness rather than other locations closer to the Thames estuary, but bomber pilots tend to be "a law unto themselves" and often ignored the oft-reiterated warnings that "everything over such and such area will be fired at tonight". Despite the failure of Santa Claus to put in an appearance, the second wartime Christmas was observed in traditional style with the officers serving the men their festive dinner.

In the late afternoon of the 28th S/L Tait, F/O Crawford and Sgt Wareing took off from Newton to deliver five 500 pounders and two SBCs of incendiaries each onto the oil storage tanks at Rotterdam, a frequent target for freshman crews, which these experienced airmen were in terms of Wellington operations. It was a moonless evening and identification was a challenge, but S/L Tait established his position and dived from 11,000 down to 5,000 feet to release his load in the face of intense but inaccurate anti-aircraft fire. Sgt Wareing and F/O Crawford preferred to remain at high-level and delivered their bombs from 10,000 and 14,000 feet in what proved to be the final operation of the year. December's tally was two operations and six sorties, completed without loss.

It had been a curious year for the squadrons which were formerly of the AASF. It had begun with stagnation during the great freeze of January and February and the continuing "Phoney War" and had then erupted into unbelievable savagery for the six weeks it took the blitzkrieg to subjugate the Low Countries and France, before descending once more into semi-retirement until the departure of the Battles and the working up to operational status on Wellingtons was completed. In truth, the Command could do little more than present a defiant face to an all-conquering enemy and help in the battle for survival. The fact that Britain was still in the war at the end of 1940 was a surprise to many looking on from the outside, but if the conflict were eventually to be won, the fight had to be taken to Germany itself, and Bomber Command was the only offensive arm capable of achieving this. Sadly, and worryingly, the coming year would find it seriously wanting in this respect, and it would prove to be a year of failure and setbacks, and one in which few positive advances were made.

January 1941

January would be devoted almost exclusively to attacks on German and French ports, both coastal and inland, and it was to the port of Bremen that the majority of the 141 aircraft detailed for operations on the night of the 1/2nd was assigned for a two-wave assault. Among important targets in the city were the Deutsche Schiff und Maschinenbau A G shipyards, abbreviated to Deschimag, which had been formed in the mid-twenties as a co-operation of eight shipyards to compete with the Blohm & Voss and Bremer Vulkan yards, the latter located at Vegesack on the bank of the Weser to the north-west of Bremen. The largest of the Deschimag shipyards was the A G Weser company, which, after six of the others had fallen by the wayside before the outbreak of war, was partnered now only by the Seebeckwerft, and would soon be swallowed up by the Krupp empire, when that organisation was handed a controlling interest in the coming months. The briefings for this night covered two targets, the Korff A.G. oil refinery, which the ORB suggested was also a depository for food stocks, and the Focke-Wulf aircraft factory situated on the eastern bank of the Weser in the south-eastern district of Hemelingen.

1 Group detailed a dozen Wellingtons for this operation, three each from 103 and 150 Squadrons at Newton and the Polish 300 and 301 Squadrons at Swinderby. The 103 Squadron trio consisting of the crews of F/Ls Blome-Jones, Havers and Kelly took off at 16.30 on a bitterly cold evening and selected their own route to the target area, the Blome-

Jones and Kelly crews preferring to follow the coast via the Frisians, while F/L Havers cut across Holland to approach the target over land from the south-east. The temperature at 10,000 feet was found to be -32 degrees and this affected engine performance, which led to F/L Blome-Jones and crew turning back after around two hours with low oil pressure leading to overheating. F/L Havers and crew experienced an identical problem and recognising the need to turn back at the first opportunity, reached what they hoped was the south-eastern suburbs of the city and dropped the incendiary part of the load on e.t.a. through ten-tenths cloud that topped out at 6,000 feet. F/L Kelly also located the target area and was able to release only one SBC after the bomb release system failed. Local sources confirmed accurate bombing by the first wave, which caused damage to the Focke-Wulf factory and the bombing spread eventually to the central districts, where some residential damage occurred.

This city was also the objective on the following two nights, and 103 Squadron was involved again on the 3/4th when the crews S/L Tait, F/Ls Blome-Jones and Kelly and F/O Max departed Newton between 16.30 and 17.00, each sitting on two 500 pounders and two SBCs of incendiaries. They were part of an overall force of seventy-one aircraft that flew out over cloud at 7,000 feet until it dispersed over enemy territory to leave clear skies. F/L Blome-Jones and crew had selected the coastal route and at 18.12 watched as an enemy aircraft approaching from six hundred feet below on the starboard bow made a climbing turn to engage them from two hundred yards before passing astern. The rear gunner fired two bursts of twenty rounds and the enemy dived down through cloud not to be seen again, leaving the wellington to continue on to the target and bomb from 13,000 feet under clear skies. S/L Tait crossed the target from north-east to south-west and attacked with a stick from 14,000 feet, while F/L Kelly and crew delivered a salvo from 9,000 feet, before exiting the coast over Bremerhaven and attracting a flak response. F/O Max and crew took the land route, avoiding much of the flak and observed one of their bombs hit a bridge. Bremen sustained further damage and Hamburg also reported fires after some crews attacked the Blohm & Voss shipyards on Finkenwerder Island in the Elbe as an alternative target.

The Ruhr city of Gelsenkirchen was selected as the target on the 9th, and a force of 135 aircraft assembled, which included a contribution from 1 Group of ten Wellingtons. The specific target was the Gelsenkirchener Bergwerke AG synthetic oil refinery, which was known to Bomber Command as the Nordstern plant and to the Germans as Gelsenberg AG (AG = Aktien Gesellschaft or production company) and was located in the Horst district to the north-west of the city centre. By this time, F/L Blome-Jones had been elevated to acting squadron leader rank to enable him to assume command of B Flight and he and his crew joined those of F/L Crawford and Sgts Crich, Ralston and Wareing at briefing to learn of their part in the night's activities. They departed Newton between 16.55 and 17.05 with W/C Littler flying as second pilot to S/L Blome-Jones and each Wellington carrying five 500 pounders. They all arrived in the target area to find six to eight-tenths cloud with tops at 4,000 feet, through which the Ralston crew delivered their bomb load from 12,000 feet without observing the results, while the crews of Sgts Crich and Wareing attacked from 13,000 feet and observed bursts on the eastern side of the city and among factory buildings. F/L Crawford's bombs were dropped from 14,000 feet and undershot to fall to the right of a bridge some distance to the north-west between Gelsenkirchen and Wesel and S/L Blome-Jones attacked a factory, believed to be in Oberhausen, from 13,000 feet. Sgt Crich and crew were long overdue when a message eventually came through to 1 Group HQ at 00.40 that they had been forced to land at Abergavenny in South Wales after running short of fuel while trying to establish a homing signal. At this stage of the war, it proved almost impossible to pinpoint a particular town or city in the Ruhr, as a blanket of industrial haze settled permanently over the region and hid it from view even on a clear night. This night was typical and resulted in bombs being scattered over a wide area, with few falling where intended.

On the 15th, a new Air Ministry directive pointed to a critical period ahead for the German oil industry, and a list of seventeen production sites was drawn up for attention, the top nine of which represented around 80% of total output. The Nordstern and Scholven-Buer sites were at Gelsenkirchen in the Ruhr, while Böhlen, Leuna, Lützkendorf and Zeitz were located close to Leipzig, with Ruhland and Magdeburg in the east and Politz in the north-east near the Baltic coast. The German synthetic oil industry relied on two main production methods, the Bergius process, which involved the hydrogenation of highly volatile bituminous coal to manufacture high-grade petroleum products like aviation fuel, and the Fischer-Tropsch process, which produced lower-grade diesel-type fuels for vehicle, Tank, U-Boot and shipping requirements. It would be February before the directive was put into effect, but it would not be exclusive, and French and German ports would continue to feature, along with other urban targets in Germany.

It was also on the 15th that S/L Mellor was posted to the squadron from 15 O.T.U. and was appointed A Flight commander in place of S/L Tait, who was about to leave the squadron on detachment to HQ 1 Group pending a permanent posting to Syerston, home to the Polish 304 and 305 Squadrons. The target for that night and already for the fourth time since the turn of the year was the naval and shipbuilding port of Wilhelmshaven on Germany's north-western coast, where, it was believed, the battleship Tirpitz was sheltering. A force of ninety-six aircraft was made ready that included a contribution from 1 Group of ten Wellingtons, of which five represented 103 Squadron and departed Newton between 17.50 and 18.00 bearing aloft the crews of S/L Mellor, F/Ls Crawford and Kelly and Sgts Muggeridge and Ralston. Each Wellington was carrying two 500 pounders and one hundred incendiaries, and propaganda leaflets or nickels were a standard part of every load. Sgt Ralston and crew suspected a fuel leak, although faulty gauges might have been responsible, but the sensible option was to turn back, and the bombs were dropped on the Frisian Island of Borkum from 12,000 feet. Three others attacked the primary target from between 9,500 and 13,000 feet, while Sgt Muggeridge and crew bombed an alternative oil-related objective from 16,000 feet. The operation was unusually effective for the period and caused considerable damage within the town and dockyard, but there was no mention of Tirpitz.

While the bombers were away, a single Luftwaffe aircraft sneaked in and dropped a few bombs on Newton, but damage was slight and there were no casualties. The bad weather restricted operational activity for the remainder of the month, and 1 Group's stations found themselves snowbound from the 20th onwards. During the course of the month the squadron was able to conduct only four operations and dispatched eighteen sorties without loss.

February 1941

The Commander-in-Chief, Sir Richard Peirse, who had been in post since replacing Sir Charles Portal in the previous October, had set a pattern of one major operation per month against an important German city. He did not embark upon the new offensive until February, and during the early part of the month, those Bomber Command airfields remaining serviceable, dispatched small numbers of aircraft to mainly French ports. 1 Group was badly restricted by the weather conditions, and even though Newton was able to declare itself serviceable on a number of occasions during the first nine nights, operations were cancelled.

On the 10th a new record force of 222 aircraft was assembled to target the northern city of Hannover, located south-east of Bremen and at the midpoint between the Dutch frontier and Berlin. The city was a major contributor to the German war effort and was home among others to the Accumulatoren-Fabrik A G, manufacturers of lead acid batteries for U-Boots and torpedoes, the Continental tyre and rubber factory at Limmer, the Deurag-Nerag synthetic oil refinery at Misburg, the VLW (Volkswagen) metalworks, and the Maschinenfabrik Niedersachsen Hannover and Hanomag factories, which were producing guns and tracked vehicles. On this night, however, the aiming points were the main post office and telephone exchange, in other words, the city centre at a time when it was not admitted publicly that residential and commercial areas were being targeted. The crews of W/C Littler, S/L Mellor, F/L Kelly and Sgts Crich, Elliott and Ralston departed Newton between 18.43 and 18.53, each sitting on three 500 pounders and two SBCs of incendiaries. Ten-tenths cloud over the Dutch coast diminished as the force headed inland, but S/L Mellor was unable to maintain height and speed and turned back shortly after crossing the Dutch/German frontier, dropping his load first onto the town of Rheine from 11,000 feet. The others reached the target under moonlight and clearing skies and found fires already burning to act as a guide. W/C Littler ran across the aiming point in a shallow dive from 13,000 to 11,000 feet, but a frozen distributor prevented the full load from falling away and a second run from 12,500 to 10,500 was necessary. F/L Kelly and crew attacked from 8,000 feet without observing the results and Sgt Elliott and crew from 11,000 feet, for some reason without fusing the bombs, despite which, two were observed to detonate. Sgt Ralston released his load from 7,000 feet after gliding down from 11,000 feet and a signal was received from Sgt Crich and crew to the effect that they had carried out an attack and were on their way home.

The above were among more than 180 crews claiming to have reached and bombed the primary target, while thirty others reported bombing alternatives. T2610 failed to return with Sgt Crich and crew, who were posted missing until the news came through from the Admiralty forty-eight hours later that they had been forced by engine failure to ditch in the North Sea. Their dinghy had been spotted by the S S Tovelil at 22.00 hours on the 12th and they had been pulled to safety suffering from exposure and one broken collarbone. They reported that their port engine had cut out in a shower of sparks at 23.30 when they were at 5,000 feet fifteen minutes out from the Dutch coast, and unable to maintain height on one engine, ditched at 23.50.

In a demonstration of the burgeoning power of the Command, the contribution by 3 Group of 119 aircraft to Hannover and Rotterdam was the first time that any group had exceeded one hundred aircraft in a single night. Among them, as part of the Rotterdam force, were the first three sorties by the new four-engine Stirling, the first of the new generation of bombers to enter service.

After the heavy snow of January, it was now the February rains that made Newton unfit for operations and it would remain out of commission until the 22nd. In the meantime, Sgt Ralston was commissioned on the 13th and the oil campaign opened at Gelsenkirchen and Homberg on the night of the 14/15th in what turned out to be a wasted effort with few aircraft reaching their respective target areas. Homberg actually referred to the Rheinpreussen (Meerbeck) synthetic oil refinery at Moers/Homberg located across the Rhine opposite Duisburg on the western edge of the Ruhr. Twenty-four hours later a smallish force attacked the Homberg plant again, while greater numbers went for the Ruhr-Chemie refinery at Sterkrade-Holten, a suburb of Oberhausen, but neither produced results worthy of mention. On the 22nd, seven 103 Squadron Wellingtons were bombed up, and with a minimum fuel load flew over to Lindholme with the intention of taking part in a raid on Brest. However, a heavy snowfall and change of wind direction prevented Lindholme from operating and the 103 Squadron participants returned to Newton on the following day.

Newton was fit for operations again in time for a raid on Düsseldorf on the night of the 25/26th, when six 103 Squadron crews joined six others from 1 Group in an overall force of eighty aircraft. They departed Newton between 18.10 and 18.18 with S/Ls Blome-Jones and Mellor the senior pilots on duty and set course to exit the English coast at Lowestoft and make landfall on the Dutch coast at the Scheldt estuary. They encountered no flak until approaching the western Ruhr between Krefeld and Mönchengladbach and arrived in the target area to find poor weather conditions and a blanket of ten-tenths cloud. F/L Kelly and S/L Mellor deployed a flare each to aid visibility, but to no avail and they delivered their five 500 pounders and SBC of incendiaries each from 9,000 and 11,000 feet respectively on estimated positions on the evidence of flak. The crews of F/L Crawford, F/O Max and S/L Blome-Jones bombed from 11,000, 12,000 and 12,500 feet respectively without knowing what was beneath them, and all returned safely to report on searchlight and flak activity and the occasional appearance of an enemy night-fighter. P/O Ralston and crew were absent from debriefing after T2621 apparently exploded in mid-air in the target area with total loss of life. An analysis of this raid and local sources revealed that only around seven bomb loads had fallen within the city.

Briefings on the 26th revealed Cologne to be the target for a force of 126 aircraft, for which 1 Group contributed just nine Wellingtons from the Polish squadrons at Swinderby. The Admiralty continued to maintain pressure on the Command to deal with the enemy's capital ships, and it was the Tirpitz at Wilhelmshaven that featured in briefings on the 28th. A force of 116 aircraft from all heavy groups was assembled, and among them at Newton was the entire 1 Group contribution of nine Wellingtons. The six 103 Squadron crews of W/C Littler, S/Ls Blome-Jones and Mellor, F/Ls Crawford and Kelly and F/O Max attended briefing to learn the details and took off between 21.20 and 21.30, each with three 500 pounders and two SBCs beneath their feet. They found the target area to be mostly cloud-covered, but a few chinks appeared later on for those at the tail end of the raid, which enabled them to pick out some ground detail. Not so for the 103 Squadron crews, however, who bombed from between 8,000 and 15,000 feet largely on the flashes from flak and any view of the ground was obliterated by the glare from thirty to fifty searchlights. S/L Blome-Jones and crew were afflicted by icing and electrical discharges producing a glow on various parts of the aircraft, but all returned safely to bring to an end a month of limited opportunities, in which just three operations had been undertaken and eighteen sorties launched for the loss of two Wellingtons and one crew. During the course of the month the squadron took on an additional eight Wellingtons and by the end had sixteen examples of the Wellington Mk Ic on charge along with two of the Mk Ia.

Ten months after it had begun, an assessment of the efficacy of mining operations by Bomber Command revealed that seventeen enemy vessels had been sunk in the Baltic's Great and Little Belts and eighteen damaged. It was believed that a further eighteen had probably been sunk and it was considered safe to estimate that for every known case of a sinking or damage, another would have occurred without news of it reaching England. Among the known sinkings was that of a troopship carrying three thousand men, of whom fewer than four hundred survived.

March 1941

The new month began with a return to Cologne on the 1st by a force of 131 aircraft, which inflicted considerable damage for the period on both banks of the Rhine in the city centre, but only a pinprick in comparison to what lay in store for this city in the years to come. 1 Group was not involved but contributed ten Wellingtons from Newton to a force of seventy-one aircraft assigned to the Rhineland capital on the night of the 3/4th. The 103 Squadron crews of S/Ls Blome-Jones and Mellor, F/O Max, Sgt Wareing and P/O Chisholm, who was flying as crew captain for the first time, departed Newton between 19.35 and 19.50 and set course for the Scheldt estuary, each sitting on four 500 pounders, one 250 pounder and four SBCs of incendiaries. They encountered seven to ten-tenths cloud in the target area with tops at around 7,000 feet and identified the Rhine by the light of flares on approach, before delivering their attacks on e.t.a. and evidence of flak from between 11,000 and 14,000 feet in the face of intense and sometimes accurate flak. All returned safely unconvinced that they had delivered an effective attack and local sources confirmed that only slight superficial damage had been achieved in western suburbs.

F/L Crawford and F/O Max left the squadron on the 8th on detachment to Wilmslow in preparation to travel to California to ferry back American aircraft. F/O Thorougood was also posted away to Doncaster from where he would proceed eventually to the Far East.

On the 9th, yet another new Air Ministry directive was received, which changed the emphasis of the Command's operations from oil to maritime matters. Unacceptably high shipping losses to U-Boots in the Atlantic forced the War Cabinet to order an all-out assault on this menace, and its partner in crime, the long-range reconnaissance bomber, the Focke-Wulf Kondor. They were to be hunted down at sea, in their bases, and at the point of their manufacture, and a new list of targets was drawn up accordingly. This was headed by Kiel,

Hamburg, Bremen and Vegesack (Bremen), wherein lay a total of seven shipyards, while Bremen was also home to a Focke-Wulf factory in the Hemelingen district. Included in the target list were Lorient and St-Nazaire on the Biscay coast, where the main U-Boot bases were situated. The first phase of the massive construction project on the Keroman peninsula on the southern extremities of Lorient had begun just weeks earlier, and would continue until January 1942, by which time the K1, K2 and K3 structures would be completed and capable of sheltering thirty vessels and their crews under cover. The complex would boast a revolutionary lift system, which could raise U-Boots from the water and transport them across the facility to repair and servicing bays. The thickness of the concrete rendered the structures impervious to the bombs available to Bomber Command at the time, and attacks would be directed predominantly at the town and its approaches to prevent access by road and rail, while mining would inhibit access by sea.

Heavy and persistent rain rendered 1 Group's airfields unserviceable after the Cologne operation, and during this period on the 10th, Halifaxes went to war for the first time, when six belonging to 4 Group's 35 Squadron were assigned to the docks at Le Havre. The new campaign began at Hamburg on the night of the 12/13th, by which time the condition of 1 Group's airfields had improved. Three raids were planned, the largest by eighty-eight aircraft on Hamburg, while eighty-six were to go to Bremen and seventy-two to Berlin. 1 Group supported the Hamburg operation with sixteen Wellingtons, six of them made ready by 103 Squadron, and they departed Newton between 19.25 and 19.45 with S/Ls Blome-Jones and Mellor the senior pilots on duty, each carrying five 500 pounders and one SBC of incendiaries. They flew out over the Lincolnshire coast and those adopting the recommended route made landfall on the Frisian Island of Texel, before heading eastwards across northern Holland to enter Germany north of Meppen on track for the turning point at Bergen. From there they flew north to Bergedorf on Hamburg's south-eastern corner, before swinging round to approach the target from the north-east. S/L Mellor and F/L Kelly preferred a direct route, and by whichever means, all arrived in the target area to find excellent weather conditions and an almost full moon to provide good visibility. They carried out their attacks from 10,000 to 14,000 feet through intense anti-aircraft fire and despite searchlight glare preventing an accurate assessment of results, the consensus of returning crews was of a successful operation. Among five shipyards hit was Blohm & Voss, at which a number of U-Boots under construction were damaged on their slipways, and eighteen large fires had to be dealt with.

Hamburg was posted as the target again on the 13th, for which a larger force of 139 aircraft was assembled, of which seven represented 1 Group. The 103 Squadron crews of W/C Littler, F/O Harper and Sgt Crich departed Newton between 19.00 and 19.20, each sitting on four 500 pounders and one SBC, and all reached the target area under clear skies and a bright moon to be greeted by an intense searchlight and flak defence. F/O Harper and crew failed to locate the primary target and dropped their bombs on a flak concentration that was plotted later to be at Vechte in Holland, while W/C Littler and Sgt Crich delivered their loads from 13,000 feet and contributed to another successful attack. The Blohm & Voss shipyard sustained further damage and this time thirty-one of 119 fires were classed as large.

A force of 101 aircraft was made ready on the 14th to operate against the Hydrierwerke-Scholven synthetic oil refinery in the Buer district of Gelsenkirchen in a nod to the oil campaign. 1 Group supported the operation with a dozen Wellingtons from Newton, eight of them belonging to 103 Squadron and taking off between 19.00 and 19.30 with W/C Littler and the two flight commanders the senior pilots on duty. They arrived over the central Ruhr to find excellent weather conditions but industrial haze and smoke impairing the vertical visibility, which created challenges for aiming point identification. They carried out their attacks on the built-up area generally from around 12,000 to 13,500 feet in the face of accurate anti-aircraft fire from batteries co-operating with searchlights and took note of barrage balloons tethered at 12,000 feet to the north. F/L Havers and crew were attacked from astern by a BF110 at 12,000 feet and both aircraft opened fire at the same time at a range of three hundred down to one hundred yards. As each banked to starboard, the Wellington's gunners were able to fire beam shots from four hundred to six hundred yards range and tracer was seen to enter the enemy's fuselage. The Wellington sustained no damage, and the night-fighter was not seen again. The oil refinery was hit by an estimated sixteen bomb loads that caused extensive damage to the site.

The first raid on the port of Lorient took place on the night of the 15/16th and involved twenty-six Wellingtons from 3 Group and eleven 4 Group Whitleys. Haze prevented accurate bombing, but no aircraft were lost and there would be many further opportunities to try again in the months and years ahead. 1 Group became involved at this target on the 21st, when contributing fifteen Wellingtons from Newton to an overall force of sixty-six aircraft. 103 Squadron made ready eight of its own and loaded them with fourteen 250 pounders each, three of them in each load semi-armour-piercing (SAP). They took off between 18.20 and 18.40 with S/L Mellor the senior pilot on duty and lost the services of F/O Barrett and crew, who turned back from a position fifty miles from the English coast because of an inability to climb beyond 9,000 feet. They brought their bombs home after failing to find a suitable target on the French coast, while the others reached the target area to find themselves hampered by poor visibility and dropped their bombs on the west bank of the river below Pont-de-Cauden from between 9,500 and 14,000 feet, some observing bursts and flashes but little detail.

The heavy rains returned thereafter, and the soggy 1 Group airfields were unable to launch aircraft for the ensuing week. On the 29th, the German cruisers Scharnhorst and Gneisenau were reported to be off Brest, and by the following day, they had taken up residence, thus beginning an eleven-month-long saga, which would prove to be a major distraction for Bomber Command. The first concerted attempt to disable them was launched on the night of the 30/31st and involved 109 aircraft, including fourteen Wellingtons of 1 Group at Newton. Eight 103 Squadron Wellingtons were loaded with seven 500 pounders each and dispatched between 19.00 and 19.20 with W/C Littler the senior pilot on duty supported by both flight commanders. All reached the target area, where most found the port to be easily identified and attacks were carried out in the face of an intense flak defence from the vessels themselves and batteries around the port. Bombing was carried out from between 10,000 and 13,000 feet, W/C Littler making four dummy runs across the target and three more to deliver his bombs, while F/L Kelly and crew dropped theirs on their third pass over the aiming point. On the way home over the Channel, R1043's engines began to falter, and they finally cut out at 10,000 feet over south-western England. P/O Auliff took over the controls for an emergency landing at what would have been an unfamiliar airfield, and was confronted by a house, which he banked steeply to avoid and collided with a tree. The Wellington crashed at Manor Farm, Mudford, two miles north-east of Yeovil in Somerset and burst into flames, trapping W/C Littler with fatal consequences, while the remaining crew members escaped with minor injuries and burns. B Flight commander, S/L Mellor, was on final approach to Newton when his Wellington was pounced upon by an enemy intruder at around 00.25, forcing him skilfully to put W5612 onto the ground in a field a mile from the airfield, from where all on board were able to walk away.

During the course of the month, the squadron took part in six operations and dispatched thirty-eight sorties for the loss of two Wellingtons and the commanding officer.

April 1941

The first week of the new month brought further misery for 1 Group in the form of waterlogged airfields. This provided the new commanding officer, W/C Lowe, with an opportunity to settle in following his arrival on the 4th from 12 Squadron at Binbrook, where he had been a flight commander during the somewhat lengthy conversion from the Battle to the Wellington. Had he remained at Binbrook for five more days, it is highly likely that he would have been appointed to command 12 Squadron, following the loss of W/C Blackden on the squadron's maiden operation on Wellingtons. The presence of the Scharnhorst and Gneisenau at Brest would occupy much of the Command's attention during the new month and would continue to do so until the infamous "Channel Dash" episode in February 1942 finally resolved the matter. The British press decided to have fun with the initials of the German cruisers and dubbed them as Salmon & Gluckstein, in a comic reference to the country's largest tobacconist, established in 1873 by a German Jewish émigré and his English partner.

The assault on Brest began with 5 Group launching a dozen Hampdens from St Eval in Cornwall for a daylight attack on the 1st, when all but one turned back in the absence of cloud, and the one that continued on failed to return. A force of ninety aircraft was drawn from 2, 3 and 4 Groups on the 3rd, and returning crews reported difficulty in locating the vessels. During the course of the 4th, Gneisenau entered a dry Dock, which was to be drained on the 5th to allow an inspection of the vessel to take place. That night, fifty-four Wellingtons and Hampdens from 3 and 5 Groups tried their hand, although, in keeping with the policy in force at this stage of the war, were probably not over the target at the same time. 5 Group conducted a low-level assault, and one Hampden crew claimed a direct hit on Scharnhorst. The Continental Hotel in the town was also struck by bombs just as dinner was being served, and a number of naval officers were killed. When Gneisenau's dry dock was drained on the 5th, a single unexploded 500lb bomb was found nestling at the bottom, and the ship's captain, Kapitän-zur-See Otto Fein, decided to move his vessel out into the harbour while it was dealt with. The dock was refilled to allow Gneisenau to vacate it, and she was spotted by a reconnaissance aircraft at some point, which led to an operation being planned by Coastal Command to be carried out at first light on the 6th. It took place in poor weather conditions, which led to the six Beauforts becoming separated while outbound, and F/O Kenneth

Campbell and his crew alone pressed home an attack, which caused damage to Gneisenau that would require six months to repair. In the face of the most concentrated anti-aircraft fire, the Beaufort stood little chance of getting away with it and was shot down without survivors, F/O Campbell receiving the posthumous award of a Victoria Cross for his actions.

By the time that six 103 Squadron Wellingtons lined up for take-off for Brest from the forward base at Bodney on the evening of the 6th, it was already the sixth attack to be launched against the port since the turn of the month. Seventy-one aircraft were involved in this latest attack, of which twenty were 1 Group Wellingtons from Newton and Swinderby, the six belonging to 103 Squadron taking off between 21.20 and 22.00 with F/Ls Havers and Kelly the senior pilots on duty. Each Wellington carried a bomb load of five 500 pounders and one SBC, but adverse weather conditions prevented many crews from identifying the target and those from 103 Squadron delivered their loads onto flak concentrations from between 10,000 and 13,000 feet, and apart from P/O Anderson's port engine cutting out for ten minutes on the way home, there was little of consequence to report.

Two major operations were mounted against Kiel on consecutive nights, the first by 229 aircraft on the 7/8th representing the largest number of aircraft yet sent to a single target. The Polish squadrons were on duty on behalf of 1 Group for this one, while 103 Squadron remained at home. It was a highly effective raid, carried out in clear conditions with bright moonlight, and the Krupp-controlled Deutsche Werke and Germania Werft shipyards, both of which were building U-Boots, were put out of action for a number of days. A force of 160 aircraft was assembled for a return to Kiel on the following night, and among them were eighteen Wellingtons representing 1 Group, seven of them made ready by 103 Squadron. They departed Newton between 20.30 and 21.20 with S/L Blome-Jones the senior pilot on duty and loads of either a 1,000 pounder, two 500 pounders and sixteen 25lb incendiaries or three 500 pounders and 240 x 4lb incendiaries. All reached the target area to find clear skies, ground haze and an increase in the number of searchlights, and they delivered their bombs from between 9,000 and 14,000 feet, P/O Chisholm and crew having arrived forty-five minutes behind schedule after a delayed take-off caused by W/T issues. Smoke was rising through 6,000 feet as the last of the bombers turned away from another successful raid, which local sources reported had centred this time more upon the town, where much damage occurred and 125 people lost their lives.

1 Group was not involved in a raid by eighty aircraft on Berlin on the 9th but welcomed 12 Squadron back to the front line with a freshman foray by four crews to the port of Emden, from which, in an inauspicious start to its new career, the commanding officer, W/C Blackden, failed to return. The warships at Brest were the objectives for fifty-three Wellingtons, Blenheims and Manchesters on the 10th, while 1 Group remained at home, and four bombs hit the Gneisenau, killing fifty men and injuring ninety. A return to Brest on the night of the 12/13th involved a force of sixty-six aircraft of which eleven Wellingtons were provided by 1 Group, all from Newton. The five-strong 103 Squadron element consisting of the crews of F/L Kelly, F/Os Barrett and Harper, P/O Anderson and Sgt Muggeridge took off between 01.05 and 01.15 on the 13th, each sitting on six 500 pounders, and all reached the target area to find it concealed beneath cloud with tops at 6,000 feet. Flak was spasmodic and

erratic as they delivered their bombs from between 9,000 and 12,700 feet through small gaps, some picking out their point of impact without being able to determine the results.

The Polish squadrons at Swinderby represented 1 Group at Brest on the following night as part of a force of ninety-four aircraft, the efforts of which were again hampered by cloud. Kiel was the destination for ninety-six aircraft on the night of the 15/16th, when 1 Group detailed a dozen Wellingtons from Newton, seven of them provided by 103 Squadron. S/Ls Blome-Jones and Mellor were the senior pilots on duty as they took off between 20.30 and 20.40, each with a 1,000 pounder, two 500 pounders and 4lb and 25lb incendiaries in the bomb bay. S/L Blome-Jones and crew were forced to turn back by an engine problem, leaving the others to press on over cloud that was at ten-tenths as they crossed the western coast of Schleswig-Holstein and persisted all the way to the Baltic coast, where tops were at around 14,000 feet. The 103 Squadron crews bombed flak concentrations from between 11,000 and 14,500 feet, P/O Chisholm and crew releasing only the incendiaries, before flying north to drop the high explosives from clear skies onto Flensburg. F/O Barrett found an aerodrome at Flensburg to attack from 11,000 feet, and observed strikes among buildings followed by fires.

1 Group continued to alternate its fire power and the Polish squadrons were detailed to take part in an operation against Bremen on the night of the 16/17th which was conducted by a force of 107 aircraft. However, when Berlin was posted as the target for the 17th, it was necessary to harness the resources of both Newton and Swinderby to contribute seventeen Wellingtons to the overall force of 118 aircraft. Horsham-St-Faith was employed as a staging post for the 1 Group contingent, which allowed the Wellingtons to dispense with overload tanks and carry an increased bomb load. Of the seven 103 Squadron Wellingtons, only five departed Horsham-St-Faith between 20.50 and 21.05, after two were found to be unserviceable. S/Ls Blome-Jones and Mellor were the senior pilots on duty as they lifted into the air with some difficulty from a short runway in a crosswind, carrying three 500 pounders each and an assortment of incendiaries. Sgt Muggeridge and crew turned back shortly after crossing the Dutch coast when an engine began to falter, but the others arrived in the Berlin area to be greeted by a hostile searchlight and flak defence and ground features hidden by thick haze. They carried out their attacks from between 11,000 and 16,000 feet without observing the results, before returning after seven or eight hours aloft with little to pass on to the intelligence section at debriefing.

No major operations were mounted over the ensuing week, during which 2 Group was the busiest, conducting operations against coastal targets and power stations. The campaign against Kiel continued on the night of the 24/25th, when a force of sixty-nine aircraft included a 1 Group contribution of six Wellingtons each from 103 and 150 Squadrons at Newton. The 103 Squadron element consisting of the crews of S/L Blome-Jones, F/L Kelly, P/Os Anderson and Chisholm and Sgts Muggeridge and Wareing took off between 20.35 and 20.45 and all reached the target area to find largely clear skies and good visibility, despite the absence of moonlight. They delivered their 1,000 pounder, two 500 pounders and incendiaries each from 9,000 to 13,500 feet, but haze and searchlight glare prevented an assessment of the results, and F/L Kelly and crew were aware that their bombs had undershot and had fallen into open country.

The Polish 300 and 301 Squadrons represented 1 Group with five Wellingtons each at Kiel again on the following night as part of a force of sixty-two aircraft. When the Poles first arrived in Bomber Command, they had had to work hard to establish themselves as equal in ability to their RAF counterparts, but now, having greatly impressed the authorities with their skill and determination to get at the hated enemy and avenge the rape of their homeland, they had become an indispensable part of 1 Group. It was the Poles again who represented 1 Group at Mannheim on the night of the 29/30, in what turned out to be a disappointing effort that caused only modest damage.

In the meantime, 12 and 142 Squadron's at Binbrook were now ready to take their place in the front line and between them contributed seven of the twenty Wellingtons detailed by 1 Group on the 30th for yet another attack on Kiel, this time by a force of eighty-one aircraft. 103 Squadron briefed the crews of S/L Blome-Jones, F/L Kelly, F/O Harper, P/O Chisholm and Sgt Muggeridge and sent them on their way from Newton between 20.55 and 21.10, each carrying a 1,000 pounder, two 500 pounders and incendiaries. F/O Harper and crew turned back with technical problems, leaving the others to arrive at the target to find ten-tenths cloud completely obscuring the ground and forcing them to bomb on flak concentrations from between 14,000 and 16,000 feet.

During the course of the month the squadron carried out seven operations and dispatched forty-four sorties without loss. F/L Havers DFC was posted to 20 O.T.U. at Lossiemouth at the end of his tour.

May 1941

Persistent problems with the Halifax would prevent the type from participating in any operations during the month and the 35 Squadron pilots were detached to 58 Squadron to learn how to fly the Whitley. However, the grounding order on 5 Group's Manchesters had been lifted so at least they and the Stirlings of 3 Group would be available to provide an increase in bomb-carrying capacity. The new month began with the posting of an operation to Hamburg on the 1st, but this was subsequently cancelled, only to be reinstated on the following day and a force of ninety-five aircraft assembled. The Polish squadrons represented 1 Group with sixteen Wellingtons in what was only a moderately effective raid, which, according to local sources, caused twenty-six fires, half of them large, but no significant incidents.

Cologne was posted as the target for a force of a hundred aircraft on the following night, of which twenty-three Wellingtons represented 1 Group from the stations at Newton and Binbrook. The six-strong 103 Squadron element took off between 21.00 and 21.10 with S/L Blome-Jones the senior pilot on duty and each crew sitting on a 1,000 pounder, three 500 pounders and an assortment of incendiaries. They arrived over the Rhineland capital to find it covered by cloud with tops at 4,000 feet and above, and bombing took place by five of them on evidence of flak from between 11,500 and 18,000 feet. Sgt Henderson and crew decided to seek an alternative target and bombed Aachen from 14,000 feet having found it to be relatively free of cloud. Local sources in Cologne confirmed that few bombs had fallen within its boundaries, adding to the long list of disappointing raids that were the hallmark of Bomber Command's efforts at this stage of the war.

The teleprinters on 1, 3, 4 and 5 Group stations began churning out the orders of the day on the 5th, to reveal that Mannheim was to be the destination for a force of 141 aircraft, of which 1 Group's contribution amounted to twenty-eight Wellingtons from all of its operational stations. The 103 Squadron crews of F/L Kelly, F/O Harper P/Os Anderson and Chisholm and Sgts Henderson and Muggeridge departed Newton between 22.05 and 22.20, each carrying five 250 pounders and four SBCs of 90 x 4lb incendiaries. The outward flight was attended by ten-tenths cloud, which persisted in the target area and forced crews to bomb on evidence of flak, five of those from 103 Squadron from 14,000 to 15,000 feet, while the Anderson crew found an alternative target under partial cloud cover and bombed it from 12,000 feet. Despite the claim by 121 crews that they had attacked the city, local sources reported some twenty-five bomb loads falling within its boundaries and causing only minor damage.

The Polish squadrons represented 1 Group in a return to Hamburg on the 6th, when results were once more disappointing, for which poor visibility was blamed. While a force of eighty aircraft attacked Brest and its lodgers on the night of the 7/8th, fifteen Wellingtons from Newton represented the entire force sent to St-Nazaire, another of the ports housing a U-Boot base, where the U-Boots and tankers were the specific targets. S/L Blome-Jones was the senior pilot on duty and had W/C Lowe on board as second pilot as the five-strong 103 Squadron element took off between 23.20 and 23.30 carrying six 500 pounders each. All reached the target area, where, for a change, the skies were clear and the visibility good, and all crews identified and bombed from between 12,000 and 15,000 feet and observed sticks straddle the target area, particularly docks 4 and 5. On the way home, F/O Harper and crew were attacked by an enemy night-fighter, which the pilot evaded skilfully by diving at 200 mph and then pulling the nose up and throttling back. This forced the enemy to overshoot, and while it was in a vulnerable stall situation, the Wellington's rear gunner managed to fire a long burst from at around one hundred yards range, after which it dived out of sight and was claimed as probably destroyed.

Two major operations were mounted on the night of the 8/9th in pursuit of the latest directive and would call upon the services of a record-breaking 364 aircraft. The larger endeavour, involving 188 aircraft, was directed at Hamburg's Blohm & Voss shipyards, while 133 aircraft, including a new record by 1 Group of forty-nine Wellingtons, went for industrial objectives, particularly the Weser A G U-Boot construction yards in Bremen. The increase in 1 Group's offering was partly made possible by the availability now for bombing operations of two more Polish squadrons, 304 and 305, who were stationed at Syerston, a short distance up the A46 from Newton. The 103 Squadron element of six took off between 23.05 and 23.15 with F/L Kelly the senior pilot on duty, having been briefed to attack the industrial centre of the city with their single 1,000 pounder, two 500 pounders and three SBCs of incendiaries. The squadron ORB employed the word "blitz", which signified, perhaps, that at least part of the force was to deliver an area attack on the city centre. P/O Anderson and crew were outbound over the North Sea when attacked at 11,000 feet by a BF110, which came in first from above on the starboard quarter at 00.40 and opened fire from five hundred yards.

P/O Anderson turned into the attack forcing the enemy to break away and make a second pass from the port quarter, during which cannon shells burst in the port wing. The enemy disappeared and the bombs were dropped from 10,000 feet onto the aerodrome on the Frisian Island of Texel. The others reached the target to find little cloud and some fires already burning, the smoke from which would hamper later arrivals. They carried out their attacks from between 14,000 and 19,000 feet, F/L Kelly's R1217 having been ensnared in a cone of searchlights and targeted by flak, which inflicted damage to flying surfaces, while Sgt Wareing's front turret developed a leak that caused hydraulic fluid to spread across the windscreen. Many fires were reported by returning crews and local sources confirmed extensive damage in the city but no hits on the Weser A G U-Boot construction yards. Meanwhile, sixty miles to the north-east, Hamburg was undergoing a destructive attack that left almost forty large fires burning.

A force of 146 aircraft was assembled on the 9th for that night's operation against the twin cities of Mannheim and Ludwigshafen, which face each other across the Rhine in southern Germany. 1 Group made available fourteen Wellingtons from Swinderby and Binbrook, while the Newton squadrons remained at home. One of the aiming points was the Badische Anilin & Soda-Fabrik (BASF) works in Ludwigshafen, which was part of the infamous I G Farben company, the largest manufacturer of chemicals and synthetic oil products in the world and major employer of slave workers.

Hamburg was posted to host its fourth raid of the month on the 10th, for which a force of 119 aircraft was assembled and the crews briefed to aim for the Blohm & Voss shipyards, the nearby Altona power station (Tiefstack) and the general city area. 1 Group detailed twenty-one Wellingtons from Newton and Syerston for the main event and six freshman crews from the same stations to attack Emden. 103 Squadron briefed the crews of F/L Kelly, F/O Harper, P/O Anderson and Sgts Henderson and Wareing to aim for the main railway station in Hamburg and loaded their Wellingtons with four 500 pounders and three SBCs each before sending them on their way between 21.55 and 22.10. P/Os Ball and Eccles followed them into the air at 23.30 and 23.35 respectively bound for Emden with similar but not identical bomb loads. On a bright moonlit night, in which conditions were favourable to attackers and defenders alike, the Luftwaffe sent night-fighters to patrol their boxes and a number of engagements would take place. Searchlights were coning as high as 15,000 feet and co-operating with heavy flak and Sgt Henderson and crew were held for twenty minutes as they and the other 103 Squadron crews delivered their attacks from 14,000 to 16,500 feet. Hamburg suffered what was for the period a heavy blow, which this time left over a hundred fires burning, almost fifty of them classed as large. F/L Kelly brought back a photograph of the aiming point, showing fires burning around the station.

A little later, 115 miles to the west, the two 103 Squadron freshman crews watched from around 15,000 feet as their bombs set off fires in Emden, before setting course for home having gained valuable experience. P/O Ball and crew were set upon by a succession of four enemy night-fighters, a BF109, two BF110s and a Ju88 and a dramatic fight for survival ensued, during which one BF110 was shot down in flames and the Ju88 broke off the engagement at 1,000 feet with smoke and flames issuing from its starboard engine. The Wellington's starboard engine was damaged and lost power and anything portable was thrown out to save weight, but R1395 brought the crew home to a wheels-up landing at base and would eventually be returned to flying condition.

There would be no respite for Germany's second city as plans were already in hand to send ninety-two aircraft back there twenty-four hours later, while eighty-one others sought out one of the Deutsche Schiff und Maschinenbau A G shipyards in Bremen. 1 Group detailed twenty-three Wellingtons from Swinderby and Binbrook for the former, which resulted in eighty-eight fires, twenty-six of them large, but no significant industrial damage. A force of 105 aircraft, divided 65/40, was made ready for a return to Mannheim and Ludwigshafen on the 12th and was supported by 1 Group with a contribution of twenty Wellingtons from Newton and Syerston assigned to the former. The 103 Squadron crews of S/L Blome-Jones, F/O Harper, P/O Anderson and Sgts Henderson and Wareing took off between 22.45 and 22.55 each sitting on a 1,000 pounder, one 500 pounder, one 250 pounder and assorted incendiaries. They crossed the North Sea over ten-tenths cloud, which diminished as they traversed Belgium and some were able to pick up the Rhine and follow it to the target, where thick haze obscured ground features and combined with intense searchlight and flak activity to prevent some crews from identifying the aiming point. S/L Blome-Jones and crew had already turned back by this stage because of excessive fuel consumption, and they bombed a searchlight concentration at Gillenfeld from 16,000 feet. The crews of F/O Harper and Sgts Henderson and Wareing bombed from between 10,000 and 16,000 feet, while the Anderson crew dropped their load on Koblenz from 16,500 feet.

The weather precluded operations on the following two nights, and it was the 15th when the northern city of Hannover was posted as the target for 101 aircraft, for which 1 Group detailed a dozen Wellingtons from Newton. The briefed aiming points were the main post office and telephone exchange, which in reality, identified this as an area attack. The six-strong 103 Squadron element flew over to Swanton Morley as a forward launching pad and took off from there between 22.30 and 22.50 with F/L Kelly the senior pilot on duty and each Wellington carrying four 500 pounders and two SBCs of 4lb incendiaries. Towering cumulus cloud was encountered outbound, and the night was intensely cold, -33 degrees at 17,000 feet, which forced the crew of 103 Squadron crew to turn back when their heating system failed, and to drop their bombs on the town of Wildeshausen to the south-west of Bremen. P/O Ball and crew were compromised by an unserviceable rear turret and the observer's parachute deploying inside the fuselage, and they also abandoned their sortie. P/O Anderson and crew were over northern Holland when their electrical system began to exhibit signs of failure, and they bombed Eelde aerodrome from 14,000 feet as a last resort target, observing hits. The others had to contend with ten-tenths cloud that obscured the ground and rendered accurate navigation something of a challenge, but the skies had partially cleared to leave five-tenths over Hannover, which they identified by the River Leine to the north-west and the Maschsee to the south-east. The crews of P/O Chisholm and F/L Kelly carried out their attacks from 13,000 and 14,000 feet respectively but despite the improving conditions, were unable to observe the burst of their bombs, and typically for Hannover, no local report was forthcoming to confirm the level of damage. A message was received from P/O Eccles and crew to the effect that they had lost the port engine, and when they failed to arrive back at Newton, it was believed that R1494 had come down in the sea forty miles off the English coast. In fact, it had crashed five miles east of Veendam in northern Holland after being hit by flak over nearby Emden, and P/O Eccles RNZAF and his rear gunner were killed, while the four survivors fell into enemy hands. It was just their second operation with the squadron.

On the 18th, the battleship Bismarck and heavy cruiser Prinz Eugen put to sea from the Polish port of Gotenhafen and headed for Norway to begin operation "Rheinübung", which for Bismarck, would be her first offensive action. They were shadowed by Coastal Command aircraft as they slipped out of Bergen, heading for the Denmark Straits between Greenland and Iceland and preparations were put in hand by the Admiralty to intercept. During an engagement on the 24th, HMS Hood, the unsinkable pride of the Royal Navy, was hit by a shell from Bismarck, which ignited the magazine and blew the vessel apart with the loss of all but three of her complement. In the knowledge that elements of the Royal Navy were steaming from all directions to avenge this shocking loss, Bismarck and Prinz Eugen headed for sanctuary at Brest, Prinz Eugen eventually breaking away to create a diversion. In fact, the Bismarck's rudder would be crippled by a Fleet Air Arm torpedo during the 26th, rendering her unable to manoeuvre and restricted to a top speed of ten knots. At first light on the 27th, multiple units of the Royal Navy closed in on the helpless Bismarck, and from 08.47, engaged her with guns and torpedoes until she slipped beneath the waves at 10.39. This left her consort, Prinz Eugen, at large and looking for the opportunity to sneak into Brest to join Scharnhorst and Gneisenau.

Cologne and Kiel were the principal targets during the remainder of the month, but neither suffered more than modest damage as raids continued to be largely ineffective. Flight commander S/L Blome-Jones was posted to 12 O.T.U at Benson on the 26th at the conclusion of his tour, while S/L Lane came in the opposite direction as his successor. The squadron was involved in just one more operation before the end of the month, a freshman sortie by P/O Ewart to attack the docks and shipping at Boulogne on the night of the 27/28th. They departed Newton at 01.30 carrying four 500 pounders, one 250 pounder and two SBCs, which were released over the target from 14,000 feet and were back home within four-and-a-half hours. During the course of the month operations were mounted on eight nights, forty-two sorties were dispatched, and one aircraft and crew were missing.

June 1941

June and July were to be significant months for the Command, as its performance began to be monitored in order to provide an assessment of its effectiveness for the War Cabinet. The project was initiated by Churchill's chief scientific advisor, Lord Cherwell, who handed the responsibility to David M Bensusan-Butt, a civil-servant assistant to Cherwell working in the War Cabinet Secretariat. The new month would be dominated by operations against Cologne, Düsseldorf and Bremen, with Kiel and Brest also receiving their share of attention. During the second half of the month Cologne and Düsseldorf would be attacked simultaneously on no fewer than eight nights by forces of varying sizes, and Bremen, including the shipbuilding yards at Vegesack, would host six raids. On the 1st, the Hipper Class cruiser Prinz Eugen, arrived at Brest having evaded detection by the Royal Navy following the sinking of Bismarck. She would now join Scharnhorst and Gneisenau to form a powerful battle group that would continue to be perceived as a constant threat by the Admiralty and on its instigation, a major distraction for Bomber Command.

June would bring a slight increase in activity for 103 Squadron, which began on the night of the 2/3ʳᵈ, when the industrial city of Duisburg was posted as the target for twenty-five Wellingtons from Newton and Syerston, while the main effort on this night, by 150 aircraft, was directed at Düsseldorf, fifteen miles due south on the Ruhr's southern edge. Perched on the eastern bank of the Rhine, Duisburg was a major centre for iron and steel production and the chemicals industry, boasted the largest inland docks in Germany in the Ruhrort complex and was hugely important to the war effort. Each of the six 103 Squadron Wellingtons was loaded with two 500 pounders and an assortment of incendiaries each and took to the air between 23.34 and 23.45 with F/L Kelly the senior pilot on duty and S/L Lane flying as second pilot with P/O Anderson. From the Dutch coast inland for thirty miles clear skies prevailed, but they were greeted in the target area by patchy cloud up to 17,000 feet and by the ever-present industrial haze that protected the entire Ruhr Valley. F/L Kelly and crew arrived at 02.20 and found a large fire already burning to guide them as they bombed from 14,000 feet and observed bursts. The crews of P/Os Chisholm and Anderson also attacked from 14,000 feet and the newly commissioned P/O Wareing and his crew from five hundred feet higher, while P/O Ewart and crew glided down to 15,000 feet before releasing their load and Sgt Muggeridge and crew topped out from 16,000 feet. Neither operation produced worthwhile results as the Command settled into an extended period of disappointment and underachievement.

Minor operations then held sway until the night of the 10/11ᵗʰ, when 104 aircraft, including twenty-three 1 Group Wellingtons, were dispatched to Brest for another crack at Scharnhorst, Gneisenau and Prinz Eugen. 103 Squadron was not involved in this operation, or in the major efforts against Düsseldorf and Duisburg twenty-four hours later, but on the latter occasion sent the freshman crew of P/O Purcivall to bomb the docks and shipping at Boulogne in company with twenty-eight others from 1, 3 and 4 Groups. Running into the moon at 11,500 feet, the bombs were released at around 01.10 and were seen to burst, but could not be plotted, and a safe return was completed at 02.50 after three hours and fifty minutes aloft.

A busy night of operations against marshalling yards was planned for the 12ᵗʰ, when 4 Group detailed eighty Whitleys and four Mk II Wellingtons to target those in the town of Schwerte, situated at the eastern end of the Ruhr, south-east of Dortmund, while 5 Group attacked yards at Soest, to the north of the one-day-to-be-famous Möhne reservoir. Other forces consisting of eighty-two 3 Group and sixty-one 1 Group Wellingtons attended to similar objectives at Hamm and Osnabrück respectively, also north of the Ruhr, while at the same time, eleven Halifaxes and seven Stirlings would be attempting to hit the "Buna" synthetic rubber works at Marl-Hüls some ten miles north of Gelsenkirchen. 103 Squadron supported the 1 Group endeavour with nine Wellingtons, which departed Newton between 23.00 and 23.10 with F/L Kelly, who was now acting as B Flight commander, the senior pilot on duty and S/L Lane again accompanying P/O Anderson. They set course for the Den Helder peninsula, and shortly after making landfall, T2996 was shot down at 00.37 by the night-fighter of Ofw Hans Rasper of 4./NJG1 and crashed six miles west of Enkhuizen with no survivors from the crew of P/O Chisholm. The others all located the target and delivered their loads of one 1,000 pounder and five 500 pounders from between 11,500 and 15,000 feet and observed fires as they turned for home. F/Sgt Henderson and crew ran into an electrical storm at 4,000 feet off

Cromer, which scrambled the wireless and compasses, persuading them to circle off the coast until daylight enabled them to map-read their way to Nottinghamshire.

The main operation on the 13th was against Brest and its resident warships, for which a force of 110 aircraft was drawn from 1, 3 and 5 Groups, while 4 Group detailed thirty-six Whitleys and six Wellingtons for a return to the railway yards at Schwerte. 1 Group detailed twenty-three Wellingtons from Newton and Syerston, including five from 103 Squadron, which took off between 23.10 and 23.30 led for the first time by S/L Lane. Four of the Wellingtons were carrying seven 500 pounders, while one was loaded with a single 1,000 pounder and five 500 pounders. The route for Brest followed a familiar track from the Dorset coast, normally passing to the west of the Channel Islands to make landfall somewhere in the region of St Malo, before traversing the Finistere peninsula. All of the 103 Squadron participants reached the target to find seven-tenths cloud at 15,000 feet and good visibility but also a smoke generator in operation. The crews of S/L Lane, F/L Scott and P/Os Ewart and Muggeridge carried out high-level bombing runs from 12,500 to 15,000 feet, mostly after spending a considerable time planning their approach, while P/O Anderson and crew, having spent thirty minutes studying the defences to find the best way in, glided down to three thousand feet to attack the torpedo boat station. They experienced no opposition until opening up the throttles to race away, whereupon they were immediately caught in searchlights and subjected to intense flak, which forced them down to 900 feet.

From this point and for the remainder of the month Cologne and Düsseldorf became the main focus of attention. The former was the objective for a force of Hampdens on the 14/15th, and thereafter, the two cities were attacked simultaneously on no fewer than eight occasions from the night of the 15/16th. While 105 and sixty-five aircraft respectively were being prepared to attack these locations on the night of the 16/17th, thirty-nine 1 Group Wellington crews from Newton, Swinderby and Syerston were briefed for Duisburg. The seven-strong 103 Squadron element took off between 22.50 and 23.05 with S/L Lane and the newly-promoted S/L Kelly the senior pilots on duty, having been briefed to target the Ruhrort docks complex, for which each was carrying three 500 pounders, a single 250 pounder and four SBCs of 4lb incendiaries. They found weather conditions and visibility in the target area to be good, but as always, intense searchlight activity and flak made for an uncomfortable time as all from the squadron carried out their attacks from between 10,000 and 16,000 feet either side of 01.30. Just one aircraft failed to return from Duisburg, 103 Squadron's N2849, which contained the crew of S/L Kelly and crashed in Belgium without survivors. S/L Kelly was an officer of great experience, who had been promoted from within the squadron, and had three times been Mentioned in Despatches. He and his crew would be keenly missed by the squadron and Newton communities.

Cologne, Düsseldorf and Duisburg were back on the target list twenty-four hours later, when 1 Group detailed twenty-six Wellingtons from Newton and Binbrook for a return to Duisburg. Five 103 Squadron Wellingtons were loaded with a 1,000 pounder, three 500 pounders and three SBCs of 4lb incendiaries each and took off between 22.45 and 23.10 with F/L Scott the senior pilot on duty. They were followed into the air at 23.30 by the freshman crews of Sgts Addy and Munro, who were bound for Boulogne to join others in an attack on the docks and shipping. P/O Ball and crew were unable to climb above 12,000 feet and dropped their load on Texel as a last resort target, leaving the remainder to reach the western Ruhr in good conditions, although prevented by thick industrial haze from identifying the docks area aiming point. Bombing was carried out from between 14,500 and 16,000 feet on the general built-up area, aided by the light from flares, and bursts were observed among buildings and railway tracks. On the way home, F/L Scott and crew were stalked by two enemy aircraft, both of which were evaded, although one did attack from four hundred yards range without effect. Meanwhile, Sgt Addy and crew had abandoned their sortie to Boulogne almost immediately after taking off because of engine trouble, but Sgt Munro and crew delivered their sixteen 250 pounders from 13,500 feet and watched them burst in the target area.

A force of 115 aircraft was assembled on the 20th to send to Kiel in search of the battleship Tirpitz, the new pride of the German fleet since the sinking of her sister ship, Bismarck. 1 Group contributed thirteen Wellingtons from Newton, seven of them provided by 103 Squadron, whose crews had been briefed to leave the target area no later than 02.15 in order to vacate enemy territory before dawn. Sadly, when S/L Lane led them away between 22.40 and 22.50, most had not been allowed sufficient time to reach the target and bomb the main telegraph office before the deadline expired. Ten-tenths cloud lay across the entire Schleswig-Holstein peninsula, with tops at 5,000 feet in the target area, and this prevented anything but an area attack from taking place on largely estimated positions. S/L Lane and crew arrived at 01.50 and bombed flak concentrations from 15,500 feet, while Sgt Munro and crew were the only others from the squadron to turn up and delivered their 1,000 pounder and 500 pounders from 15,000 feet at 02.08. Sgt Muggeridge and crew had turned back when an hour out over the North Sea, while the others simply ran out of time and attacked flak concentrations on the Island of Sylt and the towns of Schleswig and Niebüll from between 14,000 and 18,000 feet. While the above was in progress, Sgt Addy and crew attacked the docks and shipping at Boulogne with sixteen 250 pounders from 11,000 feet and watched them burst, before returning safely to land at 03.40 after four-and-a-quarter hours aloft.

A force of sixty-two Wellingtons and Whitleys assembled on the 23rd for the next assault on Cologne included a 1 Group contribution of fifteen of the former from Newton, while elements of 5 Group attended to Düsseldorf. Seven 103 Squadron aircraft took to the air between 23.00 and 23.15 with F/L Scott the senior pilot on duty and each carrying two 500 pounders, one 250 pounder and six SBCs of 4lb incendiaries. They made landfall on the Belgian coast, from where thunder cloud began to build and the target was found under layer cloud with tops at 4,000 feet, which combined with ground haze to hamper their efforts to identify the aiming point in the industrial heart of the city on the eastern bank of the Rhine. Bombing was carried out from 14,500 to 15,500 feet and bursts, explosions and fires were observed, but local sources reported little damage and no casualties.

Small-scale operations were mounted against Cologne, Kiel and Düsseldorf on the night of the 26/27th and involved a 1 Group contribution of fifteen Wellingtons from Newton. 103 Squadron was responsible for six of them, which were to target the last-mentioned in concert with a contingent of 5 Group Hampdens. They were loaded with a 1,000 pounder, three 500 pounders, a single 250 pounder and two SBCs and took off between 23.05 and 23.20 with F/L Scott the senior pilot on duty. He and his crew were among three to be persuaded by appalling weather conditions to curtail their sortie, having run into icing conditions and a violent snowstorm at 14,000 feet south of Liege in Belgium. They had spotted Knokke aerodrome on the way in and backtracked to attack it from 12,500 feet at 03.15. P/O Ewart and crew pushed through the same storm area to reach the primary target, but after searching for thirty minutes were compelled by ice accretion to head for home and bombed the aerodrome at Haamstede on Zeeland Island at the mouth of the Scheldt from 14,000 feet at 02.40. By this time, Sgt Addy and crew had turned back from the Dutch coast because of a technical issue, leaving the others to bomb the primary on e.t.a from around 15,000 feet. While this operation was in progress the freshman crew of Sgt Bucknole attacked the docks at Emden from 14,000 feet at 01.40 in more favourable weather conditions.

Binbrook and Syerston represented 1 Group on the night of the 27/28th, when Bremen was the target for 108 Wellingtons and Whitleys, while 5 Group Hampdens operated against the shipyards in Vegesack further downstream of the Weser. The night's activities resulted in fourteen failures to return, the heaviest loss yet in a single night, and eleven of these were 4 Group Whitleys, 31% of those dispatched. Luftwaffe night-fighters were probably largely responsible, and the disproportionately high losses among the Whitley brigade was a concern that perhaps pointed to the increasing vulnerability of the type compared with its contemporaries. However, as events were to prove, sporadic losses now belonged to the past as the enemy defences became more organized and adept in the face of greater Bomber Command activity and a steady rate of attrition would afflict all front-line squadrons from now on, with multiple losses from a single operation a regular feature.

Two nights later it was the turn of Swinderby at the same target, while a modest mixed force of just twenty-eight assorted aircraft delivered a surprisingly effective attack on Hamburg. The last night of the month saw further small-scale attacks on Cologne, Duisburg and Düsseldorf, for which 1 Group put up nine Wellingtons from Newton for the last mentioned. The four 103 Squadron participants took off between 23.00 and 23.05 with S/L Lane the senior pilot on duty and the main railway station as the aiming point but lost the services of P/O Purcivall and crew to port engine trouble as they traversed Belgium, and they bombed the aerodrome at Nivelles to the south of Brussels. The others found clear skies and good visibility and S/L Lane and crew approached from the north to bomb from 17,000 feet at 01.34, and P/O Ball and crew followed up from 15,500 feet and observed their bombs fall onto a large building close to the aiming point and set off explosions and a bright fire that illuminated their aircraft. Sgt Greey and crew carried out their attack from 17,000 feet at 02.02 and all were enthusiastic about the explosions and fires observed in the target area, although it is unlikely that significant damage was achieved.

During the course of the month, operations had been conducted against thirteen targets on ten nights and sixty sorties were dispatched for the loss of two aircraft and crews.

July 1941

The main focus of operations during July would be upon manufacturing centres in the Ruhr, including Cologne, and at other locations in the Münsterland between the Ruhr and north-western Germany. The major cities of Bremen, Hamburg and Hannover would continue to attract attention, and it would not be until the final third of the month that targets in southern Germany, principally, Frankfurt and Mannheim, found themselves in the bomb sights of moderately sized forces. Bremen, Cologne and Duisburg hosted fairly small-scale operations on the night of the 2/3rd, for which 1 Group detailed the Binbrook and Syerston squadrons.

The briefing of sixty-one Wellington and twenty-nine Whitley crews on the 3rd revealed that they were to participate in that night's main operation, which was against the Krupp complex in Essen and its dedicated marshalling yards, although they were unlikely to be over the target at the same time. The Krupp organisation had been the largest manufacturer of weapons in Europe since before the Great War, had a hand in all aspects of German war production from tanks to artillery and ship and U-Boot construction, and was given a controlling share in all major heavy engineering companies in Germany and the occupied countries. It also built manufacturing sites in other parts of Germany, many situated close to concentration camps, and employed vast numbers of forced workers in all of its factories. Once known as "Die Waffenschmiede des Reichs", the weapon-forge of the realm, its manufacturing sites in Essen included the Friedrich Krupp steelworks, the Friedrich Krupp locomotive and general engineering works, the Altenberg zinc works, the Presswerk plastics factory, the Goldschmidt non-ferrous metals smelting plant, six coal mines and ten coke-oven plants, all situated either within or close to the four Borbeck districts, in a segment radiating out from near the city centre as far as the Rhine-Herne Canal on the north-western boundary on the banks of the Emscher River. The steel and engineering works alone employed in the region of eighty thousand people, and the company's sites covered an area of more than two thousand acres, of which three hundred acres were occupied by factories and workshops. All of that production capacity required massive rail and canal access in the form of marshalling yards and its own harbour, and energy from at least four nearby power stations.

At the same time, 1 Group would be attacking shipyards in Bremen with twenty-nine Wellingtons from Newton and Swinderby in concert with Hampdens of 5 Group. While the seven 103 Squadron Wellingtons were being made ready at Newton, a new station at Elsham Wolds, fifty miles away in northern Lincolnshire, was officially opening for business as the main body of station staff moved in to prepare the way for the arrival of 103 Squadron a week hence. They took off for north-western Germany between 23.00 and 23.30 with S/L Lane the senior pilot on duty and P/O Purcivall and crew already compromised by a delayed departure, which may have been related to the inability of their chariot to climb beyond 12,500 feet. Having crossed into Germany with no prospect of catching up the lost time, they bombed a searchlight concentration in the Meppen area and headed home. On landing, they would find S/L Lane and crew had arrived ahead of them after their port engine had begun to show signs of stress at the Dutch coast. The others pressed on, free to adopt whichever route suited them, some of the force preferring to remain over the sea and pinpoint on Heligoland or the uninhabited Scharhörn Island located nine miles north of Cuxhaven, while others made landfall on the Dutch coast and flew directly to the target. All, though, encountered the same conditions of ten-tenths cloud over the sea and the additional challenge of haze over land. Cloud in the target area was reported to be at between 8,000 and 15,000 feet, which completely obscured all ground references and left the crews reliant on evidence of flak to guide them to the general area of the primary target and the briefed alternatives at Bremerhaven and Wilhelmshaven. Bombing by the 103 Squadron crews took place from

12,000 to 16,000 feet between 01.36 and 02.20, but they were unable to assess the effectiveness of their efforts.

F/L Max returned to the squadron on the 4th, after his release from ferrying duties and would find many new faces to get to know. There was no briefing at Newton on that day as 1 Group was not involved in the main event, against Brest, or more accurately, the cruisers Scharnhorst, Gneisenau and Prinz Eugen, which were to be left to 3 and 4 Groups, while the stations at Binbrook and Syerston represented 1 Group at Lorient and Cherbourg. When twenty-seven crews attended briefings at Newton and Swinderby on the 5th, they learned that they would be attacking a new target, the gas works and power station at Bielefeld, situated north of the Ruhr to the east and south-east respectively of Münster and Osnabrück, both of which were also to be targeted on this night, the former by elements of 3 and 4 Groups and the latter by 5 Group. 103 Squadron made ready seven Wellingtons and sent them off between 23.00 and 23.10 with S/L Lane the senior pilot on duty, and they were followed into the air at 23.25 by the freshman crews of P/Os Petrie and Lund, who were bound for Rotterdam to attack the docks and shipping. All involved in the main event arrived in the target area to find largely clear skies and good visibility and most favoured a glide approach to release their bombs from 9,000 to 17,000 feet between 01.30 and 01.50 and most observed bursts in the built-up area and fires developing as they turned away. Returning crews were enthusiastic about the outcome, and the gas works is believed to have blown up. Meanwhile, the freshman crews carried out glide attacks from 10,000 and 13,500 feet and the Petrie crew saw their bombs impact on Zalmhaven.

Newton sat out the following night's raid on the enemy warships at Brest, which was conducted by eighty-eight Hampdens and nineteen 1 Group Wellingtons from Binbrook and Syerston and failed to produce the hoped-for results in the face of an effective smoke screen.

Four main targets were posted on stations across the Command on the 7th, Cologne, Osnabrück and Münster for Wellingtons and or Whitleys, while forty Hampdens were to target marshalling yards in the town of Mönchengladbach on the south-western rim of the Ruhr. 1 Group was called upon for a maximum effort and mobilised all stations to come up with fifty-seven Wellingtons as part of an overall force of 114 for the main event at Cologne and five for a freshman attack on the docks and shipping at Boulogne. 103 Squadron dispatched ten aircraft between 23.00 and 23.10 with S/L Lane and F/L Scott the senior pilots on duty and all arrived in the target area to find ideal conditions to exploit. Briefed to aim for the industrial area on the eastern bank of the Rhine, they carried out their attacks from 12,000 to 16,500 feet between 01.55 and 02.25 and contributed to what was a relatively rare event for 1941, a highly effective attack on a German city. Not only was there the expected residential destruction, but a number of industrial premises were severely damaged, three railway lines were cut, and sixty large fires required attention.

Thirty-five Wellington crews attended briefings at Newton and Swinderby on the 8th to learn that they would be returning to Bielefeld that night to target its power station and any remaining serviceable parts of the gasworks. 103 Squadron prepared nine of its Wellingtons and dispatched them between 22.40 and 23.00 with S/L Lane and F/L Scott the senior pilots on duty and benefitting from favourable conditions as they made their way towards the east.

Sgt Addy and crew had taken off last, slightly behind schedule and, unable to make up time, attacked an already burning last resort target from 16,000 feet. All but two of the others delivered their bombs from 12,500 to 15,000 feet between 01.25 and 02.13, mostly following a glide approach and observing bursts among buildings and fires, while the crews of Sgt Munro and P/O Lund headed for Osnabrück and contributed to the raid in progress there from 16,000 and 14,000 feet respectively.

A new Air Ministry directive issued on the 9th signalled an end to the maritime diversion, which had been in force since March. It was now assessed that the enemy's transportation system and the morale of its civilian population represented the weakest points, and that Peirse should direct his main effort in these directions. A new list of targets was drawn up that included all of the main railway centres ringing the industrial Ruhr, the destruction of which would inhibit the import of raw materials and the export of finished products. Railways were relatively precise targets, and were to be attacked during the moon period, while on moonless nights, the Rhine cities of Cologne, Düsseldorf and Duisburg would be easier to locate for "area" attacks. During periods of less favourable weather conditions, Peirse was to launch operations against more distant objectives in northern, eastern and southern Germany, while still making the occasional concession to the U-Boot campaign and continuing to divert a proportion of the Command's resources to the ongoing situation of the enemy "fleet in being" at Brest.

S/L Ingram was posted in from 12 O.T.U at Benson on the 9th to take up a role as flight commander, and he would have a brief time to settle in before sitting in on the briefing on the 10th for a return to Cologne that night by a force of ninety-eight Wellingtons and thirty-two Hampdens. They were to attack a number of aiming points in the industrial heart of the city, among them the Klöckner-Humboldt mechanical engineering works in the Deutz district, situated on the East Bank of the Rhine in the city centre. 1 Group detailed forty Wellingtons from Newton and Swinderby, eleven representing 103 Squadron, which also made ready two others to take the freshman crews of Sgts Hare and Kitney to Boulogne. S/L Lane was the senior pilot on duty as the main-eventers took to the air for the last time in anger from Newton between 22.40 and 22.55, and they were followed by the freshmen at 23.10. They crossed the enemy coast between Ostend and Dunkerque and flew direct to the target, which they found largely hidden beneath eight-tenths cloud and thick haze extending up to 12,000 feet. This forced them to search for a pinpoint, some picking up the Rhine, while others were guided to the general area by searchlights and flak, spending up to forty minutes trying to establish their precise position. Only the crews of F/L Scott, P/Os Ewart, Lund and Purcivall and Sgt Munro attacked the primary target, or believed that they had done so, from 12,500 to 16,000 feet between 01.37 and 02.15, while the others went for alternatives, S/L Lane and crew delivering their bombs on Ostend on the way home, P/O Ball and crew starting a fire at marshalling yards south of Brussels, Sgt Bucknole and crew hitting Aachen and Sgt Addy and crew the town of Brühl to the west of the Rhine south of Cologne. Meanwhile the freshman duo had successfully targeted the docks at Boulogne from 14,000 and 15,500 feet at 01.20 and gained valuable experience in the process.

On the 11th, 103 Squadron moved to Elsham Wolds in north-east Lincolnshire, where it would remain until war's end, and with which it would forever be associated. It was the first resident of this former WWI airfield, which had been extensively redeveloped with a two-thousand-yard main runway, three hangars and twenty-seven concrete dispersal pans. For the majority of new arrivals, the gateway to the site was Barnetby Junction railway station, an out-of-the-way stop-off, given a new lease of life by the war and Bomber Command's insatiable appetite for humankind. The road to Elsham was uphill all the way, straight-on at a major crossroads and then left at the next one to bring into view the table-top flatness of the aerodrome at the highest point of the Wolds. Its exposed, raised location made it a bleak home to the many Australians who were posted there, accustomed as they were back home to balmy breezes, and they bemoaned the chill winds sweeping across the airfield off the North Sea and the dank fogs that rolled in from the same direction. The trip down the hill on nights off in Scunthorpe or at the start of leave was a joyous occasion full of promise of life, but the trudge back up the hill on return was heavy with tension and foreboding.

Three days after arriving at its new home 103 Squadron was back on the order of battle and briefed six crews to join twenty-five others from Swinderby and Syerston in an overall force of seventy-eight Wellingtons from 1 and 3 Groups and nineteen 4 Group Whitleys to target three aiming points in Bremen, the shipyards, the goods station and the Altstadt. The 103 Squadron element departed Elsham Wolds for the first time with hostile intent between 22.55 and 23.05 with S/L Lane the senior pilot on duty and lost the services of S/L Lane and Sgt Hare and their crews to engine issues, the former when close to or over enemy territory. The others delivered their attacks at the primary target from 15,000 to 17,000 feet between 02.05 and 02.29 in the face of some low cloud, haze and an intense searchlight and flak response, and observed bursts and fires but no detail.

Syerston became a 5 Group station on the 20th on the departure of 304 and 305 Squadrons to Lindholme and Cologne was posted as the target on that day for a force of 113 aircraft, among which were thirteen Wellingtons from Elsham Wolds and Binbrook, seven of them provided by 103 Squadron. A further four Wellingtons were made ready to take freshman crews to attack the docks and shipping at Rotterdam in company with seventeen others, and among them was that of F/L Max, who was undertaking his first sortie since returning to the squadron. Those involved in the main event took off between 23.00 and 23.15 with S/L Lane and F/L Scott the senior pilots on duty, and they were followed into the air by the freshmen between 23.30 and 23.50. After enjoying favourable conditions as far as the Dutch coast, cloud began to build to create a more challenging situation in the target area, where ten-tenths cloud at 7,000 feet forced them to bomb on estimated positions based on e.t.a. and searchlight and flak activity. Most of the Elsham crews carried out their attacks from 10,000 to 18,000 feet between 01.45 and 02.08 and observed nothing more than bursts and the glow of burning incendiaries through occasional breaks in the cloud. Sgt Bucknole and crew decided to look elsewhere and bombed at Aachen from 14,500 feet at 01.50, while Sgt Munro and crew attacked a self-evident-military-objective (SEMO) from 15,000 feet at 03.07. The freshmen, meanwhile, benefitted from ideal conditions at Rotterdam and delivered their bomb loads from 10,000 to 15,000 feet between 01.04 and 01.40.

The southern cities of Frankfurt-am-Main and Mannheim were named as the targets for a mini-campaign on three consecutive nights from the 21/22nd, and it would be the former's first taste of a major Bomber Command assault. Thirty-seven Wellingtons and thirty-four

Hampdens were made ready, nineteen of the former at Hemswell and Snaith, while thirty-six Wellingtons and eight Halifaxes were prepared to attack Mannheim city centre some forty-five miles to the south. The two operations were repeated on the following night, this time with sixty-three Hampdens, Whitleys and Wellingtons assigned to Frankfurt and twenty-nine Wellingtons to Mannheim. 1 Group detailed thirteen Wellingtons from Elsham Wolds and Lindholme, the 103 Squadron crews of F/Ls Max and Scott, P/O Purcivall and Sgts Bucknole and Greey taking off between 22.45 and 22.55 and all reaching the target area to find clear skies and only ground haze to impair the vertical visibility. F/L Max and crew were over the target from 02.01 to 02.14 and probably made a number of passes over the aiming point, releasing their bombs from 13,000 feet, shortly before Sgt Bucknole and crew delivered their load from 15,000 feet at 02.15. F/L Scott and crew followed up from 14,000 feet at 02.26 and were the last from the squadron to attack the primary target. Bursts were observed, but intense searchlight and flak activity prevented a detailed assessment of the results and scant information from local sources suggested an ineffective raid. The crews of P/O Purcivall and Sgt Greey were unable to locate the target, but the former spotted a railway through a gap in the clouds twenty-five miles to the north, while the latter bombed the aerodrome at Nivelles on the way home over Belgium. For the first time, in addition to their standard bomb loads, they had been carrying "deckers", an incendiary device also known as "razzle", which was designed to set fire to forests and arable land. It was not destined to be a successful weapon, but its use would continue until its limitations were recognised and resulted in its consignment to the "It was worth a try" file.

On the 23rd, thirty Whitleys were sent to attack the dry dock at La Pallice, the deep-water port located west of La Rochelle on the Biscay coast between St-Nazaire to the north and Bordeaux to the south. It was home to the 3rd U-Boot Flotilla that was feeding wolfpacks into the Atlantic to savage Allied convoys bringing vital supplies to Britain. However, the objective for this operation was the cruiser Scharnhorst, which had slipped away from Brest unnoticed and was feared to be about to break out into the Atlantic for a campaign of surface raiding. A most complex plan under the codename Operation Sunrise had been developed during the preceding week to target Scharnhorst and Gneisenau at Brest in daylight on the 24th, but the discovery that Scharnhorst had slipped away and was now at berth at La Pallice, some two hundred miles further south, demanded a last-minute alteration. It was decided to send the 4 Group Halifax element to attend to her, while the original plan went ahead at Brest. This called for three Fortress 1s of 2 Group's 90 Squadron to open proceedings at 30,000 feet to draw up the enemy fighters, while eighteen 5 Group Hampdens acted as further bait under the umbrella of a Spitfire escort, somewhat in the manner of a 2 Group "Circus" operation to allow the RAF fighters to get amongst the BF109s and FW190s. This was intended to leave the way clear for the seventy-nine Wellingtons from 1, 3 and 4 Groups to sneak in and attack the objectives unescorted. The 1 Group Wellingtons were to attack in eight sections of three, with 150 Squadron constituting sections 1 and 2, 103 Squadron forming sections 3 and 4 and the final four sections consisting of Binbrook's 12 and 142 Squadrons. The 103 Squadron sections were to be led by S/L Lane, with W/C Lowe acting as second pilot, and F/L Max, and they departed Elsham Wolds at 11.00 to fly with a reserve aircraft to a forward base at Tangmere near the Sussex coast. The main force was completed by a further thirty-six Wellingtons from 3 Group and nineteen Merlin-powered Mk II variants from 4 Group.

According to the 1 Group ORB, zero-hour was set for 14.00, but this may be GMT rather than the BST as it was around 15.00 when the 1 Group element approached the French coast and prepared to begin their attack. At this point it became apparent that the flak and fighter opposition was going to be much more intense than had been expected, with many engagements taking place between fighters and bombers. S/L Lane's section attracted the attention of a BF109 shortly before reaching the target and came under attack from astern and from the beam, while all three Wellingtons returned fire and, it appears, scored hits. The fighter finally focussed on Sgt Bucknole's N2770, which had fallen back slightly and was seen to slip away from the formation with an engine on fire and the fighter in pursuit. The engine fire was observed to go out, but the Wellington was unable to regain the formation and was last seen at around 8,000 feet still sinking towards the sea, into which it ultimately crashed with fatal consequences for the crew. It seems that the BF109 had also been mortally wounded and was seen to enter a spin before hitting the ground with the pilot still inside. F/L Max's formation sighted two BF109s shortly after crossing the French coast at 16,000 feet at 15.05 and both closed in, one to be shot down at a range of 250 yards and from which the pilot was seen to bale out. The second fighter received a direct hit at one hundred yards range and was last seen corkscrewing nose down towards the sea. The 103 Squadron Wellingtons were carrying 500lb SAP bombs and S/L Lane and crew delivered theirs from 15,500 feet at 15.16, observing them to straddle the docks with at least one exploding close to the bows of one of the ships. F/L Scott and crew suffered the frustration of a complete hang-up and would jettison their load into the sea on the way home. F/L Max led the second section in to attack from 14,800 feet at 15.20 with the crews of P/O Ball and Sgt Greey in tow and some bomb bursts were observed in a line from south-west to north-east along the western dry dock. Ten of the Wellingtons were brought down, in exchange for which were a number of unconfirmed hits on Gneisenau, but Scharnhorst suffered more severely at La Pallice, while inflicting heavy casualties on the attacking Halifaxes, and she was forced to return to Brest to take advantage of the superior repair facilities on offer.

That night forty-seven Whitleys and Wellingtons targeted the port of Emden, for which operation 1 Group detailed sixteen Wellingtons from Elsham Wolds and Lindholme. 103 Squadron dispatched six aircraft between 23.25 and 23.40 with no senior pilot on duty and the freshman crew of Sgt Gorrie at 23.45 to attack the docks and shipping at Cherbourg. All of the main element reached the target in favourable conditions and carried out their attacks from 11,000 to 16,000 feet between 01.45 and 02.08 in the face of an intense flak response. R1397 sent a "NGZ" signal to confirm attacking the target, but failed to arrive back at Elsham Wolds, and no trace of it or the crew of P/O Lund was ever found. Sgt Gorrie and crew were unable to identify Cherbourg, and to their credit, if the ORB is to be believed, flew three hundred miles to the north-east to deliver a glide-attack on the Luftwaffe aerodrome at Gilze-Rijen from 12,000 feet at 02.20. Sadly, three 250 pounders hung-up but the incendiaries set off a fire.

During the course of the month the squadron took part in nine night operations and one in daylight and dispatched eighty-three sorties for the loss of two Wellingtons and crews.

August 1941

The policy of dispatching small numbers of aircraft to various targets simultaneously rarely produced effective results, but it would be persisted with throughout the remainder of the year, and in fact, until a new Commander-in-Chief arrived in 1942 to provide a different direction. Germany's capital and second cities and the port of Kiel were posted as the targets for the first night of operations on the 2nd, for which forces of fifty-three, eighty and fifty aircraft respectively were assembled. 1 Group assigned fifteen Wellingtons from Elsham Wolds and Lindholme to target Hamburg's railway system and eight from Binbrook for Berlin. 103 Squadron made ready nine Wellingtons for the main event and another to take the newly-arrived crew of F/O Leslie to Cherbourg, all of which departed Elsham Wolds between 22.15 and 23.00 with S/L Lane the senior pilot on duty. F/L Scott and crew turned back shortly after crossing the English coast, but the ORB entry is too indistinct to determine the cause. The others encountered six to nine-tenths cloud at 10,000 feet over the target and were guided to the mark by intense searchlight and heavy flak at between 11,000 and 17,000 feet. Bombs were delivered by most from 11,000 to 16,000 feet between 01.42 and 02.12, while P/O Purcivall and crew were persuaded by ten-tenths cloud to seek out an alternative target and flew to the south-west to Bremen, where they glided down from 14,000 to 12,000 feet and watched their bombs burst in the centre of the town. On the way home, Sgt Kelsey was forced to ditch a fuel-starved X3204 at 07.06 some forty miles off Spurn Point on the Humber, from where he and his crew were picked up safe and sound at 20.30 by a rescue launch. Meanwhile, F/O Leslie and crew had bombed the docks at Cherbourg from 12,000 feet at 01.20. The Hamburg operation was reasonably effective for the period and the prevailing conditions and resulted in five large fires and the de-housing of more than seven hundred people.

F/L Roy Max was posted to 11 O.T.U at Bassingbourn on the 5th, but his operational career was not over and on the 19th of August 1943 he would be appointed to command 75(NZ) Squadron, a post in which he would remain until the following May. During that winter, once the Stirling had been withdrawn from operations over Germany, he would take part in SOE operations and later, interdiction raids in France as part of the pre-invasion campaign.

His presence at Elsham Wolds would be missed for a time, but the war continued and bomber stations across the Command were a hive of activity on the 5th as preparations were put in hand for three operations that night against targets in southern Germany. Ninety-eight Wellingtons and Hampdens were assigned to Mannheim, while ninety-seven aircraft, including some 4 Group Halifaxes, attended to railway targets in Karlsruhe, and forty-six Whitleys and twenty-two Wellingtons tried their hand against an unidentified "special" target at Frankfurt, which, according to the 102 Squadron ORB, was the post office. Elsham Wolds, Snaith and Lindholme provided the 1 Group element for what would be the second of three raids on Frankfurt in the space of four nights. The eight 103 Squadron Wellingtons took to the air between 22.15 and 22.45 with S/L Lane the senior pilot on duty and W/C Lowe flying as second pilot with S/L Scott, but the effort was reduced to seven when S/L Lane had to abort his sortie almost immediately because of control problems. The others found the target area to be relatively free of cloud and the good visibility assisted both attacker and defender alike, the searchlight cones ensnaring aircraft and the intense flak inflicting damage on many. The crews of F/O Leslie and Sgt Hare carried out level bombing runs from 15,000 and 17,000 feet respectively, while the others preferred a glide approach to release their bombs from 10,000 to 14,000 feet between 01.07 and 01.27. The "NGZ" signal, "target attacked", was received from Sgt Greey and crew, but W5656 failed to return, and it was established eventually that it had crashed without survivors some nine miles south-west of Calais. Although returning crews claimed an accurate attack, the only local report came out of Mainz twenty miles away, and reported bombs falling there.

The same three main targets were posted again on the 6th for much reduced forces, and Hemswell and Snaith were responsible for the 1 Group contribution of sixteen Wellingtons for Frankfurt. Having been grounded again, the troublesome operational career of the Manchesters resumed on the night of the 7/8th, when three from 207 Squadron and fifty-four Hampdens were made ready to join forces with forty-nine other aircraft to attack the mighty Krupp complex in Essen. 1 Group detailed twenty-eight Wellingtons from Binbrook and Lindholme and seven from Elsham Wolds, the last mentioned taking off between 00.01 and 00.40 with S/L Lane the senior pilot on duty. At 01.45, the crew of Sgt Kitney departed Elsham as the sole 1 Group representatives among six freshmen raiding the docks and shipping at Boulogne. The main element adopted a course to the Scheldt estuary, pinpointing on Tilburg as they crossed Holland to enter Germany near Wesel. The region was criss-crossed with waterways, including the Rivers Rhine, Ruhr and Lippe, each providing strong navigation references through the industrial haze once the cloud had diminished to three to four tenths at 8,000 to 10,000 feet as the target area drew near. P/O Purcivall and crew had already turned back by this stage after being attacked by a Ju88 at 10,000 feet over the Dutch coast at 01.35 and sustaining a hit on the rear fuselage that cut the oxygen and hydraulic feed to the rear turret. The gunners had managed to fire off a few rounds that were seen to hit the enemy aircraft, which dived away and was not encountered again. At the same time, P/O Ball and crew lost the use of their oxygen system, and after failing to locate Rotterdam docks as a last resort target, brought their bombs home. The others carried out their attacks between 02.18 and 02.55 from 15,000 to 18,000 feet, exactly the height at which the intense heavy flak shells were bursting. Local sources reported only thirty-nine high explosives bombs and two hundred incendiaries falling in the city, causing little useful damage, while other Ruhr locations received the rest. Meanwhile, Sgt Kitney and crew had encountered seven-tenths cloud at 12,000 feet over Boulogne and glided down from 15,000 to 13,500 feet to deliver their bombs at 03.42, observing them to straddle docks 4 and 5 and cause fires.

F/L Cross arrived from 11 O.T.U at Bassingbourn on the 9th as flight commander elect, once promoted to acting squadron leader rank. 1 Group operated infrequently and in small numbers during the week after Essen, and it was the 14th before major activity returned with the posting of Hannover as the target for 150 aircraft, Braunschweig (Brunswick) for eighty and Magdeburg for fifty. These three northern cities lie in a line east-south-east from Hannover with fifty miles between Hannover and Braunschweig and Magdeburg a further fifty miles beyond. The targets in Braunschweig included machine and munitions factories, inland docks, research institutions, canneries, railway maintenance works and the German Research Centre for Aviation. Targets near the city included the Reichswerke Hermann Göring steelworks at Salzgitter and the KdF-Stadt Volkswagen works near Fallersleben. Magdeburg had been a regular destination for small forces as far back as the summer of 1940, when the Command targeted a ship lift at the eastern end of the Mittelland Canal at its junction with the River Elbe, and the Bergius-process Braunkohle AG synthetic oil refinery (hydrogenation plant), both located in the same Rothensee district to the north of the city centre.

Eight Wellingtons departed Elsham Wolds for Hannover between 21.30 and 22.00 with S/L Lane the senior pilot on duty and the main railway station as their briefed aiming point. P/O Purcivall and crew had struggled to climb as they crossed the North Sea and having reached an inadequate 11,300 feet at the Dutch coast and failed to locate Rotterdam docks as a last resort target, turned for home. On discovering that their oxygen supply was running low, P/O Ball and crew attacked Soesterberg aerodrome near Utrecht in Holland from 12,000 feet at 22.32, leaving the others to press on over diminishing cloud to find Hannover under clear skies. Searchlight cones of up to twenty beams each ringed the city and co-ordinated with flak batteries to provide a hostile reception, into which the Elsham Wolds crews ventured to deliver their attacks from 10,000 to 15,000 feet between 00.13 and 00.50, many after a glide approach and some having spent twenty minutes or more in preparation. The operation cost seven Wellingtons, two belonging to 1 Group's 150 Squadron, and four Whitleys, and as usual, no local report was forthcoming from Hannover.

Railway installations in Cologne, Düsseldorf and Duisburg were posted as the targets for operations on the 16th, the Rhineland capital for a predominantly 4 Group force, while 5 Group dealt with the second-mentioned and 1 and 3 Group Wellingtons went for Duisburg with Binbrook, Hemswell and Lindholme providing the 1 Group contribution. According to the 1 Group ORB, fourteen Wellingtons were detailed from Snaith and Elsham Wolds on the 17th to take part in that night's raid by forty-one of the type on railway installations again in Duisburg. However, the 103 Squadron ORB records this operation as taking place on the 18th, when, in fact, Hemswell provided all of the 1 Group participants in a force that also numbered forty-one Wellingtons. Further proof that the 103 Squadron raid took place on the 17th is that Duisburg was covered by cloud on this night and only one aircraft positively identified it through a gap, while clear skies prevailed on the 18th and good bombing results were claimed. The eight-strong 103 Squadron element departed Elsham Wolds between 00.05 and 00.40 with S/L Lane the senior pilot on duty on what was to be a night of underachievement, caused largely by the unfavourable weather conditions. P/O Leslie and crew turned back after around thirty minutes because of an issue with the front turret, and S/L Lane and crew were some forty miles south-east of Cromer when icing caused the port engine to falter and persuaded them to jettison their load into the sea. P/O Purcivall and crew brought their bombs home after the rear turret became unserviceable and Sgt Gorrie and crew returned theirs to store also having failed to locate the primary target or a suitable alternative. This left just four Elsham Wolds crews to deliver an attack on estimated positions from 12,000 to 17,000 feet between 02.25 and 02.45 and return safely with little of value to report at debriefing. While they were away, Elsham Wolds had been attacked by a single enemy aircraft with small calibre bombs, which caused little damage but apparently, a number of fatal casualties.

On the 18th, the Butt Report on the Command's operational effectiveness was released, and it sent shock waves reverberating around the War Cabinet and the Air Ministry. Having taken into account around four thousand bombing photos produced during night operations in June and July, it concluded that only a fraction of bombs had fallen within miles of their intended targets, and the poorest performances had been over the Ruhr. It was a massive blow to morale and demonstrated that thus far the efforts of the crews had been almost totally ineffective in reducing Germany's capacity to wage war. The claims of the crews were shown to be wildly optimistic, as were those of the Command, and Sir Richard Peirse's tenure as Commander-in-Chief would forever be blighted by the report's revelations.

While the report was being digested that evening, railways remained the main interest, and installations at Cologne and Duisburg were posted as the targets for sixty-two and forty-one aircraft respectively, for which the Polish Squadrons at Hemswell represented 1 Group. On the 19th, orders were received by all heavy groups to provide aircraft for an attack on Kiel's railway infrastructure, and a force of 108 aircraft was assembled accordingly. 1 Group detailed fifteen Wellingtons from Binbrook and Elsham Wolds, but this number would be reduced and only the five 103 Squadron crews of P/Os Allen, Leslie, Petrie and Purcivall and Sgt Hare presented themselves for take-off between 21.10 and 22.00. S/L Ingram had been scheduled to fly as second pilot to Sgt Kitney, but theirs was one of the sorties to be scrubbed and this was the second time that S/L Ingram had been thwarted in this way and was still to register his first operation with 103 Squadron. There was also a small-scale freshman raid on the docks and shipping at Le Havre, for which the crews of P/O Westlake and F/L Crawford departed Elsham Wolds at 20.45 and 21.35 respectively. Weather conditions were unfavourable with thick cloud and icing during the outward flight and nine-tenths cloud in the target area with tops at up to 16,000 feet. P/O Purcivall and crew turned back early because of intercom and R/T failure, leaving the others to carry out their attacks from 14,300 to 18,000 feet between 00.26 and 01.01, and they were among fewer than seventy crews to report bombing in the target area, where heavy rain was falling. Meanwhile, the freshmen had carried out glide attacks at Le Havre from 9,000 and 10,000 feet at 23.03 and 00.28 respectively.

A series of three operations against Mannheim began on the night of the 22/23rd, for which a force of fifty-six 1 and 3 Group Wellingtons joined forces with forty-one 5 Group Hampdens, 1 Group providing fifteen of the Wellingtons, nine of them made ready by 103 Squadron and taking off between 21.25 and 21.55 with F/Ls Crawford and Scott the senior pilots on duty. They were preceded into the air at 21.25 by S/L Ingram and crew bound for Le Havre as he finally undertook his first sortie since joining the squadron. P/Os Ball and Westlake were unable to coax more than 10,500 feet out of their reluctant Wellingtons and the latter bombed Ostend docks at 23.16, while the former, having penetrated deeper into enemy territory, attacked a beacon near an undecipherable aerodrome at 00.30. P/O Petrie and crew brought their bombs home after contending with an overheating engine and the failure of their intercom and picked up flak damage over Ostend. The others arrived in the target area to find four to eight-tenths cloud with tops at up to 10,000 feet, but F/L Crawford and crew claimed ten-tenths cloud and abandoned their attempt to attack the primary target. On the way home, they spotted some lights near the port of Nieuwpoort, a mile inland from the Belgian coast, and dumped their bombs on it from 10,000 feet at 03.35. F/L Scott and crew had dropped their 1,000 pounder at the primary target on estimated position from 13,000 feet at 00.45 and retained the rest of the load perhaps to employ against a target of opportunity, and they also bombed Nieuwpoort from 15,000 feet at 02.56. This left the crews of Sgts Gorrie and Hare, P/O Allen and F/O Leslie to attack the primary from 13,000 to 15,000 feet between 00.21 and 00.50, mostly after glide approaches. Returning crews reported bomb bursts and fires, but local sources claimed that only one house had been destroyed and five others lightly damaged. S/L Ingram and crew fared better at Le Havre, where, in good visibility, they glided down from 12,000 to 10,500 feet to release their load at 23.18 and watched them burst across the docks.

W/C Lowe was posted to Hemswell on the 25th, and W/C Ryan moved in the opposite direction as his successor. Binbrook and Hemswell took care of 1 Group business at Cologne on the 26th as part of a force of ninety-nine aircraft, which wasted much of its effort to the east of the city. Orders arriving on the 1 Group stations of Elsham Wolds and Snaith on the 27th revealed a return to Mannheim for ninety-one aircraft from all heavy groups, which were to target the main railway station and other aiming points within the city. The seven 103 Squadron Wellingtons participating in the main event took off between 20.30 and 20.45 with F/L Scott the senior pilot on duty. S/L Ingram had been first away at 20.30 on a freshman trip to bomb the docks and shipping at Boulogne and S/L Lane and crew set off for the same destination at 21.50. Meanwhile, F/L Scott and his crew lost the use of their intercom during the North Sea crossing and unloaded the contents of their bomb bay on Flushing aerodrome on Zeeland at the mouth of the Scheldt after a glide to 11,000 feet at 22.30. Sgt Gorrie and crew experienced elevator problems and selected Ostend as their last resort target, bombing it from 12,600 feet at 22.58. The other Mannheim-bound crews arrived in the target area to find a small amount of cloud but ground haze to compromise the search for aiming points, and when F/O Leslie and crew identified the junction of the Rhine and Neckar rivers to the north of the city centre, they opted to bomb there from 17,500 feet at 23.30 and claimed to have set off two medium fires and four smaller ones. The others delivered their attacks from 11,000 to 14,000 feet between 23.43 and 00.06 and returned safely from a raid which achieved little significant damage, despite the enthusiastic claims by some crews. S/L Lane and crew were back home after three hours having executed a glide approach from 11,000 down to 9,000 feet at 22.50 and observing a number of bursts across the northern end of Boulogne's tidal harbour and a large spreading fire. S/L Ingram and crew, in contrast, failed to pinpoint the target and brought their bombs back after a trip of almost five hours.

Duisburg was the main target on the following night for a force of 118 aircraft, in which Binbrook represented 1 Group, while the 103 Squadron Wellington containing the crew of P/O Jones also took off from Binbrook at 23.50 to attack the docks and shipping at Ostend. They encountered eight-tenths cloud at the French coast and were unable to locate the target, and after spending a considerable time in searching for an alternative, came upon something of interest about ten miles south-west of Rotterdam and bombed it from 11,000 feet at 02.10.

On the afternoon of the 29th, the call went forth on the stations of 4 and 5 Groups for crews to gather in the briefing rooms to learn of their part in what would be the largest raid yet sent against Frankfurt. A total of 143 aircraft was made ready out on the dispersals, while their crews were informed that railway and inland harbour installations were to be the aiming points. At the same time, 1 and 3 Groups were ordered to prepare for yet another operation against Mannheim and put together a force of ninety-four Wellingtons, 1 Group detailing twenty-eight from Elsham Wolds, Snaith and Lindholme, not all of which would take-off. 103 Squadron made ready eight Wellingtons, which got away between 20.20 and 20.31 with F/L Scott the senior pilot on duty and lost the services of P/O Westlake and crew to the failure of their gyro and wireless. P/O Murchie and crew were unable to climb beyond 12,000 feet and bombed an unidentified alternative target from 10,000 feet at 22.09, while F/O Leslie and crew ran into an electrical storm that prevented them also from climbing. They had reached 10,000 feet by the time they arrived in the frontier region between Luxembourg and Germany and dropped their bombs at 22.55 when some ten miles south of the city of Trier. The crews of F/L Scott, F/O Wardhaugh, P/O Purcivall and Sgt Gorrie arrived over the Mannheim area to encounter eight to ten-tenths cloud with tops at 12,000 feet and carried out their attacks from 11,000 to 17,000 feet between 23.25 and 23.40. It seems that P/O Oldfield and crew had abandoned their sortie and were homebound at around 23.00 when R1213 was struck by lightning and crashed near Vlissingen (Flushing) on Zeeland at the mouth of the Scheldt. P/O Oldfield and his rear gunner were the only survivors, and they were taken into captivity. As these events were unfolding, the freshman crews of S/L Cross and Sgt Koslowski departed Elsham Wolds for Le Havre to bomb the docks and shipping, but neither was able to locate it through ten-tenths cloud, and while S/L Cross brought his bombs home, the Koslowski crew let theirs go over what looked like a flare-path located south-south-east of the port from 8,000 feet at 01.40.

The month's final operations were posted on the 31st and involved 103 aircraft at Cologne and seventy-one to target the Krupp complex at Essen, 1 Group supporting the latter with a detail of thirty-two Wellingtons from Binbrook, Elsham Wolds and Hemswell, not all of which would take off. 103 Squadron made ready eight of its own and sent them on their way between 20.10 and 20.50 with S/L Cross the senior pilot on duty for the first time. *(The ORB entries for this period are mostly undecipherable and the following is what can be made out.)* They arrived over the central Ruhr to find ten-tenths cloud, through which F/O Leslie and crew bombed the general area from 14,000 feet at 22.22 without a clue as to what was beneath them at the time. Sgt Hare and crew made a level run at 14,000 feet at 22.30, while S/L Cross and crew bombed from 16,000 feet at 22.35 and somehow observed bursts. At the same time F/O Wardhaugh and crew released their load after gliding down to 12,000 feet and P/O Murchie and crew chanced upon a gap in the cloud, through which they identified the target and saw a large fire to aim their bombs at from 15,000 feet at 22.48. Sgt Gorrie and crew glided down to release their load from 13,000 feet at 23.02 and the last of the Elsham Wolds gang to arrive at the primary target, Sgt Koslowski and crew, attacked at 23.19 from 14,000 feet. F/L Scott and crew had been unable to identify the target and on the way home bombed an unidentified aerodrome from 11,000 feet at 23.12. According to local sources and in keeping with the general performance characterizing the year to date, the operation was a failure that caused damage to one house. The squadron ORB placed this operation in the September record of activities, rather than those for August.

During the course of the month the squadron operated against seventeen targets on eleven nights and dispatched eighty-seven sorties for the loss of a single Wellington and crew.

September 1941

September began for 103 Squadron with the posting of S/L Lane to Snaith, the home of 150 Squadron, on the 1st and it was Snaith and Lindholme that took care of 1 Group business at Frankfurt on the 2nd. Brest and its lodgers had been left in relative peace since July, and this situation was to be rectified by a force of 140 aircraft from all groups on the 3rd, 1 Group detailing nineteen Wellingtons from Binbrook and seven from Elsham Wolds. Six 103 Squadron aircraft actually took off between 19.15 and 19.30 with S/L Ingram flying as second pilot to Sgt Hare, but all from 1, 4 and 5 Groups were recalled because of deteriorating weather conditions in their station areas and four returned to Elsham Wolds as instructed. Sgt Koslowski and P/O Murchie failed to respond and continued on to the target along with the 3 Group contingent, whose stations in Cambridgeshire were unaffected by fog, and found clear skies over the target but an effective smoke screen in operation. The Koslowski crew dropped their bombs from 12,000 feet at 22.30 and the Murchie crew from 11,500 feet at 22.42 after a glide approach, but it proved impossible to assess what was happening on the ground. They landed at Abingdon on return and were among fifty-three crews claiming to have bombed the estimated positions of the warships.

A busy night of operations on the 7th would require 303 sorties, two thirds of them, amounting to 197 aircraft from all groups, assigned to Berlin, where a government building in the Alexander Platz and the Schlesinger railway station were among the aiming points. 1 Group detailed nineteen Wellingtons from Binbrook and four each from Elsham Wolds and Snaith, those from 103 squadron containing the crews of S/L Cross, F/L Scott, F/O Wardhaugh and Sgt Giles and taking off between 21.00 and 21.04. They had been preceded into the air between 19.36 and 19.49 by the freshman crews of P/Os Hughes and Keefer and Sgt Rex, who were bound for Boulogne to attack the docks and shipping, and by the crews of P/Os Jones and Murchie and Sgt Koslowski, whose destination in company with forty-eight others was the Baltic port of Kiel and the Deutsche Werke shipyard.

Dealing with them in chronological order, the freshman trio benefitted from clear skies and ideal conditions and delivered their attacks from 9,000 to 11,000 feet between 21.09 and 21.17. The Kiel-bound Sgt Koslowski and crew soon noticed that they were flying starboard-wing-low and were persuaded to turn back, leaving the remaining pair to reach the western coast of Schleswig-Holstein in favourable conditions with diminishing cloud. P/O Murchie and crew were halfway across the peninsula on course for Kiel when they ran into a nest of searchlights and flak that forced them to take violent evasive action. They were thrown off course and abandoned their attempt to reach the Baltic coast, bombing instead a nearby aerodrome, believed to be Jagel, from 14,000 feet at 01.30. P/O Jones and crew alone from Elsham Wolds attacked the primary target from 17,000 feet at 23.15 and observed bursts on the northern end of the inner dockyard basin. Meanwhile, the Berlin brigade had become depleted by the early return of F/L Scott and crew, who were forced off track by heavy flak north of the Ruhr and dropped their bombs from 14,000 feet at 01.15 somewhere near Essen on the way home. S/L Cross and crew also turned back, in their case when just short of the target after being hit by flak, and they dropped their bombs to the south-west of the city. Those reaching the target found good conditions with just two-tenths cloud, Sgt Giles and crew bombing from 14,000 feet at 00.28 and F/O Wardhaugh and crew after gliding down to

12,000 feet at 01.08. Sixty crews failed to carry out an attack on Berlin, however, and according to local sources, many of those claiming to have done so, missed the city centre and deposited their bombs to the north and east. Some significant damage resulted and almost three thousand people were de-housed, but at a heavy cost of fifteen aircraft. The eighteen aircraft lost from all of the night's operations represented a new record for a single night, but there were no empty dispersal pans at Elsham Wolds.

The first large Bomber Command attack on the city of Kassel was briefed to crews of all groups on the afternoon of the 8th, and would involve ninety-five aircraft, including eleven Wellingtons from Binbrook to represent 1 Group. Located some eighty miles to the east of the Ruhr, the city was home among other war industry concerns to the Henschel aircraft factories, where the Dornier Do17Z bomber was built under license, the Henschel tank works, the main producer of the Panzer III tank and the much-feared Tiger I and II, and the Henschel narrow-gauge locomotive works. Altogether, the company employed some eight thousand workers in its Kassel plants in addition to a large number of slaves from a nearby sub-camp of the infamous Dachau concentration camp. The Fieseler factory was building Messerschmitt and Focke-Wulf aircraft under licence and would also be responsible for the design and construction of the V-1 flying bomb that would be unleashed on London in the summer of 1944 and become known as the "Doodlebug" or "Buzzbomb". The briefings for this night's operation revealed railway workshops and a munitions factory as the specific targets, which pointed almost certainly to Henschel.

A trip to the city of Turin on the night of the 10/11th would be a new experience for six 103 Squadron crews, who were to represent 1 Group in company with four crews from 150 Squadron at Snaith. They were to be part of an overall force of seventy-six aircraft from 1, 3 and 4 Groups who were given the Fiat steelworks and marshalling yards as their aiming points. Located in the Piedmont region of northern Italy, Turin was an industrial powerhouse and home to Fiat's Lingotto and Mirafiori car plants, the Lancia motor works, the Arsenale army munitions factory, the RIV submachine gun factory, the Nebioli foundry and plants belonging to the American Westinghouse company. The 103 Squadron element flew over to Honington as a forward base and took off from there between 20.02 and 20.10 with S/L Cross the senior pilot on duty and S/L Ingram flying as second pilot to F/L Crawford. The flight across France took place over seven-tenths low cloud and Sgt Hare and crew were some thirty miles south-east of Dijon when rising engine temperatures convinced them that they would not be able to climb high enough to clear the Alps. They turned back, and on the way home bombed a searchlight concentration at Gravelines on the French coast from 5,000 feet at 02.05. The others traversed the Alps under clear skies that persisted to the target, where thick ground haze compromised the vertical visibility and created challenges for aiming point identification. F/O Wardhaugh and crew arrived first of the Elsham Wolds element and glided down from 14,000 to 9,000 feet to deliver their attack at 23.50, before spending forty minutes in the target area regaining height for the trip back across the Alps. The crews of S/L Cross, P/O Allen and F/L Crawford bombed from 12,000 to 16,000 feet either side of midnight and reported very large fires around the marshalling yards that were still visible from the Alps. P/O Petrie and crew failed to return in R1396, and no trace of them has ever been found.

Three Baltic ports, Kiel, Rostock and Warnemünde, hosted attacks on the night of the 11/12th, while freshman crews were sent to the French coast. Four 103 Squadron crews took off for Le Havre between 21.45 and 22.25 and encountered nine-tenths cloud over the French coast, which hampered their attempts to identify the aiming point. P/O Peck and crew spent forty minutes in a vain search before bringing their bombs home, while Sgt Rex and crew jettisoned theirs and the crew of P/O Lawson attacked Dieppe as an alternative target from 9,000 feet at 00.15. Just one crew, that of Sgt Gosman, bombed the primary target, doing so from 6,000 feet at 00.43 and reported bursts, explosions and red fires in the southern part of the port area.

A force of 130 aircraft was assembled for an operation to Frankfurt on the 12th, 103 Squadron alone representing 1 Group with nine Wellingtons, which took off from Elsham Wolds between 19.38 and 21.04 with S/L Cross and F/L Scott the senior pilots on duty. They had been briefed to aim for the main post office, which was code for an attack on the city centre, but this ceased to be of interest to F/L Scott and crew when they were unable to coax more than 11,000 feet out of their aircraft, and as an alternative, bombed Haamstede aerodrome on Zeeland after a glide down to 9,000 feet at 22.00. Sgt Giles and crew had already turned back by this stage because of a port engine issue and F/L Crawford and crew also failed to reach the primary target for an undisclosed reason, but found an aerodrome at Lesquin in north-eastern France on the way home and attacked it from 11,000 feet at 01.08. Unfavourable weather conditions including ten-tenths cloud at 7,000 feet in the target area rendered any precision impossible, and ultimately only the crews of F/O Wardhaugh and P/Os Hughes and Keefer bombed in the general target area from 12,000 to 17,000 feet between 22.35 and 23.19. P/O Wallis and crew were sent to bomb the docks and shipping at Cherbourg on this night, taking off at 20.11 and returning at 01.26 with their bomb load intact after failing to locate the target through ten-tenths cloud.

Elsham Wolds sat out an operation by 147 aircraft targeting the enemy warships at Brest on the 13th, for which 1 Group contributed twenty-seven Wellingtons from Hemswell and Snaith. Two nights later, with Elsham Wolds still inactive, a force of 169 aircraft was assembled to send to Hamburg, 1 Group providing seventeen Wellingtons from Binbrook. Finally, after three nights on the ground, seven 103 Squadron crews were briefed for an operation against the southern city of Karlsruhe in company with ten from 150 Squadron at Snaith as part of an overall force of fifty-five Wellingtons. The Elsham Wolds element took off between 19.11 and 19.39 with F/L Crawford the senior pilot on duty, and they were well on their way to the target by the time that the crews of F/O Wardhaugh and Sgt Rex followed them into the air at 21.15 and 21.25 respectively bound for the docks at Le Havre. P/O Allen and crew turned back early on with an engine issue and bombed a flare-path, believed to be at Vlissingen (Flushing) on Walcheren Island at the mouth of the Scheldt from 6,000 feet at 21.02. P/O Lawson and crew lost their oxygen supply and also bombed an aerodrome, believed to be near Ijmuiden, from 9,000 feet at 22.06, and P/O Jones and crew attacked an unidentified last resort objective between Strasbourg and Karlsruhe from 16,000 feet at 23.05. The others reached the primary target, where intense darkness prevailed, and in the absence of flares it proved impossible to make out ground detail. The crews of F/L Crawford, F/O peck and P/Os Keefer and Wallis carried out attacks on estimated positions from 11,000 to 16,000 feet between 22.50 and 23.40, and fires could be seen burning twenty minutes into the return trip. Meanwhile, Sgt Rex and crew had delivered two sticks of bombs at Le Havre from 14,000 feet at 23.35 and watched the first one burst across docks 5 and 6, while F/O Wardhaugh and crew glided down to 6,000 feet to release their load at 23.37.

Orders arrived at Elsham Wolds on the 20th to prepare for two operations that night, one involving five Wellingtons as the sole representatives of 1 Group in an overall force of seventy-four aircraft targeting Berlin, while four others joined forces with eight from 150 Squadron at Snaith to attack Frankfurt with twenty-two other aircraft. The latter element consisting of the crews of F/O Peck, P/O Wallis and Sgts Koslowski and Rex took off first between 19.00 and 19.06 and were followed into the air between 19.08 and 19.16 by the Berlin-bound quintet of F/L Crawford, F/O Wardhaugh, with S/L Ingram as second pilot and P/Os Allen, Keefer and Murchie, on what was to be a black night for the squadron. Weather conditions were bad, and a recall signal sent to both forces was not picked up by ten of the Berlin contingent and some of those heading for Frankfurt, and they pressed on. In the event, perhaps only the crews of P/O Allen and F/L Crawford reached Germany's capital city to find clear skies, the former carrying out a glide approach to release their bombs from 9,000 feet at 23.25, while the latter searched for an hour before heading back towards the west and bombing an aerodrome some ten miles south-west of Amsterdam from 14,000 feet at 02.30. P/O Keefer and crew attacked what they believed was the garrison city of Münster from 18,000 feet at 23.24. The crews of F/O Wardhaugh and P/O Murchie failed to return in X9609 and X9665 respectively, the former having crashed four miles west-south-west of Hengelo in eastern Holland, killing the pilot and rear gunner and delivering the others, including A Flight commander, S/L Ingram, into enemy hands. The latter came down somewhere near the Ruhr defence zone and there were no survivors from the crew of P/O Murchie. Returning from Frankfurt and short of fuel P/O Wallis and crew encountered foggy conditions and were forced to abandon L7886 near Market Rasen in Lincolnshire at 04.10. They all made it safely to the ground, but their colleagues, Sgt Rex and crew, were less fortunate when attempting an emergency landing near Holbeach in R1539. It resulted in a crash with fatal consequences for all but the rear gunner who, when interviewed later, revealed that the Wellington had been damaged by flak, and that it, too, was running out of fuel. It was the squadron's worst night to date, made sadder by the fact that neither operation achieved anything of value.

The 22nd brought S/L Oliver Godfrey to the squadron from 12 O.T.U at Benson as the new A Flight commander. Operations planned for the 26th involved diverse targets from Cologne just south of the Ruhr to Emden in the north-west, Mannheim in the south and Genoa on Italy's north-western coast, for which a total of 104 aircraft was made ready. 1 Group detailed fourteen Wellingtons for Cologne, ten from the Polish squadrons at Lindholme and four belonging to 103 Squadron for the crews of S/L Cross, F/L Crawford and P/Os Keefer and Lawson. They departed Elsham Wolds between 19.00 and 19.10 and were about ninety minutes into the outward flight, when P/O Keefer and crew received a recall signal because of the anticipation of fog over the stations for the time of landing. They were just south of Brussels at the time and brought their bombs home after failing to locate any of the Channel ports as alternative targets. F/L Crawford and crew had also reached enemy territory and jettisoned their load into the Channel, while S/L Cross and crew bombed Ostend from 12,000 feet at 20.36. This left P/O Lawson and crew to press on to Cologne after failing to pick up the recall, and they encountered ten-tenths cloud with tops at 15,000 feet, the height from which they bombed at 22.19 without observing the results.

On the 29th, 139 aircraft were detailed to attack the port city of Stettin, located on the River Oder some thirty miles inland of the Baltic coast, while ninety-three others targeted Hamburg. 1 Group detailed eighteen and twenty-one Wellingtons respectively with just two representing 103 Squadron. The crews of S/L Cross and P/O Allen departed Elsham Wolds at 19.02 and 19.05 respectively bound for the former, which is now in Poland and called Szczecin. P/O Allen and crew were forced to turn back within an hour after the starboard engine failed, leaving S/L Cross and crew to press on over ten-tenths cloud until reaching the western coast of Jutland at 7 degrees east. From that point, with 270 miles still to travel, the cloud began to break up to leave clear skies in the target area, where they bombed from 13,000 feet at 23.06 and observed bursts around three-quarters of a mile from the briefed aiming point. They returned safely and were among ninety-seven crews to report an effective operation.

The same two cities were selected for further attention on the last night of the month, and forces of eighty-two and forty aircraft were assembled respectively for Hamburg and Stettin. 1 Group supported both operations, assigning five Wellingtons to Stettin and ten to Hamburg, all provided by Elsham Wolds and Lindholme. 103 Squadron briefed the crews of F/L Crawford and P/O Allen for Stettin and those of F/O Peck, P/O Jones and Sgts Giles and Kitney for Hamburg and dispatched them together between 18.45 and 19.00. F/L Crawford turned back within ninety minutes because of an engine issue, but P/O Allen and crew continued on to find three to six-tenths cloud in the target area and excellent visibility with just a little ground haze to contend with. They carried out a level bombing run at 12,000 feet and released their bombs at 23.09, observing them to burst one mile north-west of the aiming point and set off fires.

Meanwhile, those bound for north-western Germany ran into severe icing conditions at 15,000 feet, and this persuaded P/O Jones and crew to seek out an alternative target, which they found in the form of a bridge over a river at Zoutkamp close to Holland's northern coast. They attacked it from 3,300 feet at 22.12 and were over the sea and on their way home within seconds. Those reaching Hamburg found up to nine-tenths cloud topping out at 7,000 feet, which combined with ground haze to compromise the vertical visibility and prevent Sgt Kitney and crew from identifying the aiming point. They turned their attention upon Cuxhaven, a port at the mouth of the River Elbe forty-five miles to the north-west, and bombed it from 16,500 feet at 21.45, observing bursts in the marshalling yards. The crews of Sgt Giles and F/O Peck attacked the primary target from 15,000 and 14,000 feet at 22.00 and 22.35 respectively, the latter after a glide approach, and observed fires following the burst of their bombs. F/O Peck's R1667 was hit repeatedly by flak and was engaged by a BF109, which was evaded by flying into cloud.

While the above operations were in progress, the freshman crews of Sgt Gosman and P/O Williams carried out an attack on the docks and shipping at Cherbourg, having departed Elsham Wolds at 19.40 and 19.00 respectively. They delivered their bombs from 9,000 and

14,000 feet at 20.46 and 21.30 and observed them to burst across the docks, before returning safely home, a tad more experienced than when they left it.

During the course of the month the squadron took part in sixteen operations and dispatched sixty-seven sorties for the loss of six Wellingtons, three complete crews and five members of another.

October 1941

The adverse weather conditions that had characterised the second half of September and frustrated C-in-C Peirse continued into the new month and caused the recall of a modestly-sized mainly 5 Group force bound for Karlsruhe on the evening of the 1st, while the predominantly 4 Group raid on target "A" at Stuttgart was allowed to continue. F/L David Holford was posted in from 11 O.T.U at Bassingbourn on the 3rd, and he would assume the role of flight commander in time. Small-scale operations were carried out against the cruisers at Brest and the docks at Dunkerque on the nights of the 2/3rd and 3/4th, after which, the inhospitable weather conditions kept the Command on the ground until the 10th.

The main event on this night was an operation against the Krupp complex in Essen, which would involve a force of seventy-eight aircraft, while a second operation undertaken by a force of sixty-nine aircraft targeted Cologne. In addition to these, a flurry of minor raids aimed at ports along the occupied coastline would raise the number of sorties for the night to 234. 1 Group detailed twenty-two Wellingtons from Snaith and Binbrook to support the raid on Cologne, and thirteen freshman crews to attack the docks and shipping at Ostend, among which, those of P/Os Wallis and Williams departed Elsham Wolds at 20.44 and 21.00 respectively. They were greeted at the target by a little cloud and good visibility, and bombed from 12,000 feet at 22.10 and 22.30, observing bursts across the north and centre of the docks.

A busy night of operations was announced across the Command on the 12th, which would bring the first major raid of the war on Nuremberg, the scene of massive Nazi Rallies during and after Hitler's rise to power in the 1930s. A force of 152 aircraft was assembled and their crews briefed to aim for the Siemens-Schuckert Werke aero-engine factory. While this operation took place in southern Germany, ninety-nine aircraft were to target Bremen in the north-west, while ninety 5 Group Hampdens and Manchesters tried their hand at the "Buna" synthetic rubber works at Marl-Hüls in the Ruhr. Together with a number of minor operations, this would bring the night's sortie tally to a new record of 373, an improvement of nine on the previous record set in May. 1 Group supported the Nuremberg operation with ten Wellingtons and the Bremen raid with forty-seven and detailed a further ten to take freshman crews to Boulogne. 103 squadron dispatched the crew of Sgt Gosman to Boulogne at 18.28 and welcomed them home at 23.15, having bombed the target under clear skies from 13,000 feet at 21.00 but prevented by searchlight dazzle from observing the results. The Bremen-bound element of nine had been briefed to aim for the Deutsche Schiff und Maschinenbau shipbuilding yards, which were actually in the Seebeck yard in Bremerhaven, and departed Elsham Wolds between 19.00 and 19.51 with S/L Godfrey flying as second pilot to F/O Peck. They lost the services of Sgt Gorrie and crew to an engine issue immediately after take-off, leaving the others to cross the North Sea under clear skies until reaching the German coast, where they encountered ten-tenths cloud at around 5,000 feet with occasional gaps that afforded only the briefest glimpse of the River Weser. This forced them to bomb on e.t.a. and the intense searchlight and flak activity from 12,000 to 16,500 feet between 21.59 and 22.33.

On the following day a force of sixty aircraft was assembled from 1 and 3 Groups for an operation against Düsseldorf, for which 1 Group detailed eighteen aircraft, nine each from 103 and 150 Squadrons. They departed Elsham Wolds between 18.13 and 18.34 with F/O Peck the senior pilot on duty, W/C Ryan flying as second pilot with Sgt Gorrie and F/L Holford performing a similar role in P/O Allen's crew. They crossed the English coast under clear skies that persisted all the way to the target in the southern Ruhr, but Sgt Gosman and crew were fifty miles short when their starboard engine failed, and they had to turn back. The others reached the target to face an intense searchlight and flak response, the searchlights operating in cones of forty to fifty beams with heavy flak bursting at the apex at between 14,000 and 16,000 feet. The Elsham Wolds crews bombed from 11,000 to 16,000 feet between 20.43 and 21.49, Sgt Giles and crew on the other side of the Rhine at Neuss, and bursts and fires were observed that appeared to be developing as the bombers retreated to the west. On return, P/O Jones and crew reported bombing Krefeld from 14,000 feet at 21.35, having been thwarted at the primary target by searchlight glare. Local sources confirmed a scattered and largely ineffective raid.

A force of eighty aircraft was assembled for a return to Nuremberg on the 14th and contained a 1 Group contribution of eight Wellingtons from 12 Squadron at Binbrook. Sixteen 1 Group crews were called to briefing on the afternoon of the 16th and learned that Duisburg was to be their target that night for a raid by a force of eighty-seven aircraft on the city centre. 103 Squadron made ready five Wellingtons for the crews of F/O Peck, P/Os Jones and Keefer and Sgts Giles and Kitney and two others to take the crews of F/L Holford and S/L Godfrey to attack the docks and shipping at Dunkerque. The latter took off first, at 18.40 and 19.20 respectively, and arrived at the French coast to find only small amounts of cloud and excellent visibility, in which they delivered their bomb loads from 15,000 and 14,000 feet at 20.15 and 21.00 and observed them to explode across the docks area. They arrived home before midnight after a trip of fewer than four hours, in time to watch those involved in the main event take off from Elsham Wolds between 00.49 and 01.17. P/O Keefer was unable to coax more than 10,000 feet out of R1445 and at 02.25, dropped a stick of bombs on Oostvoorne aerodrome at the northern mouth of the Scheldt, across the water from the Hook of Holland. The others all reached the Ruhr, which was concealed beneath seven to ten-tenths cloud, and bombing was carried out largely on estimated positions. The crews of Sgt Kitney, P/O Jones and F/O Peck bombed from 13,500 to 16,500 feet between 03.05 and 03.25 aiming at the source of the volumes of flak coming up at them, and the Kitney crew reported a fire spreading rapidly followed by three yellow explosions. Sgt Giles and crew were unable to pinpoint on the primary target and attacked Haamstede aerodrome in the Scheldt estuary from 15,000 feet at 04.00 on the way home. R1217 was hit by flak on the first run over the target and the port-engine caught fire soon after crossing the Dutch coast homebound, but P/O Jones and crew nursed it home, where it was ultimately declared a write-off.

Ports dominated the target list on the 20th, Bremen, Wilhelmshaven and Emden in north-western Germany, while freshman crews practiced their craft at Antwerp in Belgium. A force of 153 aircraft drawn from 3 and 5 Groups was assigned to Bremen, while the attack on Wilhelmshaven was to be an all-4 Group show. 1 Group contributed thirty-three Wellingtons to the force of thirty-six aircraft assigned to Emden, the eight representing 103 Squadron departing Elsham Wolds between 18.11 and 19.02 with S/L Cross the senior pilot on duty. They arrived in the target area to find five-tenths cloud with tops at 12,000 feet and moderately good horizontal visibility, but extreme darkness and ground haze concealing ground features. Sgt Giles and crew spent twenty-five minutes trying to locate the target, before giving up and gliding down from 16,000 to 13,000 feet at 20.20 to bomb Petkum on the northern bank of the mouth of the River Ems. The others attacked Emden from 13,000 to 16,000 feet between 20.07 and 21.14 and returned with little of value to pass on to the intelligence section at debriefing.

Mannheim was posted as the target for 123 aircraft on the 22nd, to which 1 Group contributed eight Wellingtons from Elsham Wolds and eleven from Snaith, while detailing a further eleven Wellingtons to take freshman crews to Le Havre. The two 103 Squadron elements took off together between 18.07 and 18.57 with F/Ls Crawford and Holford the senior pilots on duty for the main event and S/L Godfrey leading Sgt Tett and crew to the Normandy coast. The latter pair found up to four-tenths cloud and good visibility in which to deliver their bomb loads from 12,000 and 15,000 feet at 19.28 and 20.26 respectively, and some bursts were observed in the docks area. Conditions for the Mannheim-bound force were unfavourable with thick cloud, electrical storms and icing during the North Sea crossing, which persuaded many crews to bomb alternative targets. F/L Crawford was unable to climb out of the icing clouds and jettisoned his bombs into the sea after turning for home. P/O Keefer and crew were still struggling to break free of the icing belt at 18,000 feet over Holland, when T2506 fell out of the air and plummeted to 13,000 feet, where the pilot regained control, but not before the rear gunner had baled out. They also turned for home and bombed Haamstede aerodrome from 8,000 feet at 20.40, observing bursts on the intersection of the runways. At 19,000 feet, Sgt Gorrie's starboard engine burst into flames forcing him to jettison the bombs off the Dutch coast and nurse his aircraft and crew home. The remainder pressed on and carried out their attacks from 11,500 to 17,000 feet between 20.35 and 21.15 but were unable to deliver an effective blow on this important industrial city. Three crews returned home to report that engines had suddenly cut out, causing them to lose height rapidly and in each case the engines had picked up again once at a warmer altitude, in the case of F/L Holford at a lowly 4,000 feet. R1459 suffered engine problems all the way home and struck a balloon cable near Hull, damaging the port wing. P/O Wallis maintained control and brought the wounded Wellington back to a crash-landing at base, eventually to return to flying duties.

Orders were received across the Command on the 24th to prepare for that night's operation against railway workshops and marshalling yards in Frankfurt-am-Main, which would involve a force of seventy aircraft, fourteen of them Wellingtons provided by 1 Group from the stations at Elsham Wolds and Snaith. The 103 Squadron crews of F/L Holford, F/O Peck and P/Os Keefer, Lawson and Williams took off between 20.40 and 21.22 and lost the Williams crew to intercom failure before reaching the English coast, while the Lawson crew was approaching the Dutch coast when the failure of the oxygen system ended their interest in proceedings also. The others ran into ten-tenths cloud at around 8,000 feet shortly after crossing the enemy coast and this persisted all the way to the target, by which time it had thickened to ten-tenths with tops at 15,000 feet, preventing all but eight crews of the entire force from locating it. F/O Peck and crew dropped one stick of bombs from 17,500 feet at 00.30 and a second stick on Haamstede aerodrome from 14,000 feet at 02.05, observing bursts to the left of the flare-path followed by a small fire. F/L Holford bombed the primary target from 18,000 feet at 00.50 and somehow observed one high explosive bomb to hit the railway station and cause a large flash. On return, they collided with a balloon cable in the Cardiff area but landed safely at Colerne in Wiltshire. P/O Keefer RCAF and crew became lost on the way home, and either overflew England or passed straight up the English Channel with diminishing reserves of fuel. Running on fumes, Keefer crash-landed T2506 as soon as he found land and discovered that they were in the neutral Republic of Ireland, where he and his crew were interned for a period. The dismal failure of the operation was typical for the period and heaped further frustration on C-in-C, Sir Richard Peirse.

The Polish squadrons from Hemswell and Lindholme took care of 1 Group business at Hamburg's Blohm & Voss shipyards on the 26th, and just one 103 Squadron aircraft was required for duty on the evening of the 28th, when joining thirteen others from 1 Group to target the docks and shipping at Cherbourg. Sgt Telfer and crew departed Elsham Wolds at 18.48 and encountered five-tenths cloud over the target with good visibility beneath, and having bombed from 14,000 feet at 21.45 without observing the results, returned safely to a landing at Marham after four-and-a-half hours aloft.

The month ended with a return to the Blohm & Voss shipyards at Hamburg on the 31st, for which a force of 123 aircraft was assembled, 1 Group calling upon the services of Binbrook, Elsham Wolds and Lindholme to provide between them thirty-one Wellingtons in addition to a dozen others to take freshman crews to Dunkerque. 103 Squadron briefed the crews of F/L Holford, F/O Peck, P/O Williams and Sgts Giles and Gosman for the main event and S/L Godfrey, P/O Jones and Sgts Lewis and Telfer for the freshman raid and dispatched them together between 18.45 and 19.50. F/O Peck and crew were back in the circuit after an hour with an engine issue, and Sgt Giles and crew, having crossed the North Sea over ten-tenths cloud, pinpointed on Wilhelmshaven and bombed there from 17,000 feet at 22.25. F/L Holford, meanwhile, had found four-tenths cloud over Hamburg with tops at 6,000 feet and had bombed from 11,000 feet at 22.25, observing bursts and fires set off by incendiaries. P/O Williams and crew attacked at the same time from 17,000 feet and believed their bombs to have fallen into a built-up area to the north of the docks, probably in the Altona district. No details were recorded of Sgt Gosman's sortie other than that he and his crew were afflicted by severe icing and had to contend with a fire in the fuselage as they neared the Lincolnshire coast homebound. They landed on the coast at Donna Nook, between Mablethorpe and Grimsby, and extinguished the fire before any major damage had occurred.

An analysis of the raid revealed that fewer than half of the force had attacked the primary target, for which poor visibility was blamed and local sources reported fourteen fires, seven of them large. The fact that F/L Holford was among those to fulfil their briefs demonstrated the press-on spirit and determination that would characterise his career. Some 360 miles to the south, the Dunkerque contingent had found their target under almost clear skies and attacked it from 10,500 to 17,000 feet between 21.20 and 21.40, observing bursts and fires.

During the course of the month, the squadron took part in thirteen operations and dispatched sixty-one sorties for the loss of two Wellingtons, one crew in temporary internment and one rear gunner.

November 1941

There is little doubt that the Command was still treading water in the wake of the Butt Report, and an extended period of bad weather had prevented Peirse from making any significant gains. Recent operations had produced scant rewards for the effort invested, and many valuable aircrew lives had been frittered away for this poor return. Typical was a raid on Kiel on the night of the 1/2nd of November, which involved twenty-five 1 Group Wellingtons from Snaith and Hemswell in an overall force of 134 aircraft. Only half reached the target area, which was covered by heavy cloud, and local sources reported hearing the force overhead, but no bombs falling in the town. Only minor operations occupied the following five nights as adverse weather conditions continued to control Peirse's options.

No doubt as a result of the frustrations caused by his inability to deliver a telling blow on Germany during the extended period of unfavourable weather, and almost certainly eager to rescue the besmirched reputation of the Command after the damning Butt Report, Peirse planned a major night of operations for the night of the 7/8th. The original intention was to send over two hundred aircraft to Berlin, but continuing doubts about the weather prompted the 5 Group A-O-C, AVM Slessor, to question the wisdom of it going ahead, and he was allowed to withdraw his force and send it instead to Cologne. A third operation, involving fifty-three Wellingtons and two Stirlings from 1 and 3 Groups was also to take place with Mannheim as the target. A force of 169 aircraft from 1, 3 and 4 Groups eventually took off for Berlin, while sixty-one Hampdens and fourteen Manchesters set off for the Rhineland capital. In addition to the above, other small-scale operations would raise the number of sorties to a record 392. 1 Group contributed twenty-two Wellingtons to the Berlin force, forty-six to Mannheim and a dozen to take freshman crews to Boulogne.

103 Squadron briefed the crews of F/O Lawson, P/Os Allen, Jones and Wallis and Sgts Giles and Lewis for Mannheim and sent them on their way between 18.09 and 18.40. There were no early returns, but the omens were not good as they traversed Luxembourg over ten-tenths cloud, which diminished as the target drew near to leave five tenths with tops at 8,000 feet and ground haze below to impair the vertical visibility. P/O Wallis and crew were unable to identify the primary target and bombed a nearby aerodrome from 16,000 feet as an alternative at 20.55, while the others delivered attacks on Mannheim from 14,000 to 17,000 feet between 20.50 and 21.37. A message was received from P/O Lawson and crew in the early hours of the 8th, after which nothing further was heard, and it was believed initially that they had landed in unoccupied Vichy France and had been interned. However, news eventually arrived to reveal that X9794 had crashed near Choloy in north-eastern France and that F/O Lawson and three members of his crew had been captured, one had been killed and one had retained his freedom after being spirited away by the French Resistance.

Once every aircraft from the night's endeavours had landed, it became clear that a record thirty-seven were missing, more than twice the previous highest loss in a single night. An analysis revealed that fewer than half of the Berlin force had managed to reach their objective, and twenty-one had failed to return. The Cologne force came through without loss, but left behind just two destroyed houses, and the Mannheim contingent missed its target altogether, while losing seven Wellingtons. This was the final straw for the Air Ministry, and Sir Richard Peirse was summoned to an uncomfortable meeting with Churchill at Chequers on the 8th to make his explanations. On the 13th, he would be ordered to restrict future operations while the future of the Command was considered at the highest level. In the event, unfavourable weather conditions for the remainder of the month largely took matters out of his hands.

Attention switched to the Ruhr on the following night with the Krupp complex in Essen as the target for fifty-four aircraft including thirteen provided by 1 Group from Binbrook and Snaith. Hamburg was posted as the main target on the 9th, for which a force of 103 aircraft was assembled, while their crews were being briefed to employ the Blohm & Voss shipyards on Finkenwerder Island as the aiming point. 1 Group detailed twenty Wellingtons from Elsham Wolds, Hemswell and Snaith for the main event and four others from Elsham Wolds to take freshman crews to Ostend. The two 103 Squadron elements consisting of the Hamburg-bound crews of F/L Holford, P/Os Jones and Williams and Sgts Giles and Telfer and the freshman crews of S/L Cross, P/O Ward and Sgts Gorrie and Pugh took off together between 17.45 and 18.22, S/L Cross and Sgt Gorrie acting as mentors and P/O Ward operating as crew captain for the first time. T2921 was intercepted by night-fighters at 12,000 feet over the North Sea while outbound and P/O Jones ordered the bombs to be jettisoned "live" some forty miles North of Cuxhaven. He and his crew turned for home and were passing south of Darlington when the starboard propeller fell off, prompting a landing at Linton-on-Ouse. Despite good visibility and the absence of low cloud, P/O Williams and crew were unable to locate the primary target after a forty-five-minute search and blamed a faulty compass. They came upon an aerodrome at Rotenburg, situated some eighteen miles to the east of Bremen and attacked it from 16,000 feet at 23.10. The others delivered their bombs on Hamburg from 11,000 to 16,000 feet between 20.45 and 21.00 and were among seventy-one returning crews to report attacking the primary target and leaving a number of fires burning in the docks and the city.

Meanwhile, the freshmen had arrived over the French coast to find clear skies and good visibility, which the crews of S/L Cross and Sgt Gorrie exploited to deliver their bomb loads onto the Ostend docks, the former from 12,000 feet at 19.22 and the latter from 9,000 feet at 20.10. The crews of P/O Ward and Sgt Pugh failed to locate the primary target and attacked Dunkerque instead from 7,000 and 10,000 feet at 20.15 and 21.00 respectively.

Aside from a number of small-scale freshman operations in mid-month, 1 Group remained inactive for the ensuing two weeks while the weather and operational restrictions held sway. Another freshman operation on the 25th brought the first 1 Group operational activity since the 15th, but it was on the 26th, the day on which 142 Squadron exchanged Binbrook for Grimsby (Waltham), when 103 Squadron's enforced rest came to an end. 1 Group contributed twenty-four aircraft from Elsham Wolds and Hemswell to the overall force of eighty Wellingtons and twenty Hampdens assembled for the main event at the naval port of Emden, and six Wellingtons, all from Elsham Wolds, for a freshman raid on Ostend. 103 Squadron briefed nine crews for Emden and six freshman crews for Ostend and dispatched them over an extended period between 17.17 and 18.51 with S/L Godfrey and F/L Holford the senior pilots on duty. The arrived at their respective target areas, separated by 230 miles, at around the same time, at Ostend to find six to ten-tenths cloud and at Emden eight to ten-tenths, both topping out at 6,000 feet. Sgt Bray and crew were unable to locate Ostend and brought their bombs home, leaving the others to carry out their attacks from 10,000 to 13,000 feet between 19.52 and 20.58. S/L Holford experienced similar challenges at Emden and also returned his ordnance to the bomb dump, while seven of the others bombed from 12,000 to 16,000 feet between 19.26 and 20.50. Sgt Giles and crew carried out three passes, releasing a salvo on each and were over the target from 20.32 to 20.40, while F/O Peck dropped a single stick and brought the rest home. Sgt Telfer failed to locate Emden and came upon the same Rotenburg aerodrome as P/O Williams earlier in the month and bombed it as a last resort target from 6,000 feet at 20.40. T2999 was forced down to sea level on the way home after its port engine failed, but P/O Ward managed to coax it as far as the Elsham circuit, where it crashed at 22.05 and burned out, happily after P/O Ward and his crew had walked away. In the light of the failure of 45% of crews to bomb at Emden, the performance of the 103 Squadron crews was worthy of praise.

A force of eighty-six aircraft assembled for an operation against Düsseldorf on the 27th was achieved without the support of 1 Group. However, when Hamburg was posted as the main target for 181 aircraft on the 30th, the number included a contribution from 1 Group of thirty-nine Wellingtons from Binbrook, Lindholme and Snaith, while eleven others at Binbrook, Hemswell and Elsham Wolds were made ready to take freshman crews to Emden. 103 Squadron briefed the crews of F/Sgt Fulbrook and Sgts Dainton and Tett and sent them on their way to Emden between 16.54 and 16.59, all arriving in the target area to find clear skies and excellent visibility, despite which, Sgt Dainton and crew overshot Emden and found themselves forty miles too far east over Wilhelmshaven, where they bombed from 17,000 feet at 19.52. Sgt Tett and crew bombed the primary target from 16,000 feet at 20.10 and F/Sgt Fulbrook and crew twenty minutes later from 12,000 feet, both observing bursts among buildings and fires.

During the course of the month, the squadron took part in six operations and dispatched thirty-three sorties for the loss of two Wellingtons and one crew.

December 1941

The dominant theme during December would be the continuing presence at Brest of Scharnhorst, Gneisenau and, sometimes, Prinz Eugen, and no less than fifteen operations of varying sizes would be mounted against the port and its guests during the month, some by daylight. The weather kept the entire Command on the ground for the first six nights of the new month, and it was not until the 7th that a posted operation would actually go ahead. The target for a force of 130 aircraft was Aachen, Germany's most westerly city, perched on the frontiers with both Holland and Belgium. The briefed aiming-point was the Nazi Party HQ, which had no special significance other than the fact that it was situated in the city centre, at a time when it was still not yet admitted publicly that population centres were being bombed. 1 Group provided fourteen Wellingtons from Binbrook, Grimsby, Holme-on-Spalding-Moor (458 Squadron RAAF) and Lindholme. A second target on this night involved 3 Group Wellingtons and Stirlings against Brest, during which the Stirling element conducted the first operational trials of Oboe, a game-changing blind bombing device which would not enter service for almost thirteen months. The Aachen operation was compromised by adverse weather conditions and the city escaped serious damage.

Daylight operations were a matter of course for 2 Group squadrons, and some, known as "Circus" and "Ramrod" had the purpose of tempting enemy fighters into the air to face RAF Spitfires in a war of attrition. These were, however, very different from the unescorted daylight operations known as "moling", conducted by the other groups, which relied on cloud and surprise to protect the crews. It was utter madness to put crews' lives at risk for a very small potential gain, but it was 5 Group's turn to order small numbers of Hampdens into the air daily from the 10th to the 13th to target ports and aerodromes in Germany and Holland.

There was no operational activity for 103 Squadron until the 16th, when eleven of its Wellingtons were detailed to join twenty others from Binbrook and Grimsby to target Wilhelmshaven as part of an overall force of eighty-three aircraft. A freshman operation by thirty-two aircraft against the docks and shipping at Ostend involved the crews of P/O Brookes and Sgt Morris, and they departed Elsham Wolds first at 17.03 and 17.07, to be followed into the air by the main element between 17.11 and 17.57 with S/L Cross the senior pilot on duty and W/C Ryan flying as second pilot to P/O Williams. The freshmen found two to five-tenths cloud in the target area, but ground haze proved to be the greater challenge, and P/O Brookes and crew spent thirty-five minutes searching, even dropping flares, before taking their bombs home. Sgt Morris and crew also searched diligently, and believing that they had identified Ostend, delivered an attack from 12,000 feet at 18.30. R1588 crashed on return to base but would be repaired and returned to duty and an analysis of the crew's navigation charts revealed that they had probably bombed Bruges in error for Ostend.

Meanwhile, Sgt Dainton and crew had abandoned their sortie when fifty miles out over the North Sea because of a problem with their starboard engine and had jettisoned their bombs. Sgt Gosman and crew turned back also after losing their heating system, and they dropped their load on the Frisian Island of Borkum from 14,500 feet at 19.24. The others were greeted by two to five-tenths cloud over Wilhelmshaven, but it was the extreme darkness and ground haze that created the greatest difficulties for target identification. Sgt Martin and crew were unable to identify the primary target but came upon an active aerodrome some twenty miles to the west and attacked it from 15,000 feet at 21.20. S/L Cross and crew searched in vain before spotting dim lights, which, after consideration, they bombed from 13,500 feet at 19.34, and their bombing photo would reveal it to be the town of Aurich, also some twenty miles to the west of Wilhelmshaven. The others carried out their attacks from 12,500 to 15,000 feet, some from estimated positions, between 19.30 and 20.04 and returned from what they assessed as an effective raid that left fires burning across the target area. The optimism was not borne out by local reports, which mentioned only slight damage.

Another raid on Brest on the 17th involved thirty-two 1 Group Wellingtons from Snaith and Hemswell in an overall force of 121 aircraft, the crews of eighty of which claimed to have attacked the estimated positions of the warships. On the 23rd, the Polish squadrons contributed thirty-one Wellingtons to a force of sixty-eight to target Cologne, but the conditions were again unfavourable and local sources made no mention of an attack taking place. The third wartime Christmas came and went and the 27th brought a return to hostilities with the posting of Düsseldorf as the target for a force of 132 aircraft, including forty-one 1 Group Wellingtons from Snaith, Hemswell and Holme-on-Spalding-Moor. Ninety-six returning crews claimed to have attacked the primary target, but only a few bomb loads hit the city and caused minor damage.

103 Squadron's latest long layoff came to an end on the 28th, when Wilhelmshaven was named as the target for eighty-six Wellingtons, forty-nine of them to be provided by 1 Group. A new squadron and station record was set when sixteen Wellingtons departed Elsham Wolds for the main event along with the Emden-bound freshman crew of Sgt Gilby. The latter took off first at 17.01 on a rare night of ideal weather conditions and reached the Frisian Island of Borkum, before concerns about excessive fuel consumption persuaded them to bomb there from 12,000 feet at 19.20. The main element took to the air between 17.30 and 18.28 with F/L Holford the senior pilot on duty and the station commander, G/C Constantine, on board. They reached the target area to find visibility that was described as perfect, topped off by bright moonlight and snow on the ground as a backdrop. Fourteen 103 Squadron crews carried out an attack from 7,500 to 17,000 feet between 19.33 and 21.04 and all returned, more or less safely, to report an accurate attack, which local sources confirmed caused widespread damage. F/Sgt Fulbrook and crew landed in a flak-damaged DV452 with its bomb doors hanging open after the hydraulic fluid had drained away, and this preventing them from deploying flaps and forced them to hand-crank the undercarriage down. At debriefing they reported overshooting Wilhelmshaven and eventually bombing Cuxhaven from 12,000 feet at 21.09 after a circuitous flight to the Baltic coast and Trischen Island off the mouth of the Elbe. P/O Ward and crew reported that they had bombed Bremerhaven in error for the primary target from 14,000 feet at 20.40.

During the course of the month, the squadron took part in four operations and dispatched thirty-sorties without loss. As the year ended, Bomber Command could not look back with any great sense of achievement, and in fact, it had largely failed to make any advances on its performance of the previous year, despite the introduction of three new aircraft types. Each had fallen short of expectations and had been grounded for extended periods while modifications were undertaken. It had been those types in existence at the start of the war, the Wellington, Whitley and Hampden, that had borne the greatest responsibility for carrying the offensive to the enemy, and in that regard, they had not been found wanting. The very existence of an independent bomber force was hanging in the balance as the year turned, with calls from the Admiralty and the Middle East Command for bomber aircraft to be diverted to them. The coming year did not promise much in the way of an improving situation, although its salvation was waiting in the wings in the shape of the Lancaster, a type born out of the failure of the Manchester, examples of which had already been delivered to 5 Group's 44 Squadron.

January 1942

As far as most crews were concerned, the incoming year would look and feel exactly like the outgoing one, and still under the restrictions of the November directive, the Command's activities reflected the continuing obsession with the German raiders at Brest, against which a further eleven operations would take place during January, eight in the first eleven days and three more during the last week. As for 103 and the other squadrons, it was a simple case of pressing on with the equipment available to them, and through the calibre of their leadership, maintaining the esprit de corps. The long-serving F/L Crawford was posted to 15 O.T.U on the 2nd at the conclusion of his tour and the presence of him and his crew would be missed. The first operation of note against Brest was mounted on the night of the 5/6th, for which 1 Group contributed forty-eight Wellingtons from Snaith, Hemswell and Lindholme as part of an overall force of 154 aircraft. A proportion of the force was briefed to attack the Scharnhorst and Gneisenau, while the remainder went for the dock facilities, but an effective smoke screen made accuracy difficult, and although many fires were claimed across the target area, there was no confirmation of damage.

On the following day, the responsibility was put upon 1 Group to attack the vessels, for which fifteen of the thirty-one Wellingtons from Binbrook, Elsham Wolds and Grimsby were provided by 103 Squadron. They took off between 16.39 and 17.14 with S/L Godfrey and F/L Holford the senior pilots on duty and each carrying six 500 pounders, half of them SAPs, not all of which would find their way to the target. P/O Wallis and crew lost their intercom after an hour and then their oxygen system and turned back, while Sgt Telfer and crew were coned in searchlights and had to take violent evasive action, which culminated in the dumping of their bombs in the sea. The others encountered five-tenths cloud with tops at 5,000 feet and an intense searchlight and flak defence, in which an unidentified aircraft was seen to be coned and shot down in flames and crash about five miles from the target. Fourteen of the Elsham Wolds crews bombed as briefed from 9,000 to 16,000 feet between 19.25 and 21.00, observing detonations across the docks area, although there were no specific claims. One bomb had, in fact, exploded close to Gneisenau and breached the hull, allowing two compartments to flood.

AM Sir Richard Peirse left his post as C-in-C Bomber Command on the 8th to be succeeded temporarily by AVM Baldwin, the A-O-C 3 Group. In February, Peirse would take up a new appointment as C-in-C Allied Air Forces in India and South-East Asia, but the sense that he had been "sacked" from Bomber Command would linger, and perhaps unjustly tarnish his legacy. That afternoon, briefings were held in preparation for the next round in the campaign against Brest, for which a force of 151 aircraft was assembled, 1 Group contributing forty-five Wellingtons from Binbrook, Elsham Wolds, Grimsby and Lindholme. It was not until 03.26 on the 9th that the departure of thirteen 103 Squadron aircraft began and all bound for the main event were airborne by 04.02, led by S/Ls Cross and Godfrey and the seemingly ever-present F/L Holford. They left behind them the freshman crew of P/O Brookes, who would follow them into the air at 04.37 to bomb the docks and shipping at Cherbourg. They exited the English coast at Bridport and headed for Ouessant (Ushant) Island to the west of the Brest peninsula, taking two-and-a-half hours to reach the target area in the Finistere region of Brittany. They found it to be under a wedge of eight-tenths cloud at between 2,000 and 8,000 feet, through which some crews caught a glimpse of the sea and the docks area. Ten 103 Squadron crews delivered an attack from 11,000 to 14,000 feet between 05.45 and 06.50, while Sgt Giles and crew were thwarted by a complete hang-up and had to bring their bombs home. The crews of S/L Godfey and P/O Jones also returned their bombs to the dump after failing to locate the target. Meanwhile, 150 miles to the north-west, P/O Brookes and crew found Cherbourg to be concealed beneath thick cloud and headed east to try their hand at Le Havre, only to be beaten by the conditions there also and jettison their bombs into the Channel.

Snaith and Hemswell took care of 1 Group business at Brest on the night of the 9/10th, the fifth night in a row that the port and its lodgers had been attacked and the seventh in eight nights since the turn of the year. Wilhelmshaven was posted as the target for 124 aircraft on the 10th, for which 1 Group detailed forty-five Wellingtons from Binbrook, Elsham Wolds, Grimsby and Lindholme. Fourteen 103 Squadron Wellingtons took off between 17.09 and 17.32 with S/L Godfrey and F/L Holford the senior pilots on duty, the latter accompanied by W/C Ryan as second pilot and a Major Albrecht as a passenger. They flew out over Mablethorpe and skirted the Frisians before arriving at the target to encounter up to eight-tenths cloud with a base at 5,000 feet. P/O Williams and crew were led astray by a navigational error and had lost their heating system by the time that they decided to bomb Emden as an alternative target, attacking from 12,000 feet at 20.55 and observing the development of a large fire in the centre of the town. Sgt Tett and crew were defeated by the failure of a bomb-release switch and brought their load home, while Sgt Ward and crew had to contend with an overheating engine and the failure of their internal heating system. They bombed the southern Frisian Island of Terschelling from 14,000 feet at 19.20, and an hour later, Sgt Giles and crew attacked the flare-path at Nordholz aerodrome from 10,000 feet. Ten minutes after that, the crew of Sgt Dainton mistook Jever for the primary target and bombed it from 14,000 feet. Nine of the 103 Squadron crews would report attacking the primary target from 10,000 to 14,500 feet between 20.03 and 21.05 and with the exception of one, all were diverted on return because of fog over Elsham Wolds. Sgt Bray landed at Waltham (Grimsby) at 22.10 and emerged with just one member of his crew from a severely damaged Z1142. At debriefing they reported believing that some bombs had hung up on their first pass, and at the point of release on the second run, an exploding flak shell had dislodged a flare from its rack and ignited it amidships. Fumes prevented the crew from extinguishing it, and in what seemed to be a hopeless situation, Sgt Bray ordered the crew to abandon the aircraft. Four did so, but the second pilot, Sgt Spooner, failed to hear the order after managing to reach the fire and spray it with an extinguisher. Two geodetic sections burned away, allowing the flare to fall out, and Sgt Spooner put out the burning fabric with his gloves before taking the controls as Sgt Bray attended to the navigation. Between them they brought the Wellington safely back home, and in recognition of their presence of mind and devotion to duty, both men received the immediate award of the DFM. It was learned later that their crew mates had fallen into enemy hands.

Briefings on the 14th revealed that night's targets to be Hamburg's Blohm & Voss shipyard and the Hamburger Flugzeugbau aircraft factory, both situated in Finkenwerder Island in the Elbe to the west of the city centre. The latter was a subsidiary of the Blohm & Voss and was building subassemblies on a contract basis for Messerschmitt, Dornier, Heinkel, Junkers and

Focke-Wulf. 1 Group provided thirty Wellingtons from Binbrook, Grimsby and Lindholme in a force of ninety-five aircraft for what would be the first of two operations against these targets on consecutive nights. In the event, barely half of the force reached the target, and they caused seven large fires.

103 Squadron's turn came on the following night, when a dozen of its Wellingtons were detailed, only for two to be scrubbed because of technical problems and six because they could not be bombed up in time. This left just four 103 Squadron participants in a 1 Group element of twenty-one aircraft provided by Elsham Wolds, Hemswell and Snaith in an overall force of ninety-six aircraft. The crews of F/L Holford, F/O Peck and Sgts Dainton and Martin took off between 17.25 and 18.00, F/L Holford carrying a large number of flares, with which to illuminate the target for those following behind. They flew out over Mablethorpe on a direct course for the uninhabited Trischen Island off the mouth of the Elbe, and F/L Holford and his crew spent thirty minutes searching for the aiming point in conditions of extreme darkness and ground haze. They eventually bombed a searchlight concentration from 15,000 feet at 20.50 and released thirty-six flares, which provided excellent illumination of a circular area estimated at a radius of twenty miles. Sgt Martin and crew bombed on the north-eastern outskirts of Hamburg from 11,000 feet at 22.10, while F/O Peck and crew attacked a searchlight concentration to the north of the city from 14,500 feet at 20.45 and a railway track ten minutes later. The raid failed to produce significant damage and according to local sources, only three of thirty-six fires were classed as large. The squadron suffered its first casualty of the year when R1395 failed to return after crashing in north-western Germany, taking the lives of Sgt Dainton and four of his crew, while the sole survivor was taken into captivity.

The squadron sat out a medium-size raid on Bremen on the 17/18th and a small effort against Emden three nights later for which 1 Group detailed thirty-two Wellingtons from Grimsby and Lindholme and nine from Binbrook and Grimsby respectively. Briefings on the 21st revealed Bremen to be the target again for fifty-four aircraft, while a smaller force targeted Emden, which was designated as 1 Group's alternative target. 1 Group put up nineteen aircraft from Elsham Wolds and Snaith, the 103 Squadron element of ten taking off between 17.19 and 18.21 with S/L Godfrey the senior pilot on duty and six of the Wellingtons loaded with five 500 pounders and the others with 4lb or 30lb incendiaries. They exited the English coast over Mablethorpe and set a course for Jade Bay and Bremervörde to approach the target from the north-east, but only four reached the primary target, where they found varying amounts of cloud up to eight-tenths and carried out attacks from 12,000 to 14,500 feet between 20.01 and 20.54. Of the others, P/O Wallis and crew lost their heating system and made for Emden, where they attempted to release flares a mile south of the town, only for one to hang up and ignite after the bomb doors had been closed. This caused a fire at the aft end of the bomb bay, which was extinguished when the doors were re-opened to allow the incendiaries and flare to fall away from 14,000 feet at 20.45. Sgt Martin and crew also went for Emden after a turret became unserviceable, and dropped their incendiaries from 15,000 feet at 20.00, observing them to set off four fires about half a mile north-east of dock 6. Sgt Gilby and crew attacked a flak concentration in the Emden area from 13,000 feet at 20.40, while Sgt Pugh and crew were prevented by searchlight glare and haze from identifying anything on the ground and attacked a last resort target (untraced) from 14,000 feet at 20.29.

Sgt Lewis and crew found a small town ten miles north of Oldenburg to target from 14,000 feet at 20.47, and this left just P/O Brookes and crew to complete the squadron's business by dropping their 500 pounders on Emden from 15,000 feet at 21.18.

The first operation of the year against an inland German target was directed at the garrison town of Münster on the 22nd by a force of forty-seven aircraft, including sixteen Polish Wellingtons from Hemswell representing 1 Group. Scharnhorst and Gneisenau were to be in the bombsights again on the 25th, for which a force of sixty-one aircraft was assembled, twenty-one of them provided by 1 Group from Elsham Wolds and Snaith. The eleven 103 Squadron Wellingtons took off between 17.06 and 17.46 with S/L Godfrey and F/L Holford the senior pilots on duty and each crew sitting on a load of 500lb SAP bombs. P/O Ward and crew turned back before crossing the south coast at Bridport, when the navigator became indisposed, and Sgt Gilby was closing on the French coast when his port engine developed a leaky exhaust ring that ended their interest in proceedings. The others followed the usual route to Ouessant Island, from where they lined up for the bombing run, F/L Holford and crew carrying thirty-six flares in addition to their bomb load. They dispensed them twelve at a time during three passes, the last of which were accompanied at 20.28 by the bombs from 14,000 feet. P/O Brookes and crew were struggling to climb and jettisoned two 500 pounders to lessen the weight, before spending seventy-five minutes in a vain attempt to locate the target and ultimately dumping the rest of the bomb load. The others carried out attacks largely on estimated positions from 12,000 to 14,500 feet between 19.58 and 21.10, but the smoke-screen from a dozen generators, haze and five to eight-tenths cloud prevented an assessment of results. Sgt Lewis and crew were thwarted by cloud and bombed a heavy flak concentration as a last resort, believed to be at Kerjean on the Roscanvel peninsula, and Sgt Pugh and crew were forced to land at Exeter in a flak-damaged Z1140 that was running short of fuel.

On the following night it was the turn of Elsham Wolds and Snaith to stand down, while the other four stations dispatched aircraft to Hannover and Emden.

All 1 Group stations were active on the 28th, when Elsham Wolds, Lindholme and Snaith provided thirty-two Wellingtons to join an overall force of fifty-five Wellingtons and twenty-nine Hampdens from 3 and 5 Groups to target Münster, while twenty freshman crews went to Boulogne to bomb the docks and shipping. Ten 103 Squadron Wellingtons were assigned to the main event and nine of them were loaded with a 1,000 pounder and three 500 pounders, while the recently promoted W/O Fulbrook and his crew carried thirty-six flares instead of the 1,000 pounder. They took off between 17.48 and 18.28 with F/L Holford the senior pilot on duty, leaving Sgt Potts and crew on the ground pending their departure at 19.22 to deliver fifteen 250 pounders onto the docks and shipping at Boulogne. Under clear skies and in excellent visibility, the latter glided down to 11,000 feet at 21.15 and observed their bombs burst on the docks. Meanwhile, the Münster-bound element had adopted a route via Mablethorpe to Elburg in Holland and then to a point to the north-west of the target for the final run-in but encountered ten-tenths cloud topping out at 15,000 feet and in places extending to 20,000 feet. Nine crews bombed on e.t.a, or dead reckoning (DR), not all at Münster, from 6,000 to 18,000 feet between 19.50 and 20.21, the low altitude that of W/O Fulbrook and crew, who brought the flares home after deeming it pointless to deploy them.

Sgt Pugh and crew withheld their bombs in the hope of finding a last-resort target on the way home and came upon an aerodrome in the Haarlem area some three miles from the Dutch coast, which they attacked from 7,500 feet at 20.30.

During the course of the month, the squadron conducted seven operations and dispatched eighty sorties for the loss of a single Wellington and its crew and four members of another crew, who were in captivity.

February 1942

There were no operations for 1 Group or, indeed, most of Bomber Command during the first five days of the new month as the weather kept the aircraft on the ground and all available personnel were press-ganged into snow-clearing duties. Orders were received on the 6th to prepare for a 1 and 3 Group raid on Brest involving fifty-seven Wellingtons and three Stirlings, for which 1 Group detailed forty-two of the former. 103 Squadron dispatched ten aircraft between 16.58 and 17.35 with S/L Cross and F/L Holford the senior pilots on duty, and they adopted the standard route to the target via Peterborough, Bridport and Ouessant Island. There were no early returns, and all reached the target to be faced by ten-tenths cloud with tops at around 6,000 feet, through which the crews of Sgt Lewis, F/Sgt Gosman, P/O Jones and F/L Holford bombed on e.t.a. or DR from 13,000 and 15,000 feet between 19.30 and 19.56. The others were among thirty-nine to either jettison their loads or bring them home to Elsham Wolds or Exeter, West Raynham, Steeple Morden and Tempsford.

Bremen was posted as the target for a force of fifty-five aircraft on the 10th, while Brest was to be the destination for a small-scale effort by twenty aircraft from 3 Group. 1 Group supported the former with thirty-three Wellingtons, only twenty-four of which attacked the primary target through up to six-tenths cloud. 103 Squadron had not been called into action but was alerted on the 11th to prepare seven Wellingtons for another small-scale raid on Brest in company with eleven from 150 Squadron at Snaith. F/Sgt Kitney's T2617 was loaded with forty-two flares in addition to 500lb SAP bombs and departed Elsham Wolds with the others between 17.44 and 17.57 with W/C Ryan flying as second pilot to P/O Williams. They were followed into the air at 18.27 by F/Sgt Bray and crew, who were on their way to Le Havre to attack the docks and shipping in company with thirty-other mostly freshman crews. The Brest-bound contingent would have been unaware that they were the last to engage in this seemingly endless saga against the German warships that had been a constant draw on resources since the previous March. They found small amounts of cloud at 6,000 feet in the target area and moderate to good visibility and carried out their attacks from 11,500 to 16,500 feet between 20.10 and 20.40, some observing bursts and others not in the glare from searchlights and flares. Sgt Pugh and crew were held for ten minutes in a searchlight cone and were down to 4,000 feet when eventually compelled to bomb a flak position sone two miles south-west of Brest at 21.00. Meanwhile, F/Sgt Bray and crew had managed to drop eight of fifteen 250 pounders on Le Havre docks from 12,000 feet at 20.30, but the others hung-up and had to be brought home.

As the sound of RAF engines receded into the eastern cloud-filled skies, Vice-Admiral Otto Cilliax, the Brest Group commander, whose flag was on Scharnhorst, put Operation Cerberus into action at 21.14, Scharnhorst, Gneisenau and Prinz Eugen slipping anchor, before heading into the English Channel under an escort of destroyers and E-Boats. It was an audacious bid for freedom, covered by bad weather, widespread jamming and meticulously planned support by the Kriegsmarine and the Luftwaffe, all of which had been rehearsed extensively during January. The planning, and a little good fortune, allowed the fleet to make undetected progress until spotted off Le Touquet by two Spitfires piloted by G/C Victor Beamish, the commanding officer of Kenley, and W/C Finlay Boyd, both of whom maintained radio silence and did not report their find until landing at 10.42 on the morning of the 12th.

The British authorities had prepared a plan in advance for precisely this eventuality under the Codename, Operation Fuller, and once the enemy fleet was spotted in the late morning, frantic efforts were made to deploy Bomber and Coastal Command and Fleet Air Arm aircraft, when only elements of 5 Group had been put on four hours readiness. It was after 13.00 before the first sorties took off, 1 Group launching thirty-seven Wellingtons in waves of twenty-five and twelve aircraft, the first, largely from Binbrook and Grimsby, taking off at 13.30 to attempt to meet the enemy fleet off the Belgian coast. Some aircraft made contact in the most challenging weather conditions of squalls and low cloud with a base at 300 feet and carried out attacks while under fire from shipborne flak and Luftwaffe fighters. The 103 Squadron crews of S/L Cross, F/L Holford, F/Sgt Kitney and Sgts Lewis and Pugh departed Elsham Wolds between 14.51 and 15.30 and set course for the Dutch coast off Rotterdam, each sitting on six or seven 500 pounders. F/Sgt Kitney and crew located the fleet and shadowed it for some time broadcasting fixes to assist others in locating it, but were unable themselves to deliver an attack in the conditions. F/L Holford and crew also made contact with the enemy but were unable to achieve a suitable position from which to attack and returned to base after five hours and thirty-eight minutes aloft. The crews of Sgts Lewis and Pugh failed to locate the fleet and returned with their bombs after a little more than three hours in the air. A request for a fix was picked up by Sealand from S/L Cross DFC and crew at 16.57, but nothing further was heard and Z8714 failed to return home. It was learned eventually via the Red Cross that the Wellington had ditched and that S/L Cross and three of his crew had been picked up by the enemy, while two others had lost their lives. S/L Cross was one of those involved in the epic "Great Escape" from Sagan PoW camp on the 24th of March 1944. He was recaptured and was among fifty officers murdered by the Gestapo on Hitler's orders on the 30th.

The 103 Squadron crews had been part of the largest commitment of aircraft by daylight in the war to date, amounting to 242 sorties, but the Germans had expertly timed their break-out to exploit the weather conditions and there had been little chance of a successful outcome for the British forces. Operation Fuller cost Bomber Command fifteen aircraft, 5 Group alone posting missing nine Hampdens and crews, all lost in the North Sea, six of them without trace, and they could be added to all of those sacrificed to this endeavour over the past eleven months. The enemy fleet made good its escape into open sea, although, its own trials and tribulations were not yet over. Scharnhorst struck a mine in the late afternoon and began to fall back, and at 19.55, a magnetic mine detonated close enough to Gneisenau, when off Terschelling, to open a small hole in the starboard side, and temporarily slow her progress also. Later still, at 21.34, when passing through the same stretch of water, Scharnhorst hit another mine which stopped both engines and damaged steering and fire control. The vessel got under way again at 22.23 using its starboard engines and making twelve knots, while carrying an additional one thousand tons of seawater. The day's activities were not yet over for 5 Group, and the crews of fourteen Hampdens and nine Manchesters were briefed to lay mines in the Nectarine garden off the Frisians through which the enemy fleet would have to pass to reach safety.

Gneisenau and Prinz Eugen reached the Elbe Estuary at 07.00 on the 13th, and tied up at Brunsbüttel North Locks at 09.30, while Scharnhorst arrived at Wilhelmshaven at 10.00 with three months-worth of damage to repair. The mines had been laid almost certainly by 5 Group Hampdens over the preceding nights and demonstrated the remarkable effectiveness of this war-long campaign. The "Channel Dash" as it came to be known was a huge embarrassment to the government and the nation, but if nothing else, this annoying itch had been scratched for the last time and the Command could now focus its energies on the strategic targets to which it was better suited. Binbrook, Hemswell and Lindholme were on duty on behalf of 1 Group on the night of the 13/14th, while Elsham Wolds, Grimsby and Snaith enjoyed a night off. The targets were Cologne and Le Havre, which 1 Group supported with seventeen and eleven Wellingtons respectively, but thick cloud and icing conditions wrecked any chance of a successful outcome.

A new Air Ministry directive, issued on the 14th, was to change the emphasis of bomber operations from that point until the end of the war. Lengthy consideration having been given to the Butt Report and the future of an independent bomber force, the new policy authorized the blatant area bombing of Germany's industrial towns and cities in a direct assault on the morale of the civilian population, particularly its workers. This had, of course, been going on since the summer of 1940, but no longer would there be the pretence of claiming to be attacking industrial and military targets. Waiting in the wings, in fact, at this very moment, four days into his voyage from the United States in the armed merchantman, Alcantara, was a new leader, a man well-known to 5 Group, who not only would pursue this policy with a will, but also possessed the self-belief, arrogance and stubbornness to fight his corner against all-comers on behalf of his beleaguered Bomber Command.

That night, Mannheim was posted as the target and a force of ninety-eight aircraft assembled accordingly, 1 Group providing thirty-seven Wellingtons from Elsham Wolds, Grimsby, Lindholme and Snaith. The seven-strong 103 Squadron element took off between 18.07 and 18.24 with F/O Peck the senior pilot on duty and exited the English coast at Orfordness on course for Dinant in Belgium. Ten-tenths cloud with tops at up to 10,000 feet accompanied the bombers all the way to the target, which F/Sgt Gosman and crew would not reach after turning back from a position thirty miles south-east of Ostend because of an inability to climb beyond 11,500 feet. Sgt John and crew were within thirty miles of the frontier with Luxembourg when a technical problem persuaded them also to abort their sortie, leaving the others to press on and attempt to locate the target in challenging conditions. W/O Fulbrook and crew were carrying thirty-six flares in addition to three 500 pounders but were unable to locate the target and dropped the bombs at ten-minute intervals from 21.15 from 13,000 to 14,000 feet, observing bursts through the cloud. F/O Peck and crew bombed from 11,500 feet at 21.35, while the crews of F/Sgt Bray and P/O Brookes spread their efforts over extended periods, the former loitering over a searchlight and flak concentration in the Mannheim area and releasing bombs at intervals between 20.59 and 21.22. The latter dispensed their bombs in three lots at ten-minute intervals from 13,500 feet at 21.25, 21.35 and 21.45, respectively on a row of lights north-east of Mannheim, a small town in the Mosel Valley and a group of buildings twenty-five miles north of Trier. Mannheim was barely touched by the raid, which cost a Hampden and a Whitley, while all from 1 Group returned safely having dispensed propaganda leaflets (nickels) to the residents of the Rhine Valley.

The following week was devoted to small-scale "roving commission" operations and mining, which only involved 103 Squadron on the night of the 21/22nd. Destinations for the dozen Wellingtons from Elsham Wolds and ten from Snaith were Karlsruhe, Mannheim, Darmstadt, Frankfurt and Giessen, all in southern Germany, and their brief was to create as big a nuisance as possible. The 103 Squadron contingent took off between 18.07 and 19.25 with S/L Godfrey the senior pilot on duty and exited the English coast at Orfordness en-route to Fumay on the Franco-Belgian frontier, from where they would go their separate ways. Once over enemy territory the skies cleared, and crews were able to map-read in excellent visibility. Sgt Lewis and crew abandoned their sortie because of a starboard engine issue when close to the French coast, while P/O Gilby and crew lost their intercom and bombed Ostend as a last resort target. S/L Godfrey and crew stooged around searching for a worthwhile target and selected the main railway station in Ludwigshafen, Mannheim's twin city over on the west bank of the Rhine. They delivered their bombs from 15,000 feet at 22.25, observing bursts across the aiming point, before heading home with a concerned eye on the fuel gauge. They were relieved when Manston appeared on the horizon and landed with almost empty tanks after eight-and-three-quarter hours in the air. The crews of F/Sgt Tett, Sgt Potts and F/Sgt Bray all located their briefed target of Mannheim and attacked it from 12,000 to 14,500 feet between 22.15 and 23.28 and P/O Ward and crew targeted Karlsruhe from 12,000 feet at 22.40. The others found alternative objectives to bomb from 13,000 to 15,000 feet between 21.50 and 23.52 and returned safely.

Air Chief Marshal Sir Arthur Harris took up his post as the new Commander-in-Chief of Bomber Command on the 22nd. He was a man well-known to 5 Group, having served as its A-O-C until November 1940, when he became second deputy to Sir Charles Portal, the Chief-of-the-Air-Staff. Harris arrived at the helm with firm ideas already in place on how to win the war by bombing alone, a pre-war theory, which no commander had yet had an opportunity to put into practice. It was obvious to him, that the small-scale raids on multiple targets favoured by his predecessor served only to dilute the effort, and that such pin-prick attacks could not hurt Germany's war effort. He recognized the need to overwhelm the defences and emergency services by pushing the maximum number of aircraft across the aiming-point in the shortest possible time, and this would signal the birth of the bomber stream and an end to the former practice, whereby squadrons or even crews determined for themselves the details of their sorties. He knew also that urban areas are most efficiently destroyed by fire, rather than blast, and it would not be long before the bomb loads carried in his aircraft reflected this thinking. Harris also needed to bolster his resources, and he would become a constant thorn in the flesh of the Ministry of Aircraft Production as he demanded more and more aircraft and improved quality control.

On the night of his appointment Harris sent fifty Wellingtons and Hampdens to bomb the floating dock at Wilhelmshaven, at which, it was believed, Scharnhorst was under repair, and it was the Polish squadrons from Hemswell that represented 1 Group. The target area was found to be covered by dense cloud and the bombing that took place on estimated positions missed the target altogether and failed to elicit any comment from local sources. F/L Saxelby was posted to the squadron from 18 O.T.U on the 25th to fulfil the role of deputy flight commander as successor to F/L Holford, who had been promoted to acting squadron leader rank to fill the void left by the loss of S/L Cross. As Elsham Wolds had completed its operational activities for the month, both would be allowed plenty of time to settle in to their new jobs. That night, sixty-one aircraft took off to attack another floating dock, this time at Kiel, where Gneisenau was thought to be at berth and 1 Group supported the operation with thirty-five Wellingtons from Binbrook, Grimsby and Hemswell. Among them were two 12 Squadron Merlin-powered Mk II Wellingtons carrying the group's first 4,000lb high-capacity blockbusters, that came to be known as "cookies". Bombs fell into the town and docks area, hitting an accommodation ship in which up to 130 people lost their lives.

Twenty-four hours later the operation was repeated by a force of forty-nine aircraft, 1 Group represented by Polish crews from Lindholme, and this time the brief named Gneisenau as the principal target. A high explosive bomb struck her bow, and not only did it kill 116 of her crew, it also ended her sea-going career for good. It was ironic that within two weeks of entering what was supposedly a safe haven after enduring eleven months of constant bombardment at Brest, this magnificent vessel should succumb in this way. Her main armament was removed for use in coastal defence, and she was towed to Gdynia, where she remained unrepaired for the remainder of the war. The British authorities were unaware of the success, however, and sent another raid of sixty-eight aircraft on the 27th. For the third consecutive night Kiel was the objective on the 27/28th, for which the 1 Group effort of thirty-four Wellingtons was provided by Binbrook, Grimsby and Hemswell. Conditions on this night were poor, and the raid missed the town altogether.

During the course of the month the squadron took part in six operations on four nights and the daylight "Channel Dash", dispatching forty-two sorties for the loss of a single Wellington and its crew.

March 1942

On the 1st of March W/C Ryan was posted on paper to Gibraltar but reposted to 103 Squadron as a supernumerary pending the arrival of his successor as commanding officer. Bomber Command's evolution to war-winning capability was to be long, arduous and gradual, but the first signs of a new hand on the tiller came early on in Harris's reign with what was a template for future operations and a sign of things to come. The Renault lorry factory was located in a loop of the Seine in the district of Billancourt to the south-west of the centre of Paris and was capable of producing 18,000 lorries per year, which was a massive boon to the German war effort. An Air Ministry request prompted the meticulous planning of an operation, which would be conducted in three waves, led by experienced crews, and would involve extensive use of flares to provide illumination. In the face of what was expected to be scant defence, crews were briefed to attack from as low a level as practicable, both for the sake of accuracy and in an attempt to avoid civilian casualties. In time, such operations would be led by aircraft equipped with the new Gee or TR1335 electronic navigation device, but the 3 Group squadrons already employing it were forbidden from taking part, lest an example fall into enemy hands. *(For the purpose of this book, the terms Gee and TR are interchangeable.)* A force of 235 aircraft was assembled on the 3rd, a new record for a single target, of which thirty-five Wellingtons were provided by 1 Group from Binbrook, Elsham Wolds, Grimsby and Snaith.

This would be 103 Squadron's first operation for a week-and-a-half, and its ten Wellingtons took off between 17.40 and 18.25 with S/Ls Godfrey and Holford the senior pilots on duty and G/C Constantine accompanying the latter. The outward route bypassed Reading on the way to exit the English coast at Beachy Head and make landfall on the French side of the Channel at Abbeville, but P/O Brookes and crew were back on the ground in a little over an hour after experiencing a lack of engine power. The others found eight-tenths cloud over the target with a base at 8,000 feet, and this enabled them to come below and obtain a clear view of the aiming point. The Elsham Wolds crews delivered their attacks from 1,500 to 4,000 feet between 21.02 and 21.40 and observed their 1,000 and 500 pounders demolish buildings within the factory area, before returning safely to report smoke rising through 1,000 feet and what was clearly a highly effective operation. Post-raid reconnaissance revealed that 40% of the factory had been destroyed at a cost to the Command of just one aircraft and to the Germans of a month's production amounting to 2,300 vehicles. The success was marred only by the deaths of 367 French people in adjacent residential districts, and this question of collateral damage would never satisfactorily be addressed. It was paradoxical, that Harris, a champion of area bombing, should gain his first major success via a precision raid. Information was received, that despite the casualties, the French were delighted with the raid and regarded it as the most important occurrence in France since the signing of the armistice.

The following days were blighted by snow falls, which prevented operations from taking place. As an industrial centre of enormous significance and home to the giant Krupp concern, Essen was to feature heavily in Harris's future plans. The first of three raids on the Borbeck districts on consecutive nights was posted on the 8th, for which a force of 211 aircraft was assembled, forty of the Wellingtons provided by 1 Group from Binbrook, Elsham Wolds, Grimsby, Hemswell and Snaith. The plan called for 3 Group's Gee-equipped aircraft to go in first to find the aiming-point and start fires to attract those following behind, the second wave to deliver incendiaries and the third wave, consisting of the heavy brigade, to drop high explosives. There was a late departure for the ten 103 Squadron Wellingtons, and as F/L Gillespie and crew taxied towards the runway, a tyre burst and ended their interest in proceedings. The others took off between 00.21 and 01.02 with S/L Holford the senior pilot on duty, accompanied by F/L Saxelby, and flew out over Southwold on course for the Scheldt estuary. From there they were to head eastwards to a point north of Cologne, where they turned to the north on a direct course to the central Ruhr. Decoy fire sites in open country south of the target lured away much of the effort, and hundreds of flares igniting at 10,000 to 12,000 feet created a glare, which, together with that from searchlights, rendered aiming-point identification something of a challenge. The Elsham Wolds crews delivered their 1,000 and 500lb high explosive bombs and 250lb incendiaries from 11,000 to 15,000 feet between 02.45 and 03.40, and it was discovered later that Sgt Potts and crew had bombed Duisburg and F/Sgt Martin and crew an unidentified built-up area. Local sources described a light raid with some housing damage in southern districts, and this was achieved at a cost to the Command of eight aircraft. It was a disappointing outcome, and it would soon become clear that despite Gee's effectiveness as a navigation tool, it could not be relied upon as a blind-bombing device.

W/C J.F.H du Boulay DFC was posted in from 27 O.T.U on the 9th and installed as the new commanding officer. Born in Burma in 1913 he had been awarded the DFC, gazetted 31st of May 1940, while serving with 115 Squadron. Shortly afterwards he was posted away and had been occupied with instruction duties ever since. A force of 187 aircraft was made ready to return to Essen on the 9th, this time adopting the northerly route to the Ruhr via the Dutch coast near Haarlem, Elburg and Wesel to leave a run of some twenty miles to the target. 1 Group ordered a "Goodwood" or maximum effort and contributed sixty-two Wellingtons, eleven of them representing 103 Squadron and departing Elsham Wolds between 19.30 and 20.07 with S/L Godfrey the senior pilot on duty. The exited the English coast over Mablethorpe and all reached the Wesel area, where P/O Gilby and crew bombed a searchlight and flak concentration from 12,000 feet at 21.33 after experiencing engine and flying instrument issues. Sgt Lewis and crew also bombed at Wesel from 15,000 feet at 21.36 after the pilot's instrument panel went dark. The others arrived over Essen to find five-tenths cloud with tops at around 8,000 feet and the vertical view onto the target compromised by the usual industrial haze. The 103 Squadron crews carried out their attacks from 12,500 to 15,000 feet between 21.31 and 22.19, Sgt John and crew jettisoning theirs when the bomb-release system failed. P/O Smith and crew were thrown off course by the need to take evasive action, and ultimately bombed two lights some six miles south-east of Essen. Returning crews reported a large number of incendiaries burning in the centre of Essen, when in fact, the bombing had been scattered over twenty-four other Ruhr towns and cities, with Hamborn and Duisburg the chief beneficiaries. The Essen authorities reported the destruction of two buildings, with seventy-two others damaged, and this was another hugely disappointing outcome.

A smaller-scale operation by 126 aircraft on the following night involved just five Wellingtons from 103 Squadron in a 1 Group contingent of thirty-one from all stations but Snaith. The Elsham Wolds quintet took off between 19.32 and 19.42 with S/L Godfrey and F/L Saxelby the senior pilots on duty and adopted the same route as twenty-four hours earlier. They ran into eight to ten-tenths ice-bearing cloud at the Dutch coast and after shedding two thousand feet, P/O Ward and crew were unable to climb beyond 10,000 feet and jettisoned their load when forced to take evasive action south of Amsterdam. Those reaching the Ruhr were greeted by three-tenths cloud, but it was the searchlight glare and industrial haze that prevented crews from making a positive identification of Essen. P/O Brookes and crew carried out three passes at 14,500 feet between 21.50 and 22.03, while F/L Saxelby and crew were driven off course by the defences and bombed a built-up area five miles south-west of the city from 15,000 feet at 21.45. S/L Godfrey and crew bombed fires on DR and P/O Smith and crew the general area on a night when fewer than half of the crews reached the primary target and thirty-five bombed alternatives. The nearest any bombs fell to the Krupp complex was on a railway line serving the area and this confirmed the limitations of Gee as anything more than an aid to navigation.

Kiel's Deutsche Werke and Germania Werft U-Boot construction yards were posted as the targets for a force of sixty-eight Wellingtons on the 12th, for which 1 Group detailed twenty-six from Binbrook, Grimsby and Hemswell, while nineteen others from Elsham Wolds, Grimsby, Lindholme and Snaith were briefed to attack the docks and shipping at Emden in an overall 1 and 4 Group force of forty Wellingtons and Whitleys. The 103 Squadron crews of F/Sgt Bray and Sgts John and Staniland departed Elsham Wolds between 19.28 and 19.51 each with six 500 pounders beneath their feet and flew out over Mablethorpe to pinpoint on the Frisian Island of Juist. Nine-tenths cloud over the target prevented a definitive identification of Emden, and bombs were delivered on estimated positions from 8,000 to 14,000 feet between 21.48 and 21.55, as it was discovered later, missing the target by five miles. Meanwhile, 140 miles to the north-east, conditions in the Baltic coast region were excellent and bombs were observed to explode across the port area and naval dockyard, and both the Deutsche Werke and the Germania Werft yards sustained damage.

Orders were received across the Command on the 13th to prepare a force of 135 aircraft of six types for a Gee-led operation to Cologne. 1 Group contributed forty-one Wellingtons from Elsham Wolds, Lindholme and Snaith and a further twelve for freshman crews to take to Dunkerque. Among the latter were the first sorties by the latest unit to form in 1 Group, 460 Squadron RAAF, which was stationed for the time being at Breighton in Yorkshire. 103 Squadron made ready eleven Wellingtons and dispatched them from Elsham Wolds between 18.50 and 19.28 with S/L Holford and F/L Saxelby the senior pilots on duty and each crew sitting on a 1,000 pounder, three 500 pounders, a single 250 pounder and a 250lb incendiary bomb. They exited the English coast at Orfordness and made for Charleroi in Belgium and those arriving in the target area offered the usual diverse opinions as to the cloud conditions. The consensus was that ten-tenths medium cloud hovered to the west and east of the city, while a gap existed right over it in which two to five-tenths cumulus topped out at 11,000 feet. The weather was favourable, and rivers, bridges and Autobahns stood out in the partial snow-cover to provide ground features to assist with navigation. Illumination flares were described as being of great assistance, and searchlight beams also provided a reference for the 103 Squadron crews, who carried out their attacks from 11,000 to 16,000 feet between 22.13 and 22.44. The last bombing time was that of Sgt Tett and crew, who had been contending with engine issues on the way out but to their credit had carried on to make an attack. P/O Lewis noticed his petrol gauge winding back fifty gallons every ten minutes and bombed on e.t.a at 21.47, which suggests that he and his crew were some way short of the target at the time. Returning crews reported fires to the west and north-west of the city centre and local sources confirmed that this had been one of the most destructive raids yet against the Rhineland capital, causing a loss of production at a number of war industry factories, while setting off 260 fires and damaging fifteen hundred houses, albeit the majority only lightly.

The weather prevented all but small-scale and mining operations from taking place over the next eleven nights, but once normal service resumed on the 25th, Harris returned to his unfinished business with Essen. The largest force yet for a single target of 254 aircraft stood ready, which included a new record contribution by 1 Group of 109 Wellingtons, fourteen of them representing 103 Squadron. They departed Elsham Wolds between 20.15 and 20.47

with S/L Godfrey and F/Ls Gillespie and Saxelby the senior pilots on duty and each Wellington loaded with one 1,000 pounder, four 500 pounders and one of 250lbs. F/L Gillespie and crew abandoned their sortie during the climb-out when the Gyro failed and landed to find that Sgt Gosman and crew had preceded them by six minutes after experiencing electrical issues, both returning their bombs to the dump. The others flew out over Cromer on course for the Scheldt estuary and it was in this area, five miles west of Voorne, that F/Sgt Bray and crew were forced to turn back when the starboard engine exhaust pipe came adrift and emitted flames that not only risked a fire but also made them highly visible. P/O Ward was struggling for height and jettisoning a 250 pounder over the sea enabled him to coax an extra four thousand feet out of R1393 so that they were at a healthier 13,000 feet as they crossed the Dutch/German frontier due west of Duisburg. Horizontal visibility in the target area was good, but ground features were rendered indistinct by industrial haze and the 103 Squadron crews delivered their attacks mostly from estimated positions from 10,000 to 14,500 feet between 22.30 and 23.04. R1393's petrol tanks were holed by flak over the target and finally ran dry five miles out from Orfordness, but Sgt John pulled off a textbook ditching and he and his crew were soon picked up, put ashore and taken to Martlesham Heath. Sgt Pugh's DV452 was intercepted by a BF110 on the way home, and raked from stem to stern, to which the rear gunner responded with a burst of eighty rounds into the enemy night-fighter from twenty yards, and it was last seen going down. At debriefing, 181 crews claimed to have bombed the city with good results, but in reality, a decoy fire site at Rheinberg had lured most of the bombing away, and there was hardly any damage in Essen.

Like a dog with a bone, Harris would not leave Essen alone and on the following night planned a return with a reduced force of 104 Wellingtons and eleven Stirlings, of which thirty-four of the former were provided by 1 Group from Binbrook, Grimsby and Hemswell. The outcome was the same, but many night-fighters were lying in wait and together with heavy flak in the target area, accounted for eleven bombers, a 10% loss rate. The war against Essen was one that Harris would win, but not before he had endured twelve months of failure and frustration waiting for the "silver bullet", Oboe.

An audacious raid on the dry dock gates at St-Nazaire by naval and commando units was mounted on the night of the 27/28th, and Bomber Command provided sixty-two aircraft to bomb German positions around the port. The plan was that the destroyer, HMS Campbeltown, her bows filled with explosives on a timer, would ram the gates and embed herself, while a small party of commandos conducted demolition work. 1 Group provided twenty-seven Wellingtons from Elsham Wolds, Lindholme and Snaith and they were to join forces with thirty-five 4 Group Whitleys. The 103 Squadron element of twelve flew to Pershore as a forward base, and eleven of them took off from there between 22.10 and 23.13 with S/Ls Godfrey and Holford the senior pilots on duty, exiting the English coast at Bridport on course for the Ile-de-Brehat on the northern approach to the Finistere peninsula and Belle Isle off the Biscay coast. They arrived in the target area to find ten-tenths cloud that offered no chance of effectively supporting the land and sea elements and only S/L Godfrey and crew caught a glimpse of the ground through a gap in the clouds and bombed at one end of the target area, while the remaining ten crews gave up and brought their bombs home.

Harris must have given great thought to the inability of his crews to locate and hit a target as big as Essen but believed that if he could give them clearly visible pinpoints on the ground, they would do the rest. He realised that coastlines could be the answer, and he began a series of attacks on urban areas located on the Baltic coast. On the night of the 28th, orders went out to stations across the Command to prepare for a major operation against the ancient and historic city of Lübeck, located on an island in the River Trave some forty miles south-east of Kiel. Lübeck was and remains by name a Hansastadt, a member of the medieval Hanseatic League of northern European free trade cities, along with the likes of Hamburg and Bremen and others in England. It contained a wealth of half-timbered buildings arranged in narrow streets, and not expecting to be attacked, was inadequately defended against a bomber force with fire-raising intent. A force of 234 aircraft was assembled, fifty-one of the Wellingtons provided by 1 Group and just five by 103 Squadron, who were informed at briefing that the operation would be conducted along the lines of the successful Renault raid at the start of the month.

The crews of P/Os Martin and Ward, W/O Fulbrook and Sgts Potts and Pugh departed Elsham Wolds between 20.51 and 21.06, each sitting on 2,250lbs of incendiaries, and flew out over Mablethorpe on course for Husum on the western coast of Schleswig-Holstein. The final turning point was a dozen miles north-west of the target, which all reached under clear skies and in excellent visibility and bombed from 2,000 to 6,100 feet between 00.25 and 01.00. The early time and low altitude belonged to Sgt Martin and crew, who, five minutes after bombing, descended to 1,500 feet and strafed a seaplane base at Travemünde. As anticipated, the defences were weak and uncoordinated and failed to protect the city and its inhabitants. At debriefing, crews reported that the glow from the burning city had remained visible for a hundred miles into the return journey and 191 of them claimed to have bombed the primary target. Post-raid reconnaissance and local sources confirmed that enormous damage for the period had resulted, in what was the first major success for the area bombing policy. More than fourteen hundred buildings were destroyed and almost two thousand others seriously damaged, and this amounted to around 30% of the built-up area. This huge success was gained for the loss of twelve aircraft, among which was 103 Squadron's R1061. A W/T message was received from P/O Ward and crew at 01.07, stating that a petrol tank was on fire, and that they were still under attack. A fix was obtained, but there was no further acknowledgement from the Wellington, which is presumed to have crashed into the sea and only the remains of P/O Ward came ashore for burial on the Frisian Island of Langeoog on the 12th of June. This was an experienced crew, who, it will be recalled, had survived a crash in November and their loss would be keenly felt by the squadron and Elsham Wolds communities. There was an outcry following this unexpected attack on Lübeck, which was a vital port for the Red Cross, and an agreement was struck that, in theory, although not entirely in practice, ensured its future protection from bombing.

During the course of the month the squadron took part in nine operations and dispatched seventy-nine sorties for the loss of two Wellingtons and one crew.

April 1942

The new month began for 1 Group on the 1st with an operation involving five Wellingtons from Binbrook against the Matford (Ford) motor works in Paris's north-western district of Poissy in company with a dozen other Wellingtons and twenty-four Whitleys from 4 Group. At the same time, fifteen freshman crews targeted the docks and shipping at Le Havre. Twenty-four Whitley and three Wellington crews returned from the main event with claims of accurate bombing, which was not backed up by photographic reconnaissance, but in truth, it was difficult to assess damage to a specific factory nestling among others in an industrial area. Elsewhere, it turned into a disastrous night for 3 Group, whose railway targets were at Hanau and Lohr to the east of Frankfurt, and from which five out of twelve 57 Squadron Wellingtons failed to return and seven of fourteen belonging to 214 Squadron.

The operations against the Matford plant and Le Havre were repeated on the following night and were supported by 1 Group with twenty-seven and six Wellingtons respectively from Binbrook, Breighton, Elsham Wolds and Snaith. 103 Squadron put up a dozen Wellingtons for Poissy, which took off between 19.45 and 19.56 with S/L Holford the senior pilot on duty. They were part of an overall force of fifty Wellingtons and Stirlings, which flew out over Beachy Head on a direct course via Dieppe for the target, where they arrived to find clear conditions, a bright moon and good visibility. The Elsham Wolds crews carried out their attacks from 1,500 to 4,000 feet in the face of an intense flak response and four of them returned in flak-damaged Wellingtons. At debriefings, crews were unanimous in their belief that the factory had been severely damaged, and there were no reports to the contrary.

The first major operation of the new month was directed at Cologne on the night of the 5/6th and involved a new record force of 263 aircraft, which included a maximum effort from 1 Group of seventy-nine Wellingtons. The aiming point was the Klöckner-Humboldt engineering works in the Deutz district on the East Bank of the Rhine in the city centre, which manufactured aero-engines and a wide range of military vehicles. 103 Squadron supported the operation with ten Wellingtons, which departed Elsham Wolds between 22.49 and 23.26 with F/L Saxelby the senior pilot on duty and each aircraft carrying a maximum load of incendiaries. They exited the English coast at Southwold to head via the Scheldt estuary to a point on the Rhine between Bonn to the south and Cologne to the north and arrived in the target area to encounter bright moonlight, which penetrated the initially modest amount of cloud. However, a large patch of cumulous with tops at 17,000 feet was advancing from the south and would reach the city before the raid ended. The glint of moonlight off an S-bend in the Rhine to the south of the city centre assisted some crews to establish a position for the bombing run, in spite of which, many failed to identify Cologne. Nine of the 103 Squadron crews carried out an attack, but there was a temporary absence of bombing heights and times on the ORB Form 541, and we know only that Sgt Pugh and crew were coned by searchlights and down to 3,500 feet by the time they jettisoned their load west of the aiming point on the way home in a flak-damaged T2921 to land at Middle Wallop. Returning crews reported fires and bursts but found it difficult to distinguish the genuine articles and decoys, and local sources claimed that the bombing was scattered right across the built-up area, destroying or seriously damaging ninety houses but nothing of industrial significance.

On the following night, Harris turned his attention back upon Essen, with the first of three raids against it in six nights, to which 1 Group contributed forty-one Wellingtons from Binbrook, Elsham Wolds, Grimsby, Hemswell and Snaith. The seven-strong 103 Squadron element had to wait until after midnight before taking to the air between 00.08 and 00.31 with F/L Gillespie the senior pilot on duty. They adopted the southerly route to the central Ruhr via Southwold, Blankenberg on the Belgian coast and Namur, to then swing south of Bonn before heading north to the target. They encountered electrical storms and severe icing conditions in cloud over the North Sea that extended to 13,000 feet, threatening to destroy lift and forcing many crews to abandon their sorties. Among them were twenty-seven of the 1 Group participants including the 103 Squadron crews of F/L Gillespie, P/O Tett, P/O Gorrie and W/O Fulbrook, who returned to base between 03.01 and 03.23, leaving the crews of P/Os Smith and Martin and Sgt Lewis to battle on and reach the enemy coast. P/O Smith was becoming concerned about excessive fuel consumption and ordered the bombs to be jettisoned over enemy territory, while Sgt Lewis and crew bombed what they believed to be Düsseldorf, some twenty miles short of Essen. Only P/O Martin and crew pressed on to the primary target on DR based on a pinpoint on the Rhine gained when south of Cologne. Where their bombs fell is unknown, but they returned safely after almost six hours aloft, albeit in a flak-damaged R1667.

Hamburg was posted as the target on the 8th, and yet another record force, this time of 272 aircraft, was assembled, which included a 1 Group contribution of seventy-eight Wellingtons, eleven of them representing 103 Squadron. They departed Elsham Wolds between 21.53 and 22.50 with S/L Holford the senior pilot on duty accompanied by W/C Du Boulay and a W/C Simmons flying as second pilot to F/L Saxelby to gain up-to-date operational experience before being handed command of 142 Squadron at Grimsby. They flew out over Mablethorpe on course for a point over the North Sea east of Heligoland, where they were to turn to the south-east to make landfall and approach the target from the south-west. They encountered one of the towering electrical storms with icing conditions that frequently built up over the North Sea to bar the approaches to north-western Germany, and on this night, not all who set out would reach their intended destination. Sgt Lewis and crew lost their heating system shortly after taking off and battled the intense cold to drop the bombs on a built-up area south-east of Oldenburg. By the time they landed at Elsham Wolds at 04.25, the pilot was suffering from frostbite. P/O Smith and crew believed that they had attacked Wilhelmshaven, while the others could only claim to have bombed at Hamburg, but as all nineteen of the squadron's bombing photos showed nothing but cloud, it was all conjecture. Local sources estimated that around fourteen bomb loads had hit the city, causing three large fires but no damage of significance.

Harris's personal war against Essen continued on the 10th, when orders were received across the Command to assemble another large force, this time of 254 aircraft, of which seventy-five of the Wellingtons were provided by 1 Group. Ten were made ready at Elsham Wolds and took off between 21.50 and 22.44 with S/L Godfrey and F/Ls Gillespie and Saxelby the senior pilots on duty and W/C Simmons accompanying W/O Fulbrook. Sgt Staniland and crew were soon compromised by an electrical issue that would end their interest in proceedings and they returned their bomb load to the dump. The others flew out under starlight with cloud below them and adopted a northerly route from Mablethorpe to Deventer in central Holland, before swinging to the south-east to pinpoint on Haltern some twenty miles north of the target, where they were greeted by up to nine-tenths cloud with tops at 6,000 to 8,000 feet. Thirty flare carrying aircraft preceded the main force with a brief to drop green flares if they could make a positive identification of the aiming point. Those equipped with Gee established their approximate positions electronically, while the remainder employed DR, e.t.a. and evidence of searchlights and flak. S/L Godfrey and crew failed to locate the primary target and continued on a southerly heading to release their all-incendiary load on e.t.a. over Cologne. P/O Tett and crew were contending with a troublesome port engine on the way out, which cut out over the target, possibly as the result of flak, but they delivered their attack and returned on one engine. The rest of the 103 Squadron contingent bombed built-up areas, mostly from between 12,000 and 15,000 feet and some observed within the glow of incendiaries but saw nothing of the ground and had nothing of use to pass on to the intelligence sections at debriefing.

Undaunted, Harris ordered another raid on the 12th, for which 251 aircraft were made ready, 1 Group contributing seventy-Wellingtons for the main event and fourteen for a freshman raid on the docks and shipping at Le Havre. Among the latter were the first eight sorties by the new Mk III Wellington in the hands of 150 Squadron, whose crews were mightily impressed by the upgrade in performance over the Mk Ic. 103 Squadron launched nine aircraft from Elsham Wolds between 21.06 and 21.42 with F/Ls Gillespie and Saxelby the senior pilots on duty, and they exited the English coast over Orfordness on course for Dunkerque and a somewhat circuitous southerly route to the target via Dinant in Belgium and Sinzig, a town to the south of Bonn. F/O Wallis and crew were closing on the French coast when the rear turret became unserviceable, and P/O Smith and crew dropped out at around the same time when an engine-driven generator failed. Those reaching the target area found clear skies but were prevented by extreme darkness and industrial haze from identifying ground features, some picking up distinctive bends in the River Ruhr to the south of the city and employing already developing fires as a guide. Some crews spotted green flares dispensed by the lead aircraft, but most were guided by an intense flak barrage and bombed on estimated positions. On return, P/O Gilby and crew reported being ensnared by forty searchlights and plummeting out of control from 15,000 feet, before pulling out at 200 feet, by which time the bombs had been jettisoned. The front gunner shot out at least six of the beams from low level before they raced away and climbed back up to 11,000 feet for the rest of the journey to a landing at Manston. F/L Gillespie and crew failed to return, and it is believed that W5664 crashed in the North Sea, this based on the washing ashore in Holland of the remains of the rear gunner. A total of 173 crews claimed to have bombed in the general area of the Krupp-occupied Borbeck districts, but bombing photos revealed many Ruhr locations, while local sources confirmed a slight improvement in accuracy, a large fire in the Krupp complex and the destruction of twenty-eight dwelling units. This brought to an end a series of eight heavy raids against the city since the night of the 8/9th of March, during which 1,555 sorties had resulted in fewer than two-thirds of the crews claiming to have bombed in the target area. A paltry twenty-two bombing photos had been plotted to within five miles of Essen and in exchange for this, sixty-four aircraft and crews had been lost, industrial damage had been slight, and housing damage modest in the extreme.

Attention on the 14th switched to Dortmund, another industrial giant located at the eastern end of the Ruhr, where it was home among other war-industry supporters to the synthetic oil-producing Hoesch-Westfalenhütte AG, the Hoesch-Benzin GmbH (Gesellschaft mit beschränkter Haftung or limited company) and the Zecha Hansa plant and was also a centre for steel, coal and beer production. The force of 208 aircraft represented by far the largest effort yet against this target and included a contribution from 1 Group of sixty-eight Wellingtons, all but one carrying an all-incendiary load, while a single Merlin-powered Mk II variant had a 4,000lb "cookie" winched into its bomb bay. The seven-strong 103 Squadron element departed Elsham Wolds between 21.36 and 22.19 with S/L Godfrey the senior pilot on duty accompanied by W/C Simmons, and they crossed the English coast at Orfordness for a southerly approach to the target via the Calais area, Dinant in Belgium and south of Sinzig in Germany. P/O Gilby's rear turret became unserviceable when two hours out, while Sgt Potts and crew failed to locate the target and forty minutes after e.t.a. turned back and bombed in the vicinity of Aachen. S/L Godfrey lost his starboard engine over the target and had to jettison his load, before returning home on the good engine to land at West Malling. A change in the wind caused many crews to arrive too late to benefit from green flares, causing the bombing to take place on estimated positions and spread itself liberally around the Ruhr.

A reduced force of 152 aircraft was assembled for the same target twenty-four hours later, this time supported by 1 Group with forty-six Wellingtons, six of them representing 103 Squadron. They departed Elsham Wolds between 22.47 and 23.45 with F/O Wallis the senior pilot on duty and set course for the target via Orfordness, Knokke on the Belgian coast and Bonn. Thick cloud and icing conditions prevented almost half of the force from reaching the target, and among those turning back were P/O Gilby and crew, who had been last to take-off. While debating the fact that they would be unable to reach the target in time, the rear gunner became indisposed and this settled the matter and persuaded them to turn back at 02.50. Those reaching the target area bombed on e.t.a, red flares and evidence of searchlights and flak, but none had a genuine fix on Dortmund and the bombing was again spread over many Ruhr locations. P/O Gosman and crew bombed on e.t.a. and were homebound when the starboard engine caught fire and shed its propeller at 06.55, forcing them to crash-land R1344 five minutes later at a spot which would become Metheringham airfield, the future home of the Lancasters of 5 Group's 106 Squadron.

Among minor operations mounted on the night of the 16/17th was an attack on the docks and shipping at Le Havre, for which 103 Squadron contributed a single Wellington bearing aloft the freshman crew of P/O Winchester. They departed Elsham Wolds at 21.05 carrying fourteen 250 pounders and ten bundles of nickels to provide reading matter, or according to Harris, toilet paper, for the residents of the Bayeux and Caen regions. Exiting the English coast at Littlehampton, they crossed the Channel in extreme darkness on a moonless night and failed to locate the target despite a search and in accordance with instructions brough their bombs home.

Hamburg was posted as the target on the 18th and a force of 173 aircraft assembled, 1 Group represented by seventy-three Wellingtons, the ten provided by 103 Squadron departing Elsham Wolds between 22.56 and 23.34 with S/L Godfrey the senior pilot on duty. All but one was carrying an incendiary load and the experienced crews illuminator flares as they headed for Mablethorpe to begin the North Sea crossing under clear skies to make landfall at Sankt Peter-Ording on the west coast of Schleswig-Holstein. Sgt John and crew lost their port engine when twenty miles north of the Frisian Island of Borkum, but once the bomb load had been jettisoned, it picked up again and behaved impeccably all the way home. As the others headed south to the target they were subjected to an intense searchlight and flak response and haze and searchlight glare prevented most from establishing a clear view of the ground. Any built-up area and searchlight position became a suitable target and consequently damage within the city was useful but not significant and local sources estimated that around fifty aircraft had taken part in the raid, causing seventy-five fires, thirty-three of them large, this despite claims by 107 crews to have attacked the primary target.

A period of misty weather curtailed operations over the following few nights until the 22/23[rd,] when an experimental operation was directed at Cologne. All sixty-four 1 and 3 Group Wellingtons and five Stirlings were equipped with Gee, for yet another attempt to test its viability as a blind bombing device. 150 Squadron represented 1 Group with six Mk III Wellingtons on a night of unfavourable weather conditions that included cloud over the target, which would not have been critical had Gee been up to the task. Local sources estimated up to fifteen bomb loads had hit the city causing modest damage, while locations up to ten miles away also reported bombs falling.

In an attempt to repeat the success gained at Lübeck, Harris selected another Baltic port, Rostock, situated sixty miles east along the coast, for a series of four raids on consecutive nights from the 23/24th, with the old town and the Heinkel aircraft factory on its southern outskirts the specific aiming-points. A force of 161 aircraft was assembled, forty-three of them 1 Group Wellingtons from Binbrook, Elsham Wolds, Grimsby, Hemswell and Lindholme, while the crews were informed at briefing that 143 of them were to attack the town and eighteen from 5 Group the factory. The 103 Squadron contingent of eleven took off between 21.42 and 22.05 with S/L Godfrey and F/L Saxelby the senior pilots on duty and flew out over Mablethorpe bound for a point north of Rømø Island in the Waddenzee off the western coast of Jutland. Each Wellington was carrying 540 x 4lb incendiaries and 750 gallons of petrol for the 1,100-mile round trip, which not all from Esham Wolds would complete. Sgt John and crew turned back from the midpoint of the North Sea crossing when the rear turret fell out of commission at 23.28 when they were at 5,000 feet. The skies were clear from around 3 degrees east all the way to the target, which F/L Saxelby and crew reached first of the 103 Squadron element at 01.50 to bomb from 12,300 feet. W/O Fulbrook and crew brought up the rear from 11,500 feet at 02.18, and in between the others delivered their attacks from 8,000 to 13,500 feet between 01.53 and 02.10. Each pinpointed on a ground feature on the coast or on the Unterwarnow River leading south from the sea to the town and most observed large fires that remained visible for up to a hundred miles into the return flight and led to the belief that the raid had been an outstanding success. Sadly, this proved to be untrue, and an analysis revealed that most of the bombing at both aiming points had fallen between two and six miles away.

Preparations were put in hand on the 24th for that night's "round 2" at Rostock, for which a force of 125 aircraft was assembled, ninety-one assigned to the town and thirty-four from 5 Group to the Heinkel factory. 1 Group contributed fifty-eight of the Wellingtons, eleven of them representing 103 Squadron, which departed Elsham Wolds between 21.34 and 21.59 with no senior pilots on duty and each crew sitting on five SBCs of 90 and fifteen of 60 x 4lbs incendiaries. They adopted the same route as for the previous night and all reached the target area to find good conditions in which they were able to pinpoint on the estuary and the town and bomb from 9,600 to 13,500 feet. Returning crews were confident that they had inflicted enormous damage, and on this occasion, they were right, the town having, indeed, sustained heavy damage, although the Heinkel works narrowly escaped. While this operation was in progress the freshman crew of Sgt Winchester took off at 21.54 carrying ten 250 pounders and joined with others from the group in an attack on the docks and shipping at Dunkerque. They exited the English coast at Orfordness and arrived at the French coast in moonlight, which was enhanced by the deployment of flares. The bombs were delivered from 13,000 feet at 23.31 and bursts and fires were observed.

The night of the 25/26th brought "round 3" at Rostock, which involved 110 aircraft to attack the town, while eighteen 5 Group Manchesters went for the Heinkel works led by the 106 Squadron commanding officer, W/C Guy Gibson, who was destined to become a household name a year hence. 1 Group contributed twenty-two Wellingtons to the main event, six of them belonging to 103 Squadron, which departed Elsham Wolds between 21.42 and 21.51 with S/Ls Godfrey and Holford and F/L Saxelby the senior pilots on duty. Each crew had 90 x 4lb and 56 x 30lb incendiaries beneath their feet as they flew out over Mablethorpe to adopt the familiar route to this target, at which S/L Godfrey and crew were the first from the squadron to arrive. They were able to make out ground detail and bombed the aiming point in the old town from 7,800 feet at 02.02 but were prevented by smoke and haze from assessing the results. The others carried out their attacks from 10,000 and 11,000 feet between 02.05 and 02.15 and five returned safely home to pass on their impressions at debriefing. Absent from that process was the crew of F/Sgt Bray DFM RCAF, who disappeared without trace in DV579, presumably finding a final resting place in the Baltic or North Sea. They had become experienced members of the squadron, and it will be recalled that F/Sgt Bray had been awarded the DFM for his actions on the night of the 10/11th of January. Also, on this night, the crew of Sgt Staniland had taken off at 22.30 to join eight others from the group to bomb the docks and shipping at Dunkerque but returned their fourteen 250 pounders to the bomb dump after failing to locate the target through cloud and ground haze.

The force of 106 aircraft assembled for the fourth and final raid of the Rostock series on the 26th was divided equally between the town and the Heinkel factory and included a contribution from 1 Group of forty-two Wellingtons, eight of them provided by 103 Squadron. They departed Elsham Wolds between 22.00 and 22.12 with no senior pilots on duty and each carrying a maximum load of incendiaries as they settled onto the standard route for this target. All reached the target area to be greeted by moonlight, excellent visibility and existing fires to aid target location, and delivered effective attacks before returning home safely to make their reports, confident in the effectiveness of their work. Sgt Staniland and crew returned to Dunkerque on this night, taking off at 21.47 and returning at

00.56 to reported dropping fourteen 250 pounders across the docks from clear skies. An analysis of the Rostock campaign revealed it to have been highly successful, destroying 1,765 buildings and seriously damaging five hundred more, which represented 60% of the town's built-up area. All of this was achieved for the remarkably modest cost to the Command of eight aircraft. In his diaries, Propaganda Minister Göbbels used the phrase "Terrorangriff", terror raid, for the first time.

The squadron was not invited to take part in an operation against the Klöckner-Humboldt-Deutz works in Cologne on the 27th, for which 1 Group put up thirty-four Wellingtons from Grimsby, Hemswell, Lindholme and Snaith. Fifteen hundred houses and some industrial premises were hit and damaged to some extent in what was an effective raid, but even so, many bomb loads missed the city altogether.

Kiel was posted as the target for eighty-eight aircraft on the following night, of which twenty-eight Wellingtons were provided by the 1 Group stations of Binbrook, Breighton and Elsham Wolds. The 103 Squadron element of nine took off between 21.57 and 22.35 with no senior pilots on duty and six SBCs of 4lb incendiaries in each bomb bay and flew out over Mablethorpe on a course identical to that employed for Rostock. They all arrived in the target area to find excellent conditions and good visibility marred only by an effective smoke screen that made pinpointing difficult. However, most identified the Selenter Lake a dozen or so miles east-south-east of the target and the Kielhafen docks area and delivered their attacks from 11,000 to 14,000 feet between 02.24 and 02.45 in the face of a spirited defence by searchlights in cones of up to twenty beams and red tracer reaching 16,000 feet. Sgt Pugh and crew had been forced to switch to the spare aircraft and took off late, which delayed their arrival and persuaded them to bomb the port of Flensburg some forty miles to the north-west as an alternative from 10,000 feet at 02.55. Returning crews were enthusiastic about their night's work and were disappointed to learn that no fresh damage had been inflicted, although all three shipyards had been hit as had the hospital in the naval academy. At debriefing, Sgt Potts and crew reported bombing from 12,000 feet at 02.41 and by 02.50 were flying up the Kiel Estuary at 250 feet under fire from a destroyer. Front and rear gunners raked the deck with machine-gun fire, and the Wellington escaped into the darkness.

The Gnome & Rhone aero engine factory at Gennevilliers in Paris was selected for attention on the night of the 29/30th, for which 1 Group contributed twenty-nine Wellingtons from Binbrook, Elsham Wolds, Hemswell and Snaith. The nine 103 Squadron participants took off between 20.55 and 21.14 with station commander, G/C Constantine, taking over P/O Gilby's crew to be the senior pilot on duty ahead of S/L Godfrey. All aircraft were carrying incendiaries and as always, nickels, and set course via Reading for Beachy Head and landfall on the French coast near Dieppe. They arrived in the target area in fine conditions with a bright moon and P/O Gorrie's DV699 was hit by light flak at the start of the bombing run, forcing them to jettison the load from 200 feet to fall on the riverbank opposite the factory. The others attacked from an average of 2,000 feet and were confident that they had hit the Gnome & Rhone factory and others nearby, almost all describing their bombs falling across the aiming point or very close, and bomb release photos initially seemed to confirm the accuracy of the attack. Despite this, the Gnome & Rhone plant escaped damage, although other factories in the immediate vicinity, the Goodrich tyre plant and the Thompson-Houston electrical components works were hit, and as a huge bonus, no French civilians were hurt.

During the course of the month the squadron took part in eighteen operations on sixteen nights and dispatched 139 sorties for the loss of two Wellingtons and their crews.

May 1942

The 3rd of May was the centenary of the Great Fire of Hamburg, of which the Bomber Command planners may well not have been aware when they posted the city as the primary target for that night. A force of eighty-one aircraft was made ready, which included twenty-nine 1 Group Wellingtons from Binbrook, Hemswell, Lindholme and Snaith. Those reaching the target found ten-tenths cloud that forced them to bomb on estimated positions and despite the fact that a third of the force failed to reach the target, a disproportionately large amount of damage resulted, and half of the 113 fires were classed in local reports as large. 103 squadron was not entirely inactive on this night and sent the crews of Sgt Pugh and Sgt Little on their way from Elsham Wolds at 00,03 and 00.12 in company with five others from the group to bomb the docks and shipping at St-Nazaire. They exited the English coast at Bridport and made landfall on the other side of the Channel at the Ile-de-Brehat, before traversing the Brest peninsula and pinpointing on Belle Isle for the run to the target. Under clear skies they each delivered ten 250 pounders, Sgt Little and crew from 10,500 feet at 03.18 and Sgt Pugh and crew from five hundred feet lower at 03.45, before returning home safely.

The highly industrialized city of Stuttgart, dubbed the "Coventry" of Germany because of its focus on car production at the Daimler and Porsche factories, also boasted among its many war-industry supporters the Robert Bosch electronics and SKF ball-bearing factories and had not yet been attacked in numbers by Bomber Command. The first of three raids upon it on consecutive nights was posted on the 4th and a force of 121 aircraft assembled, which called upon the services of twenty-four Wellingtons from Breighton, Elsham Wolds and Hemswell. The eight 103 Squadron crews were briefed like most to aim for the Bosch works at Feuerbach on the north-western extremities of the city, while some from 4 Group were assigned to a special aiming-point within the city. The first seven departed Elsham Wolds between 21.35 and 21.55 with S/L Holford the senior pilot on duty, leaving Sgt Potts and crew to take off at 22.23 after being called in to substitute for an indisposed crew. All were carrying two 1,000 pounders and a single 250 pounder and set course via Orfordness for the French coast near Dunkerque for an outward flight under clear skies. There are major discrepancies in the accounts of weather conditions, the 1 Group ORB describing complete cloud cover, while the 103 Squadron ORB reports clear skies over the target, but thick ground haze that prevented the pinpointing of an aiming point. Whatever the truth, the crews of S/L Holford, W/O Fulbrook, P/O Smith and Sgt John bombed in the general vicinity of the primary target, while the crews of P/O Tett and Sgt Potts bombed in the Karlsruhe area from 7,000 and 12,000 feet at 01.28 and 01.42 respectively. Sgt Lewis and crew found an aerodrome near Baden-Baden and attacked it from 11,000 feet at 01.36 and P/O Brookes and crew homebound approaching the French frontier when bombing in the Saarbrücken area from 10,000 feet at 02.46. By the time they crossed the English coast they were running low on fuel and P/O Brookes ordered his crew to take to their parachutes, while he belly-landed

DV612 at RAF Tibenham in Norfolk. Shortly after midnight, F/Sgt Arrowsmith and crew had departed Elsham Wolds to bomb the Loire inland docks and shipping at Nantes in north-western France and drop nickels to bolster the morale of the populace. On the way home, Z8833 became the latest from the squadron to find the sea, and when the dinghy was recovered by the Germans one week later, only the two gunners were alive to be taken into captivity. A post-raid analysis of the Stuttgart raid and local sources confirmed that the Bosch factory had escaped damage and the bombing had been scattered over a wide area, some possibly attracted by a decoy fire site at Lauffen, fifteen miles to the north, which was cleverly defended by around thirty-five searchlights.

Later, on the 5th, X9816 landed short of the runway at Elsham Wolds while training, crashed through a fence and burned out, Sgt Blandford and three others on board managing to scramble clear with various injuries, while the rear gunner lost his life. That night, a reduced force of seventy-seven aircraft was made ready for the return to Stuttgart and included a 1 Group contingent of thirty-two Wellingtons from Binbrook, Grimsby, Hemswell, Lindholme and Snaith. Despite the benefit of clear skies, the presence of ground haze and the Lauffen decoy site prevented any bombs from falling within the city and the operation was a complete failure.

A force of ninety-seven aircraft was detailed for the third Stuttgart raid on the 6th, for which 1 Group detailed seventeen Wellingtons from Breighton and Elsham Wolds, 103 Squadron dispatching seven Wellingtons between 21.40 and 21.58 with F/L Saxelby the senior pilot on duty. They flew out over Orfordness aiming to make landfall on the French coast to the north of Dunkerque, before heading south-east across France to enter Germany via the Strasbourg area. Sgt Staniland and crew turned back twenty miles out from Orfordness because of a starboard engine problem and they were followed home by P/O Winchester and crew, who abandoned their sortie also as a result of an engine issue when twenty-five miles short of the French coast. Largely clear skies over the Continent persisted to the target, where ground haze made aiming point identification a challenge, but crews were able to pick up the River Neckar as a reference and Sgt John and crew actually employed the Lauffen decoy site as the starting point for their bombing run. Four crews delivered two 1,000 pounders and a 250 pounder each from 8,000 to 12,000 feet between 01.05 and 01.12 and observed them to fall into the town area. F/L Saxelby was over Karlsruhe at 01.00 when his starboard engine appeared to burst into flames, apparently having been hit by flak. In fact, it was the dinghy that had caught fire in its wing stowage and caused the pilot to believe that the engine was burning, at which point he shut it down. Once the dinghy had burned out, the engine was restarted, and a safe return completed. It was discovered later that the damage had been caused by an incendiary dropped by another aircraft. Despite the confidence of returning crews that the raid had been effective, it had entirely missed Stuttgart, and fell largely upon Heilbronn, twenty miles away and close to the decoy fire site.

The recent successes at Lübeck and Rostock may have encouraged the posting of another Baltic coast target on the 8th, this time, Warnemünde, situated on the West Bank of the Warnow estuary ten miles north of Rostock. The docks were the site of U-Boot crew training, and also supplied German forces on the Russian front, but, equally important was the Heinkel aircraft factory, the destruction of which was handed to a specific element, while the rest of the overall force of 193 aircraft targeted the town and docks and engaged in searchlight suppression. 1 Group put up thirty-four Wellingtons for the town and a dozen to attack the Heinkel works, of which 103 Squadron contributed eight and sent them on their way from Elsham Wolds between 21.10 and 22.05 with F/L Saxelby the senior pilot on duty. They flew out over Mablethorpe on course for Fanø Island off Jutland's western coast, before setting course from there to the southern tip of Denmark's Lolland Island. Three of the 103 Squadron aircraft were carrying five 500 pounders each and the others nine SBCs containing eight 30lb incendiaries, and all were now routinely equipped with a camera. Most were able to map-read their way to the target, where the bomb-carrying 103 Squadron crews delivered theirs from 3,000 to 7,000 feet before descending to between 300 and 800 feet to strafe searchlight positions at some point within a time window between 01.08 and 02.10. The incendiary element carried out their attacks from 7,000 to 11,000 feet between 01.37 and 02.15 and all returned safely from what was at best a modestly successful operation that cost nineteen aircraft, including four 44 (Rhodesia) Squadron Lancasters, one captained by its newly appointed commanding officer.

Thereafter, a ten-day break in major operations ended on the 19th, when orders were received across the Command to prepare for an attack that night on the city of Mannheim, for which a force of 197 aircraft was assembled. 1 Group contributed sixty Wellingtons to the main event, twenty-eight to St-Nazaire and six each for mining duties in the Artichoke garden off the port of Lorient and nickelling in the Paris region. 103 Squadron made ready fifteen Wellingtons, eight for Mannheim, four for freshman crews to employ against the docks and shipping at St-Nazaire, one to deliver propaganda leaflets to the residents of Paris and two for the squadron's first foray into the dark and mysterious world of mining.

Thus far, 103 Squadron had not been involved in mining operations, for which each crew was given a grid reference as a release point after a timed run from an identified landmark, and this would result in a chain of mines that would be difficult to avoid. At first, gardening was conducted from very low level, usually from between 400 and 800 feet, which exposed the aircraft to light flak from shore and shipboard batteries. Even so, losses were relatively low, and, in time, gardening became an ideal way to introduce freshman crews to operations before unleashing them on Germany. Later, the planting of vegetables would be conducted from high level, reducing the danger from flak but increasing the risk of fighter attack.

The first departure from Elsham Wolds was that of Sgt Tew and crew at 22.00 bound for Paris, where they fulfilled their brief by dispensing bundles of reading matter under favourable conditions from 14,000 feet at 00.45, having pinpointed on the River Seine and following its course to the French capital. Those assigned to Mannheim took off between 22.08 and 22.43 with S/L Godfrey and F/L Saxelby the senior pilots on duty, while the St-Nazaire quartet followed them into the air between 22.40 and 22.54, leaving the gardeners, the crews of W/O Fulbook and Sgt Pugh, to bring up the rear at 22.57 and 22.59 respectively. The gardeners exited the English coast at Bridport on course for the St-Malo region and pinpointed on Belle and Groix Islands before conducting timed runs to the release point and planting their vegetables from 800 feet at 03.10. The point of exit for the St-Nazaire crews was Littlehampton, from where they set course for St-Malo and Nantes, before turning west for the run to the target. F/Sgt Apperley and crew pinpointed on the headland and river and carried out their attack from 10,000 feet at 02.44, observing their bombs to fall in the docks area. They were the only successful crew as two brought their bombs home after failing to locate the target through haze and Z1141 was shot down in flames in the target area, killing F/L Rees and his predominantly RCAF crew, who had arrived on posting from 150 Squadron only ten days earlier.

Meanwhile, the Mannheim contingent had headed out over Southwold on course for the southern tip of Walcheren in the Western Schelde and continued on to cross the Belgian/German frontier in the St-Vith area. They found a little high cloud at 18,000 feet and good visibility below and were able to establish their positions by ground features and green flares. They carried out their attacks from 8,000 to 14,000 feet between 01.17 and 01.50, observing bursts and developing fires which remained visible for up to seventy miles into the return journey. Local sources described the sound of aircraft overhead searching for the target, and a delay before bombing began, after which, most of the effort was wasted on open and wooded country, and very few bombs fell in Mannheim itself. There now followed another lull in major operations as Harris prepared for his master stroke and it was during this period that F/L Morison was posted in from 20 O.T.U. on the 25th to replace the missing F/L Rees.

At the time of his appointment as C-in-C, the figure of four thousand bombers had been bandied around as the number required to wrap up the war. Whilst there was not the slightest chance of procuring them, Harris, with a dark cloud still hanging over the existence of an independent bomber force, needed to ensure that those earmarked for him were not spirited away to what he considered to be less-deserving causes. The Command had not yet achieved sufficient success to silence the detractors, and the Admiralty was still calling for bomber aircraft to be diverted to the U-Boot campaign, while others demanded support for the North Africa campaign. Harris was in need of a major victory, and perhaps, a dose of symbolism to make his point, and out of this was born the Thousand Plan, Operation Millennium, the launching of a thousand aircraft in one night against a major German city, for which Hamburg had been pencilled in. Harris did not have a thousand front-line aircraft and required the support of other Commands to make up the numbers, which was forthcoming from Coastal and Flying Training Commands, and in the case of the former, a letter to Harris on the 22nd promised 250 aircraft. However, following an intervention from the Admiralty, the offer was withdrawn and most of the Flying Training Command aircraft were found to be not up to the task, leaving the Millennium force well short of the magic figure. Undaunted, Harris, or more probably his able deputy, AM Sir Robert Saundby, scraped together every airframe capable of controlled flight, or something resembling it, and pulled in the screened crews from their instructional duties. He also pressed into service aircraft and crews from within the Command's own training establishment, 91 Group. Come the night, not only would the thousand mark be achieved, but it would also be comfortably surpassed.

During the final week of the month, the arrival on bomber stations from Yorkshire to East Anglia of a motley collection of aircraft from training units gave rise to much speculation among crews and ground staff alike, but as usual, only the NAAFI staff and the local civilians knew what was really afoot. The most pressing remaining question was the weather, and as the days ticked by inexorably towards the end of May, this was showing no signs of complying. Harris was aware of the genuine danger, that the giant force might draw attention to itself and thereby compromise security, and the point was fast approaching when the operation would have to take place or be abandoned for the time being. Harris released some of the pressure by sanctioning operations on the night of the 29/30th, for which the Gnome & Rhone aero-engine and Goodrich tyre factories at Gennevilliers in Paris were the main targets. A force of seventy-seven aircraft included a contribution from 1 Group of twenty-one Wellingtons, four of them provided by 103 Squadron, which departed Elsham Wolds between 23.29 and 23.49 bearing aloft the crews of W/C Du Boulay, S/Ls Godfrey and Holford, the former accompanied by F/L Morison, and P/O Gorrie. They exited England over Beachy Head aiming for Abbeville on the opposite coast and followed the Seine to the target, where they encountered five to ten-tenths cloud with tops at 15,000 feet. W/C Du Boulay and crew spent forty-five minutes in a vain search for a pinpoint and abandoned the attempt when the fuel reserves dictated. The others bombed from 6,000 and 6,400 feet between 02.37 and 02.56 and found it difficult to gain an accurate picture of the outcome. Despite some claims of a successful operation, the only damage caused was to eighty-seven houses, in which thirty-four French civilians were killed and 167 injured.

It was in an atmosphere of frustration and hopeful expectation that "morning prayers" began at Harris's High Wycombe HQ on the 30th, with all eyes turned upon the civilian chief meteorological adviser, Magnus Spence. After careful deliberation, he was able to give a qualified assurance of clear skies over the Rhineland, while north-western Germany and Hamburg would be concealed under buckets of cloud. Thus, did the fickle fates decree that Cologne would bear the dubious honour of hosting the first one thousand bomber raid in history. At briefings, crews were told that the enormous force was to be pushed across the aiming point in just ninety minutes, an unprecedented tactic that gave rise to the question of collisions as hundreds of aircraft funnelled towards the aiming point. The answer, according to the experts, was to observe timings and flight levels, and they calculated also that just two aircraft would collide over the target. It is said that a wag in every briefing room asked, "do they know which two?"

At briefings, crews were assigned to three aiming points covering the central districts on the West Bank of the Rhine, most importantly A, located right at the commercial heart of the city from Nippes in the north to Zollstock in the south, an area containing the cathedral, main railway station and the Neumarkt. Aiming points X and Y adjoined A on its western side, the Hohenzollern Ring to the north of the centre line and the Hohenstauffen Ring to the south. Aiming point A was assigned to 1 and 3 Groups and all aircraft from the other groups and Commands operating from their stations, X to 4 Group and all aircraft from the other groups and Commands operating from its stations, plus Army Co-operation Command and 92 Group, and Y to 5 Group and all aircraft from the other groups and Commands operating from its stations plus 91 Group. The route for all aircraft was direct to the target, crossing the enemy coast over the Scheldt estuary, with a parallel return course a few miles to the south of the outward track.

1 Group was able to assemble a significant force of 181 Wellingtons along with twenty-seven others from the training units, 12 Squadron making the greatest contribution of the night when putting up a magnificent twenty-eight Wellingtons from Binbrook. In addition to the

nineteen 103 Squadron aircraft at Elsham Wolds were ten representing 22 O.T.U., which had flown in on the 27th from Wellesbourne Mountford in Warwickshire. Late that evening, the first of an eventual 1,047 aircraft took off to deliver the now familiar three-wave-format attack on the Rhineland capital, the older training hacks struggling somewhat reluctantly into the air, lifted more by the enthusiasm of their crews than by the power of their engines, and some of these, unable to climb to a respectable height, would fall easy prey to the defences or would simply drop from the sky through mechanical breakdown. The Elsham Wolds contingent took off between 22.41 and 23.30 with G/C Constantine and W/C Du Boulay the senior pilots on duty, the station commander, it is believed, having stepped in when S/L Holford reported sick. Among his crew was navigator, W/O "Dizzy" Spiller, who had the reputation of being the scruffiest bod on the squadron and a real "Jack-the-lad", who forever after would regale his drinking companions with the story that it was solely because of his guidance that "Connie" had managed to get to the target and back in one piece. Although not recorded, it is believed that each Wellington was loaded with eight SBCs containing a total of 720 x 4lb incendiaries.

There were no 103 Squadron early returns and as they pressed on across Belgium, the crews were drawn on for the last seventy miles by the glow from the already burning city, on arrival at which, they were greeted by precisely the weather conditions of clear skies and bright moonlight predicted by Magnus Spence. The squadron scribe was less than gushing in his sharing of the crews' reports and recorded only an average bombing height of 12,000 to 14,000 feet. At debriefings, returning crews described a city on fire from end to end and never-before-witnessed scenes, which were the result of 1,400 tons of bombs raining down into the confines of the city. The operation was an outstanding success by any standards and brought about the destruction of more than 3,300 buildings, with a further two thousand seriously damaged. A new record of forty-one aircraft failed to return, but in conditions favourable to both attackers and defenders alike, and in the context of the size of the force and the scale of the success, this was an acceptable loss of 3.9%. 1 Group posted missing six aircraft, but it was the training units that sustained the greatest losses amounting to twenty-one aircraft.

103 Squadron was not exempt from the casualties, Sgt Onions and crew failing to return in DV452, which crashed in Germany with no survivors. Perhaps the most poignant death was that of a newly-arrived pilot, Sgt Roberts, who was a complete stranger in the crew of S/L Saxelby with which he was flying as second pilot. DV704 was attacked by a night-fighter twenty miles west of Roermond in Holland on the way home and Sgt Roberts was killed during the engagement while in the astrodome, the only fatality in an aircraft, which, despite a fierce fire in the fuselage, made it back in one piece to a crash-landing at Honington. Sgt Flowers and crew diverted to Kirmington in R1234 and took off on the following morning to return to Elsham Wolds. Almost immediately, an engine failure caused the Wellington to stall and crash, killing the pilot and three of his crew.

During the course of the month the squadron took part in eleven operations on seven nights and dispatched sixty-four sorties for the loss of five Wellingtons, three complete crews and five additional airmen.

June 1942

A congratulatory message was sent by the A-O-C to all stations, and another received by Harris from Prime Minister Churchill was circulated. While the Millennium force remained assembled, Harris wanted to exploit its potential again immediately, and was no doubt excited about the prospect of visiting upon the old enemy of Essen a similar ordeal to that just experienced by Cologne. A force of 956 aircraft was the best that could be achieved during the 1st, 1 Group managing to come up with 137 Wellingtons from its front-line squadrons and two from 1481 Target Towing Flight at Binbrook, while a further forty-two sorties by 18, 21 and 22 O.T.Us would be launched from 1 Group stations. Each of the seventeen 103 Squadron Wellingtons had eight SBCs containing ninety 4lb incendiaries winched into their bomb bay before departing Elsham Wolds between 22.45 and 23.25 with S/L Godfrey the senior pilot on duty accompanied by F/L Morison. They began the North Sea crossing at Mablethorpe, from where they set a direct course to the target, making landfall on the Dutch coast in the vicinity of The Hague and encountering increasing volumes of cloud as they made their way inland. S/L Godfrey and crew were one of a small number to misinterpret a recall signal after around ninety minutes and landed shortly after F/O Frith and crew, who had returned for the same reason. The remaining crews bombed on e.t.a. and DR from 10,000 to 14,000 feet roughly between 01.00 and 02.00, aiming mostly at areas illuminated by flares, but none knew exactly where they were or what was happening on the ground. It was a typical attack on Essen, only on a much larger scale, and bombs fell in many Ruhr locations as cloud and industrial haze obscured ground detail. According to local sources, only eleven houses were destroyed in Essen, and fewer than two hundred were damaged, and Harris's frustrations with this city continued. Thirty-one aircraft failed to return, but 103 Squadron's participants all made it back.

A follow-up raid was planned for the 2nd, and a force of 195 aircraft assembled, for which 1 Group contributed forty-six Wellingtons from Binbrook, Breighton, Elsham Wolds, Grimsby and Snaith. 103 Squadron dispatched seven Wellingtons between 23.25 and 23.57 with S/L Godfrey the senior pilot on duty. They adopted the same route as for the previous night and lost the services of P/O Firman and crew to an engine issue after around ninety minutes, leaving the others to continue on during what proved to be a night of cloudless skies over the Ruhr, with the usual industrial haze and a low moon providing some illumination. Most crews would describe the visibility as good, and reported being further aided by flares, which highlighted the Rhine over to the west. Those equipped with Gee confirmed their positions over what they believed to be the Krupp district aiming point and those from Elsham Wolds delivered their all-incendiary loads from 11,000 to 14,500 feet between 01.45 and 01.57. S/L Godfrey and crew were among three from the squadron to be carry nickels, which they delivered over Moers/Homberg, the oil town on the western bank of the Rhine opposite Duisburg. Despite the apparent confidence of the crews at debriefing that they had attacked Essen, local authorities reported just three high explosive bombs and three hundred incendiaries falling in the city to cause only minor damage. Such was the density of the Ruhr, with overlapping town and city boundaries, it was difficult not to hit something urban, but concentration was the key to success, and the scattering of bombs over a wide area was never going to achieve a knock-out blow. Harris was stubborn and would keep trying, but it would be a further nine months before the means were to hand to make a genuine impact.

While the above was in progress, the crews of F/L Morison and Sgts Smith, Tew and Vickery departed Elsham Wolds between 00.39 and 00.51 to attack the docks and shipping at Dieppe in company with two crews from 150 Squadron. They flew out over Worthing on the Sussex coast and made directly for the target under clear skies, but lost Sgt Tew and crew to an engine issue, leaving the others to take advantage of the excellent visibility over the target. Sgt Vickery and crew bombed from 9,000 feet at 03.12 and F/L Morison from 10,000 feet two minutes later, while Sgt Smith and crew failed to locate the target until passing over it on the way home, by which time it was too late with the dawn fast approaching.

For the next operation, on the 3rd, Harris turned his attention upon Bremen, which, along with Essen and Emden, would share the bulk of the Command's attention for the remainder of the month. A force of 170 aircraft was made ready for the first major attack on the port-city since the previous October, and fifty-seven of the Wellingtons were provided by 1 Group from all of its operational stations. Six 103 Squadron Wellingtons departed Elsham Wolds between 22.40 and 22.54 with F/L Saxelby the senior pilot on duty and set course from Mablethorpe to make landfall on the Dutch coast near Alkmaar, before heading to a point on the River Weser fifteen miles to the north-west of the target for the final run-in. Sgt Staniland and crew were contending with an intercom issue, which could not be rectified, and they returned to land within an hour, leaving the others to reach the target, where the good vertical visibility was spoiled by a little ground haze, through which the river, its bridges and the distinctive shape of the docks could be identified by the light from flares. The 103 Squadron crews delivered their 720 x 4lb incendiaries each from 12,000 to 13,000 feet between 01.20 and 01.31 and observed bursts across the docks and Old Town, while numerous fires sent black smoke rising through 10,000 feet as the last crews turned away. Local reports confirmed this to be the most destructive raid yet at this target, with damage inflicted on the docks and residential districts, as well as on the shipyards and the Focke-Wulf factory in the Hemelingen district.

A force of 180 aircraft was prepared for the next intended assault on Essen on the 5th, for which 1 Group contributed forty-eight Wellingtons from Binbrook, Elsham Wolds, Hemswell, Ingham and Lindholme, ten of them representing 103 Squadron. They took off between 22.51 and 23.12 with S/Ls Godfrey and Holford the senior pilots on duty, the latter after reuniting with his crew including "Dizzy" Spiller. They exited the English coast at Mablethorpe on course for Alkmaar and lost the services of P/O Gosman and crew to an overheating starboard engine. The others reached the target, where some identified a bend in the River Ruhr to the south-east of the target, while others relied on a TR-fix, flares or evidence of searchlight and flak concentrations to establish their positions in conditions of poor vertical visibility. Searchlights were operating in cones of up to thirty beams, but not all were located within the city, and were, therefore, not a reliable guide for the purposes of navigation. The 103 Squadron crews bombed from 10,000 to 14,000 feet between 01.19 and 01.35, and many observed one large fire that sent smoke rising through 10,000 feet, otherwise, returning crews reported only small blazes. The ORB hailed this as another very successful operation, but in truth, it was yet one more scattered and ineffective attack, which caused no significant damage. DV699 failed to return with the others and the crew of F/L Morison was posted missing. In time, the Red Cross confirmed that F/L Morison was in enemy hands as the lone survivor of his crew following a mid-air collision, which resulted in the Wellington crashing near Geldern, a town close to the Dutch frontier to the north-west of the Ruhr.

While the above operation was in progress, the crews of F/Sgt Tilley and Sgt Tew departed Elsham Wolds at 23.13 and 23.52 respectively to join other freshmen for mining duties in the Nectarine I garden off the Frisian Island of Terschelling. The Nectarine region encompassed the entire Frisian chain and was divided into three gardens, Nectarine I from Texel to the eastern tip of Ameland, Nectarine II, from east of Ameland to Memmert, and Nectarine III, Juist to Wangerooge. They arrived in the target area to find little cloud and good visibility and pinpointed on Terschelling before conducting a timed run to the drop zone to release their mines from 700 and 500 feet at 01.21 and 01.35.

Before Harris tried again at Essen, he ordered an attack on Emden, the naval port situated on the northern bank of the Ems estuary opposite northern Holland. A force of 233 aircraft was made ready during the afternoon and evening of the 6th, which included fifty-nine Wellingtons of 1 Group drawn from each of its operational stations. The ground crews toiled under a blazing sun to prepare the aircraft, the armourers at Elsham Wolds loading thirteen Wellingtons with nine SBCs each of 4lb incendiaries, while the aircrews attended briefing to learn of their part in the night's activities. The narrow window of darkness during the summer months required late departures, and it was 23.09 when S/L Holford and crew began their take-off run, followed over the ensuing thirty-four minutes by the rest, among which W/C Du Boulay and S/L Godfrey were the other senior pilots on duty. They flew out over Mablethorpe in excellent conditions and made landfall on the other side of the North Sea over the Frisian Island of Schiermonnikoog, before arriving in the target area, where the coastline provided a perfect pinpoint for orientation and target location. The estuary and docks stood out clearly in the light of flares, and the Elsham Wolds crews carried out their attacks from 8,000 to 14,000 feet between 01.20 and 01.45, observing many bomb bursts and fires across the town. Reconnaissance confirmed the effectiveness of the operation, which destroyed around three hundred houses and seriously damaged a further two hundred. Harris would attempt to capitalize on this success with three further raids later in the month, but each would fall well short of the success achieved by this one.

By this time, it had been decided to convert the whole of 1 Group to the Halifax, and 103 Squadron was selected as the first in line. A little later 460 Squadron would also begin training on the type but would not achieve operational status before a change in policy decreed that the group would operate Lancasters instead. S/L Holford was posted to the newly-formed 103 Squadron Conversion Flight on the 7th, where he was joined by S/L Robinson, an experienced instructor, to begin the conversion programme. P/O Potts and W/O Fulbrook were also posted across at this time as the first two pilots to begin training. The Halifax was a troubled aircraft, which had been operating since March 1941 but had been available in only small numbers because of the constant round of modifications required to make it fit for purpose. It was not suited in most cases to retrospective modifications, which meant that new variants were required each time something major was upgraded. It had also suffered a spate of unexplained accidents involving unrecoverable spins and confidence in the type was at an all-time low when the disquieting news reached Elsham Wolds that its future lay with the Halifax. The cause of the accidents was traced to rudder-lock, in which the rudders on the triangular fins suddenly deployed and froze and the solution was found in a redesigned square fin. The Rolls Royce Merlin engines that were so successful in other types, proved to be less efficient when attached to the Halifax, and this was largely due to Handley Page's insistence that they install the engines utilizing their own nacelle mounts.

Essen was posted once more as the target on the 8th, and a force of 170 aircraft made ready, 103 Squadron responsible for ten of the Wellingtons in a 1 Group contribution of fifty of the type drawn from all stations. They were loaded with six SBCs of 4lb incendiaries and three of the 30lb variety and departed Elsham Wolds between 23.05 and 23.39 with S/L Holford the senior pilot on duty. They set course via Mablethorpe for the Dutch coast at Katwijk, north of The Hague, having been preceded into the air at 22.40 by Sgt Tew and crew bound for Dieppe, but engine trouble forced them to turn back when over the Channel. Meanwhile, F/L Saxelby and crew were caught in a searchlight cone at 16,000 feet as they ran in on Essen and were compelled to jettison their load "live" at 01.12 as they took evasive action. Conditions in the target area were generally good, with the usual range of cloud estimates at between zero and ten-tenths with tops up to 12,000 feet. Some crews pinpointed first on Duisburg, while others were guided by the flak coming up at them, and a few benefitted from the light cast by flares, but thick haze concealed all ground detail and most of the bombing by the 103 Squadron crews was carried out on estimated positions from 10,000 to 15,000 feet between 01.05 and 01.36. The glow of igniting incendiaries and fires was evident below the cloud, but no detailed assessment was possible, and it was established later that it had been another disappointing raid that caused only slight damage at a cost of nineteen aircraft. P/O Firman and crew failed to return after an encounter with a night-fighter over Holland sent DV773 crashing into the ground four miles north-east of Helmond at 02.30, killing all five occupants.

The 9th brought an end to the standard practice of carrying a second pilot, who would now be replaced by the new crew trade of flight engineer. It would be his job to monitor the aircraft's systems from his own panel of dials, principally fuel consumption, engine temperatures and revolutions, oil pressures and hydraulics etc., and to assist the pilot as required at take-off and landing with throttle controls, flaps, and undercarriage. Because of the technical nature of the job, many of the new recruits were volunteers drawn from the RAF engineering school at Halton, and for the next two years at least, the majority of flight engineers, irrespective of the nationality of the crew or the air force to which the squadron belonged, would be exclusively "Halton Brats".

Minor and mining operations occupied the ensuing ten nights, and 103 squadron next ventured forth on the 11th to plant vegetables in the Nectarine I garden, for which nine of its Wellingtons were loaded with two mines and two 250 pounders each, the latter for use against targets of opportunity. They departed Elsham Wolds between 23.25 and 00.04 with no senior pilots on duty and headed out over Mablethorpe to pick up an initial pinpoint on Terschelling or Ameland, and it was off the latter that the vegetables were planted from 600 to 800 feet between 01.39 and 02.32. F/L Fox was posted in from 25 O.T.U on the 13th, having previously served with 83 Squadron in 5 Group and earning for himself the coveted DFM. Twelve crews were posted to 1652 Conversion Unit at Marston Moor in Yorkshire on the 15th for training on the Halifax, and they would return on the 21st ready to carry out operations.

The squadron was effectively off the order of battle during this period as was 460 Squadron RAAF, whose Conversion Flight, formed at Holme-on-Spalding-Moor on the 22nd of May, took on two Halifax IIs on the 16th. Essen was posted as the target for that night, but only 150 Squadron of 1 Group was called upon to contribute fourteen Wellingtons to the force of 106 aircraft. The operation degenerated into another wasted effort in which fifty-six crews bombed alternative targets, mostly Bonn, and only sixteen claimed to have attacked Essen. This was the final one of five raids mounted against the city during the month, in the course of which, 1,607 sorties had been dispatched for the loss of eighty-four aircraft, all for the destruction of a few houses and no industrial damage. It would be three months before Harris tried again.

There was still a full complement of Wellingtons at Elsham Wolds, and six crews with sergeant pilots were briefed for a return to the Nectarine I garden off Ameland in the early hours of the 19th, taking off between 00.35 and 01.06. Despite good visibility beneath the cloud base at 2,000 feet, the crews of Sgts Coombes and Staniland were unable to locate a suitable pinpoint and returned their mines and bombs to store, leaving the crews of Sgts Bowker, Day, Emmott and Moriarty to fulfil their briefs from 600 to 800 feet between 02.24 and 03.20.

Hoping to build on a highly effective raid on Emden early in the month, Harris decided to return there later, on the 19th, for what would turn out to be the first of three operations against the port in the space of four nights. A force of 194 aircraft was assembled, which included a contribution from 1 Group of fifty-nine Wellingtons from all of its stations, 103 Squadron making ready five and loading each with nine SBCs, six containing 90 x 4lb incendiaries and three containing 8 x 30lb. With the exception of the Coombes crew, it was the same order of battle as for the previous night and they departed Elsham Wolds between 23.21 and 23.29, setting course via Mablethorpe for Schiermonnikoog and then the target. On arrival over Germany's north-western coast, they found nine to ten-tenths cloud with tops ranging from 6,000 to 12,000 feet, and most crews, unable to positively identify the port, employed the heavy flak over Borkum as a pinpoint for a DR run, while a few caught a glimpse of the North Bank of the River Ems through a gap. Bombing was carried out by the 103 Squadron crews mostly on estimated positions in the light of flares from 10,000 to 14,000 between 01.25 and 02.26, and few bursts were seen, although there was a hint of fire beneath the clouds. An analysis of the raid established that part of the flare force had started an attack on Osnabrück, some eighty miles to the south, and this had attracted a proportion of the force. Local sources in Emden reported that just five high-explosive bombs had landed in the town, along with a few hundred incendiaries, and damage was negligible.

Emden was posted as the target again on the 20th, and a force of 185 aircraft prepared, forty-one of the Wellingtons provided by 1 Group from all stations but Breighton, Elsham Wolds and Grimsby. They flew out over the Lincolnshire coast on a direct course for Schiermonnikoog, finding excellent horizontal visibility, and most were able to identify the target, or other pinpoints, through occasional gaps in the otherwise ten-tenths cloud that topped out at around 11,000 feet. The distinctive shape of Dollard Bay was a help, as was the heavy and light flak detonating at up to 16,000 feet, and most crews believed that they had at least hit the built-up area, aided by the light of flares. Local sources confirmed that a proportion of the force had, indeed, caused damage to around a hundred houses, while the remainder had missed the mark altogether.

After a night's rest, Emden was once more posted as the target on the 22nd, for the fourth and final time during the month. This time a force of 227 aircraft was assembled, and 1 Group called all of its stations into action to contribute between them sixty-eight Wellingtons, fifteen of them at Elsham Wolds, where each was loaded with six SBCs of 4lb incendiaries and three containing the 30lb denomination. They took off between 23.08 and 23.40 with S/L Godfrey and the newly promoted S/L Saxelby the senior pilots on duty, and there was also a maiden sortie with the squadron for the F/L Fox. They set course via Mablethorpe for the Waddenzee in excellent weather conditions, which would persist throughout the operation, and lost the services first of Sgt Moriarty and crew to a problem with the front turret as they began the sea crossing and then F/Sgt Tilley and crew to intercom failure when thirty miles out. The others arrived in the target area to pinpoint on the coastline, the estuary and the town, where the waterways and docks stood out clearly in the light of accurately placed flares. They had to run the gauntlet of intense light flak coming up at them in a curtain to 16,500 feet and a cone of six to eight searchlights co-operating with a heavy flak battery to the north of the town, while a further ten individual beams were operating independently on the outskirts of the built-up area. Bombing was carried out by the 103 Squadron crews from 7,000 to 12,000 feet between 01.18 and 01.44, but most were unable to distinguish the bursts of their bombs and could only report that fires were taking hold as they withdrew. Confidence was high among 196 of the returning crews that a telling blow had been struck, but decoy fire sites had been activated, and according to local sources, only fifty houses were destroyed and a hundred damaged. The return of S/L Godfrey DFC and crew was awaited in vain, and news eventually arrived via the Red Cross concerning the rear gunner, who alone had survived the crash of DV818 off the Dutch coast and was now in enemy hands. The remains of S/L Godfrey and Sgt Porteous, the front gunner, were recovered later for burial, the former in Holland and the latter in Germany. The loss of the highly experienced crew was a bitter pill for the squadron and station communities to swallow, but life and the war went on and F/L Fox would soon be elevated to acting squadron leader rank to fill the vacancy for A Flight commander.

Mining operations were now a constant feature of 1 Group activities, particularly for freshmen crews, and Ameland in the Nectarine I garden was the destination for nineteen crews from Elsham Wolds, Hemswell and Lindholme on the 23rd. The eleven-strong 103 Squadron element took off between 23.23 and 23.39, having been preceded into the air at 22.33 by the St-Nazaire-bound crews of Sgts Moriarty and Tilley. The latter flew out over Bridport with the intention of pinpointing on Belle-Isle, but both failed to locate the target area through ten-tenths cloud and a spirited flak defence, and eventually ran out of time. At the limit of their fuel reserves, they dumped their bombs off Minard Point and turned for home. The gardeners, meanwhile, also encountered eight to ten-tenths cloud in the target area with a base at 1,000 feet and thick haze below, but most were able to establish a pinpoint from which to carry out a timed run. The crews of Sgt, Bowker and Little were unsuccessful and returned their mines and bombs to the dump, leaving the others to plant their vegetables from 650 to 750 feet between 01.16 and 02.12. Still coming to terms with the loss of S/L Godfrey and crew, the squadron was faced with the failure to return of two more crews on this night, T2921 crashing into the sea with no survivors from the crew of Sgt Emmott, and Sgt Vickery and crew disappearing without trace in DV831, presumably in the same area.

The time had now arrived for the final deployment of the Thousand Force, and, indeed, for 5 Group's Avro Manchester in operational service, and it was an indication of the scale of the failure of the Manchester, that the aircraft it had been intended to replace, the Hampden, would continue to serve 5 Group in small numbers until mid-September. A force of 960 aircraft was assembled, 111 of the Wellingtons provided by 1 Group, in addition to which, seven aircraft from 1481 Target-Towing Flight and eleven from 20 O.T.U would depart from its stations. To the above numbers were added five aircraft from Army Co-operation Command and 102 aircraft from Coastal Command, the latter having been ordered by Churchill himself to take part, although, its contribution was to be deemed a separate operation. However, the 1,067 aircraft from all sources would represent a larger combined force than that sent to Cologne at the end of May. 103 Squadron made ready fifteen Wellingtons, loading each with eight SBCs of 4lb incendiaries and sent them on their way from Elsham Wolds between 22.58 and 23.43 with W/C du Boulay, S/L Saxelby and F/L Fox the senior pilots on duty.

They exited the English coast over Mablethorpe and set course for Egmond on the Dutch coast south of Den Helder but lost the services of Sgt Day and crew to a sluggish X9675 that refused to climb beyond 10,000 feet. Sgt Moriarty and crew also abandoned their sortie after surviving an encounter with an enemy night-fighter and experiencing a shudder during violent evasive action. The others pressed on, and, above the ten-tenths cloud that persisted all the way from the English coast to the target area, the sky was extremely bright, courtesy of a full moon and the Northern Lights. A band of nine to ten-tenths cloud lay over Bremen at between 3,000 and 10,000 feet, completely obscuring ground detail, which precluded any chance of picking up the individual aiming points, and positions were established by TR-fix, the glow of fires on the ground and the volume of flak coming up through the cloud and detonating at 16,000 to 20,000 feet. F/L Fox and crew bombed from 7,000 feet at 01.39 over what they believed was Vegesack, where shipyards existed on the banks of the Weser to the north-west of the city, while P/O Winchester and crew descended to 1,000 feet on the way home and attacked Cuxhaven at 02.14. The others delivered their attacks on estimated positions from 5,000 to 13,000 feet between 01.39 and 02.03 and returned safely to offer what little information they had to the intelligence section at debriefing. The low height was that of S/L Saxelby and crew, who saw fires burning in a built-up area through a rift in the cloud and decided to bomb there.

Local sources confirmed a number of hits on the Focke-Wulf aircraft factory and some shipyards, along with the destruction of 572 houses, and damage to more than six thousand others, mostly in southern and eastern districts, but this was credited by local sources to an estimated bomber force of around eighty aircraft. The level of success fell well short of that achieved at Cologne, but surpassed by far the failure at Essen, albeit at a new record loss of forty-eight aircraft, which represented 5% of those dispatched. The O.T.Us of 91 Group suffered the highest casualty rate of 11.6%, largely because they were employing tired, old Whitleys, Wellingtons and Hampdens, which were not up to the task. The training units had been particularly hard-hit during all three Thousand raids, with twenty lost at Cologne, twelve at Essen and thirty-three now at Bremen. 103 Squadron, in contrast, operated without loss, and had now finished operations for the month.

The first of three follow-up raids on Bremen spanning the turn of the month was mounted on the night of the 27/28th, when 144 aircraft were involved, and 150 Squadron alone represented 1 Group with fifteen Wellingtons equipped with special navigation aids. Some useful damage was inflicted on the Atlas Werke shipbuilding yards and the Korff refinery, which had been hit two nights earlier. A force of 253 aircraft was raised on the 29th to send back to Bremen, and this time, 1 Group contributed sixteen Wellingtons from 150 Squadron at Snaith. Among five war-industry premises to sustain extensive damage were the Focke-Wulf aircraft plant in the Hemelingen district and the A G Weser U-Boot construction yards.

Further crews were packed off to 1652 Conversion Unit on the 28th and 29th to continue the squadron's conversion to the Halifax. During the course of the month, the squadron took part in fifteen operations on twelve nights and dispatched 122 sorties for the loss of five aircraft and crews.

July 1942

As Bremen had closed the June account, so it fell to this much bombed city to open that of July on the night of the 2/3rd, for which a force of 325 aircraft was made ready. 1 Group called all of its stations into action to enable it to contribute ninety-one Wellingtons, just five of them made ready by 103 Squadron and loaded with SBCs of incendiaries. They departed Elsham Wolds between 23.00 and 23.27 with G/C Constantine the senior pilot on duty, and "Dizzy" Spiller looking after him to make sure he got there and back in one piece. They exited the English coast over Skegness and headed for Texel on a direct course to the target to enter Germany in the region of Papenburg, some fifty miles west of Bremen, and noted evidence of increased night-fighter activity over Holland. They approached the target area in good weather conditions, although, patches of high cloud above 20,000 feet occasionally blotted out the moonlight and allowed the darkness to hide ground detail. This was of little consequence, as fires were already visible fifteen minutes before arrival at the target, and the River Weser and the docks would provide sufficient pinpoints for the bombing run. The 103 Squadron crews of G/C Constantine, W/O Telfer and Sgt Frith (not to be confused with F/O Frith) carried out their attacks from 10,000 to 14,000 feet at 01.47 and 02.02, the first-mentioned having map-read from the Dümmer See after selecting their own course rather than the recommended one. Many fires were observed through the haze and drifting smoke, and large fires were reported on the aerodrome attached to the Focke-Wulf factory and another at Delmenhorst to the south-west. It was noticed also that bombs were bursting up to ten miles to the west, in spite of which the consensus was of an effective operation. Among thirteen missing aircraft were nine from 1 Group, one of which ditched and the Polish crew rescued safe and sound. 103 Squadron's R1617 was caught by a night-fighter over north-western Germany, and Australian pilot, Sgt Spooner DFM, and two of his crew were killed, while the two survivors were taken into captivity. DV611 crashed in the Lingen-Ems region of the Münsterland, well to the south-west of the target, and P/O Little RAAF and one of his mixed RCAF and RAF crew survived to be taken into captivity. As events were to prove, these were the squadron's final losses on Wellingtons. Both crews had been with the squadron for some time and would be missed. Post-raid reconnaissance and local sources revealed that a thousand houses had been damaged, along with dock installations and seven ships in the port.

The Wellington era had now ended, and the squadron was withdrawn from the operational scene to focus on Halifax training. F/L Kennard was posted in from 12 Squadron on the 12th, and he, like F/L Fox, was another who would soon find himself assuming greater responsibility. During the squadron's absence from the operational scene, 1 Group supported a major operation against Wilhelmshaven on the night of the 8/9th and the first four of a series of five on Duisburg, the industrial giant perched on the Rhine on the westerly edge of the Ruhr Valley. Compressed into a space of twelve nights from the 13/14th, these attacks were blighted by generally cloudy conditions, and bombing was carried out mostly on approximate positions, which led to scattered attacks, in which residential districts sustained the bulk of the modest damage. The first of two operations on Hamburg took place on the night of the 26/27th, when four hundred aircraft were involved and clear weather over the target allowed for an effective attack. Widespread damage was inflicted upon predominantly residential districts, where more than eight hundred houses were destroyed and five thousand more damaged to some extent, and more than five hundred large fires had the local authorities calling for outside help for the first time. Two nights later the weather forced a cancellation of the 1, 4 and 5 Group contributions to the second raid on Germany's second city, and the training group crews were recalled. Those reaching the target produced ineffective bombing, and little further damage resulted. The first major attack on Saarbrücken in the coal-rich Saarland region bordering the frontier with France in south-western Germany was mounted on the 29/30th, and severe damage was caused in central and north-western districts.

103 Squadron shared no part in these operations but was now on the brink of regaining its place in 1 Group's front line. Rarely was conversion training accomplished without accidents, and the squadron's first loss of a Halifax had occurred on the 28th, when W1218 stalled and crashed at Ludborough, six miles north-north-west of Louth in Lincolnshire, during an air-to-sea firing exercise, and Sgt Stockford and his crew were killed.

The Halifax operational era began for the squadron on the last night of the month with a major assault on the Ruhr city of Düsseldorf, for which a record non-1,000 force of 630 aircraft was assembled, the numbers bolstered by a large contribution from the training units. 1 Group provided seventy-seven Wellingtons and six 103 Squadron Halifaxes, the latter departing Elsham Wolds between 00.34 and 00.59 bearing aloft the crews of S/Ls Fox and Saxelby, F/Ls Frith and Kennard and P/Os Gilby and Winchester, "Dizzy" Spiller now looking after the welfare of S/L Fox. They crossed the English coast at Cromer on course for the Scheldt estuary and P/O Gilby and crew were some eighteen miles short of the target at 10,000 feet when the failure of their starboard-outer engine persuaded them to drop the bombs at 02.40 and turn for home. The others found the southern Ruhr and the target under clear skies with sufficiently good visibility to enable most to identify the Rhine and its bridges as they ran in to bomb. The 103 Squadron crews attacked from 7,500 to 12,000 feet between 02.35 and 02.49, and although not able to identify individual bomb bursts among the fires, confidence was high that they had landed within the built-up area. More than nine hundred tons of bombs had been delivered by the 484 crews claiming to have attacked the target area, but a proportion of that had been wasted in open country. Local sources confirmed a heavy raid, reporting that the bulk of bombing had been scattered across all parts of the city and neighbouring Neuss, resulting in the destruction of 453 buildings, damage to fifteen thousand more, the majority of them only slightly afflicted, and sixty-seven large fires. The success came at the heavy cost to Bomber Command of twenty-nine aircraft, only one of which was from 1 Group. It was a reasonably promising start for 103 Squadron's Halifax career, but sadly, it would prove to be a case of flattering to deceive. The type would not be popular, and no crews would complete a tour during its time with the squadron.

During the course of the month, the squadron took part in two operations and dispatched five Wellington and six Halifax sorties for the loss of two Wellingtons and their crews and a Halifax and crew as a result of a training accident.

August 1942

There was a gentle introduction to operations for the new month, and it was the 4th before 1 Group was called into action to provide ten Wellingtons for a small-scale raid on Essen and thirty-six others for gardening duties. 1 Group's contribution to the fifth and final operation of the three-week campaign against the Ruhr city of Duisburg amounted to thirty-eight Wellingtons and four Halifaxes, which were part of an overall force of 216 aircraft assembled on the 6th. The 103 Squadron crews of S/L Fox, P/Os Gilby and Winchester and F/Sgt Tilley departed Elsham Wolds between 00.47 and 00.55 and headed for Southwold on course for the Scheldt estuary. F/Sgt Tilley found his controls to be unstable and he was struggling to gain height when he abandoned the sortie after ninety minutes and turned for home. The others reached the target to find cloud reported variously of between zero and ten-tenths with tops at 10,000 feet and barrage balloons tethered as high as 12,000 feet. Positions had to be established by TR-fix confirmed by visual reference aided by fires, flak and flares, and the bombs were delivered by most more in hope than expectation. S/L Fox and crew identified the Rhine and the Ruhrort docks complex from six miles away and bombed on e.t.a. from 10,000 feet at 02.46. The photo-flash began to ignite in the flare chute and the wireless operator withdrew it by hand, before jettisoning it through the entrance hatch a second before it detonated. P/O Winchester and crew carried out their attack from 11,000 feet at 02.50 and observed the bursts of their bombs. There was no report from the crew of P/O Gilby, who all lost their lives when their homebound W1225 crashed into the Humber at around 05.00. According to local sources, eighteen buildings were destroyed in Duisburg and sixty-six seriously damaged, giving a sum total over the five raids of 212 houses destroyed, 741 seriously damaged, and significant industrial damage resulting from just one raid. In return for this modest gain, Bomber Command had lost forty-three aircraft.

The 11th brought a well-deserved and hard-earned DSO for S/L Holford, who had now left the squadron at the conclusion of his tour. Following a period as an instructor he would be appointed to command 100 Squadron at Grimsby in November 1943 in time for the resumption of the Berlin campaign and would lose his life a month later in one of many Lancasters crashing in foggy conditions on return from Germany's capital. The squadron was not involved in operations to Osnabrück on the 9/10th and Mainz on the 11/12th and 12/13th, all of which were supported by 1 Group and produced some useful damage.

A new era for Bomber Command began on the 15th with the formation of the Path Finder Force, and the arrival on their new stations in Huntingdonshire and Cambridgeshire of the four founder heavy squadrons. Each would represent and draw manpower from its former group, the Stirling-equipped 7 Squadron at Oakington for 3 Group, 35 (Madras Presidency) Squadron at Graveley with its Halifaxes to represent 4 Group, 83 Squadron at Wyton, the Path Finder HQ, for 5 Group operating Lancasters, and 156 Squadron at Warboys with Wellingtons for 1 Group. When 3 Group's 40 Squadron was sent overseas early in 1942, the home echelon was renumbered 156 Squadron, and thus had no previous association with 1 Group. In addition to the above, 109 Squadron was posted in to Wyton, where it would spend the next six months developing the Oboe blind-bombing device and marrying it to the Mosquito under the command of W/C Hal Bufton. The new force would occupy 3 Group stations, falling nominally under 3 Group administrative control and receiving its orders through that group, which was commanded by AVM Baldwin, whose tenure, which had lasted since just before the outbreak of war, was shortly to come to an end.

A "Path Finder" force was the brainchild of the former 10 Squadron commanding officer, G/C Sid Bufton, Hal's brother, and now Director of Bomber Operations at the Air Ministry. He had used his best crews at 10 Squadron to find targets by the light of flares and attract other crews by firing off a coloured Verey light, and, it could be said, that the concept of target-finding and marking had been born at 10 Squadron. Once at the Air Ministry, Bufton promoted his ideas with vigour, and gained support among the other staff officers, culminating with the idea being put to Harris soon after his enthronement as Bomber Command C-in-C. Harris rejected the principle of establishing an elite target-finding and marking force, a view shared by the other group commanders with the exception of 4 Group's AVM Roddy Carr. However, once overruled by higher authority, Harris gave it his unstinting support, and his choice of the former 10 Squadron commanding officer, and still somewhat junior, G/C Don Bennett, as its commander, was both controversial and inspired and ruffled more than a few feathers among more senior officers. Australian, Bennett, was among the most experienced aviators in the RAF, a pilot and a Master Navigator of unparalleled experience, with many thousands of hours to his credit. He also had the recent and relevant experience as a bomber pilot through his commands of 77 and 10 Squadrons and had demonstrated his strong character when evading capture and returning from Norway after being shot down while attacking the Tirpitz in April. Despite his reserve, total lack of humour and his impatience with those whose brains operated on a lower plane than his, he would inspire in his men great affection and loyalty, along with an enormous pride, once qualified, in wearing the Path Finder badge. He would forge the new force into a highly effective weapon, although this would not immediately be apparent.

On the night of the new force's formation, 1 Group contributed thirty-six Wellingtons and six Halifaxes drawn from all of its stations as part of an overall force of 131 aircraft detailed for another attack on the Ruhr city of Düsseldorf. 103 Squadron briefed the crews of S/L

Saxelby, F/L Kennard, W/O Edwards, F/Sgt Tilley and Sgts Davies and Smith and sent them on their way from Elsham Wolds between 00.14 and 00.33 each sitting on seven 1,000 pounders. P/O Jack Douglas had been posted in from the conversion flight earlier in the day, and he was on board W1219 with the Saxelby crew to gain his first taste of operations in a Halifax. Douglas would rise rapidly through the ranks to command both 460 and 467 RAAF squadrons, before losing his life in February 1945 after amassing more than a hundred sorties. They exited the English coast over Mablethorpe and set course for Katwijk, Sgt Davies trying desperately to coax his Halifax to a respectable height and dumping three 1,000 pounders in the process only to admit defeat and turn back from a position only fifteen miles out from the English coast. The others ran into a severe electrical storm at the Dutch coast that rendered F/Sgt Tilley's compass unserviceable and left him with no choice but to turn back also. It was possibly at the same time that S/L Saxelby lost his wireless and electrical system and became the third 103 Squadron "boomerang". The others arrived over the southern Ruhr to encounter two layers of ten-tenths cloud between 6,000 and 8,000 feet and 10,000 and 12,000 feet, through which it was impossible to catch a glimpse of the ground. They were among the many forced to bomb on a combination of Gee, DR, e.t.a. and flak and searchlights and did so from 10,000 to 12,000 feet between 02.18 and 02.31. On return, crews reported at least six cones of ten to fifteen beams each operating in and around the city but had little to say about what was happening beneath the cloud.

On the 16th, a signal was received from 1 Group HQ instructing 460 Squadron to withdraw one flight from operations to enable the crews to begin Halifax conversion training, leaving the other flight to continue the fight on Wellingtons. Harris had intended to "blood" the Path Finder Force on the night of the 17/18th, when Osnabrück was selected to receive its second visit of the month, but the commanding officers declared their units to be unready, and a standard operation was mounted instead by a force of 139 aircraft. 103 Squadron contributed three Halifaxes to the 1 Group element of twenty-nine Wellingtons and loaded them with seven 1,000 pounders each before sending them on their way from Elsham Wolds between 22.12 and 22.19, bearing aloft the crews of S/L Saxelby, F/L Kennard and P/O Winchester. The recommended route took them via Mablethorpe to the Frisian Island of Vlieland, then across northern Holland to the Dümmer See located twenty-five miles to the north-east of the target, some noting the Ems-Weser Canal or perhaps the Mittelland Canal, which provided a good navigation point, as did known dummy fire sites lit to the west of the city. They were greeted at the target by three to five-tenths cloud at between 11,000 and 14,000 feet with haze at 4,000 feet to compromise the vertical visibility, despite which some crews were able to identify the river and railway lines. Not all crews were positive of their positions as they opened their bomb bay doors, and P/O Winchester and crew were reduced to aiming at fires from 11,000 feet at 00.37 and S/L Saxelby and crew a block of buildings from 11,500 feet at around the same time. F/L Kennard and crew suffered the frustration of a complete hang-up and had to return the bombs to the dump. Local reports confirmed a moderately destructive raid, which fell mainly into northern and north-western districts, and thereby, built on the damage inflicted eight nights earlier.

It was on the following night, the 18/19th, that the fledgling Path Finder Force led its first raid on Germany, for which the port of Flensburg was selected. A force of 118 aircraft included thirty-one Path Finders and seventeen aircraft representing 1 Group, among them a single 103 Squadron Halifax containing the crew of S/L Fox. They departed Elsham Wolds at 21.02

with six 1,000 pounders in the bomb bay and set course from Mablethorpe to Amrum, one of the islands off the western coast of Schleswig-Holstein, before traversing the peninsula to reach the target on the Baltic coast just south of the Danish frontier. The brief for Path Finder crews in the early days was simply to lead a force to a target and illuminate it with flares, with none of the complex procedures and pyrotechnics that would evolve over time, and Flensburg had been selected because it would be easy to find. Sadly, the planners had not factored in an incorrect wind forecast, which pushed the bomber stream north of the intended track and over southern Denmark, a situation that the Path Finders failed to notice. As a result, in conditions of haze and two-tenths cloud at 6,000 feet, they illuminated an area of similar coastal terrain north of where they believed themselves to be, which led to a scattering of bombs across Danish territory up to twenty-five miles north of the frontier and into the towns of Abenra and Sønderborg. S/L Fox and crew delivered their bomb load from 6,800 feet at 23.30 and observed bursts a few hundred yards from the apparent aiming point but were unable to assess the results. On return, sixteen Path Finder crews claimed to have marked the target and seventy-eight main force crews reported bombing it in what was an inauspicious operational debut by the new target-locating and marking force.

The second Path Finder-led operation was directed at Frankfurt on the night of the 24/25th, for which 1 Group put up fifty Wellingtons in an overall force of 226 aircraft. This was a much-reduced effort from the originally planned force of some 330 aircraft, including 102 representing 1 Group, and was brought about by doubts about the weather and the consequent withdrawal of the less experienced crews. The Path Finders reached the target area after following the River Main from Koblenz to Mainz and finally Frankfurt, where varying amounts of cloud between six and ten-tenths hung over at least part of the city, with tops in places as high as 12,000 feet. They enjoyed good horizontal visibility but a very restricted view vertically, and there was an element of uncertainty as the main force crews released their loads. Opinions at debriefing were mixed, some satisfied with the results and others not. Certainly, a number of fires were observed across the built-up area, but no detailed assessment was possible, and it was established eventually that the main weight of bombs had fallen into open country and outlying communities to the north and north-west of the city.

Three days later, on the 27th, a force of 306 aircraft was assembled for a Path Finder-led raid on the city of Kassel, for which eighty-one Wellingtons and a dozen 103 Squadron Halifaxes were provided by 1 Group. Eight of the latter were loaded with fifteen SBCs of incendiaries and the remaining four with seven 1,000 pounders each and took to the air between 20.35 and 21.01 with S/Ls Saxelby and Fox the senior pilots on duty, along with the deputy flight commanders, F/Ls Frith and Kennard. They headed for the exit point at Mablethorpe under clear skies and moonlight, and soon lost the services of W/O Telfer and crew to a failed port-outer engine. The others pressed on across the Dutch coast at Castricum to a pinpoint at Edam, from where they tracked south-east across the Münsterland to the target, benefitting throughout from the excellent conditions. The Path Finders were able to illuminate the city successfully for the main force crews following on behind, and in turn, the main force crews exploited the opportunity to deliver their bombs predominantly into the south-western districts of the city, causing much damage and many large fires. The 103 Squadron crews bombed from 6,000 to 11,000 feet, and fires were beginning to take hold as they turned away, confident in the effectiveness of their work. Returning crews praised the efforts of the Path Finders in illuminating the target area with their well-placed flares, but it soon became clear that it had not been a one-sided affair and that the bomber force had suffered a 10% loss amounting to thirty-one aircraft. The 1 Group casualty figure was disproportionately high at fourteen aircraft, including five 142 Squadron Wellingtons and the first Halifax to be lost by 103 Squadron. W1270 was shot down on the way home by the night-fighter of Hptm Wolfgang Thimmig of III./NJG1 and crashed at 23.54 in northern Holland with no survivors from the crew of F/L Frith. Local sources confirmed the effectiveness of the operation and catalogued the destruction of 144 buildings across the city, with more than three hundred others severely damaged. Among the industrial sites afflicted were all three Henschel factories, and seventy-three large fires had to be dealt with.

On the following day, orders were issued to stations across the Command to prepare for two operations, one involving 159 aircraft to attack Nuremberg in southern Germany, while 113 others were to target Saarbrücken, the city perched on the frontier with France 180 miles to the west. The latter was made up of oddments, including 4 Group Halifaxes, which were being rested from main force operations after a spate of crashes caused by rudder-lock. 1 Group assigned seven 103 Squadron Halifaxes to Nuremberg and two to join fifty-nine Wellingtons for the Saarbrücken raid, but two of the former were found to be unserviceable and had to be scrubbed, thus delaying the first sortie for Jack Douglas as captain of his own crew. The Saarbrücken-bound crews of W/O Telfer and P/O Rose departed Elsham Wolds first at 20.04 and 20.06 respectively, each carrying thirteen SBCs containing ninety 4lb incendiaries, and they were followed into the air by the others between 20.27 and 20.42, each crew with four 1,000 pounders and a single 500 pounder beneath their feet. The Saarbrücken force flew out over Dunwich on the Suffolk coast, and crossed the French coast near Abbeville, before following major waterways parallel to the Franco-Belgian frontier towards Germany. Clear skies and good visibility aided map-reading, but ground haze obscured some detail, and it seems that the target was approached from a variety of directions. W/O Telfer RCAF and crew must have turned back early, because three hours after taking off, when the rest of the force was closing on the target 120 miles away, BB204 was shot down from 12,000 feet by Hptm Wilhelm Herget of II./NJG4 and crashed at 23.04 five miles south-west of the Belgian town of Dinant. The pilot and three others lost their lives, and the three survivors were taken into captivity. P/O Rose and crew reached and identified the target by a loop in the River Saar and observed their incendiaries ignite one mile south of the aiming point and set off fires.

Meanwhile, the 103 Squadron participants in the Nuremberg raid had taken off between 20.27 and 20.42 with S/L Saxelby the senior pilot on duty and lost W/O Edwards and crew to an unserviceable starboard-inner engine as they approached Ostend. They jettisoned their bombs "safe" before turning back at 22.50, leaving the others to press on and complete the six-hundred-mile outward leg across France to the target area, which was found to be under clear skies. The Path Finders were to employ target indicators (TIs) for the first time in adapted 250lb bomb casings and the light from a four-fifths moon enabled them to identify the aiming point and deliver them with great accuracy. The Elsham Wolds crews pinpointed on waterways and autobahns leading into the city, and then the sports stadium and marshalling yards came into view, the crews of F/L Kennard and P/O Winchester bombing from 8,000 and 9,000 feet respectively at around 23.45. S/L Saxelby and crew experienced a testing time after discovering that their bomb doors had failed to open during the bombing run. They spent thirteen minutes outside of the target pumping the doors open by hand, before making a second run at 8,200 feet, during which all but a single 1,000 pounder bomb fell away. The hang-up was eventually released by hand, and the next twenty minutes was spent pumping the doors closed. There was no question in their minds of most crews as they withdrew, that they had hit the target, a belief confirmed by fires remaining visible for some seventy miles into the return flight. Twenty-three aircraft failed to return, 14.5% of the force, and the Wellingtons were hit particularly hard again, losing a third of their number. 103 Squadron's BB214 was shot down by a night-fighter, and four of the mixed RAF, RAAF, RCAF and RNZAF crew lost their lives, while the pilot, Sgt Drysdale, and two others survived in enemy hands. Local reports suggested that about a third of the force had landed bombs within the city, causing damage to the Altstadt, but that others had wasted their effort on communities up to ten miles to the north.

During the course of its first month as a Halifax unit, the squadron took part in eight operations and dispatched thirty-nine sorties for the loss of four aircraft and crews.

September 1942

The first half of the new month would distinguish itself through an unprecedented series of effective operations, although, it would begin ignominiously for the Path Finder Force, when Saarbrücken was posted as the target on the 1st. The details were briefed out to 231 crews, forty-seven of them on all 1 Group stations but Breighton, while at Elsham Wolds, six Halifaxes were made ready, three loaded with six 1,000 pounders each and the others with fourteen SBCs containing ninety 4lb incendiaries. F/L Kennard's aircraft became unserviceable late on and was scrubbed, leaving the crews of S/L Saxelby, P/Os Douglas and Rose, F/Sgt Tilley and Sgt Davies to take off between 23.20 and 23.36 with station commander, G/C Constantine, flying with the Saxelby crew and P/O Douglas in command of his own crew for the first time. They were routed out over Orfordness, but Sgt Davies and crew were immediately in trouble as W1187 became uncontrollable and the order was given to jettison the bombs and bale out. The rear gunner complied, but once the bulk of the bomb load had gone, some semblance of control was regained, and the bale-out order rescinded. However, it proved to be a temporary respite and a belly landing was ultimately carried out on the grass adjacent to the runway without injury to the occupants. The rear gunner had landed safely and walked the three miles home minus his flying boots, which had come off during the descent.

The others reached south-western Germany to find the target under clear skies with good visibility, and established their positions by TR, confirmed by visual identification of the River Saar and other ground features and Path Finder flares. They bombed from 7,000 to 9,800 feet at around 02.00 onwards and most observed the bursts of their high explosives, while some crews from other squadrons reported the entire area of the North Bank of the Saar to be on fire and commented on a very large explosion occurring in the midst of the conflagration. There was no question in the minds of the crews as they retreated to the west, that this had been an outstandingly accurate attack, and some claimed to be able to see the glow of fires from up to 140 miles into the return flight. It was only later that the truth emerged, that the Path Finders had marked not Saarbrücken, but the non-industrial town of Saarlouis, situated thirteen miles to the north-west, which lay in a loop of the river similar to that at the intended target. Much to the chagrin of its inhabitants and those in surrounding communities, the main force bombing had been particularly accurate and concentrated, and heavy damage had been inflicted.

This could have been seen as an ill-omen for the month's efforts, but in fact, the Command now embarked on a two-and-a-half-week run of unusually effective operations, beginning at Karlsruhe on the 2nd. A force of two hundred aircraft was made ready, the 4 Group Halifax brigade having now returned to operations following intensive training to restore confidence in the type after the previously mentioned period of above average losses and design-flaw accidents. 1 Group put up forty-four Wellingtons and two Halifaxes, captained by P/O Douglas and F/L Kennard, who departed Elsham Wolds at 22.55 and 23.21 respectively, the former carrying fourteen SBCs of 4lb incendiaries and the latter six 1,000 pounders. They adopted the familiar route for this region, following the course of the Franco-Belgian frontier to cross into Germany north of Strasbourg, where they picked up the River Rhine leading northwards to the target. Both reached the target to find excellent conditions of clear skies and good visibility and identified the castle, the docks and the town by the light of Path Finder flares. They carried out their attacks from 9,000 and 8,500 feet and watched as the city appeared be swallowed by a sea of flames, before becoming obscured by smoke. Returning crews reported as many as two hundred fires burning, the glow from which remained visible for a hundred miles into the homeward journey, and there was praise for the performance of the Path Finders. Post-raid reconnaissance confirmed much residential and some industrial damage, and local reports mentioned seventy-three fatalities.

A National Day of Prayer was held on the 3rd to mark the third anniversary of the outbreak of war and was broadcast across the Nation. Bremen was posted as the target on the 4th, for which a force of 251 aircraft was assembled, 1 Group contributing fifty-three Wellingtons and five 103 Squadron Halifaxes. Crews learned at briefing that the Path Finders would be rolling out their new three-phase system based on illuminating, visual marking and backing-up, which if successful, would form the basis of Path Finder operations for the remainder of the war. The crews of S/L Saxelby, F/L Kennard, P/O Rose, F/Sgt Tilley and Sgt Davies departed Elsham Wolds between 00.01 and 00.19, each sitting on seven 1,000 pounders, and exited the English coast over Mablethorpe on course for the southern tip of Vlieland for a direct run across northern Holland to the final pinpoint at Cloppenburg. They arrived in the target area under clear skies and in bright moonlight, in which ground detail stood out clearly, and delivered their attacks onto the marker flares from 9,700 to 11,700 feet, observing explosions and fires in the built-up area, but prevented by the glare from picking out individual bursts. Twelve aircraft failed to return from this successful operation, and among them was 103 Squadron's W1220, which was homebound when crashing close to the night-fighter aerodrome at Leeuwarden in northern Holland, the famed "Wespennest" or Wasp's Nest residence of some of the Luftwaffe's leading Aces, and there were no survivors from the crew of Sgt Davies. The debriefing reports of fires in the central districts were confirmed by local sources, which listed 460 dwelling houses, six large/medium industrial premises and fifteen small ones destroyed, and a further fourteen hundred buildings seriously damaged.

Following a night off, Duisburg was announced as the target on the 6th, and a force of 207 aircraft made ready, of which thirty-three Wellingtons and four 103 Squadron Halifaxes were provided by 1 Group. S/L Saxelby's aircraft had eight 1,000 pounders winched into its bomb bay, while those earmarked for the crews of P/Os Douglas and Rose and F/Sgt Newitt were loaded with fifteen SBCs of 4lb incendiaries before departing Elsham Wolds between 00.56 and 01.06. They adopted the southern route to the target via Orfordness and the Scheldt estuary and crossed south-eastern Holland to enter Germany near Mönchengladbach. They arrived at the target under clear skies and with sufficiently good vertical visibility through the industrial haze to enable them to recognise the River Rhine and its massive Ruhrort docks complex, aided by the light from Path Finder flares. The incendiary-carrying trio delivered their loads from 10,000 to 11,500 feet and observed many scattered fires, but no clear point of concentration. The searchlight and flak defence was up to its usual proficient standard, with a main concentration to the north-west of the city that involved some forty beams in a cone co-operating with flak batteries. The return route was over northern Holland, and three of the 103 Squadron participants made it back safely to pass on their impressions at debriefing, but absent from that process was the crew of S/L Saxelby, with which F/L Pipkin was flying, and had been on a regular basis before being granted captaincy of his own crew. News was eventually received via the Red Cross that W1219 had crashed in Holland, and the rear gunner had failed to survive, while S/L Saxelby and five others had been taken into captivity and the bomb-aimer had managed to evade a similar fate. Bomber Command's record at Duisburg was little better than at Essen, and the bombing was scattered, despite which, 114 buildings were destroyed and more than three hundred others damaged, which represented a modest success at this target.

On the 7th, a letter was received at Breighton from HQ 1 Group stating that 460 Squadron crews were to be withdrawn from operations as and when the Conversion Flight was able to accept them, estimated at six crews per fortnight. The remaining crews, both converted and not, were to continue operations on Wellingtons, and the squadron would not begin Halifax operations until eight crews were fully capable.

There had been no pattern to the choice of targets thus far in the month, southern and north-western Germany and the Ruhr all featuring during the busy first week, and Frankfurt in south-central Germany was posted as the latest target on the 8th, for which a force of 249 aircraft was assembled. 1 Group contributed forty-five Wellingtons and five 103 Squadron Halifaxes, three of the latter loaded with fourteen SBCs of 4lb incendiaries and two with six 1,000 pounders. The crews of S/L Fox, P/Os Douglas and Rose, F/Sgt Newitt and Sgt Claridge departed Elsham Wolds between 20.36 and 20.52 and exited the English coast over Orfordness on course for the Belgian coast. P/O Douglas and crew ran into flak at 22.15 when at 6,000 feet over Kortrijk (Courtrai) and a hit left all of the instruments fused and both inner engines damaged, forcing them to jettison the load and return home. The others continued on a course parallel to the French frontier as far as Mons, from where they headed eastwards in favourable conditions to enter Germany to the north of Luxembourg. According to some, the skies over Frankfurt were clear of cloud and the visibility good, while others reported up to eight-tenths cloud at 2,000 feet and poor to moderate visibility. Another factor determining the accuracy of the raid was the intensity of the searchlight and flak activity, which should, perhaps, have helped to guide the Path Finders to the aiming point, but surprisingly, they failed to locate the city. Path Finder flares were in evidence, but scattered over a wide area, and it was clear that they were by no means certain of their proximity to the target. The 103 Squadron crews delivered their attacks from 7,200 to 10,500 feet between 23.40 and 23.46, before returning to report many fierce fires and a successful night's work. Local sources, however, reported only a handful of bomb loads hitting the intended target, the majority having fallen to the south-west of Frankfurt as far as Rüsselsheim, fifteen miles away. The Rüsselsheim authorities confirmed damage to the Opel tank works and a Michelin tyre factory, which compensated in small measure for the failure to hit the primary target. This halted the run of successes thus far in the month, but it would be re-established.

On the 9th, W/C Du Bulay concluded his tour as 103 Squadron's commanding officer and was posted to HQ 1 Group, whence came W/C Robert Carter DSO as his successor, an experienced operational officer, who had commanded 1 Group's 150 Squadron between June and December 1941 having served it as a flight commander, and was about to celebrate his thirty-second birthday.

The Path Finder Force was constantly evolving in tactics and equipment and had a new weapon in its armoury for the next operation, which was to be against the Ruhr city of Düsseldorf on the 10th. "The Pink Pansy", which weighed in at 2,800lbs, was the latest attempt to produce a genuine target indicator, and used converted 4,000lb cookie casings. A force of 479 aircraft included a contribution from the training units of 91, 92 and 93 Groups, and fifty-four Wellingtons and eight 103 Squadron Halifaxes representing 1 Group. At Elsham Wolds each of the latter was loaded with fifteen SBCs of 4lb incendiaries and sent on their way between 20.35 and 20.58 with S/L Fox the senior pilot on duty and P/O Douglas the only other commissioned pilot. They set course via Cromer for the Scheldt estuary and pressed on towards the southern Ruhr under clear skies, arriving at the target to encounter unusually good vertical visibility with just a little haze, and some were able to identify the distinctive five-fingered dock layout in Neuss on the South Bank of the Rhine, aided by the many red and green flares. The 103 Squadron crews let their incendiaries go from 6,800 to 11,800 feet between 22.33 and 22.59 and some observed bursts, while other impacts were lost in the kaleidoscope of flak and fire. Returning crews were confident of a successful outcome and reported the glow of fires visible from the Dutch coast homebound, while also offering complimentary comments about the performance of the Path Finders. Post-raid reconnaissance and local reports confirmed this operation to have been probably the most successful since Operation Millennium at the end of May. Other than the northern districts, all parts of the city and its neighbour, Neuss, had been hit, and 911 houses had been destroyed with a further fifteen hundred seriously damaged. In addition to the destruction also of eight public buildings, fifty-two industrial firms in the two cities sustained damage sufficient to cause a total shut down of production for varying periods. It had been an expensive victory for the Command, however, with thirty-three failures to return, of which sixteen were from the training units and four from 1 Group.

The tannoys called the faithful to prayer in the briefing rooms on stations across the Command on the 13th, to learn that Bremen was to be their target for that night, and for the second time during the month. A force of 446 aircraft was made ready, again bolstered by aircraft and crews from the training groups, and there was a contribution from 1 Group of fifty Wellingtons and seven 103 Squadron Halifaxes. Each of the latter had fifteen SBCs of 4lb incendiaries winched into its bomb bay, before taking to the skies above Elsham Wolds between 00.08 and 00.38 and heading for Mablethorpe to begin the North-Sea crossing to the northern tip of Texel. Sgt Smith's escape hatch blew open shortly after take-off and he proceeded directly to the jettison area off the coast and at around the same time, Sgt Porter and crew turned back because of unserviceable guns in the rear turret. While landing at Grimsby, the starboard undercarriage leg collapsed, but no injuries were reported and W1182 would eventually be returned to flying condition. F/L Kennard was the senior and sole commissioned pilot on duty as the others tracked under clear skies towards north-western Germany, and many fires were already burning in Bremen to draw them on for the final forty miles. Haze and smoke marred to an extent the vertical visibility, but the River Weser pointed the way into the heart of the city and the layout of the docks provided a further pinpoint. The 103 Squadron crews carried out their attacks from 8,500 to 11,700 feet between 02.35 and 02.50, and the larger fires remained visible for some forty-five minutes into the return flight. An encounter with an enemy night-fighter on the way home resulted in extensive damage to W7705, but it was able to limp back in the hands of F/L Kennard and crew and landed safely at Waterbeach. Enthusiastic reports of a punishing raid were confirmed by reconnaissance and local sources, which revealed that the damage inflicted by far exceeded the destruction resulting from June's Thousand Bomber raid. A total of 848 houses had been destroyed, and much damage had been inflicted upon the city's industry, including to the Lloyd Dynamo works, where two weeks production was lost, and to parts of the Focke-Wulf factory, which were put out of action for between two and eight days. Of the twenty-one aircraft lost, fifteen belonged to the training units.

The 103 Squadron crews of S/L Fox, F/Sgt Tilley and Sgts Berry and Smith attended briefing at Elsham Wolds on the afternoon of the 14th to learn of their part in that night's operation. It had been planned to send a large force to Hamburg but concerns about the weather prompted a reduction in the size of the force to 202 aircraft and a change of target to the naval and shipbuilding port of Wilhelmshaven. Forty Wellingtons from Binbrook, Grimsby, Hemswell, Ingham, Lindholme and Snaith completed the 1 Group contribution, and all would carry nine SBCs of 4lb incendiaries, while the Halifaxes were loaded with fifteen. S/L Fox and crew were forced to pull out at the last minute, leaving three to take off between 20.07 and 20.20 and head to the exit point over Mablethorpe. F/Sgt Tilley and crew turned back from the midpoint of the North Sea because of W/T, TR and engine issues, leaving the others to establish their positions first on the Frisian islands and then Jade Bay. As usual, opinions were divided as to the amount of cloud and haze in the target area, ranging from nil to nine-tenths with tops at 14,000 feet, while the state of the vertical visibility was described as anywhere between good and poor. Some identified ground features, like the docks, in the light from flares, while others relied on DR, and the bombing by the 103 Squadron crews took place from 10,000 feet at 22.00 and 22.13. Some bursts and fires were observed, and one enormous explosion, but it proved difficult to make an effective assessment. Post-raid reconnaissance and local sources confirmed that this had been the most successful raid yet visited upon the town, with much damage inflicted on housing and city-centre-type buildings. It was also the last raid in which the trusty old Hampden took part, leaving 5 Group now fully equipped with Lancasters.

While 369 aircraft were being prepared for Essen on the 16th, 103 Squadron was stood down from operations to embark on a period of intensive training, the intention of which was to thoroughly familiarize crews with the Halifax and its characteristics. There had been a large influx of new crews at a time when, as previously highlighted, the Halifax had gained a bad reputation for falling out of the sky for no apparent reason. The problem had been solved by replacing the triangular fins with a larger rectangular design, and further modifications to the Mk II Halifax would improve its all-round performance. Happily, such matters would soon not be relevant to 103 Squadron. The training consisted largely of "bullseye" long-range cross-country exercises, which at night would include spending time over large cities to report on the effectiveness of the blackout. If coned by searchlights or approached by night-fighters, they were permitted to use evasive tactics. There was also bombing and photography practice, circuits and landings and fighter affiliation, and this period of training continued through to the 27th.

While 103 Squadron was away from the operational scene the above-mentioned raid on Essen went ahead on the night of the 16/17th, and in the context of the Command's personal battle with this city, was, perhaps, the most destructive attack on it to date. The Krupp works was hit by fifteen high explosive bombs and a crashing bomber, much residential property was damaged, and over a hundred large and medium fires had to be tackled by the emergency services. Other Ruhr towns were also hit, including Bochum, where fifty fires were started, but the defenders fought back to claim a massive thirty-nine aircraft, or 10.6% of those dispatched. This concluded the succession of highly effective operations, and if any period in Bomber Command's development could be seen as a turning point, then these first sixteen nights of September 1942 qualified. It can be no coincidence that these encouraging results came at a time when the Path Finder crews were beginning to get to grips with the intricacies of their complex task and the new target marking techniques being introduced. It was just a start, however, and failures would continue to outnumber successes until the coming spring.

Minor and mining operations dominated the remainder of the month and the only large-scale undertaking to involve 1 Group was a raid on Saarbrücken by a force of 118 aircraft that included thirty-five Wellingtons on the 19th. During the course of the month the squadron took part in eight operations and dispatched thirty-nine sorties for the loss of two Halifaxes and crews.

October 1942

October was to provide a grim reminder of the Halifax's vulnerability but would also hold the promise of better things to come. There was promotion for F/L Kennard to fill the shoes of S/L Saxelby as a flight commander, and it was also during this month that the Maddern crew arrived at Elsham Wolds to begin their first tour of operations. Geoff Maddern was from western Australia, his navigator, Don Charlwood, from Melbourne, and wireless operator Max Burcher from New South Wales, and together with their RAF colleagues they would reflect the life of every crew finding themselves on a windswept bomber airfield in the autumn of 1942. After the war Charlwood would write a book about his experiences, and No

Moon Tonight would become a classic of wartime literature, a "must-read" for anyone who wants to know what it was like.

The ranks of 1 Group had been swelled by the recent arrival at Holme-on-Spalding-Moor of 101 Squadron on transfer from 3 Group, and as an experienced operator of the Wellington, it was immediately available for operations. However, it had been earmarked for conversion to the Lancaster in the first phase, alongside 103 and 460 Squadrons, and ten crews had been packed off to 1654 HCU at Wigsley on the 30th of September to begin training. On the 2nd, a letter dated the 1st was received at 460 Squadron, from which the following extract was taken and recorded in the ORB. *"Pending re-arming with Lancaster aircraft, the O.C. 460 Squadron is to be prepared to operate Halifax aircraft as soon as eight crews are fully converted"*. The squadron, and indeed, all but 103 Squadron in 1 Group, had dodged a bullet in being spared conversion to the much disliked "Halibag". The 103 Squadron crews shed no tears on learning of its imminent departure, although they would have to endure a further three weeks of operations until the day arrived.

The new month began for 1 Group with a call to arms on the 2nd, when the Ruhr city of Krefeld was posted as the target for a force of 188 aircraft, for which forty-nine Wellingtons and nine 103 Squadron Halifaxes were detailed. Located at the western edge of the Ruhr, a few miles to the south-west of Duisburg, Krefeld's industry had been based on silk and velvet textiles, but the presence of a Thyssen-Krupp steelworks was sufficient to attract the attention of Bomber Command. The 103 Squadron element departed Elsham Wolds between 18.49 and 19.21 with S/L Kennard the senior pilot on duty and each Halifax carrying two 1,000 pounders and a dozen SBCs containing ninety 4lb incendiaries. They set course from Mablethorpe to make landfall on the Dutch coast north of The Hague and lost the services of F/Sgt Tilley and crew to the failure of their IFF equipment at 20.03, when, according to the map reference, they were over Norfolk, which was many miles south of the recommended track. The failure of IFF did not constitute operational unserviceability, and on return it functioned perfectly, as a result of which, one imagines, the crew faced a carpeting from the commanding officer. Sgt Porter's rear gunner tested his four Browning .303s over the sea and found them to be unserviceable, and this crew also turned for home. The others encountered dense industrial haze in the target area, which thwarted the late-arriving Path Finders' best efforts to provide a reference for those following behind and most crews were reduced to bombing on estimated positions based on DR and isolated Path Finder flares. They carried out their attacks from 7,000 to 11,000 feet between 20.49 and 21.06, and on return reported some scattered fires but no detail. Local sources confirmed that three streets in the northern part of the city had sustained damage, but nothing commensurate with the size of the force and the effort expended.

On the 5th, a force of 257 aircraft was assembled to raid Aachen, Germany's most westerly city, perched on the frontiers of both Holland and Belgium south-west of the Ruhr. Forty-seven of the Wellingtons and ten 103 Squadron Halifaxes were provided by 1 Group, the latter each loaded with two 1,000 pounders and a dozen SBCs of 4lb incendiaries. They departed Elsham Wolds between 18.52 and 19.16 with S/L Fox the senior pilot on duty and W/C Carter undertaking his first operation with the squadron, flying as second pilot to Sgt Austin. They flew out over the Kent coast at Dungeness on course for Le Crotoy and ran into unfavourable weather conditions in the form of electrical storms and icing. The stormy weather extended inland, which encouraged some of the force to descend for the rest of the journey to the target, on arrival at which flares were visible, but up to nine-tenths cloud at between 8,000 and 14,000 feet with haze below created poor visibility and challenging conditions. The 103 Squadron element arrived intact, and S/L Fox and crew watched their bombs fall from 6,000 feet across a factory with a large cooling tower and four chimneys at 21.30, while the others carried out their attacks from 6,900 to 9,600 feet between 21.26 and 21.54 and also had a built-up area in their bomb sights. However, many crews from other squadrons searched in vain through cloud for a reference on the ground and reported bursts and at least one large fire. Local sources confirmed that Aachen's southern district of Burtscheid had suffered quite extensive damage to housing and industry, and five large fires had required attention. Even so, they estimated the attack to have involved only around ten aircraft. Some bombs fell seventeen miles away onto the small Dutch town of Lutterade, and this would have minor consequences for the trials of the Oboe blind-bombing device in late December. 103 Squadron's W1216 was shot down on the way home over Belgium by the night-fighter of Lt Hans Autenrieth of II./NJG1 at 22.47 German time, around 02.00 GMT, and crashed seven miles north-east of Tongeren. The long-serving W/O Edwards died along with two of the other seven men on board and it seems likely that he had remained at the controls to give his crew time to bale out. The rear gunner was too badly wounded to comply with the bale-out order and went down with the aircraft and one man failed to survive his descent by parachute. Of the five men arriving safely on the ground, four were taken into captivity and one ultimately evaded capture.

Osnabrück was posted as the target on the 6th, for which 237 aircraft were made ready, including forty-seven Wellingtons and seven 103 Squadron Halifaxes representing 1 Group. At Elsham Wolds the armourers loaded each aircraft with two 1,000 pounders and a dozen SBCs of 4lb incendiaries and watched them take off between 19.12 and 19.28 with P/Os Douglas and Rose the only commissioned pilots on duty. They adopted the familiar route out over Mablethorpe and crossed the North Sea to the northern tip of Texel and were assisted by Path Finder route marker flares dropped over Makkum in Holland and the Dümmer See to the north-east of the target. These proved to be very effective in guiding the main force in, although, inevitably, some bomb loads were released early during the twenty-mile leg from the Dümmer See to the town. Four to eight-tenths cloud lay over the target area at 8,000 feet, and provided challenging conditions for accurate bombing, although opinions varied as to the quality of the visibility. The 103 Squadron crews attacked from 9,000 to 10,000 feet between 21.30 and 21.37, and six of them returned to express confidence in the effectiveness of the raid and describe many fires and a glow visible by some from the Dutch coast homebound. Six aircraft failed to return home and absent from debriefing at Elsham Wolds was the crew of Sgt Porter, who had been homebound in W1189 when intercepted by the night-fighter of Oblt Herman Greiner of IV./NJG1. The Halifax crashed at 23.27 into the North Sea off the Frisian island of Ameland, and the remains of the two gunners were eventually washed ashore for burial, one on Ameland and the other on Teschelling. According to local sources, 149 houses and six industrial buildings had been destroyed, 530 houses seriously damaged and more than 2,700 others slightly damaged.

There followed a week of minor operations that did not involve Elsham Wolds, which came to an end when the naval and shipbuilding port of Kiel was posted as the target for a force of 288 aircraft on the 13th. 1 Group weighed in with thirty-seven Wellingtons and a dozen 103 Squadron Halifaxes, the latter each loaded with a single 1,000 pounder and thirteen SBCs of 4lb incendiaries. The plan called for the Path Finder target-locaters and illuminators to fly out over the Baltic, before turning back onto a westerly heading to drop special markers over the Selenter Lake, the second largest body of water in Schleswig-Holstein, situated some eight miles east of Kiel. The locaters were to lay sticks of flares across the target area at the opening of the attack at 21.09, or if the aiming-point had been positively identified, to act as illuminators and drop their flares onto it along with the designated illuminators, who had a time-on-target between 21.10 and 21.18. This would then leave the way clear, and the aiming point primed for the main force element to do their job.

The Elsham Wolds contingent took off between 18.11 and 18.46 with S/L Kennard the senior pilot on duty and flew out over Mablethorpe on course for Mandø Island off Jutland's western coast. The crews of P/O Rose and Sgt McGown returned early, respectively because of starboard-outer engine failure and an unserviceable rear turret, leaving the others to reach the target area after an outward flight of around three hours and find almost clear skies and good visibility. The target was illuminated and marked by the Path Finders, to which the defenders responded with an effective smoke screen and intense searchlight and flak activity, one cone alone, situated in the south-eastern corner of the town, consisting of fifty to sixty beams. The 103 Squadron crews carried out their attacks from 8,000 to 14,000 feet between 21.18 and 21.40 and turned for home confident that they had participated in an effective raid. W/O Taylor and crew were homebound when DT513 was attacked by a FW190, which inflicted severe damage upon the Halifax and wounded the navigator. The encounter ended with the fighter going down on fire after a burst from the rear turret and W/O Taylor coaxing the Halifax back across the North Sea without navigational and wireless aids and losing height on just two good engines. Down to fifty feet, he abandoned hope of reaching land and ordered his crew to ditching stations, at which point, lights were spotted ahead, which turned out to be Acklington aerodrome on the north-east coast, and this persuaded him to push on the final few miles for a successful landing. A post-raid analysis of the raid and local sources revealed that a decoy fire site had been successful in drawing off half of the bomb loads and damage in Kiel, although substantial, was less than might otherwise have been.

A force of 289 aircraft was assembled on the 15th to send against Cologne, which had been left in peace for a considerable time, and the operation was supported by 1 Group with fifty-four Wellingtons and eleven 103 Squadron Halifaxes. The latter were loaded with two 1,000 pounders and thirteen SBCs of 4lb incendiaries and departed Elsham Wolds between 18.53 and 19.24 with F/Ls Parker and Winchester the senior pilots on duty. They flew via Mablethorpe to Ouddorp in the Scheldt estuary and from there to the target, encountering stronger-than-forecast winds, which created difficulties for the Path Finders as they attempted to establish their positions. The leading Path Finders found the Rhineland capital to be concealed beneath a layer of five to ten-tenths cloud with visibility so poor that few crews were able to establish a firm position in relation to it. Apart from throwing the operation behind schedule, this ruined the marking sequencing, with the result that there was insufficient marking to attract the main force crews, although the Path Finder flares did illuminate the Rhine to provide something of a reference point. However, the presence of a large decoy fire site was a more powerful lure, and most crews were persuaded by that to waste their effort in open country. The 103 Squadron crews carried out their attacks from 6,000 to 11,500 feet between 20.47 and 21.09, and on return described a scattered and ineffective raid. Local reports mentioned 224 houses sustaining slight damage from the single 4,000 pounder and three other high-explosive bombs and 210 incendiaries that landed within the city, and this was out of a total of seventy-one 4,000 pounders, 231 other high explosive bombs and more than 68,000 incendiaries. The disappointment was compounded by the loss to the Command of eighteen aircraft, which included the two Halifaxes from Elsham Wolds containing the deputy flight commanders. Winchester. W1213 was captained by New Zealander, F/L Parker, and crashed in Germany, probably close to the frontiers with Holland and Belgium without survivors, while W7850 came down near Mönchengladbach, killing F/L Winchester and five of his crew, including the forty-three-year-old rear gunner, Sgt Vaughan DFM. The navigator alone survived and he fell into enemy hands.

The squadron would remain on the ground for the next seven nights, while minor and mining operations occupied other elements of the Command in the lead-up to a new campaign against Italian cities in support of land operations in North Africa under Operation Torch. It began with a 5 Group attack on the night of the 22/23rd against the city of Genoa and the naval dockyard, where part of the Italian fleet was sheltering. It was the eve of the opening of the Battle of El Alamein, which, after twelve days' fighting, would see Montgomery push Rommel's forces all the way back to Tunisia and out of the war. This first raid was followed up twenty-four hours later by elements of 3 and 4 Groups, but they would hit the coastal town of Savona in error. A highly successful daylight operation by 5 Group Lancasters against Milan on the 24th was also to be followed up after dark by a force of seventy-one aircraft representing 1 and 3 Groups and the Path Finders. The city was home to many war-industry factories, including the Isotta Fraschini luxury car works, which had been converted to military vehicle and aero engine manufacture, the Pirelli rubber works, Alfa Romeo, the Caproni aircraft plant, the Breda locomotive, armaments and aircraft works and the Innocenti machinery and vehicle factory.

1 Group contributed ten 103 Squadron Halifaxes and a dozen Wellingtons from 142 and 300 Squadrons at Grimsby and Ingham respectively, the Halifaxes each loaded with two 1,000 pounders and seven SBCs of 4lb incendiaries. This, to the unbounded joy of the crews, would prove to be the 103 Squadron Halifax swansong, and in No Moon Tonight, Don Charlwood describes the lead up to this operation, talking about S/L Fox, the young flight commander, whose life was about to end and who had been the one to announce to an ecstatic and uproarious briefing room that the Halifax was about to be replaced by the Lancaster. Charlwood would later admit that the belief in the invulnerability of the Lancaster was somewhat misplaced, but the type would prove to be a considerable improvement on the Mk II Halifax. They departed Elsham Wolds between 18.28 and 18.48 with S/Ls Fox and Kennard the senior pilots on duty and exited the English coast over Dungeness lighthouse on course for landfall on the French coast at Le Treport. They lost the services of Sgt Smith and crew within the hour to a fault that would be identified later as air in the fuel pipes, and they were followed home by Sgt Bayliss and crew after the testing of the guns found three in the rear turret and two in the front to be unserviceable. The others pressed on across France and

P/O Rose and crew were some thirty miles south-east of Besaçon when attacked at 8,000 feet by a twin-engine fighter, which inflicted extensive damage upon W7819. The gunners found that five of six guns had frozen, preventing them from offering a defence, and the only option was to jettison the bombs and descend quickly into cloud. The engines were unaffected, and a safe return was made to Manston. They had probably run into the huge weather front barring the approaches to the Alps, but once negotiated, around forty aircraft remained to traverse the mountain range under clear skies, only to encounter ten-tenths cloud on the Italian side, which completely obscured the ground. The only reference for the 103 Squadron crews was the glow of fires on the ground, at which they aimed their bombs from 11,000 to 17,500 feet between 22.27 and 22.49. Seven aircraft failed to return, and among them were three 1 Group aircraft including two 103 Squadron Halifaxes. W1223 crashed twelve miles north-east of Compiègne in north-eastern France, almost certainly on the way home, and there were no survivors from the crew of Sgt Claridge. It was in the same general area and probably at around the same time that W1188 was intercepted by a night-fighter over France and shot down to crash near Bar-le-Duc, killing S/L Fox DFM and four others on board. Three survived, two in enemy hands, while the irrepressible "Dizzy" Spiller retained his freedom and on his return to the squadron some months later, found that the Maddern crew was one of only two left who had been present at S/L Fox's final briefing.

During the course of the month the squadron took part in six operations and dispatched fifty-nine sorties for the loss of six Halifaxes and their crews. While the squadron had been operating Halifaxes, fifteen operations had been conducted between the 31st of July and the 24th of October, not one crew had completed a tour and a dozen had been lost.

November 1942

Charlwood describes the elation of watching the Lancasters arrive to replace the detested Halifaxes, whilst admitting that the superiority of the one over the other was insufficient to warrant such enthusiasm. Lancaster W4318 was the first to be taken on charge, arriving on the 1st of November, registering 103 Squadron as the thirteenth operational unit to equip with the type. Training began with lectures and eight-hour cross-country exercises with the final three hours in darkness. The route was Base – Kinnaird's Head - Bardsey Island – Andover – Base, with a slight deviation from course to photograph St Tudwals Island, and each crew had to complete the route successfully before passing out. There was also formation flying, searchlight co-operation, along with standard beam approach and bombing practice. S/L Powdrell, a New Zealander serving in the RAF, was posted in from 25 O.T.U. on the 5th to fill the vacancy for a flight commander following the loss of S/L Fox.

While the squadron was away from the operational scene the Command carried out a number of further attacks on Genoa and Turin, and the only effort of note against Germany targeted Hamburg on the night of the 9/10th, for which 1 Group provided forty-five Wellingtons. The 20th was a momentous day in the history of 1 Group, and despite the fact that 460 Squadron RAAF had got its hands on Lancasters a few days before 101 and 103 Squadrons, it was 101 Squadron which won the unofficial race to carry out the first 1 Group Lancaster operation that night. The target was Turin, for which 1 Group contributed eight Lancasters and thirty Wellingtons to the overall force of 232 aircraft, and a successful operation ensued.

By the 21st a full complement of Lancasters sat on the ground at Elsham Wolds, and this enabled the squadron to be declared operational after just three weeks. S/Ls Powdrell and Kennard were the senior pilots on duty, the former undertaking his first operation with the squadron, while the newly-promoted F/O Jack Douglas was also on duty and had W/C Carter on board as second pilot. The other crews on this notable occasion were those of F/Sgt "Roly" Newitt and Sgts Berry and Cook and each was sitting on four 1,500lb parachute mines as they departed Elsham Wolds bound for the Elderberry garden off Biarritz on France's south-western coast, close to the frontier with Spain. They began the Channel crossing at Selsey Bill and set course for Coulon to the north of Bordeaux, before arriving in the target area to establish pinpoints on the estuary of the River Adour and Pointe-St-Martin, from which to conduct a timed run to the release point. Excellent conditions prevailed in the target area beneath the 1,500-to-3,000-foot cloud base, and their mines were dropped from 650 and 1,000 feet between 23.18 and 00.06.

Attention returned to Germany on the following night, when 460 Squadron would finally go to war in Lancasters as part of a 1 Group contribution of twenty-five Lancasters and twenty-seven Wellingtons in an overall force of 222 aircraft bound for the difficult target of Stuttgart. 1 Group was almost back to full strength, with only 12 Squadron now side-lined as it began its conversion to the Lancaster. While a dozen 103 Squadron Lancasters were being loaded with ten SBCs of 4lb incendiaries and two 1,000 pounders each, the crews attended briefing to learn of their part in proceedings, the navigators taking careful note of the route that exited the English coast at Rye, before traversing the Channel to make landfall on the enemy coast near Le Crotoy. By the time that they departed Elsham Wolds between 18.21 and 19.00, with S/L Powdrell the senior pilot on duty, two crews had been scrubbed, leaving the others to benefit from reasonable conditions as they tracked south-east towards the turning-point into Germany. Those arriving at their briefed destination were greeted by a bright, full moon, and, despite the thin layer of three-tenths cloud at 6,000 feet, most declared the visibility to be sufficiently good to support map-reading. Landmarks were highlighted by Path Finder reconnaissance and marker flares, and the River Neckar became a useful pinpoint as bombing by the 103 Squadron crews took place from 6,500 to 12,000 feet between 21.56 and 22.30. On the way home, the recently promoted F/L Rose and his crew strafed a train near Compiègne and watched the locomotive become enveloped in steam, before all three gunners turned their attention upon light flak batteries in nearby fields and silenced them. S/L Powdrell and crew also attacked a train but lost it as it entered a tunnel. Returning crews were confident that they had delivered an effective attack, but reconnaissance and local sources revealed that the Path Finders had failed to identify the city centre, and much of the bombing had fallen into suburbs and outlying communities to the south and south-west. It was established later that a modest eighty-eight houses had been destroyed at a cost to the Command of ten aircraft.

Avro's chief test pilot, Roy Chadwick, wrote to the 1 Group A-O-C, AVM Oxland, on the 23rd, to thank him for the kind remarks about the Lancaster, express his appreciation for the trust in and approval of the Lancaster by the crews and to congratulate the group for its speed in getting three squadrons so quickly and efficiently to operational status.

Mining operations dominated for the remainder of the month until the 28th, when another attack on Turin was scheduled, for which a force of 228 aircraft was assembled, twenty-six of the Lancasters provided by 1 Group. 103 Squadron made ready a dozen of its own, loading four with a 4,000lb "cookie" and two 1,000 pounders and the others with fourteen SBCs of 4lb incendiaries. This was to have been the maiden operation for Geoff Maddern and his crew, but their Lancaster became bogged down while taxiing to the runway and was one of three scrubbed from the operation. The remaining nine departed Elsham Wolds between 18.34 and 19.25 with S/L Kennard the senior pilot on duty, some having been delayed by the Maddern incident, and Jack Douglas having risen now to acting flight lieutenant rank. They crossed the English coast at Bognor Regis and made landfall on the French coast at Cabourg, by which time F/Sgt Newitt and crew had turned back because of a blockage in the hydraulic feed to the rear turret. The others pressed on over cloud that persisted as far as the Alps and reached the target area under clear skies with just a little haze to mar the vertical visibility. Most were able to establish their positions by visual reference of the River Po assisted by Path Finder flares, and having done so, the 103 Squadron crews bombed from 8,500 to 15,000 feet between 22.30 and 23.05, observing bursts in the town and on the Fiat works. A crew from another squadron counted forty-seven fires when they were fifteen minutes into the homeward journey and others confirmed that the city was a mass of flames and commented on a particularly large blaze in the centre and some others around the Royal Arsenal. W/C Gibson and F/L Whamond of 106 Squadron dropped the first two 8,000 pounders to fall on Italy, and all indications were that the operation had been entirely successful.

All 103 Squadron crews returned safely, and thus twenty-seven Lancaster sorties had now been launched on three operations without loss. In the minds of the crews the Lancaster was beginning to repay their faith in it, but it was, of course, a faith built on optimism rather than reality.

December 1942

1 Group opened the new month's account on the 2nd when contributing seventeen of its Lancasters to an overall force of 112 aircraft for a raid on Frankfurt, for which 103 Squadron made ready a dozen Lancasters, loading eleven with eleven SBCs containing ninety 4lb incendiaries and one, for S/L Powdrell, with three 1,000 pounders and fewer incendiaries. There was a late take-off from Elsham Wolds beginning at 01.14 with S/L Powdrell and concluding at 01.47 with F/Sgt Austin, the latter preceded into the air by the Maddern crew in W4333, B-Beer, on their first sortie. They climbed into a clear sky and headed for the exit point at Rye on course to meet the French coast at Cayeux-sur-Mer and lost F/Sgt Moriarty and crew to the failure of the pilot's blind-flying panel. The others traversed France and arrived in the target area some three hours after take-off to encounter cloud and patches of thick haze, which severely impaired the vertical visibility. Three or four searchlight cones of fifteen beams each combined with the haze to create an impenetrable glare, which would render aiming-point identification impossible for most crews. Those in the vanguard of the Path Finder element were already late when they established a pinpoint on a bend in the Rhine at Oppenheim to the south-west of the target and dropped white flares over the city, some of which were observed to be illuminating open country to the north-west and south-

east. This condemned the raid to a scattered and ineffective affair and the Elsham Wolds crews could only estimate their positions and bomb what they believed to be Frankfurt or unidentified built-up areas from 5,300 and 14,000 feet between 04.22 and 04.55. F/Sgt Austin and crew were attacked by two Ju88s shortly before reaching the target, one displaying white lights acting as a decoy for the other, but six passes failed to inflict damage and the assailants were shaken off, leaving the Austin crew to deliver their attack. On emerging from the target towards the same piece of sky, they were again set upon by two Ju88s, probably the same ones, upon which F/Sgt Austin performed a very tight turn to starboard and passed within seventy-five yards of the decoy aircraft. A burst of two hundred rounds from the mid-upper turret and four hundred from the rear turret extinguished the decoy's lights and as it passed the tail of the Lancaster, the rear gunner loosed off a further 150 rounds. The enemy burst into flames and rapidly lost height, before impacting the ground in a flash some twenty seconds later to be claimed by the Lancaster crew as destroyed. Returning aircraft were diverted because of fog at Elsham Wolds and most lobbed down at Middleton-St-George in County Durham, among them the Maddern crew, and it was a further two days before they could get back to Lincolnshire. Among six aircraft failing to return was the inevitable first 103 Squadron Lancaster to go missing, W4339 having crashed somewhere in southern Germany with no survivors from the crew of F/O Cumming.

Mannheim was posted as the target for a force of 272 aircraft on the 6th, forty-nine provided by 1 Group in the form of twenty-seven Lancasters and twenty-two Wellingtons, 103 Squadron loading eleven Lancasters with a cookie and eleven SBCs of 4lb incendiaries and one with fourteen SBCs. They departed Elsham Wolds between 17.08 and 17.27 with F/Ls Douglas and Rose the senior pilots on duty and adopted the same route as for Frankfurt four nights earlier. Sgt Greig and crew turned back after an hour because of a hydraulics leak that rendered the rear turret inoperable, leaving the others to press on across France and enter Germany south of Luxembourg. Those reaching the target area found ten-tenths cloud with tops at 7,000 feet, and could only bomb on estimated position, the 103 Squadron crews from 5,000 to 11,000 feet between 20.14 and 20.35. Returning crews expressed their doubts about the effectiveness of the attack, which was confirmed by local sources as scattered and resulting in just five hundred incendiaries and propaganda leaflets falling within the city boundaries. Don Charlwood described reaching the target area after "meandering" across Europe, before becoming lost on the way home, a nightmare scenario that Charlwood, as navigator, had dreaded. They were beginning to worry about fuel reserves when a voice came through from Thorney Island near Portsmouth, after which they landed at Waddington shortly before 01.00, and flew on to Elsham Wolds later in the morning.

The Maddern crew arrived home too late to be involved in that night's operation, a mining trip to the Nectarine I garden off Terschelling in the Dutch Frisians, for which the crews of S/L Powdrell, F/Sgt Newitt and Sgt Greig took off between 17.51 and 17.53 and F/L Temperley eighty minutes later. They crossed the English coast at Cromer and pinpointed visually on the eastern tip of the island, confirming their positions by Gee, before conducting timed runs to plant their vegetables according to brief.

On the 8th S/L Kennard presented himself at Buckingham Palace to receive his much-deserved DFC and was absent from Elsham Wolds when seven Lancasters set out that night to lay mines in various regions of the Baltic in company with fifteen other 1 Group Lancaster crews and three from 199 Squadron in Wellingtons. The gardens were Asparagus (Great Belt south), Silverthorn (Kattegat), Broccoli (Great Belt south), Verbena (Copenhagen), Quince (Kiel Bay), Daffodil (The Sound south or Oresund), Nasturtium (The Sound north) and Forget-me-not (Kiel Harbour). The ORB is not specific as to which the 103 Squadron crews were assigned as they departed Elsham Wolds between 16.59 and 17.35 with F/L Douglas the senior pilot on duty, but the fact that W/O Taylor and crew pinpointed on Helsingborg on Sweden's western coast tell us that the Nasturtium garden at the northern end of The Sound was their likely destination. The Maddern crew was first away at 16.59 in W4338 L-London, a Lancaster with an evil reputation that only behaved in the hands of "Roly" Newitt and crew. They covered the four-hundred-mile leg from Mablethorpe to Kobing Fjord without incident, and then the 150 miles to the target area, where the parachute mines were delivered. Turning back towards Kobing Fjord, all seemed well until they realized that they should have been over water long ago. Suddenly they were among searchlights and flak as they stumbled into the defences at Esbjerg, and a near miss sent shrapnel tearing through the skin to hit Max Burcher, the wireless operator. He sustained a serious wound to his right arm, and cuts to his face and chest, but despite this, after being bandaged by Don Charlwood and taking a short rest, he did his best, although in vain, to repair the damaged radio set. Without being able to announce themselves at Elsham Wolds, they fired flares, which were soon answered and on landing they were met by two medical officers and the commanding officer, the latter showing great concern over Burcher's condition. Burcher had lost a third of the muscle tissue in his arm, and it was clear that he would not return to his crew. He was determined to fly again, however, and persevered with his recovery, and he was rewarded with a posting to 460 Squadron RAAF, with which he would lose his life while attacking Hamburg during the third raid of Operation Gomorrah on the 29/30th of July 1943. The others all returned safely to report planting their vegetables from between 600 and 800 feet.

While the 103 Squadron crews had been attending to gardening duties on this night, 5 Group and a Path Finder element had been active over Turin, and 227 aircraft were detailed to return there on the following night, in what would be the penultimate operation in the current campaign against Italy. 103 Squadron made ready a dozen Lancasters as part of the 1 Group contribution of twenty-six Lancasters and thirteen Wellingtons and loaded eleven of them with fourteen SBCs of 4lb incendiaries and S/L Powdrell's with a cookie and five SBCs. They departed Elsham Wolds between 17.24 and 18.11 and lost the services of F/Sgt Newitt over Peterborough when his instruments failed, leaving the rest to exit the English coast at Rye and arrive over the opposite coast at Cayeux-sur-Mer. They traversed France without incident and crossed the Alps under clear skies to find the target area partially obscured by haze and smoke from the previous night's very destructive attack, which created challenging conditions for the Path Finders in their quest to provide consistent marking. The crews were unable to pick out ground detail as they began their bombing runs from west to east or north-west to south-east and dropped their loads into the rising smoke from 6,500 to 14,000 feet between 21.36 and 22.10. By the time that they turned away, the entire centre of the city was hidden by smoke, which had risen through 8,000 feet leaving the outskirts exposed and clearly visible. Returning crews reported that the glow from the burning city remained on the horizon for sixty miles into the return trip, and some made mention of ten to fifteen searchlights to the west and north-west of the city, and intense but inaccurate light and heavy flak.

The Italian campaign closed at Turin on the night of the 11/12th with an operation that involved 101 and 460 Squadron Lancasters as 1 Group's representatives and was ruined by severe icing conditions that forced half of the participants to turn back early. The weather closed in at this point, and although operations were posted over the ensuing days, all were cancelled, on one occasion after the crews had gone out to their aircraft. It was not until the evening of the 17th that a single 103 Squadron crew actually took off, on a night the Command would regret, as many aircraft and crews were sacrificed for no return. 5 Group sent twenty-seven Lancasters to eight small towns in Germany, and nine failed to return, while 3 Group targeted the Opel motor works at Fallersleben with Stirlings and Wellingtons and lost eight.

Meanwhile, fifty aircraft conducted mining operations in gardens from Denmark to the Bay of Biscay, and P/O Smith and crew of 103 Squadron were among six 1 Group Lancasters assigned to the Asparagus and Broccoli gardens in the Great Belt and Nasturtium at the northern end of The Sound (Oresund). They departed Elsham Wolds in W4786 at 17.35 bound for the Broccoli garden and set course via Mablethorpe for Ringkoping Fjord on Jutland's western coast. As they headed inland from there, they were intercepted by a night-fighter that sent the Lancaster crashing into a built-up area nine miles west of Toftlund at 20.15, killing all on board. One of the mines exploded on impact, shattering thirteen houses and injuring some local civilians. The following two days were beset with fog, which lifted after AVM Oxland, the 1 Group A-O-C, had visited Elsham Wolds earlier in the day. The Australians hated the cold, dank, foggy weather and when it cleared late on, the rain set in.

Apart from isolated "moling" daylight operations, the Ruhr had been left in peace since Krefeld at the start of October, while attention had been focussed on Italian targets. Now, on the 20th, Duisburg was posted as the objective for a force of 232 aircraft, of which twenty-eight Lancasters were provided by 1 Group, ten of them representing 103 Squadron. Not mentioned to the crews at briefing was the fact that this operation would mask another of great significance for the Command that was taking place at the same time over Holland. Although, in the event, not all would proceed according to plan, it would be a mere blip in the development of the Oboe blind-bombing device. The 103 Squadron element departed Elsham Wolds between 18.11 and 18.36 with S/L Kennard the senior pilot on duty, all loaded with a dozen SBCs of 4lb incendiaries supplemented either by a cookie or two 1,000 pounders. They headed out over Mablethorpe in a clear sky that would persist all the way to the target and lost F/L Douglas and crew to a dead intercom caused by a blown valve, and he jettisoned his 4,000 pounder "safe", only to see it detonate on impact. The others benefitted from bright moonlight, which enabled them to map read from the Ijsselmeer to the western Ruhr, where the slight industrial haze proved to be no impediment to establishing a firm visual reference on the River Rhine and the Ruhrort docks complex. The 103 Squadron crews carried out their attacks from 9,000 to 11,000 feet between 19.51 and 20.12, observing some detonations on or close to the aiming point, and counted at least fifteen fires as they retreated, many of them large. At debriefing, many crews reported combats with night-fighters, and there was much confidence that Duisburg had been "blitzed" but absent from the process was the crew of F/Sgt Moriarty RCAF, whose W4334 had been shot down and crashed some five miles south-south-east of Alkmaar in western Holland. It was not until 1952 that the remains of this crew were recovered from the crash site and interred at Bergen op Zoom.

While the above was in progress, some fifty miles away to the south-west, six 109 Squadron Oboe-equipped Mosquitos had targeted a power station at Lutterade in Holland in a test to gauge the device's margin of error. The target had been selected in the belief that it was free of bomb craters so that the Oboe-aimed bombs could be plotted, but, unfortunately, three of the Mosquitos suffered Oboe failure and went on to bomb Duisburg instead, leaving W/C Hal Bufton and two other crews to fulfil the brief. What they hadn't bargained for was a whole carpet of bomb craters left over from the attack on Aachen, seventeen miles away, in October, and it proved impossible to identify those aimed by Oboe. The calibration tests would continue, however, and, come the spring, Oboe would be ready to unleash with devastating effect against the Ruhr.

A force of 137 aircraft was made ready on the 21st for an operation that night against Munich, the birthplace of Nazism deep in southern Germany. 1 Group contributed twenty-seven Lancasters, ten of them made ready at Elsham Wolds, where two 1,000 pounders and ten SBCs of 4lb incendiaries were winched into each cavernous 33-foot-long bomb bay. The Maddern crew was supposed to be on duty, but B-Beer's blind-flying panel had become unserviceable and there was no reserve aircraft available. The others took off between 17.26 and 17.42 with W/C Carter the senior pilot on duty, who had a special reconnaissance to carry out, and set course via Rye to Cayeux-sur-Mer at the start of the long slog across enemy territory. Sgt Morris and crew turned back after losing their port-inner engine over the Channel, leaving the others to push on across France and arrive at their destination after a three-and-a-half-hour outward journey.

They found the Bavarian capital city to be concealed beneath ten-tenths cloud with tops at a lowly 2,000 feet, but the Path Finders illuminated the Ammersee to the south-west of the city, and the 5 Group crews carried out a time-and-distance run from there to the aiming point. The 103 Squadron crews pinpointed on the nearby Wörthsee and followed the Autobahn to the city to deliver their attacks from 9,500 to 12,000 feet between 21.16 and 21.37. There were plenty of flashes below the cloud, which, together with the glow of fires convinced the crews that they had found the mark, but it is likely that a decoy site was operating to lure the bombing away and most of the bombing photos revealed open country. Twelve aircraft failed to return, and two of them belonged to 103 Squadron to put a dampener on the forthcoming Christmas festivities. W4787 and W4820 both crashed in north-eastern France on the way home, the latter near Bar-le-Duc with fatal consequences for all on board but the pilot, Sgt Bayliss RAAF, who was taken into captivity. The fact that he alone survived suggests that the Lancaster broke up in the air flinging him clear already attached to his seat parachute. The former came down further north near Maubeuge and there were no survivors from the experienced and popular crew of F/L Rose DFC, RAAF. Sgt Bayliss had been a close friend of Geoff Maddern, and Don Charlwood recalls the loss in No Moon Tonight. Sgt Greig landed on three engines after losing his port-outer and starboard trimming tab to flak. As events were to prove, this was the final operation of the year as the weather closed in again and the fourth wartime Christmas was celebrated in traditional fashion, with officers serving dinner to the lower ranks, and officers' and sergeants' messes being raided in the search for alcohol.

One wonders what it was like for the Australians, of whom there were many at Elsham Wolds. Their Christmases back home took place in the burning heat of mid-summer, perhaps even on the beach, and now here they were, trapped on a freezing, fogbound, windswept airfield contemplating the loss of friends and countrymen, and the prospect of a similar fate for themselves. The Oboe trials programme resumed at Düsseldorf on New Year's Eve and involved two Mosquitos marking for eight Lancasters of 5 Group.

During the course of the month the squadron conducted eight operations and dispatched sixty-nine sorties for the loss of five Lancasters and crews, which gave lie already to the fragile belief in the invulnerability of the Lancaster. It had been a testing year for all and was but a foretaste of things to come in 1943, when Bomber Command would embark on a series of major campaigns against industrial Germany. As the New Year beckoned, a great responsibility lay on the operational Lancaster squadrons of 1 and 5 Groups to carry the war to the enemy. There was no question that the Stirling and Mk II and V Halifaxes were inferior aircraft, and their limited availability and restricted bomb-carrying capacity meant that the Command still had to rely very much on the trusty but aging Wellington to make up the numbers if the defences were to be overwhelmed. That said, the advent of Oboe and the ground-mapping radar, H2S, would greatly enhance the Command's ability to deliver a telling blow and 1943 would see the balance of power shift massively in the Command's favour.

103 Squadron pilots pictured pre-war at Abingdon L to R: F/L James Leyden RAF (PoW 26ᵗʰ May 1940), F/O Barry Morgan-Dean (KIA 12ᵗʰ May 1940), F/L Maurice Wells RAF (PoW 10ᵗʰ May 1940), S/L Carl Kelaher RAAF (KIA 3ʳᵈ September 1943, 460 Squadron), F/O Thomas Fitzgerald RAF a New Zealander. After the Battle of France, Fitzgerald transferred to Fighter Command and fought in the Battle of Britain. He finished the war as a Wing Commander fighter ace with a DFC (BMD).

L-R: F/L Arthur Vipan (KIA 16ᵗʰ October 1944 as S/L, 12 OTU), P/O O'Shaunessy or possibly Colman O'Shaunessy Murphy RAF, S/L John Coverdale RAF (KIA 22ⁿᵈ June 1943 as W/C with 431 Squadron) and P/O Thomas Pugh RAF (MIA 2ⁿᵈ August 1943 as W/C DFC with 182 Squadron) (BMD).

Back Row - 103 Squadron Officer Group late April 1940. L to R - P/O J C F Hayter, F/O T B Fitzgerald. F/O MacDonald (IO), F/O M C Wells, P/O E E Morton, P/O K J Drabble, P/O Rhyce Price (Servicing Unit), F/O D D A Kelly. Middle Row L to R - P/O T Pugh, P/O V A Cunningham, F/O J R Havers, Doc Mahon (MO), P/O Taylor (Equipment Officer), F/O A L Vipan, F/O J N Leyden, F/O G B Morgan-Dean. Front Row L to R - F/O Rayne (Adjutant), F/L J A Ingram, S/L H G Lee AFC, W/C T C Dickens, F/L C E R Tait, F/L Fallowfield (IO) (Crown).

Sgt O J C Poole RAF KIA 10th May 1940. Observer in the crew of Sgt C H Lowne who survived the crash as a PoW.

F/O Barry Morgan-Dean, KIA 12th May 1940.

A group portrait of 103 Squadron officers during the unit's three-week stay at Rheges / St. Lucien.

(Above) Sgt Charles Perry RAF (right) with an unidentified colleague.

(Left) F/L James Leyden at Unsworth pre-war. On the 26th May 1940, Leyden managed to bale out of his Battle which had been attacked by a Bf109. He was shot and wounded by German soldiers as he descended in his parachute. Subsequently he was very badly beaten and left for dead in an orchard. Amazingly he survived this ordeal and was collected by the Germans later that day and taken to a field hospital. He spent the rest of the war as a PoW. (DF)

Oil storage tanks, Rotterdam c.1940

A salvo of bombs explodes on the hard standing at Schiphol airport, Amsterdam in a later attack than the one carried out by 103 Squadron in 1940.

P/O Ron Hawkins in his flying kit. After being shot down he managed to return to England despite a period of internment in Spain (Hawkins family).

A group of 103 Squadron WOP/AGs pictured at Newton. These airmen had all taken part in the Battle of France with 103. L to R – F/Sgt E J Lisle, F/Sgt A Werner, F/Sgt R Critchley, F/Sgt V Wall and F/Sgt F F Barker DFM.

German barges at Boulogne ready for Operation Sealion.

The remains of P/O Edgar Morton's Battle P2193 at Bouillon.

Sgt Charles Perry's Battle PM-J, which force landed near Betheniville. Perry was awarded a DFM but sadly died of wounds in the UK on the 10th June 1940.

Fairey Battle K9264 PM-L was an early casualty of 103 Squadron's war. P/O Kenneth Drabble and his crew were lost when K9264 was shot down 10th May 1940, attacking German columns advancing through Luxembourg. Crew: Sgt T D Smith and LAC P J Lamble.

The air gunner of a Battle mans the aircraft's defensive weapon, a single pintle-mounted rapid firing Vickers K machine gun, France, 1940.

L to R. P/O Ron Hawkins with F/O Roberts – 103 Squadron Gunnery Leader and F/L Charles Tait – Flight Commander.

A youthful F/O Roy Max pictured at Rheges with S/L Harold Lee in the background. Max rose to command 75 (NZ) Squadron later in the war and enjoyed a long and impressive post-war RAF career.

Sgt Brumby's Battle which force landed adjacent to the main road between Laval and Morannes. Norman Brumby returned to the UK and transferred to Fighter Command. He served with both 615 and 607 Squadrons in the Battle of Britain and was KIA 1st October 1940.

A pre-war photo of a 103 Squadron Fairey Battle (BMD).

P/O Allen and crew

F/L Desmond Fifield who was rear gunner in P/O Allen's crew, July 1941 is pictured with Wellington N9792 at Elsham Wolds. He went on to 57 Squadron and carried out a total of 25 operations.

103 Squadron Wellington, possibly R1588 PM-W.

Blohm & Voss shipyard, Hamburg, Germany which 103 Squadron attacked March 1941. (Launching of Bismark 1939).

Splendid nose art from a 103 Squadron Wellington, 1941. (Geoffrey Kelly)

S/L Dermot Kelly was Mentioned in Despatches three times. Newly-promoted as commander of 'B' Flight, he and his crew lost their lives on 16th/17th June 1941 on a raid to Duisburg (Geoffrey Kelly).

Ofw (later Leutnant) Hans Rasper's sixth victim was Wellington T2996, flown by F/O Chisholme and crew, which he shot down over Holland on 12/13th June 1941 (Andreas Wachtel).

S/L K J Mellor DSO DFC on the left with F/L J R Havers DFC. (DF)

S/L Tony Ingram DFC pictured pre-war. He became a PoW on 21st September 1941. (BMD)

Sgt John Bucknole, KIA on 24th July 1941 when his Wellington N2770 fell victim to a German fighter whilst attacking the Gneisenau at Brest. (DF)

P/O E Lawson. As a Flight Lieutenant, he crashed in northern France on 7th November 1941. Handed over to the Nazis, he became a PoW (DF)

L to R – S/L O Godfrey DFC, W/C Ryan, S/L I K P Cross DFC, F/L D W Holford DFC. S/L Ian Cross was captured after being shot down on the 21st February 1942. In Stalag Luft III, he was involved in what became known as the 'Great Escape' and was subsequently murdered by the Gestapo.

P/O Taffy Jones on the right with his co-pilot P/O Donald Smith. (Smith family)

Squadron photograph taken c. August 1941.

ACM Sir Arthur Harris, Commander in Chief   *AVM Sir Edward Rice KBE CB CBE*
of Royal Air Force Bomber Command   *MC*

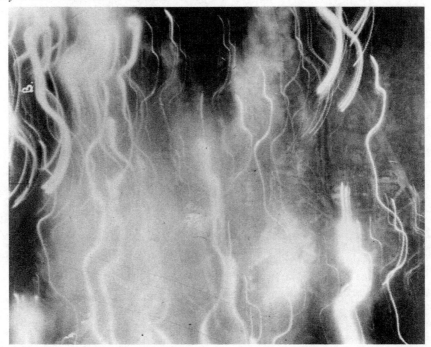

Vertical aerial photograph taken over the centre of Düsseldorf at 11 pm on 10th September 1942, at the height of the major night raid by 479 aircraft including 103 Squadron. Most of the area photographed is covered with widespread incendiary fires, from which flame and smoke are rising to obscure the target.

Group Captain Hugh 'Connie' Constantine's role as Station Commander at Elsham Wolds did not stop him taking part in a number of operationss with 103 Squadron. His wartime career culminated in his appointment as AOC No. 5 Group in 1945. He retired in 1964 as Air Chief Marshal and Commandant of the Imperial Defence College.

103 Squadron aircrew group, early 1942. (DF)

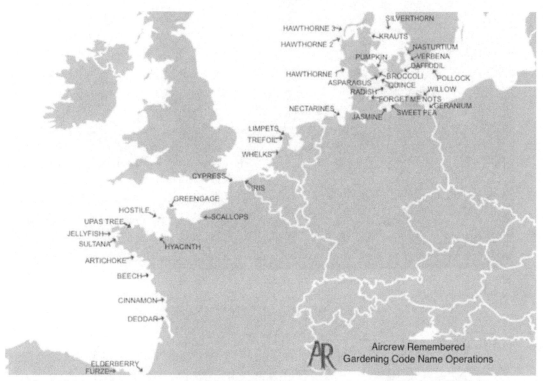

Mining area codenames

P/O Harry Smith and crew were killed when their LancasterW4786 was shot down by Major Günther Radusch on a Gardening operation to Denmark on 17th December 1942. Sgt G T Canterbury, Sgt N Frater, F/O S T Hewitt, P/O H B Smith, Sgt A D MacDonald RCAF, Sgt J A Hollingsworth RCAF and Sgt F R Collins.

Sgts L C Bray and D W Spooner. DF

L to R – S/L David Holford and Australian P/O Donald Smith. (Smith family, Australia)

Heavy cruiser Scharnhorst in 1939

Heavy cruiser Gneisenau in 1939

145

W/O Reginald Fulbrook DFC. (DF)

W/O Herbert "Dizzy" Spiller DFM. (Spiller family).

Destruction at the Renault Billancourt factory after the March 1942 attack.

Sgt H G Dryhurst, pilot of BB214 and taken PoW August 1942. (Dryhurst family).

F/L Leonard Pipkin DFC and Bar with his dog Bobby. Pipkin was navigator in S/L Clive Saxelby's crew and successfully evaded after they were shot down. He died in a shooting accident in 1944. (Pipkin family).

Geoff Maddern's crew – L to R: Sgts Frank Holmes, Max Burcher, Doug Richards, Geoff Maddern, Ted Batten, Don Charlwood and Arthur Browett. (DF)

147

Leutnant (later Hauptmann) Hans Autenrieth accounted for the Halifax W1216, PM-Q of W/O Kenneth Edwards. Autenrieth would claim 22 nighttime victories before being shot down himself and taken prisoner on 3/4th August 1944. (Theo Boiten)

S/L Sidney Fox DFM, who was shot down and killed during the Milan raid on 24/25th October 1942 (Jackson family).

103 Squadron personnel pose for a squadron photo in front of a Halifax at Elsham Wolds 1942.

Before and after images of the Gnome-Rhone Factory at Gennevilliers, France. Attacked several times by Bomber Command including 103 Squadron on 29/30th April 1942.

Bremen. Concentrated heavy and light flak over Bremen 13th September 1942.

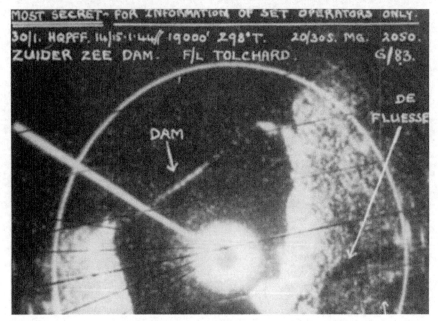

Large areas like the Zuiderzee made excellent targets for the H2S navigation system. The resolution of the system is evident in the appearance of the Afsluitdijk (labelled "dam"), which is about 90 metres (300 ft) across. (Not 103 Squadron).

H2S Fishpond display (square grey box with circular screen) mounted in radio operator's position aboard an Avro Lancaster.

The improved scanner introduced on the Mark IIC Lancaster removed the metal filet from the reflector and replaced the dipole antenna with a waveguide. These were easier to produce because the angular focusing was in the waveguide, allowing the reflector to be linear.

January 1943

The year began with the official formation on New Year's Day of the Canadian 6 Group, and the handing over to it of the former 4 Group stations in North Yorkshire on which its squadrons had been lodging. Eventually, all Canadian squadrons would find a home in the group, which was financed by Canada and controlled by Harris, but, initially, there were eight founder members, including 408 (Goose) and 420 (Snowy Owl) Squadrons, which had left 5 Group during the autumn. Further south, a continuation of the Oboe trials would occupy the first two weeks, during which 109 Squadron marked for small forces of 1 and 5 Group Lancasters at Essen on seven occasions and Duisburg once. For the first time, the cloud cover and ever-present blanket of industrial haze would have no bearing on the outcome of the raid as reliance on e.t.a., DR and Gee was cast aside in favour of Oboe, at least, that is, at targets within the device's range. Until the advent of mobile transmitter stations late in the war, Oboe would be restricted by the curvature of the earth and the altitude at which Mosquitos could fly, but this meant that the entire Ruhr lay within range of Harris's bombers. That said, the success of a raid would still rely on the ability of the Path Finders to back up the initial Oboe markers and maintain a supply of target indicators (TIs) on the aiming point.

The first of the Oboe trials against Essen was conducted on the night of the 3/4th and employed three Mosquitos and nineteen 5 Group Lancasters as the main force. On the following night, four Mosquitos were to mark for twenty-nine 1 Group Lancasters, of which seven belonged to 103 Squadron. While they were in the hands of the armourers loading each with a cookie and ten SBCs of 4lb incendiaries, the crews attended briefing to be told that this was the first operation of a kind for 1 Group. They were not given an aiming point, but were instructed to maintain a strict altitude, speed and course, and to aim their bombs at target indicators of a specific colour laid over the aiming point by the Mosquitos. They departed Elsham Wolds between 17.25 and 17.52 with S/L Powdrell the senior pilot on duty and set course via Mablethorpe for the Dutch town of Enkhuizen. On the way they lost F/Sgt Austin and crew to frozen and inoperable guns in the rear turret, and then later the Maddern crew, who were in sight of the cloud-covered target when it was discovered that the oxygen tube to "Shag" Browett, the rear gunner, had been severed by the rotation of the turret. In trying to rescue him the flight engineer also came close to collapse, so Maddern was forced to abandon the sortie, turn for home and quickly shed some height. The others pressed on to reach the central Ruhr, which was lying under five to eight-tenths cloud, with tops in places as high as 15,000 feet, and this would prevent an accurate assessment of the outcome. The 103 Squadron crews carried out their attacks from far higher than they had ever previously reached, 20,000 to 20,500 feet, between 19.42 and 19.44 and all returned safely to pass on their impressions to the intelligence section.

Snow lay on the ground at Elsham Wolds, and the next few days brought mostly PT and ultra-violet treatment for the crews. Nineteen 5 Group Lancasters provided the main force for the next Oboe trial on Essen on the night of the 7/8th, and thirty-eight for the switch to Duisburg twenty-four hours later, the day on which the Path Finder Force was granted group status as 8 Group, and the stations it occupied were transferred from 3 Group. For the purpose of this book, the titles Path Finders and 8 Group are interchangeable. On the 9th, 1

Group called upon all four Lancaster squadrons to provide between them twenty-five aircraft for the next Oboe attack on Essen, for which 5 Group also put up twenty-five. 103 Squadron loaded nine of its own with a cookie and ten SBCs of 4lb incendiaries and dispatched them from Elsham Wolds between 16.52 and 17.02 with S/L Kennard the senior pilot on duty. They adopted the same route as for the previous raid and soon lost the services of the crews of F/Sgt Burgess and Sgt Cook to issues with their rear turrets. The others pressed on to find the target under clear skies with remarkably good vertical visibility, and this enabled them to establish their positions in relation to the city centre. The operation was another test of the "Wanganui" skymarking system employing parachute flares, and although released a minute late, they allowed the main force to bomb with a degree of accuracy, the 103 Squadron crews from 19,500 to 21,000 feet between 19.23 and 19.26. Fires were observed as they turned away, and there was praise for the performance of the Path Finders. Sgt Morris and crew failed to return from this operation, and it emerged later that ED384 had been homebound when crashing near Cologne without survivors.

The largest Oboe trial force yet of seventy-two 1 and 5 Group Lancasters was assembled on the 11th for that night's assault on Essen, where the marking was in the hands of four Oboe Mosquitos. Thirty-three Lancasters represented 1 Group, eleven of them at Elsham Wolds provided with the standard bomb load before taking to the air between 16.45 and 17.18 with S/L Powdrell the senior pilot on duty. A change in the route had them exit England over Aldeburgh to make landfall on the Belgian coast at Knokke and approach the target from the south, but on a night of poor serviceability for the squadron, S/L Powdrell and crew turned back at the English coast after losing both starboard engines, F/L Kitney and crew dropped out after an hour through an overheating port-outer engine, F/L Douglas and crew followed them home because of a lack of engine power and Sgt Attwood and crew were beaten by the failure of the oxygen feed to the navigator, who became unconscious. The others found Essen hidden by a complete cloud cover with tops at between 6,000 and 10,000 feet, but it no longer mattered as marker flares delivered by Oboe had a margin of error of around four to six hundred yards, which represented pinpoint accuracy at an urban target. On this night the initial flares were described as good, but the marker flares failed to materialise after the Mosquitos all suffered technical breakdowns, and this caused the main force to overshoot and have to turn back on a reciprocal course to deliver their attacks. They bombed on estimated positions based on e.t.a., and DR, those from 103 Squadron from 20,000 feet between 19.23 and 19.36 and returned with little to report other than the glow of a few fires reflected in the clouds. It was a disappointing night all-round, but on the credit side, they were all back home at Elsham Wolds by 21.34, so there was time to wind down before bed.

In contrast, it was the graveyard shift for the eleven 103 Squadron crews detailed to take part in the next round, although only six ultimately lined up for take-off between 03.15 and 03.47 on the 13th. A main force of fifty-five 1 and 5 Group Lancasters eventually presented themselves of which twenty-one were provided by 1 Group. It had been intended to send a larger contingent, but thirteen aircraft failed to take off after the taxiways became obstructed at two stations, including Elsham Wolds, by aircraft becoming bogged down. S/Ls Kennard and Powdrell were the senior pilots on duty as they adopted the southern route to the Ruhr via Aldeburgh and Knokke, and for a change there were no early returns. They arrived over Essen to find ten-tenths cloud with tops at between 8,000 and 20,000 feet and the ground completely concealed, a situation compounded by the late and sparse marking by the Mosquito element, again because of technical failures and timing issues. This compelled many crews to bomb on DR and e.t.a., those from 103 Squadron delivering their attacks from 20,000 feet between 06.16 and 06.30, while others found urban areas to bomb up to twenty miles away. This time at debriefing there were grumblings about the Path Finder performance.

The last crew back to Elsham Wolds landed at 08.37, and the first crew took off for the same target that afternoon at 16.54, just eight hours and seventeen minutes later. These were the five crews who had been scrubbed from the morning operation, and two others, and they were part of an overall force of sixty-six Lancasters, eighteen of them belonging to 1 Group. The 103 Squadron element was on its way by 17.11 with F/Ls Douglas and Kitney the senior pilots on duty and they had been briefed to adopt the northern route to the target via Mablethorpe and Enkhuizen. Sgt Maddern and crew lost their port-inner engine during take-off and proceeded directly to the jettison area, while F/L Kitney and crew turned back from a position over the North Sea when the rear gunner's oxygen mask iced up and left him incapacitated. Sgt Burton and crew were the third "boomerang" as a result of frozen guns and a mechanical issue with the rear turret. Two of the three Oboe Mosquitos were forced to return early, and the skymarkers from the third one failed to ignite, leaving the door open for the Luftwaffe to confuse the issue with dummy flares. Those of the main force that reached the target found it under eight to ten-tenths cloud and struggled again from the lack of marking, but three 103 Squadron crews attacked from 19,000 and 20,000 feet between 19.32 and 19.38. Despite the challenges, enough bombs found their way into Essen to destroy fifty-two buildings and prompt local sources to register this as a useful raid. W4338, the L-London bemoaned by the Maddern crew, had been borrowed by the 12 Squadron crew of Sgt Atwood RCAF and was brought down by flak near Krefeld, killing all but one of the occupants.

A new Air Ministry directive was issued on the 14th, which authorised the area bombing of the French ports with concrete bunkers and support facilities providing a home for U-Boots. A list was drawn up accordingly, headed by Lorient and included St-Nazaire, Brest and La Pallice. As mentioned earlier, between February 1941 and January 1942, the Germans had built three giant concrete structures K1, K2 and K3 on the southernmost point of Lorient's Keroman Peninsula. They were capable of housing and servicing thirty U-Boots and providing accommodation for their crews and were impregnable to the bombs available to Bomber Command at the time. The purpose of this new campaign, therefore, was to render the town and port uninhabitable and block or sever all road and rail communications to them. The first of the series of nine attacks on the port over the ensuing four weeks took place that very night at the hands of a force of 122 aircraft, of which fifteen Wellingtons were provided by 1 Group, and despite accurate marking by the Path Finder element, the main force bombing was scattered and destroyed a modest 120 buildings.

Harris planned two operations against the "Big City", Berlin, beginning on the 16th, for which a force of 201 aircraft was made ready. This would be the first raid on Germany's capital for fourteen months and would bring with it the first use of custom-designed target indicators. The main force consisted predominantly of 5 Group Lancasters, with forty-seven others from 1 Group, while eleven Halifaxes of 35 (Madras Presidency) Squadron were included in the Path Finder element. Those reaching the target would share the airspace over it with the broadcaster, Richard Dimbleby, who was in a 106 Squadron Lancaster captained by W/C Guy Gibson. *(In some of my previous books, I have fallen into the trap of repeating the errors of others by recording Dimbleby's participation during the second Berlin raid that took place on the following night. This could not be the case, as Gibson was not involved in the second Berlin raid.)* 103 Squadron made ready eleven Lancasters, loading some with a cookie and eight SBCs and the others with fourteen SBCs and sent them on their way from Elsham Wolds between 16.38 and 17.22 with S/Ls Kennard and Powdrell the senior pilots on duty. The flew out over Mablethorpe and headed for Mandø Island off the west coast of Jutland, from where the route took the bomber stream across southern Jutland to the western Baltic, and from there along the coastline eastwards until reaching the final turning point at Swinemünde, from where they would swing to the south for the one-hundred-mile run on the target. F/L Temperley and crew were back on the ground within ninety minutes after a rear turret issue ended their interest in proceedings and they were followed home by Sgt Greig and crew after a frustrated pilot had been unable to drag more than 10,000 feet of altitude out of W4827. Finally of the "boomerangs", F/Sgt Burgess and crew had been the last to take off, twenty-three minutes behind the last of the others, and felt that they would be unable to reach the target within the allotted bombing window.

The remainder pressed on to reach the target under moonlight, with good visibility above six-tenths cloud at 10,000 feet, through which the built-up area could be seen clearly. The 103 Squadron crews mostly failed to observe the red warning flares and picked up the lakes and autobahns to reach the city, and it was then that red and green TIs could be seen bursting on what was assumed to be the aiming point. They dropped their cookie and incendiary bomb loads from 14,000 to 19,000 feet between 20.19 and 20.42, not all with a clear view of the ground, although some recognised that they were over the southern outskirts of the city, where the Tempelhof district could be identified. At debriefing, some crews reported black smoke rising through 5,000 feet as they turned away, but many were unconvinced of the effectiveness of the raid, and this was borne out by local sources. It should be remembered that Berlin was beyond the range of Oboe and Gee, and the new H2S radar device was not yet ready. One notable scalp was the ten-thousand-seater Deutschlandhalle, the largest covered venue in Europe, which was hosting the annual circus as the bombers approached and was efficiently emptied of people and animals with only a few minor injuries. Shortly afterwards, incendiaries set fire to the building and reduced it to ruins. Remarkably, only a single Lancaster failed to return from this operation, but the balance would be redressed somewhat twenty-four hours later.

170 Lancasters and seventeen Halifaxes were made ready on 1, 4, 5 and 8 Group stations for the return to Berlin that night, when they would follow the same route as twenty-four hours earlier with a three-and-a-half-hour outward flight ahead of them, stalked constantly by night-fighters once they reached western Denmark. Among 1 Group's forty-five Lancasters were a dozen belonging to 103 Squadron, which departed Elsham Wolds between 16.50 and 17.30 with S/Ls Kennard and Powdrell the senior pilots on duty. Eight crews were sitting on a cookie and eight SBCs and five on fourteen SBCs and only F/Sgt Roper's bomb load would fail to reach the target after he lost his starboard-outer engine some ninety minutes into the flight. The others pressed on across southern Jutland and bypassed the searchlights and flak in the Kiel defence zone on the western shores of the Baltic. Those reaching the target area

were greeted by eight to ten-tenths cloud with tops at between 10,000 and 14,000 feet, through which it was possible for most to pick out the Müggelsee to the south-east of the capital, from where a timed run was carried out to the aiming point. Some crews failed to see any flares, which was understandable as the Path Finders arrived thirty-seven minutes late, and so were forced to bomb on e.t.a. or DR. Some did benefit from target marking, which sadly, was once more concentrated over the southern fringes of the city rather than over the centre. The 103 Squadron crews carried out their attacks predominantly from 18,000 feet, although S/L Powdrell and crew dropped their load from 17,600 feet and Roly Newitt and crew from 21,000 between 20.34 and 21.10, and by the later stages, some Path Finder flares were evident. Little was seen of the results of the bombing, which local sources confirmed had not been effective and no significant damage had occurred. The disappointment was compounded by the loss of twenty-two bombers, 11.8% of those dispatched, and many of these disappeared without trace in the Baltic or North Sea.

A force of seventy-nine Lancasters and three Mosquitos was detailed to resume the Oboe trials programme at Essen on the 21st, for which 1 Group contributed twenty-nine Lancasters, ten of them representing 103 Squadron. They departed Elsham Wolds between 17.12 and 17.43 with F/L Temperley the senior pilot on duty and each Lancaster carrying a cookie and twelve SBCs. They flew out over Mablethorpe to make landfall on the Dutch coast north of Alkmaar and cross the Den Helder peninsula to Enkhuizen, before turning to the south-east to pinpoint on Noordijk. Sgt Burton and crew lost their port-outer engine before reaching the Dutch coast and turned back, while the others continued on and reached the target area, noting that condensation trails were forming at 18,000 feet to advertise their presence to the German defences. There was a question as to the cloud conditions, some reporting clear skies and others ten-tenths cloud, neither of which would have mattered if the Oboe marking had worked and been visible to all. In the event, the entire Ruhr was concealed beneath thick industrial haze, which proved to be impenetrable, and the 103 Squadron crews could only estimate that they were over Essen when they let their bombs go from 19,000 to 21,000 feet between 19.45 and 19.54 in the face of an intense flak barrage. The crews of Sgts Berry and Greig remained in the target area for an additional eighteen minutes to carry out a reconnaissance and returned safely with all but two of the others from Elsham Wolds. Four Lancasters failed to return, and two of these belonged to 103 Squadron, W4340 disappearing without trace with the crew of F/Sgt Burgess, while W4335 succumbed to an encounter with the night-fighter of Feldwebel Theodor Klein Henz of III./NJG1 and crashed at 19.35 near Enschede in east-central Holland with no survivors from the crew of Sgt Laing. Ted Laing and three of his crew were Australians, and close friends with the Maddern crew, who had just discovered that other friends at 12 Squadron had been lost on the recent Berlin operation. As far as many returning crews were concerned, there had been no Path Finder markers to point the way and the outcome of the raid remained undetermined.

The Oboe trials programme moved to Düsseldorf on the 23rd, the huge industrial city situated on the Rhine some fifteen miles south-south-east of Essen, for which 1, 5 and 8 Groups assembled a force of eighty Lancasters and three Mosquitos. Twenty-eight 1 Group Lancasters were prepared for battle, eight of them at Elsham Wolds, where they were loaded with a cookie and twelve SBC and dispatched between 17.14 and 17.26 with S/L Kennard the senior pilot on duty. They headed out over Cromer on course for the Belgian coast to enter Germany south of Aachen before swinging to the north for the run on the target. S/L Kennard lost all of the coolant from his starboard-inner engine on take-off and proceeded directly to the jettison area, leaving the others to reach the target and find ten-tenths cloud at 12,000 feet, heavy, accurate flak and Path Finder release-point flares drifting towards the cloud tops. The 103 Squadron element bombed on these from 18,000 to 20,000 feet between 19.50 and 20.04 but saw nothing of the outcome through the cloud.

Lorient had faced another assault on this night with a token Lancaster presence in a force of 121 aircraft, which inflicted further heavy damage. The fourth raid took place on the night of the 26/27th at the hands of an initial force of 157 aircraft, of which fifty-one Wellingtons and three 460 Squadron Lancasters were provided by 1 Group. 1 Group welcomed a new squadron to the front line on this night, 166 Squadron having been formed on Wellingtons at Kirmington from the remnants of 142 and 150 Squadrons, which had flown out to the Middle-Eastern theatre in December. The attack on Lorient took place in poor weather conditions and probably caused little damage.

Düsseldorf was selected again as the primary target on the 27th, when the Path Finders were to use ground marking for the first time, rather than skymarking. Ground markers, which were TIs fused to burst and cascade at 3,000 feet, could be seen through thin or partial cloud and industrial haze, and were much more reliable than the previously-employed parachute flares that drifted in the wind. However, skymarkers would remain an indispensable part of target marking techniques on nights of heavy cloud or to use in combination with ground markers. From this night onwards, Path Finder heavy aircraft would back-up the Mosquito-laid Oboe markers, to ensure that the aiming point remained visible throughout the operation. A heavy force of 124 Lancasters and thirty-three Halifaxes was made ready on 1, 4, 5 and 8 Group stations, 1 Group contributing twenty-six Lancasters, of which seven were made ready by 103 Squadron. They departed Elsham Wolds between 17.44 and 17.57 with S/L Kennard the senior pilot on duty and the newly-arrived S/L Barker flying as second pilot to F/L Temperley, and began the North Sea crossing five miles west of Cromer on course for the Dutch coast to the north of The Hague. There were no early returns and on reaching the target they encountered a thin layer of five to ten-tenths cloud at 10,000 feet, through which the red and green TIs could be seen burning on the aiming point. The 103 Squadron crews were guided by red warning flares and delivered their cookie and twelve SBCs each from 16,000 to 19,000 feet between 20.03 and 20.17. Returning crew were impressed by the potential of ground marking and confident that if the TIs had been accurate, the aiming point had been hit. The success of the operation was confirmed by local reports, which spoke of widespread destruction in southern districts, amounting to 456 houses, ten industrial premises and nine public buildings destroyed or seriously damaged, and many others had been affected to a lesser extent.

W/C Carter took part in a three-hour high-level cross-country exercise on the 29th, which was probably related to the imminent operational baptism of a new electronic aid to bombing, for which he intended to put himself on the order of battle. The ground-mapping H2S radar was to be employed operationally for the first time at Hamburg on the 30th, and a force of 135 Lancasters of 1, 5 and 8 Groups was duly assembled and would be joined by thirteen H2S-equipped Path Finder Stirlings and Halifaxes of 7 and 35 Squadrons respectively. The H2S equipment was housed in a cupola aft of the bomb bay and projected an image of the terrain onto a cathode-ray tube in the navigator's compartment. It was the job of the operator to interpret what he was seeing, and guide the pilot to the aiming point, but this was no easy task, particularly with this early Mk I set, and it proved difficult to distinguish particular ground features in the jumble of images presented to him. It would take much practice and experience to master the device, but in time, and once the Mk III set became available, it would become an indispensable tool, which ultimately would become standard equipment for main force as well as Path Finder aircraft.

1 Group contributed twenty-five Lancasters, eight of them belonging to 103 Squadron, which were loaded with a cookie and twelve SBCs of 4lb incendiaries and sent on their way from Elsham Wolds between 00.05 and 00.39 with W/C Carter the senior pilot on duty accompanied by the freshman crew of Sgt Young. F/Sgt Roper and crew failed to get off the ground after swinging during the take-off run and coming to grief, although without injury to the crew or terminal damage to W4323. The others set course from Cromer to Egmond on the Den Helder peninsula and ran into north-western Germany's "gatekeeper", one of the massive weather fronts that formed frequently over the North Sea and which on this night produced ten-tenths cloud with tops at 20,000 feet and beyond and contained severe icing conditions and violent electrical storms for the bombers to negotiate. The Maddern crew turned back within two hours after the rear turret froze, while F/L Temperley and crew found themselves in the thick of searchlights and flak over Bremen and lost so much time in evasive action that they released their bombs there from 16,000 feet at 02.32. Those reaching Hamburg at the head of the main force observed green warning flares at 02.58 as they approached over six-tenths cloud that topped out at 12,000 feet, and the red TIs became visible at 03.00. The 103 Squadron crews bombed from 18,000 to 20,000 feet between 03.06 and 03.09 but observed no bursts among the burgeoning fires that were visible as they turned away. W/C Carter carried out a reconnaissance after bombing and declared the work of the Path Finders to be excellent. Some returning crews reported a scattered raid, while others believed it to have been effective and the latter view was partially confirmed by local reports that mentioned seventy-one large fires. However, much of the bombing had fallen either into the Elbe or into marshland outside of the city, and the destruction of a railway bridge, which brought the city's network to a standstill for two days, was an unanticipated bonus. The outcome would have been disappointing to the raid planners, as Hamburg, with the nearby coastline and wide River Elbe, was an ideal target for H2S and should have been easy to identify on the cathode-ray tubes.

During the course of the month, the squadron took part in eleven operations and dispatched ninety-six sorties for the loss of four Lancasters and three crews.

February 1943

The new month began with the departure from 103 Squadron of a number of highly experienced and respected members of aircrew at the conclusion of their tours. Jack Douglas and Roly Newitt were posted off to the newly-opened 1662 Conversion Unit at Blyton, and Ken Berry was also on his way having just been awarded the DFM. His recently commissioned bomb-aimer, P/O Hopkins, had received the DFC at the same time and was immediately reposted to the squadron in the rank of acting flight lieutenant to take over as bombing leader.

It was a time of honing and refining for Bomber Command in preparation for the launching of a major campaign a month hence and February opened with the posting of Cologne as the target for an experimental operation on the 2nd, in which two marking methods were to be employed. Situated on the Rhine just to the south of the Ruhr, Cologne lay within range of Oboe Mosquitos, and these were to be supplemented by Path Finder aircraft relying on H2S. A force of 159 heavies included twenty-six 1 Group Lancasters, five of them provided by 103 Squadron, while two Path Finder Mosquitos of 109 Squadron carried the Oboe markers. At Elsham Wolds the armourers winched the standard bomb load of a cookie and twelve SBCs into each Lancaster and watched them lift themselves into the air between 18.13 and 18.20 with F/L Temperley the senior pilot on duty. They crossed the English coast at Southwold on course for the Scheldt estuary, from where they headed for the town of Jülich to the east of Aachen for an approach to the target from the south. The severe cold caused countless guns to freeze solid within the bomber stream, but those reaching the target found a layer of two to five tenths thin cloud up to 8,000 feet and patches above as high as 15,000. The main force crews were guided by green Path Finder route-marker flares dropped fifteen miles from the target, by which time they already had a clear sight of the red and green skymarkers falling over the aiming point. There was some debate as to the accuracy and concentration of the markers, which a few crews from other squadrons would report as five to ten miles to the north-west of the city, while others described them as scattered. In good vertical visibility, the 103 Squadron crews picked up the cascading red and green TIs burning on the ground and had them in the bomb sights as they delivered their loads from 16,000 to 20,000 feet between 21.03 and 21.14. Although few were able to observe their own bombs burst, many scattered fires were evident, the glow from which could be seen from a hundred miles into the return journey. As they left the target area, F/L Temperley and crew had a close head-on encounter with a Ju88, which passed a mere ten feet over their heads. The consensus among returning crews was of a successful attack, but this was not supported by a local assessment, which reported scattered bombing right across the city, the destruction of sixty-five houses and blast damage to fifteen hundred more caused by just fifteen cookies. Nowhere was the necessary concentration achieved, and the result was not commensurate with the size of the force and the effort expended. Five aircraft failed to return, but none was from 1 Group.

Hamburg was posted as the target on the 3rd, for which a force of 263 aircraft was made ready, unusually, with Halifaxes representing the most populous type followed by Stirlings. 1 Group contributed six Lancasters each from 101 and 460 Squadrons and twenty-three Wellingtons, and while they were being prepared for the operation, their crews were being warned of a cold front across the North Sea with towering cloud and icing conditions. The Wellington captains were advised to turn back if unable to climb to clear air and as events turned out, twenty-one 1 Group crews turned back on encountering the meteorological brick wall, and most of them cited frozen guns as the primary cause. Over the target, nine to ten-tenths cloud topped out at an estimated 7,000 to 8,000 feet, although some reported the cloud to be at 17,000 to 20,000 feet. Scattered red and green Path Finder H2S-laid skymarker flares were in the bomb sights of many, but no results were observed, and the impression was of an ineffective attack. This was confirmed by local reports, which mentioned forty-five large fires but no concentration or significant damage, a disappointing outcome in exchange for the loss of sixteen aircraft, but only two from 1 Group. The losses by type made interesting reading and would reflect the trend for the remainder of the year, with the Stirlings suffering the highest numerical and percentage casualties, followed by the Halifaxes and Wellingtons, with the Lancasters clearly at the top of the food chain.

A return to Italy was posted on the 4th with Turin the target for a force of 188 aircraft, while 128 others, mostly Wellingtons, were prepared to continue the assault on Lorient. 1 Group contributed twenty-one Lancasters to the former, including seven representing 103 Squadron, and a single 103 Squadron Lancaster and twenty-five Wellingtons to the latter. Those involved in the main event departed Elsham Wolds between 17.49 and 18.03 with F/L Temperley the senior and only commissioned pilot on duty and three of the Lancasters carrying a cookie and seven SBCs and the others fourteen SBCs. They exited England over Selsey Bill to make landfall on the other side of the Channel over the Normandy beach near Ouistreham, which would be the scene of the British and Canadian D-Day landings seventeen months hence. Sgt Greig and crew had already turned back by this time because of an overheating starboard-outer engine. Meanwhile, the freshman crew of P/O Lee-Brown, who had arrived from 1656 Conversion Unit only days earlier, had taken off at 19.09 bound for Lorient and would arrive at the French coast further to the west somewhere near Paimpol. As the main bomber stream adopted the usual route across France, the Lee-Brown crew dropped their cookie and twelve SBCs of 4lb incendiaries on the target from 10,000 feet at 21.19, before turning for home content that their maiden sortie had been successful. After crossing the Alps in cloud at 21,000 feet, the others found conditions on the Italian side much improved with clear skies and excellent visibility, which facilitated a visual confirmation of the accuracy of the Path Finder TIs. An estimated one hundred searchlights were active, reaching up to 17,000 feet, and the flak defence had also been "beefed-up" but was still inaccurate and in keeping with expectations at an Italian target. *(Following a raid on a German target, a bomb symbol was painted on the forward fuselage below the glasshouse, but after a raid on an Italian target, the symbol was an ice-cream cone.)* Red TIs were much in evidence in the city centre as the 103 Squadron crews carried out their attacks from 16,000 to 18,000 feet between 21.37 and 21.44, and returning crews were enthusiastic about the effectiveness of their work. Local sources confirmed later that serious and widespread damage had resulted.

The seventh raid in the series on Lorient was posted on the 7th, and was by far the largest to date, employing 323 aircraft, of which twenty of eighty Lancasters were provided by 1 Group along with twenty-six Wellingtons. It was to be conducted in two waves, an hour apart, and 103 Squadron supported the second phase with the freshman crews of F/O Bickers, P/O Blumenauer and Sgts F Cook and Lay, who departed Elsham Wolds between 1931 and 20.20 each sitting on a cookie and twelve SBCs. Faulty navigation led Sgt Cook and crew astray and by the time that they had established their position over southern England it was too late to continue. The others began the Channel crossing at Bridport and having made landfall on the Brittany coast found the fiercely burning port acting as a beacon to draw them on for the final part of the outward leg. They located the target area with ease, noting marker flares on the West Bank of the river and the aiming point confirmed by Path Finder TIs. They carried out their attacks through haze and drifting smoke from 9,000 to 12,500 feet between 21.43 and 22.16 and set off for home entirely satisfied with their night's work, leaving behind them a glow in the sky visible from the English coast.

Before the penultimate raid took place on Lorient, attention was switched to the important naval port of Wilhelmshaven, situated on the north-western coast of Jade Bay some sixty miles to the west of Hamburg. A force of 177 aircraft was assembled on the 11th, of which 129 were Lancasters, forty-two of them representing 1 Group, and at Elsham Wolds the armourers set about winching a cookie into each of ten bomb bays along with three SBCs of 30lb incendiaries and nine of 4lbs. The 103 Squadron element took off between 17.51 and 18.15 with S/L Kennard and F/L Temperley the senior pilots on duty and set course via Mablethorpe for a turning point over the North Sea to the north-west of the target. Sgt Young and crew lost their starboard-inner engine within an hour and turned back, while B-Beer and the Maddern crew were only minutes from the target when attacked from the port-quarter above by a BF109. The enemy's fire missed, while that from the Lancaster's mid-upper and rear turrets probably did not and the fighter was last seen diving vertically into cloud to be claimed as probably damaged. On reaching their destination the main force crews found ten-tenths cloud with tops at up to 10,000 feet and the least reliable marking method, H2S skymarking, in progress. On the credit side, at a smaller, more compact urban target like Wilhelmshaven, it was easier to interpret the images on the cathode-ray screens and on this night great accuracy was achieved. The red and green flares were right over the aiming point as the 103 Squadron crews delivered their attacks from 14,000 to 18,500 feet between 20.02 and 20.19, but it was impossible to assess what was happening beneath the cloud until an enormous explosion took place, the glow from which lingered for ten minutes. Many crews commented on this at debriefings across the Command, and there must have been much speculation about the source, which turned out to be the naval ammunition depot at Mariensiel, situated to the south of the town. It blew itself into oblivion, devastating 120 acres and causing widespread damage in the dockyard and built-up area. S/L Kennard had conducted a reconnaissance after bombing and assessed that the marking had worked like clockwork.

It was back to Lorient for ten 103 Squadron crews on the 13th, who learned at briefing that they were to be part of the largest force yet sent against the port of 466 aircraft, forty-four of the Lancasters contributed by 1 Group along with forty-two Wellingtons. It was to be another two-phase affair, with the Elsham Wolds contingent taking the early shift and becoming airborne between 17.54 and 18.25 with S/Ls Kennard and Powdrell the senior pilots on duty and each Lancaster carrying five 1,000 pounders and a mix of 4lb and 30lb incendiaries. They headed out over Start Point on the Devon coast and pinpointed on Groix Island for the bombing run and there were no early returns to deplete the squadron's impact. The target was located with ease in excellent visibility under clear skies and a high moon, which allowed crews to make a visual identification of the U-Boot pens on the Keroman Peninsula and the town. They delivered their attacks from 10,000 to 16,000 feet between 20.35 and 20.49, and both aiming points were left burning fiercely and emitting a pall of black smoke into the night sky. By the end of the second phase attack, more than a thousand tons of bombs had laid waste to the port and town, and this was a record for a non-1,000 force. F/L Kennard again conducted a reconnaissance and reported that the Path Finder flares had lit up the target like day and the main force bombing had been accurate and concentrated within the target area.

Orders came through to 1, 5 and 8 Group stations on the 14th to make ready for a return to Italy that night for a crack this time at Milan, the home, as previously mentioned, to many war industry factories. A force of 142 Lancasters was assembled to carry out the attack, while 243 Halifaxes, Stirlings and Wellingtons were made ready to try their hand at Cologne. Among the forty 1 Group Lancasters were nine representing 103 Squadron, each of which was loaded with a 2,000 pounder and ten SBCs of 4lb and 30lb incendiaries, before departing Elsham Wolds between 18.48 and 19.25 with S/L Powdrell the senior pilot on duty. Sgt Young and crew lost their hydraulics system during the climb-out and spent a considerable time burning off fuel, before belly-landing W4337 at base at 22.01 and walking away unscathed. The Lancaster would be repaired and put back into service, but this crew had just used up its ration of good fortune. The route took the others via Dungeness to Cayeux-sur-Mer and then Troyes and Lake Bourget, before crossing the Alps to pinpoint on Lake Maggiore on the Italian side from where they carried out a timed run, guided to the aiming point also by green and red Path Finder route-marker flares. They were able to identify the aiming point visually and those from 103 squadron ran in on the target at 12,500 to 15,000 feet between 22.32 and 22.45, some observing their own bursts and others not in the haze and general glare of many fires. A glow from the burning city remained visible for at least a hundred miles into the return journey and the operation was hailed as a major success, although no local report was forthcoming to confirm or deny. F/L Temperley carried out the reconnaissance, and he reported the city well-blitzed following accurate and timely Path Finder marking. Only two Lancasters failed to return, and one of them was W4362, which contained the crew of S/L Powdrell and was hit on the bombing run by incendiaries from above that destroyed the instrument panel. The flight engineer, navigator and bomb-aimer managed to save themselves and were taken into captivity, but S/L Powdrell and the others lost their lives. F/L Temperley was immediately promoted to the rank of acting squadron leader to succeed S/L Powdrell as a flight commander.

The ninth and final raid of the series on Lorient was announced across the Command on the 16th, and a force of 363 aircraft was assembled, which included a 1 Group contribution of forty-one Lancasters and eighteen Wellingtons, eleven of the former representing 103 Squadron. Each crew was sitting on a cookie, and up to a dozen SBCs of 4lb and 30lb incendiaries as they departed Elsham Wolds between 18.43 and 18.59 with S/L Temperley the senior pilot on duty, before they set course for Start Point and landfall on the French side of the Channel at Treguier. They all reached the target among the earlier arrivals to find clear conditions and an almost full moon and identified the Keroman peninsula visually, aided by red TIs. Bombs were delivered by the 103 Squadron participants from 10,000 to 13,200 feet between 20.47 and 20.55, the main weight of the attack falling in the form of incendiaries onto the town, which, after nine raids, 1,926 sorties and four thousand tons of bombs, was now a desolate and deserted ruin. Only one Lancaster failed to return, ED380, which crashed in the target area with no survivors from the crew of Sgt Young RAAF.

Preparations were put in hand on the 18th to make ready 195 aircraft for the second of four raids on Wilhelmshaven during the month. 1 Group contributed thirty-nine Lancasters, including eleven belonging to 103 Squadron, which were each loaded with a cookie and twelve SBCs of 4lb and 30lb incendiaries and sent on their way from Elsham Wolds between 18.26 and 18.38. F/L Stanhope was the senior pilot on duty and was undertaking his first sortie since arriving from 1656 Conversion Unit on the 10th. They exited the English coast over Mablethorpe and made for the usual final turning point over the North Sea some ninety miles north-west of the target. All reached the target area, which was identified visually in excellent conditions including bright moonlight, and red TIs were also in some bomb sights as the 103 Squadron bomb bays were emptied from 13,000 to 20,000 feet between 20.35 and 20.52. Bombs were observed to burst and fires to spring up, and most returning crews were confident that an accurate and concentrated attack had taken place. The reconnaissance appraisal by Geoff Maddern and crew was less positive and made clear that neither the Path Finder nor the main force had achieved concentration and there was stray bombing to the north. Bombing photos confirmed that view and revealed that the operation had been a failure that deposited the main weight of bombs in open country to the west of the town, thus demonstrating how easy it was to be misled by what the eye saw. Local reports admitted to a number of bombs hitting the town but causing no serious damage or casualties.

Twenty-four hours later, a force of 338 aircraft set off to return to Wilhelmshaven, with Wellingtons and Halifaxes accounting for 230 of the number and Stirlings and Lancasters the rest. 1 Group dispatched thirty-three Wellingtons and left the Lancasters on the ground, and those reaching the target once again found the conditions to be excellent, with visibility that enabled crews to identify the coastline and line themselves up on the target, which was marked by green TIs. Bomb bursts and fires were observed in the docks area and the town and left the crews with the impression that another successful raid had taken place. However, bombing photos told a different story, and revealed that the Path Finder marking had fallen to the north of the built-up area, partly through reliance upon outdated maps, which would now be replaced. Of the twelve missing aircraft five were Stirlings and represented 8.9% of those dispatched, thus confirming the type's vulnerability compared with the Lancaster and Halifax.

An all-Lancaster main force from 1 and 5 Groups was made ready on the 21st to attack the U-Boot construction yards of the Bremer Vulkan A G company at Vegesack, situated on the River Weser to the north-west of Bremen city centre. The marking was to be provided by Path Finder Lancasters, Halifaxes and Stirlings in an overall force of 143 aircraft, forty-two of which were 1 Group Lancasters. At Elsham Wolds, a dozen 103 Squadron crews attended briefing, while a cookie and twelve SBCs were winched into their Lancasters out on the dispersal pans. They took off between 18.36 and 18.58 with S/L Kennard the senior pilot on duty and headed for the coast at Mablethorpe for the North Sea crossing to the Frisian Island of Juist. They reached the target area after attempting to follow scattered route-marker flares and were greeted by ten-tenths cloud at 3,000 feet, above which, red and green skymarker flares drifted down, also in a somewhat scattered manner and up to nine minutes late to join the TIs burning dimly on the ground. The 103 Squadron crews carried out their attacks from 16,000 to 18,000 feet between 20.47 and 21.06, and a considerable glow from beneath the clouds suggested a successful outcome. Bombing photos depicted only cloud, and no local report was available to provide details of damage.

It was left to 115 aircraft of 6 and 8 Groups to conclude the current series of raids on Wilhelmshaven on the night of the 24/25th with indeterminate results, and the port would now be left in peace until October 1944. A major operation against Nuremberg was posted on stations across the Command on the 25th, and a force of 337 aircraft assembled, 1 Group responding with a maximum effort of forty-five Lancasters, thirteen of them made ready by 103 Squadron at Elsham Wolds and each loaded with a cookie and a dozen SBCs of 4lb and 30lb incendiaries. They took off between 19.41 and 20.18 with S/Ls Kennard and Temperley the senior pilots on duty and headed for the Kent coast at Dungeness at the start of the sea crossing to Cayeux-sur-Mer. Sgt F Cook and crew turned back within ninety minutes because of an unserviceable rear turret, leaving the others to press on to the target area, which they found to be under cloudless skies but cloaked by extreme darkness and haze, and those arriving in the vanguard had to wait for the Path Finder element to turn up, some sixteen to twenty minutes after the raid was due to begin. The 103 Squadron crews were further back in the bomber stream, arriving after the Path Finders had begun to mark, and were guided to the aiming point by red marker flares and red and green TIs, which they bombed from 14,500 to 18,000 feet between 23.22 and 23.55. All indications, including what looked like an oil-depot exploding, suggested a concentrated attack, which fell predominantly in northern and western districts. This was confirmed by local reports, which mentioned damage to three hundred buildings, but also revealed that bombs had fallen onto other communities and open country up to seven miles to the north.

When Cologne was posted as the target on the 26th, 1 Group responded with forty-three Lancasters and twenty-eight Wellingtons, eleven of the former made ready by 103 Squadron at Elsham Wolds as part of an overall force of 427 aircraft. They were loaded with the usual cookie and twelve SBCs of 4lb and 30lb incendiaries and took off between 18.51 and 19.04 with no senior pilots on duty, before heading out over the Norfolk coast at Sheringham bound for landfall at Noordwijk-aan-Zee to the north of The Hague. F/O Lee-Brown and crew turned back at the English coast when the rear gunner was found to be unconscious through oxygen starvation, but the remainder reached the Cologne area to encounter clear skies and good vertical visibility in which some of the bomb-aimers were able to identify the bridges over the Rhine. It seems from some comments from other squadrons that a proportion of the force bombed before the Path Finders had a chance to mark, but once the red flares and red and green TIs were seen on the ground, the 103 Squadron crews took advantage of them to release their loads from 14,000 to 17,000 feet between 21.13 and 21.23. Returning crews estimated a hundred searchlights in operation with intense light and heavy flak, and fires were reported in the city centre, as were decoys to the west of the city. Bombing photos showed fire tracks and smoke that suggested an effective raid, but, in fact, a large proportion of the effort had fallen to the south-west of the city and perhaps only a quarter had landed in the built-up area, causing much damage to housing, minor industry and public buildings. Ten aircraft failed to return and among three missing Lancasters was 103 Squadron's W4336, which crashed somewhere in the Ruhr area with no survivors from the crew of Sgt F Cook.

The 27th was a warm and sunny day on which the squadron was stood down from operations and assigned to fighter affiliation and gunnery training. F/O Lee-Brown and crew took off in W4857 with F/L Stubbs DFC, DFM of the Fighter Circus on board as their instructor. He was an experienced pilot, who had earned his DFM in 1941 while serving on Wellingtons with 3 Group's 75(NZ) Squadron. During the course of violent evasive manoeuvres part of the Lancaster's tail assembly failed, and observers saw one fin and rudder assembly hanging loose. F/L Stubbs ordered the eight other occupants to bale out and one of these fell six thousand feet upside-down, attached to his parachute by just one leg after the harness slipped. F/L Stubbs attempted to land but lost control of the aircraft on final approach and crashed into a wood near Brigg with fatal consequences.

Having dealt with Lorient under the January Directive, attention now turned upon St-Nazaire, situated further south along the Biscay coast. The force of 437 aircraft assembled on the 28th included a contribution from 1 Group of forty-five Lancasters and twenty-six Wellingtons, of which thirteen of the former represented 103 Squadron. They departed Elsham Wolds between 18.16 and 18.47 with S/L Temperley the senior pilot on duty and each crew resting their feet on a cookie and twelve SBCs. They flew directly from Start Point to the target, passing to the west of the enemy-occupied Channel Islands on the way and all arrived to find clear skies and good visibility, with only a little ground haze to contend with, and bombed on red TIs from 10,000 to 15,000 feet between 21.14 and 21.35. It was clear from the many explosions and at least forty fires in the docks that the port was undergoing an ordeal of destruction, and post-raid reconnaissance revealed the marking and bombing to have been concentrated and accurate, to the extent that local sources confirmed 60% destruction of the town.

During the course of the month the squadron took part in thirteen operations and dispatched 117 sorties for the loss of four Lancasters and three crews.

March 1943

March would bring the addition of a third or C Flight for 103 Squadron and a consequent influx of new personnel, and it would also see the opening rounds of the Ruhr campaign, the first for which the Command was adequately equipped and genuinely prepared, with a predominantly four-engine bomber force to carry an increasing weight of bombs and Oboe to provide accuracy. First, however, the crews would have to negotiate operations to Germany's capital and second cities, and it was the "Big City" itself, Berlin, that opened the month's account on the 1st for which a force of 302 aircraft was assembled, made up of 156 Lancasters, eighty-six Halifaxes and sixty Stirlings. 1 Group put up a "Goodwood" or maximum effort of forty-two Lancasters, of which a dozen representing 103 Squadron were loaded with a cookie and twelve SBCs of 4lb and 30lb incendiaries. They departed Elsham Wolds between 18.39 and 19.27 with S/Ls Kennard and Temperley the senior pilots on duty and set course via Mablethorpe for Mandø Island off the western coast of Jutland.

There were no early returns among the Elsham Wolds contingent and after a three-and-a-half hour outward flight, they arrived at the target under clear skies with only haze to impair the vertical visibility. However, reliant upon H2S, the Path Finder navigators experienced great difficulty in establishing their positions based on the images on their cathode-ray tubes over such a massive urban sprawl and this led to scattered marking and the main weight of the attack falling into south-western districts. The 103 Squadron crews bombed on red and green TIs from 12,000 to 17,000 feet between 22.02 and 22.40, and S/L Kennard's reconnaissance report would refer to a "colossal success" with more than seventy fires and an estimated 250 to 300 searchlights, adding the comment, "flak pitiful, fires plentiful". The glow from the burning city, according to some, remained visible on the horizon for two hundred miles into the return flight. A post-raid analysis based on bombing photos revealed the attack to have been spread over an area of a hundred square miles, but, because of the increasing bomb tonnage now being carried, more damage was inflicted on the city than on any previous raid. 875 buildings, mostly houses, were destroyed, and twenty factories seriously damaged, along with railway workshops in the Tempelhof district. Seventeen aircraft failed to return, just two of which belonged to 1 Group, and both belonged to 103 Squadron, W4361 lost without trace with the crew of F/Sgt Austin DFM, now, since the departures of Jack Douglas, Roly Newitt and Ken Berry a month earlier, one of the senior crews. They had been, in fact, on their twenty-ninth and penultimate operation, and the loss so late on of any crew was a body-blow to the others, who needed to witness a crew surviving just to demonstrate that, although seemingly unlikely, it was possible to come through. Also missing was W4880, which crashed while homebound eleven miles west-south-west of Bremen with no survivors from the crew of F/L Stanhope.

A force of 417 aircraft was assembled on the 3rd to send against Hamburg, of which forty-three Lancasters and thirty-one Wellingtons were provided by 1 Group, eleven of the former by 103 Squadron at Elsham Wolds, where each had a cookie and twelve SBCs of incendiaries winched into its bomb bay. They took off between 18.39 and 18.57 with S/L Kennard the senior pilot on duty and set course via Mablethorpe for the usual turning point over the North Sea that would take them on to Heide on the western side of Schleswig-Holstein to approach the target from the north. For the third operation in a row, there were no early returns and the 103 Squadron crews arrived in the target area under clear skies and benefitting from good visibility. They carried out their attacks from 15,000 to 17,000 between 21.23 and 21.33, aided by the H2S-laid Path Finder TIs and numerous fires were observed in the docks area along with black smoke rising to meet the bombers as they turned away. What was not appreciated, was the fact that some markers had fallen onto the town of Wedel, situated some thirteen miles downstream of the Elbe, and they had attracted perhaps the bulk of the bombs, while those hitting the primary target had caused a hundred fires that needed to be dealt with before the fire services could go to the aid of their neighbour. Ten aircraft failed to return, two of them belonging to 1 Group and once again 103 Squadron had the sad task of posting missing one of its most experienced crews. Sgt Greig's W4788 had crashed near Hohenaspe on the Schleswig-Holstein peninsula, and all eight men on board had perished.

On the following afternoon, Yugoslavian F/O Kujundzic, who had only arrived from 1656 Conversion Unit on the previous day, was killed while flying Geoff Maddern's favourite Lancaster, W4333 B-Beer. It caught fire in the air during a training flight and crashed near Peterborough, the rest of the crew having taken to their parachutes and arrived safely on the ground.

The decks were now cleared for the opening of the Ruhr offensive, which, over the ensuing months, would change the face of bombing and provide for the enemy an indication of the burgeoning power of the Command. This was a momentous occasion, a culmination of all that had gone before during three and a half years of Bomber Command operations. The backs-to-the-wall desperation of 1940, the tentative almost token offensives of 1941, the treading water and gradual metamorphosis under Harris in 1942, when failures still far outnumbered successes, had all been leading to this night, from which point would begin the calculated and systematic dismantling of Germany's industrial and population centres. The only shining light during these dark years had been the quality and spirit of the aircrew, and this had never faltered. The new era would begin on the 5th at Essen, Harris's nemesis thus far and the home of the giant armaments-producing Krupp complex occupying the Borbeck districts, and for the first time since the war began, the Command would have at its disposal a device which would negate the industrial haze protecting this city and its neighbours. It required only that the high-flying Path Finder Oboe-equipped Mosquitos could pick up the electronic guidance system beamed from England, and that their colleagues in the Path Finder heavy brigade could keep the aiming point marked. The magnificent pioneering work on Oboe by W/C Hal Bufton and his crews at 109 Squadron was about to bear fruit in spectacular fashion, and the towns and cities of Germany's arsenal would suffer destruction on an unprecedented scale.

A force of 442 aircraft assembled for this three-wave attack included forty-one Lancasters and thirty-eight Wellingtons representing 1 Group, 103 Squadron contributing ten of the former, each loaded with a cookie and twelve SBCs of incendiaries. At the head of the snaking line of Lancasters making their way along the perimeter track to the threshold at Elsham Wolds was W/C Carter and his crew followed by those containing the crews of S/L Temperley in W4363, F/Os Bickers and Crich in W4337 and ED528 respectively, P/O Cook in W4821, F/Sgts Maddern and Roper in W4363 and W4828, and Sgts Burton, King and Lay in W4901, W4318 and ED389. They lifted into the air between 19.12 and 19.44 and set course via Mablethorpe for the Dutch coast at Egmond for the northern approach to the Ruhr, and the recent excellent record of serviceability continued on this night as not one 103 Squadron aircraft was among the unusually large number of fifty-six that turned back early for whatever reason. Together with those bombing alternative targets, this would reduce the size of the force reaching Essen and bombing as briefed to 362 aircraft. The Path Finders dropped yellow route markers to guide the main force in, and the 103 Squadron crews were able to exploit the good visibility to bomb through the industrial haze onto red and green TIs from 15,000 to 18,500 feet between 21.21 and 21.26. Several returning crews reported a very large explosion that lit up the sky and a pall of smoke hanging above the dull, red centre of the conflagration. The overwhelming impression was of a concentrated attack, which left a glow in the sky reported by some to be visible from the North Sea homebound. Post-raid reconnaissance revealed 160 acres of devastation and damage to fifty-three buildings within the Krupp districts, and the success of the operation was confirmed by local reports of 3,018 houses destroyed and more than two thousand others seriously damaged. The operation cost the Command an acceptable fourteen aircraft, just a single one from 1 Group, and it was a most encouraging start to what would become a five-month-long offensive.

There were changes at 103 Squadron as S/L Kennard had finished his tour of operations and was now on leave pending his posting to 1656 Conversion Unit on the 15th. Coming in the opposite direction on the 8th was S/L O'Donoghue, whose time with the squadron would be relatively brief. He had previously served in India, where operations had been conducted in daylight, and his crew confided in their new colleagues that he had a distinct dislike of night operations.

A week would elapse between the first and second Ruhr operations, and in the meantime, Harris turned his attention upon southern Germany, beginning with Nuremberg on the 8th, for which a force of 338 aircraft was assembled that included forty-eight Lancasters of 1 Group. Among them for the first time were six Lancasters belonging to 100 Squadron at Waltham (Grimsby), while 103 Squadron was represented by ten, which departed Elsham Wolds without incident between 19.46 and 20.21 with S/L Temperley the senior pilot on duty. Each crew was sitting on a cookie and ten SBCs as they made their way south to begin the Channel crossing at Dungeness on course for Cayeux-Sur-Mer and yet again there were no early returns. The bomber stream traversed France to enter Germany between Saarbrücken and Stuttgart and the main force element reached the target by following the Path Finders' yellow route markers. They were greeted by clear skies and good horizontal visibility, but ground haze and extreme darkness impeded the Path Finders' ability to locate the city centre blind by H2S, and the main force crews experienced the same difficulty in identifying ground detail. They allowed themselves to be guided to the aiming point by a few red and green TIs, which appeared to lack concentration and soon burned out, but the 103 Squadron crews had them in the bombsights as they carried out their attacks from 15,000 to 18,500 feet between 23.31 and 23.51. The initial impression was of a scattered raid, however, a concentration of fires developed and the glow from these was reported by some to be visible for two hundred miles into the return journey. Local reports confirmed the marking and bombing of Nuremberg to have been spread along a ten-mile stretch, half of it falling short of the city boundaries, while the rest destroyed six hundred buildings and damaged fourteen hundred others, including a number of important war-industry factories.

On the following day, preparations were put in hand to return to southern Germany to attack the city of Munich, situated deep in the Bavarian mountains of south-eastern Germany, a round-trip of more than 1,200 miles. A force of 264 aircraft included forty-seven Lancasters of 1 Group, of which the nine belonging to 103 Squadron were each loaded with a cookie and nine SBCs of incendiaries. They departed Elsham Wolds between 19.59 and 20.20 with no senior pilots on duty and headed directly for landfall on the French coast north of Dieppe, arriving at the target after following a course similar to that of the previous night. They were greeted by clear skies and good visibility, which enabled them to observe the Path Finders' green and white TIs burning within the built-up area. The Ammersee to the south-west had also been marked for the 5 Group crews to employ as the starting point for their favoured time-and-distance runs. The 103 Squadron crews released their loads from 12,000 to 20,000 feet between 00.12 and 00.28, and some witnessed an enormous explosion in the city centre at around 00.16. Another huge explosion at 00.25, described by some as the largest they had ever witnessed, lit up the sky for twenty seconds and illuminated an area of ground with a ten-mile radius. Another particularly large one occurred at 00.43, by which time the Elsham Wolds crews were well on their way home, leaving behind them fires and a large pall of smoke rising above the city. As the last of the main force aircraft withdrew to the west, some counted eighteen blazes in or close to the city centre. A relatively modest eight aircraft failed to return, only two of them from 1 Group, but again there would be an empty dispersal pan at Elsham Wolds. W4860 crashed eight miles north-east of Reims in France, probably while homebound, and F/Sgt Roper died with all but one of his experienced crew, the navigator alone surviving to fall into enemy hands. A post-raid analysis concluded that a strong wind had pushed the attack into the western half of the city, where 291 buildings had been destroyed and 660 severely damaged. The aero-engine assembly shop at the B.M.W factory was put out of action for six weeks, and many other industrial concerns also lost vital production.

The trio of operations to destinations in southern Germany concluded with the highly industrial city of Stuttgart, for which a force of 314 aircraft was assembled on the 11th, 1 Group contributing forty-one of 152 Lancasters. Eight of these were made ready by 103 Squadron at Elsham Wolds, where they were loaded with a cookie and a dozen SBCs of incendiaries before being sent on their way between 19.41 and 19.57 with S/L Temperley the senior pilot on duty and S/L O'Donoghue flying as second pilot to P/O Cook. They set course via Rye for the French coast north of Dieppe, rendezvousing with the rest of the bomber stream on the way and following a similar course to that of the previous operation. F/O Lee-Brown and crew turned back when south-east of Reims when their oxygen system failed and S/L Temperley and crew were further along the route near Nancy when they lost their port-outer engine. The others pressed on and arrived late at the target to find excellent visibility and the Path Finder TIs already burning out on the ground, leaving the way clear for dummy TIs to lure the bombing away from the city centre. In this endeavour the enemy was largely successful, although to the bomb-aimers high above, the green TIs appeared to be legitimate and were bombed by the 103 Squadron crews from 15,500 to 17,500 feet between 23.11 and 23.24. Most of the effort was wasted in open country, but the south-western suburbs of Vaihingen and Kaltental were hit and 118 buildings, mostly houses, were destroyed. It was a disappointing outcome, which cost eleven aircraft, but none on this occasion from 1 Group.

Round two of the Ruhr campaign was posted on the 12th, when 457 crews learned at briefing that Essen was once more to be their destination. 1 Group detailed forty-five Lancasters and thirty-nine Wellingtons, of which six of the former were made ready by 103 Squadron at Elsham Wolds and loaded with a cookie and twelve SBCs. They took off between 19.39 and 20.02 with no senior pilot on duty and set course via Mablethorpe for Egmond on the Den Helder peninsula with a final turning point at Haltern to the north of the Ruhr. ED419 was nine miles short of that mark when brought down and there were no survivors from the crew of F/O Dugard. The others reached the target and found the aiming point to be well marked by red and green Path Finder TIs, with only smoke to mar the vertical visibility, and carried out their attacks from 17,500 to 21,000 feet between 21.33 and 21.41. Most crews gained a clear impression that the bombing was accurate and concentrated around the TIs, and this time the Krupp complex found itself in the centre of the area of destruction. The defences fought back to claim twenty-three bombers, five belonging to 1 Group, in return for which, post-raid reconnaissance confirmed another highly successful assault on this centre of war production. Substantially fewer buildings had been destroyed compared with the raid of a week earlier, but greater concentration had been achieved and 30% more damage inflicted upon the Krupp complex.

Thereafter, the weather caused a lull in operations for nine nights, during which a number were scheduled but cancelled, sometimes at the last minute. This was the case on the 19th, when it seems that S/L O'Donoghue had been due to carry out his first operation with his own crew since joining the squadron. He decided to go alone, and at 04.06 on the 20th took off with his crew into foul weather conditions and flew out over Mablethorpe bound for the town of Leer, a target of his own choosing, situated just inside Germany at its northern-most border with Holland. They bombed from 3,200 feet, releasing eleven 1,000lb bombs, at least one of which had a six-hour delay fuse, in two sticks, one falling close to the railway station and the other parallel with the main street in a built-up area.

Operations resumed on the 22nd, when orders came through to prepare for the next assault on St-Nazaire under the January Directive. A force of 357 aircraft was assembled, including a contribution from 1 Group of thirty-seven Lancasters, of which eight were provided by 103 Squadron. They departed Elsham Wolds between 18.53 and 19.16 with S/L Temperley the senior pilot on duty, four loaded with eleven 1,000 pounders and the others with fourteen SBCs of incendiaries and exited the English coast at Start Point to make landfall on the French coast between St-Malo and St-Brieuc. The good visibility in the target area was impeded only by ground haze, which did not prevent a visual identification of ground features. Red and green Path Finder TIs confirmed the location of the aiming point, and the 103 Squadron crews emptied their bomb bays from 14,000 to 17,000 feet between 21.30 and 21.57. Fires were taking hold as they turned away, and, despite the recall of the Stirling element, to which fifty-five crews responded, the town and its port facilities sustained massive damage.

Duisburg was selected as the host for the third operation of the Ruhr offensive and the details were transmitted to bomber stations by teleprinter on the 26th. A force of 455 aircraft was assembled, of which fifty-two Lancasters and forty-three Wellingtons were provided by 1 Group, eleven of the former made ready by 103 Squadron at Elsham Wolds, where each was loaded with a cookie and twelve SBCs of incendiaries. They took off between 19.42 and 19.54 with S/L O'Donoghue the senior pilot on duty, having learned at briefing that marking would be by "Musical Wanganui", the code for Oboe skymarking to be carried out by nine Mosquitos of 109 Squadron. They flew out over Sheringham and made landfall on the Dutch coast over cloud at Egmond, before heading for the final turning point at Elburg. They encountered ten-tenths cloud over the western Ruhr with tops at 10,000 feet and good visibility above and were guided to the aiming point by Oboe parachute flares, which were in the bomb sights as the 103 Squadron crews delivered their attacks from 17,000 to 20,000 feet between 22.00 and 22.28. The flash of a large explosion was witnessed at 21.53, but it was impossible to assess the outcome, and most doubted the effectiveness of the raid. What the crews couldn't know, was that five of the Oboe Mosquitos had returned early with equipment failure and a sixth had been shot down, leaving just three to deliver what could only be sparse marking. This was insufficient, and led to a scattered and ineffective attack, which, according to local reports, caused only minor damage. Fortunately, the failure cost a modest six aircraft,

Among the new arrivals on the 27th was W/O Nick Ross, who was already something of a veteran, having completed a tour of operations on Wellingtons with 40 Squadron at Wyton and Alconbury between November 1941 and July 1942, during which period he took part in all three Thousand Bomber raids. Born in Greenock, Scotland on the 1st of August 1917, Ross followed his father into banking, but was drawn by the prospect of war into joining the RAFVR in July 1939. On screening at the end of his first tour, he was posted as an instructor to 27 O.T.U at Lichfield, which was where Australians were trained, and now at 103 Squadron he was about to embark on his second tour.

Orders were received on stations across the Command on the 27th to prepare for a trip to the "Big City" that night, and a force of 396 aircraft was duly assembled, which included fifty-one Lancasters from 1 Group, thirteen of them made ready by 103 Squadron at Elsham Wolds. They were loaded with a cookie each and twelve SBCs of incendiaries and took off between 19.45 and 20.29 with F/L England the senior pilot on duty for the first time since his posting from 1656 Conversion Unit on the 14th. They exited the Lincolnshire coast over Mablethorpe and crossed the North Sea to Texel, before traversing northern Holland and threading their way through the defence zones at Bremen and Hannover. F/O Blumenauer and crew took a beating over the latter and sustained extensive damage to their Lancaster, but the engines were undamaged, and they pressed on to the target. By this time, having passed the midpoint of the North Sea crossing, F/Sgt Maddern and crew had abandoned their sortie because of fluctuating revolutions on the port-inner and starboard-outer engines. Those completing the outward flight approached the city from the south-west, with the Path Finders ahead of them again reliant upon H2S to locate the city-centre aiming point. However, the sheer size of Berlin thwarted the attempts of the H2S operators to establish their positions accurately, and this resulted in the marking of two areas at least five miles short of the centre. Crews reported three-tenths cloud at 13,000 feet and five tenths stratus at 19,000 feet with moderate to good visibility, and those from 103 Squadron delivered payloads on red and green TIs from 18,000 to 20,000 feet between 23.01 and 23.30. From bombing altitude, the attack appeared to be effective, but local reports confirmed that the main weight of the attack had fallen between seven and seventeen miles short of the target, and 25% of the bombs hitting the city had failed to detonate. Nine aircraft were missing on a night when many crews commented on the paucity of the Berlin defences, and just one of the absentees was from 1 Group.

There would be an opportunity to rectify the failure two nights hence, but in the meantime, St-Nazaire would face its third heavy assault under the January Directive, for which a force of 323 aircraft was made ready on the 28th. 1 Group detailed twenty Lancasters and thirty-three Wellingtons, eight of the former made ready by 103 Squadron and loaded with ten 1,000 pounders each. They departed Elsham Wolds between 19.30 and 19.42 with S/L O'Donoghue and F/L England the senior pilots on duty and W/O Nicky Ross and crew undertaking their maiden sortie with the squadron. S/L O'Donoghue was beset with engine problems from take-off and proceeded directly to the jettison area, leaving the others to fly south to begin the Channel crossing at Start Point and make landfall on the French coast between St-Malo and Saint-Brieuc. They reached the target area to encounter good visibility and carried out their attacks from 16,000 to 19,000 feet between 22.16 and 22.32, observing concentrated fires around the aiming point resulting from their bombing of the red and green Oboe-laid TIs. Post-raid reconnaissance confirmed the accuracy and effectiveness of the raid, which was achieved for the loss of one Halifax and one Lancaster.

On the following day, a force of 329 aircraft was assembled for the return to Berlin that night, night, for which 103 Squadron made ready ten of the twenty-six Lancasters provided by 1 Group and loaded each with a cookie and twelve SBCs of 4lb and 30lb incendiaries. They departed Elsham Wolds between 21.20 and 21.56 with S/L O'Donoghue the senior pilot on duty and no fewer than five others of flight lieutenant rank. They adopted the familiar route for this target, which would take them from Mablethorpe to Mandø Island, rendezvousing with the bomber stream on the way, before traversing Schleswig-Holstein to the Baltic and heading south across the Bay of Mecklenburg to the coast near Wismar. F/L Blumenauer and crew turned back from the midpoint of the North Sea crossing because of a lack of power and inability to climb, possibly after running into icing conditions that caused technical problems for a number of crews. In fact, an alarming eighteen 5 Group and nine 1 Group crews abandoned their sorties for a variety of causes, leaving the remainder to reach Berlin behind schedule because of inaccurately forecast winds. Visibility was described by most as good, which enabled them to identify the target visually, aided by red TIs burning on the ground. Bombing was carried out by the 103 Squadron crews from 16,000 to 20,000 feet between 00.52 and 01.12 and the attack appeared to be generally scattered. This was confirmed later, when bombing photos revealed that most of the effort had fallen into open country south of the city, a disappointment compounded by the loss of twenty-one aircraft.

During the course of the month, the squadron took part in thirteen operations and dispatched 120 sorties for the loss of five Lancasters and crews.

April 1943

April would prove to be the least rewarding month of the Ruhr campaign, but this was partly because of the number of operations directed away from the region and beyond the range of Oboe. There were promotions to the rank of flight lieutenant for a number of the senior pilots, and as a three-flight unit, the squadron would now be expected to support major operations with increasing numbers. The month began in inauspicious fashion, with what would appear to be the senseless loss of a flight commander on the 1st. S/L O'Donoghue and crew took off in ED626 at 04.29 loaded with ten 1,000 pounders to drop on Emmerich, a small town with oil storage facilities nestling on the east bank of the Rhine on the border with Holland north of the Ruhr. It is known that S/L O'Donoghue carried out his attack and was last heard of shortly after 07.00 seeking a fix while over Holland in broad daylight. On the same day German radio reported that a Lancaster had been shot down by Ofw Timm of 3./JG1 and had crashed at 07.22 three miles east of Harderwijk in central Holland, and all on board had lost their lives.

The new month began for a small number of other 1 Group crews with the detailing of ten Lancasters and four Wellingtons to take part on the 2nd in the final raids under the January Directive against St-Nazaire and Lorient. Five Lancasters and two Wellingtons were part of an overall force of fifty-five aircraft assigned to the former, while forty-seven aircraft, including five Lancasters and two Wellingtons dealt with the latter. Little post-raid information was forthcoming, but both targets were by now in a state of ruin and largely devoid of civilians.

The Lancaster and Halifax stations received orders on the 3rd to prepare for an operation against Essen that night, for which the Krupp complex was designated as the aiming point for a force of 225 Lancasters and 113 Halifaxes. 1 Group contributed seventy-two of the Lancasters, and this would be the first time that more than two hundred of the type were involved in a single operation. 103 Squadron loaded a record seventeen participating aircraft with a cookie and six SBCs each of 4lb and 30lb incendiaries and dispatched them from Elsham Wolds between 19.32 and 19.50 with no fewer than six pilots of flight lieutenant rank taking the lead. They set course via Sheringham for Egmond on the Dutch coast to approach the target from the north, and there were no early returns to reduce the squadron's impact. Almost clear skies prevailed over the central Ruhr, and because of uncertainty by the meteorological section of the likely weather conditions, the Path Finders had prepared both sky and ground marking plans, which led to a degree of confusion among the main force crews as to which they should direct their bombs. Most picked up the red skymarkers when a dozen miles north of the target over Dorsten, before responding to red and green release-point flares supplemented by TIs on the ground. The bombing by the Elsham Wolds crews was carried out from 12,500 to 20,000 feet between 22.04 and 22.22, and many explosions were witnessed as were fires emitting large volumes of smoke. Sgt Ryan and crew landed at Manston minus their ailerons, which had fallen off over the target causing a debate over whether violent evasive action or flak had been responsible. The glow from the burning city was reported as still visible to some from the Dutch coast homebound, and the consensus was of a successful raid. This was confirmed by bombing photographs and local reports, which spoke of widespread destruction in central and western districts, where 635 buildings had been reduced to rubble and many more seriously damaged. The searchlight and flak defence had been intense, and it became an expensive night for the Command, which registered the loss of a dozen Halifaxes and nine Lancasters, representing 6% of those dispatched, but it was the respective loss rates of the types that was most telling, with the Halifaxes suffering 10.62% compared with 4% for the Lancasters.

The largest non-1,000 force to date of 577 aircraft was made ready on the 4th for an attack that night on the naval and shipbuilding port of Kiel, for which 1 Group put up sixty-seven Lancasters and twenty-seven Wellingtons, fifteen of the former representing 103 Squadron. Each was loaded with eleven 1,000 pounders before departing Elsham Wolds between 20.30 and 20.47 with five pilots of flight lieutenant rank leading the squadron into battle. They began the North Sea crossing at Mablethorpe and headed on an east-north-easterly track to Mandø Island before traversing southern Jutland to reach the Baltic for an approach to the target from the North. P/O Crampton and crew reached the midpoint of the North Sea contending with excessive fuel consumption and an inability to climb beyond 15,500 feet and decided not to continue, while F/L England and crew made it all the way to Nordborg at the start of the bombing run, before being forced by two ailing starboard engines to jettison the load and turn for home. The remainder reached the target area, where they were guided towards the aiming point by yellow route marker flares released by the Path Finder heavy brigade either side of 23.00. On arrival, Kiel was found to be concealed beneath ten-tenths cloud with tops at around 6,000 feet and good visibility above, and the bombing was carried out by the 103 Squadron crews on the glow of fires below the cloud from 16,500 to 20,000 feet between 23.02 and 23.23. A dozen aircraft failed to return, just one belonging to 1 Group, and crews had little to report at debriefing having been unable to assess the outcome.

Bombing photos revealed only cloud, and it was left to a post-raid analysis to conclude that decoy fires were operating, and probably lured away a proportion of the effort. The strong wind had also played its part by causing the markers to drift, leading astray a proportion of the main force to miss the target altogether. According to local reports, only eleven houses were destroyed, and this was a major disappointment in view of the size of the force involved.

Before the next operation was announced, a number of postings took place on the 5th. Acting S/L Temperley was posted out to 1503 BAT Flight, almost certainly to shed his acting rank, F/O Cook RAAF went to 156 Squadron of the Path Finders and S/L Prickett came in from 1656 Conversion Unit to assume the role of flight commander.

Gale-force winds kept much of the Command on the ground for the ensuing three days, when gusts of up to 80 m.p.h. caused minor damage to buildings at a number of locations. The wind remained strong on the 8th, but it would not be allowed to disrupt the continuation of the Ruhr offensive and the targeting that night of Duisburg. A mixed force of 379 Lancasters, Wellingtons, Halifaxes and Stirlings was assembled as the heavy element, while ten Oboe Mosquitos were to provide the initial marking. 1 Group was responsible for thirty-eight of the Lancasters and twenty-nine Wellingtons, ten of the former belonging to 103 Squadron, each of which was loaded with a cookie and twelve SBCs of 4lb and 30lb incendiaries before departing Elsham Wolds between 21.00 and 21.14 with F/Ls Bickers, Blumenauer, Crich, Day, England and Lee-Brown the senior pilots on duty. They set course for Egmond via Sheringham and reached the western Ruhr to encounter ten-tenths cloud with tops in places as high as 20,000 feet. Such conditions completely nullified the Path Finders' attempts to mark either the route or the target, and the bombing had to be carried out on e.t.a., some crews embarking on a time-and-distance run from as far away as the Dutch coast as the last visual reference. The 103 Squadron crews attacked from 17,000 to 20,500 feet between 23.25 and 23.43 and had nothing of value to pass on to the intelligence section at debriefing. When ED701 landed at Elsham Wolds at 02.12, the Maddern crew was declared tour-expired, and they were the first to complete a tour for seven months. So many of their contemporaries had perished between the twentieth and thirtieth operations, Greig, Roper and Austin among them, and it was a boost to the whole squadron to finally cheer them through the main gates on their way to the station at Barnetby Junction and the promise of a further six months of life before their recall for a second tour. Nineteen aircraft were missing, two Lancasters and three Wellingtons from 1 Group in return for which, according to local sources, a widely scattered raid had hit at least fifteen other Ruhr locations and destroyed just forty buildings in Duisburg.

Not content with the outcome, Harris ordered another raid twenty-four hours later, only this time employing a much-reduced force of 104 Lancasters and five Mosquitos. 1 Group detailed thirty-four Lancasters, of which the eight representing 103 Squadron departed Elsham Wolds between 20.40 and 21.16, the late take-off that of W/O Denwood and crew, who would succeed in making up the deficit. The newly-promoted S/L England was the senior pilot on duty as they settled onto the same northerly route to the target as twenty-four hours earlier, via the Dutch coast at Egmond. There were no early returns, and the main force crews were guided to the target by red route-marker flares and then red and green skymarkers over the aiming point, which was hidden by ten-tenths cloud with tops at 5,000 to 15,000 feet. The 103 Squadron crews delivered their cookie and twelve SBCs each from 19,200 to 22,000 feet between 23.02 and 23.06, some observing a large red glow reflected in the clouds. F/L Bickers and crew came back with a badly shot-up ED724 and a mortally wounded rear gunner, Sgt Howell, after an encounter with a night-fighter near Alkmaar on the way home. A forced-landing near Bodney at 01.16 completed the destruction of the Lancaster, happily though, without further casualties among the crew. W/O Denwood's ED701 was attacked by a BF109 as it left the target, but all three gun turrets opened up and scored strikes on the assailant's belly. Half an hour later, when a second BF109 tried its luck, the rear gunner poured rounds into it causing pieces to fly off, and ultimately it went down in a vertical dive before exploding at 8,000 feet. Local sources confirmed that this was another highly scattered raid, which spread bombs over a wide area of the Ruhr and destroyed only fifty houses in Duisburg.

Frankfurt was posted as the destination for 502 aircraft on the 10th, on a night when Wellingtons represented the most populous type, demonstrating that this trusty old warhorse still had an important part to play in Bomber Command operations. 1 Group provided forty-six of 136 Lancasters and twenty-eight Wellingtons, fourteen of the former made ready by 103 Squadron at Elsham Wolds and given the standard payload of a cookie and twelve SBCs. They took off between 23.42 and 00.01 with the recently arrived F/L Brown the senior pilot on duty and flew out over Dungeness to make landfall on the French coast between Dieppe and Cayeux-sur-Mer. P/O Ewer and crew turned back within the hour because of engine issues leaving the others to enter Germany south of Luxembourg, pinpointing finally on Oppenheim to the south-west of Frankfurt, leaving a final leg to the aiming point of some twenty miles. Ten-tenths cloud had formed a backdrop all the way, and crews had to carry out time-and-distance runs from green route marker flares, those from 103 Squadron delivering their loads from 16,500 to 20,000 feet between 02.49 and 03.10. No one saw anything other than an apparent glow of fires beneath the cloud, and bombing photos would reveal nothing, while local reports suggested that most of the bombing had missed the city altogether.

208 Lancaster crews were notified on the 13th of a change of scenery for their next operation, which was to be against the docks at La Spezia on Italy's northern coast some forty miles south-east of Genoa. 1 Group detailed seventy-five Lancasters, with the remainder provided by 5 and 8 Groups, the latter also sending three Halifaxes as part of the marker force. 103 Squadron loaded twenty of its Lancasters with five 1,000 pounders and two SBCs each of 4lb and 30lb incendiaries and sent them on their way from Elsham Wolds between 20.13 and 20.33 with W/C Carter and S/Ls England and Prickett the senior pilots on duty. They rendezvoused with the rest of the bomber stream as they made their way south to begin the Channel crossing at Selsey Bill on course for Cabourg on the French coast, before setting course for Lake Bourget, at which pinpoint they were to turn south, traverse the Alps and adopt a south-easterly track to the target. S/L England and crew were led astray by a defective compass, a problem discovered as they approached Marseilles, by which time it was too late to reach the target in time.

The others arrived on the Italian side of the Alps to find almost cloudless skies and only haze and smoke to mar the vertical visibility, but the Path Finders lit up the aiming point with white flares to enable main force crews to establish their positions in relation to it by visual reference of ground detail, such as rivers and the docks. The 103 Squadron crews delivered their attacks from 7,000 to 16,000 feet between 01.40 and 02.14 and observed that three large vessels tied together east of the outer harbour appeared to be on fire, and the naval oil stores was also in the firing line. By the later stages of the raid, many fires had added to the smoke obscuring the town, and a number of large explosions encouraged the crews' belief that a successful operation had taken place, which ultimately, would be confirmed. Sgt Stoneman and crew had their wireless damaged by flak over the target and their fuel tanks holed by intense light flak as they crossed the French coast homebound. They were forced to ditch some fifty miles off Falmouth and waited in the dinghy until rescue came after just four hours. Remarkably, W4318 remained afloat for more than thirty hours, and an attempt was made to tow it to land, but the tow rope broke, and the gallant Lancaster slipped beneath the waves. Three aircraft from other squadrons landed on recently captured airfields in North Africa and were the first to do so before so-called "shuttle-raids" became a feature of operations to the Mediterranean region. Only W/C Carter landed back at Elsham Wolds, while the others were spread around a number of diversionary airfields, and their late return ensured that the squadron would not participate in that night's attack on Stuttgart. W4828 failed to return with the crew of F/L Lee-Brown, and it was established eventually that the Lancaster had been on the way home when brought down near Le Mans with fatal consequences for the occupants.

The busy round of non-Ruhr operations continued at Stuttgart, for which a force of 462 aircraft was made ready on the 14th, fourteen of the Lancasters and thirty-two of the Wellingtons provided by 1 Group. They adopted the standard route across France, hugging the Belgian and Luxembourg frontiers until turning east near Strasbourg to approach the city from the north-east. They were greeted by clear skies, but haze, aggravated by smoke rising through 8,000 feet, made ground detail indistinct. The aiming point was established by the green and red Path Finder TIs, but few crews were able to make out the impact of their own bombs and noted only a concentration of fires and considerable amounts of smoke. Post-raid reconnaissance revealed that the Path Finders had marked the centre of the city, but that a "creep-back" had developed, which had spread back along the line of approach. Creep-back was a feature of many large raids and was caused by crews bombing the first fires they came upon, rather than pushing through to the planned aiming point. It could work for or against the effectiveness of the attack, and on this night, worked in the Command's favour by falling across the industrial district of Bad-Canstatt, before spreading further back along the line of approach onto the residential suburbs of Münster and Mühlhausen. It was here that the majority of the 393 buildings were destroyed and more than nine hundred others severely damaged.

When Germany took Czechoslovakia under its wing, it acquired for itself the important Skoda armaments work at Pilsen, which was to be the main target on the 16th for a force of 327 Lancasters and Halifaxes, while a force of 271 aircraft, consisting predominantly of Wellingtons and Stirlings, created a large-scale diversion at Mannheim some 240 miles to the west. 197 Lancasters and 130 Halifaxes were detailed for Pilsen, of which sixty-eight of the former were provided by 1 Group. The plan of attack called for the Path Finders to drop route markers at the final turning point, seven miles from the target, which the crews were to then locate visually in the anticipated bright moonlight, and bomb from as low a level as practicable. It was a complicated plan that invited confusion and failure, and the outcome would question the quality of some of the briefings. 103 Squadron made ready sixteen Lancasters, loading them with a cookie and three 1,000 pounders each, before dispatching them from Elsham Wolds between 20.58 and 21.24 with S/L England the senior pilot on duty.

Ahead of them lay a round-trip of some 1,500 miles, most of it over the same route adopted forty-eight hours previously but passing north of Stuttgart and Nuremberg as they tracked east towards the Czech frontier. They had been briefed to cross the fighter belt at 1,500 feet before climbing gradually to a bombing height of around 7,000 feet. Those reaching the target area on this night of confusion found the forecast favourable weather conditions, with a layer of eight-tenths cloud at between 8,000 and 15,000 feet, below which, visibility was good and ground features could be identified. The briefings should have made clear that the bombing was to be carried out visually from below the cloud base after making a timed run from the turning-point, which had been marked by TIs. Many main force crews reported bombing from 7,000 to 10,000 feet visually and on TIs between 01.42 and 01.55, proving that they had failed to understand and comply with the instructions at briefing, and had bombed the turning point. Crews made reference to yellow and green TIs and white illuminator flares, but all described difficulty in locating and identifying the factory buildings, some after spending time searching and dodging searchlights and flak. The 103 Squadron crews carried out their attacks from 6,000 to 9,000 feet between 01.42 and 02.35 and reported many cookies bursting in open country and intense night-fighter activity in the Mannheim area on the way home. The details of the crew reports demonstrated that they could not have related to the Skoda works.

Post-raid reconnaissance revealed the truth, that despite the claims of returning crews, no bombs had fallen within miles of the factory, and had been concentrated instead around an asylum at Dobrany, some seven miles to the south-west. On return, Sgt Steel and crew reported being hit by flak over Stuttgart and letting their bombs go there, the cookie setting off a fire. Sgt Ryan and crew lost the use of their navigational aids and, failing to locate the primary target, also bombed in the Stuttgart area. Sgt Pettigrew and crew were almost on top of the target when ensnared in a cone of some thirty searchlights and hit by flak, which persuaded them to dump the bombs "safe" and head for home. The disappointment at the scale of the failure of this operation was compounded by the loss of thirty-six aircraft, split equally between the two types, and eighteen aircraft were also missing from the Mannheim contingent, which had, at least, achieved the destruction of 130 buildings and damage to some degree to three thousand others. The combined casualty figure of fifty-four aircraft represented 11% of those dispatched and a new record for a single night, although fourteen of these came down in the sea and a proportion of the crews were rescued. 103 Squadron was represented among the missing by the crew of Sgt Mooney RNZAF in W4848, which crashed somewhere in southern Germany, delivering the flight engineer and bomb-aimer into enemy hands as the only survivors.

On each station, a small team belonging to the Committee of Adjustment was on hand to remove all trace of missing men from their billets and gather their belongings to pass on to relatives. Within hours, the accommodation would be occupied by someone new, and this process would become part of the fabric of life on a bomber station, the faces of the missing soon fading from the memory. Some of the lucky ones who evaded capture to return to a squadron within weeks or months, were generally astounded at how few faces they recognised.

W/C Carter concluded his tour as commanding officer on the 17th and was appointed station commander at Elsham Wolds. He was succeeded at 103 Squadron by W/C Slater, who came in from 1656 Conversion Unit on the same day, having served earlier in the war with 150 Squadron. He presided over his first operation on the following night, when a return to the docks in the Italian naval base at La Spezia was notified to the Lancaster squadrons of 1, 5 and 8 Groups, and 8 Group would also contribute five Halifaxes to the overall force of 178 aircraft. The sixty-two 1 Group Lancasters included seventeen representing 103 Squadron, which were loaded with five 1,000 pounders and two SBCs each of 4lb and 30lb incendiaries, before departing Elsham Wolds between 20.54 and 21.08 with S/L Prickett the senior pilot on duty. Sgt Burton's starboard-outer engine burst into flames shortly after taking off and he and his crew proceeded to the jettison area, to be followed soon afterwards by Sgt Rudge and crew, who also experienced engine issues, leaving the others to adopt the familiar route to this region via Selsey Bill, Cabourg, Lake Bourget and the Alps. On the way near Chartres, P/O Carey and crew turned back after the navigator became unwell, but the remainder negotiated the outward flight and found the weather to be ideal with bright moonlight and good visibility in the target area, although an effective smoke screen partially obscured the town and docks until it drifted to the south to hang over the gulf. The aiming point was identified visually and confirmed by red Path Finder TIs, on which the 103 Squadron crews bombed from 8,000 to 10,000 feet between 01.51 and 02.07. The fires were becoming concentrated as they turned away and set course for home, completely satisfied with their night's work. Photographic reconnaissance revealed that the marking and bombing had missed the dockyards to the north-west but had caused extensive damage to the railway station and public buildings in the town centre.

Orders were received on the 20th to prepare for another long-range operation that night, this one against the port of Stettin, situated 640 miles away as the crow flies at the midpoint of Germany's wartime Baltic coast. 1 Group contributed seventy Lancasters to the force of 339 aircraft, sixteen of them belonging to 103 Squadron, whose crews learned at briefing that the route would take the bomber stream across the North Sea to a point north of Esbjerg on the Danish coast, before traversing Jutland at 5,000 feet to avoid night-fighters and to then head south-east towards the target. They would be sitting on a cookie and fourteen SBCs of 4lb and 30lb incendiaries as they departed Elsham Wolds between 21.30 and 21.43 with S/L England the senior pilot on duty and W/C Slater flying as second pilot to F/L Day. It was a night of clear skies and good visibility, which assisted the Path Finders in delivering a perfect marking performance, which was exploited by the main force crews to devastating effect. The Elsham Wolds contingent arrived to find the city laid out before them with the river, built-up area and the docks clearly defined, and the aiming point marked by green TIs. They carried out their attacks from 10,000 to 12,300 feet between 01.10 and 01.20, and on return reported fires raging across the built-up area and the glow from the burning port-city visible for a hundred miles into the return journey. Twenty-one aircraft failed to return, eight of them 1 Group Lancasters, and 103 Squadron was represented by ED614, which was shot down by a night-fighter at the Danish coast while outbound and crashed four miles south-west of Ribe at 00.22 with fatal consequences for the crew of Sgt Pettigrew. There were targets, like Duisburg, that seemed to enjoy something of a charmed life, and managed to dodge the worst ravages of a Bomber Command attack, but Stettin was not among them, perhaps because of its location near an easily identifiable coastline. It was thirty-six hours before a reconnaissance aircraft captured photographs of the still-burning city, and these revealed an area of one hundred acres of devastation across the centre. Local reports confirmed that thirteen industrial premises and 380 houses had been destroyed.

Orders on the 26th signalled a return to the Ruhr and Duisburg, for which a large force of 561 aircraft was assembled, the numbers bolstered by the inclusion of 135 Wellingtons, while 215 Lancasters represented the largest contribution by type. 1 Group was responsible for sixty-two Lancasters and thirty-one Wellingtons, sixteen of the former representing 103 Squadron and departing Elsham Wolds between 23.59 and 00.35 with S/Ls England and Prickett the senior pilots on duty and each Lancaster carrying a cookie and a dozen SBCs of 4lb and 30lb incendiaries. They set course to make landfall on the Dutch coast north of The Hague and reached the target area after approaching from the north-east, finding largely clear skies and good visibility. They were guided to the aiming point by red and green TIs, before delivering their payloads from 17,000 to 21,000 feet between 02.18 and 02.49 in the face of a hostile defence which included two to three hundred searchlights combing the sky, and a flak barrage up to the usual standard of ferocity. Sgt Egan's ED773 was hit by flak, which caused damage to the port-inner engine, the rear mainplane and flap, the windscreen, rudders and bomb doors, but they would make it home to a safe landing. Bomb bursts gave rise to many fires, although opinions were divided as to the degree of concentration achieved. A large orange explosion was witnessed to the east of the aiming point at 02.34, but fires had not fully gained a hold by the time that the force withdrew, although black smoke was rising through 7,000 feet. Seventeen aircraft failed to return, but none on this occasion from 1 Group. Post-raid reconnaissance revealed that the attack had fallen short of the city centre and had been focussed on the north-eastern districts under the line of approach, thus sparing Duisburg yet again from the full weight of a Bomber Command raid. Even so, local reports confirmed the destruction of more than three hundred buildings, which represented something of a telling blow upon this target.

The 27th was devoted to the largest mining operation of the war to date, which involved 160 aircraft targeting the waters off the Brittany and Biscay coasts and the Frisians. Sixteen Wellingtons and fifteen Lancasters were detailed by 1 Group, five made ready at Elsham Wolds for the crews of F/Ls Brown and Crich and Sgts Powell, Steel and Winchester. They departed Elsham Wolds between 21.45 and 21.58 at the start of a seven-hundred-mile outward flight to the Furze garden, located off St-Jean-de-Luz, almost at the frontier between France and Spain. Each Lancaster was carrying five 1,500lb mines as they flew out over Selsey Bill and headed for the Normandy coast and all arrived in the target area to encounter cloud, which defeated F/L Crich and crew despite a search lasing forty-five minutes and they brought their vegetables home. Sgt Powell and crew were hit by light flak during the timed run, lost their starboard-outer engine and sustained other damage, but they and the other three crews fulfilled their briefs before returning safely.

The following night brought an even larger gardening effort involving 207 aircraft, of which twenty-five Lancasters and a dozen Wellingtons were provided by 1 Group, seven of the former by 103 Squadron. Their destinations were in the Baltic, the 103 Squadron contingent assigned to gardens in the Gulf of Danzig, Privet and Tangerine, the latter off Baltiysk, now in Russia, the most distant of all mining areas. Taking into account the routing via the west coast of Denmark, this constituted a round-trip of 1,600 miles, for which they departed Elsham Wolds between 20.57 and 21.06 and lost the services of Sgt King and crew immediately to a failed port-outer engine. The others all reached their assigned target areas and delivered four mines each from 1,000 to 1,500 feet between 01.18 and 01.58, but Sgt Nicholson and crew were shot down by a night-fighter while homebound from Tangerine, and crashed without survivors at 02.20 at Jordrup in Jutland. Stern opposition was encountered by the rest of the mining force and twenty-two aircraft failed to return, six of them belonging to 1 Group. This would be the largest-ever loss to result in a single night from mining, but on the credit side, the number of mines delivered, 593, was also a record for one night and would not be surpassed.

Essen was posted as the target for a "blind" bombing raid on the 30th, as attention swung once more towards the Ruhr, and would remain upon it almost exclusively now until well into July. A force of 305 aircraft included sixty-five Lancasters from 1 Group, of which sixteen were each loaded with a cookie and twelve SBCs of 4lb incendiaries at Elsham Wolds and took off between 23.48 and 00.50 with S/Ls England and Prickett the senior pilots on duty. P/O Carey and crew dropped out because of engine issues while climbing over the station, leaving the others to fly out over Sheringham on course for the Dutch coast at Egmond. F/L Brown and crew were beyond the midpoint of the North Sea crossing when a fluctuating starboard-outer engine persuaded them to turn back, saving them from having to negotiate a layer of ice-bearing cloud across the bomber stream's path. Those reaching the target were greeted by ten-tenths cloud with tops in places as high as 21,000 feet, and red and green Oboe-laid Wanganui flares (skymarkers) identifying the aiming point. Some 5 Group crews carried out a time-and-distance run from green tracking markers, and all of the Elsham Wolds crews had some kind of flare in the bomb sight or at least the glow of one, as they released their loads from 19,000 to 23,000 feet between 02.37 and 02.44. Returning crews reported the glow of fires beneath the cloud and a number of large explosions, but it was impossible to determine whether concentration had been achieved, particularly as bombing photos showed only cloud. Post-raid reconnaissance and local sources confirmed a lack of concentration and the liberal distribution of bombs onto ten other Ruhr locations, particularly Bottrop to the north, but 189 buildings were destroyed and 237 severely damaged in Essen, and manufacturing units in the Krupp districts sustained further damage.

During the course of the month, the squadron took part in fourteen operations and dispatched a record 177 sorties for the loss of six Lancasters, five complete crews and a rear gunner. Nine sorties had been abortive, and this represented a continuation of the excellent serviceability rate achieved by the squadron, for which the ground staff deserved enormous credit.

May 1943

May would bring a return to winning ways, with a number of outstanding successes and new records as the Ruhr offensive expanded its horizons to include targets other than Essen and Duisburg. The first of these "new" targets was Dortmund, which had been attacked many times before, but not on the scale that it was about to face on the 4th, when a force of 596 aircraft represented the largest non-1,000 effort to date. 1 Group made available seventy-six Lancasters and thirty-four Wellingtons, nineteen of the former belonging to 103 Lancasters, each with a cookie and twelve SBCs of 4lb and 30lb incendiaries in its bomb bay. They departed Elsham Wolds between 21.56 and 22.34 with S/L Prickett the senior pilot on duty and the "Mad Belgian", P/O Van Rolleghem undertaking his first sortie since arriving from 1656 Conversion Unit on the 28th. They flew out over Mablethorpe to pinpoint on the northern tip of Texel before turning to the south-east to a point just inside Germany for the final leg to the target. S/L Prickett and crew returned early with an unserviceable rear turret, while the others pushed on across Holland and made their way to the eastern end of the Ruhr, where they found clear skies, good visibility, and only industrial and smoke haze to spoil the vertical view. Yellow Path Finder tracking skymarkers were useful as the starting point for a timed run to the target, while the defences responded with many searchlight cones and intense heavy flak, and much evasive action would be required after bombing to vacate the target area intact.

The initial Path Finder marking was accurately placed around the city centre, but some of the backing-up fell short, and a decoy site was also successful in luring away a proportion of the bombing. The 103 Squadron crews bombed on red or green TIs from 18,000 to 21,000 feet between 01.04 and 01.51, and on return reported many sizeable explosions, including a particularly large on at 01.12, which may have been the one reported by a 50 Squadron crew that threw flame to a height of 2,000 feet and burned for ten seconds. They also described developing fires, the glow from which could be seen, according to some, from 150 miles into the return flight. Post-raid reconnaissance revealed that approximately half of the force had bombed within three miles of the aiming point and the rest had been lured away by misplaced back-up markers and a decoy fire site. Post-raid reconnaissance and local sources confirmed the destruction of 1,218 buildings, with serious damage to more than two thousand others and a death toll of 693 people, which was a record resulting from a Bomber Command attack. It was not a one-sided affair, however, and the loss of thirty-one aircraft was a foretaste of what was in store for the bomber crews operating over "Happy Valley". 1 Group posted missing five aircraft, but all from Elsham Wolds returned safely.

The heavy squadrons were rested during the ensuing week until the 12th, when Duisburg was posted as the target for a heavy force of 562 aircraft with ten Oboe Mosquitos to take care of the initial marking. 1 Group was responsible for sixty-one of the 238 Lancasters, and they would be accompanied by 142 Halifaxes, 112 Wellingtons, thirty-two of them representing 1 Group, and seventy Stirlings. Twenty-one 103 Squadron Lancasters were made ready, nineteen loaded with the standard cookie and incendiary mix and two with three 2,000 and six 1,000 pounders, before departing Elsham Wolds between 23.33 and 00.24 with S/L England the senior pilot on duty. They began the North Sea crossing at Sheringham to make landfall on the other side over Egmond and soon lost the services of F/Sgt Rose and crew to severe icing. The others reached the target area guided by yellow tracking flares and found ideal bombing conditions with no cloud and good visibility, which helped the Path Finders to mark with great accuracy and focus. The main force crews were able to identify ground features and exploited the opportunity by producing a display of unusually concentrated bombing. The 103 Squadron crews released their loads onto red and green TIs from 17,000 to 22,000 feet between 02.04 and 02.36, contributing to a bomb tonnage greater than that delivered by the "Thousand" force at Cologne a year earlier. For the first time at this elusive target the attack proceeded according to plan and the city finally succumbed to a devastating assault. Returning crews described a large explosion at 02.30, streets outlined by fire and a highly successful outcome, the best yet witnessed by some, and their impressions were confirmed by photo-reconnaissance, which revealed extensive damage in the city centre and the Ruhrort Rhine docks, the largest inland port in Germany. 1,596 buildings were totally destroyed and the Thyssen steelworks was hit, while sixty thousand tons of shipping was sunk or damaged. However, many crews were absent from debriefing at stations across the Command, and it soon became clear that the success had been gained at the heavy cost of thirty-four aircraft. The loss rates by type again made interesting reading and confirmed the established food chain, the Lancasters sustaining a 4.2% loss, compared with 8.9% for Wellingtons, 7.1% for Stirlings and 6.3% for Halifaxes. Such was the level of destruction that Duisburg would now be left in peace for a year.

While 5 Group and elements of 8 Group were briefed on the 13th for a return to Pilsen to attempt to rectify the recent failure at the Skoda works, Bochum was selected to host the latest round in the Ruhr campaign. A force of 442 aircraft included eighty-four Lancasters and thirty-three Wellingtons provided by 1 Group, a record twenty-two of the former made ready at Elsham Wolds, where seven were loaded with three 2,000 and six 1,000 pounders each and the remainder with the standard city-busting cookie and twelve SBCs. They took off between 23.08 and 23.44 with S/L England the senior pilot on duty and adopted a southerly route into the central Ruhr via Southwold and the Scheldt estuary, followed by passage across Belgium in what was a kind of "back door" approach over Mönchengladbach and between Düsseldorf to the north and Cologne to the south. It was believed at the time that a corridor existed through the flak belt, but this proved not to be the case, and some crews experienced a torrid time crossing the Rhine. The crew of Sgt Presland abandoned their sortie because of an engine issue before reaching enemy territory and F/L Bickers and crew were well on their way when let down by an unserviceable rear turret. Sgt Stoneman and crew were four miles south of the target at 18,000 feet when all four engines were hit by flak and one burst into flames, upon which the bombs were jettisoned "live" at 02.28. Sgt Rudge and crew jettisoned their bombs in the target area from 2,000 feet, and we must assume that they had shed around eighteen thousand feet of altitude in evading searchlights. The remainder benefitted from good weather conditions and approached Bochum under clear skies and with good visibility, the 103 Squadron crews delivering their bomb loads onto red target indicators from 18,000 to 25,000 feet (P/O Ewer) in the face of a spirited flak defence between 02.03 and 02.35. The usual large explosions were observed, one in particular that sent a pall of black smoke skyward, suggesting that someone had "struck oil". The effects of the raid were visible from the Dutch coast, and all of the Elsham Wolds crews returned very satisfied with their night's work. It was established later, that decoy markers had drawn off a

182

proportion of the bombing, but the attack had destroyed 394 buildings and seriously damaged a further seven hundred at a cost to the Command of twenty-four aircraft, three from 1 Group. Meanwhile, the attack on the Skoda works had failed again to achieve the hoped-for results.

A signal from HQ Bomber Command on the 14th warned stations that, except for an emergency, there would be no major operations during the moon period. This was convenient for 460 Squadron RAAF, which had been notified a month earlier of a move to Binbrook in north-east Lincolnshire. The station was commanded by the Australian G/C Hughie Edwards VC, who had been in post since February and had twice commanded 2 Group's 105 Squadron earlier in the war. It was at this time that 617 Squadron entered bomber folklore with its epic attack on the Ruhr Dams under Operation Chastise on the night of the 16/17th.

1 Group called thirteen freshman crews to briefings at Elsham Wolds, Holme-on-Spalding-Moor and Binbrook on the 18th and informed them that they would be engaged that night in mining activities off the southern Biscay coast, respectively in the Elderberry, Furze and Deodar gardens off Biarritz, St-Jean-de-Luz and in the Gironde estuary. Assigned to Elderberry, the six 103 Squadron participants took off between 21.50 and 21.55 with F/O Shanahan the senior pilot on duty and each Lancaster carrying six mines, and lost the services of Sgt Winchester and crew to wireless failure before reaching enemy territory. The others encountered unexpected cloud in the target area, which prevented the crews of F/O Shanahan and W/O Ratcliff from locating the target area and they brought their stores home. Sgt Powell and crew delivered their vegetables into the briefed location from 2,000 feet at 01.34, and F/O Van Rolleghem and crew followed up at 02.02 from 1,200 feet after pinpointing on Cap Higuer. Sgt Presland and crew employed Pointe-de-Bravity as the starting point for their timed run and dropped the mines from 5,000 feet at 02.15.

By the time that the next major operation was launched on the 23rd, the main force squadrons had undergone an expansion with the addition to many units of a third or C Flight, which, in most cases, would eventually be hived off to form the nucleus of a brand-new squadron. The giant force of 826 aircraft was the largest non-1,000 force to date and surpassed the previous record set three weeks earlier by a clear 230 aircraft. The number of available Lancasters had leapt by eighty-eight, Halifaxes by forty-eight, Stirlings by forty and Wellingtons by forty-one, and their destination for the second time in the month was to be Dortmund. The entire Command was rested and replenished and ready to resume the Ruhr offensive, and activity on all participating stations was hectic. 1 Group detailed a record 180 aircraft, 122 of them Lancasters of which a record twenty-seven were made ready by 103 Squadron, the armourers working miracles to provide each with a bomb load of a cookie and twelve SBCs of 4lb and 30lb incendiaries. They departed Elsham Wolds in two waves, the first between 22.12 and 22.28 with S/L Prickett and the newly promoted S/L Day the senior pilots on duty, and the second between 22.46 and 23.10 with S/L England last away and set course via Sheringham for the Dutch coast north of Alkmaar. Sgt Bunten and crew dropped out with a failed a.s.i. when just a few miles out, while the others all reached the target area to find clear skies but considerable industrial haze, which, before the advent of Oboe, would have rendered the attack a lottery. Now, the thirteen Path Finder Mosquitos marked the centre of the city accurately, and the Path Finder heavy brigade backed-up to maintain the aiming point with red and green TIs, which could be seen from twenty miles away on approach, as could the yellow track markers assisting the early 5 Group arrivals for their time-and-distance runs. The 103 Squadron crews bombed largely on the clusters of red and green TIs from 18,500 to 24,000 feet between 01.01 and 01.58, observing many explosions and fires, which were merging into a large area of conflagration with thick columns of black smoke rising up through 18,000 feet as the bombers turned away.

On return, Sgt Winchester and crew reported that W4901 had its port-outer engine burst into flames during the bombing run, but the fire was extinguished, the bombs dropped on the aiming point, and a safe landing brought a happy ending. An inspection revealed .303 bullet holes in the aircraft, which demonstrated this to be a "friendly fire" incident. Sgt Breckon and crew were on their maiden operation together and were attacked multiple times by a Ju88 on the way home. Despite violent corkscrewing, the mid-upper and rear turrets sustained damage and Sgt Ferrel was reduced to rotating the mid-upper turret by hand and elevating his single serviceable gun similarly. On the ninth attack, the gunners succeeded in scoring hits, which sent the enemy aircraft into a dive, followed by an explosion on the ground that bore the characteristics of a crashing aircraft. Sgt Breckon brought the damaged W4323 to a landing at Downham Market, and on return to Elsham Wolds to tell their story, their claim of the destruction of the Ju88 was confirmed. Other returning crews reported fierce night-fighter activity over the target and on the way home, and this was reflected in the high casualty rate of thirty-eight aircraft, the largest loss of the campaign to date. Almost half of these were Halifaxes and eight were Lancasters, 1 Group posting missing a total of nine aircraft. Post-raid reconnaissance revealed the operation to have been an outstanding success, which had hit mainly central, northern and eastern districts, where almost two thousand buildings had been destroyed and some important war industry factories had suffered severe damage and loss of production. The scale of the success was such, that like Duisburg, this city would remain unmolested by the heavy brigade for a year.

The Ruhr offensive continued with the posting of Düsseldorf as the target on the 25th, for which a force of 759 aircraft was assembled, 1 Group contributing 116 Lancasters and forty-seven Wellingtons, twenty-six of the former on this occasion representing 103 Squadron. Each was given the standard cookie and incendiary bomb load and departed Elsham Wolds in two phases between 23.10 and 23.59 with S/Ls England and Prickett the senior pilots on duty. They set course via Southwold for Flushing at the mouth of the Scheldt and lost Sgt Winchester and crew to intercom failure shortly after leaving England behind. On arriving at the Dutch coast, some crews were able to observe feverish activity at the target some one hundred miles and thirty minutes flying time away. It lay beneath two layers of eight to ten-tenths thin cloud, and the generally poor visibility impacted the Path Finders' ability to back up the Mosquito-laid TIs to the extent that two red TIs were seen to be thirty miles apart. There were also decoy markers and dummy fire sites operating, which succeeded in causing confusion and prevented a concentration of bombing. The first two waves were most affected by the conditions and bombed mostly on Gee-fixes, while the third wave crews were mostly able to see green TIs clearly and would be more optimistic about the outcome than those attacking earlier. The 103 Squadron participants bombed from 19,500 to 23,000 feet between 01.38 and 02.20 and were disappointed when post-raid reconnaissance and local reports confirmed that the raid had failed to achieve concentration. It had developed into an "old-style" scattering of bombs across a wide area, leading to the destruction in Düsseldorf of fewer than a hundred buildings. Twenty-seven aircraft failed to return, and among them were seven from 1 Group.

Harris was not yet done with Essen, and the fifth visitation by the bomber force during the campaign was notified to stations on the 27th, and 518 aircraft made ready. 1 Group put up 104 Lancasters and twenty-nine Wellingtons, twenty-four of the former made ready at Elsham Wolds. They took to the skies with a standard Ruhr load between 22.22 and 23.09 with S/L England the senior pilot on duty and set course via Sheringham for the Dutch coast at Egmond. Sgt Breckon and crew lost their starboard-outer engine on take-off and proceeded directly to the jettison area, and P/O Ewer and crew aborted their sortie within an hour after becoming aware that their cookie had come loose and was resting on the bomb doors. The others pressed on to be greeted at the target by six to eight-tenths cloud with tops at 12,000 feet and tracking flares guiding them in towards the Wanganui skymarkers gently descending into the cloud tops over the aiming point. The bombing was carried out by the Elsham Wolds crews on white flares and red parachute markers with green stars from 17,500 to 23,000 feet between 00.52 and 01.33, and several large explosions were witnessed. Post-raid reconnaissance revealed that much of the bombing had fallen short, but 488 buildings had been destroyed, mostly in central and northern districts, and ten nearby towns reported themselves to be victims of collateral damage. Twenty-three aircraft failed to return, and the Halifaxes again represented almost half of the casualties. 1 Group posted missing four aircraft, but there were no empty dispersal pans at Elsham Wolds.

A force of 719 aircraft was assembled on the 29th to pitch against a new Ruhr target, the conurbation known as Wuppertal, perched on the southern rim of the Ruhr Valley east of Düsseldorf. It consisted of the towns of Barmen and Elberfeld, which were built on the proceeds of the rich coal deposits and the aiming point for this night's attack was the Barmen half at the eastern end. 1 Group contributed ninety-six Lancasters and thirty-one Wellingtons, the 103 Squadron contingent of twenty-six Lancasters departing Elsham Wolds between 22.22 and 23.27 with S/L Prickett senior pilot on duty and the standard Ruhr bomb load on board. They adopted the southern approach to the Ruhr via Southwold and the Scheldt estuary and lost the services of F/O Finlay and crew to an unserviceable rear turret within the first hour. The others ran the gauntlet of searchlights and flak in the Cologne and Düsseldorf corridor to be greeted by clear skies over the southern Ruhr, with the usual industrial haze extending up to 10,000 feet. However, the yellow tracking flares clearly identified the final turning-point, and concentrated green TIs initially marked out the aiming point before they were backed up with reds. The 103 Squadron crews carried out their attacks from 18,000 to 23,800 feet between 00.48 and 01.35, and it was clear to all that something extraordinary was taking place as the built-up area beneath them became a sea of explosions and flames with smoke rising very quickly through 15,000 feet. Post-raid reconnaissance revealed this to be the most awesomely destructive raid of the campaign thus far, which devastated by fire a thousand acres, or around 80% of the built-up area, and destroyed almost four thousand houses, five of the six largest factories and more than two hundred other industrial buildings. It would be some time before the human cost could be established, but it is now accepted that 3,400 people lost their lives during this savage Saturday night. The defenders had their say also, and fought back to claim thirty-three bombers, seven of which were Lancasters, three belonging to 1 Group.

During the course of the month, the squadron undertook eight operations and dispatched 171 sorties without loss, of which just nine were abortive, and this compared more than favourably with the 178 sorties from fourteen operations in the previous month. A number of NCO pilots received commissions, and acting F/L Blumenauer DFC and crew completed their first tour and he was packed off to 24 O.T.U. on the 28th.

June 1943

There were no major operations at the start of June in part because of the moon period, but mostly because of adverse weather conditions, and although most Lancaster stations were alerted frequently during the first ten days, no operations other than mining actually took place. On the 9th ED879 swung out of control while taking off for a night-flying test, and ended up in a ditch, where it caught fire and burned out. F/Sgt Egan and his crew emerged unscathed, but as so often happened, an accident seemed to portend a loss a short time later. The operation for which the air test was required was cancelled fifty minutes before take-off.

The Path Finder and main force crews were kicking their heels on the ground until the 11th, when Düsseldorf was briefed out to 783 crews. 1 Group was responsible for 128 of the 326 Lancasters and fifty Wellingtons, and 103 Squadron surpassed its record when making ready twenty-eight of its own and filling their bomb bays with a cookie and SBCs of incendiaries. In the event, twenty-seven departed Elsham Wolds between 22.51 and 23.27 with S/Ls Day and England the senior pilots on duty and set course via Sheringham for Walcheren Island in the Scheldt estuary. The bomber stream had to negotiate icing, static and lightning conditions in towering cloud with tops in places as high as 24,000 feet as they made their way across the North Sea, and this proved sufficient on its own or caused malfunctions that persuaded many crews to abandon their sorties. Sgt Powell's port engines cut out intermittently, P/O Carey's navigator became unwell, F/O Finlay's port-outer engine caught fire and Sgt Wishart's instrument panel iced up, but the remaining 103 Squadron participants pressed on and were rewarded as the cloud dissipated to leave just small amounts at 2,000, 5,000 and 10,000 feet, dependent upon the time of their arrival on final approach to the target.

Those in the vanguard of the main force were drawn on by yellow tracking flares from 01.05, and red skymarkers with green stars at 01.16, while those a little further back in the bomber stream were guided by red and green skymarkers. The 5 Group crews carried out time-and-distance runs to the aiming point five minutes away, noting that fires were beginning to build and join together. The Paramatta marking (ground-marking TIs) did not seem to appear until these crews were turning away, but they were clearly visible to those in the rear-guard, who described a sea of flames covering a massive area and columns of smoke rising through 21,000 feet. The 103 Squadron effort was spread throughout the duration of the raid, and attacks were carried out from 18,500 to 23,500 feet between 01.23 and 02.21. Returning crews passed on their impressions to the intelligence section at debriefing, but there were many absentees, and when all aircraft had been accounted for, thirty-eight were found to be missing, a figure that equalled the heaviest loss of the offensive to date. 103 Squadron posted missing the crew of Sgt Scholes in ED914, which had been shot down when homebound by the night-fighter of Lt Hans-Heinz Augustein of III./NJG1 and had crashed at 02.53 four miles south-south-east of Raalte in north-central Holland. Four of the crew lost their lives, while the pilot, bomb-aimer and mid-upper gunner survived to fall into enemy hands. Post-raid reconnaissance revealed an area of fire across central districts measuring eight by five kilometres, and local reports confirmed 8,882 individual fire incidents. More than seventy war-industry factories suffered a complete or partial loss of production, 140,000 people were bombed out of their homes and 1,292 lost their lives. Had it not been for an errant Oboe marker attracting a proportion of the bombing onto open country some fourteen miles to the north-east, the destruction would have been greater.

Bochum was selected to face its second heavy visitation of the campaign on the 12th, for which a force of 503 aircraft was made ready, 1 Group contributing 105 Lancasters, twenty-four of them representing 103 Squadron. Each was loaded with a cookie and fourteen SBCs of 4lb and 30lb incendiaries before departing Elsham Wolds between 22.21 and 23.04 with S/L Day the senior pilot on duty and heading for the northern tip of Texel via Mablethorpe. The crews of Sgts Wishart, Powell and Chesterton turned back early because of serviceability issues, leaving the others to continue on to the target, passing over central Holland and entering Germany to the west of Münster, before turning south for a direct run on Bochum, situated between Essen to the west and Dortmund to the east. It is believed that night-fighters were waiting over Dutch airspace and the frontier region, and a number of bombers fell victim at this stage of the operation. According to the superb book, the Bomber Command War Diaries, by Martin Middlebrook and Chris Everitt, Bochum was completely covered by ten-tenths cloud, but, according to many crew reports, they encountered three to six-tenths patchy cloud and good visibility in bright moonlight. Yellow tracking markers were helpful in guiding the main force crews to the aiming point, and the 103 Squadron crews had green or red TIs in the bombsights as they let their loads go from 20,000 to 24,000 feet between 01.18 and 01.56. Returning crews reported concentrated fires, the glow from which was visible for up to a hundred miles into the return flight, and photo-reconnaissance revealing 130 acres of devastation was backed up by local reports that 449 buildings had been destroyed and more than nine hundred severely damaged. The cost to the Command was twenty-four aircraft, at least nine of which had fallen victim to night-fighters and 1 Group posted missing five, among them 103 Squadron's ED916. Shot down while homebound by the night-fighter of Oblt Werner Rapp of III./NJG1, the Lancaster crashed at 02.30 near Hoogeveen in northern Holland, killing two members of the crew and delivering P/O King and four others into enemy hands. They had been on the final sortie of their first tour of operations.

Following a night's rest, the Ruhr offensive continued at Oberhausen, a major centre of oil production situated between Duisburg to the west and Essen to the east. An all-Lancaster heavy force numbering 197 aircraft contained eighty-nine provided by 1 Group, a reduced number in the absence of 101 Squadron, which was in the process of moving to Ludford Magna. 103 Squadron loaded twenty-seven of its own with a cookie and fifteen SBCs and sent them on their way from Elsham Wolds between 22.05 and 22.42 with F/L Brown the senior pilot on duty. For the third operation running, Sgt Powell and crew abandoned their sortie, on this occasion during the climb-out because of an unserviceable rear turret. F/Sgt

Egan and crew were defeated by an engine issue also while still in the circuit and it was not long before Sgt Dash and crew returned with an engine coolant leak. The others set course via Southwold for the Scheldt estuary to bypass Antwerp on their way to the Belgian/German frontier, from where they were to thread their way through the formidable defences at Mönchengladbach, Düsseldorf, Duisburg and Mülheim-an-der-Ruhr. By this time, F/L Rawstorne and crew had abandoned their attempt to climb beyond 16,500 feet and were on their way home, just one more of an alarming nineteen 1 Group aircraft to return early. The others were propelled through the flak belt by a strong tail wind and achieved a ground speed of 300 m.p.h, most to reach the other side unscathed and find three to ten-tenths cloud over the target with tops in places at 18,000 feet. Very bright moonlight greeted the arrival of the main force crews, who observed tracking flares drifting down over the starting point of the time-and-distance runs, while the aiming point was marked by red flares with green stars and white skymarkers dropped by the six Oboe Mosquitos and the backing-up 8 Group heavy brigade. Bombing by the Elsham Wolds crews took place from 18,850 to 24,600 feet between 01.12 and 01.46 in the face of intense heavy flak, which continued to chase them out of the target area into the guns of night-fighters. On the way home ED389 was confronted by a Ju88 emerging from a patch of cloud and firing tracer, to which the rear gunner replied with a well-aimed burst of his own and watched the enemy aircraft dive down with smoke pouring from its port engine. A flash on the ground seemed to confirm its end, but Sgt Hardman and crew could only claim it as a probable. Between them, the defenders accounted for seventeen Lancasters, seven of them belonging to 1 Group squadrons, and this represented 8.4% of the force. There were two empty dispersal pans at Elsham Wolds, which should have been occupied by ED396 and ED612, the former having crashed at Duisburg-Ruhrort with no survivors from the crew of Sgt Whitehead, while the latter came down near Mönchengladbach with fatal consequences for F/L Brown and crew. Local sources confirmed that the Wanganui flares had been right over the city centre, where 267 buildings had been destroyed and 584 seriously damaged.

On the 16th, 1, 5 and 8 Group stations were notified that Cologne was to be the target for that night, for which a force of 202 Lancasters and ten Halifaxes was made ready. They learned at briefings that there would be no Oboe Mosquitos on hand to mark the target, as that role was to be undertaken by the Path Finder Halifax element and six Lancasters employing H2S. 1 Group detailed seventy-six Lancasters, 103 Squadron making ready twenty-two at Elsham Wolds and loading eighteen with a cookie, four 500 pounders and six SBCs each of 4lb and 30lb incendiaries and four without the 500 pounders for rookie crews. They took off between 22.10 and 22.55 with S/L Day the senior pilot on duty and flew out over Southwold on course for the Scheldt, losing the services of Sgt Stoneman and crew to an engine issue within ninety minutes, and later the crews of F/L Rawstorne and F/Sgt Steel, who were over enemy territory when the failure of the oxygen feed to the rear and mid-upper turrets respectively forced them to turn back also. The remaining crews arrived in the target area to find six to ten-tenths cloud and green tracking flares to guide them to the aiming point. The Path Finders were five-and-a-half minutes late on target, and problems with some of the H2S sets led to sparse and scattered marking with solid white flares and reds with green stars. The 103 Squadron crews bombed from 21,000 to 25,850 feet between 01.05 and 01.19, and a number witnessed a large orange explosion at 01.08, although they were mostly unable to assess the outcome. The impression was gained that a proportion of the bombing had been concentrated where intended, but that some crews had been lured away by dummy markers, and local sources, which suggested that only around a hundred aircraft had been involved, tended to support the latter view. Residential districts bore the brunt of the raid, and 401 houses were destroyed, with 13,000 others sustaining damage to some extent, mostly lightly, while sixteen industrial premises and nine railway stations were hit, along with public and utility buildings. Fourteen Lancasters failed to return, five of them 1 Group aircraft, and 103 Squadron had the sad task of posting missing two more of its own. Sgt Winchester's W4901 was hit by a Luftwaffe flak battery as it crossed the Scheldt estuary outbound and crashed further east near Veghel, while ED945 fell victim to the night-fighter of Hptm Manfred Meurer of I./NJG1 and crashed in the same area on the way home at 01.55. There were no survivors from the crews of Sgt Winchester and P/O Dexter respectively, their loss meaning that six crews had now gone missing in the space of just five nights, and three more would be added to the toll before the month ended.

The recent successes in the Ruhr had been aided by the sheer size of the urban areas below, which all but guaranteed that the bombs would hit something useful, even after smoke had obscured the aiming point TIs. It was a different matter at a small or precision target, however, which would rapidly be enveloped in smoke from the first bombs before the rest of the attacking force had a chance to draw a bead on the aiming point. When, on the 20th, therefore, an attack was mounted under the codename Operation Bellicose against the production site of the Würzburg radar sets, which the enemy was employing very successfully to warn of and intercept Bomber Command raids, a plan was already in place to combat the problem by adopting the oft-used and still-under-development 5 Group time-and-distance method. It was a 5 and 8 Group show involving sixty Lancasters to attack the factory housed in the old Zeppelin sheds at Friedrichshafen, situated on the shore of Lake Constance (Bodensee) on the frontier with Switzerland, which represented a very small target. The operation employed a designated "Master of Ceremonies" to direct the bombing, much in the manner of Gibson at the Dams, and was an outstanding success, after which the force flew on to landing grounds in North Africa in what became known as a "shuttle" raid.

A hectic round of four major operations to the Ruhr in the space of five nights began at Krefeld on the 21st, for which a force of 705 aircraft was assembled. 1 Group contributed 111 Lancasters and thirty-eight Wellingtons, twenty-five of the former representing 103 Squadron, sixteen of which had four 500 pounders in the bomb bay in addition to the usual cookie and twelve SBCs. They departed Elsham Wolds between 22.59 and 23.42 with S/Ls Day and Prickett the senior pilots on duty and set course via Southwold for the Scheldt estuary. The oxygen supply in S/L Kelaher's aircraft had leaked out of a fractured pipe and was exhausted after thirty minutes, forcing him to turn back, while F/Sgt Munsch and crew had to fend off an attack by a BF109 at the Dutch coast with no working guns in the rear turret to bring to bear. Somehow, they shook their assailant off and returned safely. The others reached the target, situated a short distance to the south-west of Duisburg, and on the opposite side of the Rhine, and found conditions to be ideal, with small amounts of thin cloud between 6,000 and 10,000 feet and bright moonlight, which would benefit attacker and defender alike. The Path Finders delivered a near-perfect marking performance, dropping red TIs in concentrated fashion to clearly identify the city centre aiming point for the main force crews. The 103 Squadron crews carried out their attacks from 18,000 to 22,000 feet between

01.33 and 02.18 and described a sea of red fire giving off masses of smoke, with one particular jet-black column rising through 18,000 feet as they turned away. All were convinced of the success of the operation, and one crew likened it to the Wuppertal-Barmen raid. There was no hint of troublesome flak or night-fighters, and yet, forty-four aircraft failed to return, the heaviest casualties of the campaign to date, and many of these were lost to the Nachtjagd. There were seven missing 1 Group Lancasters, but none on this occasion from Elsham Wolds, and 35 (Madras Presidency) Squadron of the Path Finders lost six of its nineteen Halifaxes. Three-quarters of the bombing photos were plotted within three miles of the aiming point and the 2,306 tons of bombs wiped out by fire an estimated 47% of the built-up area, destroying 5,517 houses, the largest number to date at a single target, while more than a thousand people lost their lives.

This was the eighteenth and final operation of W/O Nicky Ross's second tour, and he was commissioned soon afterwards and awarded a DFC on the 5th of July. During his time away from the operational scene, he and his crew took a Lancaster to the United States, where they found themselves at Wright Field, near Dayton, Ohio, carrying out experimental parachute drops of M29 Weasel tracked carrier vehicles from a variety of altitudes onto a target zone. The Americans lacked an aircraft capable of performing this task, and it was the first time that a Lancaster had visited the States.

The medium-sized town of Mülheim-an-der-Ruhr, a close neighbour of Duisburg, Oberhausen and Essen, lies around a dozen miles to the north-east of Krefeld, and it was here that the red ribbon terminated on the target maps at briefings across the Command on the 22nd. A force of 557 aircraft was prepared, of which 102 of the Lancasters were provided by 1 Group, twenty-two of them representing 103 Squadron, sixteen of which were to carry the additional four 500 pounders. They departed Elsham Wolds between 22.51 and 23.37 with S/L England the senior pilot on duty to make their way via Sheringham and Noordwijk to cross into Germany near Bocholt for the final leg south to the target. Sgt Brown and crew aborted their sortie during the climb-out after smoke poured from their Gee-box and F/L Rawstorne and crew dropped out at the same time after their port-outer engine failed. The others arrived at the target to find small amounts of cumulostratus cloud at between 5,000 and 10,000 feet, with red and green TIs clearly visible and defining the aiming point. The Elsham Wolds crews bombed from 18,500 to 22,000 feet between 01.22 and 01.54 and witnessed the development of a concentrated area of fire, which was visible from the Dutch coast homebound. Returning crews commented on the intense searchlight and flak response, and the number of night-fighters, and reported that Krefeld was still burning from the night before. Local sources confirmed that the town had suffered severe damage, particularly in the northern districts, where 1,135 houses had been destroyed and more than 12,000 others damaged to some extent. The road and telephone communications to Oberhausen had been cut, preventing any passage out of the town other than on foot, and in fact, some of the bombing had spilled into the eastern districts of Oberhausen, which was linked to Mülheim for air-raid purposes. It was another expensive night for the Command, however, which registered the loss of thirty-five aircraft, with the Halifaxes and Stirlings representing two-thirds of them and suffering a respective loss rate of 7.7% and 11.8%. 103 Squadrons ED773 went down into the sea off the Dutch coast on the way home, and there were no survivors from the crew of F/L Spurr, who had only arrived at Elsham Wolds from 1662 Conversion Unit on the 17th.

Having destroyed the Barmen half of Wuppertal at the end of May in one of the most devastating attacks to date, it was time to visit the same catastrophe upon the western half, Elberfeld, for which a force of 630 aircraft was made ready on the 24th. 1 Group supported the operation with ninety-five Lancasters and thirty-three Wellingtons, twenty-one of the former provided by 103 Squadron, the majority loaded with a cookie, four 500 pounders and six SBCs each of 4lb and 30lb incendiaries and a few with a cookie and thirteen SBCs. They departed Elsham Wolds between 22.36 and 23.15 with S/L Day the senior pilot on duty and made landfall over the Scheldt estuary, heading towards Antwerp, Sgt Douglas and crew struggling to escape ensnarement by a searchlight cone when ten miles west of the port. Forced down to 8,000 feet with no prospect of regaining bombing altitude, they let their bombs go "live" at 01.10 and turned for home. The bomber stream ran the usual gauntlet of searchlights and flak from the Cologne and Düsseldorf defence zones, the enemy aided by the formation of condensation trails at between 18,000 and 21,000 feet. There seemed to be fewer guns firing at them over the target, where small amounts of cloud with tops at 17,000 feet were insufficient to obscure the ground. Yellow tracking flares guided the spearhead of the main force to the aiming point, where cascading red and green TIs were clearly evident, and the 103 Squadron element bombed on them from 19,000 and 22,000 feet between 01.04 and 01.46. Those arriving at the tail end of the attack, when the built-up area was well-alight, described thick columns of smoke already passing through 19,000 feet and the glow of fires visible from the Dutch coast.

Post-raid reconnaissance revealed another massively concentrated and accurate attack, which had reduced to rubble an estimated 90% of Elberfeld's built-up area, including three thousand houses and 171 industrial premises. It had also severely damaged 2,500 houses and dozens of important factory buildings, and the fact that more buildings had been destroyed than damaged, provided a telling commentary on the conditions on the ground. The number of fatalities stood at around eighteen hundred, and some of the survivors might have been cheered to know that thirty-four bombers, containing 240 of their tormentors, would not be returning to England that night. 1 Group registered the loss of five of its aircraft, but 103 Squadron enjoyed a loss-free night and near perfect serviceability.

Orders went out to stations across the Command on the 25th to prepare for that night's raid on the synthetic oil production centre of Gelsenkirchen in the north-eastern Ruhr, for which a force of 473 aircraft was assembled. This would be the first major attack on this city since 1941, when it had been a regular destination under the Oil Directive, and crews were briefed to focus on the Nordstern synthetic oil plant (Gelsenberg A.G.), which was a Bergius-process manufacturer of high-grade petroleum products, particularly aviation fuel. 8 Group was to provide seven Oboe Mosquitos plus two in reserve to drop route markers and skymark the aiming-point, and two others to bomb after the main force had finished, but none of its heavy aircraft was to be involved. 1 Group supported the operation with eighty-eight Lancasters and ten Wellingtons of 166 Squadron, twenty-four of the former provided by 103 Squadron, two-thirds of them receiving the full payload and one third the additional SBC instead of 500 pounders. They departed Elsham Wolds between 22.42 and 23.47 with S/L England the senior pilot on duty and lost the services of Sgt Powell and crew during the climb-out for an undisclosed reason. The crews of P/O Hopps, Sgt Lee and W/O Ratcliff also abandoned their sorties, respectively to an inability to climb beyond 18,000 feet, an engine fire and turret issues.

The others reached the target area to find ten-tenths stratus lying over the region with tops at 10,000 to 15,000 feet, which would not have been a problem for Oboe, had five of the twelve participating Mosquitos not suffered equipment failures. This caused tracking flares to be late and to drop in the wrong sequence in a somewhat scattered manner, at a time when the crews were contending with an intense flak barrage. Searchlights illuminated the cloud as those from 103 Squadron bombed on red flares with green stars from 19,000 to 24,000 feet between 01.21 and 01.50, and some witnessed a large explosion at 01.43. The glow from the target was visible from the Dutch coast, to which the returning bombers were chased by a large deployment of enemy night-fighters. Post-raid reconnaissance and local reports confirmed that the operation had failed to achieve accuracy and concentration, and in an echo of the past, bombs had been sprayed all over the Ruhr, leaving Gelsenkirchen largely untouched. Thirty aircraft were missing, seven of them from 1 Group, and two of them belonged to 103 Squadron, ED528 crashing on the northern rim of the Ruhr on the way in, and F/Sgt Egan RAAF, who, it will be recalled, had been involved in an accident earlier in the month, survived with two of his crew to be taken into captivity. W4827 came down eight miles south of Haarlem in Holland during the return flight, and F/L Langille RCAF also survived with four of his crew and joined the growing list of 103 Squadron members on extended leave in Germany. This was another crew who had arrived from 1662 Conversion Unit as recently as the 17th.

A series of three operations against Cologne would span the turn of the month and began on the night of the 28/29th, when 608 aircraft were prepared for a late evening take-off to deliver what would be the Rhineland capital's greatest ordeal of the war to date. 1 Group contributed eighty-nine Lancasters, including twenty-one representing 103 Squadron, and twenty-seven Wellingtons, those at Elsham Wolds divided fifteen and six between the two standard bomb loads. Two Lancasters developed last-minute technical issues and were withdrawn, leaving nineteen to take to the air between 22.47 and 23.23 with S/L Day the senior pilot on duty. F/Sgt Bass and crew dropped out while still in the circuit because of engine and turret issues, while the remainder set course via Orfordness for the Belgian coast to swing round Bruges and pass south of Antwerp with the target 110 miles away. They main force crews encountered ten-tenths cloud below them at 8,000 to 10,000 feet, with good visibility above, but were unaware that five of the Oboe Mosquitos had turned back and a sixth was unable to drop its skymarkers. This meant that just six were available to fulfil the initial marking role, and they were running behind schedule by seven minutes, and could manage only intermittent flares. The omens for a successful attack were not good, particularly as skymarking was the least reliable method because of drift, but by the time that most of the Elsham Wolds crews arrived, they were greeted by red and white flares. They delivered their attacks from 18,500 to 23,000 feet between 01.40 and 02.16 and deduced from the glow beneath the clouds and the presence of smoke rising through them that they had contributed to a successful operation. This was confirmed by post-raid reconnaissance and local reports, which provided details of forty-three industrial buildings and 6,374 others completely destroyed, and a further fifteen thousand sustaining damage to some extent. The death toll was put at 4,377, the greatest by far from a Bomber Command attack, and 230,000 others had lost their homes for varying periods. By recent standards, the figure of twenty-five missing aircraft could be considered moderate, but that was no consolation to the individual stations with an empty dispersal pan. 1 Group posted missing four aircraft and had fourteen "boomerangs".

During the course of the month the squadron participated in nine operations and dispatched 211 sorties for the loss of ten Lancasters and nine crews. It was a startling contrast to the loss-free May and graphically demonstrated the dangers of operating over the Ruhr. The campaign, although now in its later stages, was not yet over, and the region would claim more lives.

July 1943

The first two days of the new month were beset by poor weather conditions, which kept all but a few gardeners and Mosquitos on the ground. S/L Day was posted to 1667 Conversion Unit for instructional duties on the 2nd at the end of his tour and would revert to acting flight lieutenant rank. It was not unusual for the more senior operational officers to carry an acting rank a number of steps higher than their war substantive rank, which in the case of S/L Day was flying officer.

The mini-campaign against Cologne provided the first major bombing operation of the new month, for which a force of 653 aircraft was assembled on the 3rd. 1 Group's contribution amounted to ninety-four Lancasters and twenty-seven Wellingtons, twenty-three of the former made ready by 103 Squadron and given a bomb load consisting either of a cookie, four 500 pounders and twelve SBCs or an additional SBC in place of the 500 pounders. They departed Elsham Wolds between 22.25 and 23.10 with S/Ls England and Prickett the senior pilots on duty and lost F/Sgt Bass and crew to engine failure during the climb-out. The others set course via Southwold for Knokke on the Belgian coast, and all reached the target, which they found clearly visible under two to three-tenths cloud at 8,000 feet and protected by many searchlight cones and a moderate flak defence. Green tracking flares guided the first wave crews to the aiming point, which the Path Finders marked with red skymarkers with green stars and red and green ground markers, achieving great accuracy and concentration, while later crews were drawn on for the final one hundred miles by the sight of the already fiercely burning city. The 103 Squadron crews bombed on the red and green TIs from 19,000 to 23,000 feet between 01.15 and 01.55, and on return reported the city to be a mass of flames, the glow from which had remained visible for 170 miles into the return journey. The operation cost the Command thirty aircraft, six of them from 1 Group and two empty dispersal pans at Elsham Wolds on the following morning were evidence that JA672 and W5012 were not coming home. The former disappeared without trace with the crew of F/O Bradshaw, while the latter fell victim to the night-fighter of Oblt Wilhelm Telge of V./NJG1 while outbound and crashed ten miles south-east of Namur with no survivors from the crew of F/O Oldham. Post-raid reconnaissance and local sources confirmed another stunningly accurate and concentrated attack, in which twenty industrial premises and 2,200 houses had been destroyed, 588 people had lost their lives and 72,000 others had been bombed out of their homes.

Some crews commented on the presence of day fighters over the target, and this was clear evidence of a new tactic being employed by the Luftwaffe. The newly formed JG300 was operating for the first time, employing the Wilde Sau (Wild Boar) tactics, which was the brainchild of former bomber pilot, Major Hans-Joachim (Hajo) Herrmann. The unit had been formed in June with borrowed standard BF109 and FW190 single-engine day fighters to operate directly over a target, seeking out bombers silhouetted against the fires and TIs. On this night, the unit would claim twelve victories, but would have to share them with the flak batteries, which claimed them also. Unaccustomed to being pursued by fighters over a target, where they risked being hit by their own flak, it would take time for the bomber crews to work out what was happening, and until they did, friendly fire would often be blamed for damage incurred by unseen causes.

An operation against Essen was posted and cancelled on the 6th, and 1 Group took the opportunity to blood some freshman crews by sending them to the Biscay coast on gardening duties, six assigned to the Cinnamon garden off La Pallice/La Rochelle and a dozen to Deodar in the Gironde estuary leading to the port of Bordeaux. It was for the latter that the 103 Squadron crews of F/Sgts Barr, Bass and Bunton and Sgt Warren departed Elsham Wolds between 22.28 and 22.32 and set course via Selsey Bill for the Ile-de-Re off La Rochelle, some fifty miles north of the target area. The mighty Gironde estuary narrows as it leads inland towards the south-east, before dividing to become the Garonne River to the west and the Dordogne to the east. Its banks and islands were home to a number of important oil production and storage sites at Pauillac, Blaye, Bec-d'Ambes and Bordeaux itself, and the region was a frequent destination for gardening activities. Bordeaux, a gateway to the Atlantic, was vitally important to the enemy and was a base for U-Boots, which meant that it was heavily defended along the entire length of the waterway. F/Sgt Bass and crew spent twenty minutes searching for a pinpoint but were thwarted by heavy rain from ten-tenths cloud at 1,500 feet and brought their six mines home. F/Sgt Bunton and crew delivered their mines from 4,500 feet at 01.51 and Sgt Warren and crew followed up from 1,000 feet at 02.05, both arriving home safely after more than six hours aloft and leaving the crew of F/Sgt Barr RAAF unaccounted for. This is how they remained as no trace of them or W4363 was ever found.

The final raid of the series against Cologne was posted on Lancaster stations on the 8th, and a heavy force of 282 aircraft drawn from 1, 5 and 8 Groups, with six Oboe Mosquitos to carry out the initial marking. 1 Group put up 104 Lancasters, of which twenty-one were made ready at Elsham Wolds and loaded with a cookie, three 1,000 pounders and six SBCs each of 4lb and 30lb incendiaries, before taking off between 22.18 and 22.46 with S/Ls England and Prickett the senior pilots on duty. They set course via Orfordness to make landfall on the Belgian coast at Knokke and flew through the tops of towering cumulonimbus cloud as they made their way to the target, where a layer of ten-tenths white stuff at around 10,000 feet concealed the ground from view. Tracking flares guided the main force crews to the aiming point, but the release-point flares were late, and some crews bombed on e.t.a. before they were deployed. The 103 Squadron crews carried out their attacks almost exclusively on release point flares from 19,500 to 23,000 feet between 01.14 and 01.28 in the face of an intense flak barrage, and a very large orange explosion was witnessed at 01.23. Post-raid reconnaissance and local sources revealed another highly successful operation, which had caused extensive damage in north-western and south-western districts, where nineteen industrial premises and 2,381 houses had been destroyed at the modest cost to the Command of seven Lancasters, two of them from 1 Group. When the dust had settled over Cologne, the local authorities catalogued the destruction over the three raids of more than eleven thousand buildings, and a death toll of almost 5,500 people, with a further 350,000 rendered homeless.

The Ruhr campaign was winding down by the time that Gelsenkirchen was posted across Lancaster and Halifax stations as the target on the 9th, for which a heavy force of 408 aircraft was made ready supported by ten Oboe Mosquitos. The main targets were the Bergius-process synthetic oil refinery known to Bomber Command as Nordstern and to the Germans as Gelsenberg AG, and the Hydrierwerke-Scholven coal liquefaction plant, which between them produced thousands of tons of aviation fuel for the Luftwaffe. Twenty 103 Squadron Lancasters were among the eighty-two representing 1 Group, and they were each given a bomb load of a cookie, two 1,000 pounders and thirteen SBCs, before departing Elsham Wolds between 22.35 and 23.08 with S/L England the senior pilot on duty. They flew out over Mablethorpe and headed for Texel, on the way losing the services of the crews of P/O Hopps and F/Sgt Bass respectively to port-inner engine and oxygen system failure. They were two of eight 1 Group "boomerangs" as the bomber stream made its way to the target above ten-tenths cloud, which stretched over the Ruhr at around 16,000 feet and topped out in places at 20,000 feet. The Path Finder skymarkers were several minutes late, partly as a result of a 50% failure rate of the Oboe equipment, while a sixth Mosquito dropped its markers ten miles to the north. The main force crews were guided to their bombing runs by red and green tracking flares, and those from Elsham Wolds were over the aiming point between 01.10 and 01.41 at 20,000 to 23,600 feet aiming for the Wanganui markers as they drifted into the cloud. Some explosions were reflected in the cloud, one particularly large one at 01.40 lighting up the area like day, however, the impression gained by most was that the raid had fallen short of the recent outstanding successes, and this was confirmed by local sources. To those on the ground, it appeared that the attack had been meant for Bochum and Wattenscheid, which received more bombs than Gelsenkirchen, where limited damage occurred in southern districts.

Although two more operations to the region would be launched late in the month, Harris was already planning his next attempt to shorten the war by bombing and was buoyed by the success of the spring offensive. He could look back on the past four and a half months with genuine satisfaction at the performance of his squadrons, and as a champion of technological innovation, take particular pride in the performance of Oboe, which had been the decisive factor. Although losses had been grievously high and the Ruhr's reputation as "Happy Valley" well earned, its most important towns and cities had suffered catastrophic destruction. In Britain, the aircraft factories had more than kept pace with the rate of attrition, while the training units both at home and overseas were pouring eager new crews into the fray to fill the gaps. With confidence high in the ability of his Command to destroy almost any target at will, Harris prepared for his next major campaign, the erasure from the map of a prominent German city in a short, sharp series of maximum effort raids to be launched during the final week of the month.

In the meantime, 1, 5 and 8 Groups were alerted to prepare for a trip to Italy to attack the city of Turin, for which 295 Lancasters were made ready on the 12th, 1 Group contributing 108 aircraft, twenty-four of them representing 103 Squadron. Most were loaded with a cookie and five SBCs each of 4lb and 30lb incendiaries and departed Elsham Wolds between 22.00 and 22.28 with S/Ls England and Prickett the senior pilots on duty, before setting course via Dungeness for Cayeux-sur-Mer and the long slog across France to the Alps. F/L Carey and crew lost their starboard-outer engine during the climb-out, while P/O Ratcliff's pitot head iced-up when at 21,000 feet between Orleans and Dijon and W/O Breckon's starboard-outer engine burst into flames as he and his crew closed on the foothills of the Alps. The others pinpointed on Lake Annecy before crossing the Alps and arriving in the target area to be greeted by clear skies, good visibility and defences up to their usual poor standard, characterised by ineffective searchlights and inaccurate light flak rising to 15,000 feet. The marking was punctual, accurate and concentrated, inviting the bombing by the 103 Squadron crews to be carried out from 16,000 to 21,000 feet between 01.52 and 02.10, and a column of black smoke was observed rising through 12,000 feet as they withdrew. The return route involved a low-level circumnavigation of the Brest peninsula, and many of the thirteen missing Lancasters disappeared without trace into the sea after running into enemy night-fighters in this area. This was certainly where W/C Nettleton VC, the veteran of the Augsburg raid and commanding officer of 44 (Rhodesia) Squadron, went down and it seems likely that 103 Squadron's ED769 suffered a similar fate, as no trace of it or the crew of F/Sgt Graham was ever found. Reconnaissance showed the main weight of the attack to have fallen just north of the city centre, and a local report stated that 792 people had lost their lives, the largest number of fatalities from a Bomber Command attack on Italy.

Aachen, Germany's most westerly city and an important railway hub between Germany and the occupied countries, was posted as the target on the 13th and a force of 374 aircraft made ready. This consisted largely of Halifaxes, Stirlings and Wellingtons, thirty-two of the last-mentioned provided by 1 Group, and just eighteen Lancasters among the 8 Group contribution. It was left to local sources to confirm the severity of the damage inflicted upon the city, which amounted to 2,927 buildings completely destroyed, with many industrial, public and cultural buildings seriously damaged.

Hamburg had been a regular target for the Command throughout the war to date, and had been attacked, amongst other occasions, during the final week of July in 1940, 1941 and 1942. It had been spared by the weather from hosting the first "One Thousand" bomber raid at the end of May 1942, but Harris now identified it as the ideal candidate for destruction under Operation Gomorrah, the intention of which was to cause the maximum impact to the enemy's morale in a short, sharp campaign employing ten thousand tons of bombs. Hamburg's political status was second only to that of Berlin, and its value to the war effort in terms of ship and U-Boot construction and other war production was undeniable, but it suited Harris's criteria also in other respects. Its location close to a coastline aided navigation and made it accessible from the North Sea without the need to spend time over hostile territory, and its relatively short distance from the bomber stations enabled a force to approach and retreat during the few hours of darkness afforded by mid-summer. Finally, lying beyond the range of Oboe, which had proved so decisive at the Ruhr, Hamburg had the wide River Elbe to provide a solid H2S signature for the navigators high above.

What the 1 Group ORB described as the "long-awaited Battle of Hamburg" would have begun on the night of the 22/23rd with Bremen as the alternative target had adverse weather not intervened to force a late cancellation at 21.50. It happened again on the following night, only this time the cancellation came at 18.30 in time to allow the crews opportunity to arrange evening activities. There had been no operations for most squadrons for nine days by the time that the 24th dawned dry but overcast and work began on stations across the Command to prepare a force of 791 aircraft, 123 of the Lancasters and thirty-five Wellingtons provided by 1 Group. The crews trooping into their respective briefing rooms probably expected the day to end with yet another scrub but listened intently as they were read a special message from the commander-in-chief, to announce the beginning of the Battle of Hamburg. They learned that they would be aided by the first operational use of "window", aluminium-backed strips of paper of precise length, which, when released in bundles into the airstream at a predetermined point, would drift down slowly in vast clouds to swamp the enemy night-fighter, searchlight and gun-laying radar systems with false returns and render them blind. The device had actually been available for a year, but its deployment had been vetoed in case the enemy copied it for use against Britain. It was not realized that Germany had, in fact, already developed its own version called Düppel, which it had withheld for the same reason.

The plan of attack called for eleven Lancasters and nine Halifaxes to drop yellow TIs as route markers, before continuing on to mark the aiming-point with yellow TIs, and if conditions permitted, illuminator flares. The route markers were to be backed up by six Stirlings, thirteen Lancasters and nine Halifaxes, and six Lancasters and two Halifaxes were to use the yellow TIs as a guide, and with the aid of flares, mark the aiming-point with red TIs, which would be backed up with green TIs by the remaining marker crews. 103 Squadron loaded most of its twenty-seven Lancasters with a cookie, three 1,000 pounders and twelve SBCs and sent them on their way from Elsham Wolds between 21.59 and 22.48 with S/L Prickett and the newly promoted S/L Carpenter the senior pilots on duty. F/Sgt Brown found W4323 to be almost uncontrollable during the climb-out and proceeded directly to the jettison area, leaving the others to set course via Mablethorpe for a position north of the island of Sylt to make landfall on the Schleswig Holstein peninsular near Heide, before turning towards the south to run in on the target. After bombing they were to continue on a southerly heading, before turning sharply to starboard, and continue in a north-westerly direction to cross the enemy coast between Bremerhaven and Cuxhaven and gain the North Sea south of Sylt. At a predetermined point over the North Sea, the wireless operators began to dispense "window" through the flare chute, beginning shortly after 00.30 and the effects appeared to be immediate as few fighters rose to meet the approaching bombers. Matters began to go awry for 103 Squadron early on in the proceedings, when ED389 and JA866 became the operation's first two casualties, both shot down into the sea off the Dutch coast by night fighters, while well off track, one by sixty miles and the other by a hundred, and one of them was flying at only 5,000 feet when intercepted. It seems likely that they were returning early with technical difficulties, and were, therefore, outside of the protection of the bomber stream and "window". The crews of W/O Hardman and F/Sgt Moore were on their seventeenth and sixth operations respectively, and all fourteen men lost their lives.

The efficacy of Window was made more apparent in the target area, where the crews noticed an absence of the usually efficient co-ordination between the searchlights and flak batteries and defence appeared random and sporadic. This offered the Path Finders the opportunity to mark the target by visual reference and H2S virtually unmolested, and although the red and green TIs were a little misplaced and scattered, they landed in sufficient numbers close to the city centre to provide the main force crews with ample opportunity to deliver a massive blow. It rarely happened that aircraft arrived in strict bands according to their task, and some main force crews were already over the target from the opening of the raid at 01.00. The 103 Squadron crews carried out their attacks from 20,000 to 22,000 feet between 01.01 and 01.47 and returning crews reported a successful operation that had left part of the city ablaze with a column of smoke rising through 20,000 feet. Post-raid reconnaissance revealed that a six-mile-long creep-back had developed, which cut a swathe of destruction from the city centre along the line of approach, out across the north-western districts and into open country, where a proportion of the bombing had been wasted. In fact, less than half of the force had bombed within three miles of the city centre during the fifty-minute-long raid, in which 2,284 tons of bombs had been delivered, despite which, the city had suffered a telling blow and fifteen hundred of its inhabitants had lost their lives. For the Command it was an encouraging start to the campaign, particularly in the light of just twelve missing aircraft, for which "window" was largely responsible. ED878 was 103 Squadron's third failure to return and the final casualty of the operation, falling victim to the night-fighter of Oblt Hermann Greiner of IV./NJG1 and crashing into the sea off the Frisians on the way home. W/O O'Hanlon and his crew were on their thirteenth operation, and all lost their lives.

On the 25th, and in the expectation that Hamburg would be covered by smoke, Harris switched his force to Essen, where he could take advantage of the body blow dealt to the enemy defensive system by "window". A force of 705 aircraft was made ready and a plan prepared, which called for Halifaxes and Lancasters of 35 (Madras Presidency) and 156 Squadrons to drop preliminary yellow warning TIs on track by H2S, which would be backed up by elements of 7 and 156 Squadrons. Ahead, fourteen Oboe Mosquitos would mark the aiming-point with red TIs, which nineteen Lancasters, nine Halifaxes and five Stirlings were to back up with greens. 1 Group detailed 109 Lancasters and thirty-nine Wellingtons, twenty-one of the former belonging to 103 Squadron, most loaded with a cookie, three 1,000 pounders and a dozen SBCs. They departed Elsham Wolds between 21.52 and 22.39 with S/Ls Carpenter and Prickett the senior pilots on duty and set course via Mablethorpe for Egmond, which P/O Ratcliff and crew reached before their starboard-outer engine caught fire to end their interest in proceedings, and they unloaded the contents of their bomb bay on an aerodrome near Alkmaar on the way home. F/Sgt Loop and crew were the others to return early having lost their intercom. They were among ten early returns from the 1 Group contingent, the remainder arriving in the target area to find four to five-tenths cloud to the west but clear skies over the aiming-point, with just the usual ground haze to spoil the vertical visibility. The Elsham Wolds crews carried out their bombing runs at 20,000 to 22,000 feet between 00.33 and 01.15 and watched a highly concentrated attack develop, which left the ground enveloped in smoke from the many fires and explosions. Returning crews reported concentrated fires around the aiming-point in a one-and-a-half-square-mile area of the city, two large, red explosions at 00.36 and 00.39 and a column of smoke rising through 20,000 feet as they withdrew to the west, the glow remaining visible from as far away as the Dutch coast. Post-raid reconnaissance confirmed the raid to be another outstanding success against this important war materials producing city, with more than 2,800 houses destroyed, while the complex of Krupp manufacturing sites suffered its heaviest damage of the war to date. Twenty-six aircraft failed to return, three of them belonging to 1 Group, among which was JA855 containing the crew of S/L Carpenter, who were on their way home over Holland at 22,000 feet, when intercepted by the night-fighter of Luftwaffe ace, Major Werner Streib of 1./NJG1. The Lancaster crashed at Elsendorp in southern Holland at 00.46 with fatal consequences for five of the eight occupants, while S/L Carpenter and two others survived to fall into enemy hands. The experienced F/L Ewer DFC, RCAF and his crew all perished, when ED884 crashed in the target area, bringing the 103 Squadron casualty figure in just two nights to five.

During the course of the 27th, a force of 787 aircraft was assembled for round two of Operation Gomorrah, for which 1 Group detailed 118 Lancasters and forty-one Wellingtons, twenty-three of the former belonging to 103 Squadron, most of them to carry the standard bomb load. Crews attended briefing to learn that yellow route markers would be dropped by H2S on the enemy coast and backed up, and that "Y" aircraft (H2S blind markers) were to deliver red TIs and a stick of flares over the aiming-point for visual markers to confirm and back up with green TIs. They departed Elsham Wolds between 21.58 and 22.59 with S/Ls England and Prickett the senior pilots on duty and set course via Mablethorpe to make landfall on the Schleswig-Holstein coast to the north of Hansastadt Hamburg. The crews of F/Sgts Annis and Carter dropped out with engine issues during the North Sea crossing, leaving the others to press on, none of them having any concept of the events that were to follow their arrival.

A previously unknown and terrible phenomenon was about to present itself to the world and introduce a new word "firestorm" into the English language. A number of factors would conspire on this night to seal the fate of this great city and its hapless inhabitants in an orgy of destruction that was quite unprecedented in air warfare. An uncharacteristically hot and dry spell of weather had left the city a tinderbox, and the spark to ignite it came with the Path Finders' H2S-laid yellow and green TIs, which fell with almost total concentration some two miles to the east of the intended city-centre aiming-point and into the densely populated working-class residential districts of Hamm, Hammerbrook and Borgfeld. To compound this, the main force, which had been drawn on to the target by yellow release-point flares, bombed with rare precision and almost no creep-back and deposited much of its 2,300 tons of bombs into this relatively compact area. The 103 Squadron crews delivered their bomb loads from 19,000 to 21,500 feet between 00.56 and 01.42 and observed many explosions and a sea of flames developing below. Those bombing towards the later stages of the raid observed a pall of smoke rising through 20,000 feet, and the glow of fires was reported to remain visible for up to two hundred miles into the return journey.

On the ground, individual fires began to join together to form one giant conflagration, which sucked in oxygen from surrounding areas at hurricane speeds to feed its voracious appetite. Trees were uprooted and flung bodily into the inferno, along with debris and people and temperatures at the seat of the flames exceeded one thousand degrees Celcius. The defences were overwhelmed and the fire service was unable to pass through the rubble-strewn streets to gain access to the worst-affected areas. Even had they done so, they could not have entered the firestorm area, and only after all of the combustible material had been consumed did the flames subside. By this time, there was no-one alive to rescue and an estimated forty thousand people died on this one night alone. A mass exodus from the city, which would ultimately exceed one million people, began on the following morning and this undoubtedly saved many from the ravages of the next raid, which would come two nights hence. Seventeen aircraft failed to return, reflecting the enemy's developing response to the advantage gained by the Command through "window". No gain was ever permanent, and the balance of power would continue to shift from one side to the other for the next year. For a change, it was the Lancaster brigade that sustained the highest numerical casualties on this night, accounting for eleven of the failures to return.

Bomber Command's heavy brigade stayed at home on the following night, while four Mosquitos carried out a nuisance raid on Hamburg to ensure that the residents' sleep was disturbed. A force of 777 aircraft was put together to continue Hamburg's torment on the 29th, while the crews attended briefings to learn of their part in the proceedings. They were told that red TIs and flares were to be employed as route markers, before seventeen Lancasters and eight Halifaxes marked the aiming-point with yellow TIs by H2S to be backed up by thirty-four Lancasters, six Stirlings and nine Halifaxes. 1 Group contributed 111 Lancasters and thirty-nine Wellingtons, of which the twenty-six of the former representing 103 Squadron were given the standard bomb load and sent on their way from Elsham Wolds between 22.03 and 22.49 with S/Ls England and Pickett the senior pilots on duty. S/L Kennard also took part as a guest while officially screened, although he would return to the squadron for a second tour in September. W/O Presland and crew lost the use of their mid-upper turret while climbing out and proceeded directly to the jettison area, leaving the others to set course via Mablethorpe for the Schleswig-Holstein coast, during which leg W/O Chesterton and crew lost their port-outer engine, which provided the power to the turrets. The vanguard of the bomber stream reached the target area to find clear skies and the city protected only by slight ground haze. The plan involved approaching from due north to hit the northern and north-eastern districts, which thus far had escaped serious damage, but the Path Finders strayed two miles to the east of the intended track and dropped their markers just to the south of the already devastated firestorm area. A four-mile creep-back rescued the situation for the Command, by spreading along the line of approach into the residential districts of Wandsbek and Barmbek and parts of Uhlenhorst and Winterhude. The 103 Squadron crews carried out their attacks from 19,000 to 22,000 feet between 00.46 and 01.42 and released their loads on yellow and green TIs, before returning home to report smoke rising through 17,000 feet and fires visible for two hundred miles into the homeward journey. It was another massive blow against this proud city, but as the defenders began to recover from the effects of "window", so the bomber losses began to creep up and twenty-eight aircraft failed to return home on this night, three of them from 1 Group.

Before the final round of Operation Gomorrah took place, the curtain on the Ruhr offensive was brought down finally with a raid on the town of Remscheid, situated on the southern edge of the region some six miles south of Wuppertal, where the main industries were mechanical engineering and tool-making. Up until this point, only twenty-six people had lost their lives in this town as a result of stray bombs, but it was now to face a modest force of 273 aircraft consisting of roughly equal numbers of Lancasters, Halifaxes and Stirlings with six Oboe Mosquitos to mark out the aiming-point with red TIs. 1 Group put up thirty Lancasters, a reduced effort after doubts about the weather, and 103 Squadron loaded just six of its own with a cookie, three 1,000 pounders and twelve and two-thirds SBCs. They departed Elsham Wolds between 22.00 and 22.07 with F/O Hammond the only commissioned pilot on duty and lost W/O Edie and crew to engine problems during the climb-out and F/Sgt Cant and crew to a similar cause as they exited England at Orfordness. The others made landfall on the Belgian coast near Veurne and reached the target area to find clear skies and good visibility and bombed on red TIs from 19,500 to 20,500 feet between 01.02 and 01.16, observing the burst of many cookies and a pall of smoke rising through 5,000 feet. They returned home with a red glow in the sky behind them that remained visible as they crossed the enemy coast homebound and gave promise of another Ruhr town in ruins. It would be left to a post-war bombing survey to establish that a mere 871 tons of bombs had laid waste to around 83% of Remscheid's built-up area, destroying 107 industrial buildings and 3,117 houses. Three months war production was lost, and the town's industry never recovered fully. Fifteen aircraft failed to return, and the Stirling brigade suffered 10% casualties.

During the course of the month the squadron took part in ten operations and launched 195 sorties, of which fifteen were abortive, for the loss of nine Lancasters and their crews.

August 1943

Briefings for the final act of Operation Gomorrah took place on the 2nd and a force of 740 aircraft was made ready, 121 of the Lancasters and thirty-two Wellingtons provided by 1 Group. 103 Squadron loaded each of its twenty-six Lancasters with a cookie, three 1,000 pounders and twelve and two-thirds SBCs before sending them on their way from Elsham Wolds between 22.54 and 00.02 with S/L England the senior pilot on duty. Sgt Buxton and crew lost their port-inner engine during the climb-out over base leaving the rest to fly out over Mablethorpe on course for a point to the west of Heligoland, from where they were to turn south-east to cross Jade Bay and reach a point due south of the target for a bombing run south to north to the west of the already devastated area. The weather conditions were good initially, until 7 degrees East, where a towering bank of ice-bearing cumulonimbus cloud was encountered with anvil tops stretching upwards to 25,000 and even 30,000 feet, which could not be circumnavigated or climbed over. Upon entering it, aircraft were thrown around by violent electrical storms with enormous flashes of lightning, thunder and electrical discharges, which sent instruments haywire, in what was a hugely terrifying experience beyond anything that most crews had ever experienced. Twenty-eight 1 Group crews abandoned their sorties, and among them were the 103 Squadron crews of W/Os Bunton and Edie and F/Sgt Bassett, who each jettisoned their load as the conditions caused engine and other technical malfunctions.

Those battling through the conditions found the target area to be concealed beneath seven to ten-tenths cloud, and while some caught a glimpse of the Elbe and isolated yellow and green Path Finder flares, the majority bombed on e.t.a., on the glow of fires beneath the cloud and the smoke rising through it. S/L England dived down to below the cloud at 10,000 feet and caught sight of a green target indicator, which he bombed at 02.27. Others spotted built-up areas as they covered the distance between the German coast and planned start of the bombing run, the Elsham Wolds crews delivering their attacks from 10,000 to 22,000 feet between 01.27 and 02.46, before returning to unanimously report an unsuccessful operation, described by some from other units as "pure hell". Little fresh damage occurred in Hamburg as bombs were sprayed over an area of a hundred miles, but that was of little consequence in view of what had gone before. The Command suffered the relatively heavy loss of thirty aircraft, eight of them belonging to 1 Group, and some of these may have fallen victim to the weather conditions. W/O Stoneman and crew, who had successfully ditched on return from La Spezia in April, lost their lives when ED645 crashed at Harburg on the southern bank of the Elbe during the bombing run. They were on their nineteenth operation and would have been considered a senior crew. There were no survivors either from the crew of W/O Dash after ED922 crashed close to the eastern bank of the Elbe after bombing, and they were on their fourteenth operation. During the course of the four raids of Operation Gomorrah, the squadron dispatched 102 sorties, the highest number by any squadron, eighty-nine of which bombed as briefed, and lost five Lancasters and crews. (The Battle of Hamburg. Martin Middlebrook).

There now followed four nights of blessed relief from operations, during which there were training exercises for freshman crews and S/L Wood was posted in from 1667 Conversion unit at Lindholme on the 5th to assume the role of A Flight commander. Italy was now teetering on the brink of capitulation and Bomber Command was invited to help nudge it over the edge with a short offensive against its major cities, beginning with attacks on Genoa, Milan and Turin on the 7th, for which an all-Lancaster force was drawn from 1, 5 and 8 Groups. With preparations already in hand for, perhaps, the most important operation of the war to date to be launched ten days hence, the Turin raid was to be used to test the merits of employing a raid controller, or Master of Ceremonies, in the manner of W/C Gibson during Operation Chastise. The man selected for the job was Group Captain John Searby, currently serving as commanding officer of 83 Squadron, and before that, Gibson's successor as commanding officer of 106 Squadron. 1 Group assigned fifty Lancasters from 101, 103 and 460 Squadrons to Turin and twenty-two from 12 and 100 Squadrons to Genoa, creating an overall Italy-bound force of 197 aircraft.

The Elsham Wolds contingent of sixteen Lancasters took off between 20.44 and 21.59 with S/L England the senior pilot on duty and S/L Wood also present, having hitched a ride with F/L Van Rolleghem. Half of the Lancasters were carrying a cookie in addition to the ten SBCs of incendiaries and half four 1,000 pounders as they headed south to Selsey Bill and thence to Cabourg and Lake Bourget in excellent weather conditions, which persisted on the Italian side of the Alps to provide good visibility for the run to the target. The aiming point was identified visually and by green TIs, and the 103 Squadron crews attacked from 16,500 to 21,500 between 01.00 and 01.09 in the face of a desultory and ineffective defence. The

Path Finder performance was described as effective and there was praise for the efforts of G/C Searby, whose calm presence gave the main force crews confidence as he directed the bombing from one aiming point to another. At debriefings, crews were enthusiastic about the outcome, which some claimed to be the best they had been part of, and although the Master Bomber experiment at Turin had not been entirely successful, experience had been gained, which would prove useful for the forthcoming Operation Hydra.

Mannheim was posted as the target on 9th and a force of 457 Lancasters and Halifaxes made ready, 1 Group contributing 112 Lancasters of which twenty-three were provided by 103 Squadron. Each was loaded with a cookie and three 1,000 pounders in addition to the SBCs of incendiaries and departed Elsham Wolds between 22.46 and 23.29 with S/Ls England and Wood the senior pilots on duty. After climbing out, they headed for the rendezvous point over Reading, before exiting England via Beachy Head on course for the French coast at Boulogne. There were no early returns as they made their way across Belgium on a direct track to the target, where they were greeted by a five-tenths layer of broken cloud at 4,000 feet and eight-tenths at 10,000 feet. Despite this, the visibility was fair, and the yellow skymarkers and green TIs sufficient to provide a reference for the bomb-aimers. The 103 Squadron participants carried out their attacks from 16,500 to 22,000 feet between 01.34 and 02.06 and returned home to report several very large fires but a generally scattered raid. In fact, according to local reports, 1,316 buildings had been destroyed, forty-two industrial concerns had lost production, and more than fifteen hundred fires of varying sizes had required attention. Six Halifaxes and three Lancasters failed to return, one of the latter, 103 Squadron's ED882, the only 1 Group loss, coming down somewhere in southern Germany with no survivors from the crew of P/O Brown.

The following night brought a return to southern Germany, this time to Nuremberg, for which a force of 653 aircraft was made ready that included Stirlings, the type usually at the bottom of the food chain. This was good news to the Halifax crews, who in a Lancaster/Halifax force, invariably came off second best. 1 Group provided 111 of the Lancasters, twenty-three of them made ready at Elsham Wolds, where the Mk I variants were loaded with a cookie and six SBCs of 30lb and seven and two-thirds SBCs of 4lb incendiaries, while the Mk III variants, powered by American Packard rather than Rolls Royce-built Merlins, were given an additional 1,000 pounder and one of 500lbs. This was born out of AVM Rice's obsession of loading each Lancaster to its absolute maximum capacity, a policy hated by the crews and one which would lead to the dumping of bombs. We will return to this topic later. Take-off was safely accomplished between 21.27 and 22.29 with S/Ls England, Prickett and Wood the senior pilots on duty, and after climbing out and forming up, they set course for Beachy Head on the Sussex coast to follow a route similar to that of the previous night. F/Sgt Rhodes and crew lost their port-outer engine within around ninety minutes and F/Sgt Carter and crew turned back at Beachy Head after their starboard-outer failed.

The others pressed on to the target area, and F/O Marshall and crew were some fifty miles short when the starboard-inner engine failed and they released their bombs on a built-up area below, which was plotted to be Bad Mergentheim. Conditions at Nuremberg reflected those of twenty-four hours earlier with eight to ten-tenths cloud at 12,000 feet, but the Path Finders had prepared a ground-marking plan, and there were no release-point flares to draw the head of the main force on. However, the green TIs on the ground were visible to most, as were the fires for those arriving later, the Elsham Wolds crews spread throughout the bomber stream and delivering their bomb loads from 19,000 to 22,000 feet between 01.04 and 01.41. They returned safely to report a good concentration of fires, the glow from which remained visible for 150 miles into the return journey. Post-raid reconnaissance and local sources confirmed that the city had sustained much housing and industrial damage in mostly central and southern districts, and a death toll of 577 people was evidence of the intensity of the bombing. The operation cost sixteen aircraft, but none from 1 Group.

The Italian campaign continued on the 12th, when Milan and Turin were the targets, the former for a force of 504 aircraft including 111 Lancasters provided by 1 Group, while 152 aircraft from 3 and 8 Groups attended to the latter. 103 Squadron loaded each of its twenty-five Lancasters according to the variant with a cookie and ten or twelve SBCs of incendiaries and sent them off from Elsham Wolds between 21.03 and 21.40 with S/Ls Prickett and Wood the senior pilots on duty and W/C Slater undertaking a rare sortie as second pilot to F/O Hammond. After climbing out they set course for Selsey Bill to begin the Channel crossing, which would terminate on the Normandy coast at Cabourg at the start of a south-easterly straight leg across central France to the northern tip of Lake Bourget. The sortie of P/O Atkinson and crew lasted two-and-a-half hours after the No 2 Fuel tank was found to be leaking fuel at the rate of ninety gallons per hour, and F/Sgt Bassett and crew dropped out some two hours into the outward flight after an overheating starboard-outer engine caught fire. The others traversed the Alps and skirted southern Switzerland before settling onto the final run-in on the target, which was conducted under clear skies with just ground mist to spoil the vertical view. On arrival, the Elsham Wolds crews bombed visually or on yellow flares and green TIs from 16,000 to 20,000 feet between 01.16 and 01.48 in accordance with the instructions of the "Master of Ceremonies". At debriefing, the crews reported large fires in the city centre, which could be seen for a hundred miles and more into the return flight, and the crews of S/L Wood, F/O Marshall and Sgt Thomas described inconclusive encounters with night-fighters. Local reports, though short on detail, confirmed that four important war-industry factories had sustained serious damage during August and most of it probably occurred on this night.

Milan would face two further attacks before the Command's interest in Italy ceased for good, and the first of these was posted on the 14th, for which 1, 5 and 8 Groups put together a force of 140 Lancasters, forty-four of them representing 1 Group, which assigned twenty-eight to the Breda & Pirelli locomotive works, a huge complex situated in the northern suburb of Bicocca, and sixteen to join in the main force attack on the city itself. 103 Squadron made ready eleven of its own, loading seven of them with four 1,000 pounders and six SBCs each of 4lb and 30lb incendiaries and the others with a cookie and same number of SBCs. The reason for the difference in loads was made clear at briefing, when seven crews learned of their part in the attack on the factory complex, while the other four were assigned to "city-busting" duties as part of the main element. They departed Elsham Wolds between 20.53 and 21.30 with S/L Wood the senior pilot on duty and F/O Hammond this time accompanied by W/C Towle, who was about to be appointed to the command of 12 Squadron. They adopted the standard route, and all reached the target under clear skies and in good visibility aided by a brilliant moon and Path Finder route markers. The Path Finders accurately marked the factory complex with flares and the city centre with green TIs in a tight concentration, and this was exploited by the 103 Squadron crews at the Breda & Pirelli works from 7,000 to 9,000 feet between 01.23 and 01.28. No details were recorded for the attack on the city, but many fires were observed to take hold as the force turned away, and the glow remained visible for a considerable distance into the return flight.

There was to be no respite for Milan as a force of 199 Lancasters was made ready later on the 15th for a return that night, for what would be the last time over Italy for main force Lancasters. 103 Squadron provided eleven of the sixty-seven 1 Group aircraft, and they were given the same bomb load as for the previous night before taking off from Elsham Wolds between 19.59 and 20.19 with S/L Prickett the senior pilot on duty. There were no early returns to reduce the squadron's impact, all reaching the target to find clear skies, the brightest possible moonlight and green Path Finder flares over lake Bourget to guide them in. Haze and smoke hung over the city from the previous night to spoil to an extent the vertical visibility, but the Path Finders marked the city-centre aiming point with green TIs, and these were bombed to good effect by the 103 Squadron crews from 17,000 to 20,000 feet between 00.01 and 00.17. The consensus of returning crews was of a concentrated attack, but no local report was forthcoming to confirm or deny.

The final raid of the war on an Italian city was carried out by 154 aircraft of 3 and 8 Groups against Turin on the following night. A successful raid was claimed at the modest cost of four aircraft, but many of the participating Stirlings were diverted on return and did not reach their home stations in time to participate in that night's highly important operation, for which a maximum effort had been planned. This would deplete the available number of Stirlings by sixty and heap an even greater responsibility upon the rest of the force to complete the job.

Since the very beginning of the war, intelligence had suggested that Germany was researching into and developing rocket technology, and although scant regard was given to the reports by some of the leading scientific experts, photographic reconnaissance had confirmed the existence of an establishment at Peenemünde at the northern tip of the island of Usedom on the Baltic coast. The activities there were monitored through Ultra intercepts and surreptitious reconnaissance flights, and the V-1, known to the photographic interpreters at Medmenham because of its wingspan as the "Peenemünde 20", was captured on a photograph. The brilliant scientist, Dr R V Jones, had been able to gain vital information concerning the V-1's range, which would ultimately be used to feed disinformation to the enemy, largely through the double agent "Zigzag", otherwise known as Eddie Chapman. Unfortunately, Churchill's chief scientific adviser, Professor Lindemann, or Lord Cherwell as he had become, steadfastly refused to give credence to the existence and feasibility of rocket weapons and held stubbornly to his viewpoint even when presented with a photograph of a V-2 on a trailer taken by a PRU Mosquito in June 1943. It required the combined urgings of Duncan Sandys and Dr Jones to persuade Churchill of the urgency to act, and Operation Hydra was planned for the first available opportunity, which occurred on the night of the 17/18th. Earlier in the day, the USAAF 8th Air Force had carried out its first deep-penetration raids into Germany to attack ball-bearing production at Schweinfurt and the Messerschmidt aircraft plant at Regensburg, and to the shock of its leaders, had learned the harsh lesson that unescorted daylight raids in 1943 were not viable. The folks at home would not be told that sixty B17s had failed to return.

A force of 596 aircraft and crews answered the call to arms for Peenemünde, 1 Group contributing 113 of the 324 Lancasters and the rest of the force comprised of 218 Halifaxes and fifty-four Stirlings. The operation had been meticulously planned to account for the three vital components of Peenemünde, the housing estate, where the scientific and technical staff lived, the factory buildings in which the weapons were assembled and the experimental site, where testing took place. Each was assigned to a specific wave of aircraft, which would attack from medium level, with the Path Finders bearing the huge responsibility of re-directing the point of aim accordingly, for which each squadron was to provide one crew as a "shifter". That apart, once route markers had been dropped on Rügen island, the Path Finder markers and backers-up were to follow the standard routine of red, yellow and green TIs. After last minute alterations, 3 and 4 Groups were given the first mentioned, 1 Group the second, and 5 and 6 Groups the third. The whole operation was to be overseen by a Master of Ceremonies (referred to hereafter as Master Bomber), and the officer selected for this hazardous and demanding role was G/C Searby of 83 Squadron, who, as already mentioned, had stepped into Gibson's shoes at 106 Squadron after Gibson was posted out to form 617 Squadron. Searby's role was to direct the marking and bombing by VHF and to encourage the crews to press on to the aiming-point, a task requiring him to remain in the target area and within range of the defences throughout the attack. Should he be shot down, his deputy, W/C Johnny Fauquier of 405 (Vancouver) Squadron RCAF, would take over.

In an attempt to protect the bombers from the attentions of enemy night-fighters for as long as possible, eight Mosquitos of 139 Squadron were to carry out a spoof raid on Berlin beginning at 23.00, seventy-five minutes before the opening of the main event, and would be led by the highly experienced and former 49 Squadron commander, G/C Len Slee. In the expectation of encountering drifting smoke as the last wave on target, the 5 Group crews were instructed to employ their oft-used time-and-distance approach to the aiming-point and had practiced this over a stretch of coast near the Wainfleet bombing range at the mouth of the Wash in Lincolnshire, progressively cutting the margin of error from one thousand to three hundred yards.

By the time that briefings took place on Bomber Command stations on the 17th, F/L Van Rolleghem had received the award of the DFC from the hands of AVM Rice, the 1 Group A-O-C. When he then took his seat in the hushed briefing room at Elsham Wolds, he and the rest of the Command's crews due to operate that night learned that what they were about to undertake was so important to the war effort, that should they be unsuccessful, they would have to keep going back until the job was done. Twelve of the 103 Squadron contingent of twenty-four Lancasters had a cookie and seven 1,000 pounders winched into their bomb bays, a further seven received ten 1,000 pounders, four had a cookie and two 500 pounders plus six hundred 4lb and fifty-six 30lb incendiaries and one a cookie, two 1,000 pounders and six hundred 4lb and forty-four 30lb incendiaries. They departed Elsham Wolds between 21.07 and 21.45 with F/Ls Prickett and Wood the senior pilots on duty on a night when many squadron commanders elected to fly, in some cases with fatal consequences, and exited the English coast at Mablethorpe. The overall early-return rate was lower than normal, suggesting that crews had taken to heart the importance of the operation, but F/L Rawstorne had no choice but to turn back having contended with a faltering port-outer engine for the entire North Sea crossing. Rather than waste the effort he and his crew bombed an aerodrome near Sylt just after an aircraft had taken off. The various groups made their way individually to a rendezvous point some ninety minutes flying time or three hundred miles from the English coast and sixty miles from Denmark's western coast, where they became a stream. Darkness had fallen as they crossed the North Sea, and twenty miles short of landfall over the southern tip of Fanø island, south of Esbjerg, "windowing" began, in order to simulate a standard raid on a northern or north-eastern city. Southern Denmark was traversed by the Lancaster brigade at 18,000 feet, twice the altitude required for the attack, but worryingly, in a band of cloudless sky under a bright moon. They adopted an east-south-easterly course and began to shed altitude gradually during the 240-mile run to the target a little over an hour away, and at the rear of the stream, the 5 Group crews focussed on the island of Rügen, the ideal starting point for their timed run to Peenemünde, which lay some fifteen miles beyond to the south-east.

The initial marking of the housing estate went awry, and some target indicators fell onto the forced workers camp at Trassenheide, more than a mile south of the intended aiming point. Many of the 3 and 4 Group bombs fell here, inflicting grievous casualties on friendly foreign nationals, who were trapped inside their wooden barracks. Once rectified, however, the attack proceeded according to plan, and several important members of the technical staff were killed. The 1 Group second-wave crews encountered strong crosswinds over the narrow section of the island where the construction sheds were located and had red and green TIs to aim at in accordance with the instructions of the Master Bomber to "not bomb last lot of greens, they are falling in the sea, bomb the greens between the reds, ignore greens on the south." The 103 Squadron crews complied from 7,000 to 11,000 feet between 00.31 and 00.46, this phase of the operation largely achieving its aims, and they were on their way home before the night-fighters arrived from Berlin, having been attracted by the glow of fires well to the north. On arrival at Rügen, the 5 Group crews began their timed run, and reached the experimental site to encounter the expected smoke and bombed on green TIs. They and the 6 Group Halifaxes and Lancasters then ran into the night-fighters, some of which were equipped with the new upward-firing cannons, known to the Luftwaffe as Schräge Musik, their term for jazz, and they proceeded to take a heavy toll of bombers both in the skies over the target and on the route home towards Denmark. Twenty-nine of the forty missing aircraft came from this third wave, seventeen of them belonging to 5 Group and twelve to 6 Group, which represented a loss rate for the Canadians of 19.7%. 1 Group posted missing just three Lancasters and their crews, among them 103 Squadron's ED725, which was brought down near Flensburg with no survivors from the crew of the newly-commissioned P/O O'Donnell, who were on just their third operation. Returning crews praised the work of the Path Finders and the Master Bomber, and F/Sgt Rule's rear gunner shot down a BF109, which was observed to burst into flames and crash. Post-raid reconnaissance revealed the raid to have been sufficiently effective to delay the V-2 development programme by perhaps a number of months, and ultimately to force the manufacture of secret weapons underground. The flight testing of the V-2 was eventually withdrawn eastwards into Poland beyond the range of Harris's bombers, and thus Peenemünde had been nullified as a threat at the first attempt.

Before the next campaign began, Leverkusen was posted on the 22nd as the target for a heavy force of 449 Lancasters and Halifaxes with 8 Group Oboe-Mosquito to provide the initial marking. Situated on the Rhine just a stone's throw north of Cologne, the city was home to a factory belonging to the infamous I G Farben chemicals and pharmaceuticals company, or to give it its full name, Interessen-Gemeinschaft Farbenindustrie, in English, Common Interest Conglomerate of chemical dye-making corporations. Formed in 1925, it was a merger between BASF, Bayer, Hoechst, Agfa, Chemische Fabrik Griesheim-Elektron and Chemische Fabrik vorm. Weiler Ter Meer and was heavily involved in the development and production of synthetic oil, employing slave labour at all of its factories across Germany, including 30,000 from the Auschwitz concentration camp, where it had built a plant. One of the company's subsidiaries manufactured the Zyklon B gas used during the Holocaust to murder millions of Jewish victims.

103 Squadron made ready twenty-one Lancasters in a 1 Group contribution of 105, loading each with a cookie, three 1,000 pounders and twelve SBS before sending them on their way from Elsham Wolds between 20.59 and 21.40 with S/Ls Prickett and Wood the senior pilots on duty. After climbing out they headed for the Belgian coast at Knokke, to follow a well-worn route to the southern Ruhr, which would require them to pass through the searchlight and flak belt near Cologne that was guaranteed to provide a hot welcome. All from Elsham Wolds made it safely through the narrow searchlight and flak corridor to reach the target, where ten-tenths cloud topped out at 18,000 feet and blanketed the area. Oboe-equipment failures forced most crews to bomb on e.t.a. in the absence of markers, until the glow of fires came to their aid as the raid developed, although a small number of crews spotted green TIs on the ground and aimed for them. Bombing was carried out by the 103 Squadron crews in the face of intense flak from 17,000 to 21,500 feet between 00.06 and 00.40, and the glow of fires and the flash of explosions was initially the only confirmation of something happening under the cloud, until a column of smoke was observed to rise through 12,000 feet. Returning crews were not optimistic about the effectiveness of the attack, and local reports revealed its scattered nature and that up to a dozen neighbouring towns had been hit, Düsseldorf suffering the destruction of 132 buildings. The loss of only five aircraft was something of bright spot in an otherwise disappointing night, but there was sadness at the loss of 103 Squadron's W/O Breckon DFM and crew, whose ED701 was shot down by the night-fighter of Oblt Heinz Strüning of I./NJG1 and crashed without survivors four miles north-east of Waalwijk as it approached the Scheldt estuary homebound. S/L Pape was posted in from 166 Squadron later in the day, for what would be a relatively brief stay. S/L Prickett had now completed his tour and would soon be posted out to leave a vacancy for a B Flight commander.

Harris had long believed that the key to ultimate victory lay in the destruction of Berlin, the seat of the Nazi government and the symbol of its power. On the 23rd, orders were received on stations across the Command to prepare for a maximum effort that night against Germany's capital city, which had not been visited by the heavy brigade since the end of March. The crews, of course, could not know that this was to be the first of an eventual nineteen raids on the "Big City", in an offensive which, with an autumn break, would drag on until the following spring. It was a campaign that would test the resolve of the crews to the absolute limit, whilst also sealing the fate of the Stirlings and the Mk II and V Halifaxes as front-line bombers. There are varying opinions concerning the true start date of what became known as the Berlin offensive or the Battle of Berlin, some commentators believing these first three operations in August and September to be the start, while others point to the sixteen raids from mid-November. However, there was little doubt in Bomber Command circles that this was it, a fact demonstrated by the comments in numerous squadron ORBs, including that of 103 Squadron, which carried the entry: "Berlin. Twenty-four aircraft were detailed to attack this target, which begins the so-called Battle of Berlin".

There would be a Master Bomber on hand for this operation and the officer chosen was Canadian W/C "Johnny" Fauquier, the tough, grizzled and one-time bush pilot and frequent brawler, who was enjoying his second spell as the commanding officer of 405 (Vancouver) Squadron, once of 4 Group, but since April, proud to be the only Canadian Path Finder unit. The route had been planned to take the bomber stream to a rendezvous point over the North Sea, before crossing the Dutch coast near Haarlem and entering Germany between Meppen to the north and Osnabrück to the south. It would then pass between Bremen and Hannover to bypass the southern rim of Berlin, before turning back sharply on a north-westerly course across the city centre. After bombing, aircraft were to pass out over the Baltic coast in the direction of the Schleswig-Holstein peninsula. Finally, seventeen Mosquitos were to precede the Path Finder and main force elements to drop route markers at key points in an attempt to keep the bomber stream on track.

A force of 727 aircraft was assembled, of which 107 Lancasters represented 1 Group, twenty-four of them belonging to 103 Squadron at Elsham Wolds, where the twenty Mk III variants were each loaded with a cookie, two 1,000 pounders, six-and-two-thirds SBCs of 4lb incendiaries and six of 30lbs, while the four Mk Is were spared one 1,000 pounder and the two-thirds-filled SBC. During the start-up procedure some incendiaries fell out of the bomb bay of W4323 and ignited, setting off a fire that caused the cookie to explode, destroying the Lancaster and damaging four others, which had to be withdrawn. Sgt Wheeler of F/L Finlay's crew was hit by shrapnel and killed. This left nineteen Lancasters available for the operation, and they took off between 20.15 and 21.00 with F/Ls Rawstorne and Van Rolleghem the senior pilots on duty. After climbing out and crossing the Lincolnshire coast, they headed for the gap in the enemy defences at Egmond and lost the services of P/O Atkinson and crew on the way when the rear gunner's oxygen tube was severed as he tested his guns. Those reaching the target area found clear skies and moonlight, but the Path Finders were unable to identify the aiming point in the centre of the city, a result of the inherent difficulties of interpreting the H2S images over such a massive urban sprawl. They marked the southern outskirts instead, and many main force crews then cut the corner to approach the city from the south-west rather than south-east, and this would result in the wastage of many bomb loads in open country and on outlying communities.

The 103 Squadron crews carried out their attacks visually and on red and green TIs from 19,000 to 21,400 feet between 23.46 and 00.24 in the face of intense searchlight activity with moderate flak. Returning crews reported large explosions and many fires, the glow from which was visible for at least 140 miles, and a pall of smoke had already risen to meet them as they turned towards the north-west. Curiously, only a few crews commented at debriefing on hearing the Master Bomber and finding his instructions helpful. Sgt Knott and crew reported that they were coned over the target and attacked by six BF109s, which inflicted extensive damage upon JA868 but were unable to bring it down. A new record of fifty-six aircraft failed to return, twenty-three Halifaxes, seventeen Lancasters and sixteen Stirlings, representing a percentage loss rate respectively of 9.1, 5.1 and 12.9, which perfectly reflected the food chain when all three types operated together. Berlin experienced a scattered raid, but because of the numbers attacking, extensive damage was caused, a little in or near the centre but mostly in south-western residential districts and industrialized areas a little further east. 2,611 buildings were reported to have been destroyed or seriously damaged, and the death toll of 854 people was surprisingly high, caused largely, perhaps, by a failure to heed the alarms and go to the assigned shelters.

The C Flight commander, acting S/L England, had now completed his tour and was posted to 1667 Conversion Unit on the 25th and would almost certainly revert to flight lieutenant rank. Orders were received on the 27th to prepare for an operation that night against Nuremberg, the plan for which included an additional ten 139 Squadron Mosquitos to provide a "window" screen in advance of the bomber stream. The Oboe Mosquitos were to mark the route with red and green TIs, backed up by H2S Lancasters, but as Berlin was beyond the range of Oboe, the aiming-point was to be marked with red TIs by H2S, backed up by greens. A force of 674 aircraft lined up for take-off in mid-evening, 1 Group contributing 105 Lancasters, the eighteen Mk IIIs belonging to 103 Squadron receiving a bomb load of a cookie, one 1,000 pounder, one 500 pounder, seven-and-two-thirds SBCs of 4lb incendiaries and six of 30lbs, while the three Mk Is were spared the 1,000 and 500 pounders. They departed Elsham Wolds between 20.57 and 21.42 with F/Ls Rawstorne and Van Rolleghem the senior pilots on duty, and after climbing out, headed for the French coast and on arrival, followed the line of the frontier with Belgium until crossing into Germany south of Luxembourg on course for the target, where clear skies and intense darkness prevailed. F/Sgt McMahon and crew were around two hours into the outward flight when the navigator's oxygen mask was accidentally knocked off and he lost consciousness. When he came round, the crew had no idea of their position, and the sortie was aborted.

The Path Finders had been briefed to check their H2S equipment by dropping a 1,000 pounder on Heilbronn, and some crews complied, while others, it seems, experienced technical difficulties. The initial marking was accurate, but a creep-back developed, which the backers-up and the Master Bomber could not correct, and this resulted in many bomb loads falling into open country, while others hit Nuremberg's south-eastern and eastern districts. The 103 Squadron crews aimed at green TIs from 19,000 to 21,600 feet between 00.30 and 01.14 and generally gained an impression of a fairly concentrated and accurate attack, which produced many fires. They reported searchlights and night-fighters to be numerous and evidence of this came with the failure to return of thirty-three aircraft, eleven of each type, which again confirmed the vulnerability of the Stirlings and Halifaxes when operating alongside Lancasters. The loss rate on this night was 3.1% for the Lancaster, 5% for the Halifax and 10.6% for the Stirlings. 103 Squadron's W4364 was shot down by a night-fighter and crashed near Emskirchen in southern Germany with fatal consequences for four of the crew, while W/O Annis and two others survived to be taken into captivity. They had been on their ninth operation together.

The main event on the night of the 30/31st was a two-phase attack on the twin towns of Mönchengladbach and Rheydt, the first time that either would experience a major Bomber Command assault. Situated some ten miles west of the centre of Düsseldorf in the south-western Ruhr, they would face an initial force of 660 aircraft of four types, in what for the crews, was a short-penetration trip across the Dutch frontier and a welcome change from the recent long slogs to eastern and southern Germany. The plan called for the first wave to hit Mönchengladbach, before a two-minute pause in the bombing allowed the Path Finders to head south to mark Rheydt. 103 Squadron made ready nineteen Lancasters as part of a 1 Group contribution of 106 and twenty-eight Wellingtons and loaded them with a cookie, four 1,000 pounders and six hundred 4lb incendiaries, before sending them on their way in two phases between 23.48 and 23.59 and 00.19 and 00.48 with F/Ls Rawstorne and Van Rolleghem the senior pilots on duty. There were no early returns to Elsham Wolds as they passed out over Sheringham to make landfall at Knokke on the Belgian coast, and they reached the target area to find good visibility above the seven to ten-tenths cloud at 8,000 feet. A near-perfect display of target-marking by Oboe-delivered red and green flares drew on the main force to bomb with scarcely any creep-back, the 103 Squadron crews carrying out their bombing runs from 18,000 to 21,000 feet between 02.02 and 02.46. On return they reported many fires, the glow from which could be seen from the Dutch coast homebound, and photo-reconnaissance confirmed a highly accurate and concentrated attack, which destroyed more than 2,300 buildings in the two towns, 171 of them of an industrial nature, along with 869 residential properties. Twenty-five aircraft failed to return, and Halifaxes narrowly sustained the highest numerical casualties.

The month ended with the second of the Berlin operations, which was scheduled for the night of the 31st, and for which a force of 622 aircraft was assembled, more than half of them Lancasters. 1 Group was responsible for 102 Lancasters, 103 Squadron loading all but two of its twenty-two with a cookie, six SBCs of 30lb incendiaries and seven of 4lbs, the two Mk Is spared a few incendiaries. They departed Elsham Wolds between 19.59 and 20.44 with S/L Wood the senior pilot on duty and F/L Rawstorne and crew accompanied by W/C Craven, who was gaining operational experience before taking command of 12 Squadron later that very day, after the failure to return the previous night of W/C Towle. The route on this night took the bomber stream on an east-south-easterly heading across Texel to a position between Hannover and Leipzig, before turning to pass to the south-east of Berlin and approach the city-centre aiming point on a north-westerly track. The return leg would involve a south-westerly course to a position south of Cologne for an exit over the French coast, but despite the attempts to outwit the enemy night-fighter controller, he would be able to predict to some extent where to concentrate his night-fighters. For the first time the Luftwaffe was observed to be employing "fighter flares" to mark out the path of the bombers to and from the target. The Path Finders encountered five to six-tenths cloud in the target area and this combined with H2S equipment failure and a spirited night-fighter response to cause the markers to be dropped well to the south of the planned aiming point. The 103 Squadron crews reported up to eight-tenths thin cloud and bombed on red and green TIs from 17,000 to 22,000 feet between 23.35 and 00.15, observing many fires over a wide area, but it was noted by some that two groups of green TIs were ten miles apart and attracting attention from the main force. The outcome of the raid was a major disappointment, brought about by woefully short marking and a pronounced creep-back stretching some thirty miles into open country and outlying communities. The result was the destruction of just eighty-five houses, a figure in no way commensurate with the effort expended and the loss of forty-seven heavy bombers. 103 Squadron posted missing the crew of F/O Philip, and no trace of them or ED646 was ever found. The percentage loss rates made alarming reading at Bomber Command HQ, the Lancasters with an acceptable and sustainable 3%, the Halifaxes with 11.3% and the Stirlings with 16%.

During the course of the month, the squadron took part in thirteen operations and dispatched a record 261 sorties, of which only twelve were abortive, and one of these bombed an alternative target before returning home. Seven Lancasters and their crews failed to return, another was lost at home and an airman killed.

September 1943

Probably because of the heavy losses recently incurred by the Halifaxes and Stirlings, an all-Lancaster force of 316 aircraft was to conclude the current series of operations against the "Big City" on the 3rd, of which 109 were provided by 1 Group. The 1 Group ORB described the operation as an experiment in the method of hitting Berlin, in which the force would fly direct to the target and cross the aiming point in eleven minutes, before intentionally violating Swedish airspace during the return flight and passing to the north of Denmark. The 103 Squadron and Elsham Wolds station ground staff worked hard to prepare twenty-two of their charges, loading each with a cookie and mix of 4lb and 30lb incendiaries, before sending them on their way between 19.46 and 20.08 with F/Ls Rawstorne and Van Rolleghem the senior pilots on duty and S/L Pape flying as second pilot to F/O Day. The crews of F/Sgts Pargeter, Campbell and Floyd abandoned their sorties and were back in the circuit within three hours, leaving the others to rendezvous with the bomber stream over the North Sea, cross the Dutch coast over the Den Helder peninsula and adopt a direct course of 350 miles, which took them north of Hannover to Brandenburg, some thirty-five miles short of the target.

Long, straight legs were rarely employed because of the risk of interception by the Luftwaffe, but the forecast heavy cloud with tops at 18,000 feet accompanied the stream all the way from the Dutch coast to the target area and helped to keep the enemy at bay. The Path Finders had been briefed to use H2S to navigate their way via the region's lakes to the city centre aiming point, but the cloud miraculously dispersed in time to leave clear skies and allow them to drop ground-marking TIs rather than the less reliable skymarkers. The first TIs fell right over the aiming point, before others crept back for between two and five miles along the line of approach from the west. Fortunately, the backers up maintained the marking as the main force Lancasters came in in a single wave, in which the 103 Squadron participants carried out their attacks on red and green TIs from 19,000 to 23,000 feet either side of 23.30. They observed that the many fires appeared to be merging as they turned towards the north for the long homeward leg towards Sweden. Despite the fact that much of the bombing had fallen short of the city centre, most of it landed within the city boundaries, principally into the largely residential districts of Tiergarten, Wedding, Moabit and Charlottenburg and the industrial Siemensstadt, where much useful damage occurred with the resultant loss of war production. The Four Mosquitos laid spoof route marker flares well away from the actual track to mislead the night-fighters, but, in the absence of the poorer performing Halifaxes and Stirlings, twenty-two Lancasters failed to return, almost 7% of those dispatched.

Whether by design, or as a result of the losses sustained, Berlin was now shelved for the next ten weeks, while Harris sought other suitable targets, of which there were many. He would shortly begin a four-raid series against Hannover stretching over a four-week period but first he focused on southern Germany, beginning on the 5th with the twin cities of Mannheim and Ludwigshafen, which face each other from the East and West Banks respectively of the Rhine. The plan was to exploit the creep-back phenomenon that attended most large operations, by approaching the target from the west and marking the eastern half of Mannheim, with the expectation that the bombing would spread back along the line of approach across western Mannheim and into Ludwigshafen. A force of 605 aircraft was assembled, which included 102 Lancasters of 1 Group, twenty-two of them at Elsham Wolds, the Mk III variants of which were loaded with a cookie, two 500 pounders, seven SBCs of 4lb incendiaries and six of 30lbs, while the Mk Is were spared the 500 pounders. They took off between 19.30 and 20.10 with S/L Pape the senior pilot on duty for the first and last time, and after climbing out, set course for Beachy Head and the Channel crossing. There were no early returns, and all tracked across France to a point five miles south of Luxembourg, where route markers established the final turning point for a direct run on the target. The Path Finders were routed in over Kaiserslautern some thirty miles due west of Mannheim, from where they were to carry out a timed run to the aiming-point.

The main force crews arrived to find clear skies and the Path Finders performing at their absolute best, and after first observing red and yellow markers, the 103 Squadron crews had green TIs in their bomb sights as they let their loads go from 19,000 to 22,000 feet between 23.06 and 23.40. Those arriving towards the later stages of the raid were drawn on by the burgeoning fires fifty miles ahead, and a number of large, red explosions were observed at 23.12, 23.23 and 23.27, the last of which was followed by a purplish-red mushroom of fire. Searchlights were numerous but the flak negligible, and it was the abundance of night-fighters that posed the greatest risk to life and limb, although most of the Elsham Wolds crews appeared to avoid any contact. Black smoke was rising through 15,000 feet as the bombers withdrew to the west, and the glow from the burning cities was visible for 150 miles and more into the return journey, which thirty-four aircraft would fail to complete. Thirteen Lancasters, an equal number of Halifaxes and eight Stirlings were missing, and the percentage loss rates continued to tell the same story. 103 Squadron posted missing the crews of W/O Cant and F/Sgt Nelson in ED751 and LM343 respectively, the former abandoned over France on the way home, and all but one managed to retain their freedom. The pilot and two others made it into Switzerland, two reached England in a French fishing boat, and another fought alongside the French resistance for a year. Sgt Thomas, the wireless operator, was reported to have been captured while trying to cross the Pyrenees into Spain. The Nelson crew became hopelessly lost in bad weather on the way home and abandoned LM343 somewhere near the Cherbourg peninsula, six members including the pilot falling into enemy hands, while the seventh managed to evade a similar fate.

Local sources confirmed that both Mannheim and Ludwigshafen had suffered catastrophic destruction, with almost two thousand fires in the latter alone, 986 of them classed as large. Mannheim's reporting system broke down completely and little detail emerged of this raid, although it would recover in time for the next assault in fewer than three weeks' time. What is known, is that the main railway station in Mannheim and three suburban stations were destroyed and the tank and military tractor factories belonging to Heinrich Lanz and Josef Vogele respectively sustained serious damage, as did the I G Farben-owned Rashig & Sulzer chemicals plant.

Munich was posted as the target on the 6th, for which 103 Squadron made ready nineteen Lancasters as part of the eighty-six-strong 1 Group element in an overall force of 257 Lancasters and 147 Halifaxes, the Stirling brigade made conspicuous by its absence. At Elsham Wolds each Lancaster received a load of a cookie, one 500 pounder and seven and six SBCs respectively of 4lb and 30lb incendiaries, before being sent on their way between 19.37 and 20.06 with S/L Wood the senior pilot on duty and F/L Van Rolleghem undertaking the final sortie of his tour. The outward route mirrored that of the previous night and only the crew of F/Sgt Bassett failed to complete it having lost their port-outer engine within ninety minutes of taking off. The others reached the Bavarian capital city under conditions that were not ideal, with cloud at between four and nine-tenths, despite which, some ground features like the River Isar could be identified and the red, yellow and green TIs were visible. The 5 Group crews carried out a timed run from the Ammersee, located twenty-one miles away to the south-west, while those from 1 Group went straight in, the 103 Squadron contingent bombing from 19,000 to 21,700 feet between 23.36 and 23.56. A large number of fires was observed to be grouped around the markers, but an accurate assessment was not possible, and local reports would suggest that the attack had been scattered across southern and western districts. The searchlights were ineffective because of the cloud, but a strong night-fighter presence was again evident, and sixteen aircraft failed to return, thirteen of them Halifaxes, a percentage loss rate of 8.8, compared with 1.2 for the Lancasters.

There now followed a two-week stand-down from operations for the main force Lancaster squadrons, during which period a number of changes took place at Elsham Wolds. A tragedy occurred on the 8th involving three Air Training Corps cadets, who were on board JB153 for air experience during an air-test. The Lancaster's nose dropped while banking round, and F/Sgt Buxton was unable to regain control before it plunged into the ground, killing all nine occupants.

That night, a series of operations against French targets began with the bombing of heavy gun emplacements near the small coastal resort of Le Portel. This was the final phase of Operation Starkey, a rehearsal for invasion, which had begun on the 16th of August, and which was intended to deceive the enemy into believing that the invasion was imminent. Harris was less than enthusiastic about allowing his squadrons to participate in what he considered to be "play-acting" and managed to restrict Bomber Command's involvement to token gestures as on this night. The batteries, codenamed Religion and Andante, were to be attacked forty minutes apart, but much confusion surrounded the marking and the subsequent inaccurate bombing caused massive destruction to the town of Le Portel and many casualties.

(For a detailed analysis of this operation, see the excellent book, The Starkey Sacrifice, by Michael Cumming, published by Sutton).

S/L Kennard returned to the squadron on the 11th after his period as an instructor at 1656 Conversion Unit and on the 16th, ACM Harris paid a rare visit to Elsham Wolds to address the crews in the gymnasium, before conducting a question-and-answer session. F/L Van Rolleghem departed the squadron on the 18th to take up a post at Bomber Command HQ, and two days later C Flight was posted under the command of S/L Pape to the satellite station at Kirmington, where it was to form the nucleus of 166 Squadron as it converted from Wellingtons to Lancasters.

It was not until the commencement of the series of raids on Hannover that 1 and 5 Groups, as a whole, were roused from their slumber. The irony of such long layoffs was that airmen, despite occupying the most dangerous jobs in the fighting services, grew listless and bored when left to kick their heels, attend lectures and take part in PT, and, no doubt, cheered when the tannoys called them to briefing on the 22nd. They learned that they were to be part of a force of 711 aircraft to attack the ancient city of Hannover, situated in northern Germany midway between the Dutch frontier and Berlin. They were told that it was home to much war industry, but what was not known at the time was that it was also the location of seven Nazi concentration camps. According to Martin Middlebrook and Chris Everitt in Bomber Command War Diaries, the first two operations produced concentrated bombing, but mostly outside of the target, while only the third one succeeded in causing extensive damage, which, if the figures are to be believed, seem to be massively out of proportion. The author contends that the reports of the crews after the first two operations suggest strongly that the damage to Hannover was accumulative over the first three raids and did not result from just one, as will be explained in the following narrative. The telling feature is, perhaps, that no reports came out of Hannover to corroborate the testimony of the crews on the first two raids, although post-raid reconnaissance by the RAF after the second one did show that some of the bombing had fallen into open country, and the Path Finders did admit to at least one poor performance.

1 Group contributed 101 Lancasters and a dozen Wellingtons to this first operation, the number including fifteen of the former representing 103 Squadron and eight from 166 Squadron making its operational debut on the type. At Elsham Wolds most of the Lancasters were loaded with a cookie, three 1,000 pounders, ten SBCs of 4lb incendiaries and six of 30lb and took off between 18.50 and 19.30 with S/L Kennard the senior pilot on duty. After climbing out and leaving Mablethorpe behind them, they joined up with the other 1 Group participants ahead of the 430-mile outward leg, before crossing the Frisian Island of Vlieland on a direct course to the target. F/O Churchill and crew lost their radio and were among five 1 Group "boomerangs", leaving the others to press on to find good visibility in the target area, but stronger-than-forecast winds pushing the marking and bombing towards the south-east. The 103 Squadron crews carried out their bombing runs from 19,000 to 20,500 feet between 21.31 and 22.07, aiming at red and green TIs and dodging the intense searchlights and heavy flak, which was bursting at around 18,000 feet. Some returning crews observed a line of fires developing from west to east, with smoke rising through 14,000 feet, while others claimed that fires ran from the aiming point in a north-north-westerly direction across the city, but all were unanimous, that the raid had been highly successful, and that the glow

of fires was still visible from the Dutch coast, a distance of two hundred miles. Twenty-six aircraft failed to return, twelve of them Halifaxes, which again sustained the highest numerical losses, and this time, at 5.3%, even exceeded the Stirling's loss rate.

Let us now examine the claim that the main weight of bombs fell two to five miles south-south-east from the city centre and that the operation largely failed. Firstly, two to five miles in any city means that the bombing fell within the boundaries and, therefore, within the built-up area. Secondly, the majority of crews, if not all, reported a highly successful raid with fires right across the city, smoke rising to 14,000 feet as they left the scene and the glow visible from the Dutch coast. It is true that crews were very frequently mistaken in their belief that an attack had been successful, but the evidence on this occasion would seem to confirm their testimony. Decoy fire-sites do not produce a glow visible from a distance of two hundred miles or sufficient volumes of smoke to reach bombing height during the short duration of a raid and be dense enough to be visible at night.

On the 23rd, and for the second time in the month, Mannheim was posted as the target and would face a force, which at take-off, numbered 628 aircraft, 104 of them 1 Group Lancasters. Fifteen of these were made ready by 103 Squadron at Elsham Wolds, where they were loaded with a cookie, two 1,000 pounders a 500 pounder and thirteen-and-a-third SBCs of 4lb and 30lb incendiaries. The crews, meanwhile, were attending briefing to learn that Mosquitos were to drop red and green route markers, before the Path Finder blind marker crews delivered flares and red TIs over the target by H2S to guide the visual markers to the precise aiming-point. This had been placed in the less-severely afflicted northern districts, which they would mark with yellow TIs, followed by the backers-up with greens. The 103 Squadron element took off between 18.56 and 19.24 with S/L Kennard the senior pilot on duty and exited the English coast at Clacton on course for Belgium, losing within ninety minutes the services of Sgt Grigg and crew to an engine issue. The bomber stream pushed on across France and into southern Germany to encounter largely clear skies and good visibility, and at the point of the spear, the Path Finders marked out the northern districts as planned. The marking was accurate and concentrated, allowing the 103 Squadron crews to attack on red, green and yellow TIs from 17,500 to 20,700 feet between 21.52 and 22.14. Later bombing spilled over into the northern fringe of Ludwigshafen and out into the nearby towns of Oppau and Frankenthal, where much damage resulted.

Returning crews reported that smoke had reached around 6,000 feet as they turned away and that the glow of fires remained visible for 150 miles into the return journey. Thirty-two crews were absent from debriefing, and this time eighteen of them were in Lancasters, compared with seven each for the Halifaxes and Stirlings, which provided a somewhat topsy-turvy and unusual loss-rate of 5.7%, 3.6% and 6% respectively. Night-fighters were reported to be present in numbers, and an FW190 was seen to be shot down. JB152 contained the senior 103 Squadron crew of F/L Finlay DFC, and was shot down on approach to the target, delivering the pilot and four of his crew into enemy hands, while the flight engineer and a gunner lost their lives. P/O Floyd's LM332 was coned in searchlights for four to five minutes and was damaged by flak before being attacked from behind by a Ju88, the fire from which killed the rear gunner and wounded the mid-upper gunner and wireless operator. Other returning crews reported that smoke had reached around 6,000 feet as they turned away, and that the glow of fires remained visible for 150 miles into the return journey. Post-raid reconnaissance and local reports revealed that 927 houses and twenty industrial premises had been destroyed in Mannheim and that the I G Farben factory in Ludwigshafen had sustained serious damage.

F/L Rawstorne had already completed his tour and was posted to 1668 Conversion Unit on the 24th. Operations were posted and scrubbed on the 26th, which allowed everyone over at Binbrook to focus on what was really important, the rumours about which entertainment stars would grace the ENSA (Entertainments National Service Association) concert to be staged that evening. The excitement was barely contained, and it was late afternoon before the tannoy confirmed that Beatrice Lillie, Vivien Leigh, John Guilguid, Kay Young, Cyril Richard, Leslie Henson and others would be not only performing but also staying the night. Much effort was put into preparing accommodation in the officers' quarters and for the after-show party, and the whole affair was a great success, the party in the officers' mess continuing into the early hours. On leaving next day, Leslie Henson expressed gratitude on behalf of the party for the hospitality extended and said that last night's show had been the first since their return from the Middle-East, during which period they had covered nine thousand miles by air. Amid the privations, losses and stresses of war, the value of the contribution by ENSA and its cast to the morale of service personnel cannot be overstated.

It had been a brief and welcome distraction from the war for the lucky few at Binbrook, but all thoughts of it were dispelled when the tannoys called the faithful to prayer on the afternoon of the 27th, to inform crews that Hannover was to be their target again that night, for which a force of 678 aircraft was being assembled. 103 Squadron answered the call with seventeen Lancasters in a 1 Group contribution of 108 and fifteen Wellingtons, and the majority received a bomb load of a cookie, three 1,000 pounders and fifteen-and-a-third SBCs of 4lb and 30lb incendiaries, before departing Elsham Wolds between 19.29 and 20.21 with S/Ls Kennard and Wood the senior pilots on duty. As they climbed out through ice-bearing cloud, some sorties fell by the wayside, and in all, nine 1 Group crews turned back early as continuing poor weather conditions over the North Sea took a toll. The 103 Squadron crews flew out over Southwold on course for Egmond and lost the crews of Sgts Lydon, Miller and Stevens to a.s.i and pneumatic system failures, leaving the others to press on in the wake of the Path Finders, who were unaware that the weather forecasts on which their performance would be based, were incorrect. The result of that would be to push the marking some five miles from the city centre towards the north, but at least the weather improved markedly over Germany to present the crews with clear skies at the target and a sight of the red and green TIs.

The 103 Squadron crews delivered their attacks mostly on green TIs from 19,000 to 22,000 feet between 22.02 and 22.27 and observed many fires with smoke rising to 15,000 feet. Returning crews again reported the glow of fires visible from the Dutch coast, and confidence in the success of the operation was unanimous across the Command, giving lie to the claim that little damage resulted. Post-raid photos did reveal many bomb craters in open country, but the fire and smoke evidence did not support decoy fire-sites, and no local report was forthcoming to shed further light. The loss of thirty-eight aircraft was probably something of a shock, but at least, common sense returned to the statistics to re-establish the status-quo after the topsy-turvy outcome of the Mannheim raid. Seventeen Halifaxes, ten Lancasters, ten Stirlings and one Wellington failed to return, giving loss-rates for the four-engine types of 9% for the Stirling, 7.3% for the Halifax and 3.2% for the Lancaster. Among them was DV221, which crashed while homebound seven miles west of Hildesheim, killing S/L Kennard and his highly experienced and decorated crew that included two holders of the DFC and three of the DFM. The best squadron and flight commanders inspired those under them by leading from the front, many paying with their lives, and the loss of this crew was keenly felt by the 103 Squadron and Elsham Wolds communities.

The month ended with an operation on the 29th against Bochum in the central Ruhr, for which a force of 343 aircraft was assembled, 1 Group contributing seventy-seven Lancasters, a dozen of them provided by 103 Squadron. They were loaded at Elsham Wolds with a cookie, three 1,000 pounders and sixteen-and-two-thirds SBCs of 4lb and 30lb incendiaries, before taking off between 18.35 and 19.08 with S/L Wood the senior pilot on duty. They flew out over Mablethorpe to make landfall on the northern tip of Texel, and all reached the target area after a two-and-a-half-hour outward flight, having been kept on track by two route-marker flares at 20,000 feet. They established their positions visually in good visibility guided by green TIs planted on the aiming point by the Path Finders and delivered their attacks from 19,000 to 21,000 feet between 20.55 and 21.08 in the face of a strong searchlight and moderate flak defence. Some returning crews described the target as a mass of flames, with smoke rising rapidly to meet them, while local reports confirmed the destruction of 527 houses, with 742 others seriously damaged.

During the course of the month the squadron took part in seven operations and dispatched 124 sorties, of which nine were abortive, for the loss of five Lancasters, four complete crews and a rear gunner.

October 1943

The start of October was a busy time for the Lancaster squadrons, which would be called upon to participate in six major operations in the first eight nights. The month's account was opened at Hagen at the eastern end of the Ruhr on the 1st, for which a moderately sized heavy force of 243 Lancasters was drawn from 1, 5 and 8 Groups, 1 Group contributing ninety aircraft, thirteen of them representing 103 Squadron. The armourers at Elsham Wolds loaded each with a cookie, two 1,000 pounders and sixteen-and-a-third SBCs of 4lb and 30lb incendiaries, while the crews attended briefing to learn of their part in the night's plan. They took off between 18.37 and 18.56 with S/L Wood the senior pilot on duty and headed out over Mablethorpe aiming for Egmond on the Dutch coast, to then skirt the northern edge of the Ruhr as far as Werl to the north of the now famous Möhne reservoir, from where they would turn sharply to the south-west to run in on the target. (The route detailed in the 103 Squadron ORB is incorrect). They arrived to find ten-tenths cloud with tops at 8,000 feet and red and green Oboe-laid skymarkers to aim at, and the 103 Squadron crews carried out their attacks from 18,000 to 21,500 feet either side of 21.00. Sgt Lydon's Lancaster was damaged by flak and Münster was bombed from 20,000 feet as an alternative. Returning crews reported a column of black smoke rising through the clouds, while some described a large bluish-green explosion at 21.03, the glow of fires beneath the cloud, and an effective Path

Finder performance. In addition to the usual housing damage, local sources confirmed the destruction of forty-six industrial firms, among them a manufacturer of accumulator batteries for U-Boots, and this would have an impact on U-Boot production.

294 crews from 1, 5 and 8 Groups were called to briefings on the 2nd to learn that Munich was to be their target for that night. 1 Group detailed ninety-three Lancasters, and the thirteen at Elsham Wolds were loaded with a cookie and fifteen-and-a-third SBCs each before taking off between 18.33 and 18.57 with S/L Wood the senior pilot on duty. They set a course via Orfordness to make landfall in the Dunkerque region, before traversing France to enter Germany south of Strasbourg. and reach the target area after an outward flight of some three-and-a-half hours. F/Sgt Graham and crew dropped out at the French coast after losing their navigational equipment, while the others pressed on to encounter cloud over the Wörthsee, situated some fifteen miles west-south-west of the centre of Munich, which was the starting point for the 5 Group time-and-distance run. The skies over the city were clear of cloud, but the marking was scattered and led to most of the early bombing falling into southern and south-eastern districts. Most 5 Group crews were unable to establish a firm fix on the Wörthsee, and this would lead to a creep-back of up to fifteen miles along the line of approach. Some 1 Group crews also carried out a DR run from the lake, and all bombed on red and green TIs, those of 103 Squadron from 18,000 to 22,000 feet from around 22.30. Returning crews suggested that the raid appeared to be concentrated on the eastern side of the city, and local authorities reported that 339 buildings had been destroyed. Eight Lancasters failed to return and three belonged to 1 Group.

Another 103 Squadron crew was lost to a non-operational accident on the 3rd, when JB346 crashed almost immediately after take-off for an air test, and Sgt Andrews and the other five occupants lost their lives. Had this tragedy not happened, they would have been participating that night in the first of two operations during the month on Kassel, the industrial city located some eighty miles to the east of the Ruhr. In addition to the Henschel, Fieseler and other war-materials producing factories, the city housed the HQ for the military's Wehrkreis IX and was the location of a subcamp of the Dachau concentration camp, which supplied slave labour to the factories. A force of 547 aircraft was assembled consisting of 223 Halifaxes, 204 Lancasters and 113 Stirlings, 1 Group supporting the operation with fifty-seven Lancasters, of which nine were made ready by 103 Squadron at Elsham Wolds. At briefings, the crews learned of the plan of attack, which called for the Mosquitos to provide route markers to guide the Path Finder H2S crews as they marked the target blind with yellow TIs and flares. The visual markers were then to identify the aiming-point and mark it with red TIs for the backers-up to maintain with greens. The 103 Squadron aircraft each received a bomb load of a cookie, two 1,000 pounders and eighteen-and-a-third SBCs before taking off between 18.46 and 19.03 with no commissioned pilots on duty.

They set course via Mablethorpe for the northern tip of Texel and lost the services of Sgt Stevens and crew within two hours after an engine caught fire, while the others arrived in the target area to find largely clear skies but thick ground haze. The Path Finder H2S "blind" markers overshot the planned aiming point, and because of the haze and possibly decoy markers, the backers-up, whose job was to confirm their accuracy by visual means, were unable to correct the error. The 103 Squadron crews identified the target visually and by green TIs and bombed from 19,500 to 21,300 feet either side of 21.30, reporting on their return what appeared to be a good concentration of fires and a pall of smoke rising to meet them. In fact, the main weight of the attack had fallen onto the western suburbs, where the Henschel aircraft and tank factories and the Fieseler aircraft plant were hit, but a stray bomb load had also detonated an ammunition dump at Ihringshausen, situated close to the north-eastern suburb of Wolfsanger, which was left devastated by the blast. F/Sgt Hinton and crew, who were in JB147 and undertaking their maiden operation, were coned in searchlights for a number of minutes and then attacked by a Ju88, which the gunners fought off and claimed as probably destroyed after watching it dive away with an engine on fire. Twenty-four aircraft failed to return, fourteen Halifaxes, six Stirlings and four Lancasters, which gave a loss-rate of 6.3%, 3.2% and 2.9% respectively.

The busy schedule of operations continued at Frankfurt on the 4th, for which a force of 406 aircraft was made ready. The American confidence in the ability of its forces to deliver daylight attacks on military and war production targets in Germany had been shaken by the high loss rates, which were not sustainable. Since the first Hannover raid, a small number of 8th Air Force B17s had been flirting with night raids alongside their RAF colleagues, and this night would bring their final involvement. It was the first time that 1 Group had operated on four consecutive nights and detailed twenty-seven Lancasters for the main event and fifty-four for a diversionary attack on the I G Farben plant at Ludwigshafen some forty-five miles to the south. 103 Squadron made ready nine of its own for the latter and loaded each with a cookie, two 500 pounders and a mix of 4lb and 30lb incendiaries, before sending them on their way from Elsham Wolds between 18.18 and 18.39 with no senior pilots on duty. They began the Channel crossing at Beachy Head on course for Cayeux-sur-Mer and followed a somewhat circuitous route, which tracked across Belgium as if heading for southern Germany, before swinging to the north-east and passing to the west of Frankfurt for the final run-in of around eighty miles. This added significantly to the mileage but avoided the flak hotspots from the Dutch coast and north of the Ruhr.

A night of doubtful serviceability afflicted 103 Squadron, and four crews abandoned their sorties, leaving the crews of F/Os Churchill, Johnston and Ready, W/O Rhodes and Sgt Bassett to reach the target under clear skies and find red and green TIs marking out the aiming point. They delivered their attacks from 17,500 to 22,000 feet either side of 21.30 and noted the activity away to the north over Frankfurt, where a large explosion was witnessed at 21.37. The impression was of a scattered attack, but this was of little consequence as long as the diversionary aspect was successful. Frankfurt, meanwhile, was undergoing an ordeal that left the eastern half of the city and the docks area a sea of flames. The large red explosion observed from Ludwigshafen threw flames up to 3,000 feet, and smoke was rising through 8,000 feet as the bombers turned away, crews reporting the glow from the burning city to be visible for 120 miles into the homeward leg. The success was gained at the modest cost of ten aircraft, half of which were Halifaxes, which confirmed the effectiveness of the diversion. There was sad news from Warboys, the home of 156 Squadron, which had posted missing the now S/L Cook DFC, DFM, RAAF and his crew from the Frankfurt operation. F/O Cook and crew had been posted from 103 Squadron to Warboys in April and all lost their lives in the crash in southern Germany. At just twenty-one years of age, S/L Cook was among the youngest pilots to be lost during 1943.

The busy first week of the month concluded with an operation against Stuttgart, for which a force of 343 Lancasters was drawn from 1, 3, 5, 6 and 8 Groups on the 7th. A new weapon in the Command's armoury was introduced for the first time in numbers on this night with the participation of a night-fighter-communications-jamming device called "Jostle" fitted in Lancasters of 1 Group's 101 Squadron. It required a specialist operator in addition to the standard crew of seven, who, though not necessarily a German speaker, could recognise the language and on hearing it, jam the signals on up to three frequencies by broadcasting engine noise over them. At 101 Squadron the device was referred to as ABC or Airborne Cigar, and once proved to be effective, ABC Lancasters would be spread through the bomber stream for all major operations, whether or not 1 Group was otherwise involved. The Lancaster would also carry a full bomb load reduced by 1,000lbs to compensate for the weight of the equipment and its operator.

1 Group put up 107 Lancasters, of which thirteen were made ready at Elsham Wolds and loaded with a cookie, one 1,000 pounder, one 500 pounder, nine SBCs of 4lb incendiaries and six of 30lb, and took off between 20.20 and 20.43 with no senior pilots on duty. They set course via Beachy Head to Criel-sur-Mer and lost Sgt Grigg and crew on the way because of the failure of their starboard-outer engine. The others reached the target area, where ten-tenths cloud at 10,000 feet concealed the ground from view and required the Path Finders to employ H2S to establish their position. This resulted in two distinct areas of marking, which led to bombs falling in many parts of the city from the centre to the south-west, the 103 Squadron crews bombing from 19,500 to 22,000 feet between 00.08 and 00.20. The impressions of returning crews were of a scattered attack, which cost a remarkably modest four aircraft, and whether or not the presence of the radio-countermeasures Lancasters was responsible, it was a promising start for RCM and would lead, ultimately, to the formation of the RCM-dedicated 100 Group in November. Local sources reported that 344 buildings, mostly houses, had been destroyed and more than four-and-a-half thousand damaged to some extent, the town of Böblingen, ten miles to the south-west, clearly having been under one set of markers and suffered damage to 350 buildings.

The third raid of the series on Hannover was posted to take place on the 8th, and a force of 504 aircraft was duly assembled, 1 Group contributing ninety-six Lancasters and a dozen Wellingtons, thirteen of the former made ready at Elsham Wolds, where each was loaded with a cookie, three 1,000 pounders and fifteen-and-a-third SBCs of incendiaries. A large diversionary raid was planned for Bremen to begin at 01.15, five minutes ahead of zero-hour at the main event and would involve seventeen 8 Group Halifaxes and seven Lancasters marking for a main force of ninety-five Stirlings. The 103 Squadron element took off between 22.49 and 23.21 with the senior pilots still conspicuous by their absence and set course via Mablethorpe for the northern tip of Texel, before traversing northern Holland and entering Germany north of Meppen. W/O Pargeter and crew had been last to leave the ground after swinging off the runway at the first attempt, and it became clear that they would not be able to make up the time. The others reached the target area to find largely clear skies and red and green TIs marking out the city-centre aiming point, and the 103 Squadron crews delivered theirs from 20,000 to 22,500 feet between 01.36 and 01.50. Having arrived in the fairly early stages of the attack, they saw fires just beginning to take hold and it became clear as they retreated westwards that they were developing into a serious conflagration. Curiously, despite the claim by some commentators that this was the one successful raid of the series, there was no mention of the glow being visible from a considerable distance, as had been the case with the first two operations. This time a local report did emerge, which described heavy damage in all districts except for those in the west, with a large area of fire engulfing the central districts. A total of 3,932 buildings was destroyed, while thirty thousand others were damaged to some extent and the death toll amounted to 1,200 people. These statistics seem somewhat excessive for a single operation by fewer than five hundred aircraft, particularly in the absence of the kind of crew reports common to the first two raids, and this adds weight to the author's contention, that the damage was accumulative over the three operations. Twenty-seven aircraft failed to return, 1 Group posting missing four Lancasters.

The ensuing ten days were spent kicking heels as the bulk of the Command remained on the ground and left the skies to the Mosquitos and gardeners. It was particularly difficult for the Australians, who found the dank and overcast conditions of an English autumn in stark contrast to the bright, hot summer that was fast approaching back home. Acting S/L Whittet arrived on posting from 12 Squadron on the 10th, and on the 13th, 1 Group welcomed 625 Squadron to its bosom, a new unit formed from C Flight of 100 Squadron at the recently re-opened old WWI station at Kelstern, 3.6 miles south-east of Binbrook, of which it was a satellite. W/C Slater's tour as commanding officer was about to end and he led a cross-country exercise on the 14th, the day on which his successor, W/C Nelson, arrived at Elsham Wolds from 1662 Conversion Unit on attachment. He was a pre-war officer, who had joined the RAF in 1931 and had attained the rank of wing commander in March 1941, but had no operational experience before his appointment at 103 Squadron. On the 18th he officially took command on W/C Slater's departure for duties at Bomber Command HQ, and on the same day, P/O Nicky Ross, who had come back to 103 Squadron after returning from America, was posted to 617 Squadron, the now famous "Dambusters". He had completed forty-nine operations thus far and would complete many more with his new unit before hanging up his flying boots for good with seventy-seven operations to his name and a DSO to add to his DFC. After the war he would return to banking, and he passed away in 2008 at the age of ninety.

There were no doubt cheers of relief when the tannoys announced briefings on Lancaster stations later on the 18th to bring an end to the enforced period of inactivity. W/C Nelson presided over his first on the afternoon of his appointment, when the wall map revealed Hannover as the target for the fourth and last time in this series, and the crews learned that this was to be an all-Lancaster affair involving 360 aircraft. 1 Group provided 108 of them, eighteen made ready by 103 Squadron, all but five of them loaded with a cookie, three 1,000 pounders and fifteen-and-a-third SBCs. Five were carrying special navigation equipment, possibly H2S, and were spared 240lbs of incendiaries. They departed Elsham Wolds between 17.20 and 17.42 with S/L Wood the senior pilot on duty and set course via Mablethorpe for landfall over the northern tip of Texel, from where they continued on an easterly track across Holland aiming for Cloppenburg and thence Nienburg and Celle, before turning to the south-west to run in on the target close to the Deurag-Nerag oil refinery at Misburg. F/Sgt Rathbone and crew were back home within ninety minutes after both compasses let them down and they left the others to press on unmolested by the defences until encountering a nest of night-fighters on crossing the frontier into Germany. At least thirteen aircraft were brought down during the ensuing forty-five minutes encompassing the approach and withdrawal phases. A layer of eight to ten-tenths cloud hung over Hannover with tops at 12,000 to 15,000 feet, which created challenging conditions for the Path Finders in establishing the aiming point. It resulted in the deployment of both sky and ground markers that lacked concentration, and this led to a scattering of the effort. The 103 Squadron crews bombed mostly on red and green TIs or on release-point flares from 16,000 to 21,500 feet between 20.16 and 20.41, and a colossal explosion was observed at around 20.19. The strong night-fighter presence dissuaded crews from hanging around to assess the outcome further, and the impression of those returning was of a scattered attack. It was established later that most of the bombs had fallen into open country, a disappointment compounded by the loss of eighteen Lancasters.

It was a bad night for 103 Squadron, which had three empty dispersal pans to contemplate in the cold light of dawn. It was learned later that JB279 had crashed at 20.10 near Nienburg between Bremen and Hannover during the outward flight, and there had been no survivors from the crew of F/Sgt Hinton. JB147 had crashed on the northern outskirts of Hannover at 20.30 during the bombing run, killing W/O Loop DFC and his crew, who were on their twenty-second operation. W/O Stevens and crew had delivered their bombs and were leaving the target area when JB349 crashed nine miles south-west of Hildesheim at 20.45, again without survivors. They were on their fifth operation, although they had been involved in two early returns. The four raids on Hannover had cost the Command 110 aircraft from 2,253 sorties, a loss rate of 4.9%, but much of the city now lay in ruins and would receive no further attention for a year, when the oil offensive and the close proximity of the Misburg synthetic oil plant to the east would return the region to prominence.

The first major attack of the war on the eastern city of Leipzig was planned for the 20th, and an all-Lancaster force of 358 aircraft representing 1, 5, 6 and 8 Groups assembled. 1 Group was responsible for 104 Lancasters, and 103 Squadron fourteen, all but the five "special" ones loaded at Elsham Wolds with a cookie and sixteen-and-one-third SBCs. They took off between 17.34 and 17.52 with F/L Ready the senior pilot on duty and ran into atrocious weather conditions during the outward flight, with a towering front of ice-bearing cumulonimbus east of Hannover extending beyond 20,000 feet, and this persuaded many crews to turn back as engines began to falter and ice-accretion destroyed lift. Those pushing on through the front reached the target after a punishing three-and-a-half-hour outward flight, only to then encounter seven to ten-tenths cloud with tops as high as 14,000 feet. The Path Finders had been unable in the conditions to establish and mark the aiming point other than with isolated red and yellow flares, leaving crews to bomb on e.t.a., on fires glimpsed through the cloud or on scattered skymarkers, the 103 Squadron crews from 16,500 to 22,000 feet between 21.02 and 21.17. Flak was negligible, but searchlights were active and lit up the clouds brilliantly. There were some night-fighters in evidence, but a spoof raid on Berlin by Mosquitos may have drawn the majority away and only F/O Morgan and crew reported an encounter with a FW190, which attacked twice but was driven off. Sixteen Lancasters failed to return, five from 1 Group, and among them was 103 Squadron's ED881, which disappeared without trace and took with it the eight-man crew of W/O Pargeter RNZAF. The crews that did make it home were mostly unable to offer any useful details at debriefing.

The "special" Lancasters referred to above were equipped with H2S, with plans afoot ultimately to make the device available to main force squadrons and training was already in progress at Elsham Wolds. Reference to H2S was always coded, the system itself usually referred to as "special navigation equipment" and the aircraft as "Y".

S/L Colin Scragg arrived from 1656 Conversion Unit on the 22nd, and he would assume the role of flight commander. Born in 1908, he was originally a "Halton Brat", serving an engineering apprenticeship, before becoming a sergeant pilot with 1 Squadron in 1931. During the course of the day preparations were put in hand for the final operation of the month, to be launched that night against Kassel for which a force of 569 aircraft stood ready to take off in the early evening, 105 of them 1 Group Lancasters, seventeen provided by 103 Squadron. They were loaded at Elsham Wolds with a cookie and nineteen-and-a-third SBCs and took off between 17.56 and 18.15 with S/L Wood the senior pilot on duty and set course via Dungeness to make landfall near Abbeville. Part of the bomber stream passed through an electrical storm over the North Sea, although this did not seem to involve the Elsham Wolds contingent, despite which, the crews of F/Sgt West and F/O Morgan turned back early with oxygen supply issues and F/Sgt Nicholls because of an indisposed navigator, which was also probably related to oxygen starvation. The others pressed on across Belgium in continuing unfavourable weather conditions, which miraculously improved in the target area to leave clear skies between the bombers and the target, but ten-tenths cloud above them at 24,000 feet. At the opening of the raid, the H2S "blind" markers overshot the city-centre aiming point, leaving the success of the operation reliant upon the visual marker crews backing up, and they did not disappoint. The red and green TIs were concentrated right on the aiming point, and the main force crews followed up with accurate and concentrated bombing with scarcely any creep-back. The 103 Squadron crews carried out their attacks from 19,000 to 21,500 feet between 21.06 and 21.12 and observed the fires just beginning to take hold as they turned away.

It was after the sound of their engines had receded that the fires joined together to engulf the city in what, in some areas, developed into a firestorm, that sent smoke rising through 12,000 feet. The massively successful operation was achieved at a high cost of forty-three bombers, twenty-five of them Halifaxes and eighteen Lancasters, seven of the latter belonging to 1 Group. Another bad night for 103 Squadron brought three failures to return, JB276 crashing near Diepholz, well to the south of Bremen on its way out of the target area, with fatal consequences for S/L Wood MiD and four members of his crew, while the two survivors were taken into captivity. JB376 was brought down by a night-fighter and crashed into a forest four miles west-south-west of Münden, east of the Ruhr also on the way home, and W/O Rhodes was killed with all but two of his crew. There were eight men on board LM314, which was captained by W/O Lee DFC, and they all died in the crash near Lügde, a town some ten miles south-south-west of Hamelin. The second pilot, F/L Blurton, also held a DFC and had only arrived from 1656 Conversion Unit on the 9th, and the navigator, P/O Miller, was the third member of the crew decorated with the DFC.

Meanwhile, in Kassel, the shell-shocked inhabitants emerged from their shelters to find their city devastated and unrecognizable. After 3,600 fires had been dealt with, it would be established eventually that more than 4,300 apartment blocks containing 53,000 dwelling units had been destroyed or damaged, some 63% of the city's living accommodation, leaving up to 120,000 people without homes and in excess of six thousand others dead. 155 industrial buildings had also been destroyed or severely damaged, along with numerous schools, hospitals, churches and public buildings.

A period of foggy weather set in at this point and kept the Command on the ground for the remainder of the month. F/L Attwater arrived on posting from 625 Squadron at Kelstern on the 24th, and he would soon attain the rank of acting squadron leader to take over C Flight. During the course of the month the squadron took part in nine operations and dispatched 122 sorties, of which twelve were abortive. Seven aircraft and crews failed to return, and this meant that thirty-six crews had been lost in the five months since the loss-free month of May.

November 1943

November brought with it the long, dark, cloudy nights which enabled Harris to return to his main theme, the destruction of Germany's capital city. The next five months would bring the bloodiest, hardest-fought air battles between Bomber Command and the Luftwaffe Nachtjagd and test the hard-pressed crews to the limit of their endurance. In a minute to Churchill on the 3rd, Harris stated, that with the participation of the American 8th Air Force, he could "wreck Berlin from end to end". He estimated that the campaign would cost the two forces between four and five hundred aircraft, but that it would cost Germany the war. This would remove the need for the kind of bloody, expensive and protracted land campaign, which he had personally witnessed during the Great War and had prompted him to "get into the air" at the earliest opportunity. It should be remembered that this was the first time in the history of air warfare, that the means had existed to prove the theory, that an enemy could be defeated by bombing alone. It is only in the light of more recent experiences that we have learned of the need, in a conventional conflict at least, to occupy the enemy's territory to secure submission. The Americans, however, were committed to victory on land, where film cameras could capture the glory and would not accompany Harris to Berlin.

Düsseldorf was selected to open the month's operational account that very night, and no doubt, while the Prime Minister was digesting Harris's epistle, a force of 589 Lancasters and Halifaxes was being prepared for action. 1 Group's contribution amounted to 140 Lancasters, of which twenty-two represented 103 Squadron, and they were each loaded with a cookie, two 1,000 pounders and sixteen SBCs of incendiaries before taking off between 17.06 and 17.48 with F/Ls Attwater, Hopps and Ready the senior pilots on duty. They set course via Sheringham for the Scheldt estuary and bypassed Antwerp, at which point W/O Frost and crew ran out of oxygen and had to turn back. The rest of the squadron approached the south-western Ruhr after flying out over Belgium and through the concentration of fifty to sixty searchlights in the Mönchengladbach-Cologne corridor, some fifteen miles from the target. Small patches of cloud below them at 12,000 feet were drifting across the target along with smoke from the early fires, despite which, the visibility remained generally good, and the Path Finders employed both sky and ground markers to good effect to identify the aiming point in the city centre. Bombing was carried out by the 103 Squadron crews on red and green TIs and skymarkers from 20,000 to 22,500 feet between 19.45 and 20.02, and fires were observed to be developing on both sides of the Rhine with black smoke rising through 6,000 feet as the bombers turned away. Eighteen aircraft failed to return, and unusually, eleven were Lancasters and only seven Halifaxes. It was on this night, that 61 Squadron's F/L Bill Reid earned the award of a Victoria Cross for pressing on to bomb the target after his Lancaster, LM360, had been severely damaged and a number of his crew either killed or wounded. Post-raid reconnaissance revealed that central and southern districts had sustained widespread damage to industry and housing, but no report came out of Düsseldorf to provide detail.

Also present among the bomber force on this night were thirty-eight Hercules-powered Mk II Lancasters of 3 and 6 Groups, which were conducting the first large scale test of the G-H blind bombing device, employing the Mannesman tubular steel works located in the northern outskirts as the target. The G-H system was based on the leadaircraft bombing on a broadcast signal, much like Oboe and the release of his bombs acted as the signal to the aircraft in the following gaggle to release theirs also. It was a system similar to that employed by the American 8th Air Force but could be employed equally effectively by night and day. On this occasion equipment failure caused the test to be inconclusive, and it would be the autumn of 1944 before the system was put fully and effectively into service with 3 Group and used to good effect in the campaign against Germany's oil industry and railway communications.

A number of operations were planned during the ensuing week, but all were cancelled because of concerns about the weather, on one occasion the scrub coming as the crews were about to leave the crew room for their aircraft. The only serious activity for 1, 5 and 8 Groups, thereafter, until the resumption of the Berlin campaign in mid-month, was an attempt to destroy railway yards at Modane, situated in the foothills of the Alps in south-eastern France. A force of 313 Lancasters was assembled on the 10th, of which 102 were provided by 1 Group, the number including the first sorties by 626 Squadron, a new unit formed at Wickenby from 12 Squadron as part of a general expansion, and to these would be added 550 and 576 Squadrons later in the month to bring 1 Group's strength going into the winter campaign to ten Lancaster Squadrons and one, the Polish 300 Squadron, on Wellingtons.

Work had actually begun that morning to prepare an unspecified number of 1 Group Lancasters in accordance with instructions via the teleprinters for a special operation against Königsberg, a Baltic port 1,870 miles distant, now Kaliningrad in Russia, that the Germans were employing to supply the Russian front. The change of target and bomb load at noon had created something of a rush across the participating stations to load each Lancaster with different ordnance, but it was achieved, and the Elsham Wolds Lancasters each received a cookie and up to four 1,000 pounders and seventeen-and-a-third SBCs according to the variant and whether or not they were carrying the "special navigation equipment". They took to the air between 20.15 and 20.42 with F/L Hopps, now one of the senior pilots, leading the way with W/C Nelson on board for his first sortie since taking command and there was also a first operation for the now acting S/L Whittet, who was flying as second pilot to S/L Attwater on board JA868. They set course for Cabourg via Selsey Bill and all completed the outward flight of more than 650 miles, which took around four-and-a-quarter hours, at the end of which they were rewarded by the presence of a full moon shining brightly from a cloudless sky. They pinpointed on Lake Bissorte, from where they carried out a time-and-distance run to the target, which they identified visually and by red and green TIs, before bombing from 18,000 to 22,000 feet between 01.02 and 01.13. The attack seemed to be concentrated around the markers and fires appeared to be taking hold, while a large explosion was observed at 01.13. Returning crews were fairly confident in the quality of their night's efforts, and two hundred bombing photos revealed extensive damage to track and installations within one mile of the aiming point, and not a single aircraft was lost.

Undaunted by the American response to his invitation to join the Berlin party, Harris would return alone, and the rocky road to the Germany's capital was re-joined by an all-Lancaster heavy force on the night of the 18/19th, while a predominantly Halifax and Stirling contingent of 395 aircraft acted as a diversion by raiding Mannheim and Ludwigshafen three hundred miles to the south-west. The Berlin-bound crews would benefit from four Mosquitos dropping dummy fighter flares, while other Mosquitos carried out a spoof raid on Frankfurt to protect the Mannheim force. The two formations would cross the enemy coast simultaneously some 250 miles apart to confuse the enemy night-fighter controllers, the route chosen for the Berlin brigade taking it via the Frisian Island of Texel to a point north of Hannover, and thence to the target to pass over the centre on an east-north-easterly heading. The return route would pass south of Berlin and Cologne, before crossing central Belgium to gain the English Channel via the French coast. An innovation for this operation was a shortening of the bomber stream to reduce the time over the target to sixteen minutes. When the first Thousand Bomber raid had taken place in May 1942, with an unprecedented twelve aircraft per minute crossing the aiming point, there was considered to be a high risk of collisions. The number had since been increased to sixteen per minute, with large raids lasting up to forty-five minutes, but on this night, twenty-seven aircraft per minute were to pass over the aiming point.

103 Squadron made ready a record twenty-two Lancasters as part of a 1 Group force of 153, the majority of them "Y" aircraft, which were carrying a cookie, twelve-and-two-thirds SBCs of 4lb incendiaries and six of 30lbs, while the others had an extra SBC of each in the bomb bay. They departed Elsham Wolds between 17.19 and 17.41 with F/L Hopps the senior pilot on duty and S/L Scragg flying as his second pilot. They flew out over Mablethorpe to rendezvous with the bomber stream over the North Sea and there were no 103 Squadron crews among the fourteen 1 Group early returns. A blanket of cloud covered the whole of northern Germany and crews were grateful for the red spotfire route marker dropped by the Path Finders north-east of Hannover, which confirmed that they were on track. F/Sgt Law and crew had their starboard-outer engine catch fire after being hit by flak from the Hannover defences, and they retaliated by dropping their bomb load onto a flak position as they turned for home. The others benefitted from good horizontal visibility despite the absence of a moon, but the cloud persisted all the way to the target with tops at 6,000 feet and was illuminated by searchlights as the main force crews arrived. The winds were not as forecast, which upset the timings, and the single Path Finder aircraft equipped with the new, improved Mk III H2S had to turn back early.

Almost three-quarters of the blind markers using the old H2S sets either suffered malfunctions or failed to identify Brandenburg, from where they were to make a timed run to the flare release point, and the flares that were deployed disappeared rapidly into the cloud.

The Elsham Wolds crews delivered their attacks on e.t.a. and H2S-laid red and green skymarkers from 20,000 to 23,000 feet between 21.00 and 21.27 and observed little of what was happening beneath the cloud. P/O Floyd and crew were homebound at 23,000 feet at 23.15 and some thirty miles south-west of Kassel when they were hit by predicted flak that knocked out the starboard-outer engine and damaged its inboard neighbour. Control of the Lancaster was lost and the order issued to bale out, but control was regained before any of the crew complied and they limped home on two-and-a-half engines to land at the emergency strip at Woodbridge with a damaged hydraulic system, inoperable mid-upper turret and a severely frost-bitten rear gunner. Returning crews had nothing useful to pass on to the intelligence section at debriefing, and most considered the bombing to have been scattered and probably ineffective. Local sources confirmed that there had been no concentration and catalogued the destruction of 169 houses and a number of industrial units, with many more damaged to some extent. The diversion at Mannheim was deemed to have been successful in its purpose, and caused some useful industrial damage, most seriously to the Daimler-Benz motor factory, which suffered a 90% loss of production for an unknown period. In addition to this, more than three hundred buildings were destroyed at a cost of twenty-three aircraft, while the losses from Berlin were encouragingly low at just nine.

The Lancasters stayed at home on the 19th, while 3, 4, 6 and 8 Groups combined to put 170 Halifaxes, eighty-six Stirlings and 10 Mosquitos into the air for a raid on the Ruhr city of Leverkusen. They were greeted in the target area by ten-tenths cloud and an absence of marking, which was caused by equipment failure among the Oboe Mosquitos. A few green TIs were spotted some five to ten miles to the north-west of the target during the approach, but the crews were left to establish their positions on the basis of their own H2S, which, over a region as densely built-up as the Ruhr, was a challenge. As a result, the operation was a complete failure, which sprayed bombs over twenty-seven towns in the region, mostly to the north of Leverkusen.

The weather closed in for the next two days, before the second operation to Berlin was briefed to the crews on the 22nd, Harris having demanded a maximum effort, which resulted in 764 aircraft answering the call. 1 Group contributed 169 Lancasters, a squadron record of twenty-eight representing 103 Squadron, which were loaded with a cookie, twelve-and-two-thirds SBCs of 4lb incendiaries and seven of 30lbs. They departed Elsham Wolds between 16.47 and 17.35 with S/L Whittet the senior pilot on duty, and after climbing out, adopted an outward route similar to that employed by the all-Lancaster force four nights earlier. This took them via Mablethorpe to Texel and then to a point north-west of Hannover, where a slight dogleg to port put them on a due-easterly heading directly to the target. Unlike the previous raid, however, rather than the circuitous return south of Cologne and out over the French coast, they would come home via a reciprocal route. This was based on a forecast of low cloud and fog over Germany, which would inhibit the night-fighter effort, while broken, medium-level cloud over Berlin would facilitate ground marking. An additional bonus was the availability to the Path Finders of five new H2S Mk III sets, while a new record of thirty-four aircraft per minute passing over the aiming point would be achieved by abandoning the long-standing practice of allocating aircraft types to specific waves. On this night, aircraft of all types would be spread throughout the bomber stream, and this was bad news for the

Stirlings, which by the very nature of their design, would be below the Lancaster and Halifax elements, and in danger of being hit by friendly bombs.

Fifteen 1 Group Lancasters turned back early and among them was the one containing the 103 Squadron crew of W/O Graham, who lost their port-inner engine. The others pressed on across northern Germany and on arriving in the target area discovered that the meteorological forecast had been inaccurate, and that the city was hidden under a blanket of ten-tenths cloud with tops at around 12,000 feet. This meant that ground marking would be largely ineffective, and that the least reliable Wanganui (skymarking) method would have to be employed. Crews ran into intense predicted flak and a mass of searchlights as they began their bombing runs, and those from 103 Squadron aimed at red and green TIs and release-point flares from 19,500 to 22,000 feet between 20.01 and 20.29. The glow of fires was observed beneath the clouds and a very large explosion lit up the sky at 20.10, leaving the crews with an impression of a successful operation, but no real idea of what was happening on the ground. Post-raid reconnaissance and local sources confirmed that this attack on Berlin had been the most effective of the war to date and had caused a swathe of destruction from the city centre through the western residential districts of Tiergarten and Charlottenburg as far as the suburb town of Spandau. A number of firestorm areas were reported, and the catalogue of destruction included three thousand houses and twenty-three industrial premises. Many thousands more sustained varying degrees of damage, costing 175,000 people their homes and an estimated two thousand their lives, and by daylight on the 23rd, the smoke had risen to almost 19,000 feet.

It had been a good night for 1 Group, despite the high number of "boomerangs", and for once there would be no casualty reports to file. This was not the case in the other groups, however, and the families of twenty-six crews had to be informed that their son, husband or brother was missing as a result of air operations, while teams from the Committee of Adjustment eradicated all trace of them from the billets. Eleven Lancasters, ten Halifaxes and five Stirlings had failed to return, which amounted to a loss-rate among the types respectively of 2.3%, 4.2% and 10.0%. The Stirling losses proved to be the final straw for Harris because of its short wing design, which restricted it to a low service ceiling and the configuration of its bomb bay to small calibre bombs. Unlike the Lancaster and Halifax, it lacked development potential and was immediately withdrawn from future operations over Germany. It would still have an important role to play on secondary duties, however, bombing over occupied territory, mining, and in 1944, it would replace the Halifax to become the aircraft of choice for the two SOE squadrons, 138 and 161, at Tempsford. Many of those released from Bomber Command service would find their way to 38 Group, where they would give valuable service as transports and glider-tugs for airborne landings.

The crews had arrived back at Elsham Wolds around midnight and were able to spend a night in bed, but the station was a hive of activity on the following day after orders came through to prepare for a return to Berlin that night. A heavy force of 365 Lancasters and ten Halifaxes was made ready with some difficulty, as back-to-back long-range operations put a strain on those charged with the responsibility of getting the aircraft off the ground. 1 Group detailed 111 Lancasters, and the Ludford Magna armourers, unable to load all nineteen 101 Squadron Lancasters with the intended weight of bombs, would send them off 2,000lb short. At Elsham

Wolds, twenty-seven Lancasters were air-tested, armed and fuelled for the night ahead and loaded with a cookie, thirteen-and-two-thirds SBCs of 4lb incendiaries and seven of 30lbs, and two SBCs fewer for the "Y" aircraft. Sadly, much of the heroic effort would be wasted as at take-off time, a wind approaching gale-force proportions was blowing across the long runway selected as most suitable for the heavily-laden Lancasters. P/O Floyd and crew got away first at 17.04 and thirteen other crews, including that of S/L Whittet, the senior pilot on duty, managed to take-off during the next twenty-six minutes, but thirteen others were either pushed off the runway by the wind or delayed, and ultimately had their sorties scrubbed.

After climbing out and exiting the English coast over Mablethorpe, they adopted a route similar to that employed twenty-four hours earlier and joined the bomber stream over the North Sea. The depletion of the force began early and ultimately involved forty-six aircraft, 12%, twenty-three from 1 Group and eighteen from 5 Group alone, which was a further indication of the strain of back-to-back long-range operations. Another was the dumping of bombs over the North Sea by crews intending to push on to the target but wanting to gain more height. It involved largely those from 1 Group, who were shedding their cookies in protest at their A-O-C's policy of loading each Lancaster to its maximum all-up weight at the expense of altitude. AVM Rice had conducted tests to ascertain the maximum weight of bombs before the undercarriage began to buckle while taxiing, and it proved to be a counter-productive move, particularly when the slogan "H-E-I-G-H-T spells safety" could be found on the walls of most bomber station briefing rooms. 103 Squadron was badly afflicted by early returns, F/Sgt Rathbone finding his Lancaster to be dangerously uncontrollable during the climb over the station and he landed at the earliest opportunity. P/O Floyd and crew turned back with a failed intercom when some sixty miles out over the North Sea, S/L Whittet and crew had reached the midpoint of the crossing only for an iced-up pitot head and an engine issue to end their interest in proceedings, and F/Sgt Law and crew were at the Dutch coast when the navigator became unwell and forced them also to abort their sortie. F/O Russell-Fry and crew were also well into the North Sea crossing and on automatic pilot (George) when their Lancaster suddenly flipped into a spiral dive and attained a speed of more than 400 m.p.h before control was regained at 7,000 feet, by which time the bomb load had been jettisoned.

The target was found to be covered by ten-tenths cloud with tops at between 10,000 and 15,000 feet but guided by the glow of fires still burning beneath the clouds from the night before and the presence of skymarkers above and red and green TIs below, the 103 Squadron crews bombed from 17,000 to 23,000 feet between 20.02 and 20.10 to contribute to another stunning blow. Returning crews described a column of smoke reaching 20,000 feet, and the glow of fires visible again from the Hannover area some 150 miles from the target. It was on this night that fake broadcasts from England caused annoyance to the enemy night-fighter force by ordering them to land because of fog over their bases, and in comical exchanges both British and German controllers insisted that they were the legitimate voice. Despite the effectiveness of the tactic, night-fighters still had a major hand in the bringing-down of twenty Lancasters. Among them was 103 Squadron's JB528, which crashed in Germany well to the north of Berlin, and one wonders if, perhaps, it had been damaged and F/O Johnston was making for Sweden. The pilot and both gunners lost their lives, but the remaining crew members survived to fall into enemy hands. Post-raid reconnaissance and local sources confirmed another outstandingly successful operation, that destroyed a further two thousand buildings and killed around fifteen hundred people.

While 1, 3 and 5 Groups enjoyed a night off on the 25th, 216 Halifaxes of 4 and 6 Groups and forty-six 8 Group Halifaxes and Lancasters carried out an operation against Frankfurt, where the blind markers established a firm H2S fix and delivered yellow TIs and red flares with green stars to coincide with the e.t.a. of the main force crews. Local reports described a modest amount of housing damage and 3,500 people bombed out of their homes, in return for which, eleven Halifaxes and a single Lancaster failed to return.

After a three-night rest for most of the Lancaster crews, 443 of them were briefed on the 26th for a return to the "Big City" for the fourth attack since the resumption of the campaign. 1 Group detailed 153 Lancasters for the main event, including the first eight to represent 550 Squadron at Grimsby, and six from 101 Squadron to provide RCM cover for a diversionary raid by a predominantly Halifax force of 178 aircraft against Stuttgart. The plan called for the two forces to follow the same route, which involved an outward leg across the French coast and Belgium to a point north of Frankfurt, where they would diverge to their respective targets. 103 Squadron made ready a record thirty Lancasters, which the ORB suggested, as far as could be ascertained, was also a Bomber Command record and loaded those in the first phase with a cookie and six 1,000 pounders and the remainder with a cookie, twelve SBCs of 4lb incendiaries and seven of 30lbs. They departed Elsham Wolds between 16.57 and 17.31 with S/Ls Attwater, Scragg and Whittet the senior pilots on duty and set course for Beachy Head to begin the Channel crossing in what was a most unusual detour for an operation to north-eastern Germany.

An indication of the beneficial effects of the three-day lay-off was a 40% reduction in early returns compared with the previous Berlin raid, but there would still be fourteen among the 1 Group participants, including the 103 Squadron crews of F/Sgt Law, W/O Graham and P/O Young. The others were spread among the first three waves in the bomber stream and found Berlin under clear skies, but despite the favourable conditions, the Path Finders overshot the city centre aiming point by six or seven miles and by a stroke of luck marked the Siemensstadt and Tegel areas well to the north-west, which happened to contain many war-industry factories. The Elsham Wolds crews bombed on red and green TIs from 16,000 (S/L Scragg) and 23,000 feet between 21.13 and 21.44 and on return spoke of a mass of fires and thick smoke rising to 15,000 feet. S/L Scragg's bombing height was caused by the need to take evasive action against two BF110s, which were shaken off at a time when the rear guns had frozen and could not be brought to bear. F/Sgt Richter and crew were also attacked by a BF110, which broke away after being hit by a long burst from the rear turret that caused smoke to issue from the port engine. It was last seen on fire but was not observed to crash and could not be claimed as destroyed. Night-fighters got amongst the bombers on the way home, and twenty-eight Lancasters failed to return, including three from 103 Squadron. JB527 was shot down as it was turning for home and crashed nine miles north-east of Berlin with fatal consequences for F/O Pugh DFM and his crew, while JB350 came down somewhere near the target killing F/O Sumner and four of his crew and delivering the flight engineer and bomb-aimer into captivity. A similar fate befell JB458 somewhere within the Berlin defence zone, and only the wireless operator from the crew of Sgt Siddall survived in enemy hands. It would be learned later that thirty-eight war-industry factories had been destroyed and many others damaged in the Siemensstadt and Tegel districts.

The danger was not over even when the tired crews arrived back over England to find themselves diverted to 6 Group airfields, which were bringing home their own aircraft from the Stuttgart diversion and were soon to be overwhelmed. The 103 Squadron crews were diverted by R/T to Middleton-St-George in County Durham, the home of 419 and 428 Squadrons RCAF, and it was while in the circuit that ED417 collided with Halifax JN966 of 428 Squadron and crashed two miles from the airfield. F/O Brevitt and five of his crew were killed, and only the mid-upper gunner survived, albeit with severe injuries, and all on board the Halifax also lost their lives. As a result of this incident, the 103 Squadron returnees were directed to land at other 6 Group stations. W/O Frost landed JB423 at Croft with battle damage so severe that it remained there to be eventually struck off charge a few weeks later.

On the 27th, the squadron donated its C Flight under S/L Attwater to form the nucleus of 576 Squadron, with which it would share Elsham Wolds until the end of October 1944. Having now spawned two new Lancaster squadrons, 103 Squadron reverted to a standard two-flight unit. Operations for the month were now complete, but it took until the 29th to return all of the diverted aircraft to Elsham Wolds. During the course of the month, the squadron took part in six operations and dispatched 133 sorties, of which fourteen were abortive, at a cost of six Lancasters and five crews, four failing to return, one lost in the collision referred to above and one written off with battle damage.

December 1943

Berlin would continue to be the dominant theme during December, and as November had ended, so December began. A heavy force of 443 aircraft stood ready to take off in the late afternoon of the 2nd, all but fifteen of them Lancasters, after the main Halifax element had been withdrawn because of fog over their Yorkshire stations. 1 Group contributed 144 Lancasters and would benefit on this night from the operational debut of 576 Squadron, which having been formed from 103 Squadron, was battle-ready immediately. 103 Squadron loaded each of its fourteen Lancasters with a cookie, 1,230 x 4lb incendiaries and fifty-six of 30lbs, and sent them into the air between 16.45 and 17.13 with S/L Scragg the senior pilot on duty and W/C Nelson flying as second pilot to W/O Townsend. After climbing out, they left Mablethorpe behind them to rendezvous over the North Sea with the rest of the force for a straight-in-straight-out route across Holland and northern Germany with no feints or diversions. First, however, the crews had to negotiate a towering front of ice-bearing cloud over the North Sea, which would contribute to a 10% rate of early returns, eighteen alone from 1 Group, although none from 103 Squadron. They pushed through the challenging conditions and made it to the target area, mostly south of track after variable winds had thrown them off course and dispersed the bomber stream. They also had to contend with large numbers of enemy night-fighters that would harass the bombers all the way to the target, after the controller had been able correctly to predict it. The Path Finders employed H2S to establish their position at Stendal, but had strayed some fifteen miles south of track and mistakenly used the town of Genthin as their reference for the run-in. The 103 Squadron crews were spread among the three waves and found good visibility as they were guided by release-point flares to the aiming point, where they encountered a thin layer of two to three-tenths cloud at around 5,000 feet but up to nine-tenths between 10,000 and 12,000 feet, which the searchlights were able to pierce. They bombed on skymarkers and red and green TIs and where possible ground detail like burning streets from 20,000 to 22,500 feet between 20.11 and 20.46 and reported scattered fires and a number of large explosions. Some claimed the glow was still visible on the horizon from 120 miles into the homeward leg.

It was a bad night for the bomber force, which lost forty aircraft, mostly in the target area and on the way home, and among them were four from Elsham Wolds, three representing 103 Squadron, not one of which produced a survivor. F/O Ready and crew were a third of the way through their first tour and were in JB400, which is believed to have crashed somewhere in the general target area. The navigator, forty-two-year-old P/O Wakefield, was one of a very small number in that age group to be serving in Bomber Command, would have been considered to be ancient by his crew colleagues and would almost certainly have been nicknamed "grandad". In JB401, F/L Hopps DFC was on the twenty-ninth sortie of an operational career stretching back to June, and he and his crew, likewise, crashed somewhere near the target as did W/O Bellamy and crew in JB403. Some returning crews made reference to the amount of light flak and "scarecrows", the latter believed by many to be anti-aircraft shells designed to simulate a bomber exploding to cause maximum disquiet among the rest of the force. In the interests of maintaining morale, the belief was encouraged, when in fact, no such shells existed and each "scarecrow" was in reality a bomber torn asunder as its bomb load went up. Bombing photographs suggested that the raid was only partially successful, causing useful damage in industrial districts in the west and east, but scattering the main weight of bombs over the southern districts and outlying communities to the south.

Having been spared by the weather from experiencing an effective visitation from the Command in October and exploiting the enemy expectation that Berlin would be the target again, Leipzig found itself at the end of the red tape on briefing-room wall-maps from County Durham to Cambridgeshire on the 3rd. A force of 527 aircraft was made ready, which included ninety-six Lancasters of 1 Group, eleven of them belonging to 103 Squadron. They each received a bomb load of a cookie and eighteen SBCs before departing Elsham Wolds between 23.50 and 00.17 with S/L Scragg the senior pilot on duty on his final outing with the squadron. On the previous night, a number of Australian war correspondents had lost their lives in 460 Squadron aircraft, and on this night the well-known American broadcaster, Ed Murrow, bravely hitched a lift in a 619 Squadron Lancaster at Woodhall Spa. The Elsham Wolds crews set course for the Dutch coast near Haarlem and lost the services of Sgt Warner and crew to an unserviceable mid-upper turret. The others rendezvoused with the bomber stream over the North Sea and headed for Berlin as a feint, passing north of Hannover and Braunschweig with ten-tenths cloud beneath them and an hour's journey to Leipzig still ahead. Then, as they turned towards the south-east, the Mosquito element continued on to carry out a diversion at the capital.

Night-fighters had already infiltrated the stream at the Dutch coast, and at sometime during the outward flight, W/O Frost and crew were attacked by one, which damaged the fuselage and a starboard engine and seriously wounded both gunners. The rear gunner poured fire into the twin-engine assailant and watched it catch fire and enter a dive, soon after which, a burning mass was observed on the ground. As the others pressed on, the Frost crew nursed JB736 back home to a belly-landing at Woodbridge. The feint appeared to have the desired effect as few night-fighters were encountered in the target area, where two layers of ten-tenths cloud prevailed with tops at around 7,000 and 15,000 feet. Meanwhile, the Path Finders had marked by H2S with green skymarkers, and the 103 Squadron crews bombed on these from 20,000 to 23,000 feet between 04.04 and 04.13, observing explosions and a strong glow beneath the clouds. The emergence through the cloud tops of black smoke suggested that an accurate and concentrated attack had taken place, and the smoke and glow remained visible for 150 miles into the return journey on a south-easterly track towards the French frontier. Had many aircraft not then strayed into the Frankfurt defence zone, the losses may have been fewer, but twenty-four aircraft failed to return, fifteen of them Halifaxes. At debriefings, there were reports that around twenty cookies had been dumped in the North Sea just beyond the convoy lanes at 01.22, and these would have involved 1 Group crews. Local reports confirmed this as a highly successful operation, which had hit residential and industrial areas, and was the most destructive raid visited upon this eastern city during the war. Sadly, for the Command, it would take its revenge in time.

Thereafter, adverse weather conditions kept most aircraft on the ground and minor operations carried the Command through to mid-month, when S/L Colin Scragg was posted to 166 Squadron at Kirmington on the 15th on promotion to acting wing commander rank to be installed as the new commanding officer. On the 16th, the Lancaster stations were roused to prepare 483 aircraft for that night's operation to Berlin for the sixth time since the resumption of the campaign. 1 Group put up 167 Lancasters, fourteen of them representing 103 Squadron, each loaded with a cookie and the usual quantity and mix of 4lb and 30lb incendiaries. They departed Elsham Wolds between 16.22 and 17.00 with S/L Whittet the senior pilot on duty, and as they climbed into cloud, F/Sgt Richter's JB670 collided with LM322 of 576 Squadron and both Lancasters crashed at Ulceby, some three miles east-north-east of the airfield without survivors. *(There are two villages called Ulceby in Lincolnshire, one near Kirmington in the north and the other near Horncastle. The reference in Bill Chorley's Bomber Command Losses to the latter is incorrect.)* What would become known as "Black Thursday" had already begun badly and would end even more tragically. Probably unaware of the incident, the others set course via Mablethorpe for the Dutch coast near Castricum-aan-Zee, joining up with the bomber stream on the way across the North Sea, before heading due east all the way to the target with no deviations. S/L Whittet and P/O Young were contending with technical issues and each bombed Texel before turning for home, while F/Sgt Rathbone and crew were defeated by an oxygen supply problem and bombed an aerodrome in Holland.

A three-quarter moon would rise during the long return leg over the Baltic and Denmark, but it was hoped that the very early take-off and the expectation of fog to keep the enemy night-fighters on the ground would reduce the risk of interception. Night-fighters were sent to meet the bomber stream at the Dutch coast, but the depleted 103 Squadron element remained unmolested and pressed on to find Berlin obscured by ten-tenths cloud with tops at around 5,000 feet. However, it could be identified by red and green skymarkers, which were bombed from 20,500 to 23,000 feet between 20.02 and 20.08, after which the return over Denmark passed largely without major incident. Unfortunately, the greatest difficulties awaited the 1, 6 and 8 Group crews as they arrived home to find their airfields covered by a blanket of dense fog. With little reserves of fuel, the tired crews began a frantic search to find somewhere to land, stumbling blindly through the murk to catch a glimpse of the ground, which for many proved fatal, while others gave up any hope of landing and abandoned their aircraft. It was a bad night for 1 Group, which, in addition to the tragic collision between the Elsham Wolds Lancasters, had twenty others return early and sixteen crash on return, 100 and 101 Squadrons each losing four with heavy loss of life and 460 Squadron three. 103 Squadron's F/O Russell-Fry and crew broke cloud over Elsham Wolds at little more than three hundred feet, but in the poor visibility failed to see the ground until only fifty feet above it. The pilot opened up the throttles, but JB551's downward momentum took it onto a ploughed field, where it skidded to a halt at 23.34 without injury to the crew. They were lucky, as not far away near Kelstern, former 103 Squadron stalwart and flight commander, W/C David Holford, now commanding officer of 100 Squadron, was losing his life as his Lancaster crashed. These casualties were on top of the twenty-five Lancasters failing to make it back from Berlin, many of them accounted for by night-fighters over Holland and Germany while outbound, but 103 Squadron's JB658 crashed on the north-western outskirts of Berlin, killing F/Sgt Campbell RAAF and his crew. In all, twenty-nine Lancasters and a mine-laying Stirling were lost in crashes at home, and more than 150 airmen killed in these most tragic of circumstances. Local sources reported that a moderately effective raid had taken place, which had fallen principally onto central and eastern districts, where housing suffered most.

A three-day stand-down allowed the crews to recover from the Berlin operation and it was the 20th when all stations were notified of a raid that night on Frankfurt, for which a force of 390 Lancasters and 257 Halifaxes was assembled. It was becoming routine for the enemy night fighter controllers to plot Berlin as the destination for large bomber fleets, and perhaps that is why Harris selected an alternative target. A southerly approach to Berlin would take the force past Frankfurt to the north, as had been the case with the recent operation, when Stuttgart had been used as a diversion. The intention was to keep the enemy guessing as to the final destination, Stuttgart, Munich, Mannheim or Frankfurt in the south, or Kassel, Hannover, Braunschweig, Magdeburg or Berlin to the north. If not deceiving the enemy entirely, the ploy might dilute the strength of the night fighter numbers brought to bear, and on this night a small 8 Group diversionary raid was to take place at Mannheim.

1 Group made ready 107 Lancasters for the main event and thirty to assist the Path Finders in the diversionary raid by forty-four Lancasters and ten Mosquitos on Mannheim forty miles to the south. At Elsham Wolds, thirteen 103 Squadron Lancasters were loaded with the standard cookie and incendiary mix and dispatched between 16.45 and 17.06 with S/L Whittet the senior pilot on duty. W/O Frost and crew suffered an electrical failure during the climb-out and proceeded directly to the jettison area, and they would be joined on the ground by the crews of P/Os Jones and Young, who had also been let down by electrical and engine issues. The others set course for Southwold and the North Sea-crossing to the Scheldt estuary, before passing north of Antwerp and flying the length of Belgium to the German frontier north of Luxembourg. The German night-fighter controller had picked up transmissions from the bomber stream as soon as it left the English coast and was able to track it all the way to the target and vector his fighters into position. Many combats took place during the outward flight, and the diversion failed to draw fighters away from the main action. The problems

continued at the primary target, where the forecast clear skies failed to materialize, and the crews were greeted by four to nine-tenths cloud at between 5,000 and 10,000 feet. This allowed some of them to pick out ground features, while others fixed their positions by H2S, if so equipped, and the main force Lancaster crews simply waited for TIs on e.t.a.

The Path Finders had prepared a ground-marking plan in expectation of good vertical visibility and dropped red, green and yellow TIs, while the Germans lit a decoy fire-site five miles to the south-east of the city. Some crews described the marking as late and erratic, and those from 103 Squadron bombed on red and green TIs from 20,000 to 23,000 feet between 19.37 and 19.51. Most thought the attack to be scattered in the early stages, becoming more concentrated as it progressed, and many commented on the new cookies detonating with a brighter flash than the old ones and the glow of fires remaining visible for 150 miles into the return journey. Any success was achieved largely as the result of the creep-back from the decoy site falling across the suburbs of Offenbach and Sachsenhausen, situated on the southern bank of the River Main. 466 houses were destroyed and more than nineteen hundred seriously damaged, rendering 23,000 thousand people homeless. Many cultural, historical and public buildings were also hit, despite which, the operation fell well short of its aims and the loss of forty-one aircraft was a high price to pay. The Halifaxes suffered heavily, losing twenty-seven of their number, a loss-rate of 10.5%, compared with 3.6% for the Lancaster. The return of 103 Squadron's JB454 was awaited in vain, and it was learned eventually via the Red Cross, that it had been shot down over southern Germany, and that F/Sgt Rathbone, his flight engineer and navigator were now in enemy hands as the only survivors. (*In Bill Chorley's superb Bomber Command Losses 1943, JB454 is said to have crashed in Saxony, close to Germany's border with Poland. This is a very great distance from the target area, and I cannot imagine any scenario that would place this Lancaster so far off course. The fact that the crew was buried in Dürnbach Cemetery confirms that it came down in southern Germany*).

Just two more operations remained before the year ended and both were to be directed against Germany's capital city. The first was posted on the 23rd and involved an all-Lancaster heavy force with seven Halifaxes among the Path Finder element and eight Mosquitos to provide a diversion. The 128 Lancasters of 1 Group included eleven representing 103 Squadron, which were loaded with a cookie and seventeen SBCs each and launched into the cold night air between 00.07 and 00.45 with F/L Griffin the senior pilot on duty. They exited the English coast at Sheringham and adopted a somewhat circuitous route that took the bomber stream in a south-easterly direction to the Scheldt estuary, before hugging the Belgian/Dutch frontier to cross into Germany south of Aachen, as if threatening Frankfurt. When a point was reached south of Leipzig, the route turned sharply towards the north and Berlin, while the Mosquito feint threatened Leipzig. The vanguard of the bomber stream reached the target to find it enveloped in up to eight-tenths cloud at between 5,000 and 10,000 feet, which might not have been critical had the Path Finders not suffered an unusually high failure rate of their H2S equipment. This resulted in scattered and sparse marking with red and green skymarker flares at which the 103 Squadron crews aimed their bombs from 21,000 to 23,000 feet between 04.03 and 04.18. Well-concentrated fires were observed and at least four large explosions, one described as orange and red and lasting for thirty seconds. A relatively modest sixteen Lancasters failed to return, and among them was

103 Squadron's JB730, which crashed on the way home, possibly close to the Ruhr, and there were no survivors from the crew of F/Sgt McMahon RAAF. A local report named the south-eastern suburbs of Köpenick and Treptow as the ones to sustain the most damage, with 287 houses and other buildings suffering complete destruction.

The fifth wartime Christmas passed in traditional fashion, and the Command remained stood-down until the 29th, when briefings took place for the first of what would be an unprecedented three Berlin operations in the space of five nights spanning the turn of the year. A force of 712 aircraft included 136 Lancasters of 1 Group, of which fourteen represented 103 Squadron and departed Elsham Wolds between 16.50 and 17.18 with S/L Whittet the senior pilot on duty and each carrying the standard cookie and incendiary bomb load. It was from this juncture that the intolerable strain on the crews of successive long-range flights in difficult weather conditions began to manifest in some squadrons through the rate of early returns, which on this night reached forty-five or 6.3%, although only a modest seven from the ranks of 1 Group. The 103 Squadron contingent flew out over Mablethorpe and joined up with the bomber stream over the North Sea to then proceed via the Dutch Frisian islands directly towards Leipzig. Having reached a point just to the north of that city, they turned to the north towards Berlin, while Mosquitos carried out spoof raids on Leipzig and Magdeburg. 103 Squadron was exempt from early returns, and its crews reached the target area to find ten-tenths cloud with tops at anywhere between 7,000 and 18,000 feet and red and green Path Finder release-point flares hanging over the city. They delivered their bombs from 20,000 to 23,000 feet between 20.04 and 20.22, and on the way home, P/O Jones and crew strayed off track and sustained severe flak damage over Osnabrück, which necessitated an emergency landing at Woodbridge. At debriefing, crews reported a considerable red glow beneath the clouds, which remained visible for a hundred miles and gave the impression of a concentrated and successful assault. This was not entirely borne out by local reports, which revealed that the main weight of the raid had fallen onto southern and south-eastern districts and also into outlying communities to the east. Local sources reported that 388 buildings had been destroyed, although none of significance, and ten thousand people had been bombed out of their homes. Eleven Lancasters and nine Halifaxes failed to return, a loss-rate of 2.4% for the former and 3.5% for the latter. 103 Squadron posted missing W/O Grigg and crew and had to wait for the Red Cross to report that all but the rear gunner had survived and were safe but in enemy hands. It transpired that JB487 had been hit by flak on the way home, almost certainly also when passing through the Osnabrück defence zone and sustained structural damage to the tail-plane and the loss of two engines. The Lancaster came down near Ibbenbüren, west of Osnabrück, after the crew had been compelled to abandon it to its fate and the cause of the rear gunner's failure to survive is unknown.

During the course of the month the squadron participated in six operations and launched seventy-eight sorties, five of which were abortive, for the loss of eight Lancasters and crews, a disturbing 10% of those dispatched. It had been a testing end to a year which had brought major successes and advances in tactics, but it had also been a year of high losses, particularly among the Stirling and Halifax squadrons. While "window" had been an instant success, it had also caused the Luftwaffe to rethink and reorganise and the night-fighter force which emerged from the ruins of the old system was a leaner, more efficient and altogether more lethal beast than that of before. As far as the crews of Bomber Command were concerned, the New Year offered the same fare as the old one, which few would view with relish and the next three months would see morale at its lowest ebb as the winter campaign ground on. Gone were the days when a new crew would be eased into battle with freshman trips. Now one's maiden operation could be to Berlin, and that was, indeed, the fate that awaited those about to leave the training units and join a frontline squadron.

P/O Neil Lambell RAAF flew as navigator with F/O Gomer Morgan DFC, pilot and C Flight Commander.

F/L George McGill RCAF. Navigator with 103 Squadron. Took part in the 'Great Escape' 1944 and subsequently murdered by the Gestapo.

Elsham Wolds, February 1943. Some of the crew of "U" for Uncle, a Lancaster of 103 Squadron. L to Right: Sgt Ryan (FE); F/L John Keith Douglas, captain (KIA 8th February 1945); F/Sgt May, (W/Op); F/Sgt Keith Hynes, (Nav) (KIA October 1944 as F/O), Sgt Cornforth, (MUG).

A Lancaster dropping Window (the crescent-shaped white cloud on the left of the picture) over Essen during a thousand-bomber raid.

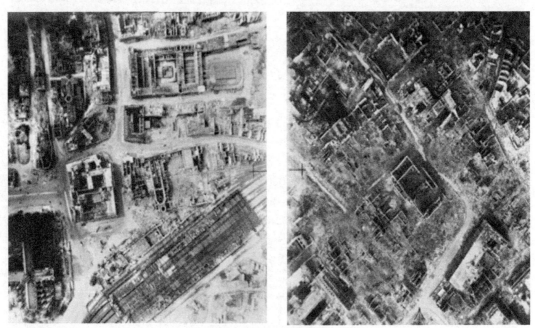

Cologne (Koln), Germany. Aerial photograph of the city showing damage after bombing by allied air forces on the night of the 30/31st May 1942 which devastated the centre of the city, destroying 600 acres. 103 Squadron was represented in this first 1000-bomber raid on the city. (Crown Copyright)

F/S W F Austin DFM and crew were reported missing on the Berlin raid of 1ˢᵗ March 1943. Crew: F/Sgt W F Austin DFM, Sgt K H Chapman, Sgt A F Reif, F/Sgt P G Roberts RNZAF, Sgt D N D Waite, Sgt D E J Boland, Sgt E J Cook.

P/O R J Edie with air and ground crews

German 8.8 cm Flak anti-aircraft gun mounted on a railway car, Hagen 1943

10.5 cm flak on the Zoo tower, Berlin

Sgt Stoneman's Lancaster W4318 afloat in the Channel on its return from Spezia 13th April 1943. It eventually sank despite attempts to recover it,

F/S J V Roper KIA 9th March 1943
(Roper family).

Sgt Bill Steel

Sgt R J Bunten with Air and Ground Crews. Navigator was Sgt E C Bailey. The other crew members were probably Sgts K B Corcoran, R T Boys, J N Ashton, A E Smith and D R Wilkinson.

Gerald Wilson and Crew

The Italian port of La Spezia on the night of 13/14th April 1943.
Annotated section of a vertical aerial photograph taken during a night raid on the docks at La Spezia, Italy. A Lancaster is silhouetted over the target area as a photoflash bomb (centre right) illuminates the docks below, revealing a 'Littorio' class battleship lying in harbour ('A').

103 Squadron Groundcrew

A railway-mounted flak battery on the coast. The white rings around the barrels of the main guns represent eleven RAF bombers claimed as shot down by this battery - a Wellington, a Stirling, six Halifaxes and three Lancasters.

245

The legendary Florent van Rolleghem and his magnificent crew pictured mid 1943 early in their tour. L to R - P/O Roy MacLeod, Sgt Philip Vickers, Sgt Harry Agar, Sgt Tom Proctor, Sgt Richard White, Sgt Bill Carlin, and P/O Florent van Rolleghem. (Carlin family).

A DFC being presented to F/L Florent van Rolleghem by AVM Edward Rice AOC 1 Group Bomber Command during a special parade at RAF Elsham Wolds on 17th August 1943. He joined the RAF on the fall of Belgium. During October 1944, he was also awarded the DSO. He returned to his homeland in 1946 and was awarded the Belgian Croix-de-Guerre. He retired in 1972 as Air Marshal and had been Belgium Air Attaché to the USA.

Lancaster ED905

In the aircraft: Van Rolleghem – pilot.

On the aircraft: The three killed were with W/C R Goodman in Lancaster ND700 on a Hasselt raid on 12th May 1944.

P/O R K McLeod (RCAF) -		Standing on port outer (KIA)
F/Sgt P O Vickers	-	Seated on port outer (KIA)
Unknown mechanic	-	seated on nacelle of port inner
Sgt G H Agar	-	Rear on port inner (KIA)
Sgt W Carlin	-	Legs dangling over wing (believed to have survived).
Sgt Tom Proctor	-	on wing, one foot on engine (survived).

On the 'cookie' from R – L: Unknown Corporal, LAC Terry Lane, LAC Joe Roberts, Sgt Bob Mason, Unknown Sergeant fitter, LAC Arthur O'Brien, LAC John Leeming, two unknown armourers. (John Lamming)

Sgt Bob Cant and Crew L-R: Sgts Sid Horton, Denys Teare, Bob Cant, Bob Parkinson, George Thomas, Bill Milburn Eric Dickson. Crashed on 5th September 1943. All members of the crew were helped to evade capture by the French population. Thomas was captured but survived.

P/O James Warren. Extract from the Daily Sketch, Monday 4th October 1943 giving details of the shooting down of an ME110 during a raid carried out by 103 Squadron. (Donated by Mr E J Ward)

P/O J D Warren with crew, Elsham Wolds

P/O Nicky Ross and crew pictured at Wright Field USA in mid-43.

Entrances to the submarine pens of Keroman III, viewed from the harbour, and at the bottom left Keroman I. Lorient port attacked 13/14th February 1943 by 103 Squadron

Hamburg, Germany. After the 1943 air raids, the port of Hamburg was strewn with sunken ships, like this Norwegian cargo vessel.

F/O L P Oldham KIA 3rd July 1943 (Oldham family).

Sgt Ken Berry DFM (Berry family)

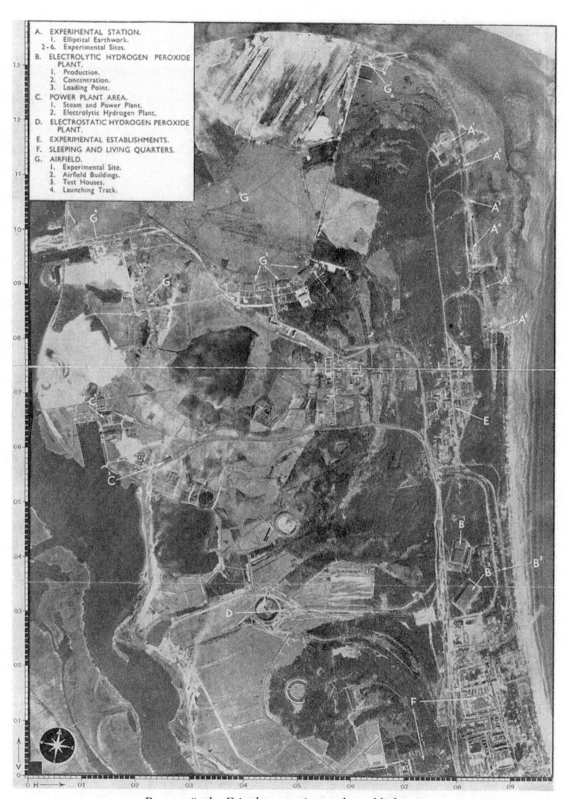

A. EXPERIMENTAL STATION.
1. Elliptical Earthwork.
2-6. Experimental Sites.
B. ELECTROLYTIC HYDROGEN PEROXIDE PLANT.
1. Production.
2. Concentration.
3. Loading Point.
C. POWER PLANT AREA.
1. Steam and Power Plant.
2. Electrolytic Hydrogen Plant.
D. ELECTROSTATIC HYDROGEN PEROXIDE PLANT.
E. EXPERIMENTAL ESTABLISHMENTS.
F. SLEEPING AND LIVING QUARTERS.
G. AIRFIELD.
1. Experimental Site.
2. Airfield Buildings.
3. Test Houses.
4. Launching Track.

Peenemünde. E is the experimental establishment.

251

12th June 1943 RAF reconnaissance photo of Test Stand VII, Peenemünde.

Aftermath of the attack on Peenemünde August 1943.

Krefeld, Germany. The centre of the town on the outskirts of the Ruhr, as the RAF left it after the heavy attack on the night of 21/22nd June 1943. Krefeld was of considerable industrial importance, being the home of the Deutsche Edelstahlwerke combine, which produced nearly 200,000 tons of special high-grade steel a year for use in Krupp and other great arms works. It was also a centre of the textile and silk manufacturing industry, with many firms making fabric for parachutes.

Target photograph of the attack on the Modane marshalling yards 10th November 1943. (Not 103 Squadron photograph)

103 Squadron personnel, along with G/C Carter, Station Commander, celebrated on 23ʳᵈ August 1943 when W4364 PM-D2 'Billie' became the first Lancaster to survive fifty operations over enemy territory. Sadly, the euphoria was short-lived as W4364 was shot down four nights later on an operation to Nuremberg with the loss of four of the crew of W/O CW Annis.

German soldier and a civilian observing fires ravaging Fieseler aircraft plant at Bettenhausen, a suburb of Kassel, Germany, possibly after bombing by RAF 22/23ʳᵈ October 1943.

F/L D W Finlay and crew: a significant loss as they were one of the most experienced crews when lost on a Mannheim operation on the 23/24th September 1943. F/O D W Finlay, Sgt R H J Rowe DFM, F/Sgt I D Fletcher DFM, Sgt J H McFarlane and F/Sgt W CC Gillespie became PoW's while Sgt W H MacDonald and FR J F Vivers were killed.

F/Sgt A W Buxton and Crew

Six killed along with three cadets on an air test 8th September 1943. Crew: F/Sgt Buxton RAAF, Sgt J Leeming, Sgt N Kidd, Sgt W S Whalley, Sgt G Sweeney, F/Sgt G A J Daldy RAAF. Cadets from 1180 Squadron ATC - P Bond (aged 14), D J Fox, E L Hall (both 17). Sgt D Roberts had just started his leave and missed the test.

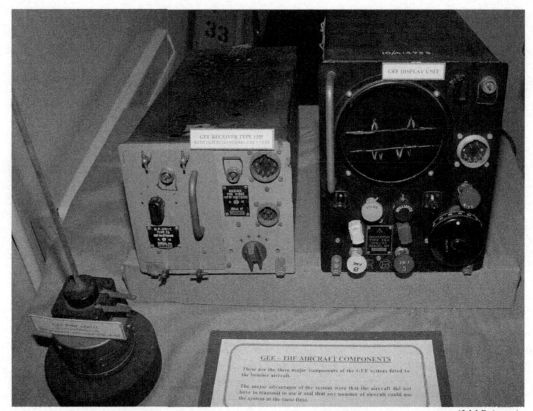

GEE airborne equipment, with the R1355 receiver on the left and the Indicator Unit Type 62A on the right.

S/L John Kennard DFC with wife and baby at the presentation of his DFC at Buckingham Palace in December 1942. Kennard and his crew failed to return from Hanover when their Lancaster DV221 PM-K, crashed near Hildesheim on the 27th September 1943. (Arthur Cook and John Dyer).

Kenneth Lee (seated) and four of his crew probably pictured at OTU. They were lost on 22na October 1943 on a Kassel operation. Crew lost: W/O K R Lee DFC, F/L P J Blurton DFC, Sgt M Sheedy, P/O B F Miller DFC, Sgts D Adams, C W Gray, C L Spink and F/Sgt G G Sveinson RCAF.

W/O Norman Frost (back row, second from right) with his 103 Squadron crew (Frost family).

The ruins of the Kaiser Wilhelm Memorial Church in Berlin, heavily damaged and preserved as a monument against destruction and war.

Canadians P/O Edgar Jones (left) and F/O Ted Hooke. Jones' crew had a very eventful tour during the winter of 1943/44. Jones was awarded a DFC and bar and Hooke a DFC (RCAF).

Care of bomb victims. Issue of hot food at a care centre Berlin.1943.

103 squadron Elsham Wolds 1943.

Fred Brownings and crew – L to R – Front Row Sgt J R Spark, F/S F G Brownings, F/O N G Barker. Back Row Sgt K G B Smart, Sgt R Thomas (KIA 25th March 1944), F/O R Walker, Sgt A Richardson. (Jack Spark).

P/O A A Moore DFC and crew.

Stuttgart, Germany. October 1944. Attacks by RAF Bomber Command caused extensive damage to Stuttgart, the most important industrial town in Southern Germany. Light and electrical engineering is carried on here while the town is also an important railway centre. Aircraft from 103 Squadron took part in these attacks.

Berlin, Germany. February 1944. Effects of an 8,000 lb bomb dropped in a suburb of Berlin during one of RAF attacks. This photograph, taken a month after the bomb was dropped, shows the crater filled in (arrow), and the visible area of destruction covering approximately 4,700 yards. The outer dotted line shows an area of approximately 14 acres over which buildings are seen to have been damaged by blast, as revealed by re-roofing and repairs.

F/L Bill Way RCAF, KIA 7th June 1944.

F/O Joe Moss and his crew were killed when their Lancaster crashed near Dijon en-route to Stuttgart on 29th July 1944. (Michael Batty)

F/O Maurice Dyer RCAF with air and ground crew. The crew, which was lost near Orleans on 26th July 1944, operating against Stuttgart were F/O Dyer, Sgt R W Nansen, F/Sgt R Dey, RCAF, F/O R J B Warren RCAF, W.O L Tommie, Sgt R J Price and Sgt R A O Blanchard.

F/O Charles Whitmore, navigator with F/O W Nixon in Lancaster LM116 was killed during a raid on Stettin 30th August 1944 along with all the crew.

The Crew, & the lads who keep the aircraft fig thay fit.

W- WILLIAM.   Terror of the Fatherland

DUSSELDORF	2	HANOVER 3
WUPPERTAL		STUTTGART.
BOCHUM		LEIPZIG
OBERHAUSEN.		KASSEL.
COLOGNE.	2	
MINELAYING.		
GELSENKIRCHEN.		
TURIN.		
HAMBURG	3	
REMSCHEID.		
MANNHEIM.	3	
NURNBERG.		

List of W-William's operations (See below)

Lancaster W-William – 'The Terror of the Fatherland'
(Unknown crews)

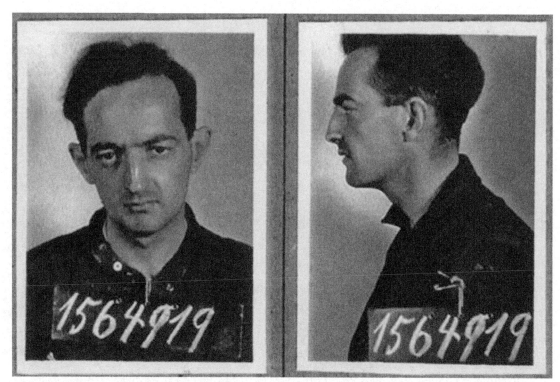

PoW ID photos of Sgt Dugald MacTaggart, Air Bomber and sole survivor of F/L Bartleet's crew.

Villeneuve St Georges, France. 1944. RAF attacks on Villeneuve St Georges, a railway marshalling area south of Paris, destroyed a large quantity of enemy motor transport, tracked vehicles and mobile guns on their way to the fighting areas as well as wrecking loading platforms.

F/L Thomas Leggett (left) was killed on 28th May 1944 when his aircraft crashed in Belgium after being hit by flak. Mid-upper gunner P/O Philip Gore DFC was the sole survivor from the crew (DF / Gore family). Crew lost: F/L Leggett, Sgt A Edwards, F/O R H Beer, F/O A A Wilkes, F/Sgt L Ireland RAAF, and F/O A V M Jones.

P/O P Furlong's Lancaster LM131 PM-V

Air Gunners squad with Sgt Ron Pilcher back row, second right

'The Furlong Scroungers' Hemswell 1944.
'Ron' (MUG), 'Mac' (W/Op), 'Johnnie' (RG), 'Ernie' (F/E), 'Alex' (Nav), 'Pat' (Pilot),
'Jack' (B/A). (Photographs by courtesy of Peter 'Jerbs' Jeffery, nephew of Sgt Ron Pilcher)

Lancaster LM131 PM-V, 2nd August 1944.
Crew: Pat Furlong DFC (Pilot), John Norman (RG), Jock Hamilton DFC (BA), Alex
Matthews (Nav), Ron Pilcher (MUG), Ernie Hall (FE). This aircraft was struck by a 250lb
bomb and abandoned on the 12th March 1945 with a different crew.

Ernie Hall (FE)

Johnny Norman (RG) 18th June 1944.

Ron Picher (MUG)

Pilot Pat Furlong in his 'office'.

January 1944

The change of year was not destined to effect a change in the emphasis of operations, and this was, no doubt, a disappointment not only to the hard-pressed crews of Bomber Command but also to the beleaguered residents of Germany's capital city. Proud of their status as Berliners first and Germans second, they were a hardy breed and just like their counterparts in London during the Blitz of 1940, would bear their trials with fortitude and humour and would not buckle under the constant assault from above. "You may break our walls", proclaimed banners in the streets, "but not out hearts", and the most popular song of the day, "Nach jedem Dezember kommt immer ein Mai", "After every December there's always a May", was played endlessly over the airwaves, its sentiments hinting at a change in fortunes with the onset of spring. Harris allowed the Berliners little time to enjoy New Year, and as New Year's Day dawned, plans were already in hand to continue the onslaught. Before it ended, the first of 421 Lancasters, 117 representing 1 Group, would be taking off and heading eastwards to arrive over the city as the clock showed 03.00 hours on the 2nd.

Take-off had actually been delayed because of doubts over the weather, and this meant that insufficient hours of daylight remained to allow the planned outward route over Denmark and the Baltic. Instead, the bomber stream would adopt the previously used almost direct route across Holland and northern Germany, but return as originally planned more circuitously, passing east of Leipzig, before racing across Germany between the Ruhr and Frankfurt and traversing Belgium to reach the Channel near the French port of Boulogne. 103 Squadron's eleven Lancasters were each loaded with a cookie and fourteen SBCs before departing Elsham Wolds between 23.45 and 00.19 and heading for Mablethorpe with S/L Whittet the senior pilot on duty. The force was gradually depleted by twenty-nine early returns, ten of them from 1 Group's ranks, but none from 103 Squadron, whose F/L Churchill and F/O Russell-Fry and their crews were to act in the new role of "windfinders". Selected crews from each group were to employ their H2S to ascertain wind strength and direction at regular intervals during the flight and transmit the findings back to HQ, where they would be collated, averaged and rebroadcast to the bombers as an aid to navigation. It would prove to be a largely useful tool but would reveal major limitations under unusual and extreme conditions.

The bomber stream covered the four-hundred-mile leg from the Dutch coast to Berlin in under two hours without once catching a glimpse of the ground through the dense cloud, and it was no different at the target, which was completely obscured by a layer of ten-tenths cloud with tops in places as high as 19,000 feet. The Path Finders had to employ skymarking (Wanganui), which was somewhat scattered, and the 103 Squadron crews aimed for these parachute flares from 20,000 to 23,000 feet between 03.03 and 03.16. They observed the glow of fires and smoke rising through the cloud tops and a huge explosion was witnessed at 03.07, which lit up the clouds for three seconds, but it was impossible to assess what was happening on the ground. It was established, ultimately, that the operation had been a failure, which had scattered bombs across the southern fringes of the city causing only minor damage, while the main weight of the attack had fallen beyond the city boundaries into wooded and open country. The disappointment was compounded by the loss of twenty-eight Lancasters, six of them belonging to 1 Group.

During the course of the 2nd, a heavy force of 362 Lancasters and nine of the new Mk III Hercules-powered Halifaxes was made ready for a return to Berlin that night. There was snow on the ground as the crews tumbled out of bed late in the afternoon to attend briefing and were still tired following the almost-eight-hour round trip the night before. Some of these were in a mutinous frame of mind at being back on the order of battle again so soon. 1 Group contributed 116 Lancasters, the thirteen belonging to 103 Squadron receiving the standard cookie/incendiary bomb load before departing Elsham Wolds in two phases between 23.28 and 00.20 with S/L Whittet and F/Ls Churchill and Griffin the senior pilots on duty. F/O Ken Berry was also back in the fold to begin his second tour, and he was on the order of battle for this night. They flew out over Mablethorpe and crossed the Dutch coast near Castricum on course for a point south-east of Bremen, followed by a dogleg to the north-west and finally a ninety degree change of course to the south-east in the Parchim area to leave a ninety-mile run to the target. The force was depleted by a massive sixty early returns, 15.7% of those dispatched, and twenty-eight were from 1 Group, fifteen of them, including the crew of 103 Squadron's Sgt Nicholls, responding in error to a recall signal sent to Polish Wellingtons on their way to the Biscay coast for mining duties. A few were defeated by severe icing conditions, while others abandoned their sorties because of minor technical problems that might have seen them carry on had they been fully rested.

The route changes worked well to throw off the night-fighters, but they would congregate in the target area after the controller correctly identified Berlin as the target forty minutes before zero-hour. Ten-tenths cloud with tops at 16,000 feet forced the bombing to take place on the red skymarkers with green stars or on the glow of fires, the 103 Squadron crews carrying out their attacks from 17,000 to 23,000 feet between 02.45 and 03.07. They reported smoke rising to 20,000 feet as they turned away, but it was not possible to make an accurate assessment of the outcome and the impression was of an effective attack, when, in fact, it had been another failure. Bombs had been scattered across the city and destroyed just eighty-two houses for the loss of twenty-seven Lancasters, most of which had fallen victim to night-fighters in the target area. 103 Squadron posted missing the crew of W/O Townsend RNZAF in JB747, which crashed about twenty miles south of Berlin after bombing, and there were no survivors.

After three trips to the "Big City" in five nights, it would now be left to the Mosquitos of 8 Group's Mosquito squadrons to disrupt the resident's sleep with cookies until the final third of the month, allowing Harris to turn his attention on the 5th upon the Baltic port-city of Stettin, which had not been attacked in numbers since the previous April. It was to be another predominantly Lancaster affair involving 348 of the type accompanied by ten Halifaxes, 1 Group putting up 113 aircraft and 103 Squadron a dozen, the latter with a cookie in the bomb bay and a slightly reduced number of incendiaries in view of the distance. They departed Elsham Wolds between 23.32 and 00.07 with F/Ls Churchill and Griffin the senior pilots on duty, and in contrast to the previous operation, a modest four from 1 Group turned back early on this night. Those continuing on found themselves in thick cloud at cruising altitude, some struggling to find a clear lane even when as high as 23,000 feet, but on the plus side, they all benefitted from a Mosquito diversion at Berlin, which kept the night-fighters off the scent. Stettin was found to be partially visible through five-tenths thin cloud with tops at around 10,000 feet, and crews were able to identify some ground features before focusing on H2S-laid flares and green TIs, which the 103 Squadron crews bombed from 21,000 to 23,500 feet between 03.46 and 03.59. Returning crews provided the intelligence section with accounts of a highly accurate and concentrated attack, which seemed to leave the entire city on fire. The Berlin diversion was successful in keeping most of the enemy fighters away, but fourteen Lancasters and two Halifaxes failed to return, among the former 103 Squadron's ND397, which crashed in the target area killing F/Sgt Nicholls and all but his flight engineer, who fell into enemy hands. Post-raid reconnaissance and local sources confirmed heavy damage in central and western districts, where 504 houses and twenty industrial buildings had been destroyed, a further 1,148 houses and twenty-nine industrial buildings seriously damaged and eight ships sunk in the harbour.

The arrival of the moon period allowed further respite from operations, and batches of crews were given a forty-eight-hour pass over the ensuing week. Snowfalls and freezing conditions made life difficult for ground personnel, but they were able to keep Lancasters flying for training purposes, while the Halifax units further north would spend three weeks in virtual hibernation apart from isolated mining forays. When briefings finally took place on the 14th, there was doubtless some relief to see the red tape on the wall maps terminate some way short of Berlin. It led, in fact, to Braunschweig (Brunswick), the historic and culturally significant city situated some thirty-five miles to the east of Hannover. It had not been attacked by the Command in numbers before, and on this night, would face a force which numbered 496 Lancasters and two Halifaxes. 1 Group supported the operation with 151 Lancasters, of which eleven represented 103 Squadron, and they each received a cookie, supplemented by 1,230 x 4lb and fifty-six x 30lb incendiaries before departing Elsham Wolds between 16.28 and 16.48 with S/L Whittet and F/L Churchill the senior pilots on duty.

They set course via Mablethorpe for Texel and entered Germany north of Meppen, where they were met by part of the enemy night-fighter response, which would harass the bomber stream all the way to the target and back. They skirted the Hannover defence zone before settling on the final leg to the target, where complete cloud cover, topping out in places at around 15,000 feet, dictated the use of red skymarkers with green stars, at which the 103 Squadron crews aimed their cookies and incendiaries from 20,000 to 22,500 feet between 19.15 and 19.30. The enemy fighters scored consistently and accounted for the majority of the thirty-eight missing Lancasters, many of which came down around Hannover. The attack almost entirely missed the city, falling mostly onto outlying communities to the south, and was reported locally as a light raid. This would be a continuing theme in future attacks up to the autumn, as Braunschweig enjoyed something of a charmed life, leading to a belief among the populace that the surrounding villages were being targeted intentionally, in an attempt to drive the residents into the city before a major operation destroyed it with them in it! News came through from Kirmington that W/C Scragg had failed to return, and it would be learned later that he had been the sole survivor of his crew. After spending the remainder of the war as a PoW, he would resume his RAF career in 1945 and retire in the rank of Air Vice Marshal in the 1960s.

The Path Finders, in particular, had been taking a beating since the turn of the year, with 156 Squadron alone losing fourteen Lancasters and crews in just three operations, four and five on Berlin, and five again on Braunschweig. This was creating something of a crisis in Path Finder manpower, particularly with regard to experienced crews, and a number of sideways postings took place between the squadrons to ensure a leavening of experience in each one. One of the solutions was to take the cream from the crews emerging from the training units, rather than wait for them to gain experience at a main force squadron.

Fog persisted from the 15th onwards, and a thaw set in on the 17th to ease conditions, but no flying took place at Elsham Wolds until air-tests on the 20th in preparation for the night's operation to Berlin. It was to be a maximum effort, and the Halifax squadrons, which had appeared to be in hibernation since late December, were roused from their slumber so that 264 of them could join 495 Lancasters to constitute the Path Finder and main force elements, while two small Mosquito elements carried out spoof raids on Kiel and Hannover. 1 Group weighed in with 144 Lancasters, a dozen of them made ready by 103 Squadron, which were loaded with a cookie, fifteen SBCs of 4lb and seven of 30lb incendiaries, before departing Elsham Wolds between 16.02 and 16.29 with S/L Whittet and F/L Churchill the senior pilots on duty. It was a rare pleasure for them to be taking off in daylight, and while climbing out they observed dozens of other Lancasters rising up into the dusk to join them from the neighbouring stations. They turned their snouts towards Mablethorpe and set course for the west coast of Schleswig-Holstein at a point opposite Kiel, rendezvousing with the other groups over the North Sea and all the time shedding individual aircraft as a hefty seventy-five crews abandoned their sorties and turned back. The remainder made landfall over the Nordfriesland coast, before turning to the south-east on a more-or-less direct course for Berlin and soon found themselves hounded by night-fighters. Since the advent of "window", the Luftwaffe Nachtjagd had been forced to develop new tactics and out of this was borne the "Sahme Sau" or "Tame Boar" system of running commentaries, which actively vectored night-fighters from their beacon assembly points to the bomber stream, rather than wait for the bombers to pass through a box as in the former "Himmelbett" system. The enemy controller had fed a proportion of his resources into the bomber stream east of Hamburg, and they would remain in contact until a point between Leipzig and Hannover on the way home, although, curiously, the 1 and 5 Group brigades experienced little of this and would lose just four Lancasters between them. The two Mosquito diversions had been completely ignored by the Luftwaffe controller, who knew well in advance that Berlin was to be the target.

The Path Finders arrived over the Müritzsee to the north of Berlin with a sixty-mile run-in to the aiming point, and they found this to be concealed beneath the same ten-tenths cloud that had accompanied them for the entire outward leg. The tops of the cloud lay beneath the bombers at up to 15,000 feet as the main force crews carried out their attacks on red skymarkers with green stars, those from 103 Squadron from 20,000 to 23,500 feet between 19.32 and 19.55. On return, the crews commented on the lack of flak activity over Berlin and reported the glow of large fires under the cloud and smoke rising through the tops. F/O Russell-Fry's JB655 was hit by heavy flak on the way home south of Hamburg, which created a large hole beneath the rear turret and cut the oxygen supply, but there were no crew casualties. Thirty-five aircraft failed to return, twenty-two of them Halifaxes, which represented an 8.3% casualty rate compared with 2.6% for the Lancasters. It took a little time for an assessment of the operation to be made because of continuing cloud over north-eastern Germany, by which time four further raids had been carried out. It seems from local reports that the eastern districts had received the heaviest weight of bombs in an eight-mile stretch from Weissesee in the north to Neukölln in the south, although no details of destruction emerged.

On the following day, the city of Magdeburg was posted to host its first major attack of the war. The city had, in fact, been a regular destination for small forces as far back as the summer of 1940, when the Command targeted a ship lift at the eastern end of the Mittelland Canal at its junction with the River Elbe and the important Bergius-process Braunkohle A G synthetic oil refinery (hydrogenation plant), both located in the same Rothensee district to the north of Magdeburg city centre. Situated some fifty miles from Braunschweig and slightly to the south of east, it was on an increasingly familiar route as far as the enemy night-fighter controllers were concerned, and within easy striking distance of the night-fighter assembly beacons. In an attempt to deceive the enemy, a small-scale diversion was planned at Berlin involving twenty-two Lancaster of 5 Group and twelve Mosquitos of 8 Group. 1 Group contributed 132 Lancasters, thirteen of them made ready by 103 Squadron and loaded with the standard cookie and incendiary mix, before departing Elsham Wolds between 19.34 and 20.21 with S/L Whittet and F/Ls Churchill and Griffin the senior pilots on duty and W/C Nelson accompanying the Churchill crew. They flew out over Mablethorpe to a point over the North Sea some one hundred miles off the west coast of Schleswig-Holstein, before turning to the south-east to pass between Hamburg and Hannover. Enemy radar was able to detect H2S transmissions during night-flying tests and equipment checks, and the night-fighter controller was, thereby, always aware of an imminent heavy raid. On this night, the night-fighters were able to infiltrate the bomber stream even before the German coast was crossed and the "Tame Boar" system provided a running commentary on the bomber stream's progress, enabling the fighters to latch onto it and remain in contact. The final turning-point was twenty-five miles north-east of the target, from where fires could be seen caused by twenty-seven main force aircraft, driven by stronger-than-forecast winds to arrive ahead of schedule and containing crews anxious to get the job done and get out of the target area as soon as possible. They bombed using their own H2S without waiting for the TIs to go down, and this, together with very effective enemy decoy markers, compromised the Path Finder efforts to achieve concentration after their initial red target indicators went down at 22.50.

The conditions over Magdeburg varied according to the time of arrival, the early birds encountering seven to nine-tenths thin cloud at around 6,000 feet, while those turning up towards the end of the raid found the northern half of the city completely clear with cloud over the southern half only. The 103 Squadron crews experienced a mixture of eight-tenths cloud and relatively clear skies, and in the face of fairly modest opposition, bombed on green TIs from 21,500 to 23,000 feet between 22.57 and 23.27, all gaining the impression that the attack was concentrated around the markers. Returning crews from other groups reported explosions and fires or their glow, and smoke beginning to rise as they turned away. A number reported a flash some twelve minutes after bombing that lit up the clouds for seven seconds, and two large explosions were witnessed at 23.15. Fires that initially seemed to be scattered, became more concentrated as the crews headed for home and the impression was of a successful operation. While all of this was in progress, the diversionary force arrived at Berlin, some seventy miles away to the north-east, and found a layer of eight to ten-tenths cloud at 10,000 feet, through which the bombing took place. The 5 Group ORB expressed the opinion that the diversion had succeeded in the early stages in reducing the impact of the Nachtjagd, although this was not borne out by the figures. In the absence of post-raid reconnaissance and a local report, the outcome at Magdeburg was not confirmed and it is generally believed now that most of the bombing fell outside of the city boundaries. A record fifty-seven aircraft failed to return, thirty-five of them Halifaxes, and this provided another alarming statistic of a 15.6% loss-rate compared with 5.2% for the Lancasters. 103 Squadron came through unscathed, but one of its former crews, that of F/L Kilvington, who had been posted to 156 Squadron in September, failed to return, but at least survived as PoWs.

The end of the month would bring the final concerted effort to destroy Berlin and involve three trips in the space of an unprecedented four nights. This hectic round of operations began on the 27th, after five nights of rest since the bruising experience of Magdeburg and involved an all-Lancaster heavy force of 515 aircraft. 1 Group put up 149, sixteen of them belonging to 103 Squadron, which departed Elsham Wolds between 17.13 and 17.42 with S/L Whittet and F/Ls Churchill and Griffin the senior pilots on duty and each carrying a cookie, ten and two-thirds SBCs of 4lb incendiaries and seven of 30lbs. After climbing out and passing over Mablethorpe to rendezvous with the rest of the group, they set course on a complex route that would take the bomber stream towards the north German coast, before swinging to the south-east to enter enemy territory over the Frisians and northern Holland. Having then feinted towards central Germany, suggesting Leipzig as the target, the force was to turn north-east to a point west of Berlin, from where the final run-in would commence. The long return route passed to the west of Leipzig before turning due east to miss Frankfurt on its northern side and traverse Belgium to gain the Channel south of Boulogne. As they pressed on towards the target, a mining diversion off Heligoland and the dispensing of dummy fighter flares and route-markers partially succeeded in reducing the numbers of enemy night-fighters making contact.

It was, therefore, a relatively intact bomber force that approached the target over ten-tenths cloud with tops at 15,000 feet, conditions which required the Path Finders to use sky-marking, and it was the red Wanganui flares with green stars that led the 103 Squadron crews to the aiming point, where all bombed from 19,000 to 23,000 feet between 20.31 and 20.54. At debriefings, crews reported the glow of fires and the appearance of a successful raid, but no detailed assessment was forthcoming. Of course, not all would make it back to tell their stories at debriefing, and thirty-three Lancaster dispersal pans stood empty in dawn's early light. Among these was the one belonging to JB277, which crashed somewhere in the target area with fatal consequences for F/O Whitehead and his crew. Reports from Berlin described bombs falling over a wide area, more so in the south than the north, and damage to fifty industrial premises, a number of them engaged in important war work, while twenty thousand people were bombed out of their homes. A feature of the campaign was the number of outlying communities suffering collateral damage, and on this night sixty-one such hamlets recorded bombs falling.

The early time-on-target had allowed crews to get a full night in bed and they were, hopefully, fully rested, when news came through on the 28th that many of them would be returning to the "Big City" that night. A heavy force of 673 aircraft was assembled, of which 432 were Lancasters and 241 Halifaxes, 125 of the former provided by 1 Group. 103 Squadron made ready eleven Lancasters, which departed Elsham Wolds between 23.35 and 00.39 with S/L Whittet and F/L Churchill the senior pilots on duty, the latter accompanied by a S/L Nicholas, and each Lancaster carrying a similar bomb load as for the previous operation. They were routed out over southern Denmark before turning south-east on a direct course for the target, with an almost reciprocal return and various diversionary measures to distract the night-fighter controller. Sixty-six crews turned back early, suggesting some adverse reaction to the back-to-back operations, leaving the remainder to reach the target area and encounter ten-tenths cloud and a mixture of sky and ground-marking to aim at. The 103 Squadron crews delivered their bombs on red and green release-point flares from 21,000 to 23,000 feet between 03.16 and 03.29, and huge explosions were reported at 03.15, 03.18 and 03.25, the second-mentioned one described by a 10 Squadron crew as lighting up the sky over a radius of fifty miles. Forty-six aircraft failed to return, twenty-six of them Halifaxes as the defenders fought back to exact another heavy toll of bombers, but all of the Elsham Wolds dispersal pans were occupied come the morning. The impression gained from returning crews at debriefing was of a concentrated and effective attack, and this was partly borne-out by local reports of heavy damage in western and southern districts, where 180,000 people were bombed out of their homes. However, as had been the pattern throughout the campaign against Berlin, seventy-seven outlying communities had also been afflicted.

After a night's rest a force of 534 aircraft was made ready on the 30th for the final operation of this concerted effort against Berlin. 1 Group contributed 129 Lancasters, thirty of which were to act as Path Finder supporters, a role requiring them to accompany the 8 Group spearhead across the aiming point to "beef" up the numbers and make it harder for flak batteries to single out individual aircraft. They would then carry out a second pass to deliver their bomb loads. 103 Squadron's thirteen Lancasters had a cookie, fourteen SBCs of 4lb and six of 30lb incendiaries winched into position and departed Elsham Wolds between 16.43 and 17.04 with S/L Whittet the senior pilot on duty. After climbing out and crossing the coast at Mablethorpe, they joined with the rest of the force over the North Sea to follow a route similar to that adopted two nights earlier. The bomber stream remained relatively free of harassment and on reaching the target was greeted by ten-tenths cloud at around 8,000 feet and the sight of Path Finder skymarking in progress. The 103 Squadron crews bombed on these from 21,000 and 23,000 feet between 20.21 and 20.33, and all commented on the smoke rising through 12,000 feet and the glow of fires beneath the cloud, which, according to some, was still visible from a hundred miles into the return flight.

P/O Jones and crew reported that they were attacked three times by an FW190 while outbound and sustained extensive damage, which persuaded them to drop their bombs on a flak position some seventy miles north-west of Berlin before turning for home. Thirty-two Lancasters and a single Halifax failed to make it back, and in return for these significant losses, according to local sources, central and south-western districts suffered heavy damage and serious areas of fire. Other parts of the city were also hit, while many bomb loads were again scattered liberally onto outlying communities, and at least a thousand people lost their lives. 112 heavy bombers and their crews had been lost to the Command as a result of these three operations, and with the introduction of the enemy's highly efficient Tame Boar night-fighter system, the advantage had swung back in the defenders' favour.

Two further heavy raids would be directed at Berlin before the end of the winter offensive, one in February and the other in March, but they would be almost in isolation. There is no question that Germany's Capital had been sorely afflicted by the three latest operations, but it remained a functioning city and showed no signs of imminent collapse. Harris had failed in his stated aim to bring an end to the war by destroying Berlin, but in truth, it was never a realistic expectation. Berlin was no Hamburg, developed over hundreds of years with tightly packed houses in narrow streets, where fire could spread more rapidly than it could be extinguished. Berlin was modern, built of concrete and steel, with wide thoroughfares and open spaces that acted as natural firebreaks. Each attack created further firebreaks and invoked the law of diminishing returns. Ultimately Berlin was too big, too far and too well-defended, and it was being attacked at a time when the weather was at its worst and the enemy night fighter force was performing at its most lethal. During the course of the month the squadron took part in nine operations, launching 115 sorties, of which only one was abortive, for the loss of three Lancasters and crews.

February 1944

Bad weather during the first two weeks of February allowed the crews to draw breath and the squadrons to replenish. Harris had intended to maintain the pressure on Berlin and would have launched a further attack had he not been thwarted by the conditions, and as a result, the time was filled with training and mining operations. The crews of F/Os Hiscock and Dyson volunteered for duties with the Path Finder Force and were accepted and were posted to 156 Squadron on the 2nd and 13th respectively. When the Path Finder and main force squadrons next took to the air, it would be for a record-breaking effort to Berlin on the 15th and would also be the penultimate operation of the campaign, and indeed of the war by Bomber Command's heavy brigade against Germany's capital city. The force of 891 aircraft represented the largest non-1,000 force to date, and, therefore, the greatest-ever to be sent against the capital, and it would be the first time that more than five hundred Lancasters and three hundred Halifaxes had operated together. The bomb bays of this huge armada would convey to Berlin the greatest-ever tonnage of bombs to any target to date. Extensive diversionary measures included a mining operation in Kiel Bay ahead of the arrival of the bombers, a raid on Frankfurt-an-Oder to the east of Berlin by a small force of 8 Group Lancasters and, finally, Oboe Mosquitos attacking five night-fighter airfields in Holland. 1 Group contributed 161 Lancasters, seventeen of them representing 103 Squadron and carrying between them seventeen cookies, 17,350 x 4lb incendiaries and 952 x 30lbs. They departed Elsham Wolds between 17.04 and 17.35 with S/L Whittet the senior pilot on duty and flew out over Mablethorpe to join up with the rest of the 1 Group squadrons on a course for the western coast of Denmark. After traversing southern Jutland, they were to enter Germany via the Baltic coast between Rostock and Stralsund on a direct heading for the target, and having delivered their bombs, return south of Hannover and Bremen and cross Holland to the gain the North Sea via the known gap in the defences at Egmond.

The force had been depleted by seventy-five early returns by the time the remainder homed in on the target, and among the twelve 1 Group "boomerangs" was 103 Squadron's F/O Floyd and crew, who were afflicted by starboard-outer engine failure. Those reaching the target encountered ten-tenths cloud at around 10,000 feet, which concealed it from their view, but those equipped with H2S, like the Elsham Wolds contingent, were able to confirm their positions, while the others relied on the Path Finders' red release-point flares with green stars and red and green TIs on the ground. The 103 Squadron crews bombed on these from 22,000 to 24,500 feet between 21.17 and 21.58 and on return reported the markers to be highly effective and well-concentrated. The burgeoning glow beneath the clouds convinced them that they had taken part in a successful operation, and this was borne out by local reports, which confirmed that the 2,642 tons of bombs had caused extensive damage in central and south-western districts but also had spilled out into surrounding communities. A thousand houses and more than five hundred temporary wooden barracks were destroyed and important war-industry factories in the Siemensstadt district were damaged in return for the loss to the Command of forty-three aircraft, made up of twenty-six Lancasters, (4.6%) and seventeen Halifaxes, (5.4%). Perhaps slightly disturbing was the fact that eight of the missing Halifaxes were Mk IIIs, only one fewer than the nine now obsolete Mk II/Vs. ND363 failed to return with the crew of F/L Ken Berry DFM, whose navigator was S/L Lindo DFC, RCAF, a native of Jamaica. They had been shot down on the way home by the BF110-G of Lt Kurt Matzak of IV./NJG1 and crashed without survivors at 22.50 local time at Oost, on the eastern shore of Texel.

Berlin had been posted as the target on the 16th and 18th, but both operations were cancelled, and when orders were received on the 19th to prepare for another major assault that night, the target was revealed as Leipzig, where four Messerschmitt aircraft factories were the principal targets. The heavy squadrons were able offer 816 aircraft, 561 Lancasters and 255 Halifaxes, 1 Group detailing 171 Lancasters, of which the fifteen representing 103 Squadron were each loaded with a cookie, thirteen-and-two-thirds SBCs of 4lb incendiaries and seven of 30lbs. They departed Elsham Wolds between 23.04 and 00.01 with S/L Whittet the senior pilot on duty and headed out via Mablethorpe to rendezvous with the rest of the force over the North Sea. They were aiming for the Dutch coast near the fishing port of Harlingen, and a 49 Squadron flight commander returning early described a scene of chaos over the North Sea, with aircraft flying in every direction, the wiser crews with their navigation lights on but most without and he witnessed three aircraft exploding, possibly as a result of collisions. F/O Russell-Fry and crew suffered electrical failure within about ninety minutes and aborted their sortie before reaching the Dutch coast. A proportion of the night-fighter force was waiting for the bomber stream as it closed on a pinpoint at Groningen, having passed close to the "wasps' nest" night-fighter aerodrome at Leeuwarden. As W/O Frost and crew approached this region, they were contending with some kind of issue that would prevent them from continuing and dropped their load onto the airfield from 16,000 feet at 02.03. Some night-fighters had been drawn away by a mining diversion off Kiel, but plenty were still available to shadow the bomber stream as it continued on south of Bremen and north of Hannover. It was at this stage, as they adopted a south-easterly course, that sections of the bomber stream became embroiled in a running battle with night-fighters that continued all the way into eastern Germany. 103 Squadron's JB745 and ND408 ran into trouble, and both crashed in the Hannover defence zone with no survivors from the crew of Sgt Bradley in the former, while only the flight engineer and bomb-aimer in W/O Law's crew escaped with their lives to fall into enemy hands.

Inaccurately forecast winds caused some aircraft to arrive at the target ahead of schedule, forcing them to orbit while they waited for the Path Finders to arrive, and the local flak batteries accounted for around twenty of these, while four others were lost through collisions. The 103 Squadron crews arrived to find ten-tenths cloud with tops at around 10,000 feet and bombed on green Wanganui flares and red and green TIs from 22,500 to 24,000 feet between 04.04 and 04.22. It seems that there was a brief period during the attack when skymarking stopped and led to some scattering of bombs, but the marker-flares were soon replenished with the arrival of more backers-up and a considerable glow beneath the cloud remained visible for some fifty minutes into the return journey, giving the impression of a successful assault. When a large forced returned to home airspace, the often-overlapping circuits could become severely congested and the potential for collision was enormous. Such was the fate of 103 Squadron's ND334 and JB530 as they arrived in the Elsham circuit and prepared to land. F/Sgt Gumbrell managed to maintain control of JB530 and crash-land on the airfield without injury to the occupants, but W/O Warner was less fortunate, and when he brought ND334 in for a landing, the impact was more severe and only he and his rear-gunner emerged alive, albeit with injuries. When all of those aircraft returning home had been accounted for, there was a massive shortfall of seventy-eight, a record loss by a clear twenty-one aircraft. Forty-four Lancasters and thirty-four Halifaxes had failed to return, with a loss-rate of 7.8% and 13.3% respectively, prompting Harris to immediately withdraw the Mk II and V Halifaxes from further operations over Germany, which at a stroke, removed a proportion of 4 Group's fire-power from the front line until they could be re-equipped with the Mk III. In the meantime, the Mk II and V operators would focus their energies for the remainder of the month on gardening duties.

The squadron bade farewell to the long-serving crew of F/L Churchill on the 20th, on their posting to 156 Squadron of the Path Finder Force. Despite the recent heavy losses and the consequent depletion of available numbers, a force of 598 aircraft was made ready on the 20th for an operation that night against Stuttgart, which would be the first of three against the city over a three-week period. 1 Group was able to offer 170 Lancasters, of which nine belonged to 103 Squadron at Elsham Wolds, where each was loaded with a cookie, thirteen-and-a-third SBCs of 4lb incendiaries and six of 30lbs, before taking off between 23.19 and 23.56 with S/L Whittet the senior pilot on duty. They flew south to exit England over Beachy Head on course to make landfall on the other side to the north of Dieppe, from where the cloud remained at ten-tenths with tops at 8,000 feet all the way into southern Germany. A North Sea sweep and a diversionary raid on Munich two hours ahead of the main activity had caused the Luftwaffe to deploy its forces early, and this allowed the bomber stream to push on unmolested to the target. By the time it hove into view, the cloud had thinned to five to eight-tenths at around 6,000 feet and the excellent visibility enabled the crews to draw a bead on the Path Finder red and green sky-markers and similar-coloured TIs on the ground. The 103 Squadron crews bombed from 22,500 to 24,000 feet between 04.00 and 04.15, observing many large fires, and on return there were reports that the glow from the burning city was still visible from 250 miles into the return flight. Despite some scattering of bombs, local sources reported that central districts and those in a quadrant from north-west to north-east had sustained extensive damage, and a Bosch factory was one of the important war industry concerns to be hard-hit. In contrast to twenty-four hours earlier, a modest nine aircraft failed to return.

In an attempt to reduce the prohibitive losses of recent weeks, a new tactic was introduced for the next two operations. A force of 734 aircraft was assembled on the 24th for an operation to the centre of Germany's ball-bearing production, Schweinfurt, situated some sixty miles to the east of Frankfurt in south-central Germany. The plan called for 392 aircraft to depart their stations between 18.00 and 19.00 and to be followed into the air two hours later by 342 others in the hope of catching the night-fighters on the ground refuelling and re-arming as the second wave passed through. While this operation was in progress, extensive diversionary measures would be put in hand that involved more than three hundred other aircraft, including 179 from the training units conducting a North Sea sweep and 110 Halifaxes and Stirlings mining in northern waters. 1 Group contributed seventy Lancasters to the first wave and eighty-six to the second, of which a dozen were made ready by 103 Squadron for inclusion in the second phase, each loaded with a cookie, ten-and-two-thirds SBCs of 4lb incendiaries and four-and-a-half SBCs of 30lbs. They departed Elsham Wolds between 19.59 and 20.33 with S/L Whittet the senior pilot on duty and W/C Nelson hitching a ride with F/L Eddy, and followed a similar route via Beachy Head to that for Stuttgart. The first phase bombers reached the target to find three-tenths cloud at 3,000 to 4,000 feet, with haze spoiling the vertical visibility for some, while others described excellent visibility and the aiming point clearly identified by red and green TIs and already established fires towards the south-western edge of the town. The bombing took place from between 23.00 and 23.30 and two columns of black smoke were observed to be rising through 5,000 feet as they turned away. At debriefings, the consensus among returning crews was of an effective, if, somewhat scattered attack.

The second phase crews picked up the glow of fires from the earlier raid at a distance of two hundred miles and the visibility in the target area remained good, despite the rising smoke, as the 103 Squadron crews bombed under almost cloudless skies onto red and green TIs from 22,500 to 24,000 feet between 01.05 and 01.22. All indications suggested an effective raid, but it was discovered after an analysis that both phases of the operation had suffered from undershooting after some Path Finder backers-up had failed to press on to the aiming point. In that regard, it was a disappointing night, but an interesting feature was the loss of 50% fewer aircraft from the second wave in comparison with the first, in an overall casualty figure of thirty-three, and this suggested some merit in the tactic.

The main operation on the following night was directed at the beautiful and culturally significant southern city of Augsburg, situated around thirty miles north-west of Munich. It was home, among other war-supporting industrial concerns, to a major Maschinenfabrik Augsburg Nuremberg (M.A.N) diesel engine factory, which had been the target for the epic low-level daylight raid by 44 and 97 Squadrons in April 1942. On this night, 594 aircraft were divided into two waves, 1 Group providing 102 Lancasters for the early shift, of which nine were made ready by 103 Squadron and loaded with a cookie and sixteen SBCs of 4lb and 30lb incendiaries. They departed Elsham Wolds between 18.06 and 18.30 with F/Ls Eddy, Griffin and Russell-Fry the senior pilots on duty, the first and last mentioned each accompanied by a newly arrived pilot. For the third operation running, the Channel crossing began at Beachy Head and terminated north of Dieppe, and it was during this leg that W/O Frost and crew turned back because of an oxygen supply issue. They were on the final operation of their tour, for which this aborted sortie was allowed to count, enabling Frost, after receiving a commission, to be posted to 5 Lancaster Finishing School on the 20th of March. The others traversed north-eastern France over ten-tenths cloud and entered Germany near Strasbourg to find the cloud dissipating to the extent, that on arrival at the target, it was possible for crews to gain a visual reference. The Path Finders' red and green TIs were in the bomb sights as the 103 Squadron crews carried out their attacks from 22,000 to 23,000 feet either side of 22.45, and fires were beginning to take hold as they turned away.

The second wave crews were drawn on by the glow in the sky from a hundred miles away and arrived to find visibility still good despite copious amounts of smoke rising through 10,000 feet. The loss of twenty-one aircraft seemed to confirm the benefits of splitting the forces, and this tactic would remain an important part of Bomber Command planning for the remainder of the war. 103 Squadron's ND417 had been homebound at 20,000 feet when hit by flak and set on fire, and F/L Eddy dived it down to 10,000 feet to successfully blow out the flames. He climbed back up to 15,000 feet, by which time the fuel situation had become critical, and he ordered his seven-man crew to take to their parachutes, only to discover that his own had been burned and was unusable. He put the Lancaster down on open ground near Bertrix in Belgium and was spirited away by the local resistance organisation to evade capture, while his crew was less fortunate and fell into enemy hands. It had been a devastatingly destructive attack on Augsburg, in which all facets of the plan had come together in near perfect harmony to spell disaster for this lightly defended historical treasure trove. Its heart was torn out by blast and fire that destroyed almost three thousand houses along with buildings of outstanding historical significance, and centuries of irreplaceable culture was lost forever. There was also some industrial damage, and around ninety-thousand people were bombed out of their homes.

During the course of the month the squadron took part in five operations and launched sixty-four sorties, four of which were abortive, for the loss of six Lancasters, four complete crews and five additional airmen.

March 1944

The new month began with the arrival on the 1st of acting S/L Bickers from 1667 Conversion Unit, and other officers would be posted in from 166, 460 and 550 Squadrons during the course of the month. March would bring an end to the winter campaign, but a long and bitter month would have to be endured first before any respite came from long-range forays into Germany. The crews had enjoyed a few nights off when the second raid of the series on Stuttgart was posted on the 1st, for which a force of 557 aircraft was made ready, including eighty Lancasters representing 1 Group, a somewhat depleted number after the station commanders at Binbrook and Elsham Wolds expressed concerns about the likely weather conditions for returning aircraft and cancelled their involvement. The Path Finders employed a combination of sky and ground-marking, which became scattered, and the bombing was directed between two main concentrations. It was not possible to assess the accuracy of the attack, although a column of smoke had reached 25,000 feet by the end of the raid and large fires were evident from the glow in the sky visible from up to 150 miles away. The presence of thick cloud all the way there and back made conditions difficult for enemy night-fighters and a remarkably modest four aircraft failed to return. It was eventually established that the raid had been an outstanding success, which had caused extensive damage in central, western and northern districts, where a number of important war-industry factories, including those belonging to Bosch and Daimler-Benz, had sustained damage.

At the end of the first week, the Halifax brigade, particularly the older variants withdrawn from operations over Germany, fired the opening salvoes of the pre-invasion campaign, the purpose of which was to dismantle by bombing thirty-seven railway centres in France, Belgium and western Germany. It began on the night of the 6/7th at Trappes marshalling yards, situated some ten miles west-south-west of Paris and continued at Le Mans in north-western France on the following night. 5 Group was in the process of developing a new low-level marking technique and would be active over the ensuing nights practicing its craft at French aircraft factories with such success, that the group would soon gain a virtual independence from the main force and be given its own target marking force. For the other groups, however, there was no employment following Stuttgart, until a return to that city in mid-month, and now that the Mk III Halifax was becoming available in larger numbers, the Command was quickly returning to full strength. The 103 Squadron crews had been told to prepare for operations on the 4th, 5th, 6th and 10th, but each was cancelled before briefings took place. Excellent flying weather on the 14th provided the opportunity for a full programme of training, and S/L Whittet took a Lancaster up for the purpose of dropping a dummy from the forward escape hatch to represent a wounded airman, to ascertain whether he would impact the H2S cupola. The experiment was considered satisfactory, as the dummy and the cupola did not make contact. The long-serving F/L Griffin and crew were posted to 156 Squadron on the 15th, while their former colleagues attended briefing for an operation that night that, at last, would take place.

A force of 863 aircraft was assembled on the 15th, a number that included a record 190 Lancasters provided by 1 Group, nineteen of them belonging to 103 Squadron. Nine of these were given a bomb load of a cookie and 600 x 4lb and 120 x 30lbs incendiaries and the rest a 2,000 pounder and 1,500 x 4lb and 48 x 30lb incendiaries, before they departed Elsham Wolds between 18.28 and 19.38 with S/Ls Bickers and Whittet the senior pilots on duty. They rendezvoused with the rest of the force as they passed over Reading on their way to the exit point at Selsey Bill, and an elongated bomber stream crossed the Normandy coast at 20,000 feet over broken cloud with clear conditions above. By this time, F/O Johnston and crew had turned back after the bomb-aimer's hatch fell away. The stream maintained a course parallel with the frontiers of Belgium, Luxembourg and Germany as if heading for Switzerland, before crossing the German border between Strasbourg and Freiburg and turning towards the north-east for the run-in to the target. It was during this final leg that the night-fighters managed to infiltrate a section of the stream and score heavily. Adverse winds were responsible for the Path Finders arriving up to six minutes late to open the attack, when they employed both sky and ground-markers in the face of seven to ten-tenths cloud at between 8,000 and 15,000 feet. The Wanganui flares drifted in the wind, marking an area to the north-east of the River Neckar, while the TIs landed far apart in the north and south of the city. The 103 Squadron crews bombed on whatever markers presented themselves, mostly red TIs, from 20,000 to 24,000 feet between 23.16 and 23.32 and observed smoke rising to bombing altitude and a spread of fires, including two large ones ten miles apart. It would be established later that some of the early bombing had been accurate, but that most of it had undershot and fallen into open country, a disappointment compounded by the loss, mostly to night-fighters, of thirty-seven aircraft.

F/L Van Rolleghem returned to the squadron from 1656 Conversion Unit to begin a second tour, but was exempt from that night's operation, the first of two in quick order against Frankfurt. A force of 846 aircraft was made ready, which 1 Group supported with a new record of 194 Lancasters, eighteen of which belonged to 103 Squadron, fifteen loaded at Elsham Wolds with a cookie and incendiaries, while the three Path Finder supporters had a cookie, six 1,000 and five 500 pounders in their bomb bays. They took off between 18.41 and 19.17 with S/L Whittet the senior pilot on duty and headed for Orfordness on course for the Franco/Belgian frontier, at which point JB744 lost both inner engines, forcing F/O Moores and crew to dump their load into the sea. They regained the Suffolk coast and crash-landed at 21.30 after hitting trees and buildings at Hill Farm a mile south of Hadleigh, the pilot, flight engineer and rear gunner sustaining injuries, while the Lancaster was damaged beyond repair. The others benefitted from favourable weather conditions as they pressed on across France and into Germany, where they encountered a layer of haze 20,000 feet thick over the target, and according to most, no more than three-tenths cloud. This allowed the Path Finders to employ the Newhaven ground marking technique (blind marking by H2S, followed by visual backing-up), and the 103 Squadron crews confirmed the accuracy of the marking by referring to their own H2S, as a result of which, they were not misled by decoy fires north of the city. The 103 Squadron crews carried out their attacks on red and green TIs from 15,300 to 23,000 feet between 21.55 and 22.16, the low height that of F/O Johnston and crew, who had lost an engine when thirty minutes short of the target and dumped their cookie in order to carry on and deliver their incendiaries. A large explosion was witnessed at 22.05, and the participants in the raid flew home confident that their efforts had been worthwhile. They had, indeed, contributed to an outstandingly successful raid, during which, 5 Group alone dropped more than one thousand tons of bombs for the first time at a single target. Local reports calculated that six thousand buildings had been destroyed or seriously damaged in predominantly eastern, central and western districts, and this was in return for the loss of twenty-two aircraft, just two of which were from 1 Group.

Frankfurt was named again on the 22nd as the target for that night, and 194 crews of 1 Group learned at briefings that they were to be part of another huge force of 816 aircraft. The eighteen 103 Squadron Lancasters were each loaded with a cookie, 1,170 x 4lb incendiaries and 108 x 30lbs, before departing Elsham Wolds between 18.35 to 19.10 with S/Ls Bickers and Whittet the senior pilots on duty. After climbing out above the station, they flew out over Mablethorpe and adopted an unusual route for a target south of the Ruhr, crossing the enemy coast over Vlieland and Teschelling, before passing to the east of Osnabrück on a direct course due south to the target. They arrived to find five to six-tenths thin, low cloud at around 4,000 feet and Paramatta marking (blind marking by H2S) in progress and focussed their attention on the release-point flares and red and green TIs marking out the aiming point. They bombed from 20,000 to 23,000 feet between 21.52 and 22.05, after which a massive rectangular area of unbroken fire was observed across the centre of the city, the glow from which could be seen, according to some, from two hundred miles into the return flight. Returning crews reported numerous searchlights lighting up the cloud, and moderate to intense flak that reached up to the bombers' flight level.

Local reports confirmed the enormity of the devastation, which was particularly severe in western districts and left this half of the city without electricity, gas and water for an extended period. More than nine hundred people lost their lives and a further 120,000 were bombed out of their homes at a cost to the Command of twenty-six Lancasters and seven Halifaxes, a loss-rate of 4.2% and 3.8% respectively. 103 Squadron was represented among the missing by ND329, which blew up west-north-west of the target while on the bombing run, flinging clear the pilot, F/Sgt McInerney RAAF, who was undertaking his first operation since joining the squadron. He would soon find himself in enemy hands as the sole survivor of a crew whose mid-upper gunner, Sgt Findlay, was just eighteen years of age. S/L Whittet landed at 00.27, concluding a magnificent tour as flight commander, and would be posted on the 28th to HQ 1 Group for a well-earned break from operations. It was a bad night for senior officers, 207 and 7 Squadrons losing their commanding officers, while Bardney's station commander, G/C Norman Pleasance, failed to return in a 9 Squadron Lancaster. What was about to happen over the next week and a half, however, would overshadow anything that had gone before and would certainly not fall within what might be considered acceptable.

It was more than five weeks since the main force had last visited the "Big City", and 811 aircraft were made ready on the 24th for what would be the final raid of the war upon it by RAF heavy bombers. 1 Group put up 184 Lancasters, of which sixteen were made ready by 103 Squadron, nine to carry crews assigned to Path Finder support duties and loaded with a cookie, six 1,000 pounders and a single 500 pounder, while four others carried a cookie and 4lb incendiaries and three a 2,000 pounder and incendiaries. They departed Elsham Wolds between 18.30 and 18.57 with S/L Bickers the senior pilot on duty and set course via Mablethorpe for the west coast of Jutland near Ringkøbing and thence to a point on the German Baltic coast near Rostock. When north-east of Berlin they were to adopt a south-westerly course for the bombing run, and once clear of the defence zone homebound, dogleg to the west and then north-west to pass around Hannover on its southern and western sides, before heading for Holland and an exit via the Castricum coast. The extended outward leg provided a time-on-target of around 22.30, but an unexpected difficulty would be encountered, which would render void all of the meticulous planning.

The existence of what we now know as "Jetstream" winds was unknown at the time, and the one blowing from the north with unprecedented strength on this night pushed the bomber stream south of its intended track. Navigators, who were expecting to see the northern tip of Sylt on their H2S screens, were horrified to find the southern end, which meant that they were thirty miles south of track and about to fly over Germany rather than Denmark. The previously mentioned "wind-finder" system had been set up for precisely this eventuality, but the problem on this night was that the wind-finders refused to believe what their instruments were telling them. Winds in excess of one hundred m.p.h had never been encountered before, and fearing that they would be disbelieved, many modified the figures downward. The same thing happened at raid control, where the figures were modified again, so that the information rebroadcast to the bomber stream bore no resemblance to the reality of the situation.

The bomber stream had by now become depleted by the early return of fifty-three aircraft for a variety of reasons, and many of those pressing on commented on the inaccurate wind information received during the outward journey. Having arrived in the target area, some were convinced that the Path Finders were up to ten minutes late in opening the raid and this was confirmed to some by the voice of the Master Bomber exhorting them to hurry up. Crews reported a variety of cloud conditions from three to ten-tenths at between 6,000 and 15,000 feet, but most were able to pick out the red and green TIs on the ground, and if not, found red Wanganui flares with green stars to guide them to the aiming point. The 103 Squadron crews confirmed their positions by H2S before bombing from 20,500 to 23,500 feet between 22.20 and 22.51 and observing what appeared to be a scattered attack in the early stages, until fires began to become more concentrated in three distinct areas and large explosions were witnessed at 22.42 and 22.54. The defences were very active with moderate flak bursting at up to 24,000 feet and light flak attempting to shoot out the skymarkers, but night-fighter activity was described by the 5 Group ORB as unusually quiet. There was a shock awaiting the Command as the returning aircraft landed to leave a shortfall of seventy-two, and it would be established later that two-thirds of them had fallen victim to the Ruhr flak batteries after being driven into that region's defence zone by the wind on the way home.

103 Squadron's ME665 crashed south of Berlin, near the PoW camp at Lückenwalde, on the way out of the target area and exploded with great force. Twenty-one-year-old S/L Ken Bickers DFC was on the third sortie of his second tour and died alongside his crew. ND572 was intercepted by a night-fighter, and during the engagement the rear gunner was killed and the aircraft badly shot-up. F/Sgt Brownings brought the Lancaster home to the American bomber airfield at Dunsfold, where the brakes failed on landing and the Lancaster slewed off the runway to collide with the wreckage of a B17, happily without further casualties. Post-raid analysis revealed that the wind had also played havoc with the marking and bombing and had pushed the attack towards the south-western districts of the capital, where most of the damage occurred, while 126 outlying communities also received bombs. During this long and bitter campaign against Germany's capital city, 103 Squadron had participated in all nineteen main force operations and dispatch 319 sorties for the loss of fifteen aircraft, the lowest loss rate in 1 Group. (The Berlin Raids. Martin Middlebrook).

1 Group captured two Berlin campaign records, both by 460 Squadron RAAF, the crews of W/O Douglas and F/L Wales having completed fourteen of the sixteen Berlin raids since the November resumption, the former the most by a first-tour crew and the latter by a second-tour crew. While the bombs had been falling on Berlin, the Great Escape was taking place at Stalag Luft III at Sagan in Poland, and seventy-six men managed to exit the tunnel before the seventy-seventh was spotted. All but three would be recaptured and fifty of them murdered by the gestapo on Hitler's orders.

Although Berlin had now been consigned to the past, the winter campaign still had a week to run, and two more major operations for the crews to negotiate. The first of these was posted on the 26th and would bring a return to the old enemy of Essen that night, for which a force of 705 aircraft was made ready. 1 Group contributed 165 of the 476 Lancasters, fifteen of them provided by 103 Squadron, which were loaded at Elsham Wolds with a cookie and 1,170 x

4lb incendiaries and 108 x 30lbs, before taking off between 19.30 and 20.38 with five pilots of flight lieutenant rank taking the lead. They climbed out over the station and set course via Mablethorpe for the Dutch coast to the north of Haarlem and Amsterdam, before swinging to the south-east on a direct run to the target. F/Sgt Whitley and crew turned back with an engine issue and on landing at 00.05, ND402's brakes failed, causing it to veer off the runway and lose its undercarriage. The crew scrambled clear before a fire took hold, and the Lancaster was damaged beyond repair. The others reached the target to find it covered by eight to ten-tenths cloud with tops in places as high as 14,000 feet, but Oboe performed well and enabled the Path Finders to mark the city with red and green TIs and Wanganui flares. The 103 Squadron crews bombed from 20,500 and 23,500 feet between 22.01 and 22.19, before returning safely, having been unable to assess the results of their efforts. The impression was of a successful raid, and this was based on a considerable glow beneath the clouds as they withdrew. Post-raid reconnaissance soon confirmed another outstandingly destructive operation against this once elusive target, thus continuing the remarkable run of successes here since the introduction of Oboe to main force operations a year earlier. Over seventeen hundred houses were destroyed in the attack, with dozens of war industry factories sustaining serious damage, and on a night when the night-fighter controllers were caught off guard by the switch to the Ruhr, the success was gained for the modest loss of nine aircraft.

The period known as the Battle of Berlin, but which was better referred to as the winter campaign, was to be brought to an end on the night of the 30/31st with a standard maximum-effort raid on Nuremberg. The plan of operation departed from normal practice in only one important respect, and this was to prove critical. It had become standard practice for 8 Group to plan operations and to employ diversions and feints to confuse the enemy night-fighter controllers. Sometimes they were successful and sometimes not, but with the night-fighter force having clearly gained the upper hand with its "Tame Boar" running commentary system, all possible means had to be adopted to protect the bomber stream. During a conference held early on the 30th, the Lancaster Group A-O-Cs expressed a preference for a 5 Group-inspired route, which would require the bomber stream to fly a long straight leg across Belgium and Germany to a point about fifty miles north of Nuremberg, from where the final run-in would commence. The Halifax A-O-Cs were less convinced of the benefits, and AVM Bennett, the Path Finder chief, was positively overcome by the potential dangers and predicted a disaster, only to be overruled. A force of 795 aircraft was made ready, of which 180 Lancasters were to be provided by 1 Group, sixteen of them representing 103 Squadron, and at briefings, crews were told of the route, wind conditions and the belief that a layer of cloud would conceal them from enemy night-fighters. Before take-off, a Meteorological Flight Mosquito crew radioed in to cast doubts upon the weather conditions, which they could see differed markedly from those that had been forecast. This also went unheeded, and from around 21.45 for the next hour or so, the crews took off for the rendezvous area, and headed into a conspiracy of circumstances, which would inflict upon Bomber Command its heaviest defeat of the war.

Nine of the 103 Squadron Lancasters had a cookie in the bomb bay, while seven had a 2,000 pounder, all supplemented with the maximum weight of incendiaries, and they departed Elsham Wolds between 21.30 and 22.31 F/Ls Russell-Fry and Hart the senior pilots on duty. They headed via Southwold for the Franco/Belgian coast, and it was not long into the flight before they and the other crews began to notice some unusual features in the conditions, which included uncommonly bright moonlight, and a crystal clarity of visibility that allowed them the rare sight of other aircraft in the stream. On most nights, crews would feel themselves to be completely alone in the sky all the way to the target, until bang on schedule, TIs would be seen to fall, and other aircraft would make their presence known by the turbulence of their slipstreams as they funnelled towards the aiming point. Once at cruising altitude on this night, however, they were alarmed to note that the forecast cloud was conspicuous by its absence, and instead, lay beneath them as a white tablecloth, against which they were silhouetted like flies. Condensation trails began to form in the cold, clear air to further advertise their presence to the enemy, and the Jetstream winds, which had so adversely affected the Berlin raid a week earlier, were also present, only this time blowing from the south. As then, the wind-finder system would be unable to cope, and this would have a serious impact on the outcome of the operation. The final insult on this sad night was, that the route into Germany passed close to two night-fighter beacons, which the enemy aircraft were orbiting while they awaited their instructions, unaware initially that they were about to have the cream of Bomber Command handed to them on a plate.

The carnage began over Charleroi in Belgium, and from there to the target, the route was sign-posted by the burning wreckage on the ground of eighty Bomber Command aircraft. F/L Allwood and crew were at least two hours into the outward flight and must have been closing on the night-fighter killing zone when the oxygen supply to the rear turret failed and they were forced to turn back. 103 Squadron's JB736 was one of a very few to be brought down by flak, having been hit by a battery at Westerburg, before crashing some five miles to the south at Bilkheim. F/O Johnston and crew were on their third operation and were the twenty-eighth to be brought down on this catastrophic night, all but the mid-upper gunner losing their lives, while Sgt Fealy managed to escape through the hole left in the floor of the fuselage where the H2S cupola had burned away. He sustained serious burns to his legs and was taken into captivity. ND572 had penetrated a further seventy miles to the east when it was shot down by a night-fighter to crash a mile south of Hünfeld as the fifty-fourth victim. P/O Tate and crew were on their first operation and there were no survivors. The wind-finder system broke down again, and those crews who either failed to detect the strength of the wind, or simply refused to believe the evidence, were driven up to fifty miles north of their intended track, and consequently, turned towards Nuremberg from a false position. This led to more than a hundred aircraft bombing at Schweinfurt in error, which combined with the massive losses sustained before the target was reached to reduce considerably the numbers arriving at the primary target.

The remaining 103 Squadron crews arrived over Nuremberg to encounter eight to nine-tenths cloud with tops as high as 16,000 feet and bombed from 20,500 to 23,000 feet between 01.11 and 01.27. They aimed at red and green TIs and sky-markers after confirming their positions by H2S and observed many fires, the glow from which, according to some reports, remained visible for 120 miles into the return journey. Ninety-five aircraft failed to return home, twenty-one of them from 1 Group, and many others were written off in landing crashes or with battle damage too severe to repair. The shock and disappointment were compounded by the fact that the strong wind had driven the marking beyond the city to the east, and Nuremberg had, consequently, escaped serious damage.

During the course of the month the squadron undertook six operations and dispatched 102 sorties, five of them aborted, for the loss of six Lancasters and four crews.

April 1944

The winter campaign had brought the Command to its low point of the war and was the only time when the morale of the crews was in question. What now lay before the hard-pressed men of Bomber Command was in marked contrast to that which had been endured over the seemingly interminable winter months. In place of the long slog to Germany on dark, often dirty nights, shorter range hops to France and Belgium in improving weather conditions would become the order of the day. However, these operations would be equally demanding in their way, and require of the crews a greater commitment to accuracy to avoid casualties among friendly civilians. Despite this, a decree from on high insisted that such operations were worthy of counting as just one third of a sortie towards the completion of a tour, and until this flawed policy was grudgingly rescinded late in the war, a sense of injustice pervaded the crew rooms. In fact, the number of sorties to complete a tour would fluctuate up and down between this point and the end of hostilities. Despite the horrendous losses of the winter campaign, the Command was in remarkably fine fettle to face its new challenge, with 3 Group gradually changing to Lancasters and the much-improved Hercules powered Halifaxes equipping 4 Group and most of 6 Group. Harris was now in the enviable position of being able to achieve what had eluded his predecessor, namely, to attack multiple targets simultaneously with enough strength to be effective. Such was the hitting-power now at his disposal, that he could assign targets to individual groups, to groups in tandem or to the Command as a whole, as dictated by operational requirements. Although invasion considerations would come first, while Harris was at the helm, his favoured policy of city-busting would never be entirely shelved.

There would be an influx of new aircrew during the course of the month, many arriving from 11 Base, which comprised the Heavy Conversion Units at Lindholme, Blyton and Sandtoft. On the 4th, Operational Instruction No 19 was issued by 1 Group HQ, stating that it was the intention to "train and operate suitable crews to act as target markers and assembly point markers for precision attacks by small forces of exclusively 1 Group aircraft". The instruction went on to state that these operations would be carried out "chiefly during moonlight periods", and generally when the bulk of the Command's main force squadrons were inactive. This mirrored in a small way 5 Group's march to independence, although, what would become 1 Group's Special Duties Flight was minor in comparison, and as events were to prove, would be relatively short-lived.

The weather at the start of the month was not conducive to operational flying, and Elsham Wolds was effectively stood down until the 9th, when the pre-invasion campaign got into full swing with the posting of two operations, one against the Lille-Delivrance goods station in north-eastern France assigned to 239 aircraft from 3, 4, 6 and 8 Groups, and the other targeting the marshalling yards at Villeneuve-St-Georges, on the southern outskirts of Paris involving 225 aircraft drawn from all groups. In addition to these operations, a large mining effort in the Baltic involved forty-seven and fifty-six Lancasters respectively from 1 and 5 Groups. Among thirty-six 1 Group Lancasters detailed for Villeneuve-St-Georges were two representing 103 Squadron containing the crews of F/L Cox and P/O Rowe, who departed Elsham Wolds at 20.51 and 20.57, each with a bomb load of a dozen 1,000 and four 500 pounders beneath their feet. They began the Channel crossing at Selsey Bill, and having rendezvoused with the rest of the force, made landfall on the Normandy coast at around 14,000 feet under clear skies. The target could be identified visually, but crews aimed for the red and green TIs that had been accurately placed by the Path Finders, and the 103 Squadron duo delivered their hardware from 13,000 and 12,000 feet in the face of little opposition at 23.57. Many bomb bursts were observed along with orange explosions, and to those high above, the raid appeared to be highly successful. In fact, many bomb loads had fallen into adjacent residential districts, where four hundred houses had been destroyed or seriously damaged, and ninety-three people killed. This was far fewer than had died in the simultaneous operation at Lille, many miles to the north-east, where over two thousand items of rolling stock had been destroyed, and buildings and installations seriously damaged, but at a collateral cost of 456 French civilian lives. Civilian casualties would prove to be an unavoidable by-product of the campaign.

Meanwhile, some eight hundred miles to the north-west, the gardeners were benefitting from excellent conditions and visibility as they employed H2S to confirm the positions for the release of their five 1,500lb parachute mines each. 1 Group had been assigned to five gardens, among them Spinach, located off the port of Gdynia in Danzig Bay, one of the most distant of all Bomber Command destinations and a frequent shelter for elements of the Kriegsmarine. It had been targeted with special bombs by W/C Guy Gibson and an element from 106 Squadron in August 1942 in an attempt to destroy the aircraft carrier Graf Zeppelin, which was not found, but was never completed anyway. The eight 103 Squadron crews had departed Elsham Wolds between 21.10 and 21.18 with F/Ls Floyd and Hart the senior pilots on duty for what would be their first taste of high-level mining. Until the advent of H2S, mining had been conducted at low-level, typically at between 500 and 1,000 feet, where pinpoints could be identified visually as the start of a timed run to the release point, but weather conditions could be challenging, and aircraft were exposed to lethal light flak from shore and ship-based batteries. H2S allowed them to establish their position from the safety of high altitude, where weather conditions were less critical, and night-fighters were the main threat. They flew out over Mablethorpe on course for the western coast of Jutland near Esbjerg, and lost F/O Young and crew to the failure of an engine, which forced them to drop their mines in an alternative garden, probably Hawthorn off Jutland's western coast. Having traversed southern Jutland and noted night-fighter activity, they reached the Baltic with a further 350 miles to cover to the target area and were discouraged by accurate Swedish flak from straying too close to neutral airspace. They arrived at Danzig Bay to find bright moonlight and only high cirrus cloud, which enabled them to establish their positions visually on Hel Point, from where timed runs of two to three minutes were carried out and the vegetables delivered from 14,000 to 15,000 feet between 01.34 and 01.40. On the way home, ND420 was intercepted by a night-fighter and crashed at 04.00 at Brande in central Jutland, killing P/O Nimmo RAAF and four of his predominantly RAAF crew, and only the gunners survived to fall into enemy hands.

On the following day, Monday the 10th, a further five railway yards, four in France and one in Belgium, were posted as the targets for that night and assigned to individual groups. 1 Group was handed those at Aulnoye in the Haut-de-France region of north-eastern France, and for the first time would be employing its own target marking element and a Master Bomber and Deputy to back up the Path Finders. 130 Lancasters were made ready, plus two more for the Master Bomber pairing, and 103 Squadron supported the operation with a dozen aircraft, which were loaded with twelve 1,000 and four 500 pounders. They departed Elsham Wolds between 23.10 and 23.45 with S/L Van Rolleghem the senior pilot on duty and set course over ten-tenths cloud for Selsey Bill and the Channel crossing. There were no early returns, and as the French coast hove into view, the cloud gradually dispersed to leave clear skies and good horizontal visibility. At the target they encountered patches of thin, drifting cloud with tops at 6,000 feet and haze that presented challenging conditions in which to identify ground detail. The Path Finders opened the attack on the northern aiming point on time with green TIs, which the Master bomber assessed before directing the main force crews. He was carrying red TIs to remark the aiming point if necessary, but the only reds to appear were employed at the southern aiming point. The 103 Squadron crews bombed mostly on green TIs from 10,000 to 11,000 feet between 02.21 and 02.37, and all but one returned safely to report too much conversation between the Master Bomber and Deputy, which apparently lasted for forty minutes, a comment echoed by others. There was little opposition from the ground, but night-fighters were active over the target and at the French coast and seven Lancasters failed to return. Among them was JB732, which was homebound at 10,000 feet when hit either by flak or a rocket projectile and crashed near Meharicourt, twenty miles east-south-east of Amiens. P/O Armstrong RNZAF and both gunners lost their lives, while two of the survivors were taken into captivity and two evaded a similar fate. It proved impossible to assess the outcome, but reconnaissance and local sources confirmed a successful raid, in which 287 bombs had landed in the yards, damaging the engine sheds and thirty locomotives. Sadly, 340 houses were either destroyed or damaged and fourteen civilians were killed, and the Germans rounded up local civilians to force into repairing the damage to get the yards working again before long.

Aachen was a major railway centre with marshalling yards at both the western and eastern ends, but the attack planned for the night of the 11/12th was clearly designed as a city-busting exercise for which a force of 341 heavy aircraft was drawn from 1, 3, 5 and 8 Groups. 103 Squadron made ready eleven of the ninety-five Lancasters representing 1 Group, and they were loaded with a dozen 1,000 pounders, two of 500lbs, three SBCs of 4lb incendiaries and one of 30lbs, before departing Elsham Wolds between 20.07 and 20.39 with S/L Van Rolleghem the senior pilot on duty. F/O Young and crew lost their starboard-outer engine after an hour and turned back, while the rest of the bomber stream climbed to between 18,000 and 20,000 feet by the time it reached the Belgian coast at 3 degrees east and maintained that altitude all the way to the target, where six to ten-tenths thin cloud was encountered that topped out at 12,000 feet. Red and green TIs identified the aiming point, and the 103 Squadron crews attacked it from 18,000 to 21,000 feet between 22.43 and 22.50, observing many bomb bursts and fires, which suggested that the attack was accurate. The crews maintained height on the way home until fifty miles from the coast, at which position they began a gentle descent to exit enemy territory at 15,000 feet or above. Reports coming out of Aachen revealed this to be the city's worst experience of the war to date, with extensive damage in central and southern districts, disruption of its transport infrastructure and a death toll of 1,525 people in return for the loss of nine Lancasters, none of which was from 1 Group. However, post-raid reconnaissance revealed that the railway yards had not been destroyed and would require further attention.

Thirty-two-year-old S/L Harold "Jock" Swanston was posted to 103 Squadron from 11 Base on the 12th to assume the role of A Flight commander. On the 14th, the Command became officially subject to the orders coming from the Supreme Headquarters of the Allied Expeditionary Force (SHAEF), under General Dwight D Eisenhower, and would remain thus shackled until the Allied armies were sweeping towards the German frontier at the end of the summer. On the 15th, 300 Squadron, the last in 1 Group to relinquish the Wellington, was declared operational on Lancasters at Faldingworth, and would bring the passion and fierce determination of Polish airmen back to the frontline after spending much of the previous eight months undertaking gardening operations. 1 Group's Special Duties Flight, or SDF as it became known, was formed officially at Binbrook on the 18th under the command of S/L Breakspear, an experienced flight commander from 100 Squadron and a man to whom taking the war to Germany was a point of principle and pride. He had recently been awarded a DFC following eleven trips to Berlin. The other crews to be posted in were those of F/L Gillam, also from 100, Squadron, F/L Hull from 101 Squadron, F/L Russell-Fry from 103 Squadron, P/O Marks from 625 Squadron and P/O Stewart from 626 Squadron. F/Sgt Daley from 460 Squadron and P/O Knowles from 625 Squadron would be added to the unit three weeks hence.

It was on this day also that 83 and 97 Squadrons were sent on what amounted to a permanent transfer from the Path Finders to 5 Group along with the Mosquito unit, 627 Squadron. They would retain their Path Finder status and privileges but would spend the remainder of the war as part of 5 Group, 83 and 97 Squadrons to fulfil the heavy target marking role, while the Mosquitos would eventually take over the low-level marking role currently performed by 617 Squadron. This was a major coup for AVM Cochrane and 5 Group and a bitter blow to AVM Bennett, the Path Finder Chief. Relations between Cochrane and Bennett had never been cordial, but this plunged them to new depths. Both were brilliant men, Bennett, an Australian, in particular, a man of the greatest intellect, who, despite his total lack of humour, commanded the deepest respect and loyalty from his men. He and Cochrane possessed vastly different opinions on the subject of target marking, Bennett believing that a low-level method exposed the crews to unnecessary danger, while Cochrane insisted that the risks in a fast-flying Mosquito were negligible and would produce greater accuracy.

The Transportation Plan continued on the 18th with the briefing of 827 Lancaster and Halifax crews for attacks on marshalling yards at four locations in France. 1 Group was assigned to Rouen in Normandy, and detailed 140 Lancasters, including seven from 300 Squadron on its Lancaster debut. 103 Squadron prepared eleven Lancasters, loading each with eleven or twelve 1,000 pounders and four 500 pounders, before sending them on their way from Elsham Wolds in two phases between 21.18 and 21.29 and 23.22 to 23.58 with S/L Swanston the senior pilot on duty for the first time. They headed south to Selsey Bill under almost clear skies, which persisted as they crossed the Channel and the French coast near Dieppe and covered the twenty miles inland to the target. In the light provided by Path Finder flares, the crews were able to visually identify the River Seine, the marshalling yards and railway track, and green warning flares guided them to the mark. The first phase attack on the southern aiming point proceeded seamlessly with the Path Finders and Master bomber fulfilling their roles faultlessly, and among numerous explosions was a particularly large one at 00.18, which lasted a few seconds. The second phase assault on the northern aiming point was only a little less effective, and the site was left in ruins and burning fiercely. At debriefing, the 103 Squadron participants reported bombing on red and green TIs from 9,000 to 11,000 feet between 00.21 and 00.22, and from 8,000 to 10,000 feet between 02.19 and 02.25.

While the assault on railways in the occupied countries continued on the night of the 20/21st, a force of 357 Lancasters and twenty-two Mosquitos was drawn from 1, 3, 6 and 8 Groups to attack railway installations in Cologne. There were several major marshalling yards within the city, those at Kalk and Gremberg on the eastern side of the Rhine and Nippes to the west, each within a relatively short distance of the city centre, which effectively turned the raid into a city-busting affair. 1 Group contributed a record 196 Lancasters, fourteen of them provided by 103 Squadron, which received loads of a cookie and SBCs containing 1,170 x 4lb incendiaries and 108 x 30lbs. They departed Elsham Wolds between 23.10 and 23.58 with F/Ls Allwood, Cox and Fortier the senior pilots on duty, and with enemy intruders active over eastern England, were advised to find alternative routes to the departure point at Southwold. They made landfall on the Belgian coast at Knokke, and all reached the target area to find ten-tenths cloud with tops at 12,000 to 16,000 feet. It would be impossible to see TIs on the ground, and they had to aim at red and yellow Path Finder release point flares, which went down late and were a little scattered. The 103 Squadron crews carried out their attacks from 18,000 to 23,000 feet between 02.05 and 02.22, and the flashes from many explosions were observed along with a red glow from the burgeoning fires. There was little opposition from the ground, but night-fighters were active over Belgium on the way home and ten combats were reported by 1 Group crews. Post raid reconnaissance and local sources confirmed an outstandingly destructive operation, during which a record 4,500 tons of bombs had been dropped mostly in northern and western districts. 1,861 houses or apartments were destroyed, and 20,000 others damaged, and there was damage to some extent also to 192 industrial premises and 725 dwelling houses with commercial units attached. Many public buildings, including schools and churches, were caught in the bombing and more than 1,200 fires had to be dealt with.

A major night of operations on the 22nd called for three forces to be made available, the largest of 596 aircraft from all but 5 Group to target Düsseldorf for the first time for a year, while 5 Group tested its low-level marking system at Braunschweig and 181 aircraft from 3, 4, 6 and 8 Groups attended to railway yards at Laon. I Group contributed 178 Lancasters to the Ruhr raid, of which the thirteen belonging to 103 Squadron were given a similar bomb load to that for Cologne, before departing Elsham Wolds between 22.10 and 23.23 with F/Ls Allman and Fortier the senior pilots on duty. The take-off was disrupted by a 576 Squadron Lancaster swinging off the runway and catching fire, which necessitated a change of runway and a delay. Once airborne, they flew out over Southwold under cloudless skies on the southern route to the Ruhr via the French coast and were greeted by high cirrus cloud above 21,000 feet in the target area, with which their heavy condensation trails merged to betray the bomber stream's presence. The first Mosquito-borne Oboe red TIs went down between 01.14

and 01.15 and were immediately joined by concentrated greens delivered by the Path Finder heavy brigade, which were clearly visible through the industrial haze. The backers-up maintained the aiming point throughout the raid, and some of the experience crews would describe the marking as the best they had witnessed.

The 103 Squadron crews carried out their attacks from 18,000 to 23,000 feet between 01.19 and 01.36 to contribute to the total of 2,150 tons of bombs and gained the impression that the entire city was on fire. By 01.23 a large volume of smoke was rising to meet the bombers and a large explosion at 01.45 was observed by some crews who were well into the homeward flight. They also reported the glow from the burning city to be still visible from the Dutch coast. Night-fighters infiltrated the bomber stream over the target and on the way home, and twenty-nine aircraft failed to return, among them seven from 1 Group including 103 Squadron's ME741, which was brought down by flak and abandoned, delivering F/O Birchall and crew into enemy hands. On return at 04.56, LL913 smacked into the side of a hill five miles south-south-west of Helmsley in Yorkshire, killing P/O Astbury and crew, while F/L Allwood's JB746 barely survived a brush with a night-fighter and landed at the emergency strip at Woodbridge. Local sources confirmed the severity of the raid, which hit predominantly northern districts and destroyed or badly damaged more than two thousand houses and fifty-six large industrial concerns and killed in the region of 1,200 people.

On the following night, 1 Group sent eight Lancasters from 103 and 166 Squadrons on mining sorties in the Baltic, specifically to the Geranium garden off the port of Swinemüde in Pomeranian Bay and Pollock, off the Swedish Island of Bornholm, located some seventy miles to the north. 103 Squadron briefed the crews of P/Os Jones, Mitchell and Whitley and F/O Brownings, assigning two to each garden, and sent them on their way from Elsham Wolds between 21.01 and 21.05. They flew out over Mablethorpe on course for landfall on the west coast of Jutland and all reached their respective target areas to plant their vegetables as briefed from 6,500 to 15,000 feet sometime after midnight.

The main operation on the night of the 24/25th was to be against Karlsruhe in southern Germany, for which a force of 637 aircraft was assembled, while 5 Group targeted Munich in another test of its low-level marking system against a heavily defended urban target. 1 Group put up 179 Lancasters, of which fifteen were made ready by 103 Squadron, five loaded with six 2,000 pounders for crews who were to act as Path Finder supporters, and six as part of the main force carrying a cookie and incendiaries. They departed Elsham Wolds between 21.36 and 22.15 with F/Ls Allwood and Cox the senior pilots on duty, and according to the ORB, were given two routes, the first via Sheringham and the second via Beachy Head, presumably to converge as they approached the target. They flew out over small amounts of medium cloud as far as the Franco-German frontier, where they encountered a band of high cloud between 18,000 and 23,000 feet, which contained pockets of icing. Thin variable cloud persisted over the target to present the Path Finders with challenging conditions for target identification and marking, and they were a little late in opening the attack. Some crews bombed on their own H2S before the first TIs went down, and the altitude of the others determined whether or not they could see the red and green TIs on the ground. Those bombing from 18,000 feet gained a clear view of the marked area, while those above did not, and the 103 Squadron crews were on both sides of the divide. They bombed from 17,000 to

23,500 feet between 00.32 and 00.54 and reported fires over a wide area and smoke rising through 12,000 feet as they turned away.

ND638 was hit by incendiaries from above and became almost uncontrollable, whereupon F/O Leggett ordered his crew to prepare to abandon ship. The mid-upper gunner was either ejected or chose to leave the aircraft, before the pilot managed to regain control and bring the Lancaster home, where it was eventually declared a write-off. JB278 was attacked by two Ju88s over the target, and although the gunners claimed one of them as destroyed, the other raked the Lancaster from stem to stern, putting both turrets out of action and causing other serious damage including holes in two petrol tanks. F/Sgt Ogden coaxed the aircraft towards the English coast and as he called up Manston to announce his arrival, the tanks ran dry and he was able to give Manston a running commentary on his ditching in Sandwich Bay. The Lancaster sank within forty seconds, but the crew members all reached the dinghy, and were eventually picked up by a lifeboat and returned to shore, apparently none the worse for their experience. An analysis of the raid revealed that a strong wind had helped to push the main weight of the attack into northern districts and beyond, where some nine hundred houses had been destroyed or seriously damaged and Mannheim also reported being under attack.

W/C Goodman was posted in from No1 Lancaster Finishing School on the 26th as the new commanding officer elect. Born in Basutoland in South Africa in 1915, Hubert Goodman joined the RAF in 1934, and passed out of Cranwell as a pilot officer two years later. He served with distinction in Egypt and Palestine until late 1942, before returning to England in 1943 to undertake various senior roles. On the day of his arrival at Elsham Wolds, briefings took place for an operation against Essen, for which a force of 493 aircraft was assembled from all but 5 Group. 1 Group contributed 175 of the Lancasters and a dozen of these were made ready by 103 Squadron at Elsham Wolds, where each received a bomb load of a cookie and 4lb and 30lb incendiaries before taking to the air between 22.26 and 23.04 with F/Ls Allwood and Cox the senior pilots on duty. They flew out over Mablethorpe and joined the bomber stream as it adopted the northern route to the central Ruhr, encountering a little broken cloud over the Frisians, but clear skies as they progressed inland to find good visibility and only a little industrial haze at the target, while the defenders were aided by the formation of condensation trails. Many crews arrived in the target area ahead of the Path Finders and not all were prepared to wait for the attack to begin, which it did at 01.24 with red TIs that were soon backed up by a concentration of greens. The aiming point was well-maintained throughout the raid, during which the 103 Squadron crews carried out their attacks from 22,000 to 24,500 feet between 01.28 and 01.38, describing a good concentration of bomb bursts around the markers and a pall of smoke rising to a considerable height. The glow from the burning city remained visible for eighty miles and more, and returning crews were in no doubt that another devastating blow had been achieved. A modest seven aircraft failed to return, among them P/O Shepard and his all-NCO crew in ND847, which was leaving the target area when brought down by flak batteries operating near Neuss, the city facing Düsseldorf from across the Rhine. Most of the wreckage fell in the Meerbusch in the city's north-western corner, and all on board lost their lives.

The 27th saw a further three operations scheduled, two against railway yards at Aulnoye in France and Montzen in Belgium, and the night's largest effort against the small city of

Friedrichshafen, situated on the northern shore of Lake Constance (Bodensee) on the border with Switzerland and close to the Austrian frontier. An all-Lancaster force of 322 aircraft was assembled, the main force element drawn from 1, 3 and 6 Groups with fifty-nine 8 Group Lancasters to provide the marking. At briefings, the 162 crews from 1 Group were told of the importance of Friedrichshafen to the German war effort as a centre of war production, particularly of tank engines and gearboxes. Five of the ten 103 Squadron Lancasters were loaded with a cookie and incendiaries and five with a 1,000 pounder, a 500 pounder and additional incendiaries and departed Elsham Wolds between 21.15 and 21.48 with F/Ls Allwood and Cox the senior pilots on duty. They exited the English coast at Shoreham-on-Sea on course for the Normandy coast, and apart from ten-tenths cloud over the Channel, the outward route was completed under clear skies, and the high-level cirrus over the target was no impediment to the crews' ability to establish their positions visually on Lake Constance. Zero hour for the main force was brought forward by ten minutes to 02.05, and the Path Finders opened the attack at 02.00 with green flares and green TIs. The 103 Squadron crews confirmed their positions by H2S before carrying out their attacks from 19,000 to 20,000 feet between 02.05 and 02.12 in accordance with the instructions of the Master Bomber. They observed an accurate and concentrated pattern of bombing and many explosions and fires and were confident that they had contributed to an outstandingly effective attack. It was not a one-sided affair, however, and having avoided to some extent contact with night-fighters on the way to the target, the bombers sustained heavy casualties at their hands in the target area. Eighteen Lancasters were lost, among them 103 Squadron's ME738, which was one of the night-fighter victims and crashed in the Black Forest some twenty miles short of the Strasbourg section of the frontier with France, killing F/L Cox AFC and three of his crew. Three men did at least escape with their lives, two of them falling into enemy hands, while the bomb-aimer ultimately evaded capture. A total of 1,234 tons of bombs had been dropped on Friedrichshafen and an estimated 67% of its built-up area destroyed. Several factories sustained severe damage and the tank gearbox plant was destroyed, thus dealing a severe blow to tank production.

S/L Ollier DFC arrived from 11 Base on the 28th to perform the role of B Flight commander, but he wasn't ready to operate and probably sat in on the briefing on the 30th, at which six 103 Squadron crews learned that this would be the first operation to be conducted exclusively by 1 Group with six Lancasters of the Special Duties Flight acting as the marker force. The target for 116 Lancasters was a Luftwaffe bomb and ammunition dump at Maintenon, situated some twenty miles to the west of Paris, for which they departed Elsham Wolds between 21.23 and 21.48 with F/O Way the senior pilot on duty and each Lancaster carrying eleven 1,000 and four 500 pounders. Apparently, W/C Goodman had impressed with his enthusiasm since arriving at Elsham, and he chose this night to operate for the first time, flying as second pilot to F/O Morrison. They flew out over Selsey Bill on course for the Normandy coast and so favourable were the conditions during the outward flight that crews were able to map-read their way to the target, where red spot fires marked out the aiming point, and when these had been obliterated by explosions, crews aimed for the centre of the smoke and flames. The 103 Squadron crews attacked from 6,500 to 8,000 feet between 23.53 and 00.12 in accordance with instructions from the Master Bomber, whose broadcasts were indistinct but sufficiently comprehensible. A number of very large explosions confirmed the attack as an outstanding success, which was achieved without loss.

During the course of the month, the squadron took part in eleven operations and dispatched 114 sorties for the loss of eight Lancasters and six crews.

May 1944

With the invasion now just five weeks away, the new month would be devoted to attacks on railway targets and coastal defences, and in the case of the latter, the focus would be on the Pas-de-Calais region of France, to try to reinforce the enemy's mistaken belief that the landings would take place there. The month began with six small-scale operations over France on the night of the 1/2nd, three directed at railway targets and three at specific factories. The target for seventy-five Lancasters of 1 Group, six of them from the SDF, was the Berliet motor works in the Venissieux district of Lyons in east-central France, which was manufacturing lorries for the benefit of the enemy. 103 Squadron loaded six Lancasters with eleven 1,000 pounders and a single 500 pounder and sent them on their way from Elsham Wolds between 21.23 and 21.31 with F/Ls Allwood and Leggett the senior pilots on duty. They set course for Selsey Bill and then Cabourg on the French coast, and the excellent conditions persisted all the way to the target, which was bathed in bright moonlight and the vertical visibility was marred only by a little ground haze as the first marker went down accurately at 00.47. However, the backer-up's first attempt fell wide of the mark, and he had to make a second pass, and this time the marker was deemed to be sufficiently accurate for the Master Bomber, S/L Breakspear, to call in the first wave of the main force at 01.02. The crews of F/Ls Leggett and Allwood bombed from 9,500 and 8,700 feet at 01.04½ and 01.06 respectively, before the second wave was called in at 01.07, by which time smoke had enveloped the aiming point and concealed the spotfires from view. Cascading TIs were then employed to guide the crews in, and those from 103 Squadron attacked from 7,900 to 10,000 feet between 01.13 and 01.15. The target was well plastered, and the operation achieved complete success without loss.

Briefings took place on 1 and 5 Group stations on the 3rd, for what would become a highly contentious operation that night against a Panzer training camp and transport depot at Mailly-le-Camp, situated some seventy-five miles east of Paris in north-eastern France. The units based there posed a potential threat to Allied forces as the invasion unfolded and needed to be eliminated. The events of the operation proved to be so controversial, that recriminations abound to this day concerning the quality of leadership provided by the 5 Group Master Bomber, W/C Laurence Deane, and marker leader, W/C Leonard Cheshire. Although the grudges by 1 Group aircrew against them can be understood in the light of what happened, they are unjust and based on emotion and incorrect information, and it is worthwhile to examine the conduct of the operation in some detail. W/C Cheshire was appointed as marker leader, and was piloting one of four 617 Squadron Mosquitos, while 83 Squadron's commanding officer, W/C Deane, was overall raid controller with S/L Sparks as his Deputy. Deane and Cheshire attended separate briefings, and neither seemed aware of the complete plan, particularly the role of the 1 Group Special Duties Flight from Binbrook, which was assigned to mark its own specific aiming point for an element of the 1 Group force provided by 460 and 625 Squadrons.

A force was assembled consisting of 346 Lancasters and fourteen Mosquitos of 1 and 5 Groups and two 8 Group Mosquitos, 1 Group providing 140 Lancasters for Target A, the military camp, and thirty-three, including four from the SDF, to attack Target B, the tank repair depot. 103 Squadron provided fourteen Lancasters, each of which was loaded with a cookie and sixteen 500 pounders before departing Elsham Wolds between 21.38 and 22.10 with S/L Swanston the senior pilot on duty. They began the Channel crossing at Beachy Head on course under clear skies and in bright moonlight to make landfall east of Dieppe, before tracking south-east to the final turning point north of the target. The excellent conditions persisted as the force arrived and began to orbit awaiting instructions, but confusion was already beginning to influence events. 617 Squadron's W/C Cheshire and S/L Shannon were in position before midnight, and as the first flares from the 83 and 97 Squadron Lancasters illuminated the target below, Cheshire released his two red spot fires onto the first aiming point at 00.00½ from 1,500 feet. Shannon backed them up from 400 feet five and a half minutes later, and as far as Cheshire was concerned, the operation was bang on schedule at this stage. A 97 Squadron Lancaster also laid markers accurately, to ensure a constant focal point, and Cheshire passed instructions to Deane to call the bombers in. It was at this stage of the operation that matters began to go awry. A communications problem arose, when a commercial radio station, believed to be an American forces network, jammed the VHF frequencies in use. Deane called in the 5 Group element, elated that everything was proceeding according to plan, but nothing happened. He checked with his wireless operator that the instructions had been transmitted and called up S/L Sparks, who was also mystified by the lack of bombing. A few crews from 9, 207 and 467 Squadrons had heard the call to bomb, and did so, but, for most, the instructions were swamped by the interference. Some 5 Group crews realised that R/T was jammed and bombed between 00.11 and 00.17 with smoke already beginning to drift across the target area.

The four SDF aircraft, led by F/L Hull, were in position by this time, but the initial green spot flare was assessed by Hull to have overshot by a thousand yards, and a second was misplaced by five hundred yards. The deputy marker leader laid a third marker which was judged to be accurate, and at 00.11, the first dozen of twenty-nine Lancasters from 460 and 625 Squadrons followed up with accurate bombing from 6,500 to 9,000 feet, before the target became obscured by smoke. As a result of this, and the fact that the 5 Group attack had commenced close by, the remaining seventeen 1 Group aircraft assigned to the "special target" were diverted to assist in that. W/C Deane then attempted to control the operation by W/T, which also failed.

Post raid reports are contradictory, and it is impossible to establish an accurate course of events, particularly when Deane and Cheshire's understanding of the exact time of zero hour differed by five minutes. Remarkably, it also seems, that Deane was unaware that there were two marking points, or three, if one includes 1 Group's Special Duties Flight. Cheshire, initially at least, appeared happy with the early stages of the attack, and described the bombing as concentrated and accurate. It seems certain, however, that many minutes had passed between the dropping of Cheshire's markers and the first main force bombs falling, during which period, Deane was coming to terms with the fact, that his instructions were not getting through. As the 1 Group crews became increasingly agitated at having to wait in bright moonlight with evidence of enemy night-fighters all around, some of them inevitably joined in the bombing.

Now a new problem was arising. Smoke from these first salvoes was obliterating the entire camp, and Cheshire had to decide whether or not to send in Fawke and Kearns to mark the second aiming point. His feeling, and that of Deane, as it later transpired, was that it was unnecessary, as the volume of bombs still to fall into the relatively compact area of the target would ensure destruction of the entire site. By 00.16, the first phase of bombing should have been completed, leaving a clear run for Fawke and Kearns across the target. In the event, the majority of 5 Group crews were still on their bombing run, a fact unknown to Cheshire, who asked Deane for a pause in the bombing, while the two Mosquitos went in. As far as Cheshire was concerned, there was no response from Deane, who would, anyway, have been confused by mention of a second aiming point. In the event, Deane's deputy, S/L Sparks, eventually found a channel free of interference, and did, in fact, transmit an instruction to halt the bombing, both by W/T and R/T, and some crews reported hearing something. While utter chaos reigned, Kearns and Fawke dived in among the falling cookies at 00.23 and 00.25 respectively, to mark the second aiming point on the western edge of the camp. At 2,000 feet, they were lucky to survive the turbulence created by the exploding 4,000 pounders, when 4,000 feet was considered to be a minimum safe height. They were not entirely happy with their work, but F/O Edwards of 97 Squadron dropped a stick of markers precisely on the mark, and S/L Sparks was then able to call the 1 Group main force in along with any from 5 Group with bombs still on board. Among these were the 103 Squadron crews who attacked from 7,000 to 8,000 feet between 00.25 and 00.32. Meanwhile, the night fighters continued to create havoc among the Lancasters, as they milled around in the target area close to a night-fighter assembly beacon just a few miles from the target, and picked off Lancasters with impunity, Hptm Helmut Bergmann alone downing no fewer than six bombers in thirty minutes. The 103 Squadron crews reported many night-fighters, particularly ME410s, with rockets well in evidence, and as burning aircraft were seen to fall all around, some 1 Group crews, particularly those from Australia, who weren't restrained by RAF protocol, succumbed to their anxiety and frustration. In a rare breakdown of R/T discipline, they let fly with comments of an uncomplimentary nature, many of which were intended for, and indeed heard by Deane.

Despite the problems, the operation was a major success, which destroyed 80% of the camp's buildings and 102 vehicles, of which thirty-seven were tanks, while over two hundred men were killed. Forty-two Lancasters failed to return, however, twenty-eight of them from 1 Group, and 460 Squadron was 1 Group's most afflicted unit with five Lancasters and crews unaccounted for. 103 Squadron posted missing three Lancasters and crews, ND905 falling victim to a night-fighter close to Chalons-sur-Marne, east of Paris and south of Reims while outbound, and there were no survivors from the crew of S/L Swanston. ME673 was milling around in the target area awaiting instructions to bomb when it was shot down by a night-fighter and crashed in the centre of Chalons-sur-Marne, with fatal consequences for P/O Rowe RAAF and his crew. P/O Holden and crew were homebound in ND411 and possibly north of track, when they crossed paths with a night-fighter and came down six miles north-east of Provins in the Ile-de-France region without survivors. At debriefing on the 5 Group station at Spilsby, the former 103 Squadron flight commander, S/L Blome-Jones, now of 207

Squadron described the situation as a complete shambles and chaos, the controller as inefficient and the discipline of some crews as bad. Others voiced the opinion that this was a trip worthy of more than one-third of a sortie. On the following day, an inquest into the conduct of the raid revealed that the wireless transmitter in Deane's Lancaster had been sufficiently off frequency to allow the interference from the American network to mask the transmission of instructions and prevent the call to bomb from reaching the main force crews. The 1 Group A-O-C, AVM Rice, decided he would not participate in further operations organized by 5 Group, which was probably not a blow to Cochrane, who was confident that his group did not need back-up.

W/C Nelson was posted out on the 6th to become station commander at Ingham, and W/C Goodman, who had been effectively in command since his arrival, now officially stepped into his shoes for what would prove to be a very brief period of tenure. Following a two-night break, 1 Group detailed fifty-two Lancasters, including four from the SDF, to attack an ammunition dump at Aubigne-Racan, situated some twenty miles south of Le Mans in north-western France. 103 Squadron briefed the crews of F/L Leggett, P/O Whitley and F/Sgt Brownings and filled their Lancasters' bomb bays with eleven 1,000 and four 500 pounders each, before dispatching them from Elsham Wolds between 00.11 and 00.28. The Binbrook station commander, G/C Hughie Edwards VC, was also flying on this night in a 460 Squadron Lancaster, as was the 13 Base commander, A/C Ivelaw-Chapman, in one belonging to 576 Squadron, the latter not destined to return until after the war. They flew out over Shoreham-on-Sea over a layer of stratus cloud at 4,000 feet from the midpoint of the Channel to the French coast, and thereafter enjoyed clear skies and bright moonlight all the way to the target. The assembly point was inadequately marked, but smoke, explosions and red spotfires clearly indicated the target without the need for instructions from the Master Bomber, and the 103 Squadron trio attacked from 7,500 and 8,600 feet between 02.42 and 02.48. Large explosions were witnessed, and smoke was rising through 9,000 feet as they turned for home confident in the success of their efforts.

The following night brought further attacks on ammunition dumps, coastal defences and airfields, for which 1 Group detailed two forces, one of fifty-one Lancasters, including one from the SDF, assigned to the aerodrome at Saint-Jacques-de-la-Lande to the south-west of Rennes and another of fifty Lancasters plus four from the SDF to attack a nearby ammunition dump at Bruz. 103 Squadron made ready seven Lancasters, loading each with a cookie and sixteen 500 pounders, and dispatched them from Elsham Wolds between 21.26 and 21.42 with no senior pilots on duty. P/O Furlong and crew turned back early because of intercom failure, leaving the others to pinpoint on Bridport and cross Torbay to begin the Channel crossing at Start Point, making landfall on the French side near Saint-Brieuc. They arrived in the target area to find clear skies and bright moonlight, despite which, the marker crews experienced difficulty in locating the aiming point and the main force had to wait to be called in. The first bombs on the western aiming point fell a little to the south, and the Master Bomber did his best to correct the aim, but the results, a few fires but no explosions, were a little disappointing in comparison with the previous night's attack. The bombing of the eastern aiming point began four minutes later and was hampered by smoke drifting across to conceal the spotfires, some of which was from the attack on the airfield. The 103 Squadron crews carried out their bombing runs from 11,000 and 12,000 feet between 00.15 and 00.17

and returned safely, uncertain as to the effectiveness of their efforts. Post-raid reconnaissance suggested that most of the bombs had fallen wide of the mark and onto a village.

The focus of more than four hundred crews on the night of the 9/10th was upon seven coastal defences, most of them in the Pas de Calais in an effort to maintain in German minds the belief that the invasion would come there. However, while one of the 1 Group targets, three light batteries on the foreshore at Mardyck, was indeed, near Dunkerque, the other, a heavy gun emplacement, was at Merville-Franceville-Plage, close to what would be Sword and Juno Beaches on D-Day. 13 and 14 Bases provided fifty-three Lancasters for the former, including eight from 103 Squadron, while fifty-six from 12 Base attended to the latter, three of them from the SDF. The 103 Squadron Lancasters each received a bomb load of eleven 1,000 pounders and four 500 pounders, which they lifted into the air at Elsham Wolds between 22.12 and 22.47 with S/L Ollier the senior pilot on duty for the first time. The route took them via Orfordness to a point on the French coast between Calais and Dunkerque, and they arrived at the target under clear skies and bright moonlight that afforded excellent visibility. The "Musical Paramatta" (blind marking by H2S) marking technique was employed to great effect and the 103 Squadron crews delivered their bombs onto the markers from 12,400 to 14,500 feet between 00.10 and 00.16. Sticks of bombs were observed to fall across the markers and one battery was seen in the flash of a nearby explosion of what was believed to be an ammunition dump.

All 1 Group bases contributed to a raid by sixty Lancasters on railway yards at Dieppe on the night of the 10/11th, one of five separate operations in the Transportation Plan involving more than five hundred aircraft. Four of the operations were concluded successfully, but there was no post-raid reconnaissance at Dieppe and the outcome remained unclear. Six 103 Squadron crews were briefed for mining duties on this night in the Rosemary garden in the Heligoland Bight, and departed Elsham Wolds between 21.58 and 22.10 with F/L Allwood the senior pilot on duty and each carrying six 1,500 parachute mines. The mines were delivered by H2S from 12,000 feet between 00.14 and 00.24, and a photograph of an H2S screen taken on a Leica camera was back-plotted to confirm the accuracy of the drops.

Six operations were mounted on the night of the 11/12th, four of them against railway yards in France and Belgium, and the largest, by 5 Group, directed at a military camp at Bourg Leopold in north-eastern Belgium. The objective for a 1 Group contingent of 105 Lancasters was the nearby marshalling yards at Hasselt, for which 103 Squadron made ready ten of its own and loaded each with eleven 1,000 and four 500 pounders. They departed Elsham Wolds between 21.40 and 22.05 with W/C Goodman the senior pilot on duty flying in ND700 accompanied by the crew of the currently hospitalized "Mad Belgian" S/L Van Rolleghem. They set a course via Orfordness to the Scheldt estuary and proceeded to the target over patches of cloud, which had dispersed by the time they arrived. The forecast winds proved to be inaccurate, causing some crews to arrive late, and all found the vertical visibility to be compromised by thick haze, which blotted out all ground detail. No TIs were seen while the 103 Squadron crews were in the target area, but flares had been dropped in large numbers and thirty-nine aircraft bombed on these. The Master Bomber was unable to establish the position of the aiming point and called a halt to proceedings at 00.07, by which time the crews of P/O Gibbons and F/O Broadbent had picked up a transmission from the Master

Bomber at a different target, telling the crews to bomb the red T.Is, and immediately, thereafter, received a message from group confirming the recall. They thought it was an enemy trick and decided to add their bombs to those from 5 Group at Bourg Leopold, doing so from 14,000 and 11,000 feet at 00.04 and 00.17 respectively. Night-fighters were active and five Lancasters failed to return, two of them belonging to 103 Squadron. JB733 was shot down by the night-fighter of Oblt Werner Baake of I./NJG1 and crashed at 02.00 some fourteen miles north-west of Antwerp on the way home over Belgium and there were no survivors from the crew of P/O Whitley. ND700 was also hit by cannon fire from a night-fighter, causing the bomb load to explode and spread wreckage over a wide area of the Belgian countryside east-south-east of Lier. There was deep sadness at the loss of S/L Van Rolleghem's crew and Van Rolleghem himself was inconsolable.

W/C St John DFC was posted in from 1656 Conversion Unit on the 12th to succeed W/C Goodman as commanding officer, and in a break from bombing operations that night, 1 Group dispatched twenty Lancasters from 12 and 13 Bases on mining sorties in the Rosemary garden in the North Sea's Heligoland Bight. 103 Squadron's F/Sgt Brownings and F/L Allwood departed Elsham Wolds at 20.20 and 20.33 respectively, setting a course via Mablethorpe that was slightly north of east to the target area, which was found to be under clear skies but concealed by haze up to 7,000 feet. Positions were established by H2S, and the six mines delivered into the briefed locations from 12,000 feet at 00.12 and 00.17.

On the 15th, the former 103 Squadron stalwart, W/C John "Jack" Douglas, arrived at Binbrook from 1662 Conversion Unit to assume command of 460 Squadron RAAF, having, it will be recalled, completed twenty-five operations on Halifaxes and Lancasters with 103 Squadron in the second half of 1942. That night, 1 Group detailed twenty Lancasters for mining operations in the Forget-me-not garden in Kiel Bay, for which 103 Squadron made ready five aircraft and sent them on their way from Elsham Wolds between 21.58 and 22.26 with F/L Allwood the senior pilot on duty. They began the North Sea crossing at Mablethorpe and made landfall on Jutland's western coast, by which time, F/L Allwood and W/O Rabchak had lost the use of their H2S and turned for home to return their mines to store. The crews of P/O Moore and F/O Way delivered their six mines each from 15,000 feet 01.07 and 01.18 before returning safely, having negotiated severe icing conditions en-route, but P/O Mitchell and crew did not arrive back, and it was established in time that LL963 had crashed on the edge of the tiny Danish Island of Avernako, and all on board had lost their lives.

Minor operations held sway until the 19th, when five railway yards and two gun emplacements were posted as the targets for that night, 1 Group assigned to the marshalling yards in the Les Aubrais district of Orleans on the northern bank of the Loire, for which it offered 105 Lancasters from 13 and 14 Bases to join forces with thirteen Lancasters and four Mosquitos of 8 Group. 103 Squadron loaded eleven of its Lancasters with eleven 1,000 and four 500 pounders each and dispatched them from Elsham Wolds between 21.42 and 22.11 with F/L Leggett the senior pilot on duty. They began the Channel crossing at Beachy Head and lost the crew of P/O Green soon afterwards to port-inner engine failure, leaving the others to benefit from excellent conditions in the target area, where accurate marking by the path Finder element was exploited by the main force crews to produce an outstandingly successful outcome. With the exception of P/O Gibbons and crew, who were unable to hear the master Bomber's instructions, the 103 Squadron crews delivered their attacks from 8,000 to 10,000 feet between 00.44 and 00.50 and returned safely.

In a complete change of objective on the 21st, Duisburg was posted as the target for the first time since the previous May, and a force of 510 Lancasters and twenty-two Mosquitos was drawn from 1, 3, 5 and 8 Groups for the task, of which a record 207 of the former belonged to 1 Group. 103 Squadron made ready eighteen of its Lancasters, each of which received a bomb load of a cookie and 208 x 30lb incendiaries and took off from Elsham Wolds between 22.06 and 22.50 with S/Ls Ollier and Van Rolleghem the senior pilots on duty. They had been instructed at briefing to adhere to the plan for the outward route, which involved a few aircraft from 3 Group gaining height as they adopted a north-westerly course as far as Sleaford, so as not to cross into enemy radar cover earlier than necessary. The groups were to rendezvous at 18,000 feet over the North Sea at 3 degrees east to cross the enemy coast via the Dutch Frisians at 20,000 feet and climb to 22,000 or 23,000 feet, before increasing speed for the run across the target. All but one of the 103 Squadron participants reached the Ruhr, ME722 having the misfortune to cross paths with the Luftwaffe Ace, Hptm Martin Drewes of III./NJG1 over Holland, who shot it down to crash at 00.50 near Zwolle, killing P/O Jones and both gunners and delivering the navigator into enemy hands. The remaining three crew members were spirited away by the local resistance network and retained their freedom. Meanwhile, the Oboe Mosquito element had suffered a 50% rate of equipment failure, leaving eleven to dispense red Wanganui markers with-yellow-stars, which disappeared into the cloud tops almost before they could be seen. A number of crews commented on the data provided by the "wind finder" system to be inaccurate, and this made it a challenge for some to establish their position. A steady stream of marker flares provided an aiming-point for the heavy brigade between 01.04 and 01.18, and the 103 Squadron crews carried out their attacks from just above the cloud tops at 20,000 to 22,500 feet between 01.07 and 01.31. Returning crews were not enthusiastic about the outcome, and post-raid reconnaissance confirmed that a modest 350 buildings had been destroyed in the southern half of Duisburg, and 665 others had been seriously damaged. Twenty-nine Lancasters failed to return, demonstrating that the Ruhr had lost none of its sting since the campaign against it a year ago.

Just like Duisburg, Dortmund had not been visited by the heavy brigade for a year when it was posted on the 22nd to face an all-Lancaster heavy force of 361 aircraft drawn from 1, 3, 6 and 8 Groups, while 5 Group targeted Braunschweig. 1 Group made available 183 Lancasters of which fourteen represented 103 Squadron and took off from Elsham Wolds between 22.03 and 22.39 with S/L Van Rolleghem and F/Ls Allwood, Leggett and Morrison the senior pilots on duty and each Lancaster loaded with a cookie and SBCs containing 1,170 x 4lb incendiaries and 108 x 30lbs. They climbed away into heavy cloud and severe icing conditions from 4,000 feet, which persuaded a considerable number of crews to abandon their sorties before reaching enemy territory. The 103 Squadron element flew out over Mablethorpe on course for the Frisian Island of Vlieland and was not represented among 1 Group's six "boomerangs". Those pressing on were rewarded with improving conditions and by the time the target hove into view, the cloud had diminished to no more than two-tenths, and the attack opened punctually with red and green TIs and red flares with yellow stars. The 103 Squadron crews delivered their bomb loads from 20,000 to 25,500 feet between 00.45

and 00.57 and observed many fires, some with oily smoke, leading to a consensus among returning crews of an accurate and effective raid. Eighteen Lancaster failed to return, eleven from 1 Group, and three empty dispersals at Elsham Wolds, two that should have been occupied by 103 Squadron aircraft, told their own story. ND629 had just crossed the frontier into Germany when shot down by a night-fighter to crash three miles north of Ahaus, north of the Ruhr on the way to the target, and there were no survivors from the crew of P/O Charles RCAF. LL946 was some twenty miles further advanced when also shot down by a night-fighter five miles east of Dülmen, and there were no survivors from this experienced crew captained by F/L Morrison DSO. Post-raid reconnaissance revealed that the main weight of the attack had fallen onto predominantly residential districts in the south-east of the city, where six industrial premises and more than eight hundred houses had been destroyed, and almost as many seriously damaged.

On the following night, the three 103 Squadron crews of S/L Ollier, F/O Way and W/O Rabchak alone represented 1 Group and were assigned to mining duties in the Kraut garden, in a stretch of the Lim Fjord between Aalborg and Hals on the Baltic side of northern Jutland. They departed Elsham Wolds between 21.37 and 21.43 and flew out over Mablethorpe to make landfall near Sønder Kettrup, from where they had a thirty-mile run south-east to the target area. They planted their vegetables as briefed from 11,700 and 12,000 feet at 00.58 and 01.02 before returning safely from uneventful sorties.

The main operation on the 24th involved 442 aircraft in a two-phase attack, ninety minutes apart, on marshalling yards at Aachen, Rothe-Erde in the east and Aachen-West. As the most westerly city in Germany, it was a major link in the railway network that would be a route for reinforcements to the Normandy battle front after D-Day. Other operations on this night were directed at coastal batteries, mostly in the Pas-de-Calais, and war-industry factories in Holland and Belgium. 1 Group contributed 116 Lancasters to the main event and fifty-four to an attack on a coastal battery at Le Clipon near Dunkerque, which was part of the deception plan. 103 Squadron's thirteen Lancasters were loaded with eleven 1,000 and four 500 pounders each, while their crews were attending briefing to learn that their aiming point was Aachen-West, for which they departed Elsham Wolds between 23.20 and 23.59 with S/L Van Rolleghem the senior pilot on duty. They exited the English coast at Orfordness and made landfall near Dunkerque, benefitting from favourable weather conditions all the way to the target, where the Path Finders employed the "Musical Paramatta" technique, blind marking by H2S, to establish the aiming point for the main force crews. Those representing 103 Squadron carried out their attacks from 18,500 to 23,000 feet between 02.21 and 02.29 in the face of a heavy flak barrage and had to dodge night-fighters as they vacated the target area. ND624 was shot down by a night-fighter and crashed some twenty-five miles south-east of Aachen, and F/Sgt Tate and his crew all lost their lives. Photographic reconnaissance revealed that the railway installations had escaped serious damage, and a second operation was deemed necessary.

In addition to the return to the Rothe Erde marshalling yards at Aachen on the night of the 27/28th was a second "return" visit, this one to the military camp at Bourg-Leopold in northern Belgium, which had been the target for an attack earlier in the month but had been abandoned because of poor visibility after half of the force had bombed. 1 Group supported both of the above with 110 and ten Lancasters respectively, while also providing fifty-seven for a return to the Merville coastal battery in the planned invasion area. 103 Squadron loaded twelve Lancasters with eleven 1,000 and four 500 pounders each and dispatched them from Elsham Wolds between 23.41 and 00.10 with S/L Ollier the senior pilot on duty supported by F/Ls Allwood, Leggett and Way. They flew out over Southwold on course for the Dunkerque area and joined up with the rest of the 1, 3 and 8 Group force, which at take-off had numbered 162 aircraft. They enjoyed excellent conditions all the way to the target area, where a new tactic was to be employed during the final leg of the outward flight from the Dutch frontier to the target. The main force was to shallow dive at 1,400 feet per minute to reach a bombing height of 10,000 feet, while a spoof raid on Düsseldorf, some fifty miles to the north-east, would provide a distraction and hopefully draw off night-fighters. The Path Finders provided punctual and accurate marking, which provided the focal point for the 103 Squadron bomb-aimers as they released their hardware from 10,000 to 16,000 feet between 02.26 and 02.35, most clearly having ignored the designated bombing altitude. Enemy night-fighters were present in numbers and contributed to the downing of a dozen Lancasters, the two belonging to 103 Squadron containing experienced crews. ND362 disappeared without trace with the crew of S/L Ollier DFC, while ND925 was hit by rail-mounted flak, which set a wing on fire and caused the Lancaster to explode. The wreckage came down near Veurne in Belgium, killing the experienced F/L Leggett and all but his mid-upper gunner, who survived as a PoW. The body of the rear gunner, F/O Jones, was washed ashore, suggesting that the Lancaster had been over the sea for a time, perhaps before turning inland to allow the remainder of the crew to bale out safely.

Among three coastal batteries briefed to 181 crews on the 28th was one described as a field battery at Eu, located south-east of Le Treport at the eastern end of the Normandy coastline. 1 Group provided six SDF markers and the main force of fifty Lancasters, all from 12 Base, while 103 Squadron remained at home having concluded its operational activity for the month. With the invasion now just a week away, operations on the 31st focussed on railway targets, signals stations and coastal batteries, 1 Group detailing ninety-seven Lancasters for an attack on the marshalling yards at Tergnier in north-eastern France in company with an element of Lancasters and Mosquitos from 8 Group.

During the course of the month, the squadron took part in fifteen operations and dispatched 133 sorties, five of which were abortive, for the loss of twelve Lancasters and crews.

June 1944

June was to be a hectic month which would make great demands on the crews, and the first week was dominated by unsettled weather, which caused concerns for the impending launch of Operation Overlord. The bombing of coastal batteries and signals stations was to be the priority during the first few days leading up to D-Day, and crews were briefed on the 1st for two sites, a battery at Brutelles and a radar-jamming station at Berneval-le-Grand, situated to the north and south respectively of the recently attacked site at Eu, well to the east of the landing grounds. In the event, both operations were cancelled, but the attack on the Berneval site was reinstated on the 2nd and handed to a 1 Group main force of 103 Lancasters, while sixty-three others targeted one of four heavy gun batteries near Calais as part of the deception plan. Fourteen 103 Squadron crews were briefed for Calais, while out on the dispersals their Lancasters were being loaded with eleven 1,000 and four 500 pounders, before taking off from Elsham Wolds between 22.23 and 23.17 with F/Ls Allwood and Way the senior pilots on duty and the W/C St John flying as second pilot with the latter. They flew out over Orfordness and made landfall near Dunkerque in poor weather conditions over ten-tenths cloud, having been told at briefing to bring their bombs home if the TIs could not be seen. In the event, eleven of the 103 Squadron crews drew a bead on what they took to be the aiming point and bombed from between 9,000 and 11,000 feet between 00.30 and 00.36, while three complied with the briefing instructions and returned their ordnance to the dump.

1 Group operations on the night of the 3/4th involved only sixty-one Lancasters from 13 Base squadrons, which were assigned to a railway-mounted heavy battery at Wimereux to the north of Boulogne in company with 113 other Lancasters and eight Mosquitos from 1, 3 and 8 Groups. The operation was in support of the deception plan, for which 103 Squadron loaded fourteen of its Lancasters with a cookie and sixteen 500 pounders and dispatched them from Elsham Wolds between 22.50 and 23.35 with S/L Van Rolleghem the senior pilot on duty. Conditions of low cloud and rain for both take-off and landing made this a testing operation, but there were no mishaps as they headed for the Kent coast near Dungeness to begin the Channel crossing, and clear skies greeted them over the target, where they bombed the TIs from 8,000 to 10,000 feet, before returning safely from another uneventful operation.

The 5th was D-Day Eve and, during the course of that night, a record number of sorties would be flown against coastal defences and in support and diversionary operations. The weather had been a source of concern for the D-Day planners, and even as Operation Overlord was given the green light, massive uncertainty attended the final decision to go. Sixteen 103 Squadron crews attended the evening briefing at Elsham Wolds, where, as at every other station, no direct reference was made to the invasion but unusually, they were given strict altitudes at which to fly and were instructed not to jettison bombs over the sea. They learned also that they would be among more than a thousand aircraft targeting ten heavy gun batteries along the Normandy coast, and that their specific objectives were at Crisbecq, on the Cherbourg peninsula to the north of the American Utah landing ground, and at St-Martin-du-Varreville, which actually overlooked it. Six crews were briefed for the former and ten the latter, while their Lancasters were receiving loads of eleven 1,000 and four 500 pounders. They were among the first to start the ball rolling and departed Elsham Wolds between 21.06 and 21.51 with F/Ls Allwood and Way the senior pilots in the Crisbecq element and F/L Marsden in the other.

They began the Channel crossing at Bridport over ten-tenths cloud with tops at around 6,000 feet and bright moonlight above and lost the services of P/O Chase and crew from the Crisecq contingent for an undisclosed reason. The cloudy conditions persisted as the others pressed on to the target, where the Path Finder Mosquitos employed the "Musical Paramatta" technique to mark the aiming point. Some TIs were seen to burst just above the cloud tops, otherwise crews focussed on the glow of red TIs beneath, which seemed to cover quite a large area, and the bombing at Crisbecq was carried out from 9,000 to 11,200 feet at 23.35 and at St-Martin from 8,500 to 10,000 feet between 23.48 and 23.58. No results were observed, and all returned safely to report a quiet, uneventful operation, which was largely unopposed from the ground and in the air. Aircraft were taking off throughout the night, and those crews returning in dawn's early light were rewarded with a glimpse through gaps in the cloud of the greatest armada in history ploughing its way sedately across the Channel below. A total of five thousand tons of bombs was delivered during the course of these operations, and this was a record for a single night.

As the beachheads were being established during the 6th, preparations were put in hand to support the ground forces by attacking nine road and railway communications centres through which the enemy could bring reinforcements. 1 Group was handed two targets, marshalling yards at Acheres, situated in a loop of the Seine north-west of Paris, and two railway bridges at Vire near the American landing grounds south-east of St-Lô in Normandy, one by the railway station and the other over the river valley. Ninety-seven Lancasters were detailed for the former and 107 for the latter, and it was for Vire that eighteen 103 Squadron Lancasters departed Elsham Wolds between 21.36 and 22.30 with S/L Van Rolleghem the senior pilot on duty and each carrying, it is believed, eighteen 500 pounders. They flew south to Bridport over eight-tenths cloud with tops at 8,000 feet, which dispersed somewhat over the sea until reforming in the target area with a base at around 6,000 feet. The visibility below was good as the SDF carried out the initial marking with red TIs, which were backed up with Path Finder greens at both aiming points, and the Master Bomber called in the main force crews at 00.37. Those from 103 Squadron bombed the red TIs from 3,000 to 5,500 feet between 00.34 and 00.38, and the usual isolated undershooting aside, the attack appeared to be accurate, although drifting smoke hampered an assessment of the outcome. There was general agreement that the Master Bomber had played a valuable part in the proceedings and that little opposition came from the ground, but night-fighters were in evidence and some crews reported watching two aircraft go down in flames, while another saw one of the bridges to be completely wrecked. 103 Squadron's NE173 failed to return with the others, and the sad news was eventually received that F/L Way RCAF and his crew had lost their lives.

Elsham Wolds was not called into action on the 7th for operations by elements of 1, 5 and 8 Groups against a six-way road junction at Balleroy, situated between Bayeux and St-Lô, and a tank unit and ammunition dump hidden in the nearby Forêt-de-Cerisy. 1 Group provided eighty Lancasters for the latter as part of a force of 112 Lancasters and ten Mosquitos, and twenty in support of an attack on the Versailles Matelots railway centre.

There were no 1 Group operations on the 8th, and it was left to 13 and 14 Bases to provide a hundred Lancasters on the 9th to join three hundred other aircraft from 4, 6 and 8 Groups to bomb airfields south of the battle area at Flers, Le Mans, Laval and Rennes to prevent their use by the enemy to bring up supplies and reinforcements. The 1 Group target was at Flers, for which 103 Squadron loaded eighteen of its Lancasters with eighteen 500 pounders each and sent them on their way from Elsham Wolds between 00.11 and 01.02 with F/Ls Gane and Nixon the senior pilots on duty. They crossed the Sussex coast at Beachy Head over low cloud and made landfall at Fécamp to the east of Le Havre, before reaching the target to find "Musical Paramatta" marking in progress, which appeared to be accurate. The crews of F/L Gane and F/Sgt Hill were unable to identify the target or see markers, and took their bombs home, while the remainder attacked from 2,000 to 4,000 feet between 03.15 and 03.25.

The squadron was stood down on the 10th, when 101 Lancasters from 12 and 13 Bases were detailed for an operation against a railway junction at Acheres, one of four similar targets for the night along with Dreux, Orleans and Versailles, involving a total of 430 aircraft. All targets were believed to have been hit, but no details emerged. 103 Squadron remained off the order of battle on the 11th, when four railway targets were earmarked for attention by elements of 1, 3, 4 and 8 Groups, among them the marshalling yards at Evreux, situated some twenty miles south of Rouen on the approaches to the battle area. A 1 Group force of 101 Lancasters carried out a successful operation based on clear and accurate Path Finder marking, and just one Lancaster failed to return.

Since beginning operations on Lancasters, a lack of Polish airmen had prevented 300 Squadron from operating two flights, as had been intended. A temporary solution was to form a second flight at Faldingworth under the command of S/L Misselbrook with ten RAF crews drawn from 101, 550, 576 and 626 Squadrons and four new crews from 1LFS. As they were settling in to their new accommodation on the 12th, 193 other 1 Group crews were attending briefings for what at this time was a rare foray over Germany involving 286 Lancasters and seventeen Mosquito from 1, 3 and 8 Groups. The target was the Nordstern synthetic oil plant at Gelsenkirchen, and this operation would begin a new oil campaign, which would continue to the last day of the bombing war. The briefing included a reference to a new method of dispensing "window", now at five bundles per minute. Nineteen 103 Squadron Lancasters were loaded with a cookie and sixteen 500 pounders each and sent on their way from Elsham Wolds between 22.31 and 23.06 with S/L Van Rolleghem the senior pilot on duty. Conditions were excellent as they headed out over Mablethorpe on course for the Scheldt estuary, losing the services of P/O Hayes and crew on the way when the navigator became indisposed. The others reached the target area, where they were greeted by clear skies with ground haze, and the first red Path Finder TIs fell at 00.55 some five miles south-south-east of the target. This was surprising and frustrating, as a new version of Oboe had been made available for this operation and the errant markers attracted a considerable number of bomb loads, before further red and green TIs identified the true aiming point to bring the operation back on track. The 103 Squadron crews delivered their attacks from 18,000 to 21,000 feet between 01.00 and 01.13, and large explosions were observed at 01.05, 01.07 and 01.12 with smoke rising through 15,000 feet as they turned away. The glow from the burning refinery remained visible as far as the Dutch coast, by which time night-fighters had taken a heavy toll of bombers, mostly as they crossed Holland, and seventeen Lancasters failed to return, 6% of those dispatched, ten of them belonging to 1 Group squadrons. All production at the plant was brought to a halt for several weeks at a cost to the German war effort of a thousand tons of aviation fuel per day. While this operation was in progress, 671 aircraft representing 4, 5, 6 and 8 Groups had been engaged in attacks on six communications targets, mostly railway-related, in France.

Minor operations on the following night enabled training to continue as new crews got to grips with H2S and "Village Inn", the code for the Automatic Gun-Laying Turret (AGLT), a radar device designed to prevent friendly fire incidents between bombers. It would not be introduced to operations until the autumn, but trials were under way in 1 Group. The 14th brought the Command's first daylight operation since the departure of 2 Group from Bomber

Command twelve months earlier. The target was Le Havre, from where the enemy's E-Boats and other fast, light marine craft were posing a threat to Allied shipping supplying the Normandy beachheads. The two-phase operation was to be conducted by predominantly 1 and 3 Groups with 617 Squadron representing 5 Group and would take place in the evening under the umbrella of a fighter escort. The plan called for 617 Squadron's twenty-two Lancasters to target the concrete U-Boot pens with their recently introduced 12,000lb Tallboy earthquake bombs just ahead of the main attack, for which 198 Lancasters of 1 Group would constitute the main force and bomb on Oboe markers provided by 8 Group. 3 Group would then follow up in the twilight to complete the destruction. The twenty 103 Squadron Lancasters each received a bomb load of eleven 1,000 and four 500 pounders, before departing Elsham Wolds into a lowering sun between 20.10 and 20.50, with W/C St John and S/L Van Rolleghem the senior pilots on duty. They were greeted at the target by clear skies and accurate marking and delivered their payloads from 18,000 to 21,000 feet between 22.32 and 22.50. Many explosions were observed, and greyish-white smoke was rising through 12,000 feet as the crews headed back across the Channel. The 3 Group attack was equally destructive and few if any craft remained to pose a threat to the Allied shipping supplying the beachhead.

Other operations on this night were directed against railway installations at three locations in France, while elements of 4, 5 and 8 Groups attended to enemy troop and vehicle concentrations, referred to as "choke points" at Aunay-sur-Odon and Évrecy near Caen. A Path Finder presence was required at five locations, in addition to which, 8 Group sent thirty-five Mosquitos to attack the Hydrierwerke-Scholven AG synthetic oil plant located in Gelsenkirchen's north-western suburb of Buer.

A force of 297 aircraft from 1, 4, 5, 6 and 8 Groups was assembled on the 15th to try to do to Boulogne what had been done to Le Havre twenty-four hours earlier. 1 Group provided 101 Lancasters in the absence of 103 Squadron, whose contribution of twenty-one Lancasters was cancelled at 19.00. Five to ten-tenths cloud lay over the target with tops at 11,000 feet and a base at around 3,000 feet, despite which, some crews were able to identify the breakwater and docks, but not the briefed aiming point. They were guided to the mark by red TIs, the first going down at 22.47 to be visible beneath the cloud, and the aiming point was backed up throughout the raid, during which a particularly large explosion occurred at 22.51 that was estimated to be on the south-western corner of the Bassin Loubet. The conditions hampered a detailed assessment of the outcome, but the raid was believed to be just as successful as at Le Havre, albeit at a cost of many civilian lives as collateral bombing hit the town.

Plans were put in hand on the 16th, to launch 829 sorties that night against a number of targets, including four flying-bomb launching sites in the Pas-de-Calais/Hauts-de-France regions of north-eastern France. Just three days earlier, the first V-1 flying bombs had landed on London, and this prompted a response in the form of a second new campaign to open during the month against this revolutionary new menace. The V-1 targets were of two types, launching sites in the form of small buildings shape like the letter J, which were attached to a launch ramp, and large concrete storage sites known in Bomber Command parlance as "constructional works", and many were, indeed, still under construction with additional work in progress to provide road and rail links. The largest single operation on this night was posted across 1, 4, 6 and 8 Group stations, which were ordered to prepare between them 321 aircraft to attack the synthetic oil plant at Sterkrade-Holten, a district of Oberhausen in the Ruhr, a plant known to the Germans as Ruhr-Chemie A G. 1 Group's contribution to this operation amounted to one hundred Lancasters from 13 and 14 Bases, while fifty-four others from 12 Base were to target the Domleger "constructional works" situated ten miles north-east of Abbeville in north-eastern France.

103 Squadron loaded twenty-one Lancasters with a cookie and sixteen 500 pounders each and launched them from Elsham Wolds between 22.45 and 23.24 with F/Ls Allwood and Marsden the senior pilots on duty. They headed for the Scheldt via Sheringham, flying out over patchy cloud, which built over the Channel to leave a blanket of ten-tenths in the target area with tops at 7,000 to 10,000 feet, into which the cascading red TIs, delivered blindly by H2S ("Musical Paramatta") disappeared quickly to leave a concentrated glow for the crews to aim at. It would be considered later that "Wanganui" parachute flare might have been a better option. The 103 Squadron crews delivered their attacks from 18,500 to 23,000 feet between 01.20 and 01.27, but their bombing photos revealed nothing but cloud. Crews returned with an expectation that the bombing had been scattered and ineffective and this was confirmed by reconnaissance and local sources that revealed little impact on oil production. Night-fighters were active and the rear gunner in the crew of P/O Hayes was wounded in both legs. Meanwhile, some two hundred miles to the west, similarly unfavourable weather conditions also compromised the attack on the V-Weapon site, and the consensus was that if the TIs had been accurate, the raid had been successful. It had been an expensive endeavour for the Command, however, which registered the loss of thirty-one aircraft, twenty-two of them Halifaxes, two-thirds having fallen to night-fighters. 103 Squadron's LM173 was among seven missing 1 Group Lancasters and was lost without trace with the crew of P/O Lambert RNZAF.

On the 17th, 317 aircraft of 1, 3, 4 and 8 Groups were assembled to attack railway targets at Aulnoye, Montdidier and St-Martin-l'Hortier, 1 Group detailing 101 Lancasters from 13 and 14 Bases for the first mentioned, located close to the Belgian frontier some forty miles south-east of Lille. 103 Squadron loaded seventeen of its Lancasters with eighteen 500 pounders, including two with long delay fuses, and sent them on their way from Elsham Wolds between 23.25 and 23.55 with S/L Van Rolleghem the senior pilot on duty. They flew out over Orfordness to make landfall a little to the south of the Scheldt, and by the time that they were approaching the target, the excellent conditions had given way to cloud. The Master Bomber descended through it to 600 feet but could see nothing and sent the force home with their bombs, those with long delay fuses being jettisoned over the sea.

Operations were posted on each day from the 18th to the 21st, only for them to be cancelled at the last minute, on one occasion when they were taxiing to the runway. It was a frustrating experience for the crews, who would have sat through a briefing and followed all of the procedures necessary before a major operation, including the build-up of tension, all for nothing and usually too late to be able to use the evening for leisure pursuits. On the 21st, 5 Group targeted the oil refineries at Wesseling, south of Cologne, and Scholven-Buer to the north-west of Gelsenkirchen, and lost forty-three Lancasters, many to night-fighters on the way to the former. Two 101 Squadron ABC Lancasters from 1 Group also failed to return.

The transportation and V-Weapon campaigns continued side-by-side on the 22nd with attacks planned for marshalling yards in north-eastern France in the evening, but first, constructional works in the same region at Mimoyecques, Siracourt and Wizernes during the afternoon. 1 Group provided one hundred Lancasters for the Mimoyecques site, located some four miles from the French coast at Wissant, which was being constructed to house a V-3 super-gun, referred to by Hitler as the "London Cannon". Originally planned as one of two sites near Cap Gris Nez, each containing twenty-five barrels angled at fifty degrees and aimed at London, test failures and delays meant that a single three-barrel shaft stretching a hundred metres into the limestone hill, 103 miles from its target, was all that existed at the time. Each fifteen-metre-long smooth-bore barrel, which was designed on the multiple-charge principle to progressively boost the acceleration of the one-ton projectile as it travelled towards the muzzle, was to be capable of pounding London at the rate of hundreds per day without let-up. It was protected by a concrete slab thirty meters wide and five-and-a-half meters thick, which was correctly believed by the designers to be impregnable to conventional bombs.

Twenty-one 103 Squadron Lancasters were loaded with eighteen 500 pounders each and departed Elsham Wolds between 13.39 and 14.31 with S/L Van Rolleghem the senior pilot on duty. They flew out over Beachy Head to make landfall east of Dieppe and were greeted at the target by largely clear skies, under which, in the absence of an abundance of TIs, they bombed visually from 12,000 to 17,000 feet between 15.45 and 15.48, achieving a reasonable degree of concentration but with little chance of success. Later that afternoon, 617 Squadron scored direct hits with 12,000lb Tallboy earthquake bombs, and provisional reconnaissance revealed four deep craters in the immediate target area, one causing a large corner of the concrete slab to collapse. The extent of the damage underground would not be apparent to the planners at Bomber Command until after the liberation of France, but the shafts and tunnels had been rendered unusable and the weapon would never fire a single shell.

The railway targets that evening were at Reims and Laon and were assigned to 1 and 4 Groups respectively, both with a Path Finder element to provide the marking. 1 Group put up one hundred main force Lancasters and two SDF markers and completed the outward flight over patchy cloud that had built to nine-tenths in the target area with tops at around 6,000 feet. The red, green and yellow TIs disappeared into the cloud tops to leave a glow for the bomb-aimers to latch onto, but returning crews were unable to offer an assessment of their efforts and suspected a scattered raid.

Flying bomb sites and railway yards provided the objectives for more than six hundred aircraft on the night of the 23/24th, and while 5 Group went for marshalling yards at Limoges, 13 and 14 Bases were ordered to provide one hundred Lancasters and Binbrook six SDF markers for a raid on marshalling yards at Saintes, an important link in the railway communications with the port of Bordeaux and located a few miles inland from the Atlantic coast, south-east of La Rochelle. 103 Squadron loaded twenty of its Lancasters with ten 1,000 pounders and two long-delay 500 pounders and dispatched them from Elsham Wolds between 21.42 and 22.15 with F/L Allwood the senior pilot on duty supported by F/Ls Gane, Marsden and Nixon. They began the Channel crossing at Bridport and skirted the Brest peninsula in favourable conditions that persisted for the entire flight, and once the Master

Bomber had cancelled an errant TI, the bombing proceeded accurately and unopposed, the 103 Squadron crews delivering their attacks from 5,500 to 8,000 feet between 01.58 and 02.09, before returning safely.

Later, on the 24th, orders were received for 1 Group to provide a hundred Lancasters, predominantly from 12 and 14 Bases for an attack on a "constructional work" at les Hayons, situated fifteen miles south-east of Dieppe, one of three sites involving a total of 321 aircraft drawn from 1, 4, 6 and 8 Groups. The marking was accurate, but the excellent visibility almost rendered it unnecessary, as most crews were able to identify the aiming point visually, and a good concentration was achieved. As they were landing, 739 other crews were preparing to depart their stations to attack seven other flying bomb sites, among them a hundred 1 Group Lancasters predominantly from 13 Base and two SDF markers from Binbrook, whose target was "constructional works" at Flers in north-western France. Twenty-one 103 Squadron Lancasters received a bomb load each of eighteen 500 pounders, including two with long delay fuses, and were dispatched from Elsham Wolds between 01.11 and 01.50 with F/L Van Rolleghem the senior pilot on duty. It was another night of fine weather conditions and moonlight, which would be ideal for target identification and marking, but would also be of help to the night-fighters. They set course via Beachy Head for the Normandy coast, passing over the battle area before reaching the target to find plenty of searchlights, but no flak, which suggested that the batteries were, indeed, working in conjunction with night-fighters. The marking was late, probably as the result of a big change in the forecast wind, but once underway it was accurate, and the 103 Squadron participants delivered their bomb loads onto the TIs from 12,000 to 13,000 feet between 03.16 and 03.26.

The squadron was stood down on the 25th, a day which began early for a hundred 1 Group Lancaster crews of 12 and 14 Bases, who had been briefed for an attack on "constructional works" at Ligescourt II, located fifteen miles inland from the coastal resort of Berck-sur-Mer. There were two targets to occupy 1 Group during the night of the 27/28th, marshalling yards at Vaires-sur-Marne, east-north-east of Paris for one hundred Lancasters and two SDF markers and "constructional works" at Chateau Bernapre for ninety-nine, including two from the SDF. Twenty-one 103 Squadron Lancasters were loaded with eighteen 500 pounders and departed Elsham Wolds for the latter in a heavy shower between 01.09 and 01.55 with the newly promoted S/L Gane the senior pilot on duty. They began the Channel crossing over cloud at Beachy Head and lost P/O MacDonald and crew to port-outer engine failure on the way, leaving the remainder to make landfall on the Normandy coast, and by good fortune, large gaps appeared in the cloud over the target to allow the TIs to stand out clearly. The 103 Squadron crews bombed from 12,000 to 14,000 feet between 03.30 and 03.38, and on return reported the TIs to be somewhat scattered and the bombing to have lacked concentration, despite which, it seems that all of the night's objectives were dealt with in a satisfactory manner.

The operation for 103 Squadron on the afternoon of the 29th was something of a rushed job after being called late and was an attack on the "constructional works" at Domleger, located a dozen miles east-north-east of Abbeville. This was one of three flying bomb-related sites to be attacked by a total of 286 Lancasters from 1 and 5 Groups, 1 Group detailing ninety-eight Lancasters and ninety-nine for a similar target at Siracourt. 103 Squadron made ready twenty of its Lancasters and loaded each with eleven 1,000 and four 500 pounders before sending them on their way from Elsham Wolds between 11.23 and 11.53 with S/L Van Rolleghem the senior pilot on duty. They headed south to begin the sea crossing at Dungeness and complied with the instructions at briefing to remain below cloud level until reaching the enemy coast. The target area was found to be relatively free of cloud and the aiming point well-marked by the Mosquito element, enabling crews to bomb visually, those from 103 Squadron from 12,000 to 14,000 feet between 13.28 and 13.33. They returned home confident in the effectiveness of their work, NE117 arriving back with a damaged undercarriage that compelled F/O Broadbent to carry out a landing on just one main wheel, a feat he executed with aplomb, and the Lancaster was back in service by the following day.

The final operation of this hectic month began at first light on the 30th, when a hundred Lancasters from 13 and 14 Bases, including nineteen representing 103 Squadron, took off to attack a flying bomb launching site at Oisemont/Neuville-au-Bois, ten miles to the south of Abbeville. The 103 Squadron contingent departed Elsham Wolds between 05.31 and 06.08 with S/L Gane the senior pilot on duty and each crew sitting on eleven 1,000 and four 500 pounders. Conditions were good initially, but on reaching the French coast the force encountered complete cloud cover and the Master Bomber issued instructions to bomb on H2S. The 103 Squadron crews complied from 12,000 to 14,000 feet between 07.58 and 08.02 but were unable to assess the results and suspected that the effort had been scattered and not fully effective.

During the course of the month, the squadron took part in fifteen operations and launched a very creditable 278 sorties, of which seven were abortive, for the modest but painful loss of two Lancasters and their crews.

July 1944

The new month began as June had ended, with flying-bomb sites providing employment for over three hundred aircraft on both the 1st and 2nd. Reconnaissance had revealed that the raids thus far on the "constructional works" at Oisemont/Neuville-au-Bois had failed to completely destroy the site, and another operation was scheduled for the afternoon of the 1st. In the event, complete cloud cover prevented any TIs from being observed by the 6 Group main force and bombing was carried out on estimated positions based on Gee and DR. Orders were received on the 2nd to return to the site in the early afternoon, for which 1 Group detailed fifty Lancasters from 12 Base, while a further 125 from 13 and 14 Bases targeted the previously attacked Domleger "constructional works". 103 Squadron loaded twenty of its Lancasters with eleven 1,000 and seven 500 pounders each, two of the latter containing long delay fuses, and dispatched them from Elsham Wolds between 11.51 and 12.36 with S/L Van Rolleghem the senior pilot on duty. They began the sea crossing at Dungeness and made landfall on the French coast near Eu, before swinging to the east for the run on the target, by which time the ten-tenths cloud accompanying them for the majority of the outward flight had dissipated to leave a large gap over the aiming point. Crews were able to bomb visually, those from 103 Squadron from 12,000 to 15,000 feet between 14.14 and 14.19 in the face of only slight opposition from flak, however, LM177 was hit on the way home and P/O Harrison's rear gunner was killed, while his bomb-aimer sustained wounds.

Orders were received on 1 Group stations on the 4th to prepare for an operation that night against the marshalling yards at Orleans in the Loire Valley, some fifty miles south-west of Paris. A 1 Group force of 156 Lancasters, including six SDF markers, was made ready, 103 Squadron contributing eighteen of them, which were loaded with eighteen 500 pounders each before departing Elsham Wolds between 21.45 and 22.17 with S/L Gane the senior pilot on duty. They began the Channel crossing at Lyme Regis and made landfall on the approaches to Abbeville, before reaching the target to find a thin layer of cloud at 8,000 to 10,000 feet with clear visibility below aided by bright moonlight. The crews easily identified the assembly point, which had been marked with green TIs, and the marking of the aiming point commenced at 01.20, only for it to be observed in the light of illuminating flares that the TIs had fallen well to the east. This prompted the SDF to drop red spotfires at 01.27, which fell in two distinct groups, those to the south assessed by the Master Bomber as "bang on" the aiming point. Within three minutes of the first wave of bombing, the aiming point became obscured and had to be re-marked for the second wave. The 103 Squadron participants released their payloads from 6,000 to 8,000 feet between 01.30 and 01.37 and all returned safely home emphatic in their belief that the marshalling yards had been severely damaged, persuaded in part by one particularly large explosion at 01.37.

The target for 154 Lancasters of 1 Group on the 5th was the marshalling yards in the city of Dijon in east-central France, for which fifteen 103 Squadron Lancasters were loaded with eight 1,000 and three 500 pounders. They departed Elsham Wolds between 20.51 and 21.17 with S/L Van Rolleghem the senior pilot on duty and all other crew captains of commissioned rank. This operation caused the Binbrook crews to miss the special dance open to all ranks and held in the airmen's dining hall in support of the "Salute the Soldier Week" campaign. They flew out over the Bridport-Lyme Regis area with ten-tenths cloud below them topping out at 7,000 feet, and this persisted until halfway across the Channel, when it began to disperse to provide crews with visibility good enough to enable them to map-read their way from the French coast, west of Abbeville, all the way to their destination. They were greeted at the target by near perfect visibility, and the attack began with cascading yellow TIs delivered blind by H2S as a guide to the SDF marker crews. They fell around a mile to the north-west of the aiming point, and the Deputy Master Bomber, who arrived ahead of the Master Bomber, dropped one red and one yellow TI to within sixty yards of the mark, and the Master Bomber then arrived to back up with red spotfires. The main force crews were called in, bombing initially with great accuracy until smoke obscured the aiming point and the attack began to creep back towards the town. It proved difficult to re-mark the aiming point in the face of a spirited light flak defence at lower levels, but the Master Bomber maintained control of proceedings and the marshalling yards stood out clearly to the main force crews flying at a higher level out of range of the light flak. The 103 Squadron crews attacked from 7,000 to 8,000 feet between 01.50 and 02.04, and all returned safely to report a successful outcome.

F/L Russell-Fry had returned to the squadron following his spell at Binbrook with the SDF, and on the 6th, he was posted to 1LFS to undertake instructional duties. Elsewhere, the 6th was devoted to daylight attacks on five V-Weapons sites involving 550 aircraft, of which a hundred Lancasters were provided by 1 Group predominantly from 12 Base for its target of "constructional works" in the Forêt-du-Croc, situated some five miles south-east of Dieppe. The Path Finders were punctual and accurate with their marking, and the initial bombing was seen to fall across the aiming point, before cloud drifted across, and crews had to aim at the glow of TIs.

During the course of the 7th, 467 aircraft from 1, 4, 6 and 8 Groups were made ready to carry out the first major operation in support of the Canadian 1st and British 2nd Armies, which were trying to break out of Caen. The target had been changed from German-fortified villages to an area of open ground north of Caen, which, ultimately, would prove to be counter-productive as it blocked access roads in the northern suburbs, rather than inflicting damage on German forces. 1 Group contributed 192 Lancasters, twenty-one of them provided by 103 Squadron, each of which had eleven 1,000 and four 500 pounders winched into their bomb bays before departing Elsham Wolds between 19.12 and 19.51 with S/Ls Gane and Van Rolleghem the senior pilots on duty. The cloud that accompanied the bomber stream over England gradually dispersed during the sea crossing to the Scheldt, leaving small amounts of broken white stuff with a base at 7,000 feet. Excellent visibility prevailed, and ground features were clearly identified as the Path Finders opened the attack on time and with great concentration, the first red TIs going down at 21.46. These were backed-up until the aiming point was ready to receive the main force bombs, and it was not long thereafter that smoke and debris concealed the markers, the Master Bomber retaining control, however, and keeping the attack on track. A series of explosions between 21.52 and 22.03 suggested a successful outcome, contributed to by 103 Squadron's efforts from 2,500 to 7,400 feet between 21.51 and 22.04. LM124 was involved in a collision with another Lancaster on the way home and sustained severe damage to the tail area, losing a fin and rudder and the rear turret, which fell away with its occupant trapped inside. P/O Moore was able to bring the aircraft home to a landing at Tangmere and it would be returned to flying condition. A message from the 2nd Army awaited the returning crews, congratulating them on the accuracy of their work and thanking them for their efforts.

Operations were posted and cancelled over the ensuing days, and it was the 12th before 1 Group crews would take to the air again in anger, when three railway targets were briefed out to 378 Lancaster crews of 1, 5 and 8 Groups, at Culmont for 5 Group, Revigny for 1 Group and Tours for 1 and 8 Groups. 1 Group committed a main force of a hundred Lancasters to each of its targets with an additional seven SDF aircraft assigned to the junction at Revigny, a town located south-east of Reims on the south-eastern edge of the Marne region. 103 Squadron loaded each of its nineteen Lancasters with seven 1,000 and four 500 pounders, before dispatching them from Elsham Wolds between 21.00 and 21.35 with S/L Gane the senior pilot on duty. They climbed out into five tenths cloud and pointed their snouts towards the south to begin the Channel crossing at Bridport on what was a circuitous route via the Channel Islands, with landfall on the Brittany coast near St-Malo. From there they headed south-east, swinging south of Le Mans and Orleans and then turning to the north-east for the final leg to the target. Thin cloud in the target area at between 4,000 and 6,000 feet and haze below created challenges for the Master Bomber's efforts to establish his bearings, particularly as his H2S had failed. He was forced to carry out a DR run to drop a green TI on the assembly point, before calling upon the illuminators to dispense their flares in the hope that this would reveal the aiming point. Neither he nor his Deputy were able to locate it despite searching for fifteen minutes, and he had little choice but to abandon proceedings and send the force home. By this time, half of the force had bombed on DR or on flares and even on what they believed were red spotfires, which must have been aircraft burning on the ground, and among them were eight from 103 Squadron, who bombed on "markers" from 2,500 to 8,000 feet.

PA999 fell victim to an enemy night-fighter and crashed at 01.50 some two-and-a-half miles west of Bar-le-Duc, killing P/O Harrison and all but his bomb-aimer, who ultimately evaded capture. Shortly afterwards, ME674 collided with LL796 of 550 Squadron and both Lancasters crashed six miles west of Bar-le-Duc with fatal consequences for F/O Phillips and his crew and for those in the other aircraft. F/O Abbott and crew were also homebound in ND993, when they came under fire from PD202 of 166 Squadron and responded in kind, the result of which was both Lancasters crashing without survivors, the 103 Squadron victim at 02.10 some twenty miles south-south-east of Bar-le-Duc. ND990 arrived at the English coast short of fuel, probably while making for the emergency strip at Carnaby in Yorkshire, and F/O Durrant RCAF was ordered by W/C St John to abandon the aircraft to its fate. This completed a bad night for 1 Group, which had ten Lancasters fail to return for no gain, and for 103 Squadron, which lost four aircraft and three crews.

A second attempt on the railway junction at Revigny was scheduled for elements of 1 and 8 Groups on the 14th, and a force of 105 Lancasters assembled on 12 and 13 Base stations with five 101 Squadron ABC Lancasters from 14 Base to provide RCM cover. 103 Squadron briefed a dozen crews, while each of their Lancasters were having seven 1,000 and four 500 pounders winched into their bomb bays, before departing Elsham Wolds between 21.02 and 21.28 with F/L Broadbent the senior pilot on duty. They climbed away through ten-tenths cloud and passed overhead unseen by the residents of Bridport as they made their way via the St-Malo coastal area following the same route as for the previous raid. The cloud broke up during the trek across France to leave three to seven-tenths in the target area with a base at 6,000 to 8,000 feet. The Master Bomber and Deputy from 8 Group's 156 Squadron experience great difficulty in establishing the location of the aiming point, despite a gap opening in the clouds right above it and the employment of numerous flares. The Deputy, S/L Davies DSO, apparently found it before being shot down by a night-fighter and, meanwhile, the main force crews orbited for a considerable time as they awaited instructions. Five aircraft bombed before the Master Bomber abandoned the operation, but those from 103 Squadron had all but their delay-fused bombs on board as they approached home airspace in broad daylight. This second failure at this target cost six 1 Group Lancasters, among them 103 Squadron's NE136, which was intercepted by a night-fighter on the way home and crashed some eighteen miles south-south-east of Bar-le-Duc, killing P/O Ogden DFC and his crew. ME773 crashed four hundred yards from the village of Magny-Fouchard to the east of Troyes, delivering P/O Anthony's rear gunner into enemy hands as the sole survivor. It was a very young crew, the pilot only twenty-one years of age and at least four of his crew just twenty. At debriefing, some crews complained that they had clearly identified the target and could have carried out an attack, but this troublesome target would now be handed to 5 Group, which would succeed where 1 Group had failed, but at a great cost in aircraft and lives.

F/L Allwood had now completed his tour of operations and was posted to 30 O.T.U on the 17th for instructional duties. Fifteen 103 Squadron crews were called to briefing at midnight on the 17/18th to learn of their part in a tactical support operation to be carried out at dawn by a force of 942 aircraft, of which 201 of the Lancasters were to be provided by 1 Group. It was the start of the ground forces' Operation Goodwood, which was Montgomery's plan for a decisive breakout into wider France as a prelude to the march towards the German frontier. The aiming-points were five enemy-held villages of Colombelles, Mondeville, Sannerville, Cagny and Manneville, all situated to the east of Caen and standing in the path of the advancing British 2nd Army. The 1 Group target was Sannerville, for which the 103 Squadron aircraft were loaded with eleven 1,000 and four 500 pounders, before departing Elsham Wolds between 03.14 and 03.45 with S/L Van Rolleghem the senior pilot on duty. They began the Channel crossing at Selsey Bill and by the time that they made landfall on the Normandy coast, the ten-tenths cloud had broken up to reveal the red and yellow TIs bang on the aiming point. Each aiming point was carefully controlled by a Master Bomber because of the close proximity of Allied troops and the 103 Squadron bomb-aimers had TIs in the bomb sights as they delivered their hardware from their briefed height of 6,500 to 8,000 feet between 05.44 and 05.57. The bombing was accurate and concentrated, and even after smoke and debris had concealed the aiming point the TIs remained visible. All 1 Group aircraft returned safely after a highly successful operation and crews reported little opposition from the ground and none in the air. Of 6,800 tons of bombs delivered by RAF and USAAF aircraft on these targets, more than 5,000 tons had been dropped by the RAF.

Many of the crews involved in the morning activity were back in the briefing room during the late afternoon to learn of their respective targets for that night. The Command would be committing almost a thousand aircraft again, principally against synthetic oil and railway objectives, but also on a variety of support and minor operations. The Wesseling synthetic oil refinery, or to give it its full title, the Union Rheinische Braunkohlen-Kraftstoff Aktien Gesellschaft, situated on the eastern bank of the Rhine south of Cologne, was to be the target for a force of 194 aircraft made up of a 6 Group main force of 153 Halifaxes and Lancasters with six ABC Lancasters from 101 Squadron, and twenty-nine Lancasters and six Mosquitos of 8 Group to provide the marking. At the same time, 153 Lancasters of 1 Group would be joined by four Lancasters and thirteen Mosquitos of 8 Group to target the Hydrierwerke-Scholven plant in the Buer district of Gelsenkirchen. The twelve 103 Squadron Lancasters were loaded with a cookie and sixteen 500 pounders each and departed Elsham Wolds between 22.56 and 23.20 with S/L Gane the senior pilot on duty. They climbed out through ten-tenths cloud, breaking into clear air at 6,000 feet, before passing over Mablethorpe on their way to landfall on the Dutch coast to the south of Zandvoort. The cloud began to disperse as they progressed towards the northern rim of the Ruhr and clear skies greeted them over the target with just a little industrial haze to compromise the vertical visibility.

The first red TIs went down a little early at 01.25 and thereafter, the aiming point was backed up to ensure a constant focal point, until, at 01.29, the markers were scattered by a huge yellow mushroom-shaped explosion, from which sheets of flame lit up the surrounding area for fifteen to twenty seconds. A column of black, oily smoke began to rise, and had reached 18,000 feet by the end of the raid. The 103 Squadron crews attacked from 18,000 to 21,500 feet between 01.30 and 01.33 in the face of moderate to intense flak and the usual array of searchlights, before leaving the target area to contend with night-fighters lurking in the darkness on the homeward route. It was assessed that 550 bombs fell into the oil plant, but curiously, according to local sources, 40% of themfailed to detonate. Despite this, the operation was successful and brought all production to a halt for a considerable period. A dozen 1 Group aircraft sustained flak damage and twelve crews reported combats, while four failed to return, a modest figure for a target in the heart of the Ruhr.

A concentrated raid at Wesseling was confirmed by local reports, which told of one thousand high explosive bombs falling within the plant, destroying 20% of the installations and causing a substantial loss of production. The town was also hit, and 151 houses were destroyed, many of them in the estate occupied by the plant's workforce. It was on this night that 5 Group finally delivered a telling blow on the marshalling yards at Revigny, but at a cost of twenty-four Lancasters hacked out of the sky by night-fighters, mostly during the outward flight. *(For an account of the three raids on Revigny, read the outstanding book, Massacre over the Marne by Oliver Clutton-Brock).*

A daylight raid on "constructional works" at Wizernes, situated twenty-five miles east of Boulogne, was scheduled for the evening of the 20th and would involve a hundred 1 Group Lancasters from 12 and 13 Bases. At the same time, six flying bomb launching sites were to be attacked by other groups for which a further 269 aircraft were detailed. The Wizernes site had already been subjected to many attacks and had, in fact, been effectively destroyed and abandoned a few days earlier after a visit from 617 Squadron, whose Tallboys had caused a landslip that knocked the dome out of alignment. This was not revealed in photographs taken from above, however, and attacks would continue for the time being. 103 Squadron made ready nineteen Lancasters, each of which was loaded with eleven 1,000 and four 500 pounders and departed Elsham Wolds between 18.50 and 19.25 with S/L Gane the senior pilot on duty. They headed towards Southwold in ten-tenths cloud with a base at 2,000 feet, which persisted as they made landfall on the Belgian coast near Knokke but broke up in the target area to leave skies clear enough for the crews to identify the aiming point visually. The bombing was carried out by the 103 Squadron crews either visually or on accurately placed TIs from 12,500 to 14,000 feet between 20.59 and 21.05, and all returned safely from what was a successful operation.

Meanwhile, ninety-three Lancasters from the group were preparing to attack the railway yards and a triangular junction at Courtrai (Kortrijk) in north-western Belgium that evening as part of a 1, 5 and 8 Group force of 302 Lancasters and fifteen Mosquitos. The first red TIs went down on time and were followed by many illuminating flares, which failed to highlight the aiming points, but their position in relation to the town suggested that they were in the right place. The first phase of bombing created so much smoke and dust that the aiming point was soon enveloped, prompting the Master Bomber to call a halt at 01.59.

On the afternoon of the 23rd, 189 crews attended briefings on all 1 Group operational stations to be told that, after a two-month break from city busting, Harris had sanctioned a major raid on the naval and ship-building port of Kiel, for which an overall force of 629 aircraft was made ready. 103 Squadron contributed nineteen Lancasters, loading thirteen with a cookie and sixteen 500 pounders and six with six J-cluster bombs in place of eight of the 500 pounders. They departed Elsham Wolds between 22.15 and 22.54 with F/Ls Broadbent and Marsden the senior pilots on duty and lost the latter to the failure of an engine soon after take-off, ending their part in the operation. After climbing out, the others headed for the coast at Mablethorpe and rendezvoused with the rest of the bomber stream over the North Sea to form up behind an elaborate "Mandrel" jamming screen laid on by 100 Group, before setting course for Denmark's western coast. When they arrived unexpectedly and with complete surprise in Kiel airspace, they rendered the enemy night-fighter controller confused and unable to bring his resources to bear. Kiel was covered by a nine to ten-tenths veil of thin cloud with tops at 5,000 feet, and a skymarking plan was put into action, which enabled the main force crews to bomb on the glow, first of the flares, and then of fires. Positions were confirmed by H2S, before the 103 Squadron crews aimed at the red and green "Wanganui" markers disappearing into the cloud tops from 19,000 to 21,500 feet between 01.21 and 01.38. Flak was mostly in barrage form and exploding at 15,000 to 22,000 feet but was not overly troublesome. It was not possible to determine the outcome, but the glow of fires remained visible for a hundred miles into the return journey, which suggested an effective raid at a cost of just four aircraft. This was confirmed by local reports, which conceded that this had been the town's most destructive raid of the war and had inflicted heavy damage on the port and U-Boot construction yards and cut off water supplies for three days and gas for three weeks. Many delayed-action bombs had been dropped, and these continued to cause problems for some time.

The first of three heavy raids on Stuttgart over a five-night period was posted on the 24th and a force of 614 aircraft assembled, 120 of the Lancasters provided by 1 Group's 13 and 14 Bases. 103 Squadron loaded each of its fifteen Lancasters with a 2,000 pounder and twelve J-clusters and dispatched them from Elsham Wolds between 21.04 and 21.31 with S/L Gane the senior pilot on duty. They began the Channel crossing at Selsey Bill, from which point the cloud began to disperse and the Normandy coast was crossed under clear skies that persisted until the German frontier was reached near Strasbourg. There it built up again to ten-tenths, with tops in the target area at 10,000 feet, which demanded the deployment of skymarkers ("Wanganui") to mark out the aiming point and the Master Bomber to exercise effective control. The 103 Squadron crews bombed from 16,000 to 17,500 feet between 01.51 and 01.59 and were unable to assess the outcome, but the large glow of fires was reflected in the clouds and the impression gained was of a successful operation. Twenty-one aircraft failed to return, and among them was 103 Squadron's LL941, which crashed in France killing all but the pilot, F/Sgt Shean. The wreckage was spread over a wide area south of Orleans, suggesting that the Lancaster had been outbound when attacked by a night-fighter, causing the bomb load to explode and fling the pilot clear attached to his seat parachute. He joined the growing complement of 103 Squadron crewmen on extended leave in PoW camps.

There was an early start on the 25th for 1 Group forces of thirty and thirty-one Lancasters from 12 Base, which were assigned to act as the main forces at two flying bomb launching sites, at Ardouval II, a dozen miles south-south-east of Dieppe and Coquereaux, situated some fifteen miles to the east, each to be marked by 8 Group Mosquitos. Both operations were carried out in accordance with instructions from a Master Bomber and appeared to be accurate, the Ardouval site becoming obscured by smoke and dust by the end. Bombing photos revealed that both aiming points had been straddled, but that the main weight of the attacks had fallen short or wide.

That night, 560 aircraft, including 108 Lancasters of 1 Group, were sent back to Stuttgart, while 114 Halifaxes of 4 Group attended to the Krupp Treibstoffwerke synthetic oil plant at Wanne-Eickel, situated between Gelsenkirchen and Herne in the Ruhr, the latter supported by three Path Finder Lancasters and eight of the ABC variety provided by 101 Squadron. 103 Squadron loaded seven of its Lancasters with a 2,000 pounder and twelve J-cluster bombs for the main event and seven others with eighteen 500 pounders for use against a flying bomb launching ramp at Bois-des-Jardins, located south of Amiens. The latter would join forces with two SDF Lancasters and fifteen of 460 Squadron RAAF, the only 1 Group unit not to contribute to the Stuttgart raid. The 103 Squadron main eventers departed Elsham Wolds between 21.21 and 21.31 with F/Ls Broadbent and Marsden the senior pilots on duty and set course for Selsey Bill, where they met seven to ten-tenths cloud. They followed the same route as for the previous Stuttgart raid and arrived in the target area under a cloud base at 17,000 feet, which was the height at which all but one of the 103 Squadron participants carried out their attacks between 01.59 and 02.07, the exception bombing from a thousand feet higher. The marking was considered to be somewhat scattered but covered the target area, and the glow remained visible on the horizon for 150 miles into the homeward journey. Twelve aircraft failed to make it home, and among them was 103 Squadron's ND903, which crashed in the vicinity of Orleans, killing F/O Dyer RCAF and his crew.

It was 00.32 before the first 103 Lancaster rolled down the runway at Elsham Wolds bound for Bois-des-Jardins and all seven were airborne by 00.48 with S/L Gane the senior pilot on duty. They began the Channel crossing somewhere near Brighton and made landfall to the north of Dieppe, before pushing the few miles inland to the target, the cloud thinning as they closed on it. The Master Bomber called the main force element down to the 9,000-foot cloud base to ensure a clear view of the red Path Finder TIs, which went down a little early and were assessed as being slightly misplaced, prompting the Master Bomber to drop four green TIs, which fell within two hundred yards of the aiming point at 02.53½. He called in the main force and instructed them to overshoot by two hundred yards, and the 103 Squadron crews complied from 9,000 to 10,200 feet between 02.55 and 02.57, before returning home to report what appeared to be a successful outcome. This confidence was not supported by bombing photos, which revealed the attack to have fallen wide of the mark.

The night of the 28/29th would prove to be busy, eventful and expensive as the Command prepared for major operations against Stuttgart and Hamburg and a number of smaller undertakings involving a total of 1,126 aircraft. The final raid of the series on Stuttgart was to be prosecuted by an all-Lancaster heavy force of 494 aircraft drawn from 1, 3, 5 and 8 Groups, of which 159 Lancasters were provided by 1 Group. The annual last-week-of-July attack on Hamburg, 320 miles away to the north, was to be conducted by 307 aircraft, consisting of a predominantly 6 Group Halifax and Lancaster main force, with six ABC Lancasters of 1 Group's 101 Squadron to provide RCM cover and 8 Group Lancasters and Mosquitos to carry out the marking. The operation would take place a year and a day after the devastating firestorm raid of Operation Gomorrah.

103 Squadron briefed sixteen crews for Stuttgart, loading each of their Lancasters with a cookie and ten 500 pounders and dispatching them from Elsham Wolds between 21.06 and 21.40 with F/Ls Broadbent and Marsden the senior pilots on duty. They flew out over the Sussex coast and followed a similar route as before for this target, crossing France in bright moonlight above the cloud layer and exposing themselves to the night-fighter hordes that had infiltrated the bomber stream from 5 degrees east and stayed in contact with it all the way to the target. It was the Luftwaffe's Nachtjagd that would gain the upper hand on this night and inflict a major blow upon 103 Squadron, as its participants passed over the Grande-Est region of north-eastern France, closing in on the German frontier near Strasbourg. PB147 was probably the first to fall, crashing at Charmes, some sixty miles west of Strasbourg with total loss of life among the crew of F/O Moss, while ME799 was shot down by a night-fighter some twenty miles further east, within three miles of Baccarat, and crashed at 01.30 with fatal consequences for F/O Armstrong and two of his crew, the other four succeeding in saving themselves, two falling into enemy hands and two managing to evade a similar fate. Two of the squadron's Lancasters crashed at the same time, at 01.45, but some distance apart as they closed in on the target. LM538 crashed near Freudenstadt, just over the frontier in Germany, with no survivors from the crew of F/O West, and NE117 was a little to the north-west of Stuttgart when the end came. It was carrying the crew of F/L Broadbent, plus a second pilot, Canadian, F/O Mitchell, and all but the pilot died in the wreckage. F/L Broadbent was found with severe injuries, to which he succumbed within hours.

A thin layer of up to ten-tenths cloud lay over the city, with tops in places at around 12,000 feet, and the Path Finders initially employed skymarker flares (Wanganui), which were quickly swallowed up. Most crews bombed on H2S, before scattered red and green TIs appeared on the ground in a line from north-west to south-east, and the Master Bomber attempted to persuade the main force crews to bomb the glow from a cluster of greens nearest to the aiming-point. A number of crews descended into clear air beneath the cloud base and reported green TIs at the southern end of the railway station at 01.56. The 103 Squadron crews carried out their attacks from 17,000 to 17,500 feet between 01.39 and 02.03, and large explosions were observed at 01.47, 01.51 and 02.05. It was impossible to assess the outcome, but most returning crews reported a scattered raid, for which they blamed the weather conditions. Thirty-nine Lancasters failed to return, seventeen of them from 1 Group, and to compound the grievous 103 Squadron losses, a night fighter-damaged PA985 was brought back by F/O Green to a crash-landing at 03.55 near Little Harwood airfield in Buckinghamshire, and all emerged from the fuselage unscathed. PB147 was badly shot up and landed at White Waltham near Maidenhead in Berkshire with just the Canadian pilot, F/O Birch, the flight engineer and navigator on board, who reported that the other four members of the crew had baled out. JB655 was another to barely survive an encounter with a night-fighter, and after P/O Henry RAAF had accomplished a safe landing at Dunsfold in Surrey, two seriously wounded members of his crew were taken to hospital. LM132 landed at Elsham Wolds in the hands of F/O Ansley RNZAF and crew, and it too bore the scars of a brush with the enemy. At debriefing, crews described the intensity of the night-fighter activity, and ten combats were reported, with one enemy aircraft claimed as destroyed, two as probably destroyed and three as damaged. Some crews also reported being fired upon by other bombers, despite flying at the correct height and briefed course. The Hamburg force was also mauled by night-fighters while homebound and lost twenty-two of its number to bring the night's casualty figure to sixty-one aircraft.

The penultimate operation of a busy month for 103 Squadron was as part of a 1 Group force of 104 Lancasters assigned to two aiming points at Cahagnes in the Caumont-Villers-Bocage region of Normandy in support of the American 2nd army. A total of 692 aircraft were to be involved at six German positions, for which 103 Squadron contributed nine Lancasters, each loaded with twenty 500 pounders and dispatched from Elsham Wolds between 06.25 and 07.05 with S/L Van Rolleghem the senior pilot on duty. They began the Channel crossing at Selsey Bill over low cloud, which persisted all the way to the target, where it became necessary for the Master Bomber to call the main force crews down to below the cloud base. The 1 Group force was divided 34/70 between aiming points "E" and "F" and the 103 Squadron crews bombed the Oboe markers from 1,800 to 3,500 feet in accordance with instructions from the Master Bomber. The marking seemed well placed and the bombing concentrated, and the attacks were delivered unopposed, most of the returning 103 Squadron Lancasters displaying the scars from the blast of their own bombs at such low level. The low cloud was responsible for only 377 aircraft bombing and just two of the six aiming points were effectively dealt with.

The final operation of the month involving Elsham Wolds was to be by fifty Lancasters from 13 Base in company with two Lancasters and five Mosquitos of 8 Group, in an attack on the port area of Le Havre and any U-Boats sheltering therein on the 31st. 103 Squadron loaded nine of its Lancasters with eleven 1,000 and four 500 pounders and sent them on their way between 17.59 and 18.16 with S/L Van Rolleghem the senior pilot on duty. They headed south to begin the Channel crossing at Brighton and arrived at the target under clear skies with excellent visibility that facilitated a visual identification of the aiming point. Moderate flak in the target area was focussed on aircraft right over the target, and F/O Furlong observed JB746 receive a direct hit, which caused a wing to break away. Two parachutes were seen to deploy and these crewmen, the navigator and bomb-aimer, landed in the arms of their captors, while F/O Avon RCAF and the others perished in the wreckage. The remaining 103 Squadron crews bombed from 13,000 to 14,000 feet between 19.59 and 20.01, and it is believed that one U-Boot was hit.

That night, ninety 1 Group Lancasters crews from 12 and 14 Bases were briefed to attack a flying bomb storage site in the Forêt-de-Nieppe, close to the Belgian frontier in north-eastern France, one of four storage and launching sites to be targeted by two hundred aircraft of 1, 6 and 8 Groups. Bombing took place on the glow of TIs through ten-tenths cloud, and post-raid reconnaissance revealed that only the 1 Group operation had been successful.

During the course of another busy month, the squadron took part in fourteen operations and dispatched 202 sorties for the loss of twelve crews and fourteen aircraft.

August 1944

August would bring an end to the flying bomb offensive, and also see a return to major night operations against industrial Germany. Flying bomb sites were to dominate the first half of the month, however, and sites would be targeted in daylight on each of the first six days. It began with the commitment of 777 aircraft to operations against thirteen flying bomb-related sites during the afternoon and evening of the 1st, although there were serious doubts about the weather conditions, which were poor over England. A 1 Group operation by fifty Lancasters of 13 Base against a "constructional works" at Belle Croix les Bruyeres involved eight 103 squadron aircraft, each loaded with a dozen 1,000 and four 500 pounders before departing Elsham Wolds between 18.48 and 19.03 with F/Ls Josey and Marsden the senior pilots on duty. They exited the English coast at Orfordness and encountered ten-tenths low cloud as they crossed the French coast near Calais and the master Bomber sent them home.

Elsham Wolds was not called into action when four small-scale operations against flying bomb sites were handed to individual 1 Group squadrons on the 2nd, the plan for which required each element to formate on two Path Finder Mosquitos, and bomb when the first Mosquito released its load. There was also a repeat of the recent attack on Le Havre for which fifty-one Lancasters were detailed.

On the following day, 1,114 aircraft were committed to attacks on flying bomb sites at Bois-de-Cassan, Forêt-de-Nieppe and Trossy-St-Maximin, and 1 Group was assigned to the last-mentioned, described in the 1 Group ORB as large "constructional works". This was one of many similar sites in the Hauts-de-France region, and it had been targeted by 5 Group on the previous day. 103 Squadron contributed fifteen Lancasters to the 1 Group force of 180 and loaded them with eleven 1,000 and four 500 pounders before dispatching them from Elsham Wolds between 11.24 and 11.51 with S/L Van Rolleghem the senior pilot on duty. They disappeared almost immediately into a very low cloud base hovering at around 300 feet, but this was in the process of breaking up as they began the Channel crossing at the Sussex coast and made landfall on the French side near Dieppe, where heavy flak brought down a 460 Squadron RAAF aircraft and damaged others, including one containing W/C "Jack" Douglas, formerly of 103 Squadron. The others were forced to run the gauntlet of flak, largely from airfields, and on reaching the target, crews were confronted by three to seven-tenths cloud in a wedge between 3000 and 7,000 feet. Most crews were able to identify the target visually through the many gaps and bombed on their own reference, while others aimed for the red TIs or to port of the yellows in accordance with the clear instructions from the Master Bomber. The 103 Squadron crews delivered their attacks visually from 11,400 to 13,500 feet between 14.16 and 14.19, and the aiming point and markers were soon obscured by smoke. Twenty-seven 1 Group aircraft sustained flak damage, and one was seen to have half a wing sliced off by bombs from above.

The Bois de Cassan and Trossy sites were to be attacked again by elements of 6 and 8 Groups on the 4th, while 288 Lancasters of 1, 3 and 8 Groups were made ready for the long flight to the Bordeaux region of France's Biscay coast. The mighty Gironde estuary narrows as it leads inland towards the south-east, before dividing to become the Garonne River to the west and the Dordogne to the east. Its banks and islands were home to a number of important oil production and storage sites at Pauillac, Blaye, Bec-d'Ambes and Bordeaux itself, and the region was a frequent destination for gardening activities. Bordeaux, a gateway to the Atlantic, was a vitally important port to the enemy, contained U-Boot pens and was heavily defended along the entire length of the waterway. The targets on this occasion were oil refineries at Pauillac and Bec-d'Ambes, and the attacks were to be carried out for the first time under the umbrella of an escort of twenty-seven "Serrate" Mosquitos provided by 100 Group. "Serrate" was a radar device that enabled the night-fighter variant of the Mosquito to home in on enemy night-fighters to turn the hunters into the hunted, and a spectacularly successful campaign was waged that spread panic through the Luftwaffe Nachtjagd and spawned the term "Moskito Panik" among its crews.

1 Group detailed 169 Lancasters for the Pauillac site, of which fourteen were made ready by 103 squadron and loaded with nine 1,000 and three 500 pounders each before departing Elsham Wolds between 13.13 and 13.45 with F/Ls Josey and Marsden the senior pilots on duty. In contrast to the previous day, the weather was exceptionally fine, and they flew out over Land's End to skirt the Brest peninsula on their way south, before arriving in the target area under clear skies and in good visibility that enabled them to identify ground features on approach. The yellow TIs went down on time and thick black and white smoke began to rise from the moment the first bombs detonated at 18.00, to be followed by those from 103 Squadron from 6,500 to 9,000 feet between 18.00 and 18.10. The entire northern half of the complex was left burning and black smoke was rising through 8,000 feet as the last of the bombers turned away.

On the following day, 1 Group issued orders for 176 Lancasters to return to the Gironde estuary, half to attack the southern section of the Pauillac refinery and half to target the oil storage site at Blaye, situated on the East Bank of the estuary further south. 103 Squadron made ready fifteen of its Lancasters for Blaye, loading each with nine 1,000 and five 500 pounders, before dispatching them from Elsham Wolds between 13.56 and 14.45 with W/C St John and S/L Van Rolleghem the senior pilots on duty. The conditions were as perfect as for the previous day's operation, and all from the squadron arrived safely in the target area drawn on by the smoke still issuing from the site but not impeding identification of the aiming point. The Yellow TIs fell a little to the north-west and the south, but any over and undershooting was quickly rectified by the Master Bomber and a huge fire soon broke out which gradually enveloped the site. The 103 Squadron crews carried out their attacks from 6,000 to 8,000 feet between 18.59 and 19.07 and witnessed a large orange explosion at 19.10, before setting course for home under the protection of the 100 Group Mosquito escort. On return, they were diverted to Ossington because of fog over northern Lincolnshire.

More than a thousand aircraft were assembled during the course of the 7th to send against five enemy strong points ahead of advancing Allied ground forces in the Normandy battle area. Two of the aiming points were west of the Caen to Falaise road and three to the east, each to be attacked by roughly two hundred aircraft under the control of Master Bombers. 1 Group was assigned to one of the western targets at Fontenay-le-Marmion to the south of the city, for which 204 Lancasters were detailed, seventeen of them provided by 103 Squadron and carrying thirteen 1,000 and four 500 pounders. They departed Elsham Wolds between 19.52 and 21.20 with F/Ls Bartleet, Forbes, Josey and Marsden the senior pilots on duty and flew out over Selsey Bill under cloudless skies which persisted all the way to the target area. As they approached at 23.17, they were greeted by green star-shells fired by the artillery as a guide to the aiming point, and green Path Finder TIs fell beneath them to mark out the area intended for destruction. The bombing began just before H-Hour, and among those delivering an attack were ten from 103 Squadron from 7,000 to 7,500 feet between 23.19 and 23.24, the bursts from which were observed to straddle the markers, before they became obscured by smoke and, eventually, obliterated altogether. At 23.25, the Master Bomber reported that no further green TIs were available and issued the code word "Greengage" to signal an end to proceedings, sending home all those with bombs still on board, including the remaining seven from 103 Squadron. Having crossed the English coast homebound, LM292 suffered an engine fire, which created control challenges for F/O Brown RCAF, who still had a full bomb load on board. He ordered five of his crew to take to their parachutes, while he and the flight engineer attempted a landing, but the Lancaster crashed at Lenton, seven miles south-east of Grantham, and the bomb load went up on impact, killing both men.

Crews at Elsham Wolds were warned of an operation in the early morning of the 8th and again in the afternoon, but both were scrubbed. Elsewhere on that day, the focus returned to oil for 170 Lancaster and ten Mosquito crews of 1, 3 and 8 Groups, who were briefed for attacks on two depots and storage dumps at Aire-sur-la-Lys and Forêt-de-Lucheux, both situated in the Hauts-de-France region in the north-east of the country. 1 Group briefed fifty crews at the 12 and 14 Base stations of Binbrook and Wickenby for the oil tankage depot at the former, and at the target observed little happening on the ground until a large red/orange explosion erupted at 23.34 in the centre of the marked area and emitted a large mushroom of oily smoke. Several fires broke out, the glow from which remained visible for seventy-five miles into the return flight, and all returned safely to their respective stations to report a successful outcome.

On the following night, Elsham Wolds provided two crews from each squadron to lay mines in the Cinnamon garden south of La Pallice/La Rochelle on the Biscay coast at a location referred to in the ORB as Pertuis-d'Antioche. The crews of F/O Gibbons and F/L Marsden took off at 21.24 and 21.26 and began the Channel crossing at Bridport, on course for landfall on the Brittany coast near Treguier. They pinpointed visually on the Ile d'Oleron and established the point of release on H2S, before letting their six mines go from 11,000 feet within half a minute of each other at 00.57 and returning safely from uneventful sorties.

The 10th brought four flying bomb targets for 1 Group, each assigned to fifteen Lancasters from individual 12 Base squadrons, but the largest operation was against an aviation fuel storage site at Dugny, a north-eastern suburb of Paris around eight miles from the city centre, for which eighty-nine Lancasters were detailed from 13 and 14 Bases. Fifteen 103 Squadron Lancasters received a bomb load of thirteen American-built 1,000 pounders and four 500 pounders and departed Elsham Wolds between 09.00 and 09.29 with S/Ls Gane and Van Rolleghem the senior pilots on duty. They climbed into cloud with a base at 2,000 feet, but conditions improved as they headed south to exit the English coast over Selsey Bill, and by the time that they made landfall to the east of Dieppe, they were benefitting from clear skies and good visibility, which facilitated an accurate attack. The first batch of markers fell short of the aiming point, but the next ones were well placed, and the attack proceeded under the control of a Master Bomber, whose communications were described as indistinct. The 103 Squadron crews bombed from 15,000 to 16,500 feet between 12.00 and 12.05, and despite the absence of a spectacular explosion and black oily smoke common to most attacks on oil-related objectives, the operation was deemed a success.

A morning briefing on 1 Group's 12 and 13 Base stations on the 11th informed 120 crews of their part in an attack on marshalling yards that afternoon at Douai, situated ten miles south of Lille in north-eastern France. They were to act as the main force and would be supported by ten Lancasters from 35 (Madras Presidency) Squadron of the Path Finders to provide the marking and Master Bomber. The fifteen-strong 103 Squadron contingent departed Elsham Wolds between 13.30 and 13.55 with S/L Gane the senior pilot on duty and each crew sitting on thirteen 1,000 and four 500 pounders. The Channel crossing began at Selsey Bill and ended south of Cayeux-sur-Mer, and on arrival at the target they found three to four-tenths broken cloud with tops at around 7,000 feet. The visibility was excellent, enabling all crews to identify the target visually and the aiming point by the red Oboe TIs in the centre of the yards and to the western edge, which were backed up by yellows. However, these were soon rendered ineffective as they became obscured by smoke, upon which the master Bomber, F/L Forde, instructed the crews to bomb the windward edge of the smoke until he was able to re-mark with yellow TIs. He inadvertently left his transmit button on, which caused some confusion and annoyance, but the bombing went ahead, the 103 Squadron crews delivering their loads from 16,000 feet between 16.15 and 16.25. A violent explosion at 16.19 was followed by a column of smoke, and direct hits were observed on rolling stock, engine sheds, depots and also on a road bridge at the northern end of the yards, which left returning crews confident of a successful outcome. This proved to be the final outing for the Special Duties Flight, which performed its final operation in a bombing rather than target-marking role and was disbanded without ceremony a few days later with little recognition for its contribution to 1 Group's war effort.

1 Group would be active throughout the 12th, beginning with a late morning take-off for twenty Lancasters from 12 Base to target U-Boot pens at La Pallice on the Biscay coast and thirty from 13 Base assigned to oil storage facilities at Bordeaux further to the south. The six-strong 103 Squadron element departed Elsham Wolds bound for the latter between 11.21 and 11.29 with S/L Van Rolleghem the senior pilot on duty and six 2,000 pounders in each bomb bay. They flew out over Bridport and traversed the Brest peninsula, before proceeding south on a course parallel to the coast and arriving at the target under clear skies and with good vertical visibility. They delivered their attacks from 10,500 to 11,500 feet between 15.10 and 15.12 in accordance with instructions from the Master Bomber to slightly overshoot and were under fire throughout by heavy flak in barrage form, which caused damage to F/L Bartleet's LM243, but hit nothing critical to prevent a safe return.

That night was to bring heavy activity, during which the principal operation was the raid by 379 Lancasters and Halifaxes from all but 8 Group on Braunschweig (Brunswick), to ascertain the ability of main force crews to identify and attack a target on the strength of H2s alone without any marking taking place. Meanwhile, a second force of 297 aircraft would attempt to hit the Opel tank works at Rüsselsheim some two hundred miles to the south-south-west, and a rush job added late on would involve 144 aircraft attacking a German troop concentration and a road junction north of Falaise. 1 Group detailed eighty-three Lancasters for Braunschweig, a city known for supporting the German war effort with a particular emphasis on aircraft components. 103 Squadron contributed just six of its Lancasters, which were loaded with a 2,000 pounder and twelve 500lb J-Type cluster bombs each, before departing Elsham Wolds between 21.31 and 21.39 with S/L Gane the senior pilot on duty. They began the North Sea crossing at Mablethorpe and made landfall on the Dutch coast in the region of Alkmaar (the route provided in the ORB is wrong), in excellent weather conditions and it was only when some fifty miles from the target that the cloud thickened to ten-tenths at around 10,000 feet to cover Braunschweig. This was an anticipated eventuality and was not critical as crews had been briefed to bomb on H2S anyway, five of the 103 Squadron participants complying from 20,000 to 21,000 feet between 00.06 and 00.09, while F/O Haldane and crew bombed visually on the centre of fires from 20,000 feet at 00.08. Night-fighters had been evident over the target and continued to harry the returning bombers, and F/O Jarratt and crew shot down a Me110 north of Hannover. Night-fighters were largely responsible for the loss of twenty-seven aircraft, 7.1% of the force, in return for a modestly effective raid, which hit the centre of the city but also other locations up to twenty miles distant. The simultaneous attack on the Opel tank works at Rüsselsheim cost a further twenty aircraft, and the effort and losses were not compensated for with a successful outcome.

As the bombers were turning away from Brunswick, three Lancasters from each of the Elsham Wolds squadrons were in the process of taking off for Falaise as part of a 1 Group force of thirty-five aircraft. The 103 Squadron crews of S/L Van Rolleghem, F/O Smith and F/Sgt March became airborne between 00.09 and 00.29 with eleven 1,000 and four 500 pounders beneath their feet and flew out over Selsey Bill to make landfall on the Normandy coast. They arrived under a cloudless sky, only for cloud to build as they progressed inland to find the target area concealed beneath a fifteen-hundred-foot layer of ten-tenths with a base at 1,000 feet. Despite this, the plentiful and concentrated red and green TIs could be seen and were bombed by the 103 Squadron trio from 7,000 to 7,500 feet between 02.16 and 02.20, after which, they returned without incident to report a few fires and explosions.

The main activity during the afternoon of the 14th was an operation in support of Canadian divisions in the Falaise area involving 805 aircraft, 130 of them provided by 1 Group. Their targets were seven enemy troop positions, and each attack was to be controlled by a Master Bomber to ensure as far as possible that no "friendly fire" incidents resulted from the close proximity of the opposing forces. One hundred of the 1 Group crews were briefed for aiming point 25, the village of Fontaine-le-Pin, and thirty for 21B, and it was for the former that fifteen 103 Squadron Lancasters departed Elsham Wolds between 13.10 and 13.31 with S/Ls Gane and Van Rolleghem the senior pilots on duty and twenty 500 pounders in each bomb bay. Cloud over England gave way to clear skies over the Channel and French coast, and smoke could be observed in the target area as the 1 Group formations approached. Smoke from Fontaine-le-Pin was rising through 6,000 feet even before some of the force had reached the French coast, and the Master Bomber brought them down to 4,000 feet, before reducing the bombing height still further to 3,000 feet. The smoke rendered map reading difficult and target identification something of a challenge, but 50% of crews were able to see TIs, and when these disappeared from sight, they were instructed to aim for the northern edge of the smoke. The 103 Squadron crews bombed on the TIs from 2,000 to 3,500 feet between 15.30 and 15.38 and left the scene satisfied that the attack had been concentrated where intended. Aiming point 21B soon became obscured by thick smoke, but the Master Bomber handled the attack expertly, and when two sticks of bombs were seen to undershoot by some three hundred yards, he was quick to admonish the culprits and no further wayward bombing occurred. Despite the most stringent efforts to avoid friendly fire incidents, about halfway through the sequence of attacks, some bombs did fall into a quarry occupied by Canadian troops, killing thirteen men, injuring fifty-three others, and destroying a large number of vehicles. One of two 13 Base Lancasters lost at Fontaine-le-Pin was 103 Squadron's ND613, which crashed in the target area after the bomb-aimer in F/L Bartleet's had parachuted into the arms of his captors as the sole survivor.

In preparation for his new night offensive against Germany, Harris called for operations against enemy night-fighter airfields in Holland and Belgium, in response to which, a list of eight such targets was drawn up. Those at Eindhoven, Soesterberg, Volkel, Melsbroek, St-Trond, Tirlemont-Gossancourt and Le Culot were to be targeted in daylight during the course of the morning and early afternoon of the 15th, and Venlo that night, involving, in all, 1004 aircraft. 1 Group ordered 202 Lancasters to be made ready to be divided equally between Volkel in south-central Holland and Le Culot, situated some ten miles south-south-east of Leuven in north-central Belgium. 103 Squadron loaded each of its sixteen Lancasters with thirteen 1,000 and four 500 pounders and dispatched them from Elsham Wolds between 09.42 and 10.11 with S/Ls Gane and Van Rolleghem the senior pilots on duty bound for Le Culot. They began the North Sea crossing at Southwold and made landfall over the Scheldt estuary in perfect conditions, which enabled them to identify the target from many miles away on approach. The Path Finder element carried out its part in the operation in exemplary fashion, dropping TIs close to the runway intersection, but most crews were able to bomb visually, those from 103 Squadron from 12,000 to 17,000 feet between 11.59 and 12.05. In a short space of time, smoke and dust obliterated the aiming point, but all bombs appeared to fall within the airfield boundaries, and the operation was declared a success. There was some opposition along the route and at the aerodrome from heavy flak, S/L Van Rolleghem's navigator sustaining a slight wound, while a strong fighter escort kept the Luftwaffe at bay to ensure no losses.

The new offensive began with simultaneous attacks on Stettin and Kiel on the night of the 16/17th, for which 1 Group contributed 134 aircraft to the overall all-Lancaster force of 461 assigned to the former. 103 Squadron made ready seven of its own for the main event, giving each a load of a 2,000 pounder and twelve 500lb J-Type cluster bombs, while six others had six 1,500lb parachute mines winched into their bomb bays for delivery to the Geranium garden of Swinemünde in the Bay of Pomerania. They departed Elsham Wolds together between 20.48 and 21.46 with no senior pilot on duty among the Stettin-bound element and S/L Gane leading the gardeners and flew out over Mablethorpe on course for Jutland's western coast. They enjoyed clear skies over the North Sea and Denmark and encountered cloud only when it began to build up over the Baltic to reach ten-tenths with tops at 17,000 feet as they crossed the German coast. It took some three-and-a-half hours to reach the respective target areas, where the crews were greeted by up to nine-tenths high cloud with a base, according to the Master Bomber's broadcast at 00.52½ at 14,000 feet, but with sufficient breaks to enable them to register clear visibility below.

At Stettin, the initial flares and green TIs were observed to be a little north and east of the built-up area, which reduced the effectiveness of the illumination, but this did not prevent the Path Finder primary visual markers from identifying the aiming point and dropping a mix of red and green TIs to form a good concentration that the visual re-centerers maintained throughout. The main force element approached from 16,000 to 20,000 feet and began to bomb the TIs from around 00.56 until 01.21 and reported fires taking hold. The 103 Squadron crews carried out their attacks from 17,000 to 18,500 feet between 00.59 and 01.10

in accordance with the Master Bomber's instructions and, according to most crews, almost unopposed from the ground. However, a moderate amount of heavy and light flak was reported by 103 Squadron crews along with searchlights and night-fighters, and F/O Henry and crew fought off two encounters without damage to either party.

Meanwhile, the gardeners had planted their vegetables unopposed by H2S from 10,000 to 12,000 feet between 01.11 and 01.25 and both elements returned home safely. While the above operations were in progress, 190 miles away to the west, severe damage had been inflicted on the docks and shipbuilding yards at Kiel, but much of the bombing had also been wasted outside of the town to the north-west. Not all crews at debriefing were confident about the outcome of the Stettin raid, some suggesting that it had been scattered, when in fact, it had been highly successful and had destroyed fifteen hundred houses, numerous industrial premises, had sunk five ships in the harbour and seriously damaged eight more.

There is confusion concerning an operation late on the 17th against an oil storage depot at Terneuzen, a northern district of the city of Ghent in north-eastern Belgium, sometimes referred to as Ertvelde-Rieme, after a location called Riemer a little to the north of Terneuzen. According to the 1 Group ORB, this operation was cancelled in mid-afternoon and all squadrons stood down for the rest of the day, and there is no mention of it either in Bomber Command War Diaries by Martin Middlebrook and Chris Everitt. However, the 103 Squadron ORB is adamant that the operation went ahead and a dozen 103 Squadron Lancasters departed Elsham Wolds between 22.10 and 22.30 with station commander G/C Sheen the senior pilot on duty supported by S/L Van Rolleghem. Each aircraft was loaded with thirteen 1,000 and four 500 pounders as they flew out over Orfordness on course for the Scheldt as part of a 1 and 5 Group force of 105 Lancasters and five Mosquitos assigned to the Ertvelde-Rieme site. Under largely clear skies, they identified the target visually and by TIs, and bombed in accordance with the instructions of the Master Bomber from 10,000 to 12,000 feet between 00.04 and 00.11. P/O Pearce landed LM293 heavily at 01.50 and burst a tyre, sending the Lancaster out of control to be wrecked, happily without crew casualties.

On the following day, 1 Group was handed five daytime targets, beginning, we are informed, with an attack in the early afternoon by thirty aircraft from 14 Base on the Ertvelde-Rieme site. The remaining four targets were all flying-bomb related and involved just four Lancasters each, at Le Nieppe for 103 and 550 Squadrons, Wemars-Cappel for 576 Squadron, Vincly for 625 Squadron and Fromental for 460 Squadron RAAF. The 103 Squadron crews of F/Os Austin and Farris and P/O March departed Elsham Wolds between 19.06 and 19.25, each carrying twenty 500 pounders, and flew out over Orfordness under favourable conditions until arriving at the French coast between Calais and Dunkerque. Here, they encountered ten-tenths cloud that forced them to descend to 5,000 feet, at which height they were able to map-read their way to the target to deliver their hardware at 21.00. PB363 was observed to be shot down in flames by flak after releasing the bombs, and F/O Austin perished with two of his crew, while the four survivors were taken into captivity. That night, major attacks on Bremen and the oil refinery at Sterkrade-Holten involved forces of 288 and 234 aircraft respectively, and by the time that the last aircraft had landed, the twenty-four hour period had generated 1,069 sorties for the loss of just four aircraft.

Most of Bomber Command's heavy brigade spent the following week in non-operational activity while a few carried out minor operations and mining. Major operations resumed on the 25th, when preparations were put in hand to make ready more than nine hundred aircraft to launch against three major targets, while four hundred others would be engaged in a variety of smaller endeavours. The largest operation was to be the all-Lancaster affair involving 461 aircraft from 1, 3, 6 and 8 Groups in a return to the Opel tank works at Rüsselsheim in southern Germany, while 334 others attended to eight coastal batteries between Brest and the islands to the south of Lorient, leaving 5 Group to focus on Darmstadt, a university city renowned as a centre of scientific research and development, and one of a few almost virgin targets considered to be worthy of attention. The Opel factory had produced motor vehicles up until October 1940 and was a wholly-owned subsidiary of the American General Motors Corporation with a sister plant manufacturing lorries at Brandenburg near Berlin. In 1942, the Rüsselsheim plant was given over to war production and began to manufacture aircraft and tank parts.

1 Group detailed 189 Lancasters, of which eighteen were made ready by 103 Squadron and each loaded with a cookie and twelve 500lb Type-14 cluster bombs, before departing Elsham Wolds between 19.53 and 20.23 with S/L Gane the senior pilot on duty. They flew out over Selsey Bill and made landfall on the Normandy coast to the east of Caen, and patchy cloud gave way to clear skies in the target area with good vertical visibility. The Path Finders opened the attack on time with illuminator flares followed by TIs, which were backed up throughout, and some crews confirmed their positions by H2S before committing themselves to the bombing run. A decoy site some ten miles west-south-west of the target attracted a few bomb loads in the early stages, but the main weight of the attack fell where intended in the face of little effective opposition from the ground. The 103 Squadron crews delivered their loads from 16,500 to 18,000 feet between 01.00 and 01.12, aiming mostly for red and green TIs and fires in the face of numerous searchlights and moderate heavy flak in barrage form. Large explosions were observed at 00.58, 01.02, 01.09 and 01.10 and smoke was seen to be rising through 11,000 feet as the force retreated, leaving a glow from the burning factory visible for eighty miles. Night-fighters were much in evidence and three 103 Squadron crews returned with claims of having each shot one down. ND632 was either short of fuel or battle damaged when F/O Westcott attempted a landing at Ford on the south coast, only to lose control and crash, killing all on board. Local sources confirmed that parts of the Opel factory had been put out of action for several weeks, although most of the machine tools escaped damage and production was not badly compromised.

The following night brought an operation by 372 Lancasters and ten Mosquitos from 1, 3 and 8 Groups against Kiel, while 174 Lancasters of 5 Group targeted Königsberg, now Kaliningrad in Russia, at the eastern end of Germany's Baltic coast. 1 Group provided 175 of the Lancasters for Kiel, fifteen of them belonging to 103 squadron, whose crews listened intently at Elsham Wolds to learn of their part in the proceedings. Out on the dispersals, the armourers were loading each of their Lancasters with a cookie and eighteen SBCs of incendiaries, which they lifted into the air between 19.43 and 20.37 with S/L Van Rolleghem the senior pilot on duty. The sound of their engines was still heavy in the air when the crews of F/Os Colvin and Gibbons and F/L Josey took off between 20.43 and 20.49 bound with nine others for the distant Spinach garden located off the port of Gdynia in Danzig Bay. Both elements set course via Mablethorpe over thin stratus cloud as far as the west coast of southern Jutland and the bombing brigade arrived in the target area at 23.00 to find eight-tenths thin, low stratus with tops at around 4,000 feet. Illuminating flares were already falling over the town to the west of the estuary and a very effective smoke screen was in operation over the southern part of the town. Only a few red and green TIs were on the ground before the rest of the primary visual marker crews were instructed not to release any more, but those already burning proved to be sufficient, and a good concentration of bombing was achieved south of the aiming-point with a very large explosion observed at 23.10. The 103 Squadron crews carried out their assigned tasks from 17,000 to 18,500 feet between 23.10 and 23.17, and all returned safely, while some 340 miles to the east, the gardeners established their positions by H2S on Hel point and delivered five mines each into the briefed locations from 13,000 feet between 01.27 and 01.40. Seventeen Lancasters failed to return from Kiel, among them five from 1 Group, and ten others sustained damage, while three gardeners were also missing. A reconnaissance Mosquito flew over Kiel at 25,000 feet at 00.18 and reported a five-mile arc of fire with a large bank of smoke rising through 15,000 feet.

The final acts of the flying bomb campaign were played out on the 28th, when 150 aircraft were detailed to carry out small "Oboe-leader" raids on a dozen sites, 1 Group assigned to four sites, at Fromental, Wemars-Cappel, Vincly and Chapelle-Notre-Dame, each to be targeted by ten Lancasters. It was for the last-mentioned, located a few miles south-east of Calais, that 103 Squadron made ready six aircraft and loaded each with thirteen 1,000 and four 500 pounders, before dispatching them from Elsham Wolds between 18.57 and 19.07 with no senior pilot on duty. They rendezvoused with four 576 Squadron Lancasters as they headed south past Reading over patchy medium level cloud, which had dissipated by the time the Channel crossing began and the skies remained clear for the remainder of the outward flight. Despite ground haze, crews were able to map-read and identify the aiming point visually, confirmed by H2S and also by red TIs dropped by the Oboe Mosquito leaders, although the squadron ORB suggests that no marking activity took place. Bombing was carried out from 9,500 to 12,000 feet between 20.43 and 20.46 and appeared to be concentrated, a fact confirmed by bombing photos. The Pas-de-Calais region was captured by Allied ground forces a few days later.

A total of 591 Lancasters were primed for action in the Baltic region on the 29th, 189 belonging to 5 Group to attack the port of Königsberg for the second time in three nights, while 402 Lancasters of 1, 3 and 8 Groups attended to the Baltic port-city of Stettin 260 miles closer to home. The seventeen 103 Squadron participants were part of a 1 Group contribution of 188 Lancasters and carried a variety of bomb loads, eight given a cookie, 660 x 4lb and 60 x 30lbs incendiaries, while eight others had a single 1,000 pounder and 500 pounder, with 1,100 x 4lbs and 80 x 30lbs incendiaries and one a 2,000 pounder, 1,150 x 4lb and 84 x 30lb incendiaries. They departed Elsham Wolds between 20.55 and 21.27 with F/Ls Forbes and Josey the senior pilots on duty and were followed into the air between 21.46 and 21.53 by the crews of S/L Gane and F/Os Colvin and Haldane, who were bound for mining duties in the Geranium garden off Swinemünde. The two elements flew out over Mablethorpe and encountered a layer of low cloud over the North Sea and part of Jutland, and this gave way to seven to eight-tenths thin cloud over the target area at between 12,000 and 19,000 feet with good visibility below. The master Bomber called "Basement 12,000", but his signal was weak and not all main force crews heard him as the attack opened with flares to illuminate the aiming-point and provide the marker crews with a visual reference confirmed by H2S. Salvoes of red and green TIs fell accurately, inviting the main force bomb loads, which fell squarely and in concentrated fashion where intended, those from the 103 Squadron aircraft from 12,000 to 18,000 feet between 02.00 and 02.13, and by 02.08, the whole area had become a sea of flames. The crew of a reconnaissance Mosquito approaching the target, but still some 250 miles away, reported a huge explosion at 02.09 and later, a large part of the town burning fiercely with a huge mushroom smoke cloud ascending through 26,000 feet.

Twenty-three Lancasters failed to return and a bad night for 1 Group was reflected in the loss of fifteen, two of them belonging to 103 Squadron. PB365 was lost in the general target area and there were no survivors from the crew of F/L Forbes RCAF, which included an American second pilot also serving in the RCAF. LM116 came down somewhere near Kiel, and F/O Nixon and his crew also all lost their lives. Meanwhile, the gardeners had fulfilled their briefs by planting their vegetables in the allotted locations by H2S from 12,000 to 15,000 feet between 02.14 and 02.23, and as before when operating in this region, landed at Lossiemouth on return. At debriefing, not all of the Stettin crews were convinced of the effectiveness of the operation, but in fact, it had caused severe damage in parts of the city previously untouched, with more than fifteen hundred houses destroyed, along with thirty-two industrial premises, and besides the industrial and residential damage, a 2,000-ton ship was sunk and seven others were hit in the docks.

The flying-bomb campaign may have ended on the 28th, but a new one against V-2 rocket storage and launching sites began on the 31st with raids on nine suspected locations at Raimbert, Lumbres North, Lumbres South, Agenville, St Riquier and Pourchinte, all located in the Hauts-de-France region of north-eastern France. 601 aircraft were made ready, 1 Group providing 149 Lancasters in roughly equal numbers for the sites of Raimbert, Agenville and St-Riquier. Fifty-two aircraft from 13 Base were assigned to the Agenville site, located some fifteen miles east-north-east of Abbeville, for which 103 Squadron loaded each of its fourteen Lancasters with thirteen 1,000 and two 500 pounders. They departed Elsham Wolds between 12.46 and 13.14 with F/L Josey the senior pilot on duty and began the Channel crossing over cloud at Worthing, having to descend to below the briefed bombing height by the time that the French coast hove into view. They were greeted at the target by intense predicted flak, which may have contributed to the scattered marking and the Master Bomber's confusing instructions led to a scattering of bombs also. The 103 Squadron crews attacked from 7,000 to 11,500 feet between 15.22 and 15.30 and turned for home without LM243, which was brought down by flak in the target area killing F/O Ryerse RCAF and all but the mid-upper gunner, who would succumb to his serious injuries ten days hence.

During the course of what had been its busiest month yet, the squadron took part in twenty-four operations and dispatched 250 sorties for the loss of six Lancasters and crews. From this point on, the squadron would enjoy an unprecedented loss free period, which, as far as human casualties were concerned, would extend for almost three months.

September 1944

The destructive power of the Command was now almost beyond belief with each of its heavy bomber groups capable of laying waste to a German city at one go, and, from now until the end of the war, this would be demonstrated in awesome and horrific fashion. Much of the Command's effort during the new month would be directed towards the liberation of the three French ports remaining in enemy hands, but operations began for 103 Squadron with an attack on Eindhoven aerodrome on the 3rd. This was one of six Luftwaffe airfields in southern Holland to be targeted in daylight, for which 348 Lancasters, 315 Halifaxes and a dozen Mosquitos were made ready across the Command. 1 Group provided ninety-nine Lancasters from all Bases for Gilze-Rijen and fifty-one from 13 and 14 Bases for Eindhoven, the 103 Squadron element of fifteen departing Elsham Wolds between 15.21 and 15.52 with F/L Josey the senior pilot on duty and each crew sitting on eleven 1,000 and four 500 pounders. The 1 Group squadrons climbed from their north Lincolnshire stations into rain-bearing low cloud, before heading for the Suffolk coast at Southwold on course for Walcheren Island at the mouth of the Scheldt. The poor weather conditions persisted until the targets drew near, at which point the cloud began to dissipate to enable the crews to establish their positions visually. At Eindhoven, the 103 Squadron crews bombed from 13,000 to 16,000 feet between 17.28 and 17.37 in the face of a weak flak defence and returned safely to report a slightly scattered but successful attack.

A force of 348 aircraft was assembled on the 5th to carry out the first operations against enemy strong points around the port of Le Havre. 313 Lancasters from 1, 3 and 8 Groups would be accompanied by thirty Oboe Mosquitos and five Stirlings of 149 Squadron, the last of the type in service with a bomber unit three days ahead of its retirement in favour of Lancasters. 1 Group provided 159 of the Lancasters, which had been assigned to three of six waves, each with a Master Bomber and Deputy to control the attacks and two marker backers-up. 103 Squadron loaded each of its seventeen Lancasters with nine 1,000 and four 500 pounders and sent them on their way from Elsham Wolds between 15.57 and 17.04 with S/L Van Rolleghem the senior pilot on duty. Nine-tenths cloud lay over England, but as the formations made their way towards the Sussex coast at Worthing, it began to break up and over the target it was no more than three-tenths with tops at around 6,000 feet. The vertical visibility was excellent and the main force crews of the first wave experienced no difficulty in identifying the aiming point visually but were told to orbit until the first red TIs were seen at 18.07. Six 103 Squadron crews, including that of S/L Van Rolleghem, bombed in the first wave from 11,000 and 12,000 feet between 18.08 and 18.11, and they were followed by the next five in the third wave from 11,000 to 11,500 feet between 18.24 and 18.26 and the final six from 11,000 to 12,000 feet between 18.40 and 18.46. The attack appeared to be concentrated where intended, despite smoke enveloping the target from time to time and hiding it from view, and a westerly breeze kept blowing it away to reveal the TIs again. A post-raid analysis suggested that around 90% of the bombs had fallen within the six defined target areas.

It was similar fare on the following evening when a force of 344 aircraft was assigned to six aiming-points around Le Havre, at which four Path Finder Lancasters and five Oboe Mosquitos would provide the marking. 1 Group made ready 160 Lancasters assigned to section I, aiming point 4, section II, aiming point 5 and section III, aiming point 6, of which fifteen were provided by 103 Squadron. They were each loaded with nine 1,000 and four 500 pounders and departed Elsham Wolds between 17.39 and 17.52 with F/L Josey the senior pilot on duty. They adopted the same route as before and those in section I reached aiming-point 4 to find ten-tenths stratus with a base at around 8,000 feet and fair visibility below. They responded in accordance with the call by the Master Bomber, F/O Mills, to come down to 7,000 feet at 18.57, while he assessed that the green TIs had missed the aiming-point by some fifteen hundred yards. He dropped his own red TIs to within a hundred yards, and these were joined by others from the Deputy and backers-up at 19.00, which fell a little closer and, later, greens falling closer still. He called in the main force crews, who produced mainly concentrated bombing with a little scatter, but the cloud base was sinking gradually and was at 6,000 feet by the time that the section II element arrived to carry out their attacks. By the time of arrival of section III, which included the 103 Squadron contingent, the cloud base had descended to 5,000 feet and the Master Bomber sent a signal to the main force crews at 19.31 and 19.32 to abandon the attack and take their bombs home.

There was an early start for crews participating in the next round of attacks on five German positions around Le Havre on the 8th, for which 1 Group put up 160 Lancasters in an overall 1, 3 and 8 Group force of 333 aircraft. The four Stirlings would be the very last to conduct a bombing operation, although the type would remain in Bomber Command service for SOE operations from Tempsford. The 103 Squadron element of fifteen Lancasters took off from Elsham Wolds between 06.05 and 06.28 in foul weather conditions with S/L Van Rolleghem the senior pilot on duty and each crew with nine 1,000 and four 500 pounders beneath their feet. They were bound for aiming-point 13 and approached the target area to find ten-tenths cumulus with a base at 10,000 feet and broken cloud at 6,000 feet. The Master Bomber broadcast the cloud base at 6,000 feet at 08.03 and issued instructions for the main force to orbit while he assessed the situation. As they circled, some observed red and green TIs on the ground, which they confirmed to themselves as being accurately placed, and on hearing no further instructions, a number of crews from other squadrons bombed, before the order was received to abandon the attack and take their bombs home. All from 103 Squadron complied with the master Bomber's instructions, and in all, only a third of those involved at the various aiming points carried out an attack.

Four aiming-points were earmarked for attention at Le Havre on the morning of the 9th, involving a total of twenty-two 8 Group Lancasters and twenty Oboe Mosquitos marking for 230 Halifaxes of 4 and 6 Groups. Poor visibility intervened again, and the operation was abandoned before any bombing took place. The weather over northern France had improved by the following day, and a massive effort involving 992 aircraft was mounted by the Command in the afternoon and evening to deal with eight enemy positions. The aiming-points were given the names of a car manufacturers, Buick 1 and 2, Alvis 1, 2, 3 and 4 and Bentley 1 and 2, and 8 Group was to provide forty Lancasters and forty-one Mosquitos to carry out the marking, with a Master Bomber and Deputy and three backers-up at each. 1 Group detailed two hundred Lancasters for Bentley 1 and 2, nineteen of them representing 103 Squadron and loaded with thirteen 1,000 and four 500 pounders each. They departed Elsham Wolds between 16.20 and 17.04 bound for Bentley 1 with F/L Josey the senior pilot on duty and followed the now familiar route in diminishing cloud conditions to find clear skies and excellent visibility in the target area. Smoke from the earlier attacks was drifting south-west across the town, but did not compromise the aiming point, which was easily identified. At 18.25, the Master Bomber ordered the main force crews to remain at their briefed height and called them in at 18.40 to bomb on red TIs, those from 103 Squadron complying from 9,000 to 10,000 feet between 18.40 and 18.50. Smoke soon drifted across the aiming point, but its location was maintained with further red TIs throughout the attack, and the Master Bomber was praised for his control and clear instructions. All indications pointed to a concentrated and accurate operation, which achieved its aims.

The morning of the 11th would bring the final attacks on the environs of the port, and involve 218 aircraft drawn from 4, 5, 6 and 8 Groups at two aiming-points, Cadillac 1 and 2. 1 Group had been alerted to the possibility of taking part but had been stood down for the day. Photo-reconnaissance confirmed accurate and concentrated bombing, and within hours of this operation, the German garrison surrendered to British forces. Elsewhere that afternoon on 3, 4, 6 and 8 Group stations in a sign of things to come, 379 crews attended briefings to learn of a daunting task facing them a little later, that would require them to present themselves over the heart of the Ruhr in broad daylight. They were told that the targets were synthetic oil refineries, the Nordstern (Gelsenberg A G) plant at Gelsenkirchen, the Klöckner Werke A G at Castrop-Rauxel ten miles to the north-east and the Chemischewerke-Essener-Steinkohle A G fifteen miles further to the east at Kamen. As previously mentioned, the German synthetic oil industry relied on two main production methods, the Bergius process for high-grade petroleum products like aviation fuel, and the Fischer-Tropsch process for lower-grade diesel-type fuels. Those mentioned above were all of the Bergius variety and were vital for maintaining a Luftwaffe fighter defence. The bomber force was to be protected by twenty squadrons of Spitfires and three each of Mustangs and Tempests, and the attacks at Castrop-Rauxel and Kamen were concluded successfully in good visibility, while the Nordstern plant was protected by a smoke screen and an assessment of the result was not possible. It mattered little as Germany's oil industry would now face increasing attention right through to the end of the bombing war.

That night, 5 Group delivered a crushing blow on the university city of Darmstadt in southern Germany, which destroyed the city centre and neighbouring districts and set off a firestorm in which more than twelve thousand people perished and seventy thousand were rendered homeless out of a total population of 120,000.

The oil offensive continued on the 12th with the briefing of 412 crews on 4, 6 and 8 Group stations for daylight raids on the Hydrierwerke refinery at Scholven-Buer to the north of Gelsenkirchen, the Krupp Treibstoffwerke at Wanne-Eickel to the east and the Hoesch-Benzin plant a dozen miles further east in the Wambel district of Dortmund. Meanwhile, 1, 3 and 8 Groups were busy assembling a force of 378 Lancasters and nine Mosquitos for the final major raid of the war on Frankfurt that night, while 195 Lancasters and thirteen Mosquitos of 5 Group focussed on Stuttgart with a sprinkling of 101 Squadron ABC Lancasters to provide RCM cover. 1 Group's contribution was two hundred Lancasters, of which eighteen were provided by 103 Squadron and loaded either with ten 1,000 pounders and one of 500lbs or a cookie, cluster bombs and incendiaries. They departed Elsham Wolds between 17.55 and 18.38 with S/L Van Rolleghem the senior pilot on duty and proceeded south to begin the Channel crossing at Beachy Head on course for landfall near Dieppe. The outward flight was conducted under clear skies and on arrival in the target area only a little haze lay between the bomb sights and the aiming point, and even this was negated by the illuminator flares that went down at 22.52½ to provide the bomb-aimers with a clear view of the ground. Red and green TIs were cascading as the first main force crews began their bombing runs, and they were seen to settle on the ground just to the south of the marshalling yards. The 103 Squadron crews carried out their attacks from 16,000 to 19,000 feet between 22.52 and 23.08 in the face of an intense searchlight and flak defence, and the bombing appeared to be concentrated, eventually drifting towards the more industrialised western districts in the final stages, by which time a dense pall of smoke was rising through 5,000 feet. Night-fighters were out in force and sixteen combats were reported by 1 Group crews, while seventeen Lancasters failed to return, six of them 1 Group aircraft. Returning crews reported many explosions and fires, and local sources confirmed the scale of destruction as severe on a night when many firemen were away helping out at Darmstadt. The Stuttgart operation had been equally destructive, and one central district may have suffered a firestorm.

A force of 490 aircraft from 1, 4, 6 and 8 Groups took off to attack the port of Kiel late on the 15th, the 1 Group contribution provided by 101 Squadron in an RCM role. Poor weather conditions improved in the target area on the eastern side of Schleswig-Holstein, where clear skies prevailed and most crews were able to pick out some ground detail, aided by illuminator flares. A smoke screen was activated, but the TIs remained visible throughout, and fires had gained a hold by the time the force retreated to the west, with the glow from the burning town still visible from Denmark's western coast 120 miles away.

While the above was in progress, nineteen 1 Group Lancasters from 13 and 14 Bases were detailed for mining duties in three gardens, Silverthorn IV in the Kattegat off Anholt island, and the distant Spinach and Tangerine gardens, respectively off the ports of Gdynia and Pillau, the latter, now Baltiysk in Russia, the most distant of all mining locations. Nine 103 Squadron crews were briefed, five for Spinach, the crew of F/O Hayes for Tangerine and three for Silverthorn IV, and they departed Elsham Wolds respectively between 21.47 and 21.52, at 21.56, and between 22.21 and 22.29, losing F/O Henry and crew from the Spinach element to an engine issue on the way. Having flown out over Mablethorpe on course for Jutland's western coast, they all arrived at their allotted target areas to plant four, five or six vegetables without difficulty from 10,000 to 12,000 feet between 01.29 and 03.04. The Hayes crew returned with flak damage to an unrecorded location, probably in Scotland, at 07.12 after more than nine hours aloft.

With Operation Market Garden about to be launched on the 17th, Bomber Command was to provide support with attacks in the early hours by 1 Group on four aerodromes. In roughly equal numbers, 201 Lancasters were detailed to target Rheine and Hopsten, located in the Münsterland to the west of the Dortmund-Ems and Mittelland Canals close to the Dutch frontier, and Leeuwarden and Steenwijk situated in northern Holland. Leeuwarden had earned its "wasps nest" reputation because of the crack fighter units based there, but the area had also gained fame as the birthplace of the famed but ill-fated WWI spy, Mata Hari. It for this objective that 103 Squadron made ready nineteen Lancasters among fifty-one drawn from all three bases, the 14 Base element consisting of 101 Squadron ABC Lancasters to provide RCM cover. They departed Elsham Wolds between 00.12 and 01.04 with F/Ls Birch, Haldane, Josey and MacLachlan the senior pilots on duty and each loaded with twenty 500 pounders and flew out via Mablethorpe in excellent conditions to make landfall on the northern tip of Texel. Clear skies and good visibility prevailed in the target area and the marking with red TIs was punctual and concentrated, providing the bomb-aimers with a clear reference for bombing from 11,000 and 11,500 feet between 02.25 and 02.30. The night was very dark, which made it difficult to assess what was happening on the ground, and it was only in the light from photo flashes that any ground detail was discernible. The consensus was that the success of the operation depended upon the accuracy of the TIs, which had been peppered with bomb bursts, and post-raid reconnaissance confirmed that all four aerodromes had sustained extensive damage.

Early briefings across the Command on the 17th prepared 762 crews for operations against enemy troop positions at seven locations around the port of Boulogne. The raids would be staggered over a four-hour period and benefit from an 8 Group contribution of five Lancasters and five Oboe Mosquito at each aiming-point. Three thousand tons of bombs was sufficient to persuade the German garrison that their time was up, and the port was returned to Allied control soon afterwards. Having already operated during the night, 1 Group was not invited to take part, but made ready 104 Lancasters to send against three coastal batteries on Walcheren Island and an ammunition dump or possibly V-1 storage depot at Eikenhorst, near Castricum on the Dutch coast, later in the day. 103 Squadron detailed ten Lancasters for Eikenhorst, loading each with thirteen 1,000 and four 500 pounders, before dispatching them from Elsham Wolds between 17.10 and 17.30 with F/L Garton the senior pilot on duty. They began the North Sea crossing at Cromer and arrived in the target area to find it well marked with red TIs, but the excellent conditions enabled them to bomb visually from 10,000 to 12,000 feet between 18.45 and 18.48, and all the indications were of a successful operation.

103 Squadron was stood down and would remain so for a few days along with most of 1 Group, and it was left to 101 Squadron to support a 5 Group operation against the twin towns of Mönchengladbach and Rheydt, for which the now famous W/C Guy Gibson VC was selected for the role of Master Bomber. His Mosquito failed to return after crashing on the outskirts of the Dutch town of Steenbergen, where he lies beside his navigator, S/L Warwick, in the Catholic cemetery. S/L Gane had now concluded his tour and on the 20th was posted to 11 Base, which was responsible for 1 Group training, to pass on his skills and experience, probably having to relinquish his acting squadron leader rank in the process.

The time had now arrived to turn attention upon Calais as the final French port still under enemy occupation and 646 crews attended briefings across the Command on the 20th, among them seventy Lancaster and forty Mosquito crews of 8 Group, who would lead attacks on five aiming-points, three of them receiving two visits. 1 Group assembled 184 Lancasters, sixty-three from 12 Base, sixty-five from 13 Base and fifty-two from 14 Base, and they were divided between two aiming points, 6C and 6D, at Sangatte, located to the west of the main town and port area. 103 Squadron loaded each of its fourteen participating Lancasters with thirteen 1,000 and four 500 pounders and sent them on their way from Elsham Wolds between 14.50 and 15.24. Whether or not S/L Gane's departure had galvanised W/C St John into action is uncertain, but the commanding officer made a rare appearance as the senior pilot on duty, climbing away with the others into poor weather conditions, which would persist throughout the operation. They flew out over the Kent coast and found the cloud dispersing somewhat over the sea to leave a thin layer of stratus at the target with a base at 3,000 to 4,000 feet. The master Bomber called the main forces down to 3,000 feet to carry out their attacks, and those assigned to 6C were able to observe red TIs on the aiming point as they approached in good visibility with ground features identifiable. At 6D, cloud and haze made it more difficult to identify the aiming point, and ccommunications problems between the Master Bomber and main force added to the difficulties. After releasing their bombs from 3,000 feet between 16.40 and 16.49, some 103 Squadron crews felt that the attack had overshot to some extent but commented on the helpfulness of the Master Bomber in trying to ensure a successful outcome. The master Bomber called a halt at 16.50 after the target area became concealed beneath smoke and debris, but the bombing appeared to have fallen within the marked area and was deemed successful.

The weather remained unfavourable over the ensuing days, keeping most squadrons on the ground or restricted to training flights. F/L Marsden had now concluded his tour of operations and was posted to 1667 Conversion Unit on the 23rd. The lull in operations ended on the 23rd, when a return to targets in Germany was communicated, and the main operation on this night was to be directed at Neuss, a city situated on the western bank of the Rhine opposite Düsseldorf, for which a force of 549 aircraft was drawn from 1, 3, 4 and 8 Groups. While this was in progress, seventy miles to the north-east, 5 Group would be engaged at two targets, the twin aqueduct section of the Dortmund-Ems Canal near Ladbergen and the nearby Handorf Luftwaffe aerodrome, for which a total of 243 Lancasters and ten Mosquitos was detailed. 1 Group contributed 204 Lancasters to the Neuss endeavour, nineteen of them at Elsham Wolds loaded with thirteen 1,000 and four 500 pounders before taking off between 18.22 and 19.11 with S/L Van Rolleghem the senior pilot on duty. The sensitivity of the Oboe equipment led to the early return of ten Mosquitos, leaving the others to drop their red TIs into the tops of the ten-tenths cloud that lay over the target at up to 10,000 feet. All but three of the 103 Squadron crews picked up the red TIs or their glow and delivered their bombs from 15,000 to 18,000 feet between 21.20 and 21.28, but the crews of F/O Henry and P/Os Scott and Wright were uncertain and returned their bombs to the dump. It was not possible to form an impression of what was happening on the ground, and Bomber Command claimed that the main weight of bombs had fallen into the Rhine docks and industrial areas. Local sources reported 617 houses and fourteen public buildings destroyed, and this was achieved at a cost of five Lancasters and two Halifaxes.

The assault on enemy positions around Calais resumed on the 24th, when five aiming-points were briefed out, the attacks upon which would follow a sequence beginning at aiming point 8, and continuing through 10, 11 and 9 before ending at 12. 1 Group's contribution amounted to just twenty-five Lancasters from Elsham Wolds, which were called to arms at such short notice, that 103 Squadron had time only to load eleven of its intended fifteen participating Lancasters with thirteen 1,000 and four 500 pounders. They took off between 15.54 and 16.41 with no senior pilot on duty and soon disappeared into the low rain-bearing cloud base as they made their way south. Conditions were no better in the target area, and bombing had to take place either visually or on Oboe skymarkers from as low as 2,000 feet. The 103

Squadron crews delivered their attacks visually from 2,000 to 3,000 feet between 17.28 and 17.36 and were lucky to collect only shrapnel damage from the lethal light flak that accounted for seven Lancasters and a Halifax.

A further attempt was made on the following morning involving 872 aircraft, 201 of them provided by 1 Group and divided between two aiming points. 103 Squadron contributed just five of its Lancasters, which were loaded with nine 1,000 and four 500 pounders and took off between 07.14 and 07.20 with W/C St John the senior pilot on duty. They headed south in perfect weather conditions, only for them to deteriorate dramatically over the Channel and French coast to leave a blanket of low cloud with a base at 2,000 feet, which would result in only 287 aircraft bombing. At 08.38, the master bomber for aiming point 2A abandoned the operation and sent the crews home with their bombs, and the master Bomber at aiming point 1B followed suit at 09.02. Despite the huge effort involved in launching so many aircraft, the 1 Group A-O-C decreed that the sorties would not count towards a tour.

Nine separate attacks were briefed out to 722 crews across the Command during the early morning of the 26th, 531 to target four coastal batteries at Cap Gris-Nez, situated some ten miles along the coast to the west of Calais, and 191 to attack enemy positions closer to the port. 1 Group supported the operation with seventy-seven Lancasters for aiming point 7A, seventy-eight for 7B and fifty-three for 7C, and while neither the 1 Group nor 103 Squadron ORBs informs us as to which the 103 Squadron element of eight was assigned, there are clues which suggest that it was 7B. They departed Elsham Wolds between 10.20 and 10.27 with F/L Peter Hague the senior pilot on duty, having just been posted in from 576 Squadron to fulfil the role of flight commander, and each bomb bay replete with thirteen 1,000 and four 500 pounders. They headed south over six to eight-tenths cloud, which gave way to clearing skies in the target area, where the smoke from earlier attacks had drifted away to enable crews to establish their positions visually. The Master Bomber's instruction to descend to 6,000 feet was not heard by all crews, but even those approaching from higher levels were able to identify the aiming point either visually or by red TIs. The 103 Squadron crews delivered their attacks visually from 9,000 to 10,000 feet between 11.41 and 11.49 and watched their hardware fall with good concentration where intended.

Crews were roused early from their beds on the 27th, and no doubt expected to be briefed for the next round of attacks on enemy positions around Calais. 341 crews from 1, 3, 4 and 8 Groups had their expectations fulfilled, while 346 others from 6 and 8 Groups discovered that they would be divided more-or-less equally between the destinations of Bottrop and Sterkrade-Holten, situated within six miles of each other on the northern edge of the Ruhr to the north of Duisburg and Essen. In all, seven aiming-points around Calais were to be targeted in the presence of twenty-four 8 Group Lancasters and thirty-five Oboe Mosquitos, and three aiming points, 12, 17 and 16, were assigned to 1 Group forces respectively of thirty-nine, forty-one and forty Lancasters. The fifteen-strong 103 Squadron element departed Elsham Wolds between 08.46 and 09.11 with F/Ls Hague and MacLachlan the senior pilots on duty and climbed out through the ten-tenths cloud that lay over the entire route with tops at 6,000 feet. The crews of F/Os Knott and Vernieuwe turned back early with engine and bomb sight issues, leaving the others to head to what clues suggest was aiming point 16. As they crossed the Kent coast, the Master Bomber issued instructions to descend to the cloud base at 5,000 feet, and they actually broke cloud at 5,500 feet, where visibility was excellent. This allowed ample opportunity to prepare for the bombing run and the aiming-points were identified visually before being marked with green and red TIs. The greens were observed to have fallen to the north-west of the aiming point and the reds to the west, but the 103 Squadron crews ignored both and bombed visually from 4,500 to 5,500 feet between 10.25 and 10.31. The bombing was both accurate and concentrated, and by the end of the attack, the target was concealed by rising smoke and dust.

The final operations to clear the enemy from the Calais area took place on the 28th, and involved 494 aircraft from 1, 3, 6 and 8 Groups, which were assigned to four positions around the port and six coastal batteries at Cap Gris-Nez. 1 Group contributed eighty Lancasters, forty each from 12 and 13 Bases to target aiming points 18 and 8, and the eight representing 103 Squadron were loaded with the usual thirteen 1,000 and four 500 pounders before departing Elsham Wolds between 07.45 and 08.09 with no senior pilots on duty. They flew out under clear skies until some five miles short of the French coast, where they were greeted by nine to ten-tenths cloud with tops at between 3,000 and 8,000 feet. Both 1 Group elements were instructed to orbit out to sea while the Master Bombers assessed the situation, and orders were issued at 09.36 and 09.48 to go home. At least, this time, the A-O-C decreed that the sorties should stand as completed. The final attacks on enemy positions took place that evening, some of them successfully, and the German garrison surrendered to Canadian ground forces soon afterwards. There was much to do to clear and repair the ports at Le Havre, Boulogne and Calais, and the port of Antwerp also needed to be liberated to speed up the supply of equipment to the front for the push into Germany.

During the course of another hectic month, the squadron operated on sixteen occasions against eighteen targets including three separate gardens in one night and launched 222 sorties without loss.

October 1944

Having now discharged his primary obligation to SHAEF, Harris would turn his attention once more fully towards industrial Germany, with a particular emphasis on oil production. He was about to launch a second Ruhr offensive and had at his disposal a massive force in which each individual group had the potential to lay waste to an entire city in one attack. The independent 5 Group had been delivering hammer blows for months and soon, in mid-month, 3 Group would be handed a measure of autonomy in the form of the G-H bombing system, which they were to employ to great effect for the remainder of the war, principally against oil and communications targets. A theme running throughout October would be a campaign against the island of Walcheren in the Scheldt estuary, where heavy gun emplacements were barring the approaches to the much-needed port of Antwerp some forty miles upstream. Attempts to bomb these positions in September had proved unsuccessful, and it was decided to flood the land, both to inundate the batteries, and to render the terrain difficult to defend when the ground forces moved in.

A force of 252 Lancasters was assembled from the ranks of 1, 5 and 8 Groups and made ready on the 3rd to attack the seawalls at Westkapelle, the most westerly point of the island.

Eight waves of thirty aircraft each were to attack at fifteen-minute intervals, with the Tallboy-carrying Lancasters of 617 Squadron standing off to be called in only if required. 1 Group contributed 120 Lancasters, which were to form waves five to eight, 12 and 14 Bases constituting one wave each and 13 Base two. 103 Squadron loaded each of its thirteen Lancasters with a cookie, eight 1,000 pounders and a single 500 pounder, and sent them on their way from Elsham Wolds between 12.50 and 13.03 with W/C St John and S/L Van Rolleghem the senior pilots on duty. At The Wash, they encountered layers of up to eight-tenths cloud between 4,000 and 9,000 feet, which persisted all the way to the target and prompted the Master Bomber to bring them down to 5,000 feet, where the visibility was good. The target was clearly visible on approach and the marking punctual but requiring corrections from the Master Bomber, and within two minutes of the start of the 12 Base attack at 14.00, water was observed to be seeping through the dike. By 14.10, a clear breach had opened, and the water was spreading into the outskirts of Westkapelle village as the 103 Squadron elements carried out their attacks from 4,000 to 6,500 feet between 14.16 and 14.21, leaving a hole in the wall that would be extended to a width of some one hundred yards by those following behind. In the event, 617 Squadron was not required and was able to take its precious and very expensive Tallboys home.

While a 5 Group force carried out a scattered attack on Wilhelmshaven on the morning of the 5th, 531 other aircraft of 1, 3 and 8 Groups were being prepared for a two-phase operation that night against Saarbrücken in south-west-central Germany, the first attack on this city since September 1942. It was in response to a request from the American Third Army, which was advancing towards the German frontier in that region. The purpose of the first phase, to be delivered by 184 Lancasters of 3 Group and a sprinkling of 101 Squadron ABC Lancasters, was to hit the marshalling yards to cut enemy rail communications, while the second phase, by 239 Lancasters of 1 Group two hours later was to be directed at the city. 8 Group's ninety-six Lancasters and twenty Mosquitos were to be divided equally between the two phases to establish and maintain the aiming-points. Each of 103 Squadron's twenty-three Lancasters was loaded with a cookie and fourteen Type 14 cluster bombs before departing Elsham Wolds between 18.08 and 19.13 with S/L Van Rolleghem the senior pilot on duty. They began the Channel crossing at Worthing and made landfall on the French coast at Le Treport, having lost F/L Garton and crew by this stage to an engine issue. The outward route was characterized by eight-tenths low cloud as far as 6°E, at which point it dissipated to leave a thin veil over the target area with haze below. Illuminating flares at 22.23 were followed by cascading red and green TIs, at which the 103 Squadron crews aimed their bombs from 14,000 to 16,500 feet between 22.29 and 22.49. Several large explosions were witnessed, a particularly large one occurring at 22.45, from which smoke rose to 12,000 feet, and the city was well alight as the last of the bombers turned away to leave a glow in the sky visible for a hundred miles. Local reports revealed that the railway lines had been cut to stop all through traffic, and 5,882 houses had been destroyed, largely in the Altstadt and Malstatt districts, but the relatively modest death toll of 344 people suggested that what was now a front-line city, had been partially evacuated.

From this point until the end of the war, German towns and cities were to be subjected to a new and terrible bomber offensive, and the opening rounds of a new Ruhr offensive began on the 6th with daylight attacks on the Ruhr-Benzin A G and Hydrierwerke-Scholven oil plants at Sterkrade-Holten and Scholven-Buer respectively by a combined 4 Group Halifax force of 254 aircraft. Later, 3, 6 and 8 Groups assembled a force of 523 aircraft to attack Dortmund, while 5 Group had its own non-Ruhr target and prepared 237 Lancasters and seven Mosquitos for what would prove to be the thirty-second and final raid of the war on the city of Bremen. A signal to all stations from Bomber Command HQ on this day brought the news of a reduction in the length of a tour from thirty-five to thirty-three sorties, and this would be an unexpected bonus for some crews, who could spend the evening celebrating in the mess rather than exposing themselves to risk over Germany. However, this was not the final word on the length of a tour, which would take on the characteristics of an elastic band.

1 Group was fully rested when orders were received on the 7th to prepare for daylight attacks on the German frontier towns of Cleves (Kleve) and Emmerich. These were prompted by the failure of Operation Market Garden, which had left the Allied right flank exposed and vulnerable to a German counter-attack. Five miles apart and separated by the Rhine, both would face large forces, Cleves of 351 Halifaxes and Lancasters from 3, 4 and 8 Groups and Emmerich of 340 Lancasters and ten Mosquitos from 1, 3 and 8 Groups. 1 Group contributed 254 Lancasters, among them the first to represent 153 Squadron, while twenty-one 103 Squadron aircraft were loaded with a cookie and sixteen SBCs of 4lb incendiaries, before departing Elsham Wolds between 11.43 and 12.27 with four pilots of flight lieutenant rank leading the way, including two F/Ls Henry. They flew out over Cromer with eight to ten-tenths cloud beneath, which lifted at the Dutch coast to allow them to map-read from the Hague area to the target, following the course of the Rhine into the built-up area of the town, where the inland docks were clearly visible. Red and Green TIs marked out the aiming point, and the 103 Squadron crews carried out their attacks visually in accordance with the Master Bomber's instructions from 10,500 to 13,000 feet between 14.19 and 14.30. Many explosions were observed, one at 14.28 sending a pall of black smoke skyward, probably from one of the oil storage facilities located in the town, and with TIs no longer visible, crews were instructed to aim at the smoke, which had reached 12,000 feet as the last of the bombers turned away. The defenders responded with accurate predicted flak, and three aircraft were seen to go down during the course of the attack. Reconnaissance confirmed the outstanding success of the operation, which destroyed more than 2,400 buildings and damaged nearly seven hundred others and local sources reported a civilian death toll of 641 along with ninety-six military personnel.

It was on this day that 15 Base came into being with the re-opening for business of its main station at Scampton, now famous as the launch pad for 617 Squadron's Operation Chastise carried out against the Ruhr Dams in May 1943. Then a 5 Group station, it had closed in August 1943 for the laying of concrete runways and had since been transferred to 1 Group. The newly formed 153 Squadron would transfer there from Kirmington eight days hence, and satellite stations at Dunholme Lodge, Fiskerton and Hemswell would also welcome further new squadrons before the end of the month as 1 Group expanded.

The 11th brought operations by 1 and 5 Groups against coastal batteries in the Scheldt estuary, at Fort Fredrick Hendrik at Breskens on the southern bank of the Western Schelde for 1 Group and at Flushing across the water on Walcheren for 5 Group. There were two aiming points for 1 Group, divided equally between 150 Lancasters, forty provided by 12

Base, sixty-two by 13 Base and forty-eight by 14 Base. It was a day of low cloud and drizzle as the fourteen 103 Squadron Lancasters departed Elsham Wolds in two phases between 14.30 and 15.39 with the newly promoted S/L Hague the senior pilot on duty and each Lancaster carrying thirteen 1,000 and four 500 pounders. As they approached the target area, the Master Bomber was contending with a wedge of cloud over aiming point A at between 2,500 and 6,000 feet, and at 15.59, he instructed the crews to orbit over the sea and await instructions, which came at 16.35 with the order to abandon their sorties and take their bombs home. One crew from another squadron did bomb after hearing no instructions and finding a gap in the clouds. Conditions were more favourable at aiming point B, where the Master Bomber called the bombers down to 4,000 feet and six from 103 Squadron attacked from 4,000 to 5,500 feet between 16.51 and 16.54. The 5 Group effort across the water to the north was also concluded without problem. Those whose sorties had to be aborted were nevertheless able to count it towards the completion of a tour.

The operation was repeated on the following morning in two phases involving forty and thirty-seven Lancasters, seven of them provided by 103 Squadron, and as usual for daylight operations, they would be well protected by a strong fighter escort. They departed Elsham Wolds between 06.24 and 06.47 with F/Ls Birch, A J Henry and MacLachlan the senior pilots on duty and flew out over cloud that gradually gave way to clear skies in the target area. The aiming point was identified without difficulty, and the 103 Squadron crews delivered their thirteen 1,000 and four 500 pounders each visually from 8,000 to 9,500 feet between 08.14 and 08.18 with sufficient accuracy to contribute to the destruction of two of the four gun positions.

The 14th was the day on which were fired the opening salvoes of Operation Hurricane, a terrifying demonstration to the enemy of the overwhelming superiority of the Allied air forces ranged against it. Bomber Command ordered a maximum effort from all but 5 Group to attack Duisburg, for which 1,013 Lancasters, Halifaxes and Mosquitos answered the call. The American 8th Air Force would also be in business on this day, targeting the Cologne area further south with 1,250 bombers escorted by 749 fighters. 1 Group briefed 245 crews for three of five aiming points, 183 for aiming point P, twelve for aiming point Q and fifty to attack the Thyssen steel works. 103 Squadron filled the bomb bays of its twenty-two Lancasters with a variety of bomb loads, fourteen with a cookie and fourteen Type-14 cluster bombs, five with a cookie and nine SBCs each of 4lb and 30lb incendiaries and three with thirteen 1,000 and four 500 pounders. They departed Elsham Wolds between 06.00 and 07.10 with F/Ls Birch, both Henrys and MacLachlan the senior pilots on duty and flew out over Cromer on course for the Belgian coast near Zeebrugge. The giant force picked up an RAF fighter escort as it made its way to the target, and at the same time lost the four 103 Squadron crews of F/L Birch and F/Os Brown, McLetchie and Scott to engine issues. The vanguard arrived over the western edge of the Ruhr to find drifting cloud in layers at between 8,000 and 14,000 feet, which prevented the Master Bomber from identifying aiming-point P. He instructed the main force crews at 08.42 to bomb the built-up area, only for the cloud to part briefly five minutes later for one minute only and allow him to redirect them to the aiming-point. The 103 Squadron crews carried out their attacks visually from 18,000 to 19,000 feet between 08.45 and 08.53, aiming at the built-up area generally in accordance with the Master Bomber's instructions. It was a similar story at the other aiming-points, and 4,500 tons of high-explosives and incendiaries fell into the city to cause unimaginable destruction, to which would be added that night.

A force of 1,005 aircraft was assembled during the day to continue Duisburg's ordeal that night, and 103 Squadron weighed in with twenty-one Lancasters in an overall 1 Group contribution of 217, 118 assigned to aiming-point Q, sixty-two to aiming point R and thirty-seven to aiming point S. Five of the 103 Squadron aircraft received a bomb load of a cookie and a dozen SBCs of 4lb cluster bombs and 4lb incendiaries, while the remainder each carried a dozen 1,000 and four 500 pounders, all of which was lifted into the air between 21.53 and 22.39 with S/L Hague the senior pilot on duty. They were bound for aiming point "Q" and flew out in fine conditions via a somewhat circuitous route according to the ORB that took them over Beachy Head before turning sharply towards the French coast to make landfall at Cayeux-sur-Mer. The crews of F/L Butts and F/O Durrant dropped out with engine issues, leaving the others to arrive at the target under almost clear skies and find it still burning from the earlier attack. They aimed at the plentiful red TIs from 19,500 to 20,500 feet between 01.28 and 01.37 and observed a large red explosion at 01.34, before turning away to leave a beacon visible from 150 miles away to draw the rest of the force on. The total weight of high explosives and incendiaries delivered in the two raids by the 2,018 participating aircraft amounted to 9,000 tons, and this massive effort in fewer than twenty-four hours was achieved without a contribution from 5 Group, which took advantage of the activity over the Ruhr to finally deliver a devastating attack on the northern city of Braunschweig.

There was no immediate respite from operations as preparations were put in hand on the 15th to attack Wilhelmshaven that night. Crews would have done their best to catch up on sleep as the work of the day went on around them, and some of those who had landed at dawn were up, briefed and fed in time to join others for an early evening take-off in an overall force of 506 aircraft drawn from all but 5 Group on what would turn out to be the last of fourteen major raids on this naval and ship-building port. 1 Group contributed seventy Lancasters to the main event, six belonging to 103 Squadron, four of which were loaded with a dozen 1,000 and four 500 pounders and the others with a cookie and an assortment of cluster bombs and incendiaries. They departed Elsham Wolds between 17.25 and 17.38 with S/L Hague the senior pilot on duty and flew out over Mablethorpe under clear skies until the midpoint of the North-Sea crossing, when, according to some, cloud gradually built-up to ten-tenths thin stuff with a base at around 12,000 feet. Typically, there was no agreement as to the conditions, and some crews reported clear skies with haze or cirrus cloud at between 16,000 and 19,000 feet, through which the red and green TIs could be seen and their accuracy confirmed by H2S, while the 8 Group ORB recorded that it was impossible to make out ground features from above 12,000 feet. What may have been spoof green TIs were reported some five miles to the west and north-west of the target, and these attracted some bomb loads. The 103 Squadron crews delivered their payloads on red and/or green TIs from 13,000 to 20,000 feet between 19.43 and 19.57 and observed little of the outcome. The bombing appeared to be scattered, and this was largely confirmed by local sources, which named only the Rathaus (Town Council HQ) as completely destroyed.

A major step forward in Bomber Command operations came with the virtual independence of 3 Group, beginning on the morning of the 18th after a year of trials with the G-H bombing system. This mirrored to an extent the American method of releasing bombs on observing the leader's fall away, but the RAF system was equally effective at night. The first massed live trial took place against the small city of Bonn, situated some twenty miles to the south-east of Cologne, which had little previous damage to cloud the assessment of the G-H performance. The operation was not entirely successful, but time and practice would lead to a highly effective means of attacking precision targets like oil refineries and marshalling yards in particular, and this would ease the pressure on 8 Group.

There were two major operations on the night of the 19/20th, both over southern Germany, one by 5 Group on Nuremberg, and the other by 565 aircraft of 1, 3, 6 and 8 Groups, on Stuttgart. The latter was to be a standard city-busting raid to be conducted in two waves, separated by four-and-a-half hours, for which 1 Group detailed 251 Lancasters, 134 to attack aiming point D and 117 to target aiming point E. 103 Squadron loaded seven of its eighteen Lancasters with a cookie and twelve SBCs of 4lb incendiaries each and sent them on their way from Elsham Wolds between 16.50 and 17.03 with F/Ls Butts and Garton the senior pilots on duty. F/O Vernieuwe and crew turned back as the others flew out via Beachy Head and Cayeux-sur-Mer over cloud, which persisted all the way across France as far as the target, where it topped out at up to 12,000 feet and required the Path Finder crews to employ H2S to establish their positions. The red and green TIs disappeared quickly into the white stuff to leave a faint, reflected glow, forcing the Master Bomber to call for skymarking. The red Wanganui flares with yellow stars fell with a reasonable degree of concentration and continuity from 20.28, and the 103 Squadron crews delivered their attacks from 14,500 to 16,000 feet between 20.32 and 20.40 after confirming their positions by H2S. A 3 Group crew described the target area as glowing as bright as day, and reported a white explosion at 20.44, while others observed black smoke emerging through the cloud tops and the glow of fires below.

The second wave element of eleven 103 Squadron Lancasters took off between 21.00 and 21.47 with S/L Hague the senior pilot on duty and each crew sitting on nine 1,000 and four 500 pounders. The effort had been reduced by two after F/O Farris had swung on take-off, and by the time he was ready to go again, it was too late, and another crew's participation was scrubbed through technical problems. They followed the same route as the first wave and were drawn on to the aiming point by the glow of fires beneath the ten-tenths cloud that topped out at 12,000 feet. Time-on-target was 00.52 to 01.10, and the attack proceeded much as that delivered earlier, the 103 Squadron crews aiming at TIs from 14,500 to 19,000 feet between 00.53 and 01.10. It was not possible to assess what was happening on the ground, but clear evidence of fire and a large explosion at 01.05 indicated a successful outcome, which local sources confirmed. The bombing had been scattered across the city and outlying communities and had caused widespread damage, with the important Bosch factory mentioned among industrial concerns to sustain damage.

The Hurricane force had lain dormant since Duisburg, but was roused from its sleep on the 23rd, when Essen was posted as the target that evening for a record 1,055 aircraft carrying 4,538 tons of bombs, more than 90% of which was high explosive. Once again, this massive effort would be achieved without the involvement of 5 Group, which would be enjoying a night off. 1 Group detailed 237 Lancasters, of which eighteen were made ready by 103 Squadron, fifteen loaded with a cookie, five 1,000 and eight 500 pounders and the others with a cookie and incendiaries. They departed Elsham Wolds between 15.55 and 16.35 with F/Ls Garton and D A Henry the senior pilots on duty and climbed out into scattered cloud before heading south to exit the English coast over Hastings on course for the French coast, from where they were to thread their way between the flak hotspots of Cologne and Mönchengladbach. The cloud thickened over the Channel until the tops were at 23,000 feet, and, by the time the target hove into view, the cloud had become ten-tenths up to 14,000 feet. The Path Finders had prepared a ground and skymarking plan, and after the Oboe TIs had been swallowed up by the cloud, red skymarker flares were released at 19.28 to be followed by greens three minutes later. The 103 Squadron crews carried out their attacks on both red and green skymarkers from 18,500 to 20,500 feet between 19.29 and 19.52 and found it impossible to observe the fall of the bombs, but an intense glow on the cloud told its own story that there was still plenty of combustible material in the tortured city. Local reports from Essen confirmed the destruction of 607 buildings and a further eight hundred seriously damaged along with a death toll of 667 people.

Harris had not yet done with his old enemy, and ordered another attack, this time by daylight on the 25th, for which 771 aircraft were made ready, including a 1 Group contribution of 229 Lancasters for aiming points J, the Krupp district, and G, the general built-up area. 103 Squadron made ready nineteen Lancasters, fifteen loaded with eleven 1,000 and four 500 pounders and the rest with a cookie and incendiaries and they departed Elsham Wolds between 12.30 and 13.08 with W/C St John and S/L Hague the senior pilots on duty. After climbing out they headed for Bradwell Bay on the Essex coast and made landfall near Knokke, before traversing Belgium to enter Germany near Aachen and proceed to the target in cloudy, but quite favourable weather conditions. They encountered ten-tenths cloud with tops at between 6,000 and 12,000 feet during the run-up to the target, but isolated breaks appeared, one a mile wide, which allowed crews to assess the accuracy of the red and yellow TIs in relation to the Krupp complex. The master Bomber ordered the red TIs to be ignored in favour of the yellows, which appeared to be a little to the north of the aiming-point, before a massive explosion close by at 15.29 created a pall of smoke, which the Master Bomber was then able to employ as the focus for the rest of the bombing. W/C St John, F/L Birch and F/O Cartwright bombed visually through gaps in the cloud, while the remainder of the 103 Squadron crews aimed at the skymarkers from 15,000 to 19,500 feet between 15.30 and 15.51, and all returned safely to make their reports. Many bomb bursts and volumes of smoke were evident through the clouds, and it was clear to all that another devastating blow had been visited upon the city, which had, by now, lost its status as a major centre of war production. Local reports confirmed the destruction of 1,163 buildings, almost twice the number resulting from the larger attack thirty-six hours earlier, and the death toll was also greater at 820 people. The Krupp complex was in a state of paralysis, and other than steelworks and coal mines, the majority of industry had been dispersed to other regions of Germany, robbing Essen of its status as a major centre of arms production.

On the following evening, the crews of S/L Van Rolleghem and F/L Birch were among ten from 13 Base assigned to mining duties in the Rosemary garden in Heligoland Bight, and departed Elsham Wolds at 17.16 and 17.21 respectively. They flew out over Mablethorpe and found the garden area under ten-tenths cloud with a base at 3,000 feet and delivered their mines by H2S from 11,500 and 12,000 feet at 19.35 and 19.50. F/L Birch's first run had been made ineffective by a faulty release switch, and on his second run he was attacked by a night-fighter, but the six mines were delivered according to brief, and he and his crew arrived home at 21.34 without damage. This was the final sortie of S/L Van Rolleghem's third tour, during which he had undertaken seventy operations in the space of eighteen months and would be awarded a DSO to go alongside his DFC. He was posted to the RAF College at Cranwell for a short spell and would return to his family in Belgium on Christmas Day.

On the morning of the 28th, 4 Group dispatched a main force of 155 Halifaxes to join forces with eighty-six Lancasters and thirty-six Mosquitos of 8 Group to continue the assault on the defences on the island of Walcheren. While that operation was in progress, preparations for the first of a three-raid mini-campaign against Cologne were already in hand. The last time that the Command had targeted Cologne in such a way was in June/July 1943, when three raids had been mounted over the course of ten nights, resulting in the destruction of 11,000 buildings, 5,500 fatalities and 350,000 people being rendered homeless. The operation was to be conducted in two phases, with one aiming-point in the district of Müllheim, to the north-east of the city centre, and the other in Zollstock to the south-west. A force of 733 aircraft included a 1 Group contribution of 249 Lancasters for aiming points G and H, 103 Squadron supporting the operation with twenty aircraft, which were loaded with either a cookie and incendiaries or a cookie, five 1,000 and six 500 pounders, before departing Elsham Wolds between 13.04 and 13.38 with S/L Hague the senior pilot on duty.

They headed for Orfordness, where F/O Farris and crew lost an engine but carried on, while F/O Cartwright turned back. The others encountered a weather front over the North Sea on their way to making landfall on the French coast in the Dunkerque region, and pressed on to the target, where six-tenths cloud topped out at around 10,000 feet, enabling some to bomb visually and others on markers from 10,500 to 19,500 feet between 15.45 and 16.10 in the face of an accurate flak barrage that caused damage to a number of aircraft. Fires and copious amounts of smoke followed the bombing, and a suspension bridge over the Rhine collapsed after receiving direct hits. No great concentration of marking was achieved, and there were periods when no flares were visible, during which time, the main force crews targeted the built-up area generally. A few red and green TIs were spotted intermittently, but they were of little use, and the bombing was scattered across the south-western districts of the city. A large explosion was reported at 16.04 following a direct hit on a factory, and smoke was rising through 15,000 feet from the other aiming point as the bombers turned away. The crews of F/L Remy and F/O Alderdice landed with flat tyres and swung off the runway, but there was no further damage and no crew casualties. Despite reservations concerning the quality of some of the bombing, both aiming-points had been devastated, local reports confirming the destruction of 2,239 blocks of flats and fifteen industrial premises, along with many other buildings of a public nature. Severe damage had also been inflicted upon power stations, transportation and railway and river docks installations.

The main theme on the 29th was the push to wrest Walcheren from the hands of the enemy, and 358 aircraft were drawn from 1, 3, 4 and 8 Groups to target eleven aiming-points on the morning of the 29th. 1 Group put up seventy-five Lancasters, twenty-five for each of three aiming points at Domburg on the north-western coast, the five 103 squadron participants departing Elsham Wolds between 11.28 and 11.37 with the two F/Ls Henry the senior pilots on duty and each Lancaster carrying thirteen 1,000 and four 500 pounders. They crossed the English coast at Aldeburgh over ten-tenths cloud, which persisted over the North Sea with tops at around 10,000 feet, but convenient gaps over the target would allow most crews to make a visual identification of their respective aiming point. The 12 Base crews were able initially to make a visual identification of their aiming point, where a red TI was observed to go down at 12.59 and fall into the sea some four hundred yards short. The Master Bomber called the main force in to bomb with a three-second overshoot, but only a proportion of the force had complied before the Master Bomber called a halt and ordered those still carrying bombs to orbit. At this point the cloud rolled in to conceal the ground and the Master Bomber decided to abandon the operation, possibly believing the task had been accomplished.

Fewer difficulties at the 13 and 14 Base aiming points allowed the bombing to go ahead unhindered, the 103 Squadron crews complying with the Master Bomber's instructions and bombing from 7,000 to 7,800 feet between 13.15 and 13.19. The operation was deemed to be a success, and the final operations against Walcheren were undertaken by 5 Group on the 30th, when two forces of fifty-one Lancasters and four Mosquitos each were sent against coastal batteries at Westkapelle and Flushing. Canadian and Scottish ground forces went in on the following day, and a week of heavy fighting preceded the island's capture. Even then, the clearing of mines from the approaches to Antwerp kept the port out of commission for a further three weeks and the first convoy arrived for unloading on the 28th of November.

A force of 905 aircraft was made ready for another massive assault on Cologne on the 30th, for which 1 Group detailed 251 Lancasters, twenty-one of them representing 103 Squadron and loaded with a cookie and either incendiaries or six 1,000 and five 500 pounders. They departed Elsham Wolds between 17.16 and 17.50 with S/L Hague the senior pilot on duty, and climbed away into ten-tenths cloud, which persisted for most of the outward flight via Beachy Head. F/O Wright and crew lost the use of their navigation equipment and turned back, leaving the others to press on over the Channel, where the cloud tops reached 20,000 feet with a bright, full moon above. As the target drew near, the cloud tops lowered to 10,000 to 15,000 feet, into which the red and white marker flares delivered by nine of the Oboe Mosquitos drifted in concentrated fashion. The main force crews confirmed their accuracy by Gee and H2S before carrying out their attacks, those from 103 Squadron delivering their bomb loads from 16,500 to 18,500 feet between 20.58 and 21.22, and although the ground was obscured, the glow in the clouds suggested a successful outcome. A post-raid analysis suspected a scattered attack, but local reports confirmed heavy damage in south-western suburbs, where housing, communications and utilities were the principal casualties.

A force of 493 aircraft from 1, 3, 4 and 8 Groups was made ready on the 31st to complete the series of raids on Cologne, 1 Group providing 219 Lancasters, of which twenty belonged to 103 Squadron. Each received one of the standard bomb loads before departing Elsham Wolds between 17.41 and 18.27 with S/L Hague the senior pilot on duty. They began the Channel crossing at Beachy Head and made their way to the target under another full moon with cloud beneath them at 12,000 feet. The cloud persisted to the target where tops were at 6,000 to 10,000 feet and the attack opened with red and white flares delivered by Oboe Mosquitos at

20.56, which were backed up in what appeared to be concentrated fashion by greens from the heavy marker element. Crews established their positions by Gee and H2S-fix before carrying out their assigned roles, those from 103 Squadron attacking from 16,500 to 19,000 feet between 21.00 and 21.12. Returning crews reported concentrated bombing and a large red glow beneath the clouds as they turned for home but absent from the debriefing process was the predominantly Canadian crew of F/Sgt Cooke RCAF. News soon came through that LL964 had been hit by flak over the target and had struggled on with damaged fuel tanks and rudder controls until reaching Allied-held territory at Namur in Belgium. Five crew members baled out to arrive safely on the ground, while the mid-upper gunner accidentally deployed his chute inside the fuselage, and by the time he located a spare the Lancaster was perilously low. F/Sgt Cooke pulled off a forced-landing, nine miles north-west of Dinant and both emerged unscathed from the wreckage. Sadly, F/Sgt Cooke's skill and courage would not reward him with a long life, although he would receive the CGM for this night's work. Local reports confirmed that the southern districts had received the main weight of bombs, but the reporting system was breaking down and precise details were not forthcoming. It is likely, that the city had been largely evacuated by this stage, and all future operations would be directed at its numerous and extensive marshalling yards.

Earlier in the day 576 Squadron had completed its move from Elsham Wolds to another former 5 Group station at Fiskerton, where it would remain until war's end. During the course of the month 103 Squadron carried out sixteen operations and dispatched 251 sorties, of which nine were abortive, for the loss of a single Lancaster and no crew casualties.

November 1944

As worthwhile targets became more difficult to find in a country so thoroughly destroyed by bombing, smaller, seemingly irrelevant towns and cities began to find themselves in the bomb sights, particularly if they happened to lie in the path of the retreating enemy forces or on a main railway line. Oil was now the overriding priority, and November began with a daylight attack by 5 Group and 8 Group Mosquitos on the Gewerkschaft Rheinpreussen AG plant, located on the west bank of the Rhine opposite Duisburg on the western edge of the Ruhr. The name of this target would strike fear into the hearts of 3 Group crews, who had suffered heavy casualties while attacking the plant during the summer, but it meant nothing to 5 Group crews, who were less familiar with it and would have found the name of Wesseling far more unsettling.

Düsseldorf's turn to face a massive force came on the 2nd, when 992 aircraft were made ready for what would prove to be the final major raid of the war on this much-bombed city, and it was one of those rare occasions when the "Lincolnshire Poachers" were invited to operate with the rest of the Command. 1 Group detailed 252 Lancasters, sixteen of them made ready by 103 Squadron and loaded with either a cookie, six 1,000 and six 500 pounders or a cookie and incendiaries, before departing Elsham Wolds between 16.15 and 16.30 with F/Ls Butts, Garton and Remy the senior pilots on duty. They adopted the circuitous route to the southern Ruhr via Beachy Head and Cayeux-sur-Mer and arrived at the target to encounter clear skies, moonlight and only ground haze to slightly mar the vertical visibility. The moonlight nullified the glare of the searchlights ringing the city, but of greater concern was the heavy flak bursting at 17,000 to 20,000 feet as they ran across the city towards the aiming-point. The attack opened early with red flares and TIs dropped by eight Oboe Mosquitos at 19.05, which enabled the crews to identify the river, railway tracks and built-up area visually, and the heavy marker element maintained the aiming-point throughout the raid with mostly well-placed green TIs. The Elsham Wolds crews carried out their bombing runs from 17,000 to 18,500 feet between 19.12 and 19.37, and by 19.20 it was clear that fires were gaining a hold. Smoke was rising through 10,000 feet as the last crews headed for home with the glow from the burning city remaining visible as far away as Charleroi in Belgium, some 115 miles away. It was established later that five thousand houses had been destroyed, along with many important war-industry factories.

The continuing campaign against Ruhr cities brought Bochum into the spotlight on the 4th, when a force of 749 aircraft was drawn from 1, 4, 6 and 8 Groups, while 5 Group renewed its acquaintance with the Dortmund-Ems Canal, which had been repaired following the successful breaching of its banks near Ladbergen in September. 1 Group detailed 235 Lancasters, the eleven representing 103 Squadron receiving one or other of the standard bomb loads and departing Elsham Wolds between 17.39 and 17.48 with F/L Pamplin the senior pilot on duty. They flew out over Orfordness and lost F/O Alderdice and crew to an undisclosed technical issue within two hours, leaving the others to cross the North Sea to make landfall on the Dutch coast in the vicinity of The Hague. There, they invited the attention of the local flak as they passed by, before pressing on for the remaining 130 miles to the target, which they found to be under a veil of very thin cloud of up to three-tenths at 5,000 feet. Red Oboe TIs were seen to cascade at 19.26, to be followed over the ensuing minutes by greens, and the aiming-point remained well marked for the duration of the attack. The 103 Squadron crews carried out their attacks from 16,000 to 18,500 feet between 19.31 and 19.48, witnessing a number of large explosions, one throwing flame a thousand feet into the air, while a reconnaissance Mosquito crew reported a circular patch of fire and one particularly intense conflagration visible from one hundred miles away. At the Elsham Wolds debriefing, there were reports of a heavy flak barrage and many night-fighters, including jets, and F/O Dale's gunners claimed an unspecified fighter destroyed, while F/O Picot and crew were coned and sustained flak damage but no crew casualties. The success of the operation was confirmed by post-raid reconnaissance and local reports, which confirmed that the city centre and industrial districts had borne the brunt of the attack, with four thousand buildings destroyed or seriously damaged, and almost a thousand people killed. However, the defences demonstrated that they were not yet spent, and brought down twenty-eight aircraft, twenty-three of them Halifaxes.

Bochum's neighbour, Gelsenkirchen, was posted as the target for a two-phase daylight operation on the 6th, for which a force of 738 aircraft was assembled. In the past, it had been the synthetic oil plants that had drawn the bombers on, but this time, part of the force was to attack the built-up area as well as the Nordstern refinery. 1 Group detailed 221 Lancasters, sixteen representing 103 Squadron, which departed Elsham Wolds between 10.49 and 11.49 with S/L Hague the senior pilot on duty and the standard loads in the bomb bays. They adopted a route similar to that for the previous operation and flew into cloud that increased to almost ten-tenths at the Dutch coast. Thereafter, it began to break up to six to eight-tenths at 9,000 feet until a gap appeared right over the target, which enabled the early arrivals to pick out the distinctive L-shaped docks in the Schalke-Nord district to the north-west of the aiming point. Bombing commenced a few minutes early on red and green TIs, the latter assessed by the 35 Squadron Master Bomber, S/L Leicester, as more accurate and he directed the crews towards them at 14.01. However, it wasn't long before thick smoke spread across the area to obscure any sight of the ground, and at 14.06 he instructed the crews to focus on the built-up area generally. The 103 Squadron crews delivered their high explosive and incendiary bomb loads either visually or on red TIs from 17,000 to 20,000 feet between 13.58 and 14.04 in the face of accurate heavy flak, which inflicted damage on a number of aircraft and was probably responsible for the failure to return of three Lancasters and two Halifaxes. Many explosions were witnessed, and the presence of a column of black, oily smoke rising through the cloud tops through 10,000 feet suggested that the Nordstern plant had been hit. The consensus among the crews at debriefing was of a concentrated attack, although it was impossible to make an accurate assessment. Local reports confirmed that a "catastrophe" had befallen the city, and that more than five hundred people had lost their lives.

Within an hour of the last Lancaster returning to Elsham Wolds, six others took off between 18.02 and 18.07 to lay mines in the Rosemary garden in the Heligoland Bight with F/Ls Garton and Remy the senior pilots on duty. They headed out over Mablethorpe, climbing through cloud that thickened over the North Sea before thinning slightly to leave six to eight-tenths in the target area with tops at 9,000 feet. Positions were confirmed by H2S before each crew delivered six mines unopposed into the briefed locations from 11,000 feet between 20.03 and 20.14. They flew home through gale-force winds, which created challenging conditions for landing, and caused NF913 to swing off the runway and sustain damage, but F/L Remy and his crew were unhurt.

The Ruhr oil industry continued to hold the Command's attention on the morning of the 9th, when the target was the Krupp Treibstoffwerke synthetic oil plant at Wanne-Eickel, situated no more than three miles east-north-east of Gelsenkirchen, for which a heavy force of 256 Lancasters was made ready. 1 Group was responsible for 226 of them and 103 Squadron twenty, which all received the same bomb load of a cookie and sixteen 500 pounders before departing Elsham Wolds between 07.31 and 08.06 with S/L Hague the senior pilot on duty. They climbed into clear skies as they headed for Orfordness and found cloud building over the North Sea to ten-tenths with tops at 20,000 feet, which persisted all the way to the eastern Ruhr with tops in places as high as 21,500 feet. There was a gap of clear air between 10,000 and 17,000 feet, but this was of no help, and the Path Finders delivered no markers. Ten minutes before H-Hour the Master Bomber ordered the crews to bomb on H2S, Gee or e.t.a., and the 103 Squadron crews complied from 16,500 to 21,000 feet between 10.40 and 10.49. It was impossible to assess the outcome, but a local report suggests that the bombing almost entirely missed the town.

Attention turned to the Hoesch-Benzin oil plant in the Wambel district of Dortmund on the 11th, for which 1 Group assembled a main force of 183 Lancasters, including fourteen provided by 103 Squadron, which each received a bomb load of a cookie, six 1,000 and six 500 pounders. They departed Elsham Wolds between 15.45 and 15.58 with F/Ls Butt, D A Henry, Holland and Murton the senior pilots on duty and joined up with the rest of the bomber stream on the flight to Berck-sur-Mer via Hastings for the southern approach to the target area. The cloud thickened from 4°E and had become ten-tenths by the time the Ruhr drew near and remained so over the target with tops at 10,000 to 15,000 feet. This provided most unfavourable conditions for the Path Finder marker crews, and those of the main force were left to try to seek out the glow of markers through the cloud or simply bomb on H2S and Gee. The 103 Squadron crews carried out their attacks from 16,500 to 19,500 feet between 19.00 and 19.07, before returning with little idea of where their bombs had fallen. Remarkably, despite the challenges, it seems that the attack was accurate, and local sources confirmed that the oil plant had been severely damaged along with housing and a nearby aerodrome.

The 16th was devoted to the destruction of the three small towns of Heinsberg, Jülich and Düren, located respectively in an arc from north to east of Aachen, and close to the German lines upon which American ground forces were advancing. A total of 1,188 aircraft was detailed, with 1 and 5 Groups providing the main force of 452 Lancasters for the last-mentioned with thirty-three Lancasters and thirteen Mosquitos of 8 Group to provide the marking, while 4 and 6 Groups were to contribute 254 Halifaxes and forty-five Lancasters between them as the main force at Jülich, supported by thirty-three Lancasters and seventeen Mosquitos of 8 Group. This left Heinsberg to be the objective for a G-H raid by 182 Lancasters of 3 Group. Fourteen of 1 Group's 238 Lancasters were provided by 103 Squadron and given either a high explosives bomb load or a cookie and incendiary mix and departed Elsham Wolds between 12.55 and 13.05 with F/Ls Butts, Pamplin, Remy and Riches the senior pilots on duty. They flew out over Bradwell Bay and made landfall on the Belgian coast over ten-tenths cloud, which cleared to three-tenths stratus above 6,000 feet as they approached the aiming-point. A red Oboe TI was dropped right on the mark at 15.26, after which the Master Bomber repeatedly called the main force crews down to 10,000 feet and instructed them to aim for this and, later, red and green TIs, which fell with similar accuracy. Not all complied with the Master Bomber's height instructions, but some from Elsham Wolds did and delivered their loads from 10,000 to 12,000 feet between 15.30 and 15.37, reporting smoke rising through 9,000 feet and drifting across the target area as they turned for home. Most were confident in the success of the attack, and although the majority of photos were unplottable, it was established soon afterwards that the operation had been a complete success at a cost of just three aircraft, and post-raid reconnaissance confirmed that the town had been all-but erased from the map. Local sources provided a death toll in excess of three thousand inhabitants, which proved to be an unnecessary loss of life when unfavourable ground conditions prevented the American advance from succeeding. The other operations were equally effective, although no report emerged from Jülich to provide details.

Briefings took place on 4, 6 and 8 Group stations on the morning of the 18th to inform 479 crews of the details for an attack on the heavily-garrisoned city of Münster, situated some twenty-five miles from the north-eastern edge of the Ruhr. The operation failed to achieve concentration and few details emerged locally to shed light on the outcome. By the time they landed, preparations were already well in hand for a return that evening to the Krupp Treibstoffwerke (fuel works) at Wanne-Eickel, for which a 1 Group main force of 253 Lancasters was assembled and an 8 Group marker element of thirty-two Lancasters and twenty-four Mosquitos. The fifteen 103 Squadron participants each received a load of a cookie and sixteen 500 pounders and departed Elsham Wolds between 15.40 and 15.52 with F/L Murton the senior pilot on duty. They climbed away through poor weather conditions of low cloud and mist and headed south to Beachy Head to begin the Channel crossing, which ended on the French coast south of Berck-sur-Mer under clearing skies.

Shortly after crossing the Rhine, however, a thin layer of stratus slid in at 8,000 feet and remained in place with occasional breaks over the target. Seven of the Mosquitos had laid a "window" screen ahead of the bombers, and four of the Oboe variety delivered red TIs, which were seen to cascade at 18.55 and were followed by others three minutes later and greens at 18.59. Few crews could pick out ground detail, but the red and green TIs were visible through the clouds, and apart from one group of greens, were well placed on the aiming-point. The bombing was focused on the main group of reds and greens, and very soon a large fire developed, which emitted a column of black smoke seemingly from the refinery. The bombers were met by heavy flak in barrage and predicted form as they carried out their attacks, the 103 Squadron crews crossing the aiming-point at 16,000 to 18,500 feet between 19.00 and 19.08. The consensus among returning crews was of a successful operation, photo-reconnaissance revealing fresh damage to the oil plant, and according to local reports, the nearby Hannibal coal mine was destroyed.

The night of the 21/22nd would be one of large-scale activity at numerous locations involving 1,345 sorties. 1 Group assembled a main force of 238 Lancasters to attack the railway yards at Aschaffenburg, situated some twenty miles south-east of Frankfurt, and they would be supported by thirty-six Lancasters and nine Mosquitos of 8 Group. In addition, a dozen 13 Base Lancasters, including five representing 103 Squadron, were assigned to mining duties in the Onion garden in Oslo harbour. Elsewhere, 273 aircraft with a predominantly 6 Group main force were assigned to an oil refinery at Castrop-Rauxel in the Ruhr, while 4 Group focused on a similar target at nearby Sterkrade-Holten as part of an overall force of 270 aircraft. 5 Group would be targeting the Dortmund-Ems and Mittelland Canals further north at Ladbergen and Gravenhorst in two forces with a combined total of 260 aircraft, while small-scale and mining operations took place at a variety of other locations.

103 Squadron made ready sixteen Lancasters for the main event, loading each with a cookie and sixteen 500 pounders and dispatching them and the gardening quintet from Elsham Wolds between 15.31 and 16.13 with F/Ls Murton and Riches the senior pilots on duty among the bombing element and F/Ls D A Henry and Remy leading the miners. After climbing out, they went their separate ways, the miners via Mablethorpe to the North Sea and the bombers to Beachy Head to begin the Channel crossing. Cloud began to build over France and was at ten-tenths with tops at 8,000 to 10,000 feet as the bomber stream reached the target area shortly after 19.00. The Deputy Master Bomber descended to 7,000 feet, but was unable to mark the aiming-point, and the Master Bomber issued instructions for the main force to bomb on navigational aids. Red, green and yellow TIs were spotted by a few of the 103 Squadron crews, but the majority aimed at the glow beneath the clouds from 12,500 to 13,500 feet between 19.15 and 19.23 in accordance with the Master Bomber's instructions. It was impossible to assess the outcome, and it was left to local sources to confirm that fifty bombs had hit the railway yards but had not severed the main access line in and out, while

the main weight of the attack had fallen into the central and northern districts of the town, destroying five hundred houses and seriously damaging three times that number.

Meanwhile, seven hundred miles to the north, the gardeners had benefitted from excellent conditions, which enabled them to establish the drop zone visually, confirm it by H2S and deliver between them twenty-eight 1,800lb and two 1,500lb mines from 11,000 feet between 19.32 and 19.45.

There would be no further operations for the majority of the heavy squadrons over the ensuing six days, despite a number being announced, but then scrubbed, while 3 and 5 Groups went about their business independently. As worthwhile targets became increasingly difficult to find, some seemingly strategically insignificant towns and cities began to find themselves in the bomb-sights. The university city of Freiburg, situated in the south-western corner of Germany with the French and Swiss frontiers to west and south, was believed to be inhabited by German troops preparing to resist the approaching American and French forces some thirty-five miles away, and found itself a target on the night of the 27/28th. 1 Group was now able to call upon the resources of fourteen squadrons with the recent addition of 150 and 170 Squadrons at Fiskerton and Dunholme Lodge respectively, but both soon to take up residence at Hemswell. This enabled a record 292 Lancasters to be assembled in an overall force with 8 Group Lancasters and Mosquitos of 341 aircraft. 103 Squadron's contribution to the main event was twenty-three Lancasters, which received a bomb load either of a cookie, five 1,000 and seven 500 pounders, or a cookie, cluster bombs and incendiaries. They departed Elsham Wolds between 15.43 and 16.08 with no fewer than five pilots of flight lieutenant rank leading the way and set course in clear skies for Orfordness. Cloud began to build over the French coast, and increased to full cover by the German frontier, but dispersed to five to six-tenths, thin and low over the target. The first flares were released at 19.55, and thanks to mobile Oboe stations operating from the liberated countries, Mosquitos were able to deliver red TIs a minute later, which were soon backed up by greens. The Master Bomber's instructions were loud and clear, and, once he had directed the main force crews to aim for the red and green TIs around the aiming-point, 1,900 tons of bombs fell in an orgy of destruction lasting twenty-five minutes. The 103 Squadron crews carried out their attacks almost totally unopposed from 12,000 to 14,500 feet between 20.00 and 20.13, and a reconnaissance Mosquito crew reported a city on fire with smoke rising through 8,000 feet. Local sources would confirm the destruction of two thousand houses and severe damage to 450 others, and a death toll of more than two thousand people with a further four thousand injured and almost nine hundred registered as missing. In contrast, the Bomber Command losses amounted to a single Lancaster.

The final major operation of the month brought a return to the Ruhr, to Dortmund at the eastern end, for which 1 Group put together a main force of 262 Lancasters, twenty-two of them provided by 103 Squadron, with 8 Group adding thirty-two Lancasters and seventeen Mosquitos to take care of the marking. The Elsham Wolds contingent received either an all-high explosives bomb load or a cookie, cluster bomb and incendiary mix and took off between 11.35 and 12.02 with S/L Hague the senior pilot on duty. They climbed into five-tenths cloud, which had dispersed completely by the time they exited the English coast at Orfordness, but built-up again at the enemy coast to become six to eight-tenths in the target area with tops at anywhere from 2,000 to 8,000 feet. The conditions prevented the Master Bomber from identifying the aiming-point, and the combination of sky and ground marking became scattered and sparse, if well-placed, to the extent that it could only be seen from directly above. The Master Bomber had little choice but to instruct the crews to bomb visually or on navigational aids, and the Elsham Wolds crews responded from a uniform 20,000 feet between 14.56 and 15.08. A hostile flak defence inflicted some shrapnel damage, but it was a collision with a 550 Squadron Lancaster over Germany that caused the loss of PB465, which went down almost immediately, taking the lives of the previously-mentioned F/Sgt Cooke CGM RCAF and all but the bomb-aimer, who fell into enemy hands. The other Lancaster managed to limp back to land at Manston. The operation was thought to have been scattered, despite which, local sources confirmed that some fresh damage had occurred.

During the course of the month, the squadron carried out twelve operations and dispatched 177 sorties for the loss of a single Lancaster and its crew.

December 1944

On the 1st of December, W/C St John relinquished command of the squadron and handed the reins over to W/C Duncan MacDonald, who was an officer with no operational experience who would be celebrating his thirty-third birthday ten days hence. W/C St John's posting to the RAF Staff College would take place on the 8th of January. December would follow a similar pattern of operations, with the accent remaining on oil and communications, but with city-busting interspersed. The new month began with a heavy attack on the town of Hagen, situated on the south-eastern edge of the Ruhr, ten miles south of Dortmund. It had never been the subject of a major raid before, and now, on the evening of the 2nd, it faced a force of 504 heavies, predominantly from 4 and 6 Groups, with Path Finder support and seven Lancasters of 101 Squadron to provide RCM cover. The result was a catastrophe for the town, which suffered the destruction of or serious damage to more than sixteen hundred houses and ninety industrial concerns, some of which lost three months production. Among the factories destroyed was one producing accumulator batteries for the new Type XXI U-Boot currently under construction in Hamburg.

The first outing of the month for 103 Squadron was announced on the morning of the 3rd, when ten Lancasters were detailed to join 147 others from 1 Group to act as the main force for an attack on the Urft Dam, situated near Heimbach in the Eifel region of Germany adjoining the Belgian frontier. With American ground forces advancing upon Germany through Belgium, it was thought that the enemy might release large quantities of water to create difficult terrain and bog them down. The 103 Squadron aircraft had fourteen American-built 1,000 pounders winched into their bomb bays and departed Elsham Wolds between 07.30 and 07.38 with F/Ls Henry, Holland, Murton and Pamplin the senior pilots on duty. They climbed away into heavy cloud that hid Orfordness from view, and although it broke up over Belgium to leave almost clear skies, a front materialised as they approached the German frontier at Aachen, and it extended beyond the target area, concealing all ground detail. As it was a precision target, the Master Bomber was left with no option but to abandon the operation at 09.51 and send the aircraft home with their bomb loads intact. There would be further attempts on this target over the ensuing days, the first by 8 Group on the following day, which failed to cause a breach.

On the evening of the 4th, 535 aircraft of 1, 6 and 8 Groups set off for an operation against Karlsruhe in southern Germany, for which 1 Group contributed 259 Lancasters, sixteen of them provided by 103 Squadron and loaded with either thirteen 1,000 pounders or a cookie supplemented by cluster bombs and incendiaries. They departed Elsham Wolds between 16.29 and 16.50 with F/Ls Butts, Pamplin and Riches the senior pilots on duty, and set course via Beachy Head for the French coast near Dieppe. The weather conditions throughout the operation were generally favourable, with cloud building and decreasing in turns across the Channel and France, and on arrival over the target, the crews found nine to ten-tenths white stuff with tops at around 14,000 feet. As they approached, a few crews were able to see red and green TIs through gaps, but the majority had to rely on the glow of greens coming through and confirm their accuracy by means of H2S or Gee. It was difficult to assess what was happening because of a scarcity of red TIs, and, although the greens were plentiful, they were scattered. However, the cloud was moving eastwards, and later arrivals were able to identify the built-up area visually. The 103 Squadron crews delivered their attacks on the evidence of TIs from 17,500 to 19,500 feet between 19.29 and 19.43 and reported fires visible from up to a hundred miles into the homeward flight. It was established ultimately, that severe damage had been inflicted upon the city, particularly in western and southern districts, at a cost of just two aircraft.

This paled into insignificance when compared with 5 Group's simultaneous assault on the virgin town of Heilbronn, situated some fifty miles east-north-east of Karlsruhe and north of Stuttgart. It sat astride the River Neckar and had the misfortune to be served by a north-south railway line, but was otherwise of no genuine strategic importance, and would not have been expecting to be attacked. The aiming-points were the marshalling yards and the town, and by the time that the force retreated westwards into electrical storms, 82% of the city's built-up area was in the process of being destroyed by what probably amounted to a firestorm. The post-war British Bombing Survey estimated 351 acres of destruction, and a death toll of at least seven thousand people.

On the following night, a force of 497 aircraft from 1, 4, 6 and 8 Groups was sent against the town of Soest, situated just to the north of the Ruhr and five miles from the now famous Möhne Reservoir and its rebuilt dam. The 1 Group element was provided by ten ABC Lancasters of 101 Squadron to provide RCM cover. The town contained one of a number of important railway hubs linking the Ruhr with greater Germany that would face attacks until the end of hostilities, and on this night suffered the destruction of a thousand houses mainly in its northern half, where the marshalling yards were situated.

Three major operations were mounted on the night of the 6/7th, against the oil refinery at Leuna (Merseburg) a dozen miles or so west of Leipzig in eastern Germany by 1, 3 and 8 Groups, railway yards at Giessen in west-central Germany by 5 Group, and Osnabrück in the north-west by 4, 6 and 8 Groups. 1 Group contributed 291 Lancasters to the attack on the I G Farbenindustrie A G Merseburg-Leuna refinery, which lay some 250 miles from the Dutch frontier and five hundred miles from the bomber bases of eastern England and was one of many oil plants located in an arc from north to south of Leipzig. 103 Squadron made ready twenty Lancasters in an overall heavy force of 475 of the type, which was unusually large for an oil target and reflected the importance of this particular one in the context of the oil offensive. The Elsham Wolds contingent took to the air between 16.34 and 16.52 with S/L Hague the senior pilot on duty and Lancasters carrying one of three loads, a cookie, three 1,000 and five 500 pounders, a cookie and twelve 500 pounders or a cookie and cluster bombs.

They climbed away into complete cloud cover over England and passed unobserved from the ground over Newhaven on their way to the French coast, from where patchy cloud accompanied them along the route to the German frontier south of Aachen. It was during this segment of the outward flight that F/O Stepharnoff and crew lost the use of their navigational equipment and had to turn back. The cloud built again as the bomber stream undertook the 250-mile final leg across Germany, but the Path Finders had prepared for "Newhaven" marking (ground), with emergency Wanganui (skymarking) if required, and this proved to be the case as ten-tenths stratocumulus was unexpectedly encountered over the target area with tops at 10,000 feet. The early arrivals observed TIs cascading into it, but they were not visible by the time the main force crews came in to bomb, and the Path Finders quickly changed to skymarking. Release-point flares were in plentiful supply, their accuracy checked by H2S, and in the absence of instructions from the Master Bomber, they provided the main reference for bombing. The skymarkers were plentiful, continuous and concentrated throughout the raid, which took place in the face of a strong flak defence that, fortunately, was exploding below the bombers' flight level. The Elsham Wolds crews carried out their attacks from 17,500 to 20,500 feet between 20.37 and 20.56 and returned to report large explosions and the glow of fires for around sixty miles into the return journey. Absent from debriefing was the crew of F/O Johnson RCAF in NG276, which had been hit by flak over the target and exploded with fatal consequences for the occupants. Post-raid reconnaissance confirmed much damage to the oil plant, but it would continue to feature on the target list right through to the final month of the bombing war.

S/L Butler was posted in from 71 Base on the 9th, and he would be allowed time to settle in before undertaking his first operation. He would almost certainly have sat in on the next briefing at Elsham Wolds, which took place on the 12th and provided seventeen crews with the details of that night's operation to Essen by a force of 540 aircraft drawn from 1, 4 and 8 Groups. The 1 Group contribution amounted to 266 Lancasters, those representing 103 Squadron loaded with a cookie, fifteen 500 pounders and a Munroe bomb, the last mentioned a weapon with a shaped charge designed to focus the detonation and achieve greater penetration. As they taxied to the runway, W/O McArthur's tailwheel broke, which left sixteen to take off between 16.10 and 16.24 with five pilots of flight lieutenant rank leading the way. They climbed into poor weather conditions with low cloud, which persisted as they passed out over Beachy Head and set course for the French coast on the southerly route to the central Ruhr. While they were heading north over Germany between Cologne and Düsseldorf, the cloud began to clear, but built-up again south of the Ruhr to leave the target completely obscured.

The Path Finders were a little late in opening the attack, and a few red TIs were seen to enter the cloud tops at up to 16,000 feet and disappear, whereupon red and yellow release-point flares were dropped at 19.27 to be followed by greens three minutes later. Initially, they appeared to be scattered, but soon became plentiful and concentrated, although some crews would complain that they ignited too high, in the region of 18,000 to 20,000 feet. Generally, however, the marking and bombing were accurate, and many large explosions lit up the clouds, followed by a column of black smoke rising up to 20,000 feet. The 103 Squadron crews bombed from 17,000 to 20,000 feet between 19.31 and 19.51, before returning with the general opinion that the attack had been scattered and probably ineffective. In fact, it had been very successful, and had caused much damage to residential and industrial buildings, including the Krupp complex, which was now effectively finished as a major producer of war materials. It is believed that the rear gunner in ME649 had been wounded and was unable to abandon the doomed Lancaster with the rest of the crew, which left F/O Picot with no option but to attempt a forced-landing. Sadly, both lost their lives, while the five survivors fell into enemy hands to spend the final few months of the war in captivity.

On the following night, 103 and 166 Squadrons loaded five Lancasters each with five 1,500lb parachute mines to send to one of the many Silverthorn gardens in the Kattegat region of the Baltic, specifically in Aarhus Bay. The Elsham Wolds quintet of S/L Hague, F/Ls Henry and Remy and F/Os Cartwright and Dobson took off between 15.18 and 15.25 and set course via Mablethorpe for landfall on the west coast of Jutland. Weather conditions were not ideal, and they were greeted in the target area by ten-tenths cloud with tops at 6,000 feet, through which they delivered their stores by H2S from 11,000 and 15,000 feet between 18.34 and 18.43. They were diverted to Lossiemouth on return, where they reported uneventful and unopposed sorties.

1 and 6 Groups combined on the 15th to prepare a main force of 327 Lancasters to send to Ludwigshafen to bomb the city's northern half and the nearby town of Oppau, both locations containing an important I G Farben factory, which were engaged in the production of synthetic oil and relying heavily upon slave labour. 1 Group contributed 224 Lancasters, of which ten belonged to 103 Squadron and received a bomb load each of a cookie with four 1,000 and seven 500 pounders and a Munroe bomb. They departed Elsham Wolds between 14.26 and 14.34 with F/Ls Butts, Holland and Murton the senior pilots on duty and flew south to begin the Channel crossing in the Newhaven area. Cloud came and went as the bomber stream traversed enemy territory until fifty miles from the target, when a bank of thick stuff appeared with tops at 20,000 feet. Fortunately, it ended abruptly just a short distance from the target, to leave clear skies and visibility marred only by ground haze. It seems that a tail-wind had propelled some aircraft to the target a little ahead of schedule, and they had to orbit to await the arrival of the Path Finder element, which dispensed the first red TIs punctually at 18.26 and backed them up with greens soon afterwards. Release-point flares were also in evidence, but they were ignored in favour of the clearly-observed TIs, which the 103 Squadron crews bombed from 17,000 to 19,000 feet between 18.20 and 18.34. All returned safely to report a concentrated raid with explosions, green and orange smoke, and fires visible for a hundred miles. The Ludwigshafen I G Farben factory sustained severe damage and fires, and the Oppau plant was put out of action completely, all for the loss of a single Lancaster.

It was on the 16th that German ground forces began a new offensive in the Ardennes, in an attempt to break through the American lines and reach the port of Antwerp in what would become known as the Battle of the Bulge. Another virgin target was the city of Ulm, situated on the Danube to the south-east of Stuttgart and west of Augsburg in southern Germany. It was similar in nature to the recently-bombed Heilbronn, and because of the catastrophic raid visited upon that city, the local Gauleiter had urged the women and children to evacuate the inner city urgently. Plans were put in place to begin evacuation on Monday the 18th, so that Advent could be observed on the Sunday, but something caused a change of plan and loudspeaker vans toured the city on Sunday the 17th, urging the population to leave at once. It proved to be a fortuitous move. Unlike Heilbronn, Ulm contained industry, including the important Magirus-Deutz and Kässbohrer lorry factories, and there were also military barracks and depots.

A main force of 263 Lancasters of 1 Group contained fifteen representing 103 Squadron, and they would benefit from the marking and support of fifty-four Lancasters and thirteen Mosquitos from 8 Group. The Elsham Wolds Lancasters were each loaded with a cookie, 420 x 4lb incendiaries and a Munroe bomb and took off between 15.10 and 15.40 led by five pilots of flight lieutenant rank. They encountered cloudy, but fairly good conditions as they headed south to rendezvous with the rest of the bomber stream as it crossed Newhaven on course for the French coast south of Dieppe, but found the weather deteriorating as they traversed France and much of the outward flight was spent in cloud. The skies became clear at the Rhine to leave excellent visibility, which allowed the crews to map-read their way to the target, until some twenty miles short, when a layer of thin stratus slid in with tops at 2,000 feet to completely obscure the ground. The Path Finders opened the attack with red TIs at 19.24, but they quickly became swallowed up in the cloud or were extinguished by the heavy snow on the ground. Release-point (Wanganui) flares were dropped at the same time, and at 19.31, the 35 Squadron Master Bomber, F/L Cook, ordered these to be bombed and orbited the target from H-3 to H+14, trying to persuade the main force crews to comply and not undershoot on a bunch of errant incendiaries. The 103 Squadron crews attacked from 10,500 to 12,500 feet between 19.32 and 19.43 and played their part in an accurate and concentrated raid, which resulted in fierce fires consuming a square kilometre of the city's built-up area. It would be established later that almost 82% of the buildings had sustained damage to some extent, including both lorry factories and twenty-seven other industrial premises. There is no question that the evacuation saved many thousands of lives and restricted the civilian death toll to around six hundred.

Operations were not yet over for the night of the 17/18th, and it was well into the early hours of the 18th when a force of 523 aircraft from 4, 6 and 8 Groups departed their stations for Duisburg, and arrived to find it completely hidden beneath ten-tenths cloud with tops at 6,000 to 8,000 feet. Two aiming-points were marked by Oboe Mosquitos, but the TIs disappeared into the cloud to leave a glow as the only reference point for bombing, and most crews confirmed their positions by H2S and Gee before releasing their loads. Despite doubts about the effectiveness of the bombing, 346 houses were destroyed and more than five hundred seriously damaged, and the likelihood is that industry also suffered to some extent.

The city of Bonn would become prominent after the war as the capital city of Western Germany, and had received a number of small-scale visits from the Command during 1944. It was now to be the objective for seventy-seven Lancasters of 1 Group on the 21st, with Path Finder Lancasters and Mosquitos to carry out the marking of the railway yards. It had been intended to send a force of 260 Lancasters but doubts about the state of the weather for their return prompted a reduction in the force to involve just 12 Base squadrons and six from 14 Base's 101 Squadron to provide RCM cover. Heavy cloud over the target created an expectation of failure, and post raid-reconnaissance confirmed that the marshalling yards had not been touched. While this operation was in progress, twenty Lancasters from 12 and 13 Bases were engaged in mining duties, according to the 460 Squadron ORB in the Geranium garden in the Bay of Pomerania, while the 103 Squadron record states Stettin Bay. There is no Stettin Bay on the map, but a large body of water between the coastal region at Swinemünde south to Stettin itself called the Stettiner Haff, provided a gateway for shipping to the Baltic, and perhaps this was the destination for the six 103 Squadron crews that departed Elsham Wolds between 15.15 and 15.18 with F/Ls Henry and Remy the senior pilots on duty. They set course over Mablethorpe for landfall on the western coast of Jutland and enjoyed favourable weather conditions, which deteriorated somewhat, before improving again to provide fair to good visibility in the target area. The mines were delivered into the briefed locations from 12,000 feet between 19.34 and 19.44, before all returned safely to a diversion airfield at East Fortune in Scotland.

The dismantling of Germany's railway infrastructure continued on the 22nd with the launching of an attack by a 1 Group main force of 156 Lancasters from all but 12 Base on the Koblenz-Mosel marshalling yards located some thirty miles south-east of Bonn. The eleven 103 Squadron Lancasters were loaded with a cookie, six 1,000 and seven 500 pounders and a Munroe bomb and departed Elsham Wolds between 15.19 and 15.35 with F/Ls Armstrong and Holland the senior pilots on duty. They made landfall on the French side of the Channel to the north of Dieppe and arrived at the target to find ten-tenths cloud and somewhat scattered skymarkers drifting over it to provide a less-than-ideal bombing reference. The 103 Squadron crews carried out their bombing runs at 18,500 to 19,500 feet between 18.52 and 19.03, and according to local sources, largely missed the mark and in company with the rest of the force, deposited the main weight of bombs onto farmland a mile or so to the west. However, the eastern fringes of the bombing found the yards and cut several main lines, while also hitting two important road bridges.

Cologne contained a number of important marshalling yards, among them Nippes, situated to the north of the city centre west of the Rhine and Gremberg and Kalk on the other side of the river. The first-mentioned, which was known to be active in supporting the transportation of men and materials to the Ardennes battle front, had been attacked unsuccessfully by a force of 136 aircraft from 4, 6 and 8 Groups on the 21st, and now, on Christmas Eve, would face eighty-one 1 Group Lancasters predominantly from 12 and 13 Bases, with sixteen Lancasters and five Mosquitos provided by 8 Group as the marker force. Eleven 103 Squadron Lancasters received a bomb load of a cookie, six 1,000 and eight 500 pounders and departed Elsham Wolds between 14.40 and 15.04 with S/L Hague the senior pilot on duty and headed southwards into clearing skies to be greeted at the French coast by a blue canopy extending all the way to the target and beyond. Despite the presence of ground haze, the crews were able to identify the target with ease and the attack opened at 18.27 with red Oboe TIs falling in a concentrated cluster right on the aiming-point. The Path Finder marker crews were right on the money and sent red and green TIs cascading into the railway yards, where they attracted the bombs of the main force Lancasters. The 103 Squadron crews carried out their attacks from 17,500 to 18,500 feet between 18.30 and 18.35 and observed smoke rising through 6,000 feet as they turned for home to be diverted to Old Buckenham in Norfolk. Absent was the crew of F/L McDonald RAAF in NG420, which was hit by flak and crashed at Sindorf some twelve miles to the west of the centre of Cologne with no survivors, thus depriving them of the opportunity to celebrate the last of the six wartime Christmases.

The festivities passed in traditional style uninterrupted by operational activity, but the peace came to an end on Boxing Day, when crews from all groups were roused from any resulting stupor to attend briefings for operations against enemy troop positions at St Vith in Belgium. The German advance towards Antwerp had ground to a halt after its initial successes, and starved of fuel and ammunition, was now attempting to withdraw back into Germany. 1 Group contributed sixty-four Lancasters from 12, 13 and 14 Bases, leaving 103 Squadron on the ground, and they benefitted from clear skies over Belgium, that enabled them to map-read their way to the target area and visually identify the town. The attack opened on time with red Oboe TIs, which were backed up by red and green TIs right on the aiming-point, and the operation appeared to be successful.

Binbrook was somewhat crowded on the 27th as fifty-one Lancasters were being prepared for an operation by two hundred aircraft from 1, 3, 5 and 8 Groups against the marshalling yards at Rheydt on the western edge of the Ruhr to the south of Mönchengladbach. The station had been playing host to Lancasters from 13 and 15 Bases following their diversion on the previous day, and forty-four had to be bombed-up and fuelled along with seven from 460 Squadron. They were to adopt what 1 Group referred to as the "Group Column" formation, which consisted of vics of three in line astern, and the formation held together satisfactorily after rendezvousing with the other groups until the final leg from Liege, when the 3 Group gaggle crossed over 1 Group and inevitably created confusion. Nevertheless, the main weight of bombs was observed to fall in the southern end of the marshalling yards, although some overshot and landed in the town to the east, and the target area was covered by a mass of fires emitting brown and grey smoke, convincing returning crews that they had fulfilled their brief.

1 Group divided its forces on the 28th to send 103 Lancasters from 12 and 13 Bases to Mönchengladbach in company with forty-six Halifaxes of 4 Group and twenty-six Lancasters and eleven Mosquitos of 8 Group, while a further 133 from 14 and 15 Bases targeted the marshalling yards again at Bonn. Following 103 Squadron's extended break during the festive period, the armourers at Elsham Wolds got to work loading nine Lancasters with a cookie, six 1,000 and eight 500 pounders or eight 1,000 and eight 500 pounders, before sending them on their way between 15.45 and 16.15 with F/Ls Armstrong, Pamplin and Riches the senior pilots on duty. Clear skies over England gave way to six-tenths stratocumulus over the Channel, decreasing slightly over France as far as 6°E, where it built again to leave nine-tenths over the target with tops at 8,000 feet. The first red TIs cascaded into the clouds at 19.01 to be followed by skymarkers a minute later, and what was initially

sparse marking became more concentrated as the raid developed. Positions were confirmed by H2S by the main force crews, those from 103 Squadron delivering their attacks from 18,000 to 19,500 feet between 19.01 and 19.10. The bombing appeared to be scattered generally with extensive undershooting and could not be assessed, but explosions at 19.06, 19.10 and 19.17 and the glow of fires suggested at least a degree of success. In fact, a modest 128 houses and nineteen public buildings had been destroyed along with forty-five houses and various other buildings in nearby Rheydt, while forty miles to the south, extensive damage had been inflicted across the city of Bonn but not on the railway yards.

Twenty 103 Squadron crews attended briefing on the 29th to learn that they would be heading to the Ruhr later that evening to target the Hydrierwerke synthetic oil refinery at Scholven-Buer in the north-western quarter of Gelsenkirchen. They were part of a 1 Group force of 239 Lancasters bolstered by fifty-seven provided by 6 Group, with twenty-eight from 8 Group with twenty-two Mosquitos to take care of the marking. The Elsham Wolds Lancasters were each loaded with a cookie and sixteen 500 pounders and took off between 14.56 and 15.25 with five pilots of flight lieutenant rank leading the way, one of which, F/L Norem, was forced to return early, the flight engineer having forgotten to pack his parachute harness. The others enjoyed favourable weather conditions on the way out over the Channel and were greeted with bright moonlight at the target over a thin veil of ten-tenths cloud topping out at 5,000 feet. Skymarkers had to be employed and the first Oboe red went down a fraction early at 18.53, followed precisely at Zero-Hour by a good concentration of others to leave their red glow clearly visible. The 103 Squadron crews delivered their payloads from 17,500 to 19,500 feet between 18.56 and 19.10, before returning safely to report numerous large explosions, smoke rising to 15,000 feet and fires visible for a hundred miles. A local report detailed three hundred high-explosive bombs hitting the area of the plant, causing fires and inflicting severe damage upon the installations. A further 3,100 bombs fell in other parts of Scholven, causing much residential and industrial destruction, and surface buildings at two coal mines were also hit and severely damaged.

The final operation of the month for 1 Group was to take place on the 31st and involve 133 of its Lancasters in an attack on the railway yards at Osterfeld, a town deep inside Germany some twenty miles south-west of Leipzig, for which the marking was to be provided by sixteen Lancasters and seventeen Mosquitos of 8 Group. The sixteen 103 Squadron Lancasters each received one of three bomb loads, a cookie and six each of 1,000 and 500 pounders, a cookie and fourteen 500lb clusters and 120 x 4lb incendiaries and a cookie and 2,070 x 4lb incendiaries and departed Elsham Wolds between 14.41 and 14.53 with F/Ls Armstrong, Norem, Pamplin and Riches the senior pilots on duty. They adopted the now seemingly standard route via Newhaven to the French coast north of Dieppe and initially enjoyed favourable weather conditions, until cloud began to build over France and Belgium and a headwind of 120 mph over the latter delayed the arrival of the force at the target. Faced with seven to ten-tenths cloud with tops at 10,000 feet, the Path Finders struggled to provide adequate concentrated marking after arriving a few minutes behind schedule and the first markers were observed at 18.45. The red TIs appeared to be fairly concentrated and the green scattered, and it was at the glow of the former that the 103 Squadron crews aimed their bombs from 18,000 to 19,500 feet between 18.47 and 19.02. Fires and several large explosions were observed, and the return flight proved to be uneventful and the landing in time to see in the New Year.

It had been a hectic and demanding year, which had seen the Command rise phoenix-like from the traumas of the winter campaign and pave the way for the land forces to sweep across the Occupied Countries to the frontiers of Germany itself, which lay in ruins, its transport system in chaos and its manufacturing base no longer able to support the war effort. It had been a year of steady losses for 103 Squadron, although the three-month loss-free spell in the autumn had been welcome. The New Year beckoned with the scent of victory in the air, but much still to be done, and any thoughts that the enemy defences were spent were misplaced. Even though they were unable to protect every corner of the Reich, they would continue to provide stubborn opposition for a further three months.

During the course of the month, the squadron took part in thirteen operations and dispatched 165 sorties for the loss of three Lancasters and crews.

January 1945

The final year of the war began with a flourish, as the Luftwaffe launched its ill-conceived and, ultimately, ill-fated Operation Bodenplatte (Baseplate) at first light on New Year's Day. The intention to destroy the Allied air forces on the ground at the recently liberated airfields in France, Holland and Belgium was only modestly realized, and it cost the German day fighter force around 250 aircraft. Many of the pilots were killed, wounded or fell into Allied hands, and it was a setback from which the Tagjagd would never fully recover, while the Allies could make good their losses within hours from their enormous stockpiles.

The old enemy of Nuremberg was posted on the 2nd as the first major urban target of the New Year and would face a main force of 445 Lancasters drawn from 1, 3 and 6 Groups with a further sixty-nine Lancasters representing 8 Group to provide the marking and bombing support. A simultaneous operation was to involve 351 Halifaxes of 4 and 6 Groups in attacks on two I G Farben chemical plants, one in Ludwigshafen and the other close by in Oppau. Both operations would also benefit from Oboe Mosquitos, seven for Nuremberg and twenty-two for Ludwigshafen, their participation made possible by the mobile Oboe stations in liberated territory. 103 Squadron made ready twenty Lancasters in a record 1 Group effort of 296, and they each received a bomb load of either a cookie and thirteen or fourteen 500 pounders or a cookie and fourteen SBCs of 4lb cluster bombs. They departed Elsham Wolds between 14.51 and 15.37 with F/Ls Armstrong, Norem and Riches the senior pilots on duty and headed via Beachy Head for the French coast north of Dieppe, losing the services of F/O Pearton and crew to the failure of two engines on the way. The two forces were to follow a similar route until diverging shortly before reaching Ludwigshafen, where the Nuremberg force would continue on towards the east for a further 140 miles.

They began the outward flight over six-tenths cloud, which thickened over the Channel and remained at ten-tenths until breaking up from 7°E to leave Nuremberg under clear skies and effectively naked to the bomb sights high above. The built-up area contrasted sharply with the snow-covered countryside, and the illuminating flares highlighted the River Pegnitz, railway tracks and buildings. Some main force aircraft arrived a little early courtesy of a tail wind, and orbited as they awaited the Path Finders, who opened the attack a few minutes early with the first salvoes of mixed red and green TIs. They fell across the marshalling yards in the city centre in good concentration and attracted the main force bombs under the guidance of the Master Bomber. The 103 Squadron crews carried out their attacks from 16,000 to 18,000 feet between 19.26 and 19.53, those at the tail end aiming at the upwind edge of the smoke in accordance with the master Bomber's instructions after the ground became enveloped. A glow from the burning city remained on the horizon for 150 miles and returning crews were confident of a successful outcome. The raid left more than 4,600 houses and apartment blocks in ruins and destroyed a further two thousand preserved medieval houses. Industrial districts and railway areas also sustained heavy damage, in return for the modest loss of six aircraft.

Meanwhile, the success of the Ludwigshafen operation was confirmed by local reports that five hundred high-explosive bombs had fallen within the confines of the two I G Farben production plants, along with many thousands of incendiaries. This had put an end to all production of synthetic oil, and adjacent industrial buildings, residential property and railway installations had also been destroyed.

Returning to Elsham Wolds following a training sortie on the 4th, ND861 ran into a blizzard and crashed at 14.40 into the Humber near Hull, killing P/O Weight and his crew. In the early hours of the 5th, Lancasters and Mosquitos of 1, 5 and 8 Groups carried out a controversial attack on the small French town of Royan on the east bank of the Gironde Estuary. Acting in response to requests from Free French forces, who were laying siege to the town on their way to Bordeaux, a heavy force of 340 aircraft almost wiped it off the map in a two-wave operation involving ninety-eight 1 Group Lancasters from 14 and 15 Bases. The tragedy was that the residents had been offered the opportunity by the German garrison commander to evacuate, but two thousand people had opted to remain, and up to eight hundred of these are believed to have lost their lives. In an ironic twist of war, the town was not taken, and the garrison would remain in place until mid-April.

Briefings took place on the 5th for the first major assault on the city of Hannover since the series in the autumn of 1943 and was to be conducted by 650 Lancasters and Halifaxes and fourteen Mosquitos drawn from 1, 4, 6 and 8 Groups. The plan called for the 4 and 6 Group Halifaxes to go in first to be followed two-and-a-half hours later by the Lancasters, the 8 Group Lancaster element split fifty-nine and thirty-one between the first and second phases with seven Mosquitos assigned to each. 1 Group detailed 163 Lancasters, of which the sixteen belonging to 103 Squadron received a bomb load of either a cookie and sixteen 500 pounders or a cookie and incendiaries, before departing Elsham Wolds between 18.55 and 19.09 with S/L Hague the senior pilot on duty. The route over the North Sea and Holland and as far as 7°E was covered by a layer of up to ten-tenths cloud between 5,000 and 12,000 feet, but from south of Bremen to the target, clear skies prevailed, and the burning city acted as a beacon to draw the bombers on for the last one hundred miles. The Halifax attack had taken place over ten-tenths low cloud with tops at between 2,000 and 5,000 feet, but good H2S returns enabled the Path Finder element to establish its position over the aiming-point in the northern half of the city, and the bombing had been accurate and concentrated. Numerous fires were spread across the city, the glare and smoke from which created challenging conditions and most TIs were soon lost to view. In truth, marking was somewhat superfluous, but the 103 Squadron crews found sufficient red and green TIs to satisfy their needs and disgorged the contents of their bomb bays from 19,000 to 21,000 feet between 21.49 and 21.57. The second phase attack added to the destruction inflicted upon Hannover, and once the fires had been extinguished and the dust had settled, the local authorities were able to assess that almost five hundred apartment blocks had been destroyed with their 3,600 individual dwelling units. P/O Barnes and crew failed to return in PB528, which had crashed at 21.59 some fifteen miles due south of Hannover, killing both gunners and delivering the rest of the crew into enemy hands.

Orders were sent out to 1, 3, 4, 6 and 8 Group stations on the 6th to prepare for operations against two marshalling yards, one in the town of Hanau-am-Main, situated a short distance to the east of Frankfurt and the other in Neuss in the southern Ruhr. A force of 482 aircraft was assigned to the former and included a contribution from 1 Group of fifty-two Lancasters from 12 and 14 Bases, which found the target under ten-tenths cloud and bombed on the glow of TIs until skymarkers were employed. Returning crews reported the glow from the target to be visible from seventy-five miles away, but it had not been possible to assess the outcome and it was left to local sources to confirm damage in the area of the railway yards and also in other parts of the town resulting in the destruction of 40% of the built-up area. Meanwhile, the raid on Neuss, which had included thirty-three 1 Group Lancasters also from 12 and 14 Bases, had destroyed or seriously damaged almost eighteen hundred buildings.

While the above operation was in progress, twenty Lancasters from 12, 13 and 14 Bases were assigned to mining duties in the Geranium I and II gardens in the Bay of Pomerania. The 103 Squadron crews of S/L Hague and F/Os Pearton, Robson and Stepharnoff departed Elsham Wolds between 16.07 and 16.24 and set course via Mablethorpe to make landfall on the western coast of Jutland. The initially poor weather conditions improved during the crossing of the North Sea and southern Denmark and the target area was found to be clear of cloud for the establishment of positions by H2S and the delivery of either five 1,800lb or six 1,500lb mines from 13,000 and 14,000 feet. PB637 failed to return with the others and was lost without trace with the crew of F/O Pearton.

A major operation against Munich was planned for the 7th, for which a two-wave force of 645 aircraft was drawn from all five of the Lancaster-equipped groups. 5 Group, which was unused to sharing this target, would lead the way with 213 Lancasters and three Mosquitos, leaving the second wave to follow two hours later, the tanks of the heavy brigade containing sufficient fuel for a nine-hour round-trip. 103 Squadron made ready seventeen Lancasters with a variety of bomb loads, each including a cookie and incendiaries and dispatched them from Elsham Wolds between 18.20 and 19.03 with S/L Butler the senior pilot on duty and undertaking his first sortie since joining the squadron. Sadly, he would be forced to turn back early after being let down by unserviceable navigation equipment, while the crews of F/Os Hart and Stepharnoff were defeated by engine issues. The others set course via Beachy Head for the French coast to rendezvous with the rest of the bomber stream, while ahead the 5 Group element was about to cross the Franco-German frontier near Strasbourg with an hour's flight still ahead of it. On arrival at Munich, the 5 Group spearhead encountered broken medium-level cloud at 14,000 feet, with haze or thin cloud below, by which time, the Master Bomber had made a visual identification of the aiming-point and sent the first two primary blind markers in to deliver their TIs at the same time thirty seconds ahead of the planned opening of the attack. The flare force went in immediately afterwards, and illuminated the city very effectively, allowing ground detail to be identified. Red TIs went down west and east of the River Isar, bracketing the aiming-point, and the Master Bomber ordered the backers up to drop their TIs between the reds, after which, the next batch of flares formed a circle around the aiming point. The main force was then called in, and as they withdrew with empty bomb bays minutes later, they left behind a burning city that would act as a beacon visible to the second phase crews from 130 miles away.

Soon after crossing the French coast, the second phase force had met an ice-bearing front extending up to 20,000 feet, and although this diminished to a layer of thin cloud at 10,000 feet, the ground remained hidden. The target itself was concealed beneath ten-tenths cloud with tops at 12,000 feet as the attack began well on time with green TIs and red flares with green stars, the former quickly disappearing into the cloud tops and leaving the skymarkers to provide a concentrated reference for the bombing element. The Elsham Wolds crews delivered their bombs from 16,000 to 18,500 feet between 22.23 and 22.44, and some observed five large explosions between 22.27 and 22.41, the last-mentioned resulting in a mushroom of smoke breaking through the cloud tops. F/O Skinner and crew lost their port-inner engine when thirty minutes short of the target but pressed on to bomb as briefed and returned safely. A dozen Lancasters landed safely at Elsham Wolds to report a successful night's work, which left substantial damage in central and industrial districts, but as usual at Munich, no local report emerged to provide details. Two 103 Squadron Lancasters remained unaccounted for, NF999 and NN766 containing the crews of F/O Mathieson RAAF and P/O McArthur RCAF respectively. The former came down without survivors somewhere in southern Germany, probably as the result of enemy action, while the latter was outbound when it smacked into high ground near the town of Munster in the Haut-Rhin region of France close to the German frontier, and again, all on board lost their lives. This proved to be the final large-scale attack of the war on Munich, but joint operations led by 5 Group would become an established format for the remainder of the war.

The following week was relatively busy for the independent 3 Group, while other groups were employed sparingly and 1 Group not at all. On the 14th, 1, 5, 6 and 8 Group stations were alerted to a major two-phase operation against the I G Farbenindustrie synthetic oil refinery situated at Leuna near Merseburg, which, as previously mentioned, was one of many similar sites situated in an arc from north to south to the west of Leipzig. They were part of an overall force of 573 Lancasters and fourteen Mosquitos, of which the 5 Group contingent of 210 Lancasters and nine Mosquitos would form the first phase and be followed up by a 306-strong main force consisting of 245 Lancasters of 1 Group and sixty-one from 6 Group three hours later. The 5 Group element began to depart their stations at around 16.00 for the three-and-a-half-hour outward flight, which would take them via the southerly route across France and into eastern Germany. They reached the target area to find clear skies but poor vertical visibility due to a layer of haze, which, in the event, was no hindrance to the primary blind markers, whose job was to establish their position over the aiming-point by means of

H2S. They delivered their TIs from 18,000 feet, after which, the first element of the flare force went in. The Master Bomber called for ground marking only, which was carried out by the low-level Mosquito element, and by 20.50, he was satisfied and sent the marker aircraft home.

As the 5 Group main force crews went in to attack, 550 miles to the west-north-west, those of the second phase were in the process of taking off, eleven at Elsham Wolds departing between 19.03 and 19.18 with F/Ls Holland, Norem and Riches the senior pilots on duty and each Lancaster carrying a cookie, ten 500 pounders and a Munroe bomb. They set course via Beachy Head for the French coast and the standard route into Germany in good weather conditions over thin cloud, which would prevail throughout the almost nine-hour round trip. The target was reached early by some crews and found to be covered by ten-tenths thin cloud or smoke, with the glow from the 5 Group raid clearly visible. The illuminating flares went down at 23.54, followed by red and green TIs, and although they could be seen, the ground itself was completely obscured and the Master Bomber experienced difficulty in identifying the aiming point, eventually instructing the main force to bomb on the red and yellow release-point flares. The Elsham Wolds crews complied with his instructions from 19,500 to 22,000 feet between 23.59 and 00.08, and large explosions were reported at 23.59 and 00.18, one of which sent dense clouds of smoke rising through the cloud tops. Many returning crews thought the operation to have been scattered and probably ineffective, when, in fact, it had been among the most devastating attacks on the synthetic oil industry of the war.

Feverish activity across the Command on the 16th prepared more than twelve hundred aircraft for action, the majority to participate in four major operations that night, three to target oil refineries and the largest to deliver an area attack on the eastern city of Magdeburg, which also contained the Braunkohle AG Bergius process hydrogenation plant, located in the Rothensee district to the north of the city centre. The independent 3 and 5 Groups were handed the refineries at Wanne-Eickel in the Ruhr and Brüx in Czechoslovakia respectively, leaving 320 Halifaxes of 4 and 6 Groups to take care of Magdeburg and 283 Lancasters of 1 and 6 Groups to ply their trade at Zeitz-Tröglitz, the location of another Braunkohle-Benzin AG plant, situated some twenty miles south-west of Leipzig. 1 Group detailed 232 Lancasters for Zeitz and 8 Group forty-five, and the eight-strong 103 Squadron contingent departed Elsham Wolds between 17.30 and 17.37 with F/Ls Norem and Riches the senior pilots on duty and each Lancaster carrying a cookie, eleven 500 pounders and a Munroe bomb. Ten-tenths cloud over England and the Channel began to disperse at the French coast and the skies were clear from 6°E for the rest of the outward flight, although extremely dark in the absence of a moon. A strong tail wind resulted in some crews arriving up to six minutes ahead of schedule and not all were prepared to wait for the marking to begin, preferring instead to bomb by H2S before heading home. The first salvoes of mixed red and green TIs fell on the northern edge of the plant and were backed up plentifully and continuously throughout the attack, which was tightly controlled by the Master Bomber, who called in the main force at 22.09. The Elsham Wolds crews delivered their loads from 15,500 to 19,000 feet between 22.12 and 22.19 and at debriefing reported a series of large explosions between 22.13 and 22.23, the largest at 22.19 sending a mushroom of black smoke to 10,000 feet and beyond. They also reported the oil plant and parts of the town to be ablaze.

While the above was in progress, the crews of F/Ls Holland and Murton and F/Os Henry and Morgan departed Elsham Wolds between 20.34 and 20.37 and flew out over Mablethorpe bound for one of the Silverthorn gardens in the Baltic, in particular, Aarhus Bay off Jutland. They arrived to find ten-tenths cloud but established their positions by H2S before planting six 1,800lb vegetables each from 12,000 and 12,500 feet between 23.46 and 23.59.

On the 22nd, 130 Lancasters from 13, 14 and 15 Bases were detailed to join forces with 156 other Lancaster of 3 and 8 Groups and sixteen Mosquitos for an attack on a benzol plant in the Hamborn district of Duisburg. The 1 Group ORB mentions a single 103 Squadron Lancaster taking part, but this is not recorded in the squadron record suggesting that the sortie was cancelled. Much damage was inflicted upon the plant and upon the nearby Thyssen steelworks, which was hit by five hundred high explosive bombs, either as the result of misidentification or by accident.

S/L Hague was posted to 582 Squadron of the Path Finders on the 27th and appears to have survived the war with a DFC to his credit. 103 Squadron had been inactive for eleven nights by the time that orders were received on the 28th to prepare sixteen Lancasters for that night's trip to Stuttgart by 602 aircraft divided into two forces separated by three hours, each with its own specific target. The first phase, by 226 aircraft, was to be directed at the marshalling yards in the town of Kornwestheim, situated just beyond the northern boundary of Stuttgart, while the second phase would target the Hirth aero-engine factory at Zuffenhausen, fewer than two miles to the south. 1 Group put up 150 Lancasters for the latter, those at Elsham Wolds receiving a load of a cookie, eleven 500 pounders and a Munroe bomb, before fifteen lifted into the air between 19.34 and 20.01 with five pilots of flight lieutenant rank taking the lead. F/O Thomson and crew lost an engine early on and proceeded directly to the jettison area, leaving the others to fly out over the Sussex coast over five-tenths cloud as far as the French coast north of Dieppe, from where they encountered large gaps until reaching the German frontier north of Strasbourg. Here, the cloud built until it was at ten-tenths over the target with tops at 10,000 feet, a situation requiring a skymarking plan. The Path Finders were three minutes late, and some main force crews arrived early and carried out their attacks before any release point flares were evident. F/L Newman and crew were attacked twice by night-fighters just before bombing and having lost both inner engines, were forced to jettison the bombs. The first red and yellow flares appeared at 23.30 and were initially sparse and scattered, but the density of marking increased as the raid progressed, and the 103 Squadron crews had adequate numbers to aim at as they delivered their attacks from 18,000 to 20,000 feet between 23.33 and 23.44. Large explosions were observed at 23.36 and 23.38 and the glow of fires beneath the clouds suggested some success, although returning crews believed the raid to have been scattered. F/L Newman skilfully nursed RA500 back to England on the two outer engines and landed at Manston. Local sources confirmed the extent of the damage, reporting that many parts of the city had been hit, while a decoy fire site had also attracted some bomb loads as the Germans fired dummy TIs into the air. Local sources admitted to damage to the railway installations and to a number of important war industry factories including the Robert Bosch works. This would prove to be the last of fifty-three major raids on this important industrial city, which had now been largely destroyed.

During the course of the month the squadron took part in eight operations and dispatched ninety-five sorties for the loss of five Lancasters and crews, one while training.

February 1945

The weather at the start of February provided difficult conditions for marking and bombing, and several operations would struggle to achieve their aims in the face of thick, low cloud and strong winds. Three major operations were laid on for the night of the 1/2nd, the largest by 382 Lancasters and fourteen Mosquitos of 1, 6 and 8 Groups against Ludwigshafen, while thirty-five miles to the north, 340 aircraft from 4, 6 and 8 Groups attended to the city of Mainz. Further north still, 5 Group's target was the marshalling yards in the town of Siegen, situated some fifty miles east of Cologne. 1 Group would be represented at Ludwigshafen by 277 Lancasters, the nineteen belonging to 103 Squadron receiving one of three bomb loads, each involving a cookie and supplemented by 500 pounders, cluster bombs and incendiaries, and departed Elsham Wolds between 15.35 and 16.14 with the newly promoted S/L Riches the senior pilot. The skies were largely clear from the Sussex coast until around 6°E, where cloud began to build and was at nine-tenths with tops at 6,000 feet by the time the spearhead of the bomber stream arrived at the target at the end of a three-hour flight. The Path Finders opened the attack punctually at 19.11 with cascading red TIs backed up by greens and followed by release point flares, and these could be seen by the approaching main force crews until the start of their bombing runs, when the ground became concealed by cloud. They then had to rely on the flares, which resulted in scattered bombing and a degree of undershooting. Small gaps in the cloud revealed incendiary fires on both sides of the Rhine, and several large explosions were observed at 19.20, 19.25, 19.36 and 19.42, the last-mentioned by crews fifty miles into their homeward flight. The Elsham Wolds crews carried out their bombing runs from 15,000 to 17,500 feet between 19.17 and 19.27 employing red and green skymarker flares as their reference, and all but one returned home safely. P/O Stepharnoff and crew were attacked by a Ju88 over the target and twice more on the way home and landed at Manston with a wounded rear gunner. Local sources confirmed that bombs had fallen right across the city and that nine hundred houses had been destroyed or seriously damaged along with the marshalling yards, and a Rhine bridge had been forced to close for repairs.

When briefings took place on the 2nd, they came with the bad news that a tour of operations for main force crews was to be increased again to thirty-six sorties. On 5 Group stations in drizzly Lincolnshire, 250 crews were told further, that the night's operation was to be against Karlsruhe in southern Germany, and that this was one of three major undertakings involving a total of 1,150 aircraft. Elsewhere, 495 crews from 1, 3, 6 and 8 Groups were informed that Wiesbaden would be their destination and that it would the first time that this city, separated from nearby Mainz to the south by the River Rhine, had been targeted by Bomber Command. The third operation on this night would bring a return to the Ruhr for 277 Halifaxes of 4 and 6 Groups with twenty-seven 8 Group Lancasters and nineteen Mosquitos to provide the marking for an attack on the Krupp Treibstoffwerke synthetic oil plant in the Wanne-Eickel district of Herne. 1 Group put up 233 Lancasters for Wiesbaden, sixteen of them made ready at Elsham Wolds, where they received bomb loads of a cookie, 1,620 x 4lb incendiaries and a Munroe bomb, before taking off between 20.35 and 20.52 with S/L Riches the senior pilot on duty. They adopted a similar course to that of the previous night and from 3°E encountered a build-up of cloud to ten-tenths in layers up to 20,000 feet, which would persist all the way to the target. F/O Ross and crew turned back after losing an engine, while F/L Anderson and crew were let down by their navigational equipment and also had to abort their sortie when deep into enemy territory. Winds were lighter than forecast, resulting in the late arrival of the force, and the cloud completely nullified the attempts to mark, leaving crews with no option but to bomb on Gee and H2S. The 103 Squadron crews carried out their attacks from 18,000 to 21,500 feet between 23.35 to 00.02, and none had a clue as to the outcome of the operation.

Two Ruhr oil production sites were the focus of attention on the evening of the 3rd, one of them the Prosper coking plant at Welheim, an eastern district of Bottrop, and situated about five miles to the north-east of Duisburg and Oberhausen, and the other was the Hansa benzol plant at Dortmund. The former was assigned to a 1 and 8 Group heavy force of 192 Lancasters, of which 1 Group contributed 164, while the latter was entrusted to 3 Group and its highly effective G-H bombing system. The nine 103 Squadron Lancasters each received a bomb load of a cookie, fifteen 500 pounders and a Munroe bomb before departing Elsham Wolds between 16.10 and 16.40 with a quartet of flight lieutenant pilots leading the way. They adopted the familiar route to southern Germany and flew out under largely clear skies until a few miles from the target, where a little low cloud began to form at 3,000 feet, but insufficient to interfere with the progress of the raid. The first red TIs appeared punctually at 19.26 and were observed to be both accurate and concentrated, and they were followed by greens which also fell right on the aiming point. Many crews were able to confirm visually the effectiveness of the marking and proceeded to bomb in a very tight pattern, those from Elsham Wolds from 16,000 to 18,000 feet between 19.33 and 19.39. Fires and explosions were evident along with much black smoke and it was clear to most that a successful operation had taken place, albeit in the face of a spirited and accurate flak defence supported by some two hundred searchlights in cones of between ten and twenty. Post-raid reconnaissance confirmed that extensive damage had been inflicted upon the plant.

Three main operations were posted again on the 4th, against the Gutehoffnunugshütte Oberhausen AG benzol plant at Osterfeld near Leipzig, the Gelsenkirchener Bergwerke AG (Nordstern) coking plant in the Ruhr and an area attack on the city of Bonn, all of which 1 Group sat out. Fifteen crews were briefed for mining operations in the Rosemary and Eglantine gardens, respectively in the Heligoland Bight and the Elbe estuary, five each at Binbrook, Elsham Wolds and Scampton, and it was for the latter that the 103 Squadron crews of F/Ls Armstrong, Dobson and Holland, F/O Morgan and P/O Stepharnoff took off between 17.40 and 17.44, two sitting on five 1,800lb mines and the others on six of 1,500lbs. They set course from Mablethorpe and enjoyed clear conditions as far as 4°E, where cloud began to build and reach ten-tenths in the target area with tops at 5,000 to 8,000 feet, through which each delivered their stores on H2S from 15,000 feet between 20.02 and 20.12.

The towns of Cleves and Goch are separated by around eight miles and lie east of the Reichswald and to the south of the Rhine and formed part of the enemy's defensive line towards which the British XXX Corps was preparing to advance. Briefings took place on the 7th at which it was learned that a 1 Group force of 250 Lancasters was to join up with forty-five Lancasters and ten Mosquitos from 8 Group to attack the former, while 464 aircraft of 4, 6 and 8 Groups attended to the latter. Sixteen 103 Squadron Lancasters swallowed up a cookie and sixteen 500 pounders each and took off from Elsham Wolds between 18.50 and 19.04 led by no fewer than seven pilots of flight lieutenant rank. The weather was good as they climbed out over the Lincolnshire Wolds and headed south to the exit point at Hastings on course for the Boulogne coastal area. The route out was virtually cloud-free, but a dozen miles from the target it began to build and was at seven to ten-tenths in a band from 5,000 to 7,000 feet when the raid began. This prompted the Master Bomber to bring the main-force crews down to 5,000 feet to provide them with a view of the red and green TIs on the brilliantly-illuminated aiming-point. He was clear and concise and maintained excellent control of proceedings, and most of the 103 Squadron crews delivered their attacks in accordance with his instructions from 4,500 to 5,500 feet between 22.01 and 22.16, while P/O Folkes and crew were among a number from other squadrons bombing from 10,500 to 12,000 feet. Returning crews reported many fires and multi-coloured explosions with smoke rising through 4,000 feet as they turned away, and post-raid reconnaissance revealed almost total destruction of the town, which had been largely evacuated by the civilian population.

The sad news was received on the 8th that the former 103 Squadron stalwart, 460 Squadron commanding officer and now commanding officer of 467 Squadron RAAF, W/C "Jack" Douglas, had failed to return from a 5 Group raid on the Dortmund-Ems canal at Ladbergen on the previous night. Leading the men under their command frequently into battle was a characteristic of the very best commanding officers and a way to inspire and create esprit de corps, but the consequence was that many paid the ultimate price. In contrast, the names of the commanding officers of 103 Squadron were rarely to be found on the order of battle.

Thirteen crews were called to briefing at Elsham Wolds on the afternoon of the 8th to learn that they were to take part in the third and what would prove to be the final raid in a series against the I G Farben-owned Wintershall synthetic oil refinery at Politz, which had begun in December. Situated to the north of Stettin in what is now Poland, it represented a long round-trip of some 1,400 miles, and was to be another two-phase attack led by a 5 Group force of 227 Lancasters and seven Mosquitos and completed two hours later by 184 Lancasters from 1 Group and fifty-seven representing 8 Group. The 103 Squadron aircraft were each loaded with a cookie and either eleven 500 pounders or nine plus a Munroe bomb and departed Elsham Wolds between 19.10 and 19.22 with F/Ls Armstrong and Holland the senior pilots on duty. They began the North Sea crossing at Mablethorpe and were accompanied by low cloud as far as 7°E, before climbing to cross the German coast under clear skies, which then persisted all the way to the target. They were drawn on by six fires resulting from the earlier 5 Group raid, and the attack opened on time with flares illuminating the plant, before marking began with red and green TIs from the Deputy Master Bomber at 23.10. These were well-placed on the aiming-point and were soon backed up by others to form an excellent concentration within the boundaries of the site. The marking was maintained throughout the attack, and the main force exploited the opportunity to deliver a decisive blow against this important contributor to Germany's war effort, the 103 Squadron crews delivering their attacks from 12,500 to 14,500 feet between 23.15 and 23.24. The entire area was soon covered by smoke, through which numerous explosions were observed, one of particular violence that lasted seconds and added another column of smoke to the pall that had reached

10,000 feet by the time that the last of the bombers had turned for home. The glow remained visible for a hundred miles, and post-raid reconnaissance confirmed that the plant's ability to produce oil had been ended for good.

Two major operations were planned for the night of the 13/14th, the first by a main force of 326 Halifaxes from 4 and 6 Groups with thirty-four Lancasters and eight Mosquitos of 8 Group to provide the marking at the Braunkohle-Benzin oil plant at Böhlen, situated some seven miles to the south of Leipzig. On the Lancaster stations, meanwhile, briefings took place for the first round of Operation Thunderclap, the Churchill-inspired offensive against Germany's eastern cities, which was devised partly to act in support of the advancing Russians, and also as a demonstration to Stalin of RAF air power, should he turn against the Allies after the war. The historic and culturally significant city of Dresden was selected to open the offensive in another two-phase affair, with a 5 Group force of 246 Lancasters and nine Mosquitos leading the way, to be followed three hours later by 529 Lancasters of 1, 3, 6 and 8 Groups. It had proved to be a successful policy thus far, with the 5 Group low-level marking system and main force attacks providing a beacon for the second force, and should it be required on this night, 8 Group would provide any necessary marking for phase two from high level. The crews involved had absolutely no concept of the ramifications of the operation, both in terms of its outcome on the ground and its hysterical aftermath. Dresden was Germany's seventh largest city and its largest remaining largely un-bombed built-up area, which, according to American sources, contained more than a hundred factories and fifty thousand workers contributing to the war effort. It was also an important railway hub, to the extent that the marshalling yards had been attacked twice in late 1944 by the USAAF.

The heavy force was two hours out when W/C Maurice Smith of 54 Base, the Master Bomber for the 5 Group attack, lifted off the Woodhall Spa runway at a few minutes before 20.00 hours in Mosquito KB401 AZ-E, a 627 Squadron aircraft, and he was followed away by eight others from 627 Squadron. The heavy brigade and the Mosquitos arrived in the target area at the same time to encounter three layers of cloud between 3,000 and 5,000 feet, 6,000 to 8,000 feet and 15,000 to 16,000 feet, but otherwise good visibility. The first primary blind marker crew delivered green TIs from 15,000 feet at 22.03 and was followed in by the flare force, which lit the way for the low-level Mosquitos. The main force Lancasters were carrying eight hundred tons of bombs, mostly in the form either of a cookie and twelve 500 pounders or one 2,000 pounder and fourteen cluster bombs, which were delivered onto the glow of red TIs in accordance with the Master Bomber's instructions. As far as the crews were concerned, this was no different from any other attack, and the fires visible for more than a hundred miles into the return journey were nothing out of the ordinary.

At Elsham Wolds, nineteen 103 Squadron Lancasters were loaded with either a cookie or a 2,000 pounder, supplemented by incendiaries and a Munroe bomb as part of a 1 Group contribution to the operation of 260 aircraft, and took off between 21.26 and 21.55 with six pilots of flight lieutenant rank leading the way. They began the Channel crossing at Hastings and made landfall near Abbeville under clear skies until 3°E, when large amounts of broken cloud reached 18,000 feet. This dispersed from 12°E to leave clear skies over the target, although a large bank of cloud threatened a short distance away to the east. By the time that this second force of 1, 3, 6 and 8 Group Lancasters arrived over Dresden three hours after 5

Group, the fires created by the earlier attack provided the expected reference point. The 103 Squadron crews delivered their attacks on green and then red TIs from 16,500 to 20,000 feet between 01.30 and 01.49, their bombs among a further eighteen hundred tons raining down onto the historic and beautiful old city, setting off the same chain of events that had devastated parts of Hamburg in July 1943 and a number of other cities since. Dresden's population had been swelled by masses of refugees fleeing from the eastern front, and many were engulfed in the ensuing firestorm, which was still burning on the following morning, when three hundred American bombers carried out a separate attack under the umbrella of a fighter escort and completed the destruction. There were claims that RAF aircraft had strafed the streets and open spaces to increase the level of terror, and such accusations abound in the city to this day. In fact, American fighters were responsible, and were trying to add to the general confusion and chaos. Initial propaganda-inspired reports from the Office of the Propaganda Minister, Joseph Göbbels, falsely claimed a death toll of 250,000 people, but an accurate figure of twenty-five thousand has been settled upon since. The operation cost only six Lancasters, including 103 Squadron's LM682, which crashed near Bensheim, a town between Darmstadt and Mannheim, and there were no survivors from the crew of P/O Rimmington.

The destruction of Dresden has been used by some in this country also as a weapon with which to denigrate Bomber Command and Harris, and label them as war criminals. Curiously, no accusations have been levelled at the Americans. It should also be understood that Harris had no interest in attacking Dresden and had to be nagged by Chief-of-the-Air-Staff Portal to fulfil Churchill's wishes. The aircrew simply did the job asked of them, and the Dresden raid was no different from any other attack on a city. The death toll at Hamburg was much higher, and yet, there has been no similar outcry. The legacy of this operation served to deny Harris and the men under his Command their due recognition for the massive part they played in the ultimate victory, and only in recent times has a monument been erected in Green Park in London and a campaign clasp awarded, sadly, far too little and far too late for the majority. Churchill, with his eyes set on a peacetime election, betrayed Harris and the Command in a typical politically motivated U-turn, in which he accused Harris of bombing solely for the purpose of inflicting terror. In the post-war honours, Harris was the only commander in the field to be omitted.

Briefings for round two of Operation Thunderclap took place across the Command on the 14th, when crews learned that the highly industrialised city of Chemnitz would be the target for 717 aircraft drawn from 1, 3, 4, 6 and 8 Groups, which would be divided into two waves separated by three-and-a-half hours. The city contained many factories manufacturing military hardware, including the Siegmar tank-engine works and an oil refinery and was home to the headquarters of the Auto Union automotive company. The Flossenbürg female forced workers camp had a subcamp in the city that provided slave labour for the Astrawerke AG factory that produced calculator machines. 5 Group would also be in the area on this night with 224 Lancasters and eight Mosquitos to target an oil refinery in the small town of Rositz, situated twenty-five miles due south of Leipzig and thirty miles north-west of Chemnitz. 1 Group put together a force of 202 Lancasters for the second phase of the main event, thirteen of them made ready by 103 Squadron and loaded with either a cookie or a 2,000 pounder supplemented by incendiaries and a Munroe bomb. 1 Group also detailed twenty Lancasters for mining duties in the Sweet Pea Garden in the Kadet Channel between Denmark's Lolland Island and Warnemünde on Germany's Mecklenburg Bay coast, which 103 Squadron supported with five Lancasters, each loaded with six mines. The gardening quintet consisting of the crews of F/Ls Armstrong, Dobson, Holland and Short and F/O Stepharnoff departed Elsham Wolds first between 17.55 and 17.58 and were followed into the air between 20.00 and 20.39 by those bound for eastern Germany with F/Ls Anderson and Newman the senior pilots on duty. F/O Armour lost his port-outer engine on take-off but managed to gain height and proceeded directly to the jettison area.

Favourable conditions prevailed for the outward flight via Hastings and Abbeville, until 11°E was reached, where cloud built to ten-tenths with tops at between 10,000 and 18,000 feet, and extended to the target and beyond. The Master Bomber issued a time check at 00.15, and he was then heard to call for markers at 00.25, to which the Path Finder blind markers responded with green TIs delivered on H2S. They disappeared quickly into the cloud, forcing the Master Bomber to call for skymarking, in response to which four aircraft released green/red flares without achieving concentration. The Master Bomber ordered the main force crews to aim for the skymarkers until 00.30, at which point, with so few remaining visible, he instructed them to bomb on navigational aids. Any marking that took place was sparse and inadequate and the subsequent bombing became scattered over a wide area. The Elsham Wolds crews carried out their attacks on H2S from 15,500 to 19,500 feet between 00.31 and 00.48 and had no clue as to what was happening beneath the clouds. Most crews returned home dissatisfied with the conduct of the raid but reported that fires appeared to be taking hold across the target area, the glow from which lingered on the horizon for at least an hour into the homeward flight. Meanwhile, the gardeners had enjoyed excellent conditions and had planted thirty mines between them on H2S from 12,000 feet between 21.06 and 21.17. Post-raid reconnaissance at Chemnitz confirmed that many parts of the city had been hit, but that much of the effort had been wasted in open country.

It was gardening duties again on the following night for the crews of F/Ls Holland Murton and Norem and F/O Morgan, this time in the Silverthorn garden off Aarhus on Jutland's eastern coast, while others from 1 Group plied their trade elsewhere in the Baltic. They departed Elsham Wolds between 16.40 and 16.42 and passed over Mablethorpe on their way to make landfall on Jutland's western coast, enjoying largely favourable conditions even if ten-tenths cloud greeted them in the target area. A total of twenty-four 1,800lb mines were delivered into the briefed locations from 10,000 and 12,000 feet between 20.00 and 20.02, and all returned safely from unopposed and uneventful sorties. It was similar fare on the 18th for the 103 Squadron crews of F/Ls Armstrong, Dobson, and the newly promoted Stepharnoff and F/Os Morgan and Mosley, who were assigned to the Eglantine garden in the Elbe estuary, while others from 1 Group were active further north in the Rosemary garden in Heligoland Bight. They departed Elsham Wolds between 17.50 and 17.54 and arrived in the target area to find ten-tenths cloud with tops at 8,000 feet, through which they delivered their six mines each by H2S from 10,500 to 12,400 feet between 20.13 and 20.22.

Preparations for the next operation were put in hand on the 20th, when a major assault was planned on the southern half of Dortmund, for which a force of 514 Lancasters was assembled from 1, 3, 6 and 8 Groups. 1 Group detailed 271 Lancasters, sixteen of them belonging to 103 Squadron and receiving a bomb load of either a cookie or a 2,000 pounder supplemented by incendiaries and in some cases by a Munroe bomb. They departed Elsham Wolds between 21.31 and 21.47 with S/L Riches the senior pilot on duty, and as they climbed away into clear skies, further north a force of 156 Halifaxes of 4 Group was climbing out over Yorkshire before heading south the join up with a Path Finder element for an attack on the Rhenania-Ossag oil refinery in the Reisholz district of Düsseldorf. As the two bomber streams made their way to their respective targets via the Sussex coast, the sky filled rapidly with cloud from 5°E and was at eight to ten-tenths over the north-eastern Ruhr, but very low and thin enough for the red Oboe TIs to be clearly visible. At 00.58, the visual centerers released green TIs, and from then onwards the ground marking was well concentrated and maintained and was supplemented by green skymarkers, which, unfortunately, tended to fall short and created a marking creep-back for fourteen miles along the line of approach. The bombing in the early stages was accurate, but as the cloud thickened and the glow through the clouds diminished, it became scattered and much of it fell short. The 103 Squadron crews carried out their attacks from 17,000 to 19,000 feet between 01.03 and 01.18, and all returned home safely to report developing fires but no detail. It was an expensive night for the Command for the period and cost fourteen Lancasters, ten of them belonging to 1 Group. The authorities in Dortmund were beyond the ability to produce an account of the raid, and the next major attack in three weeks' time would obliterate all traces of this night and leave the city totally paralysed.

Responsibility for the final heavy raid of the war on the much-bombed city of Duisburg was handed to 362 Lancasters of 1, 6 and 8 Groups on the night of the 21/22nd, for which 1 Group assembled a force of 245 Lancasters, sixteen of them made ready by 103 Squadron and loaded with a cookie and incendiaries and some with a Munroe bomb, before departing Elsham Wolds between 19.35 and 19.55 with S/L Riches the senior pilot on duty. After climbing away, they headed south to the Sussex coast in conditions of little or no cloud, which persisted until shortly before the target was reached, when a band of stratus a thousand feet thick slid over the city at 15,000 feet to cover it completely. The winds outbound were different from those forecast at briefing, and this delayed the arrival of the main force by a few minutes. As they approached, the crews could see the first red TIs cascading at 22.56, but by the time they arrived to bomb, these had disappeared below the cloud and no more were evident until 23.08. Some considerable difficulty was experienced in identifying the target, and incendiaries were seen to be dropped all the way from Krefeld to Duisburg. By 23.10, the cloud was beginning to break up, and a better concentration was achieved, and had a Master Bomber been present, he might have been able to compensate for the scarcity of the marking. The Elsham Wolds crews delivered their attacks from 14,500 to 18,500 feet between 23.03 and 23.22, and on return reported large explosions, post-raid reconnaissance eventually confirming this to have been a successful operation.

A Halifax main force of 297 aircraft from 4 and 6 Groups was made ready on the morning of the 23rd to send against Essen in the afternoon, and despite complete cloud cover and the use of skymarking, most of the bombing fell squarely into the Krupp districts. The day's operations were not yet over, however, and a force of 366 Lancasters, plus one from the Film Unit and thirteen Mosquitos was drawn from 1, 6 and 8 Groups to send against the city of Pforzheim, situated in southern Germany between Karlsruhe to the north-west and Stuttgart to the south-east. This would be the first area raid on the city, which was known as a centre for jewellery and watch manufacture but was believed by the Allies to be involved also in the production of precision instruments in support of Germany's war effort. 1 Group detailed 258 Lancasters, eighteen of them representing 103 Squadron, which received a cookie each and the usual mix of incendiaries and in some cases a Munroe bomb, before departing Elsham Wolds between 15.46 and 16.20 with S/L Butler the senior pilot on duty undertaking only his second sortie since joining the squadron, the first having ended in an early return. They climbed out through ten-tenths low cloud, which persisted until the bombers were over France, where it began to break up, leaving the skies clear under a bright moon as the target drew near. The thin veil of ground haze proved to be no impediment, and the first red Oboe TIs went down at 19.52, to be followed quickly by illuminator flares and salvoes of concentrated reds and greens. The Elsham Wolds crews delivered their attacks from an unusually low 7,000 to 9,000 feet between 20.00 and 20.10, and fires rapidly took hold until the whole town north of the river looked like a sea of flames. By 20.06, the fires were too dazzling for the TIs to be visible, after which, the Master Bomber ordered the smoke to be bombed.

The raid lasted twenty-two minutes, during which 1,825 tons of bombs fell into the built-up area, reducing 83% of it to ruins and setting off a firestorm in which 17,600 people lost their lives. This was the highest death toll to result from a single attack on a German city after Hamburg (40,000) and Dresden (25,000). It was during this operation that the final Victoria Cross was earned by a member of RAF Bomber Command. It went posthumously to the Master Bomber from 582 Squadron, Captain Ed Swales of the South African Air Force, who continued to control the attack in a Lancaster severely damaged by a night-fighter, before sacrificing his life to allow his crew the opportunity to save themselves. Two 103 Squadron crews failed to return from this operation, those of F/O Hart RAAF and F/L Dobson in NF909 and RA515 respectively. Where the former came down is unknown, but the five RAF members of the crew survived to fall into enemy hands, while the pilot and fellow Australian wireless operator are commemorated on the Runnymede Memorial. The latter crashed in southern Germany, presumably in the general target area, and the long-serving F/L Dobson lost his life along with six others, leaving just one of the eight occupants to be taken into captivity. It is believed that F/L Dobson had more than thirty sorties to his credit and was, therefore, close to the end of his tour.

The only 1 Group operational activity on the 24th was a mining operation by five Lancasters each from 103 and 153 Squadrons in the Yewtree garden located in the Baltic between north-eastern Jutland and Læso Island. The crews of S/L Riches, F/Ls Morgan, Norem and Stepharnoff and F/O Mosley took off between 17.09 and 17.12 and began the North Sea crossing at Mablethorpe on course for Jutland's western coast. They were greeted in the target area by clear skies and positions were established by H2S for the delivery of six mines each from 12,000 feet between 20.11 and 20.23.

During the course of the month the squadron took part in fifteen operations and dispatched 179 sorties for the loss of two Lancasters and crews.

March 1945

Just when the crews must have been thinking that bomber operations were becoming safer, March came along to prove them wrong. The new month would see the Command continue to bludgeon its way across Germany, concentrating on oil, rail and road targets, along with the few towns still boasting a built-up area. The penultimate month of the bombing war began with a daylight operation on the 1st and was the final one of the many visited upon Mannheim. It was a 1, 6 and 8 Group force of 372 Lancasters and ninety Halifaxes that prepared for take-off that morning, among them 248 Lancasters representing 1 Group. At Elsham Wolds, 103 Squadron loaded seventeen Lancasters with a cookie, 1,770 x 4lb incendiaries and a Munroe bomb and sent them on their way between 11.45 and 12.05 with seven crews captained by pilots of flight lieutenant rank. After climbing out, they made for the Sussex coast, joining up with the rest of the 1 Group force and forming into vics in line astern led by the Hemswell units, which were employing yellow verey lights, yellow trailing lights and light green fins to aid identification. They began the Channel crossing over five-tenths cloud and maintained good formation as the cloud built to ten-tenths from the French coast, the tailwind lighter than forecast, despite which, no attempt was made to make up time. They arrived at the target some six minutes later than planned, and at 14.47, the Master Bomber was heard to ask his Deputy if he could see the main force, to which he received a negative response and ordered the marker force to orbit above the 12,000-foot cloud tops until 15.03, when he called for release-point flares. Blue smoke-puff skymarkers went down accurately and in concentration, and the main force crews were instructed to aim for the centre of these, the Elsham Wolds crews complying and delivering their loads from 16,500 to 19,000 feet between 15.07 and 15.12. On return, they were unable to provide an assessment of the results and there was no post-raid reconnaissance or local report to provide clarity, but it is known that many bombs fell on neighbouring Ludwigshafen and its surrounds, where much damage occurred. F/O Thomson and crew failed to return in PD272, which crashed somewhere in the general target area killing all but one of the eight occupants and delivering the flight engineer into enemy hands.

With Cologne now almost on the front line, it, too, was earmarked for its final attack of the war on the morning of the 2nd, for a which a two-phase operation was planned, the first by 703 aircraft from 1, 4, 6 and 8 Groups, and the second, a G-H attack by 155 Lancasters of 3 Group. 1 Group contributed 244 Lancasters, fifteen of them belonging to 103 Squadron, each loaded with a cookie, a dozen 500 and four 250 pounders, before departing Elsham Wolds between 07.00 and 07.38 with pilots of flight lieutenant rank again the most senior. The rule of thumb across the Command generally was that a squadron commander should operate once a month and flight commanders perhaps twice, and while senior officers in a large number of squadrons frequently led from the front, the official policy appeared to be rigidly adhered to at 103 Squadron.

After climbing out, they pointed their snouts towards Beachy Head to take their place in the elongated bomber stream, before beginning the Channel crossing and reaching the target to find near perfect bombing conditions with a little cloud with tops at around 6,000 feet. A Master Bomber was on hand to tell them where to bomb, although the city's landmarks, the cathedral and nearby main railway station and the Hohenzollern railway bridge stood out in the sunshine, almost inviting the bombs to fall. The 103 Squadron crews released their bombs onto red and green TIs from 16,000 to 18,000 feet between 10.01 and 10.06, and many, for a change, were able to see the fall of their bombs. It wasn't long before a mushroom of black smoke began to conceal the ground, and later crews were instructed to bomb the up-wind edge of that. The main concentration of bombing was on the western side of the Rhine, and the western end of the Hohenzollern railway bridge appeared to have been demolished and had collapsed into the Rhine. The second wave by 3 Group was ruined by the failure of a G-H station in England and had to be halted after only fifteen aircraft had bombed. It mattered little, as the damage was done, and the once proud city fell to American forces four days later.

The night of the 3/4th brought mining sorties in one of the Silverthorn gardens of the Kattegat for fifteen 1 Group crews from 12, 14 and 15 Bases, and it was also the night chosen by the Luftwaffe for Operation Gisella, which involved some two hundred intruders stalking returning bombers as they prepared to land. They succeeded in bringing down twenty bombers, including one Lancaster from 460 Squadron RAAF returning to Binbrook from the Kattegat and two from 12 Squadron who were on training exercises.

Preparations for Operation Thunderclap to return to Chemnitz were put in hand on the 5th, and a force of 760 aircraft assembled from all but 5 Group, which itself would be active some thirty-five miles to the north, attacking the oil refinery at Böhlen. 1 Group dispatched 239 Lancasters, the fourteen representing 103 Squadron loaded with either a cookie and incendiaries or a 2,000 pounder plus incendiaries and a Munroe bomb and departing Elsham Wolds between 16.50 and 17.21 led by pilots of flight lieutenant rank. Those taking off from the more northerly stations, particularly those of 6 Group, climbed into ten-tenths cloud with severe icing conditions, which caused nine of them to crash. Aside from a slight reduction over the Channel and northern France, the complete cloud cover would remain in place all the way to the target area, and there were reports of predicted flak around Leipzig, which had probably been stirred-up by the above-mentioned 5 Group operation. The target area was concealed beneath ten-tenths cloud with tops up to 13,000 feet, and crews had to listened out for the Master Bomber's instructions as they lined up for the bombing-run. They observed cascading red and green skymarkers and were told at 21.50 to bomb them with a twelve-second overshoot from 15,000 feet. When the skymarkers went out at 21.55, they were ordered to bomb the glow in the clouds, before further skymarkers appeared and the original order was reinstated.

The 103 Squadron crews carried out their attacks from 15,000 to 17,000 feet between 21.46 and 22.04, but were unable to assess the outcome, reporting only a bright glow beneath the clouds that seemed to cover an area a mile wide. They turned south towards the Czechoslovakian frontier for the homeward flight across southern Germany, where some were pestered by enemy night-fighters, which were probably largely responsible for the failure to return of fourteen Lancasters and eight Halifaxes. F/L Short and crew were attacked by three Ju88s in the target area without sustaining damage and they returned safely, but ME392 and PB563 were absent from their dispersal pans and crews of F/O Exel RCAF and F/L Norem respectively were posted missing. It is not clear where the former came down, but the pilot and Canadian bomb-aimer have no known grave, while the rest of the crew were taken into captivity and confirmed that the bomb-aimer was observed to leave the Lancaster. The latter crashed somewhere in the Berlin defence zone and there were no survivors from among the eight men on board. It was established eventually that the operation had been a major success, which had destroyed by fire much of the central and southern districts of the city. It also resulted in damage to some important war-industry factories, and the destruction of the Siegmar tank-engine works.

The main operation on the 7th was to be undertaken by 526 aircraft of 1, 3, 6 and 8 Group against the virgin target of Dessau, a city in eastern Germany between Berlin to the north and Leipzig to the south. While this was in progress, 256 Halifaxes and twenty-five Lancasters of 4, 6 and 8 Groups were to target the Deutsche Erdöl oil refinery at Hemmingstedt on the western side of the Schleswig-Holstein peninsular, while 5 Group went for a similar target at Harburg on the south side of the River Elbe opposite Hamburg. 1 Group contributed 243 Lancasters to the Dessau raid, fifteen of them belonging to 103 Squadron and loaded with either a cookie or a 2,000 pounder supplemented by incendiaries and a Munroe bomb. They departed Elsham Wolds between 16.50 and 17.28 with S/L Butler the senior pilot on duty and climbed out through complete cloud-cover, which persisted as the stream adopted a circuitous route via the Sussex coast to make landfall north of Dieppe. F/L Anderson and crew had turned back with navigation equipment failure before the others traversed Belgium and skirted the southern Ruhr, where the cloud thinned to up to five-tenths but built again to eight to ten-tenths with tops at 10,000 feet as they headed on a north-easterly track to the target. Night-fighters had infiltrated the bomber stream from the Rhine, and flak intensified in the Braunschweig and Magdeburg defence zones.

As the main force crews approached the city, which, since 1925, had been home to the famous Bauhaus architectural school, they observed illuminating flares going down at 21.56, followed by red and green TIs, which proved not to be visible through the cloud. Release point flares soon joined the mix, and they were concentrated at first, but became scattered later, as the Master Bomber's instructions suffered from interference after someone in a main force aircraft left a transmitter on. Fortunately, a large break in the clouds at 22.04 provided a clear view of the ground and the many TIs still burning, and the main force crews were able to take advantage. A drama was unfolding on board RA500, which was attacked by night-fighters on the final approach to bomb and sustained damage to two engines, both turrets, the electrical and hydraulic systems and control surfaces, and was losing fuel fast. F/O Nightingale RCAF nursed it back to Allied lines, where the crew abandoned it to its fate, but tragically, F/O Nightingale's parachute did not deploy and he was killed, while his crew all landed safely on the ground with a number of injuries between them. The remaining 103 Squadron crews carried out their attacks from 13,000 to 15,000 feet between 22.00 and 22.10 and observed widespread fires revealing a distinct pattern of streets, and many explosions, including one producing a large bluish flash at 22.08. At 22.18, a section of the town burning with white flames suddenly erupted in a terrific red burst and continued to burn red. There was a mention at some debriefings of "scarecrows" over the Ruhr on the way home, but these mythical shells, supposedly created to simulate a bomber blowing itself to pieces to demoralise crews, did not exist, and were, indeed, some of the missing eighteen Lancasters blowing up violently.

Among the twelve 1 Group absentee Lancasters were two from 103 Squadron, including JA857, which was shot down at around 22.00 and crashed near Kölleda, some thirty-five miles west of Leipzig, killing F/O Havell and five of his crew, while the sole survivor, the rear gunner, was reported to have been shot by his captors on the following day. (Bomber Command Losses Vol 6. W R Chorley). F/O Saxe RCAF and three of his predominantly Canadian crew lost their lives when NF913 came down somewhere in the Ruhr region, and the three survivors, it is believed, were taken prisoner. The operation caused extensive damage in the town centre and residential, industrial and railway districts, all of which would have to be completely rebuilt after the war, sadly, in the Eastern Bloc style of concrete architecture.

The pace of operations refused to slacken, and what, perhaps, should have been a wind-down towards the German capitulation, became one of the most intense operational periods in the entire war. With six major operations already behind it during the first week of the month, the second week began for 8 Group with orders on the 8th to provide sixty-two Lancasters and ten Mosquitos to mark for 241 Halifaxes of 4 and 6 Groups for an attack on the Blohm & Voss U-Boot yards in Hamburg, where the new Type XXI vessels were under construction. While this operation was in progress, 235 Lancasters of 1 Group would be joining twenty-seven others and fourteen Mosquitos of 8 Group to raid Kassel, some 150 miles to the south. 103 Squadron made ready thirteen Lancasters for what would be the last major raid on it of the war and the first return to this destination since the devastating raid in late October 1943. They were loaded with either a cookie or a 2,000 pounder supplemented with incendiaries and departed Elsham Wolds between 17.14 and 17.33 with S/L Butler the senior pilot on duty. They climbed out through nine to ten-tenths thin cloud that topped out at around 5,000 feet, and this would accompany the bomber stream all the way from the Sussex coast, over France and Belgium, until it decreased slightly as they swung north of the Ruhr. However, it built again as they headed south-east for the target, which they found to be covered by eight to ten-tenths cloud topping out at 6,000 feet. The attack opened on time with both sky and ground markers, the latter clearly visible through the cloud, and although the red TIs were a little sparse, greens were plentiful. The skymarking was less accurate, but as most crews focused on the TIs, it mattered little, and when a gap opened up over the city, crews were able to assess for themselves the quality of the marking. The 103 Squadron crews attacked from 19,000 to 21,000 feet between 21.30 and 21.45 and observed fires building steadily in the western half of the city, the glow from which hung in the sky to remain visible for a hundred miles and more. No local report emerged to provide details of the damage, which would have been severe.

An all-time record was set on the 11th, when 1,079 aircraft, the largest Bomber Command force ever to be sent to a single target, was assembled to attack Essen for the last time. 1 Group contributed 240 Lancasters, fifteen of them belonging to 103 Squadron, which were loaded with a cookie, twelve 500 and four 250 pounders before taking off from Elsham Wolds between 11.33 and 11.47 with S/L Riches the senior pilot on duty. They climbed out through ten-tenths cloud, above which conditions were excellent, but the ground would remain concealed from view throughout the operation. All arrived in the central Ruhr to find the cloud tops at 6,000 feet, which required the Path Finder element to employ skymarkers in the form of blue, and later red smoke puffs, and the first of these went down at 14.59, to be backed up throughout the course of the raid. The 103 Squadron crews delivered their bombs from 16,000 to 19,000 feet between 15.00 and 15.07 as part of a total of more than 4,600 tons to complete the destruction of the already ravaged city and former industrial powerhouse. Smoke and dust emerged through the cloud tops in a tight spiral that had reached 10,000 feet as the last of the bombers retreated, and the city would still be in a state of paralysis when the American ground forces captured it unopposed on the 10th of April.

Twenty-four hours after the Essen raid, the short-lived record was surpassed by the departure from their stations in the early afternoon of 1,108 aircraft, which had Dortmund as their destination. This time 1 Group provided 244 Lancasters, eleven made ready at Elsham Wolds and loaded with a cookie, eleven 500 and four 250 pounders plus a Munroe bomb and taking off between 13.00 and 13.08 with S/L Butler the senior pilot on duty. Having adopted the southerly route, they all reached the eastern Ruhr to find it still under a blanket of ten-tenths cloud with tops again at 6,000 feet, conditions for which the Path Finders had prepared a skymarking plan based on green and blue smoke puffs. The first Oboe-aimed greens appeared at 16.26 to be followed a minute later by blues from the blind primary markers, and the Master Bomber directed the main force crews to aim for the latter. It was not long before brown smoke was observed to be climbing through the clouds to 8,000 feet from the northern end of the city, and crews also reported a ring of smoke encircling the entire area so dense that it remained visible for 120 miles into the return flight. The 103 Squadron crews carried out their attacks from 16,000 to 19,000 feet between 16.30 and 16.37 and contributed to the delivery of a new record of 4,800 tons of bombs. LM131 arrived back over Lincolnshire with a bomb lodged in its mainplane, courtesy of a higher-flying Lancaster, and was abandoned by F/O Wright RCAF and his crew. It crashed near the village of Elsham and the body of the flight engineer was found nearby, his parachute having failed to open, possibly as a result of jumping too late. Photo-reconnaissance revealed that the central and southern districts of the city had received the greatest weight of bombs and had been left in chaos with all industry silenced permanently and railway tracks torn up.

That night, five Lancasters each from 103 and 153 Squadrons were made ready for mining duties in the Silverthorn 1 garden in the Skagerrak off Sweden's Kullen point. The 103 Squadron crews of S/L Slater and F/Ls Holland, Murton, Short and Stepharnoff departed Elsham Wolds between 17.43 and 17.47 and flew north to begin the North Sea crossing at Scarborough. F/L Holland and crew were let down by their H2S equipment and turned back, while the others pressed on and traversed Jutland and the western Baltic to reach the target area and deliver their six 1,800lb or 1,500lb mines each from 12,000 feet between 20.55 and 21.00. ME449 was homebound over Jutland's western coast when it was shot down by the night-fighter of Major Werner Husemann of I./NJG3 and crashed at 21.45 at Lyne with both gunners still on board, they possibly having been killed or severely injured during the engagement. S/L Slater and the others in the forward section of the aircraft landed safely and were spirited away by the local resistance to retain their freedom.

Elements of 1 and 8 Groups joined forces on the evening of the 13th, to attack two benzol producers in the Ruhr, the Erin plant at Herne, located between Bochum and Gelsenkirchen, and the Dahlbusch AG plant, south of the Gelsenkirchen city centre. 1 Group detailed seventy-eight Lancasters from 12 and 13 Bases for the former and eighty-one from 14 and 15

Bases for the latter, the fourteen representing 103 Squadron departing Elsham Wolds between 17.15 and 17.36 with S/L Riches the senior pilot on duty and each Lancaster carrying a cookie, twelve 500 and four 250 pounders or a Munroe bomb instead of one 500 pounder. The partial cloud cover over England gave way to clear skies during the Channel crossing from Hastings to Le Touquet and as far as the Rhine, where cloud built to nine-tenths with tops at 10,000 to 12,000 feet with considerable haze below. The first red and green TIs went down three-and-a-half minutes late at 20.29½ and were visible only by their feint glow beneath the cloud, as a result of which, most crews bombed on H2S or Gee, those from Elsham Wolds from 14,200 to 16,000 feet between 20.30 and 20.32. A large white explosion was witnessed at 20.31, but an assessment of the raid was impossible, and the impression was that much of the bombing had under and overshot the aiming point. This was confirmed by post-raid reconnaissance, which also revealed the Gelsenkirchen raid to have been successful.

Benzol plants at Bottrop and Castrop-Rauxel in the Ruhr would occupy elements of 4, 6 and 8 Groups during the afternoon of the 15th, while 1 and 8 Group stations were conducting briefings for the evening operation against the Deurag-Nerag oil refinery at Misburg, on the north-eastern rim of Hannover. 1 Group detailed a main force of 212 Lancasters supported by forty-six Path Finder Lancasters and nine Mosquitos, the 103 Squadron element of fourteen departing Elsham Wolds between 17.10 and 17.23 with S/L Butler the senior pilot on duty and each crew sitting on a cookie, ten 500 and three 250 pounders and a Munroe bomb. The Channel crossing outbound terminated at Le Treport in what was a most circuitous route for a target in northern Germany, that crossed France, Belgium and Holland, before entering Germany to the north of Duisburg and swinging towards Hannover from the south. The passage across enemy territory both out and in benefitted from cloudless skies, and this enabled crews to identify the target visually by the light of illuminator flares. The raid began punctually with red TIs, backed up by mixed reds and greens in great concentration right on the aiming-point, and the Master Bomber called in the main force at 21.12. Almost immediately the target was engulfed in flames, and smoke was observed to rise through 10,000 feet following an explosion at 21.13. The Elsham Wolds crews delivered their bomb loads from 17,000 to 19,000 feet between 21.14 and 21.30 and returned home to report a highly successful operation, characterised by many explosions and fires visible from a hundred miles into the return journey. There was particular praise from the main force crews for the performance of the Master Bomber and the Path Finder element generally.

Nuremberg was posted as 1 Group's target on the 16th, for which a force of 231 Lancasters was assembled, and it would be supported by forty-six Lancasters and sixteen Mosquitos of 8 Group. A simultaneous operation by 225 Lancasters and eleven Mosquitos of 5 Group would take place at Würzburg some fifty miles to the north-west, and the presence of more than five hundred aircraft was likely to draw a Luftwaffe night-fighter response despite the shortage of experienced pilots and aviation fuel. 103 Squadron launched fifteen Lancasters from Elsham Wolds between 17.14 and 17.30, each carrying a cookie and incendiaries and some a Munroe bomb. Partial cloud cover increased to ten-tenths at the French coast near Abbeville with tops at 14,000 feet, but this broke up slowly to leave four to six-tenths in the target area with tops at 7,000 to 9,000 feet. A stronger than forecast wind drove the spearhead of the main force to the target ahead of schedule, and half a dozen of these bombed five minutes before H-Hour and before the appearance of any markers. The Path Finder illuminator crews officially opened the attack on time at 21.24, and a large gap opened up in the cloud to reveal the red and green TIs on the ground. The master Bomber provided clear instructions with which the 103 Squadron crews complied as they bombed from 16,000 to 18,000 feet between 21.30 and 21.37, and as smoke began to obscure the ground at around 21.35, the Master Bomber instructed crews to aim for bomb bursts. By this time smoke had risen through 7,000 feet and developing fires were outlining streets before merging into a single conflagration that produced a glow on the horizon for 150 miles.

The flak was relatively ineffective, but night-fighter activity was intense from the Stuttgart area to the target and back as far as the bomb line, and a shocking twenty-four 1 Group Lancasters failed to return, 10.4% of those dispatched. Many 1 Group squadrons posted missing multiple aircraft, 12 Squadron alone having four unaccounted for, while three 103 Squadron dispersal pans stood empty at Elsham Wolds. It was a particularly sad night for the squadron's Canadian element as all three pilots and eight crew members were members of the RCAF. ME848 crashed at Schwäbisch Hall, forty miles north-east of Stuttgart and F/O Armour survived with all but one of his crew, although a number of them sustained injuries. F/L Stepharnoff and his crew were on their twenty-eighth sortie and all lost their lives when NG492 came down somewhere in southern Germany. The wreckage of NN758 was found at Laichingen, forty miles south of Schwäbisch Hall, and just one man escaped with his life from the crew of F/O Watt. Heavy damage was caused in the southern half of the city and the already devastated Altstadt and more than five hundred people lost their lives, many in one of the south-western districts ravaged by fire.

Operations continued to come thick and fast, and the next target was also in southern Germany. Hanau's railway system had been attacked in January, and now it was time for an area attack, which was to be carried out by a 1 Group main force of 230 Lancasters, supported as always by a strong Path Finder element. 103 Squadron made ready fourteen aircraft, which departed Elsham Wolds unusually late for the period, between 00.36 and 00.49 on the 19th, with S/L Butler the senior pilot on duty and each Lancaster carrying a cookie and incendiaries and some a Munroe bomb. They climbed out through layer cloud and set course for the south coast and the Channel, pressing on with cloud alternately building and dispersing all the way out until 8°E, where the skies cleared but the ground became obscured by thick haze. The first illuminating flares were seen at H-15, and these were followed immediately by both skymarkers and red and green TIs, which fell in excellent concentration and stood out clearly through the haze until obliterated by the ensuing bombing. The 103 Squadron crews carried out their attacks from 10,000 to 12,000 feet between 04.31 and 04.37, at which point the Master Bomber issued instructions to bomb the upwind edge of the smoke. Crews headed for home confident that they had contributed to a highly effective raid, which would be confirmed by post-raid reconnaissance and local sources that revealed the destruction of 2,240 houses, the devastation of the Altstadt and damage to most of the public buildings. F/O Essex and crew failed to return in NG491, and no trace was ever found of Lancaster and crew.

1 Group alerted 13 and 15 Bases on the 21st to prepare for an operation against the Deutsche Vacuum oil refinery in Bremen, for which 104 Lancasters were made ready to act as the

main force, with twenty-nine Lancasters and six Mosquitos of 8 Group to provide the marking. 103 Squadron loaded a dozen Lancasters with a cookie, eleven 500 and four 250 pounders and a Munroe bomb and sent them on their way from Elsham Wolds between 07.46 and 07.56 with S/L Butler the senior pilot on duty. They set course via Wainfleet for Egmond, and all arrived in the target area under clear skies and with the Path Finder marking punctual and concentrated on the aiming point. They carried out their attacks from 14,000 to 15,000 feet between 10.00 and 10.03 in accordance with the instructions of the Master Bomber and in the face of an intense flak barrage, which caused damage to six Lancasters. F/L Wilson sustained a head wound, but all returned safely to base to make their reports. Later, that night, 117 Lancasters of 12 and 14 Bases conducted an operation with elements of 8 Group against the benzol plant in the Bruchstrasse district of Bochum in the heart of the Ruhr.

Elements of 1, 6 and 8 Groups were selected to deliver the only heavy raid of the war on the city of Hildesheim, situated south-east of Hannover and south-west of Brunswick. The aiming-point was to be the marshalling yards, but any major operation at this stage of the war was essentially an area attack, for which a force of 227 Lancasters and eight Mosquitos was made ready on the 22nd. 1 Group detailed a hundred Lancasters from 13 and 15 Bases, the ten belonging to 103 Squadron each receiving a load of a cookie, incendiaries and a Munroe bomb, before departing Elsham Wolds between 11.25 and 11.32. They adopted the same course across the North Sea as for the Bremen operation, via Wainfleet and Egmond, and all arrived under clear skies and good visibility, which enabled ground features to be identified. In contrast to the previous operation, defence was non-existent and the 103 Squadron crews delivered their attacks from 14,500 to 15,200 feet between 14.03 and 14.08 in accordance with the Master Bomber's instructions. A large column of smoke was rising through 6,000 feet as the last of the bombers turned away, and it was established later that a highly effective raid had laid waste to 70% of the town, including 3,300 apartment blocks containing around ten thousand individual dwellings.

A daylight operation was posted on 12 and 14 Base stations on the 23rd, which involved ninety-seven 1 Group Lancasters following on the heels of twenty Tallboy and Grand Slam-carrying Lancasters of 5 Group's 617 Squadron to target a railway bridge in Bremen. On the following day, eighty crews on 13 and 15 Base stations attended briefings to learn of that afternoon's operation against the Harpenerweg benzol plant in Dortmund, for which 103 Squadron made ready a dozen Lancasters and filled their bomb bays with a cookie, twelve 500 and four 250 pounders. They departed Elsham Wolds between 12.55 and 13.04 with F/Ls Anderson and Armstrong the senior pilots on duty and set course via Hastings to make landfall near Berck-sur-Mer. Conditions were ideal, with the TIs standing out clearly on the aiming point and inviting the 103 Squadron bomb loads to fall in accordance with the instructions of the Master Bomber from 17,500 to 19,000 feet between 16.30 and 16.33. The attack again took place in the face of a spirited flak defence, which inflicted damage on a number of the squadron's Lancasters. Smoke was rising through 8,000 feet at the end of the raid and all from Elsham Wolds returned safely, F/L Hardman and crew with their bomb load intact after failing to hear the Master Bomber.

Operations on the 25th were directed at urban areas through which enemy reinforcements might pass on their way to the Rhine battle area. 4 Group detailed 131 Halifaxes to act as the main-force for an attack on the marshalling yards at Osnabrück in the Münsterland region of Germany north of the Ruhr, while 151 Halifaxes from 4 and 6 Groups were made ready for Münster, some thirty miles to the south-west, and 251 Lancasters of 1 and 6 Groups for Hannover seventy miles to the east. 1 Group put up 151 Lancasters for the last-mentioned, seven of them provided by 103 Squadron, which each received a bomb load of a cookie, incendiaries and a Munroe bomb and departed Elsham Wolds between 06.51 and 07.00 with four pilots of flight lieutenant rank taking the lead. They climbed out through ten-tenths cloud, before heading to the rendezvous point at Wainfleet, which was found to be cloud-free, but cloud began to build again halfway into the North Sea crossing, and it was around this time that F/L Price and crew turned back with an engine issue. The cloud dispersed again from 06.30°E to leave clear skies in the target area, which enabled crews to identify the built-up areas, the marshalling yards and the river visually. The attack opened with accurate bombing, although the bright sunlight made it impossible to distinguish the colours of the TIs and eventually smoke obscured the aiming-point, persuading the Master Bomber to call for the bombing to be aimed at the upwind edge. The 103 Squadron crews bombed from 17,500 to 18,500 feet between 09.46 and 09.49, and as they turned away, smoke could be seen rising through 14,000 feet. They all returned safely, confident that the main weight of bombs had fallen within the built-up area of the city.

The focus remained on the region of Germany to the north of the Ruhr on the 27th, as its encirclement by American ground forces required just the capture of the town of Paderborn, situated some thirty-five miles due east of Hamm. 1 Group provided a main force of 225 Lancasters, including fourteen representing 103 Squadron, while 8 Group contributed forty-four Lancasters and nine Mosquitos. The Elsham Wolds element took off between 14.45 and 14.57 with S/L Butler the senior pilot on duty and each Lancaster carrying a cookie and either incendiaries or cluster bombs. After climbing out, they headed via Wainfleet for the Dutch coast under fairly clear skies, but the cloud began to build over enemy territory until reaching ten-tenths over the target with tops at around 10,000 feet. This prompted the Master Bomber to call for smoke-puff skymarkers at 17.25, but the first greens did not appear until 17.28, after which, a steady supply maintained the aiming-point for the next ten minutes. The early arrivals had been forced to orbit, but the crews following behind, who had been preparing to bomb by H2S and Gee, were able now to use the skymarkers as a more reliable reference, while confirming their accuracy by means of navigational aids. The 103 Squadron crews carried out their attacks from 15,500 to 17,000 feet between 17.30 and 17.37 and returned home to report a cloud of brown smoke ascending to 2,000 feet above the clouds. The operation was an outstanding success, confirmed by a local report, which stated that three thousand separate fires had occurred, and that the town had been virtually destroyed.

The final operation of the hugely busy penultimate month of offensive activity by the Command was to end with a 1, 6 and 8 Group raid on the Blohm & Voss U-Boot yards at Hamburg, where the new Type XXI vessels were being assembled. A force of 361 Lancasters and a hundred Halifaxes was made ready on the 31st, 201 of the former provided by 1 Group, of which eight stood ready for departure at Elsham Wolds. F/Ls Holland Nicols and Price were the senior pilots on duty as they took off between 06.25 and 06.32 and climbed out through layer cloud on course for Skegness, where they were to rendezvous with the rest of the group and form into a line-astern column. The cloud prevented this, and the force was closing on the Dutch coast at 3°E, when it broke up sufficiently to allow the forming up to take place, only for it to build again from 6°E and remain at ten-tenths for the remainder of the flight to the target. When the leading aircraft of the main force were fifteen minutes out, the Master Bomber warned them to look for smoke-puff markers, and the first of these appeared at 08.43, but only in small numbers. It was a further three minutes before they became plentiful, by which time the bombing was well underway in accordance with the frequent instructions and changing aiming points coming through from the Master Bomber. It caused a degree of jostling for position over the target, but the 103 Squadron crews found red smoke puffs to bomb from 17,000 to 18,000 feet between 08.45 and 08.52. F/O Meiklem and crew suffered the frustration of a total hang-up over the aiming point caused by a defective bomb-release key, and they returned safely with the others, mostly with the impression that the raid had lacked a degree of concentration. However, local reports spoke of widespread damage in residential and industrial areas in the south of the city and across the Elbe in Harburg, with energy supplies and communications also hard-hit.

It had been a sobering month for 103 Squadron and Elsham Wolds, during the course of which, the squadron carried out seventeen operations and dispatched 213 sorties for the loss of eleven Lancasters, nine crews and two other airmen.

April 1945

April would be a time to mop up defences, cut off communications and finish off the oil industry, and it began for 1 Group with an operation against what was believed to be a military barracks at Nordhausen, situated in the Harz mountains between Hannover to the north-west and Leipzig to the south-east. The site was actually a pair of enormous parallel tunnels under the Kohnstein Hill, which had been developed originally by the BASF Company to mine gypsum between 1917 and 1934. Following the destruction of Peenemünde, smaller tunnels had been created as a link between them to form a horizontal ladder effect, and the site turned over to the Mittelwerk GmbH (Gesellschaft mit beschrenkter Haftung, or Limited Company) for the manufacture of V-2 rockets and other secret projects. The "barracks" were part of the Mittelwerk-Dora forced workers camp, where inmates existed under the most horrendous conditions and brutal treatment, while they were starved, worked to death or simply executed by an increasingly desperate regime seeking to change the course of the war. 1 Group provided a main force of 210 Lancasters, including eleven from 103 Squadron, while 8 Group added a further thirty-seven and eight Mosquitos to conduct the marking. At Elsham Wolds, the armourers winched eleven 1,000 and two 500 pounders and one Munroe bomb into each Lancaster and sent them into the air between 13.20 and 13.30 with W/C Macdonald undertaking his first operation since taking command four months earlier and supported by S/L Riches as the other senior pilot on duty. They flew out over Southwold on course for the Belgian coast, to follow the line of the frontier with France until entering Germany near St Vith, the moderate cloud thickening as the bomber stream progressed eastwards.

By the time the target drew near, there was ten-tenths cloud, and the Master Bomber issued instructions at 16.02 for the main force crews to descend to the cloud base at 8,500 feet. Four minutes later, as the bombers approached the cloud tops at around 11,000 feet, the Master Bomber rescinded his original order, and instructed the crews to climb again. This caused confusion, and all semblance of the previously coherent formation was lost. Some futile attempts were made to reform the stream as the Master Bomber called for smoke-puff markers, but these seem to have burst inside the cloud and were not visible. As a last resort, he ordered the crews to "bomb on best navigational aids", and the main force crews complied, all but two of those from 103 Squadron on H2S from 13,000 to 15,000 feet between 16.18 and 16.22, while the crews of F/Sgt Bishop and F/O Thomson failed to pick up the instructions and withheld their bombs. It was impossible to accurately assess the outcome, but a single 1 Group crew dropped beneath the cloud base to 5,500 feet and reported two small fires in the town but no bombing around the aiming point. The target and the nearby town would be attacked again twenty-four hours later by 5 Group and would sustain severe damage. Many friendly foreign nationals would lose their lives in the barracks, while those in the tunnels remained safe from bombs, but endured a hellish existence as they were systematically worked to death.

The night of the 4/5th brought a return to the oil offensive at three sites, Leuna and Lützkendorf near Leipzig, and Harburg on the South Bank of the Elbe opposite Hamburg. 1 Group detailed 238 Lancasters for Lützkendorf, situated west of Leipzig on the western edge of the Geiseltal Lake. Lützkendorf no longer exists on a map of Germany and is now known as either Mücheln or Krumpa. 103 Squadron made ready a dozen Lancasters for the main event and five to join ten others from 1 Group for mining duties in one of the Silverthorn gardens in the Kattegat region of the Baltic, and it was the latter, consisting of the crews of F/Ls Anderson, Armstrong and Murton and F/Os Hole and Mosley, that departed Elsham Wolds first, between 19.20 and 19.31, each with six 1,800lb mines beneath their feet. They flew out over Whitby and were approaching the Danish coast as the bombing brigade took to the air between 20.50 and 21.16 with F/Ls Holland, Nicol, Price and Wilson the senior pilots on duty. The gardeners reached their destination first to find good conditions but extreme darkness that hid ground detail, and they planted their vegetables by H2S from 15,000 feet between 22.44 and 22.49. They met resistance in the form of flak and night-fighters and three Lancasters were seen to go down, among them LM177, which disappeared without trace with the predominantly Australian crew of F/O Hole RAAF. This proved to be the last of the 179 aircraft lost by 103 Squadron during the war. Also missing without trace was the crew of the 153 Squadron commanding officer, W/C Powley DFC.

Meanwhile, those involved in the main event had climbed out through cloud that persisted over England but cleared at the south coast, before building up again between 5° and 11°E. It then dispersed again to leave clear skies and good visibility at the target, which was reached after an outward flight of almost four-and-a-half hours. The first Path Finder ground markers went down at 01.25 and were easily identified by the 103 Squadron crews as they delivered their cookie and ten 500 pounders each from 12,000 to 14,000 feet between 01.28 and 01.35. Some crews at the tail end of the main force were instructed by the Master Bomber to aim at the smoke, which had largely concealed the T.Is at 01.33. Returning crews reported observing fewer fires than expected, but several large explosions witnessed at 01.29, 01.31

and 01.40 and accompanied by volumes of thick smoke suggested that the attack had been at least moderately effective. In fact, the plant had not been decisively damaged, but an attack by 5 Group on the night of the 8/9th would bring an end to all production at the site.

A major operation again the Blohm & Voss U-Boot yards at Hamburg involved 440 aircraft from 4, 6 and 8 Groups on the night of the 8/9th, while 1 Group enjoyed a night off. The operation cost eleven aircraft, the last double-digit loss of the war to result from a single target. Preparations were put in hand on 1, 3 and 8 Group stations on the 9th to prepare 591 Lancasters for a raid that night on the harbour area of Kiel, the location of the major shipbuilding yards. 1 Group detailed 256 Lancasters for the main event, including fourteen representing 103 Squadron, and briefed the crews for two aiming points, D and E. In addition, thirty-four Lancasters, five belonging to 103 Squadron, were to sneak in under cover of the bombing activity to lay mines in the Forget-me-not garden in Kiel harbour and at Eckernförde in the bay to the north. The gardeners departed Elsham Wolds between 19.09 and 19.15 with S/L Butler the senior pilot on duty and began the North Sea crossing at Whitby, enjoying excellent weather conditions and visibility all the way to the target, where four delivered their six 1,800lb mines each by H2S according to brief from 14,000 and 15,000 feet between 22.31 and 22.45. F/L Hardman and crew lost their H2S, and it is believed, brought their mines home.

They bombing brigade took off between 19.26 and 19.50 with F/Ls Newman, Price and Ridd the senior pilots on duty and a cookie and sixteen 500 pounders in each bomb bay and followed in the wake of the gardening element via Whitby to make landfall at Sankt Peter-Ording on the western coast of Schleswig-Holstein, leaving them with a sixty-mile dash across the peninsula to the target. They encountered a little cloud before the enemy coast hove into sight, but the target itself lay under clear skies with good visibility, and illuminating flares allowed the Master Bombers to identify the outline of the fjord and inner harbour and the two aiming-points. Ground marking commenced at aiming-point D at 22.25 and at aiming-point E two minutes later, and both were well-marked with red TIs, backed up by greens, enabling the main force crews to aim at whichever presented the better target. Eventually, all of the TIs became obscured by smoke, and by the end of the attack, the entire area between the aiming-points was on fire, with flames spreading down to the water's edge. A particularly large explosion at 22.35 gave the impression that an ammunition dump had been hit, and hits on an oil storage depot resulted in thick, black smoke billowing up to a considerable height as the crews turned away. The Elsham Wolds crews delivered their attacks from 13,500 to 16,000 feet between 22.31 and 22.39, and photo-reconnaissance confirmed the effectiveness of the operation, revealing the Deutsche Werke U-Boot yards to have sustained severe damage and the other two shipyards also to have been hit. The pocket battleship, Admiral Scheer, had capsized, the Admiral Hipper and the Emden were badly damaged, and adjacent residential districts had suffered also.

The focus of operations on the 10th was upon railway installations in eastern Germany, the Engelsdorf and Mockau marshalling yards in Leipzig for a force of 134 Lancasters, ninety Halifaxes and six Mosquitos by daylight, and a stretch of track linked to the Wahren yards in the same city by seventy-six Lancasters and nineteen Mosquitos of 5 and 8 Groups after dark. A further operation involving 307 Lancasters and eight Mosquitos from 1 and 8 Groups would target the marshalling yards in the town of Plauen, situated close to the frontier with Czechoslovakia thirty miles south-west of Chemnitz. The 1 Group contribution of 253 Lancasters included eighteen provided by 103 Squadron, which each received a bomb load of a cookie and ten 500 pounders, before departing Elsham Wolds between 18.03 and 18.37 with S/L Riches the senior pilot on duty. They began the Channel crossing near Hastings on course for the Boulogne area and lost the services of F/Sgt Finsand and crew to an engine issue on the way.

The others traversed Belgium to enter Germany via the St-Vith region with a further 260 miles and ninety minutes flying time ahead of them and reached the target area to encounter clear skies and good visibility. The red Oboe TIs went down on time to open proceedings and were backed up by greens in a tight cluster that satisfied the Master Bomber, who then called in the main force crews to deliver their attacks, those from 103 Squadron complying with his instructions from 16,000 to 18,000 feet between 23.09 and 23.16. A large explosion was observed at 23.11, and by 23.20, the town was completely obscured by smoke rising through 12,000 feet. The glow of fires remained visible for a hundred miles into the return journey and post-raid reconnaissance would confirm the accuracy of the attack, which resulted in the destruction of 365 acres, or 51% of the town's built-up area. Tragedy struck when P/O Candler's PA217 and F/Sgt Boklaschuk's RF193 collided as they were taxiing to their dispersal pans on return, and the rear gunner in the former, F/O Mayers, was killed.

Four 103 Squadron crews were among thirty from 1 Group to attend briefings on the 13th to learn that they would be returning to the Forget-me-not garden in Kiel harbour that night under cover of a 5 Group raid on the port and its shipyards. The crews of F/Ls Armstrong, Murton and Nicol and F/Sgt Hatchard departed Elsham Wolds between 20.20 and 20.24 and climbed away into ten-tenths cloud which hid Whitby from view as they began the North Sea crossing. The cloud persisted as far as 3°E before clearing, only to build again at the Danish coast and remain at ten-tenths in the target area with tops at 2,000 feet. They dropped between them eighteen 1,800lb mines and six of 1,500lbs by H2S from 12,000 feet between 23.18 and 23.43 and returned safely after round-trips of some six hours.

The final major attack on a German city was directed at Potsdam on the night of the 14/15th, and this would be the first incursion into the Berlin defence zone by RAF heavy bombers since March 1944. In the twelve months since then, Mosquitos of 8 Group's Light Night Striking Force (LNSF) had maintained a regular presence over the city, acting as a constant menace, dropping cookies to unsettle the populace and robbing the workers of their sleep. So fast was the "Wooden Wonder", that it was not unknown for a single aircraft to make two trips to Berlin in one night after a change of crew. A force of five hundred Lancasters from 1, 3 and 8 Groups was assembled, of which 215 Lancasters were provided by 1 Group, while twenty-four others from 576 Squadron carried out a spoof raid on the port of Cuxhaven at the mouth of the Elbe. Thirteen 103 Squadron Lancasters had their bomb bays filled with a cookie and ten 500 pounders before departing Elsham Wolds between 17.36 and 17.58 with F/Ls Hardman, Price and Ridd the senior pilots on duty. They set course via Southwold for Knokke on the Belgian coast, before swinging towards the Ruhr to pass its north-western edge and continue on an east-north-easterly track to the target. The cloud that had been present in the early stages finally disappeared from the Rhine eastwards, to leave the target area under clear skies with excellent visibility.

The attack opened with illuminating flares under the watchful eyes of the designated Master Bomber, W/C Le Good, and his Deputy, F/L Douglas, both of 35 (Madras Presidency) Squadron, and the marking commenced six minutes before H-Hour with red TIs, which fell initially a little to the west of the aiming-point. These were soon corrected by other reds planted right on the mark and backed up by greens to leave the main force crews with no doubt about where to direct their bombs. The Master Bomber maintained good control throughout, changing the point of focus as required and keeping the attack firmly on the aiming point. The Elsham Wolds crews performed as briefed from 18,000 to 20,000 feet between 22.48 and 22.57, and on return reported many fires and explosions and an afterglow visible for a hundred miles into the return journey. The raid was confirmed as a success, but some bomb loads were found to have spilled into northern and western districts of Berlin.

There was good news for some main force crews to celebrate on the 17th, when the length of a tour was reduced yet again to thirty sorties, releasing many to contemplate a long future. Early briefings across the Command on the 18th informed 969 crews of an assault on the coastal batteries, naval base, airfield and town on the island of Heligoland. 1 Group assembled a force of 310 Lancasters to be divided equally between aiming points A, at the northern end of the island and B, at the southern end where the harbour and U-Boots pens were situated. A third aiming point, C, was the Luftwaffe aerodrome and would be the first to come under attack by one of the other groups. 103 Squadron made ready twenty Lancasters, loading each with a dozen 1,000 and four 500 pounders and sending them on their way from Elsham Wolds between 09.48 and 10.25 bound for aiming point A with S/L Riches the senior pilot on duty. They flew out over Mablethorpe and arrived in the target area under clear skies and in good visibility, Heligoland and its smaller neighbour, Düne, appearing as two tiny dots some thirty miles off Germany's north-western coast. Aiming point B had been attacked minutes earlier and it seems that six of the 103 Squadron crews had either arrived early or had been assigned to aiming point B, which they bombed from 17,500 to 19,000 feet between 12.33 and 12.37.

Smoke was already rising as the second-phase bomber stream covered the leg between the final turning point and the target and the Master Bomber was first heard at 12.50 issuing instructions to bomb the yellow TIs. However, these were found to have undershot, and he shifted the point of aim to the upwind edge of the smoke, by which time the remaining 103 Squadron crews had bombed the markers from 16,500 to 19,000 feet between 12.49 and 12.55. A very large explosion in the docks area at 12.47 sent a column of black smoke a thousand feet into the air and started an oil fire, and several vessels, believed to be destroyers, were observed to be heading away south-east of the harbour, one of them, it is believed, receiving a direct hit. Post raid reconnaissance revealed the surface of Heligoland to resemble a cratered moonscape, but its ordeal was not yet over, as on the following day it would face an attack by 617 and 9 Squadrons, the former carrying 10-ton Grand Slams and 6-ton Tallboys and the latter Tallboys. If not already totally evacuated, the island certainly was after this operation.

As the British XXX Corps moved in on the city of Bremen, Bomber Command was asked to bomb four enemy strong points in the south-eastern suburbs, where the attack was due to take place in two days' time. A main force of 691 aircraft was drawn from 1, 3 and 6 Groups, 270 of them provided by 1 Group, while 8 Group put up seventy-six Lancasters and sixteen Mosquitos. 103 Squadron's contribution of seventeen Lancasters departed Elsham Wolds between 14.55 and 15.22 with S/L Riches the senior pilot on duty and flew out over Mablethorpe over cloud that persisted more or less for the entire outward flight, and as the first wave element approached the target at 17.56, the crews could only catch a glimpse of the ground through gaps. The Master Bomber was heard to ask his Deputy whether the aiming point could be marked in those conditions, and a negative response persuaded him to broadcast "Marmalade", the signal to abandon that phase of the operation. The visual marker crews confirmed that they were unable to identify the aiming-points, and the attacks on aiming-points J1, J2 and G were called off at 17.58, 18.13 and 18.49 respectively, and the entire 1 and 6 Group elements returned home with their bombs. 195 aircraft bombed at aiming-point F, before that, too, was abandoned at 19.05.

The final operations of the bombing war were carried out on the 25th, beginning with what was, perhaps, a symbolic attack by a main force of 335 Lancasters of 1 and 5 Groups and twenty-four Lancasters and eight Mosquitos of 8 Group on Hitler's Eaglesnest retreat and the nearby SS barracks at Berchtesgaden in the Bavarian mountains. 1 Group provided 247 Lancasters, and none of those involved in the preparation and operation of the sixteen 103 Squadron aircraft had any notion that this would be the final offensive action of 1 Group's war. It required an early start, the Elsham Wolds crews taking to the air between 05.04 and 05.27 with S/L Butler the senior pilot on duty and each Lancaster carrying a cookie, four 1,000 pounders and single 500 and 250 pounders as gifts for the Führer. They crossed the coast near Folkestone on course for Cap Gris Nez, and a few patches of high cloud aside, the outward flight benefitted from perfect conditions. However, the attempt by the 1 Group element to form into a line-astern column became somewhat chaotic from 4°E, where two gaggles developed, and the designated leaders found themselves in the rear one. By the time 6°E was reached, a large proportion of the 1 Group force had managed to form up into a reasonable column, but about eighty remained ahead and made no effort to re-join. Some of these eventually orbited and joined the column as it passed by, but many stragglers remained and the whole 1 Group formation found itself south of track. The attempt to rectify the situation all but eliminated the turning point at 12°E and the final turn to the target was a good ten miles wide.

The vanguard of the bomber stream arrived in the target area on time, only to find that all was not proceeding according to plan. The deputy Master Bomber had been unable to mark the target, and, realising this, the leader of the first wave overshot the final turning point by two-and-a-half minutes, before bringing the force back in a wide orbit. This had the effect of splitting up the formation, and aircraft began approaching the aiming-point from a variety of headings. At 09.45 the Master Bomber ordered the crews to bomb visually if they could, but a minute later a red target indicator went down, which appeared to be accurate, and crews selected whatever was best for them, including the upwind edge of the smoke. The 103 Squadron crews carried out their attacks from 15,000 to 18,000 feet between 09.49 and 09.57 and a concentration of bombs was seen to fall across the SS barracks. Despite the lack of cohesion, it seems that most fell within the confines of the general target area, causing a column of smoke to rise to 10,000 feet.

When W/O Green and crew touched down at Elsham Wolds at 14.39, they unwittingly brought to an end the offensive wartime career of 103 Squadron. A force of 482 aircraft from 4, 6 and 8 Groups were sent against coastal batteries on the Frisian Island of Wangerooge during the afternoon, and 5 Group attacked an oil refinery at Tonsberg in southern Norway that night to effectively bring an end to the bombing war. Operation Exodus, the repatriation of prisoners of war began on the 26th and would continue on into the summer and Operation Manna, to provide food for the starving Dutch people still under enemy occupation, would run from the 29th to the 8th of May, the day on which the war in Europe ended. On the 28th of April, a dozen 103 Squadron Lancasters undertook their first sorties of Operation Exodus and flew to Brussels to bring home former PoWs to Dunsfold. The weather at Melsbroek was extremely unhelpful with low cloud and rain, and only the crews of F/L Anderson and F/Os Ross and Taylor were able to land and pick up around eighteen men each for transportation back to England.

103 Squadron was undoubtedly one of the finest in Bomber Command, and emerged from the war with a record of service which bears comparison with any. It suffered generally higher casualties than most squadrons, however, and finished the war with a loss rate of 3.1%. The Squadron was the proud owner of the highest sortie-scoring Lancaster of them all, ED888, coded PM-M, which notched up an estimated 147 sorties in all and arrived at 103 Squadron in April 1943. In December 1943, it moved across the airfield to 576 Squadron, before returning to 103 as PM-M2 and completing its mammoth service by December 1944. During the first nine months of the war, the squadron conducted the highest equal number of Fairey Battle operations in the AASF and Bomber Command, the second highest number of Battle sorties and second equal highest number of Battle losses in Bomber Command.

Off to mine Stettin Bay 21st December 1944 at 3pm. An eight hour trip with a six 1500lb bomb load.

Lancaster ME773 PM-U took off on the 14th July 1944 on an operation to bomb Revigny rail facilities. The aircraft was shot down and crashed roughly 400 metres from Magny-Fouchard, France. Wireless Operator/Air Gunner Sgt James Richards and five of his comrades were killed. All were buried in the local cemetery with full military honours. The ceremony was well attended by the villagers, and services were again carried out on November 1st and Remembrance Sunday. Local children made wreaths from the flowers laid on the six graves.

Crew: P/O H R Anthony (Pilot) Sgt E Beard (FE), Sgt H D Birkbeck (Nav), Sgt N H Maughan (BA), Sgt J A Richards, Sgt W Wass (MUG) Sgt W H Taylor (PoW).

Sgt James Richards

F/Ls John and David and P/O Gaven Henry; Australian brothers and all pilots at 103 Squadron in the second half of 1944 (Henry family)

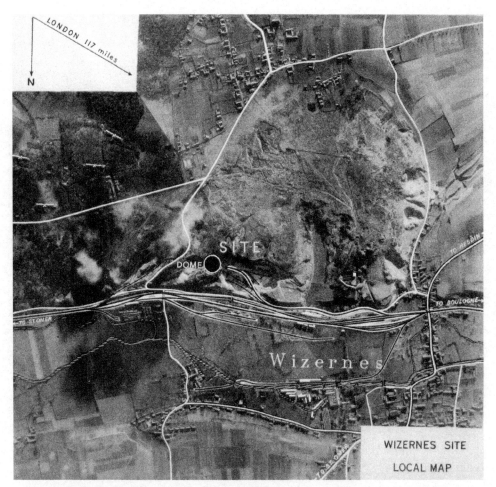

Photo map of the area around the site before the bombing campaign

A photograph taken by a British Mosquito aircraft flying only 20 metres (66 ft) above the ground shows the dome, still intact, sitting at the centre of the wrecked construction site on 6th July 1944, shortly before its abandonment.

393

Training on the quadruple anti-aircraft gun, probably of 37mm bore, a weapon used for air and ground targets because of its powerful combined fire effect.

F/L Anselme "Selmo" Verniueuwe DFC – one of the four Belgian aircrew that served with 103 Squadron.

Two Belgian crew mates: rear gunner Georges Bechoux (left) and his pilot Louis Remy DFC (Belgian War Museum).

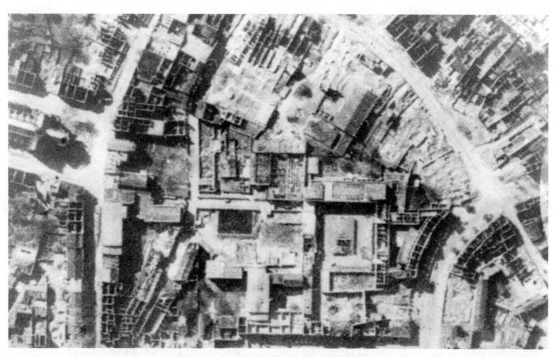

Aachen, Germany. 1944. The Post Office, telephone exchange and commercial buildings at Aachen after the attacks of RAF squadrons including 103 Squadron.

F/Sgt Jackson C Cooke CGM and crew.

Hasselt, Belgium. May 1944. A wrecked locomotive framed in the broken structure of the ruined buildings at the railway marshalling yards at Hasselt, following attacks by Allied bombers which included some from 103 Squadron.

S/L Harold Swanston and his crew were lost on the Mailly raid on 4ᵗʰ May 1944. It is believed they were one of the crews shot down whilst orbiting Chalons-en-Champagne waiting for the order to commence the attack. They crashed at Villers le Chateau and are buried in the local churchyard.

A low flying Lancaster is seen through the glare of a burning Mailly-le-Camp 3/4ᵗʰ May 1944.

P/O G W Chase 4th July 1944.

Aerial photo of Cap Gris Nez, taken by the RAF before bombing, by amongst others, 103 Squadron.

W/C H R Goodman

Sgt C L Finigan

P/O W L Vanderdasson DFM

F/Sgt G H Agar

F/O R McLeod

P/O P D Vickers

F/Sgt R White

Crew of Lancaster ND700 All lost 12th May 1944 on a Hasselt operation.

103 Squadron Lancaster PM-S

399

Damage at Pas de Calais after an attack by RAF aircraft June 1944.

The centre of Düren, fortress town near Aachen, photographed by RAF reconnaissance on 18th November 1944, two days after RAF's daylight attack which included 103 Squadron. All roads are impassable, many buildings are still burning, and the town has been blotted out under the great concentration of bombs.

The Fortress of Mimoyecques is the modern name for a World War II underground military complex built by the forces of Nazi Germany between 1943 and 1944. It was intended to house a battery of fixed V-3 cannons permanently aimed at London, 165 kilometres (103 mi) away.

It was constructed by a mostly German workforce recruited from major engineering and mining concerns, augmented by prisoner-of-war slave labour. The complex consisted of a network of tunnels dug under a chalk hill, linked to five inclined shafts in which 25 V-3 guns would have been installed, all aimed at London. The guns would have been able to fire ten dart-like explosive projectiles a minute – 600 rounds every hour – into the British capital, which Winston Churchill later commented would have constituted "the most devastating attack of all".

Left: The prototype gun in

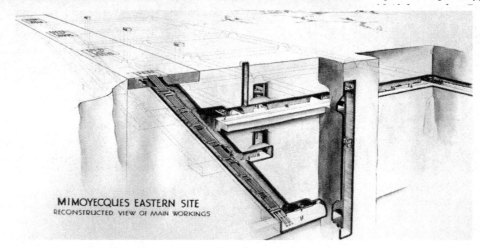

MIMOYECQUES EASTERN SITE
RECONSTRUCTED VIEW OF MAIN WORKINGS

103 Squadron Lancaster at dispersal in 1945

S/L Ken Butler and crew (Butler family).

Crew of Lancaster ND861 lost on 4ᵗʰ January 1945.
Sgt Cyril Lloyd (RG), P/O Christopher Weight (Pilot), P/O George Widdicombe (FE)), F/O Maurice Pickersgill (Nav), Sgt Henry Backway (W/Op), Sgt Clifford Hillier (MUG). Contact was lost with the aircraft after the weather deteriorated. They were believed to have flown into a blizzard and crashed into the River Humber. Only wreckage was found, and the crew are commemorated on the Runnymede Memorial.

P/O Christopher Weight who crashed into the Humber 4ᵗʰ January 1945.

F/L Charles Pearton KIA 7ᵗʰ January 1945 on a mining operation. All crew lost and commemorated on the Runneymede Memorial. (Pearton family).

The Thomson Crew

Seven crew were lost on Mannheim operation 1st March 1945, Sgt Ron Pain being the only survivor. L-R: F/Sgt D Kyle, F/Sgt A Crampin (W/Op), M/T driver, Sgt R Pain (FE), F/Sgt Bill Tromp (Nav), P/O John Peace (BA). Kneeling is F/Sgt John Rochester. Also lost were F/O F J Brickman (2nd pilot) and F/Sgt J W Grice (RG).

F/O A S Thomson

F/Sgt William Tromp, F/O A S Thomson, F/Sgt Donald Kyle. Front P/O J M Peace. F Sgt John Rochester.

A thick mass of smoke obliterates Cologne towards the end of the attack by RAF, including 103 Squadron in support of the advancing Allied ground forces. March 1945

Cologne Cathedral stands seemingly undamaged (although having been directly hit several times and damaged severely) while entire area surrounding it is completely devastated. Köln Central Station and Hohenzollern Bridge lie damaged to the north and east of the cathedral. Germany, 24th April 1945.

The Deurag-Nerag refineries Hanover after attacks including 103 Squadron 1945.

Krupps factory, Essen 1945.

ED888, here bearing 103 Squadron code PM-M2, flew more operational sorties than any other Lancaster in Bomber Command.

They wore scarves to keep away enemy fighters. F/L Joseph Albert Laviolette, Lancaster pilot, had a fancy one; F/L Gordon Campbell Nicol, on the right flaunted a white one which he never washed, lest it break the talismanic effect. It seemed to work, too, neither was ever a target for an enemy fighter. Photo PL43904 (ex-UK21317) and caption © Library & Archives Canada (used with copy and presentation permissions).

Oblique aerial view of wrecked railway repair sheds in the Rothenditmold marshalling yards at Kassel, Germany. These were hit in the last large raid on the city on the night of 8/9th March 1945, when 1,100 tons of bombs were dropped on its western parts by 262 Avro Lancasters of No. 1 Group including 103 Squadron, led by 14 De Havilland Mosquitos of No. 8 Group.

Aerial view of part of Heligoland Island in the North Sea, which was subjected to a massive air raid by nearly 1,000 British medium and heavy bombers on 18th April 1945. The population of the island took refuge in underground bunkers but almost everything above ground was destroyed.

Front Row - Extreme left S/L Butler, W/C MacDonald, 4th left S/L Riches, extreme right possibly F/L Taylor. Back Row 5th from left F/L G Nicol. F/O Monteith and extreme right F/L J A Laviolette.

Cleve, Germany. February 1945.
Aerial views from an RAF aircraft flying over the British battle front at Cleve. Left photo shows a 5.5 medium gun in action south of Cleve. Stacked ammunition and the place where charges are buried in the ground are in the foreground. Right photo shows two 5.5 medium gun in action under netting. 103 Squadron were involved in destroying the German defences as the British army moved forward.

Aircraft flying over Berchtesgaden, the target area, already billowing with clouds of dust and smoke, during the daylight attack by Lancaster aircraft of RAF Bomber Command including 103 Squadron.

After an air attack by Lancaster aircraft of RAF Bomber Command including 103 Squadron, Hitler's Chalet showing part of the main building destroyed and both wings, on the right and left. The Main Control centre (top left) for guarding Oberzalzburg has been severely damaged too.

F/O Fred Gibson and crew (Purves family).

F/Sgt S A Jeffrey bomb aimer in the crew of F/O L Hole MIA 5th April 1945. This was the squadron's last operational loss in the war (Eric McKay).

F/Sgt J M Hayward was a qualified pilot but flew as Flight Engineer in the crew of F/L W W Anderson in 1945.

Dresden 1945.

Hamburg, Germany. 1945
Over 16,000 tons of bombs were dropped, resulting in the destruction of 75% of the built-up (target) area. Aerial photograph showing the rubble and the ruined buildings. Unfinished U-boats are still on slipways.

An Avro Lancaster with a food drop over Ypenburg, Netherlands during Operation Manna 1945.

Lancaster bombers, including 103 Squadron, took part in Operation Manna, dropped thousands of pounds of food supplies in occupied Holland for the starving Dutch people. This is the total load of one Lancaster, and in the foreground are the contents of a typical sack: dried eggs, milk powder, cheese, dried yeast, chocolate, margarine, dehydrated meat, mustard, salt, luncheon meat, tea, beans and all dropped without parachutes.

Near Frankfurt, Germany. The veteran Lancaster "S" for Sugar of 467 Squadron landed without fear of enemy opposition on a German airfield near Frankfurt. The Lancaster aircraft is engaged in the repatriation of prisoners of war (POWs) from Europe after VE Day 5th May 1945 known as Operation Exodus, repeated many times after the war by 103 Squadron amongst others.

Runnymede Memorial, Surrey
The memorial contains the names of Commonwealth Air Forces war dead who have
no known grave, or are lost without trace anywhere in the world.

Memorial dedicated at former RAF Elsham Wolds to those lost on operations
from 103 Squadron and 576 Squadron RAF.

Roll of Honour

Sgt	Philip Robert	ABBAS	05.05.42.
F/O	Peter John	ABBOTT	13.07.44.
W/O	Sidney Edward	ABRAMS	07.01.45.
Sgt	Percy William	ADAMS	09.01.43
F/Sgt	Dene	ADAMS	22.10.43
F/Sgt	George Roughton Carver Gilroy	ADAMS	31.07.44.
F/Sgt	Thomas	ADCOCK	30.08.44.
P/O	Joseph Horace	ADDISON	26.06.43.
F/Sgt	Gilbert Harry	AGAR	12.05.44.
Sgt	William	AINSCOW	02.12.43
Sgt	Eric	AIREY	20.12.42
Sgt	Philip William	ALDERTON	16.12.43.
Sgt	John Edward	ALDRIDGE	19.03.45.
Sgt	Sidney Walpole	ALLEN	30.08.44.
Sgt	Frederick William	ALLEWAY	06.08.41.
Sgt	George Henry	ANDERSON	21.01.43
Sgt	William	ANDREWS	12.03.43
Sgt	Edgar James	ANDREWS	03.10.43
P/O	Henry Roy	ANTHONY	15.07.44.
F/Sgt	Kenneth	ARCHER	26.07.43.
Sgt	Stanley	ARMITAGE	19.03.45.
P/O	John Walter	ARMSTRONG	11.04.44.
Sgt	Francis Thomas	ARMSTRONG	15.07.44.
F/O	Robert	ARMSTRONG	29.07.44.
Sgt	Derek Souter	ARMSTRONG	14.08.44
F/Sgt	John Raymond St George	ARROWSMITH	05.05.42.
F/O	Eric Richard Victor	ASHCROFT	01.04.43
Sgt	Philip Kennedy	ASHCROFT	24.12.44.
P/O	Thomas Edwin	ASTBURY	23.04.44.
F/Sgt	John Edward Griffiths	ASTON	27.09.43
F/O	Kenneth Leslie	ATKINS	15.02.44
F/Sgt	William Frank	AUSTIN	01.03.43
F/Sgt	William Henry	AUSTIN	23.08.43
F/O	John Prescott	AUSTIN	18.08.44
F/O	Joseph Geonidas Gerald	AVON	31.07.44.
Sgt	Henry George	BACKWAY	04.01.45
Sgt	William John	BAGLEY	01.08.42
F/Sgt	Charles	BAGSHAW	20.02.44
Sgt	Robert James	BAILES	15.06.43.
Sgt	Peter	BAILEY	03.03.43
Sgt	George Irvine	BAILEY	25.07.43.
Sgt	Edward William	BAKER	24.06.42.

Sgt	Reginald Wilfred	BAKER	24.12.44
Sgt	Frederick William Ewart	BALL	09.06.42.
F/Sgt	William Stuart	BANCROFT	13.07.44.
F/O	George Graham	BANKS	18.10.43
F/Sgt	Frank	BARKER	24.07.41
Sgt	Peter Adin	BARNES	26.11.43
Sgt	Clarence	BARNES	14.08.44
F/Sgt	Donald Leighton Spence	BARR	07.07.43.
Sgt	James William	BARRETT	03.08.43.
F/L	John Peter Dennis	BARTLEET	14.08.44
Sgt	Kenneth Charles	BARTLETT	06.01.44.
Sgt	Thomas	BARTON	30.08.44.
Sgt	John William	BATEMAN	03.01.44.
Sgt	Richard William	BAYBUT	04.07.43.
Sgt	Charles James	BAYNES	25.07.44.
F/Sgt	Harry James	BEAKE	10.08.43.
Sgt	Eric	BEARD	15.07.44.
F/Sgt	William James Henry	BEARDSMORE	29.07.44.
Sgt	Leonard	BEAUMONT	16.06.41
W/O	Jean	BEAUPRE	07.08.42.
Sgt	George Joseph	BECKWITH	24.07.41
F/O	Raymond Henry	BEER	28.05.44.
F/Sgt	Alec Henry	BEESLEY	05.09.42.
F/O	Sydney Frank	BELBIN	05.09.42.
Sgt	James Bulman	BELL	21.09.41.
Sgt	Tom	BELL	18.10.43
F/O	Peter Anthony Charles	BELL	24.03.44
F/Sgt	Duncan Neilson	BELL	27.04.44.
W/O	John Edward	BELLAMY	02.12.43
P/O	Allan Conway	BELYEA	31.03.44.
Sgt	Peter Maxwell	BENNETT	10.09.41
F/Sgt	Thomas	BENNETT	20.12.42
Sgt	Charles Edward	BENSTEAD	06.09.42
F/Sgt	Jack	BERNALDO	10.04.44.
F/L	Kenneth Herbert	BERRY	15.02.44
Sgt	Elmer	BETTS	04.07.43.
S/L	Kenneth George	BICKERS	24.03.44
P/O	John William	BICKERTON	08.01.45.
F/Sgt	Ernest Roy	BIGGS	18.08.43.
P/O	Ronald Albert	BINGHAM	28.08.42
Sgt	Howard Derek	BIRKBECK	15.07.44.
F/Sgt	William John	BIRMINGHAM	28.07.42
F/Sgt	Claude Frederick	BISH	16.05.44.
Sgt	Albert Frank	BISSELL	24.06.42.
Sgt	Roland Edward	BLACK	02.12.43

Sgt	Allan Neil	BLACKLEY	26.06.42
F/Sgt	George Ralph	BLACKMORE	10.09.41
F/Sgt	George William	BLACKSHAW	17.03.45.
Sgt	Desmond	BLAKE	21.09.41.
F/Sgt	Walter Steward	BLAKE	20.12.43
Sgt	Raymond Arthur Oswald	BLANCHARD	26.07.44.
Sgt	Arthur Frank	BLENCOWE	25.04.42
Sgt	Peter Ivo	BLIGH	10.06.40
Sgt	Dugald	BLUE	26.11.43
F/Sgt	Barriemore Smallwood	BLUNDALL	28.08.42.
F/L	Philip Jones	BLURTON	22.10.43
Sgt	Donald Edward Joseph	BOLAND	01.03.43
Sgt	Eric	BONE	24.12.44
F/O	Geoffrey	BOOTH	26.11.43
Sgt	Reginald Patrick	BOWLER	11.04.44.
F/Sgt	Frank Lawrence	BOYD	21.01.43
W/O	Ronald Howard	BOYD	04.05.44.
F/Sgt	Brian Phillip	BOYLE	31.03.44.
W/OI	Gordon Clark	BRADLEY	03.08.43.
Sgt	William Leslie	BRADLEY	20.02.44.
P/O	Thomas Wallace	BRADLEY	10.04.44.
F/O	Dennis Charles	BRADSHAW	04.07.43.
Sgt	Neville	BRADSHAW	29.07.44.
Sgt	Gerald Charlesbeth	BRAMS	03.08.40
F/Sgt	Charles Lorne	BRAY	25.04.42
W/O	Kenneth	BRECKON	23.08.43.
F/O	Robert William	BREVITT	27.11.43.
Sgt	Stanley Charles	BREWER	21.01.43
Sgt	John Walker	BREWSTER	24.12.43.
P/O	Edward Arthur Rutherford	BRIANT	28.08.42.
F/O	Frederick John	BRICKMAN	01.03.45
Sgt	Frank	BRIGGS	15.10.42
Sgt	Joseph Allen	BRIGHT	10.08.43.
Sgt	Kenneth Lindon	BRINDLEY	18.10.43
Sgt	Alfred John	BRISTOW	20.02.44.
Sgt	Charles Alfred	BRITTON	26.06.43.
F/L	Eric	BROADBENT	29.07.44.
Sgt	Alfred George	BROADMORE	25.07.43.
F/Sgt	Kenneth Arba	BROOKE	15.07.44.
Sgt	Ronald	BROOKER	15.10.42
F/O	John Parrington	BROOKSBANK	06.12.44.
F/O	Roye Wilmott	BROWN	12.04.42
Sgt	Alfred Ernest	BROWN	20.12.42
F/L	Alan McKeand	BROWN	15.06.43.
Sgt	James	BROWN	26.06.43.

P/O	Cyril MacDonald	BROWN	10.08.43.
F/Sgt	William Richard	BROWN	22.10.43
Sgt	Harry	BROWN	02.12.43
F/O	George Chahoon	BROWN	08.08.44.
Sgt	Robert Steedman	BROWN	06.03.45.
Sgt	George	BRUCE	27.11.43.
F/O	Charles Edward Thomas	BRYAN	03.08.43.
Sgt	John Stanley	BUCKNOLE	24.07.41
F/Sgt	Francis William	BULL	13.07.44.
Sgt	Ernest	BULL	26.08.44.
Sgt	Harry Bircham	BULLEN	25.04.42
Sgt	Albert George	BURBRIDGE	13.06.41.
Sgt	Geoffrey Harry	BURCH	08.03.45.
P/O	William Edward	BURCHER	07.01.45.
F/Sgt	Norman George Albert	BURGES	26.08.44.
Sgt	Alfred Charles	BURGESS	09.01.43
P/O	Edgar Heaton	BURGESS	21.01.43
F/O	Ian Crawford	BURNS	01.04.43
Sgt	Raymond Harold	BUSSELL	26.11.43
Sgt	Leslie Charles	BUTCHER	25.02.41
Sgt	Philip Bertie Joseph	BUTCHER	06.10.42
F/Sgt	Robert	BUTLER	26.11.43.
F/Sgt	Alfred William	BUXTON	08.09.43
Sgt	Wilfred Claud	BUZAN	26.11.43
Sgt	James Edward	CALLAGHAN	01.04.43
F/Sgt	Edward Hilary	CALVERT	25.05.44.
Sgt	David Ian	CAMERON	25.07.43.
F/Sgt	Duncan	CAMPBELL	12.04.42
W/O	Hugh	CAMPBELL	16.12.43
F/Sgt	Donald Fletcher	CAMPBELL	07.01.45.
Sgt	Roy Percy	CANDY	07.01.45.
Sgt	William George	CANE	21.10.43.
F/Sgt	Dennis	CANNON	24.03.44
Sgt	Gerald Thomas	CANTERBURY	17.12.42
F/Sgt	Edward Butler	CAPIN	01.09.43.
F/Sgt	Philip John	CAPON	18.08.43.
Sgt	Douglas Eric	CARDWELL	16.02.43
F/Sgt	John Joseph	CAREY	29.08.42.
Sgt	George Robert	CARR	31.07.44
Sgt	James Maurice	CARROLL	17.06.43,
Sgt	Richard	CARSON	06.10.42
P/O	James Alexander	CARTER	12.05.44.
Sgt	Francis Edward	CARTER	13.03.45.
Sgt	Mark Watson	CARTMELL	27.11.43.
Sgt	George Francis	CASEY	04.05.44.

F/Sgt	John Melburne	CASSADY	28.01.44.
P/O	Eric Arthur	CASSIDY	07.08.42.
Sgt	Louis	CERVI	13.07.43.
Sgt	William Henry	CHAMBERS	16.12.43.
Sgt	Kenneth Herbert	CHAPMAN	01.03.43
Sgt	George	CHAPMAN	20.12.43
P/O	William James Donald	CHARLES	23.05.44.
Sgt	William Edward	CHEAL	02.12.43
F/Sgt	John Vincent	CHICOINE	03.07.42.
Sgt	Kenneth	CHILES	14.08.44
F/O	Robert Stanley	CHISHOLM	13.06.41
Sgt	Thomas Hill	CLAPP	03.10.43
Sgt	Sidney Arthur	CLARIDGE	25.10.42.
F/Sgt	Douglas	CLARK	23.11.43
Sgt	Arthur Charles	CLARK	05.01.45
Sgt	Victor Neville	CLAYTON	13.07.44.
F/Sgt	William Alfred	CLEVEY	28.05.44.
Sgt	Jack	CLIFFE	14.06.43
Sgt	Douglas Charles	COCHRANE	28.07.42
Sgt	Dennis John	COLDICOTT	04.05.44.
Sgt	Frank Reginald	COLLINS	17.12.42
Sgt	Dennis James	COLLINS	10.08.43.
Sgt	Timothy	COLLINS	29.07.44.
F/Sgt	Leonard John	COMER	24.03.44
Sgt	Albert Allan	CONISBEE	31.05.42
Sgt	William	CONNELL	16.06.41
Sgt	Francis Stewart Crichton	COOK	26.02.43
Sgt	Edward John	COOK	01.03.43
Sgt	Alexander	COOK	12.06.43.
Sgt	Samuel	COOK	05.01.45
F/Sgt	Jackson C.	COOKE	29.11.44
P/O	Walter Arthur	COOPER	09.09.40.
Sgt	Ernest	COOPER	09.01.43
Sgt	James	COOPER	21.04.43.
P/O	John Albert Basil	COOPER	26.07.43.
Sgt	Charles Joseph	COOPER	01.09.43
F/Sgt	Roger Hughes	COOPER	07.06.44.
Sgt	Peter	COOPMAN	16.12.43.
Sgt	Frederick Stanley	COPPING	16.12.43.
Sgt	John	CORLESS	08.08.44.
F/Sgt	John Edmund	COUCH	25.07.43.
Sgt	Herbert Edwin	COWLING	25.07.44.
Sgt	John James	COX	25.07.41.
Sgt	William Frederick	COX	18.10.43
F/L	Maurice Ivan	COX	28.04.44.

Rank	Name	Surname	Date
F/Sgt	John Harry	COXON	06.06.42.
Sgt	John David	CRAIG	28.08.42.
W/O	James Ferrie	CRAIG	22.10.43
F/Sgt	Patrick Joseph	CRAMER	21.04.43.
F/Sgt	Alan Joseph	CRAMPIN	01.03.45
F/Sgt	William Maurice	CRANE	07.08.42.
Sgt	Frederick Arthur	CRAWFORD	03.08.43.
Sgt	George Ernest	CRAWFORD	24.12.43.
Sgt	Ronald Gordon	CREBER	03.01.44.
F/Sgt	Ronald	CRITCHLEY	24.07.41
Sgt	James Grant	CROCKETT	05.09.42.
Sgt	Arthur Woodrow	CROOKE	29.07.44.
S/L	Ian Kingston Pembroke	CROSS	31.03.44.
Sgt	Leslie	CROSS	21.10.43
Sgt	Kenneth Denzel	CROTHERS	23.05.44.
Sgt	James Alexander	CRUICKSHANK	26.08.44.
Sgt	Peter Neller	CRUTCHFIELD	12.05.44.
Sgt	John Kenneth	CUBEY	27.11.43.
F/O	Robert Morison	CUMMING	03.12.42.
P/O	Vernon Allan	CUNNINGHAM	14.05.40
Sgt	Donald Henry James	CUNNINGHAM	20.02.44.
P/O	Leo Patrick	CURTIN	23.02.45
F/Sgt	Keith George	CURTIS	21.01.43
Sgt	Albert Henry	DAINES	20.02.44.
Sgt	John Samuel	DAINTON	15.01.42
F/Sgt	Gordon Alfred Joffre	DALDY	08.09.43
F/O	Arthur	DALEY	21.04.43.
Sgt	Thomas James	DALEY	29.04.43.
F/O	Eric John	DANE	04.05.44.
Sgt	Jack Bays	DANIEL	02.12.43
W/O	Ronald	DASH	03.08.43.
Sgt	Eric James	DAVEY	26.02.43
Sgt	Alan	DAVIDSON	27.09.43
F/Sgt	Ernest Lewis	DAVIES	05.09.42.
Sgt	Thomas Henry	DAVIES	18.10.43
Sgt	Vaughan	DAVIES	23.05.44.
F/Sgt	Alan	DAVIES	17.03.45.
Sgt	Thomas	DAVISON	23.08.43.
S/L (A)	Robert Adrian	DE SANDOVAL-SIEVIER	09.09.40.
Sgt	Carl	DEGES	05.08.41.
F/O	Keith Inger	DEXTER	17.06.43.
P/O	Robert	DEY	26.07.44.
F/O	Michael Frederick	DILLON	11.04.44.
Sgt	Thomas William	DINSDALE	01.08.42
Sgt	John Scott	DOBIE	10.03.43.

F/L	Reginald Frederick	DOBSON	23.02.45
Sgt	John Robert	DODD	28.03.42
Sgt	Peter Laird	DONALD	21.12.42
Sgt	John	DORRITY	28.04.44.
Sgt	Albert Nelson	DOWLING	15.06.40
P/O	Arthur Cyril Reid	DOWNWARD	23.06.42.
F/O	John Christopher Patrick	DOYLE	31.03.44.
P/O	Keith John	DRABBLE	10.05.40
Sgt	Fred	DRINKWATER	09.09.40.
F/O	Joseph Jean Andre	DUCHARME	31.03.44.
F/O	Harry Welland	DUGARD	12.03.43
Sgt	Walter	DUNCOMBE	28.08.42.
F/Sgt	Joseph Pearson	DUNS	07.06.44.
F/O	Maurice Ballard	DYER	26.07.44.
Sgt	Hedley	DYKE	03.12.42.
Sgt	James Stanley	EASTHAM	13.07.44.
P/O	Raymond Gordon	ECCLES	16.05.41.
F/Sgt	Henry Gordon	EDWARDS	23.06.42.
Sgt	John William	EDWARDS	03.07.42.
P/O	Kenneth Fraser	EDWARDS	05.10.42
Sgt	Cyril Bert	EDWARDS	28.08.43.
Sgt	William Austin	EDWARDS	28.05.44.
Sgt	Frank O'Kearney	EIVERS	25.04.42
F/O	Douglas Cunningham	ELDER	03.08.43.
Sgt	Raymond George	ELKINS	21.04.43.
Sgt	Charles Victor	ELLEN	03.03.43
Sgt	Thomas Alfred	ELLIOTT	03.07.42.
P/O	Stanley Brown	ELLIOTT	26.06.43.
F/O	Frank William	ELLIOTT	06.03.45.
Sgt	Thomas William Burnett	EMMOTT	24.06.42.
Sgt	George Alfred	ENGLAND	02.12.43
Sgt	Donald Fraser	ENRIGHT	31.07.44
F/O	Adrian West	ESSEX	19.03.45.
F/Sgt	Geoffrey Charles	EVANS	24.06.42.
Sgt	David Richard	EVANS	22.09.42
Sgt	David Ivor James	EVANS	26.11.43
Sgt	Eric Walter	EVANS	08.01.45.
F/L	Harold Frederick	EWER	26.07.43.
F/O	Gordon Wynne	EXEL	05.03.45
Sgt	Ronald Owen	EYNON	20.12.42
Sgt	Edward Ernest	FAIRHURST	12.04.42
P/O	Frank	FARNHAM	15.07.44.
P/O	Ivor George Arthur	FAULK	21.12.42
F/O	Ronald Norman	FAULKNER	27.09.43
F/O	Arthur James	FAULKNER	13.07.44.

Sgt	Henry	FEATHERSTONE	03.10.43
Sgt	David	FELL	07.01.45.
Sgt	Duncan Alexander Holmes	FERGUSON	15.06.43.
F/Sgt	Thomas William	FERGUSON	30.08.44.
Sgt	Edwin Carlo	FERMANIAN	12.03.43
F/Sgt	William Henry	FETHERSTON	17.03.45.
Sgt	Arthur Harry	FIGG	29.08.41
Sgt	Duncan Cameron	FINDLAY	26.03.40.
Sgt	German Francis	FINDLAY	21.09.41.
Sgt	Dennis John	FINDLAY	22.03.44
Sgt	Clifford Leslie	FINIGHAN	12.05.44.
Sgt	Alexander Edward	FINNEY	01.08.42
P/O	John Evans	FIRMAN	09.06.42.
Sgt	Frank John	FISHER	21.12.42
Sgt	Frederick Graham	FISHER	06.12.44
F/Sgt	James Richard	FITCH	26.07.43.
Sgt	Roland	FITCHETT	17.06.44.
Sgt	Lawrence	FITZSIMMONS	25.10.42.
Sgt	James Arthur	FLEMING	15.10.42
Sgt	Albert Ronald	FLEMING	24.12.43.
Sgt	Stanley George	FLETCHER	25.07.43.
P/O	Alan Noel	FLETCHER	23.02.45
Sgt	Leslie William	FLOWERS	31.05.42
F/Sgt	Kenneth William	FLOWERS	20.02.44.
W/O	James	FLYNN	03.08.43.
Sgt	Reginald Douglas	FOLEY	01.03.43
F/L	Allan Patrick	FORBES	30.08.44.
Sgt	Herbert Charles	FORD	16.02.43
Sgt	William Vernon	FORD	31.03.44.
Sgt	William John	FORGAN	03.08.43.
Sgt	Stanley	FOSTER	04.07.43.
S/L	Sidney Horace	FOX	25.10.42.
Sgt	Herbert	FOX	02.12.43
Sgt	Willoughby	FOX	06.01.44.
Sgt	William Henry	FOX	17.03.45.
Sgt	Hugh Ian	FRASER	28.03.42
Sgt	Norman	FRATER	17.12.42
Sgt	Robert	FRAZER	01.03.43
Sgt	Ronald William	FREEMAN	04.07.43.
F/L	James Rothwell	FRITH	28.08.42.
Sgt	Antony Hare	FRY	01.04.43
Sgt	Arthur George	FRY	08.03.45.
W/O	Reginald John	FULBROOK	22.09.42
F/O	Ronald Harry	FULLER	20.02.44.
Sgt	Francis Andrew	FURRIE	16.12.43.

F/O	Bertram John	FYSON	28.03.42
Sgt	Patrick	GALLAGHER	26.11.43
P/O	John Douglas	GALLAGHER	07.06.44.
F/Sgt	Vincent John	GALLOGLY	23.06.42.
Sgt	Henry	GARDNER	07.07.43.
Sgt	Ronald Francis	GARSIDE	07.07.43.
P/O	Robert Barry	GARSIDE	29.07.44.
F/Sgt	Clifford Samuel	GAY	04.05.44.
Sgt	Kenneth	GAYTHORPE	13.07.44.
Sgt	Ronald Alfred	GERRARD	12.03.43
P/O	Joseph Norman	GILBY	07.08.42.
Sgt	Evan David	GILES	03.08.43.
Sgt	George Ross	GILFILLAN	14.02.45.
F/L	Robert	GILLESPIE	12.04.42
F/O	Aaron Henry	GIPSON	17.04.43.
P/O	Alfred George	GLEESON	13.07.44.
W/C	Oliver	GODFREY	23.06.42.
F/Sgt	James Alfred	GOFF	29.11.44
Sgt	Ralph	GOODACRE	29.07.44.
F/Sgt	Frederick James	GOODALE	23.05.44.
Sgt	Stanley Victor	GOODHEW	25.10.42.
W/C	Hubert Rreginald	GOODMAN	12.05.44.
F/O	Theodore	GORAK	30.08.44.
W/OI	Harold Richmond	GRAHAM	13.07.43.
Sgt	Neil	GRAHAM	22.03.44
Sgt	William Brodie (Bill)	GRAHAM	23.04.44.
F/O	Douglas Munroe	GRANT	23.06.43.
Sgt	Hugh Kerr	GRANT	23.05.44.
Sgt	John	GRANT	17.03.45.
Sgt	John	GRASSOM	29.08.41
Sgt	Cecil William	GRAY	22.10.43
Sgt	William Henry	GREAVES	18.08.43
Sgt	George	GREEN	05.10.42
P/O	John Alexander	GREEN	06.03.45.
Sgt	Henry	GREENFIELD	27.04.44.
F/Sgt	Alan	GREENSIDES	13.06.41.
F/Sgt	Meyer	GREENSTEIN	07.01.45.
Sgt	John	GREENWAY	14.06.43
Sgt	Clement Ralph	GREENWELL	03.01.44.
Sgt	Denis Maxwell	GREEY	06.08.41.
Sgt	Charles Henry	GREGORY	19.03.45.
Sgt	Alexander	GREIG	03.03.43
F/Sgt	John William	GRICE	01.03.45
Sgt	Robert Elliot Pringle	GRIEVE	06.06.42.
Sgt	Robert Grattan Gurney	GRIFFIN	05.08.41.

F/O	Michael Francis	GRIFFIN	05.03.45
P/O	Eric	GRIFFITHS	23.06.43.
Sgt	Albert Marino	GRIMSON	26.11.43
Sgt	Edward Sandilands	GUNN	20.02.44.
Sgt	William James	GWYNNE	31.03.44.
Sgt	Dennis Allen	HADDEN	04.05.44.
Sgt	Anthony Oliver	HAINES	20.02.44.
Sgt	Horace Ronald	HALLAM	31.05.42.
Sgt	Henry	HALLIWELL	09.06.42.
Sgt	Jack	HAMER	22.10.43
Sgt	Alan Moffatt	HAMILTON	03.12.42.
Sgt	James Crane	HAMILTON	25.07.43.
Sgt	Ernest William	HAMILTON	20.02.44.
Sgt	Stanley	HAMILTON	18.08.44
Sgt	Owen Douglas	HANCOCK	01.08.42
Sgt	Peter George	HANCOCK	20.12.43
P/O	Arthur Vernon John	HARDCASTLE	13.06.41.
F/Sgt	Gilbert Peter Mallon	HARDESTY	15.01.42
F/Sgt	Benedict Joseph	HARDESTY	06.10.42
Sgt	Ronald Redfern	HARDEY	29.07.44.
F/O	William John	HARDING-HAYDON	12.06.43.
W/O	Gordon Edmund Bernard	HARDMAN	25.07.43.
Sgt	Frederick Ralph	HARDY	17.06.44.
Sgt	Sidney Harold	HARLE	25.04.42
Sgt	Robert William	HARLEY	17.04.43
Sgt	Reginald Eric Rees	HARRIES	09.01.43
Sgt	Andrew Albert Sidney	HARRIS	28.03.42
Sgt	Bernard William	HARRIS	20.05.42.
P/O	Peter Graham	HARRIS	12.03.43
Sgt	Edward Charles	HARRIS	01.09.43.
Sgt	Walter Gordon	HARRISON	05.05.42.
P/O	Arthur	HARRISON	27.09.43
P/O	John Albert	HARRISON	13.07.44.
F/O	Clifford Seymour	HART	24.02.45.
F/Sgt	Matthew	HARTLEY	16.12.43.
F/Sgt	Francis Leon Joseph	HARTNETT	28.07.42
Sgt	John	HARWOOD	23.08.43.
Sgt	Herbert Charles	HASLAM	02.12.43
F/O	William James	HAVELL	08.03.45.
Sgt	David Preston	HAWKES	21.09.41.
Sgt	Gordon Thomas	HAWKINS	21.12.42
F/O	Eric Henry	HAWKINS	13.07.43.
Sgt	Victor Barnett	HAWKINS	18.10.43
Sgt	Eric George	HAYWARD	26.05.40
Sgt	Joseph Michael	HEALEY	22.10.43

Sgt	Philip Charles	HEATH	25.10.42.
Sgt	Thomas Cook	HENDERSON	29.12.43.
Sgt	Leslie	HENDERSON	31.07.44
Sgt	Joseph Arthur	HENSON	01.08.42
W/O	John Wallace Mills	HERBERT	24.12.44
Sgt	Robert Arthur	HESLOP	17.06.43,
F/O	Samuel Tweedy	HEWITT	17.12.42
F/Sgt	James Stanley	HICKEY	17.03.45.
F/Sgt	Frederic Winston	HILL	22.09.42
F/Sgt	John Stewart	HILL	21.01.43
Sgt	Eric	HILL	18.10.43
W/OII	Francis Ignatius Roy Bruce	HILL	29.11.44
Sgt	Clifford Frederick	HILLIER	04.01.45
P/O	Ian Percival	HINTON	26.03.40.
P/O	Leonard John	HINTON	18.10.43
F/Sgt	Charles John	HODGE	05.04.45.
F/Sgt	Aubrey	HOGG	23.04.44.
P/O	John Edgar	HOLDEN	04.05.44.
F/O	Lincoln	HOLE	05.04.45.
Sgt	Raymond	HOLLAS	07.07.43.
Sgt	Robert Henry	HOLLIDAY	24.12.44
P/O	Derrick Reginald	HOLLINGSWORTH	07.06.44.
Sgt	Cyril Ernest	HOLLINGWORTH	09.01.43
W/OII	Jack Athelston	HOLLINSWORTH	17.12.42
Sgt	Ronald Leslie	HOLLYWOOD	26.06.43.
P/O	Sidney George	HOLMAN	01.09.43.
F/Sgt	Donald Richard George	HOLMES	12.02.42
Sgt	Robert	HOLMES	25.05.44.
F/Sgt	Stanley James	HONOUR	29.07.44.
P/O	Percival Gerald	HOPKINS	28.08.42.
F/Sgt	Donald	HOPKINS	23.04.44.
F/L	Francis Thomas	HOPPS	02.12.43
W/O	Millard Henderson	HORNE	07.01.45.
F/Sgt	John Knox Emslie	HORNIMAN	13.06.41.
Sgt	Harold Alfred	HORRELL	26.06.43.
Sgt	George	HOUGHTON	16.06.41
Sgt	George Watson	HOULISTON	14.04.43
F/Sgt	Ernest George	HOUSDEN	04.05.44.
Sgt	Richard Herbert	HOWELL	09.04.43
Sgt	David	HOWELLS	16.05.44.
Sgt	Henry Howard	HOWLES	13.07.44.
Sgt	Fred Carson	HOXFORD	04.05.44.
W/OII	Nickolas	HREHORAK	22.09.42
Sgt	William Frank	HUBBARD	26.05.40
F/O	Francis James	HUDSON	17.04.43.

Sgt	Ronald Leslie	HUNT	01.03.43
F/O	Kenneth Alfred Isaac	HUNT	24.12.44
P/O	Harold Joseph	HUTCHESON	07.01.45.
Sgt	Olaf Arthur	HUTCHINSON	10.05.40
Sgt	Robert Stanton	IMESON	02.12.43
Sgt	Stanley Lionel	INGLE	27.11.43.
Sgt	Roy Henry	INGRAM	04.07.43.
F/Sgt	Lawrence	IRELAND	28.05.44.
F/Sgt	Gerald Henry	ISAACS	07.07.43.
F/Sgt	Crossley	JACKSON	23.05.44.
Sgt	Eric Hartley Gordon	JACKSON	30.08.44.
F/O	Keith	JACKSON	06.03.45.
Sgt	James Frederick	JACKSON	17.03.45.
Sgt	Melville	JAMES	12.02.42
Sgt	Frank Lancelot	JAMES	14.08.44
F/Sgt	Norman Thomas	JAMES	31.08.44
F/O	Charles Reginald	JAQUES	16.12.43.
Sgt	Francis Norman	JAY	13.06.43.
F/Sgt	John Massey	JEFFERIES	21.12.42
F/Sgt	Sidney Alexander	JEFFREY	05.04.45.
Sgt	Arthur	JEFFREYS	21.12.42
Sgt	Raymond William	JEFFS	06.01.44.
Sgt	John Edward	JENNINGS	07.06.44.
Sgt	Anthony	JERVIS	23.04.44.
Sgt	Walter James	JEWISS	19.03.45.
AC1	Joseph	JOHNSON	14.05.40
F/O	Harry William	JOHNSON	06.12.44
F/O	John David	JOHNSTON	23.11.43
F/Sgt	Thomas Frederick	JOHNSTON	20.02.44.
F/O	James Guy	JOHNSTON	31.03.44.
Sgt	Ronald Sidney	JOHNSTONE	20.02.44.
Sgt	Harry Arthur	JOINT	03.01.44.
Sgt	William Kerr	JONES	31.05.42.
Sgt	Alfred	JONES	24.06.42.
Sgt	William Richard	JONES	12.03.43
Sgt	John Whyford Marsh	JONES	23.06.43.
F/Sgt	Claude William	JONES	23.08.43.
P/O	Thomas Ivor	JONES	22.05.44.
Sgt	William Ernest	JONES	22.05.44.
F/O	Albert Victor Morgan	JONES	28.05.44.
Sgt	William Kelvin	JONES	14.08.44
Sgt	David John	JONES	25.05.44.
F/Sgt	Francis Ernest	JUGGINS	26.07.43.
F/O	Ben Ingard	KALHEIM	30.08.44.
F/Sgt	Thomas Leslie Hobson	KAY	16.12.43.

Sgt	James William	KEANE	01.08.42
Sgt	James Arthur	KEIGHLEY	17.06.43.
S/L	Dermot Daly Aloysius	KELLY	16.06.41
Sgt	Hugh Alphonsus	KELLY	29.08.41
F/Sgt	William	KELLY	16.05.44.
F/Sgt	Edmund	KELLY	05.04.45.
Sgt	Ralph	KEMP-WELCH	18.10.43
S/L	John Herbert	KENNARD	27.09.43
F/O	Lancelot Stanley	KENNEDY	23.05.44.
Sgt	John James	KEREVAN	15.06.43.
Sgt	Douglas Paterson	KERR	21.01.43
Sgt	Charles	KERSHAW	22.10.43
Sgt	Peter Robert	KEWN	13.07.44.
Sgt	Keith Dawson	KIBBEY	29.07.44.
Sgt	Normand	KIDD	08.09.43
Sgt	James	KILGOUR	13.07.44.
Sgt	Charles Frederick	KILNER	25.07.43.
F/O	Gordon Patrick James	KIMMINS	28.05.44.
F/O	Brian Charles Henry	KING	06.10.42
F/O	Michael Henham	KING	26.11.43
Sgt	Clifford Clarke	KINVIG	02.07.44.
Sgt	William David	KIRTON	25.05.44.
Sgt	George Henry	KITCHEN	21.12.42
F/O	Nebojsa	KUJUNDZIC	04.03.43
Sgt	Stephen Francis	LABERN	13.07.44.
Sgt	Alexander Edwards	LAING	25.02.41
F/Sgt	Edward Vivian	LAING	21.01.43
F/O	Robert Kenneth	LAMB	04.07.43.
P/O	Maurice	LAMBERT	17.06.44.
LAC	Phillip James	LAMBLE	10.05.40
Sgt	Leslie Joseph	LANGAN	01.08.42
Sgt	Alfred Jack	LARBY	03.01.44.
F/O	Thomas Coulton	LATHAM	27.09.43
P/O	Frank	LAW	20.02.44.
Sgt	Douglas John	LAWLER	17.06.44.
Sgt	Maurice Desmond	LAWLOR	15.10.42
P/O	Joseph Willy Odessa Roger Garry	LE BROCK	18.10.43
Sgt	Alfred John	LE POIDEVIN	25.07.41.
W/OII	Donald Grant	LEASK	27.04.44.
F/Sgt	Robert Leslie	LEAVERS	08.03.45.
Sgt	John Charles	LEE	07.08.42.
Sgt	Clarence Norman	LEE	18.08.43
P/O	Kenneth Reuben	LEE	22.10.43
Sgt	Augustus Ernest	LEE	23.05.44.

F/L	Edward Claude	LEE-BROWN	14.04.43.
Sgt	Charles Henry	LEECH	18.10.43
Sgt	John	LEEMING	08.09.43
F/Sgt	Albert Edward	LEFORT	23.08.43.
Sgt	Donald Arthur William	LEFTLY	23.04.44.
F/L	Thomas Gordon	LEGGETT	28.05.44.
Sgt	Ernest George Birch	LENNON	21.09.41.
Sgt	Alexander	LESLIE	31.05.42.
F/O	Herbert Frank	LEWIS	14.06.43
Sgt	Stanley Alfred	LEWIS	22.03.44
F/O	Norman John	LEWIS	26.08.44.
Sgt	Squire	LIGHTOWLER	01.08.42
Sgt	James Charles	LILLEY	29.04.43.
S/L	Harold Lester	LINDO	15.02.44
P/O	Archie Thomas	LITTLE	03.07.42.
W/C	Charles Eric	LITTLER	30.03.41
Sgt	Cyril	LLOYD	04.01.45
Sgt	Maurice Albert	LODGE	25.07.43.
F/Sgt	Charles Alfred	LONGLAND	25.07.44.
W/O	David Halstead	LOOP	18.10.43
F/O	Ralph James	LOUGHEED	07.01.45.
W/OII	James Hawthorne	LOVE	20.12.42
W/OII	David Wesley	LOWTHER	03.03.43
F/Sgt	Jack	LUCK	20.02.44.
P/O	Mervyn Sydney	LUND	24.07.41
F/L	Torkel Torkelsson	LUNDBERG	21.01.43
Sgt	Patrick Joseph	LYNCH	31.03.44.
Sgt	Frederick Norman	MACAULEY	22.10.43
Sgt	Angus Daniel	MacDONALD	17.12.42
Sgt	Samuel	MacDONALD	28.08.43
F/Sgt	William Henry	MacDONALD	23.09.43
F/O	Allan Gordon	MacDONALD	24.12.43.
Sgt	Ronald James	MacDONALD	31.03.44.
F/O	Leonard William	MACHIN	25.07.43.
Sgt	Archibald Ian	MACKAY	21.04.43.
Sgt	John Louis	MacLACHLAN	29.08.42.
Sgt	Gordon	MACLEAN	16.05.41.
F/Sgt	John	MacQUEEN	09.06.42.
Sgt	John Douglas	MacVICAR	16.06.41
F/O	James	MAHER	29.07.44.
F/L	Denis William	MAHON	09.06.41
Sgt	James William	MALLARD	05.08.40
F/Sgt	Stephanus Francois	MARAIS	16.06.41
Sgt	Robert Alfred	MARETT	08.01.45.
Sgt	Kenneth Mark	MARTIN	12.05.44.

Sgt	West Stewart	MASON	15.10.42
F/Sgt	Arthur James Cedric	MASON	16.02.43
Sgt	Albert Henry	MASTERS	26.11.43
F/O	Milton Alexander	MATHIESON	08.01.45.
Sgt	Albert Stanley	MATTHEWS	06.01.44.
Sgt	Norman Hepple	MAUGHAN	15.07.44.
Sgt	Alexander	MAVROMATIS	26.11.43
Sgt	George William	MAWSON	29.07.44.
F/Sgt	Russell Edward	MAY	25.07.43.
F/O	Bernard	MAYERS	11.04.45.
Sgt	Peter	MAYNARD	07.07.43.
F/Sgt	Norman George	MAYO	08.03.45.
F/O	William John	McARTHUR	07.01.45.
F/Sgt	Donald Joseph	McAULAY	07.01.45.
Sgt	Kevin William	MCAULIFFE	25.10.42
Sgt	Tom	McCALL	26.02.43
Sgt	George LK	McCALLUM	29.04.43.
Sgt	Arthur Arnold	McCALLUM	04.05.44.
P/O	John Herbert Charles	McCOUBREY	29.11.44
F/Sgt	Robert Lyle	McCULLOCH	22.09.42
Sgt	William	McCULLOCH	25.05.44.
Sgt	Edwin	McCULLY	31.03.44.
Sgt	Edward Campbell	McDONALD	24.07.41
Sgt	Thomas Lindsay	McDONALD	01.08.42
F/O	Donald Ian	McDONALD	24.12.44
Sgt	George McCulloch	MCGAVIN	05.05.42
F/L	George Edward	McGILL	31.03.44.
Sgt	Donald Estcourt	McGILL	17.06.43.
F/Sgt	Keith Charles	McGINN	08.03.45.
F/Sgt	Denis	McGRATH	16.12.43.
Sgt	Edward Walter	McGRATH	29.11.44
P/O	Angus Albert	MCGRATH	24.02.45.
Sgt	William	McINTOSH	25.02.41
Sgt	Douglas Howie	McINTOSH	25.06.42
Sgt	Alexander	McKECHAN	04.07.43.
F/Sgt	Joseph Niall	McKENNA	23.05.44.
F/Sgt	George Arthur	McLEAN	05.05.42.
Sgt	John Cook	McLEAN	21.10.43.
Sgt	William Whitelaw	MCLELLAN	25.07.43.
F/O	Roy	McLEOD	12.05.44.
P/O	Michael	McMAHON	24.12.43.
Sgt	Norman Tolson	McMASTER	05.10.42
Sgt	John	McMINN	17.06.44.
Sgt	Niel Graham	McSPORRAN	30.08.44.
F/Sgt	James	MEAD	03.03.43

F/O	Leonard	MEAKIN	29.04.43.
F/Sgt	Malcolm Graeme	MEDHURST	18.08.43.
F/Sgt	Norman Alexander	MERCER	25.10.42.
Sgt	Victor John	MEREFIELD	17.04.43.
F/Sgt	Edward Arthur	METCALFE	04.05.44.
Sgt	Donald William	MILLER	18.10.43
P/O	Bruce Fitzgerald Henry	MILLER	22.10.43
Sgt	Gordon	MILLER	13.07.44.
P/O	Andrew Gordon	MILNE	21.09.41.
F/L	Guy Benedict	MILNER	13.06.43.
Sgt	Donald	MINOR	28.01.44.
Sgt	Wallace	MITCHELL	20.05.42.
P/O	Kenneth Walter	MITCHELL	16.05.44.
P/O	George Clarke	MITCHELL	15.07.44.
F/O	Charles Joseph	MITCHELL	29.07.44.
Sgt	Joseph Martin	MITCHINSON	13.07.44.
W/O	William Edward	MITTON	15.02.44
F/Sgt	James	MOLESWORTH	25.10.42.
P/O	James Owen Beggs	MOONEY	17.04.43.
F/Sgt	Robert Arthur	MOORE	25.07.43.
Sgt	Thomas Watson	MOORE	16.12.43.
Sgt	James Ernest	MOORE	04.05.44.
F/Sgt	William Linkous Cameron	MORAN	23.06.43.
F/O	Stanley Allan	MOREY	27.09.43
Sgt	Christopher Hubert	MORGAN	01.08.42
Sgt	Iorwerth Beynon	MORGAN	27.11.43.
F/O	George Barry	MORGAN-DEAN	12.05.40
W/OII	Louis Edmund	MORIARTY	20.12.42
Sgt	Edgar Harry	MORLEY	15.06.43.
Sgt	Reginald Henry	MORRIS	09.01.43
Sgt	Donald	MORRIS	13.03.45.
P/O	Vincent Merrill MacDonald	MORRISON	29.08.42.
F/L	Godfrey Arnold	MORRISON	23.05.44.
F/O	Alexander John	MORRISON	13.07.44.
P/O	Edgar Elliot	MORTON	12.05.40
Sgt	Cerris	MOSELEY	12.04.42
Sgt	Stanley	MOSELEY	14.04.43.
Sgt	John William	MOSS	24.06.42.
F/O	Joseph Barker	MOSS	29.07.44.
Sgt	Jack	MOULES	06.08.41.
F/Sgt	Bernard	MOXHAM	27.04.44.
F/O	Michael	MULLIGAN	18.10.43
Sgt	Joseph	MULLIN	10.08.43.
Sgt	William Alfred	MUNDAY	22.03.44
Sgt	Andrew McKenzie	MUNN	14.04.43.

F/O	Douglas Philip	MUNNS	15.10.42
Sgt	John	MUNRO	01.08.42
P/O	Ian	MURCHIE	21.09.41.
P/O	David Beveridge	MURDOCH	15.10.42
F/Sgt	Harold Sidney	MURTON	06.01.44.
Sgt	Dennis William	MUSGROVE	25.04.42
F/Sgt	Frederick Charles	MUSTOE	28.05.44.
Sgt	George Henry	NAIRN	29.07.44.
Sgt	Reginald William	NANSON	26.07.44.
Sgt	William George	NEALE	02.12.43
P/O	Wilfred Ronald	NEVILLE	16.02.43
Sgt	James Paterson	NEVILLE	21.10.43.
Sgt	George Henry	NEWBOLT	26.07.43.
Sgt	Gwilym	NICHOLLS	21.12.42
F/Sgt	Edwin Clifford	NICHOLLS	06.01.44.
F/Sgt	Arthur Leslie	NICHOLS	27.04.44.
F/O	Charles Edward	NICHOLSON	14.02.43
Sgt	Arthur Dennis	NICHOLSON	29.04.43.
F/O	William Edwin	NIGHTINGALE	08.03.45.
P/O	James Andrew Harold	NIMMO	10.04.44.
F/O	William	NIXON	30.08.44.
F/O	William	NIXON	30.08.44.
Sgt	Joseph George	NOLAN	14.02.43
Sgt	Richard	NOLAN	23.02.45
F/L	Max Raymond	NOREM	05.03.45
Sgt	John	NORGROVE	31.03.44.
F/Sgt	James Joseph	O'BRIEN	14.04.43.
F/Sgt	Eusebins William	O'CONNELL	15.06.43.
P/O	Peter Joseph	O'DONNELL	18.08.43.
S/L	Charles	O'DONOGHUE	01.04.43
Sgt	Kenneth James	OFFER	18.10.43
P/O	Cecel Harold	OGDEN	15.07.44.
W/O	Felix Francis	O'HANLON	25.07.43.
Sgt	John Leivers	OLDERSHAW	28.08.43.
F/O	Lawrence Philip	OLDHAM	04.07.43.
F/O	Michael Richard Frewin	OLIVER	29.07.44.
S/L	Leonard	OLLIER	28.05.44.
F/Sgt	George Orlando	OLSON	13.07.44.
Sgt	Charles	O'NEILL	16.12.43.
Sgt	Clifford William	ONIONS	08.11.41
F/Sgt	William	ONIONS	31.05.42.
P/O	Melvin Osborne	ORR	29.11.44.
Sgt	Frederick George Francis	OSBORNE	20.02.44.
Sgt	Clement Basil	OSBORNE	29.07.44.
Sgt	John Gregory	O'SULLIVAN	25.06.42

Sgt	Spencer	OTTY	03.10.43
Sgt	Arthur Edward	OWEN	25.07.41.
W/O	Arthur William Horace	PAGE	03.08.43.
F/O	George Stapleford	PALIN	03.01.44.
Sgt	Allan George	PALMER	28.01.44.
Sgt	Charles Henry	PALMER	07.01.45.
W/O	Aubrey Huia	PARGETER	21.10.43.
Sgt	John James	PARISH	05.09.42.
Sgt	Alexander Muir	PARK	17.06.43.
F/L	Graham Noel	PARKER	15.10.42
F/Sgt	William Glen	PARKER	03.10.43
Sgt	Anthony Keith	PARKER	23.02.45
P/O	Rowland Ira	PARKS	17.03.45.
Sgt	John	PATCH	28.08.42
F/Sgt	John Campbell	PATON	03.03.43
Sgt	Eric Stephen	PATTISON	06.12.44
Sgt	Eric George	PAUL	21.09.41.
P/O	John Montgomery	PEACE	01.03.45
F/Sgt	James John	PEACOCK	15.02.44
F/Sgt	Stanley David	PEARCE	05.04.45.
F/Sgt	Alexander Francis	PEARSON	28.07.42
F/L	Charles	PEARTON	07.01.45.
Sgt	Douglas Frank	PEGRUM	16.05.44.
Sgt	Leonard	PENDLETON	19.03.45.
Sgt	Douglas William	PERCH	03.03.43
P/O	Arthur Frederick James	PERROTT	04.07.43.
Sgt	Charles David	PERRY	14.05.40
Sgt	Sidney Edward	PERRY	21.01.43
Sgt	Ronald Leonard	PERRY	25.07.43.
Sgt	Maurice Dawbry	PETERS	29.04.43.
P/O	David Layton	PETRIE	10.09.41
P/O	George May	PETTIGREW	21.04.43.
Sgt	Albert Harry	PETTMAN	14.02.45.
F/O	David Walter Alexander	PHILIP	01.09.43.
F/O	Charles Ronald	PHILLIPS	13.07.44.
F/O	Maurice Desmond	PICKERSGILL	04.01.45
Sgt	Maurice	PICKLES	22.05.44.
F/O	Philip Mourant	PICOT	12.12.44
Sgt	Edwin George	PILBEAM	18.10.43
Sgt	James Edward	PINNOCK	29.07.44.
Sgt	Henry Lewis	PITCHFORTH	15.10.42
F/Sgt	Kenneth Henry	PITHOUSE	31.08.44
Sgt	Cyril Walter	PLAMPTON	16.12.43.
Sgt	James Wilfred	PLATT	29.08.42.
F/O	Cyril John	PLUMMER	24.03.44

P/O	Clifford Thomas	POLLARD	08.01.45.
Sgt	Albert Ernest	PONSFORD	23.06.43.
Sgt	Christopher John Stafford	POOLE	10.05.40
Sgt	James Wallace	PORTEOUS	23.06.42.
Sgt	James	PORTER	06.10.42
F/Sgt	Harvey James	PORTER	13.03.45.
F/Sgt	Peter Ernest	POULSON	20.12.42
S/L	Walter Harry	POWDRELL	14.02.43
W/OII	Oliver John Lancaster	PRATLETT	15.07.44.
Sgt	John Royal Crossley	PRATT	25.02.41
Sgt	George William	PRESCOTT	26.11.43
Sgt	Reginald Joseph	PRICE	26.07.44.
Sgt	George Kenneth	PROCTOR	21.09.41.
F/O	Richard Elwyn Vaughan	PUGH	26.11.43
P/O	Harry Clinton	PULLEY	01.03.43
F/Sgt	Thomas Andrew	PURVIS	30.08.44.
Sgt	Bertam George	RADBOURN	25.07.43.
P/O	John Kenneth Churchill	RALSTON	25.02.41
Sgt	Keith Lund	RAMAGE	12.05.44.
Sgt	Walter Dennis	RAMSAY	21.04.43.
Sgt	Jack Raymond	RANKIN	04.05.44.
Sgt	Victor Edward Richard	RAPHAEL	25.07.43.
Sgt	John	RAY	28.05.44.
F/L	Charles Peter	READY	02.12.43
F/L	Patrick Elmore	REES	20.05.42
Sgt	Derek James	REEVES	23.02.45
P/O	Alfred Frederick	REIF	01.03.43
Sgt	James Black	REILLY	23.11.43
Sgt	James	RENWICK	15.06.43.
W/OII	John William McLeod	RENWICK	28.08.43.
Sgt	Anthony Hughenden	REX	21.09.41.
W/O	John Thomas Campbell	RHODES	22.10.43
Sgt	John	RHODES	13.07.44.
P/O	Arthur Gwyn	RICHARDS	06.10.42
Sgt	James Arthur	RICHARDS	15.07.44.
F/O	Robert Edwin	RICHARDSON	31.08.44
F/Sgt	Valentine	RICHTER	16.12.43.
Sgt	Roy Cyril	RIDGWAY	17.06.43.
P/O	Dugald Geoffrey	RIMMINGTON	14.02.45.
F/Sgt	Robert Ian	ROBB	21.12.42
Sgt	Thomas Manuel	ROBBINS	02.12.43
Sgt	George Christopher	ROBERTS	31.05.42.
F/Sgt	Peter George	ROBERTS	01.03.43
P/O	Frederick John	ROBERTS	02.12.43
Sgt	Robert William	ROBERTS	20.12.43

Sgt	James Manderson	ROBERTS	10.04.44.
F/Sgt	Frederick Glyn	ROBERTS	07.07.44
F/Sgt	Humphrey Peter	ROBINSON	22.10.43
Sgt	Stanley	ROBSON	26.07.43.
F/Sgt	John Lorn	ROCHESTER	01.03.45
Sgt	Horace	ROCKNEAN	17.06.43.
Sgt	Michael Bruce	ROGERSON	31.05.42.
F/Sgt	John Victor	ROPER	10.03.43.
F/L	John Colin McIntosh	ROSE	21.12.42
Sgt	Stanley John	ROSE	10.03.43.
AC1	Alexander Strachan	ROSS	12.05.40
P/O	Sydney Lawrence	ROWE	04.05.44.
Sgt	James	ROY	08.03.45.
Sgt	Frank Alfred	RUSHWORTH	14.02.45.
Sgt	Emrys	RUSSELL	12.06.43.
F/Sgt	Isaac	RUTHERFORD	07.08.42.
F/Sgt	William Edward	RYAN	21.12.42
F/Sgt	Stanley Norman	RYDER	28.07.42
Sgt	George Stevens	RYE	10.09.41
F/O	Donald Arthur	RYERSE	31.08.44
Sgt	William Charles	SADLER	30.08.44.
Sgt	Jack Henry	SALLIS	04.05.44.
Sgt	Bernard William	SANSOM	31.05.42.
Sgt	Walter Leonard	SARGENT	02.12.43
Sgt	James Harold	SAVILLE	15.06.43.
F/O	Samuel Leo	SAXE	08.03.45.
Sgt	Alfred Brian	SCANLAN	23.06.42.
Sgt	William	SCOBIE	09.01.43
Sgt	Norman Robert	SEDGWICK	15.10.42
Sgt	Walter	SEECKTS	06.03.45.
Sgt	Abraham	SEGAL	29.04.43.
F/Sgt	Sidney Mervyn	SELWAY	05.09.42.
AC1	Horace Basil	SEWELL	12.05.40
F/O	Wilfred Tasman	SHANNON	04.07.43.
F/Sgt	Evan Frederick	SHANNON	05.04.45.
AC2	John Alexander	SHARPE	26.03.40.
F/O	Michael	SHATZKY	08.03.45.
F/O	Reginald	SHAW	24.07.41
F/Sgt	Ernest	SHAW	15.06.43.
Sgt	Michael	SHEEDY	22.10.43
Sgt	Henry Alfred	SHEPHARD	23.05.44.
Sgt	William Thomas	SHEPHERD	17.06.43.
P/O	Frank	SHEPHERD	27.04.44.
P/O	Herbert William	SHINN	01.09.43.
F/O	John Oswell	SHONE	10.08.43.

Sgt	Eric Smith	SIDDALL	26.11.43
P/O	Alexander	SIMONS	01.08.42
F/O	Leonard Harry	SIMPSON	30.08.44.
F/O	Leslie John	SLATTER	28.01.44.
Sgt	Donald	SLEEP	08.01.45.
Sgt	Brian Clifford	SLOWLY	31.05.42
Sgt	Cyril	SMALL	10.09.44.
Sgt	Philip	SMART	01.03.43
P/O	James	SMART	14.04.43.
Sgt	Thomas Daw	SMITH	10.05.40
P/O	Harry Bernard	SMITH	17.12.42
Sgt	Edward Jack	SMITH	21.12.42
Sgt	Charles Derrick	SMITH	26.02.43
Sgt	Jack	SMITH	10.03.43.
W/O	John Coates	SMITH	04.05.44.
Sgt	John William	SMITH	12.05.44.
Sgt	John William	SMITH	25.07.44.
Sgt	Joseph Gerard	SMITH	08.03.45.
Sgt	William	SNOWDON	06.12.44
Sgt	Douglas Reynold	SOUTH	26.02.43
F/O	Jack Celtic	SOUTHEY	15.02.44
F/Sgt	Alvin Leslie	SPAFFORD	03.07.42.
Sgt	William	SPEAKMAN	28.01.44.
Sgt	Charles Leonard	SPINK	22.10.43
P/O	Douglas Wilberforce	SPOONER	03.07.42.
Sgt	Leslie G	SPURGEON	03.08.43.
F/L	Alfred Eugene	SPURR	23.06.43.
P/O	Charles Patrick	St. LEGER	17.06.43.
Sgt	Sefton	STAFFORD	01.04.43
W/O	Ernest Edwin	STANDING	23.02.45
P/O	Alan Geoffrey	STANES	21.09.41.
F/L	Gilbert William	STANHOPE	01.03.43
Sgt	Philip Arthur	STANILAND	04.05.44.
Sgt	Thomas	STANLEY	03.08.43.
Sgt	Horace	STAPLES	17.06.43,
F/Sgt	Edward Voster	STAPLES	14.02.45.
F/L	Arthur Lloyd	STEPHARNOFF	17.03.45.
F/Sgt	Hugh Francis	STEPHENS	08.01.45.
W/O	Robert	STEVENS	18.10.43
F/O	Arthur	STEVENS	20.02.44.
F/Sgt	Edwin	STEWART	25.07.44.
Sgt	Arthur	STOCKDALE	15.01.42
Sgt	Stewart William	STOCKFORD	28.07.42
Sgt	Robert Blyth	STOCKS	24.12.43.
F/Sgt	Richard Grange	STOLZ-PAGE	03.12.42.

W/O	John Stafford	STONEMAN	03.08.43.
Sgt	Leonard Joseph	STOREY	28.07.42
Sgt	Thomas Frederick	STOTT	18.10.43
P/O	Harry Kenneth	STOTT	17.03.45.
F/O	Norman John	STRONELL	30.08.44.
P/O	Alexander William	STUBBS	16.02.43
F/L	Richard Noel	STUBBS	27.02.43
F/O	Anthony John	SUMNER	26.11.43.
F/Sgt	James	SUTHERLAND	18.10.43
W/OII	Glen Geoffrey	SVEINSON	22.10.43
Sgt	Bernard Dudley	SWAIN	25.10.42.
Sgt	William Henry	SWAN	14.02.45.
S/L	Harold (Jock)	SWANSTON	04.05.44.
Sgt	Gerald	SWEENEY	08.09.43
Sgt	Frederick John	SWIFT	03.08.43.
Sgt	Harry	SYKES	21.10.43.
Sgt	Terence William	SYKES	04.05.44.
F/O	William Clifford	TAFFENDER	13.06.41.
Sgt	Alan John	TAIT	03.10.43
F/Sgt	Ralph Aubrey	TAPP	16.05.44.
Sgt	Kenneth Charles	TATE	26.07.43.
P/O	Robert Richard Jack	TATE	31.03.44.
P/O	Donald Elgin	TATE	25.05.44.
Sgt	Johnston Playfair	TAYLOR	06.08.41.
F/Sgt	Leonard Clayton	TAYLOR	20.05.42.
F/Sgt	Ronald Ward	TAYLOR	25.10.42.
Sgt	Ronald	TAYLOR	21.01.43
Sgt	Nicholas Daunt	TAYLOR	26.11.43.
Sgt	Francis James	TAYLOR	20.02.44.
F/O	George Laurence	TAYLOR	06.03.45.
F/O	George Graham	TEBBLE	17.06.43.
Sgt	Allen Parker	TEBBUTT	26.08.44.
W/OI	Robert Lloyd	TELFER	28.08.42
Sgt	John Charlton	TETLEY	18.10.43
F/O	Donald Seymour	THOM	26.11.43.
P/O	Cecil Vernon	THOMAS	10.06.40
Sgt	Charles Alfred Frederick	THOMAS	20.09.41
Sgt	Ambrose Bowen	THOMAS	15.01.42
Sgt	Harold Gwyn	THOMAS	17.06.43,
Sgt	Roy	THOMAS	02.12.43
Sgt	Ronald	THOMAS	25.03.44
Sgt	Douglas Jerome	THOMAS	29.07.44.
Sgt	Ernest	THOMASON	15.07.44.
Sgt	Harry Edward	THOMPSON	21.10.43.
Sgt	Tom	THOMPSON	24.12.43.

Sgt	Edward	THOMPSON	31.08.44
Sgt	Gordon	THOMSON	31.03.44.
F/O	Alexander Stuart	THOMSON	01.03.45
Sgt	James Henry	THORNTON	26.07.43.
P/O	Andrew Thomas	THORNTON	10.04.44.
Sgt	Robert Frank	TIDMARSH	07.08.42.
Sgt	Norman Guy	TIPPIN	13.07.43.
Sgt	John Alexander	TODD	10.03.43.
Sgt	Stanley William	TOLLEY	22.03.44
F/O	Norman	TOMBS	24.03.44
Sgt	Richard Henry	TOMLIN	02.12.43
Sgt	Derrick Reuben	TOMLINSON	29.07.44.
W/O	L aurence	TOMMIE	26.07.44.
W/OI	James Willis	TOON	14.04.43.
Sgt	John Newton	TOWN	26.02.43
W/O	Edgar Thomas	TOWNSEND	03.01.44.
F/Sgt	William Lyall Edmond	TRAQUAIR	06.06.42.
Sgt	Percival Edwin	TREW	12.03.43
Sgt	Bernard Frederick	TREW	01.09.43.
W/O	Nash James	TREWAVAS	22.03.44
Sgt	Norman Frederick	TRIGG	03.03.43
Sgt	Frederick	TRIMMER	21.12.42
F/Sgt	William Henry	TROMP	01.03.45
Sgt	George Edward	TROWSDALE	13.07.43.
Sgt	Arthur	TUFFS	23.05.44.
W/O	Geoffrey Edgar	TURNBULL	07.04.45.
F/Sgt	Jean Albert Marc	TURNER	09.06.42.
Sgt	Desmond Frank Oswald	TURNER	07.07.43.
Sgt	George	TURNER	14.02.45.
F/Sgt	Eric	TWELVES	15.01.42
Sgt	Dennis William Albert	UDALL	28.01.44.
F/O	Vivian Lawrence	VALENTINE	05.04.45.
F/O	William Lorne	VANDERDASSON	12.05.44.
F/Sgt	Frederick Albert Charles	VARRALL	29.07.44.
Sgt	Bernard William	VAUGHAN	15.10.42
Sgt	Marco Joseph Henry	VEDOVATO	28.05.44.
Sgt	Aubrey Walter	VERNON	10.09.41
Sgt	John Henry	VICKERS	05.10.39.
P/O	Philip Dennis	VICKERS	12.05.44.
Sgt	Stanley John	VICKERY	24.06.42.
P/O	Robert James Francis	VIVERS	23.09.43
Sgt	John Thomas	VODDEN	04.07.43.
Sgt	William	VOELLNER	26.08.44.
F/Sgt	Joseph	WADSWORTH	24.03.44
Sgt	Ernest Solomon	WAGHORN	10.03.43.

Sgt	Charles Edward	WAGON	10.09.41
P/O	Ernest Adam	WAGSTAFF	25.10.42.
Sgt	Derrick Norman Duckers	WAITE	01.03.43
F/O	Arthur James	WAKEFIELD	02.12.43
Sgt	Raymond Victor	WAKEFIELD	06.12.44
Sgt	Frank Gordon	WALKER	25.07.41.
F/O	Reginald	WALLACE	03.12.42.
F/Sgt	Bruce Woodrow	WALLS	13.07.43.
Sgt	Ernest Desmond	WALTERS	06.06.42.
Sgt	John Arthur	WARBURTON	28.04.44.
P/O	John Edward	WARD	28.03.42
F/O	Thomas	WARDHAUGH	20.09.41
Sgt	George James	WARE	17.06.44.
Sgt	Neville Philip	WARLOW	28.05.44.
Sgt	Kenneth Robert James	WARREN	04.05.44.
F/O	Robert John Branch	WARREN	26.07.44.
Sgt	William	WASS	15.07.44.
Sgt	Reginald	WATKINSON	12.06.43.
F/Sgt	Howard Cameron	WATSON	20.05.42.
Sgt	David George	WATT	25.02.41
F/L	Alastair Clarence	WATT	17.03.45.
Sgt	William	WATTERS	23.09.43
F/Sgt	Rae McGee	WATTS	13.07.43.
F/L	Wilfred Howard	WAY	07.06.44.
Sgt	William John	WEARN	23.08.43.
Sgt	Cultra Vallance	WEBB	03.07.42.
F/Sgt	Ronald Bennett	WEBB	12.05.44.
Sgt	Kenneth Graham	WEBB	18.08.44
F/Sgt	Keith Robert	WEBBER	21.01.43
Sgt	Squire Arbuthnott	WEBSTER	28.08.42
P/O	Christopher Joseph	WEIGHT	04.01.45
Sgt	Stanley Henry	WELCH	26.07.43.
F/O	Arthur	WEST	29.07.44.
F/O	Lawrence Edward	WESTCOTT	26.08.44.
Sgt	Stanley Anthony	WESTCOTT	06.12.44
Sgt	Leonard	WHALEN	25.07.43.
Sgt	William Stephen	WHALLEY	08.09.43
Sgt	David Lumgair	WHAMOND	17.06.44.
Sgt	William Horace	WHEATLEY	10.08.43.
Sgt	Harry Sidney	WHEELER	23.08.43.
Sgt	Leo Patrick	WHELAN	13.07.44.
Sgt	Frank	WHITE	12.04.42
Sgt	Gordon Roy	WHITE	04.07.43.
F/Sgt	Richard	WHITE	12.05.44.
Sgt	John Douglas	WHITEHEAD	05.09.42.

Sgt	George	WHITEHEAD	15.06.43.
F/L	Francis Allen	WHITEHEAD	28.01.44.
F/Sgt	Wilfred	WHITEHEAD	17.03.45.
F/Sgt	Albert Edward	WHITEING	19.03.45.
P/O	Ralph	WHITELOCK	06.10.42
P/O	Richard	WHITLEY	12.05.44.
F/O	Charles Bernard	WHITMORE	30.08.44.
Sgt	Cyril	WHITTLE	23.04.44.
Sgt	John Gibson	WHITWORTH	25.07.44.
Sgt	Arthur Hugh	WHYTE	08.03.45.
P/O	George Edward	WIDDICOMBE	04.01.45
F/O	Derek Abraham	WIENER	23.05.44.
F/O	Kenneth	WILCOCK	15.02.44
Sgt	Percy Eric	WILKINS	04.07.43.
Sgt	Thomas Tweedy	WILKINSON	03.12.42.
F/O	Robert	WILKINSON	17.03.45.
F/O	Arthur Alexander	WILKS	28.05.44.
F/Sgt	Edgar Harold	WILLCOCKS	21.10.43.
Sgt	Henry Edward Arthur	WILLEY	24.06.42.
Sgt	Roy Penry	WILLIAMS	25.07.41.
Sgt	Gregory Percival	WILLIAMS	29.08.41
P/O	Maldwyn Wyn	WILLIAMS	20.05.42.
F/Sgt	Douglas George	WILLIAMS	21.01.43
Sgt	James Dennis	WILLIAMS	01.03.43
Sgt	David Dennis	WILLIAMS	25.07.43.
P/O	Derek	WILLIAMS	26.07.43.
Sgt	Cyril Percy	WILLIAMS	18.08.43.
Sgt	Stanley	WILLIAMS	02.12.43
F/Sgt	Joseph	WILLIAMS	25.05.44.
Sgt	Gwynne	WILLIAMS	07.01.45.
Sgt	James	WILLIAMSON	18.10.43
Sgt	John Paul	WILLIAMSON	22.10.43
Sgt	Anthony Marshall	WILLIS	21.01.43
Sgt	George Hunter	WILSON	28.08.42.
Sgt	Richard	WILSON	15.10.42
F/Sgt	John William Edward	WILSON	03.12.42.
Sgt	Jack William George	WILSON	26.07.43.
Sgt	Henry Robert	WILSON	22.10.43
Sgt	John	WILSON	28.04.44.
Sgt	Robert Arthur	WILSON	04.05.44.
F/L	Kenneth Frederick John	WINCHESTER	15.10.42
Sgt	Ronald Gordon	WINCHESTER	17.06.43.
Sgt	John Edwin	WINN	01.04.43
Sgt	George Charles	WITCHLOW	25.07.43.
Sgt	Thomas Edward	WITTS	25.07.43.

Sgt	John Pennington	WOLFENDEN	22.09.42
P/O	Fred Hall	WOOD	24.06.42.
Sgt	Henry Frederick	WOOD	25.10.42.
F/O	William Henry	WOOD	23.06.43.
S/L	Clifford Sinclair Farquhar	WOOD	22.10.43
P/O	Philip Ralph	WOOD	29.07.44.
Sgt	Hugh	WOODFIELD	26.02.43
Sgt	John Charles	WOODWARD	16.02.43
F/Sgt	Albert Edward	WOTHERSPOON	17.03.45.
Sgt	Erskine Peter	WRIGHT	28.03.42
P/O	Thomas Kitchener	WRIGHT	16.05.44.
F/O	Owen	WRIGHT	23.05.44.
F/Sgt	Jack Adams	WRIGHT	06.03.45.
Sgt	Eric George	WYATT	02.12.43
Sgt	William John Crozier	WYLIE	29.07.44.
F/O	Sidney Herbert	YATES	15.06.43.
F/Sgt	Prince Edward Gooderham	YATES	12.12.44
F/O	Denis	YOUNG	14.02.43
P/O	John Charles Harley	YOUNG	16.02.43
F/Sgt	Leonard William	ZINGELMANN	07.06.44.

103 Squadron

MOTTO **NOLI ME TANGERE** (No one to touch me)   Code
PM

Stations

CHALLERANGE	06.09.39. to 27.09.39.
MONTHOIS	27.09.39. to 28.11.39.
PLIVOT	28.11.39. to 15.02.40.
BETHENIVILLE	15.02.40. to 16.05.40.
RHEGES/ST LUCIEN FERME	16.05.40. to 04.06.40.
OZOUER-le-DOYEN	04.06.40. to 14.06.40.
SOUGE	14.06.40. to 16.06.40.
HONINGTON	16.06.40. to 03.07.40.
NEWTON	03.07.40. to 11.07.41.
ELSHAM WOLDS	11.07.41. to 26.11.45.

Commanding Officers

WING COMMANDER H J GEMMELL	27.01.39. to 12.03.40.
WING COMMANDER T C DICKENS	12.03.40. to 23.11.40.
SQUADRON LEADER C E R TAIT	23.11.40. to 05.12.40.
WING COMMANDER C E LITTLER	05.12.40. to 04.04.41.
WING COMMANDER B E LOWE	04.04.41. to 25.08.41.
WING COMMANDER R S RYAN	25.08.41. to 09.03.42.
WING COMMANDER J F H DU BOULAY DFC	09.03.42. to 09.09.42.
WING COMMANDER R A C CARTER DSO	09.09.42. to 17.04.43.
WING COMMANDER J A SLATER DFC	17.04.43. to 18.10.43.
WING COMMANDER E D McK NELSON	18.10.43. to 26.04.44.
WING COMMANDER H R GOODMAN	26.04.44. to 12.05.44.
WING COMMANDER J R ST JOHN DFC	12.05.44. to 01.12.44.
WING COMMANDER D F MacDONALD	01.12.44. to 07.08.45.

Aircraft

BATTLE	08.38. to	10.40.
WELLINGTON	10.40. to	07.42.
HALIFAX	07.42. to	11.42.
LANCASTER	11.42. to	11.45.

Aircrew Killed

973

Operational Record

OPERATIONS	SORTIES	AIRCRAFT LOSSES	% LOSSES
519	5840	179	3.1

CATEGORY OF OPERATIONS

BOMBING	MINING
486	33

BATTLES

OPERATIONS	SORTIES	AIRCRAFT LOSSES	% LOSSES
16	51	1	2.0

Figures do not include operations with the AASF.

WELLINGTONS

OPERATIONS	SORTIES	AIRCRAFT LOSSES	% LOSSES
144	1116	31	2.8

CATEGORY OF OPERATIONS

BOMBING	MINING
138	6

HALIFAX

OPERATIONS	SORTIES	AIRCRAFT LOSSES	% LOSSES
15	137	12	8.8

LANCASTER

OPERATIONS	SORTIES	AIRCRAFT LOSSES	% LOSSES
344	4536	135	3.0

CATEGORY OF OPERATIONS

BOMBING	MINING
317	27

A further 22 Lancasters were destroyed in crashes.

Aircraft Histories

BATTLE.	To October 1940.
K9264	FTR from attacks in Luxembourg 10.5.40.
K9265	To 8 Maintenance Unit.
K9266	To 1 Salvage Section.
K9268	To 20 Maintenance Unit.
K9269	To Advanced Air Striking Force.
K9270	FTR from attacks in Luxembourg 10.5.40.
K9271	Force-landed in France during reconnaissance operation 27.9.39.
K9295	To 3 Salvage Section.
K9297	To SF Abingdon.
K9298	To 52 Squadron.
K9299	To 8 Maintenance Unit.
K9372	FTR from attacks in Luxembourg 10.5.40.
K9374	Lost in France June 40. Details uncertain.
K9392	From 150 Squadron. To 8 Maintenance Unit.
K9404	From 52 Squadron. Abandoned in France during withdrawal 16.5.40.
K9408	From 52 Squadron. To Royal Canadian Air Force.
K9409	From 52 Squadron. DBR during operation to Vernon 10.6.40.
K9411	From 52 Squadron. To 8 Maintenance Unit.
K9456	To 8 Maintenance Unit.
K9460	From 52 Squadron via 12 OTU and 6 MU. To 27 Maintenance Unit.
K9471 PM-N	From 35 Squadron via 47 and 6 MUs. To 27 MU.
L4941	To 63 Squadron.
L4942	To 150 Squadron.
L4957	From 52 Squadron. To 8 Maintenance Unit.
L5010 PM-C	From 6 Maintenance Unit. FTR Calais 9/10.9.40.
L5011	From 3 Bombing and Gunnery School via 27 MU. To 12 Squadron.
L5038 PM-H	To 38 Maintenance Unit.
L5125	To 27 Maintenance Unit.
L5190	From 16 Squadron. FTR Sedan 14.5.40.
L5204	To 22 Maintenance Unit.
L5205	To 110 Wing.
L5206	To 6 Anti-Aircraft Cooperation Unit.
L5207	To Royal Canadian Air Force.
L5208	To 110 Wing.
L5209	To 6 Anti-Aircraft Cooperation Unit.
L5210	To South African Air Force.
L5211	To 110 Wing via 22 Maintenance Unit.
L5212	To 22 Maintenance Unit.
L5213	To 22 Maintenance Unit.
L5214	To 3 Group Training Flight.
L5234	From 15 Squadron. Abandoned in France during withdrawal 16.5.40.
L5236	From 15 Squadron. Force-landed in France while training 1/2.3.40.

L5237	From 150 Squadron. To 301 Squadron.
L5244	From 40 Squadron. To Royal Australian Air Force.
L5246	From 40 Squadron. FTR from operations against troop columns and communications in France 9/10.6.40.
L5336 PM-J	From 10 Maintenance Unit. To 22 Maintenance Unit.
L5358	From 10 Maintenance Unit. To 20 Maintenance Unit.
L5363	From 10 Maintenance Unit. To 27 Maintenance Unit.
L5381	From 235 Squadron via 10 Maintenance Unit. To a Maintenance Unit.
L5395 PM-P	From 27 Maintenance Unit. To 20 Maintenance Unit.
L5431 PM-E	From 20 Maintenance Unit. To 38 Maintenance Unit.
L5432 PM-G	From 20 Maintenance Unit. To 12 OTU via 9 Maintenance Unit.
L5433	From 20 Maintenance Unit. Crashed on approach to Cottesmore while training 3.8.40.
L5444	From 27 Maintenance Unit. To 9 Maintenance Unit via Rollason.
L5465	From 8 Maintenance Unit. Lost France June 1940. Details uncertain.
L5469	From 150 Squadron. To 18 MU after taxying accident Newton 3.8.40.
L5479	From 6 Maintenance Unit. To 9 Maintenance Unit via Rollason.
L5508	From 8 Maintenance Unit. Lost in France June 40. Details uncertain.
L5509	From 8 Maintenance Unit. Lost in France June 40. Details uncertain.
L5511	From 8 Maintenance Unit. Lost in France June 40. Details uncertain.
L5512	From 8MU. FTR Bouillon 12.5.40.
L5513	From 8 Maintenance Unit. Lost in France June 40. Details uncertain.
L5514	From 218 Squadron. FTR Roumont 26.5.40.
L5515	From 8 Maintenance Unit. FTR Roumont 26.5.40.
L5516	From 6 Maintenance Unit. FTR Sedan 14.5.40.
L5525 PM-F	From 6 Maintenance Unit. To 38 Maintenance Unit.
L5532	From 300 Squadron. To 12 Squadron.
L5792	From 18 Maintenance Unit. To 4 Group Target Towing Flight.
N2157 PM-R	From 8 Maintenance Unit. To 38 Maintenance Unit.
N2163 PM-T	From 20 Maintenance Unit. To 20 Maintenance Unit.
N2253	From 6 Maintenance Unit. FTR Poix 8.6.40.
N2255	From 6 Maintenance Unit. To 9 Maintenance Unit via Rollason.
P2163	From 6 Maintenance Unit. Lost in France June 40. Details uncertain.
P2191	From 142 Squadron. FTR Sedan 14.5.40.
P2193	From 142 Squadron. FTR Bouillon 12.5.40.
P2256	From 226 Squadron. Crashed in France while training 27.3.40.
P2278	To 4 Bombing and Gunnery School via 22 Maintenance Unit.
P2303	To 22 Maintenance Unit.
P2304	From 8 MU. To 9 MU after belly-landing 31.8.40.
P2305	From 8 Maintenance Unit. To 20 Maintenance Unit.
P2306 PM-D	From 8 Maintenance Unit. To 20 Maintenance Unit.
P2307 PM-K	From 8 Maintenance Unit. To 9 Maintenance Unit.
P2308 PM-G	From 8 Maintenance Unit. To 12 Squadron via 27 Maintenance Unit.
P2311	From 8 Maintenance Unit. To 12 Squadron.
P2312	From 8 Maintenance Unit. To 150 Squadron.
P2314	From 8 Maintenance Unit. Lost in France May 40. Details uncertain.

P2315	From 218 Squadron. FTR Poix 8.6.40.
P2320 PM-B	
P2328	From 10 Maintenance Unit. FTR Vernon 10.6.40.
P2357	From 20 Maintenance Unit. Lost in France May 40. Details uncertain.
P5237	From 27 Maintenance Unit. To 12 Squadron.

WELLINGTON.   **From October 1940 to July 1942**.

L7813	From 150 Squadron. Crashed on landing at Newton while training 13.11.40.
L7819	From 301 Squadron. To Air Sea Rescue Training Unit.
L7886 PM-X	From 305 Squadron. Abandoned over Lincolnshire on return from Frankfurt 21.9.41.
N2770	FTR Brest 24.7.41.
N2849	FTR Duisburg 16/17.6.41.
N2996	From 38 Squadron. To Central Gunnery School and back. To Central Gunnery School.
N2997	From 38 Squadron. To Central Gunnery School.
R1041	To 15 Operational Training Unit.
R1043	Force-landed in Somerset during operation to Brest 30/31.3.41.
R1061	From 300 Squadron. FTR Lübeck 28/29.3.42.
R1140	From Exeter. To 14 Operational Training Unit.
R1163	From 75 Squadron. To 16 Operational Training Unit.
R1213	From 305 Squadron. FTR Mannheim 29/30.8.41.
R1217	Damaged beyond repair operation to Duisburg 16/17.10.41.
R1234	From 12 Operational Training Unit. Crashed soon after take-off from Kirmington for transit flight 31.5.42.
R1274	From 301 Squadron. To 11 Operational Training Unit.
R1344	From 300 Squadron. To 21 Operational Training Unit.
R1347	From 300 Squadron. To 21 Operational Training Unit.
R1393	Ditched off Suffolk coast on return from Essen 25/26.3.42.
R1395	FTR Hamburg 15/16.1.42.
R1396	FTR Turin 10/11.9.41.
R1397	FTR Emden 24/25.7.41.
R1445	To 11 Operational Training Unit.
R1446	To 23 Operational Training Unit.
R1459	From 301 Squadron. To 29 Operational Training Unit.
R1467	To 20 Operational Training Unit.
R1494	FTR Hanover 15/16.5.41.
R1538	To 18 Operational Training Unit.
R1539	Force-landed in Lincolnshire during operation to Frankfurt 20/21.9.41.
R1588	To 156 Squadron.
R1617 PM-T	From 300 Squadron. FTR Bremen 2/3.7.42.
R1667	From 301 Squadron. To 21 Operational Training Unit.
R1760	To 20 Operational Training Unit.
R3215	To 18 Operational Training Unit.

T2475	To 150 Squadron.
T2506	From 305 Squadron. Force-landed in Eire on return from Frankfurt
and	interned 24/25.10.41.
T2610	Ditched in the North Sea during operation to Hanover 10/11.2.41.
T2617	To 11 Operational Training Unit.
T2621 PM-T	FTR Düsseldorf 25/26.2.41.
T2921	From 301 Squadron. FTR from mining sortie 23/24.6.42.
T2965	To 21 Operational Training Unit.
T2996 PM-C	FTR Osnabrück 12/13.6.41.
T2999 PM-P	Force-landed near Elsham Wolds on return from Emden 26.11.41.
W5612	Force-landed in Nottinghamshire following attack by intruder on
return	from Brest 31.3.41.
W5656	FTR Frankfurt 5/6.8.41.
W5664 PM-H	FTR Essen 12/13.4.42.
W5690	From 301 Squadron. To 20 Operational Training Unit.
X3204	Ditched in North Sea on return from Hamburg 3.8.41.
X3221	From 57 Squadron. To 11 Operational Training Unit.
X3414	From 115 Squadron. To 150 Squadron.
X3448	From 115 Squadron. To 150 Squadron.
X3762	To 150 Squadron.
X9609	FTR Berlin 20/21.9.41.
X9665	From 301 Squadron. FTR Berlin 20/21.9.41.
X9666	From 301 Squadron. To 20 Operational Training Unit.
X9675	To 26 Operational Training Unit.
X9792	To 11 Operational Training Unit.
X9794	FTR Mannheim 7/8.11.41.
X9813	Crashed on approach to Elsham Wolds 1.9.41.
X9816	From 150 Sqn. Crashed landing Elsham Wolds during training 5.5.42.
Z1108	From 156 Squadron. To 11 Operational Training Unit.
Z1140	To 29 Operational Training Unit.
Z1141	FTR St Nazaire 19/20.5.42.
Z1142	To 21 Operational Training Unit.
Z1152	To 21 Operational Training Unit.
Z1171	To 16 Operational Training Unit.
Z8714	From 25 Operational Training Unit. FTR from shipping strike
	(Channel Dash) 12.2.42.
Z8833 PM-L	From 150 Squadron. FTR Nantes 4/5.5.42.
Z8840	From 150 Squadron. To 15 Operational Training Unit.
Z8843 PM-U	To 16 Operational Training Unit.
DV452	FTR Cologne 30/31.5.42.
DV578	From 150 Squadron. To 29 Operational Training Unit.
DV579 PM-Z	FTR Rostock 25/26.4.42.
DV596	From 27 Operational Training Unit. To 11 Operational Training Unit.
DV611	FTR Bremen 2/3.7.42.
DV612 PM-J	To 11 Operational Training Unit.
DV697	To 26 Operational Training Unit.

DV699	FTR Essen 5/6.6.42.
DV704	To 11 Operational Training Unit.
DV773 PM-J	FTR Essen 8/9.6.42.
DV818	FTR Emden 22/23.6.42.
DV831 PM-R	FTR from mining sortie 23/24.6.42.
DV878	To 11 Operational Training Unit.
DV882	To 1481 Flight.
DV923	From 29 Operational Training Unit. To 11 Operational Training Unit.
HD946	To 16 Operational Training Unit.
HF897	To 1481 Flight.
HALIFAX.	**From July 1942 to November 1942.**
R9379	From 76 Squadron. Conversion Flt only. Crashed on approach to Elsham Wolds 1.8.42.
R9380	From 102 Squadron. Conversion Flight only. To 1656 CU.
R9390	From 102 Squadron via 460 Squadron RAAF Conversion Flight. Conversion Flight only. To 1656 Conversion Unit.
R9422	From 35 (Madras Presidency) Squadron. To 1656 Conversion Unit.
V9983	From 35 (Madras Presidency) Squadron. To 1656 Conversion Unit.
W1182	To 158 Squadron.
W1185	From 460 Squadron RAAF. To 51 Squadron.
W1187	To 1656 Conversion Unit.
W1188 PM-D	FTR Milan 24/25.10.42.
W1189	FTR Osnabrück 6/7.10.42.
W1212	To 51 Squadron.
W1213	FTR Cologne 15/16.10.42.
W1216 PM-Q	FTR Aachen 5/6.10.42.
W1217	To 158 Squadron.
W1218	Crashed in Lincolnshire while training 28.7.42.
W1219	FTR Duisburg 6/7.9.42.
W1220	FTR Bremen 4/5.9.42.
W1223 PM-U	FTR Milan 24/25.10.42.
W1224	To 51 Squadron.
W1225	Crashed in the Humber on return from Duisburg 7.8.42.
W1243	Conversion Flight only. Crashed on landing at Elsham Wolds 22.9.42.
W1251	To 158 Squadron.
W1270	FTR Kassel 27/28.8.42.
W7705	To 1656 Conversion Unit.
W7772	To 51 Squadron.
W7818	From 460 Squadron RAAF. To 51 Squadron.
W7819	From 103 Squadron Conversion Flight. To 1656 Conversion Unit.
W7846	To 1656 Conversion Unit.
W7850 PM-A	FTR Cologne 15/16.10.42.
W7860	To 51 Squadron.
W7861	To 51 Squadron.

BB202	To 1656 Conversion Unit via 103 Squadron Conversion Flight.
BB204	FTR Saarbrücken 28/29.8.42.
BB214	FTR Nuremberg 28/29.8.42.
BB219	To 78 Squadron.
BB221	To 76 Squadron and back. To 1662 Conversion Unit.
BB223	To 51 Squadron.
DG229	To 1656 Conversion Unit via 103 Squadron Conversion Flight.
DT482	From 103 Squadron Conversion Flight. To 1656 Conversion Unit.
DT483	From 460 Squadron RAAF Conversion Flight. To 51 Squadron.
DT485	To 158 Squadron.
DT495	To 1445 Flight.
DT505	To 158 Squadron.
DT506	To 51 Squadron.
DT513	To 51 Squadron.
DT523	To 1656 Conversion Unit.

LANCASTER.   **From November 1942.**

R5674	From 207 Squadron. To 1662 Conversion Unit.
W4132	From 1667 Conversion Unit. To 1 Lancaster Finishing School.
W4318 PM-C	Ditched in the Channel on return from Spezia 13/14.4.43.
W4323 PM-C	Destroyed in ground accident at Elsham Wolds 23.8.43.
W4328	No operations. To 12 Squadron.
W4333 PM-B	Crashed in Cambridgeshire during training 4.3.43.
W4334 PM-R	FTR Duisburg 20/21.12.42.
W4335 PM-F	FTR Essen 21/22.1.43.
W4336 PM-U	FTR Cologne 26/27.2.43.
W4337 PM-K	FTR Berlin 2/3.12.43.
W4338 PM-L	FTR Essen 13/14.1.43.
W4339 PM-M	FTR Frankfurt 2/3.12.42.
W4340 PM-A	First off on Squadron's first Lancaster op. FTR Essen 21/22.1.43.
W4361 PM-N	FTR Berlin 1/2.3.43.
W4362 PM-P	FTR Milan 14/15.2.43.
W4363 PM-U	FTR from mining sortie 6/7.7.43.
W4364 PM-D	FTR Nuremberg 27/28.8.43.
W4376	From 57 Squadron. To 166 Squadron.
W4786	FTR from mining sortie 17/18.12.42.
W4787	FTR Munich 21/22.12.42.
W4788 PM-O	From 12 Squadron. FTR Hamburg 3/4.3.43.
W4820 PM-S	FTR Munich 21/22.12.42.
W4821	To 9 Squadron and back. To 300 Squadron via 1656 Conversion Unit and 1 Lancaster Finishing School.
W4827 PM-W	FTR Gelsenkirchen 25/26.6.43.
W4828 PM-G	FTR Spezia 13/14.4.43.
W4845	To 1656 Conversion Unit.
W4848 PM-L	FTR Pilsen 16/17.4.43.

W4852	To 15 Squadron via 1654 Conversion Unit.
W4857 PM-V	Crashed near Elsham Wolds during training 27.2.43.
W4860	FTR Munich 9/10.3.43.
W4880 PM-H	FTR Berlin 1/2.3.43.
W4901 PM-W	FTR Cologne 16/17.6.43.
W5012 PM-O	FTR Cologne 3/4.7.43.
DV180	To 166 Squadron.
DV193	From 460 Squadron RAAF via 1 LFS. To 1 LFS.
DV220 PM-L	To 166 Squadron.
DV221 PM-K	FTR Hanover 27/28.9.43.
DV333	From 460 Squadron RAAF. To 576 Squadron.
DV342	To 576 Squadron.
ED370	From 101 Squadron. To 460 Squadron RAAF.
ED380 PM-F	From 101 Squadron. FTR Lorient 16/17.2.43.
ED384 PM-H	FTR Essen 9/10.1.43.
ED389 PM-J2	From 100 Squadron. FTR Hamburg 24/25.7.43.
ED396	FTR Oberhausen 14/15.6.43.
ED417	Collided with Halifax JN966 (428 Squadron RCAF) over County Durham on return from Berlin 26/27.11.43.
ED419 PM-X	FTR Essen 12/13.3.43.
ED528 PM-Z	FTR Gelsenkirchen 25/26.6.43.
ED612 PM-J	FTR Oberhausen 14/15.6.43.
ED614 PM-G	FTR Stettin 20/21.4.43.
ED626 PM-G	FTR Emmerich 1.4.43.
ED645 PM-W/F	FTR Hamburg 2/3.8.43.
ED646 PM-V/E	FTR Berlin 31.8/1.9.43.
ED701 PM-B2	FTR Leverkusen 22/23.8.43.
ED713 PM-N	To 576 Squadron.
ED714 PM-L	To 12 Squadron.
ED724 PM-M/R	Crash-landed on approach to Bodney on return from Duisburg 10.4.43.
ED725 PM-P	FTR Peenemünde 17/18.8.43.
ED731	To 166 Squadron.
ED733 PM-X	FTR from mining sortie 28/29.4.43.
ED751 PM-S	FTR Mannheim 5/6.9.43.
ED767	To 576 Squadron.
ED769 PM-U	FTR Turin 12/13.7.43.
ED773 PM-U	FTR Mülheim 22/23.6.43.
ED878 PM-G/V	FTR Hamburg 24/25.7.43.
ED879 PM-E	Crashed during take-off at Elsham Wolds for night flying test 9.6.43.
ED881 PM-K/S	FTR Leipzig 20/21.10.43.
ED882 PM-A	From 97 (Straits Settlement) Squadron. FTR Mannheim 9/10.8.43.
ED884 PM-L	FTR Essen 25/26.7.43.
ED888 PM-M/M2	To 576 Squadron and back. Completed 135 operations including 11 to Berlin. To 10 Maintenance Unit.
ED904	To 166 Squadron.
ED905 PM-X	To 166 Squadron.

ED913	To 576 Squadron.
ED914 PM-Z	FTR Düsseldorf 11/12.6.43.
ED916 PM-J	FTR Bochum 12/13.6.43.
ED922 PM-C	FTR Hamburg 2/3.8.43.
ED942 PM-B	To 460 Squadron RAAF.
ED945 PM-R	FTR Cologne 16/17.6.43.
EE182	From 101 Squadron. To U.S.A. July 1943.
EE196	To 166 Squadron.
JA672 PM-E	FTR Cologne 3/4.7.43.
JA704	To 166 Squadron.
JA855 PM-A	FTR Essen 25/26.7.43.
JA857 PM-M	From 576 Squadron. FTR Dessau 7/8.3.45.
JA866 PM-E	FTR Hamburg 24/25.7.43.
JA868	To 576 Squadron.
JA957	To 576 Squadron.
JA962	From 582 Squadron. To 1668 Conversion Unit.
JB147 PM-C	FTR Hanover 18/19.10.43.
JB152 PM-H	FTR Mannheim 23/24.9.43.
JB153 PM-D	Crashed soon after take-off from Wymeswold on air-test 8.9.43.
JB276 PM-F	FTR Kassel 22/23.10.43.
JB277 PM-M	FTR Berlin 27/28.1.44.
JB278 PM-L	Ditched in North Sea on return from Karlsruhe 24/25.4.44.
JB279 PM-E	FTR Hanover 18/19.10.43.
JB319	To 5 Lancaster Finishing School.
JB346	Crashed soon after t/o from Elsham Wolds during air-test 3.10.43.
JB349 PM-G	FTR Hanover 18/19.10.43.
JB350 PM-L	FTR Berlin 26/27.11.43.
JB376 PM-B	FTR Kassel 22/23.10.43.
JB400 PM-K	FTR Berlin 2/3.12.43.
JB401 PM-P	FTR Berlin 2/3.12.43.
JB403 PM-T	FTR Berlin 2/3.12.43.
JB423	From 460 Squadron RAAF. Damaged beyond repair during an operation to Berlin 26/27.11.43.
JB454	FTR Frankfurt 20/21.12.43.
JB458 PM-C	FTR Berlin 26/27.11.43.
JB460	To 576 Squadron.
JB487 PM-G	FTR Berlin 29/30.12.43.
JB527 PM-B	FTR Berlin 26/27.11.43.
JB528 PM-Q	FTR Berlin 23/24.11.43.
JB530	Collided with ND334 (103 Squadron) in Elsham Wolds circuit on return from Leipzig 19/20.2.44.
JB550	FTR Leipzig 3/4.12.43.
JB551	To 5 Lancaster Finishing School.
JB555 PM-D	To 576 Squadron.
JB655	To 1656 Conversion Unit.
JB658	FTR Berlin 16/17.12.43.

JB670	Crashed in Lincolnshire after collision with LM332 (576 Squadron) when bound for Berlin 16.12.43.
JB730 PM-P	FTR Berlin 23/24.12.43.
JB732 PM-S	FTR Aulnoye 10/11.4.44.
JB733 PM-K	FTR Hasselt 11/12.5.44.
JB736 PM-N	FTR Nuremberg 30/31.3.44.
JB744	To 576 Squadron and back. FTR Frankfurt 18/19.3.44.
JB745 PM-I	FTR Leipzig 19/20.2.44.
JB746 PM-I	FTR Le Havre 31.7.44.
JB747 PM-M	FTR Berlin 2/3.1.44.
LL913	Crashed in Yorkshire on return from Düsseldorf 22/23.4.44.
LL941 PM-E	From 166 Squadron. FTR Stuttgart 24/25.7.44.
LL946 PM-Z	FTR Dortmund 22/23.5.44.
LL963 PM-D	FTR from mining sortie 15/16.5.44.
LL964 PM-H	From 460 Squadron RAAF. FTR Cologne 31.10/1.11.44.
LM116 PM-D	FTR Stettin 29/30.8.44.
LM124	To 6 Lancaster Finishing School.
LM131 PM-V	Abandoned over Lincolnshire on return from Dortmund 12.3.45.
LM132 PM-I	To 57 Squadron.
LM173 PM-M	FTR Sterkrade 16/17.6.44.
LM177 PM-Z	FTR from mining sortie 4/5.4.45.
LM243 PM-T	FTR Agenville 31.8.44.
LM272	To 5 Maintenance Unit.
LM292	Abandoned over Lincs on return from Fontenay-le-Marmion 7/8.8.44.
LM293	Crashed while landing at Elsham Wolds on return from Ertvelde-Rieme 18.8.44.
LM295 PM-Z/W	
LM314 PM-J	From 97 (Straits Settlement) Squadron. FTR Kassel 22/23.10.43.
LM332	To 576 Squadron.
LM335	To 166 Squadron.
LM343 PM-F	FTR Mannheim 5/6.9.43.
LM381	From 460 Squadron RAAF. To 576 Squadron.
LM538 PM-H	FTR Stuttgart 28/29.7.44.
LM682 PM-O	FTR Dresden 13/14.2.45.
ME392 PM-Y	FTR Chemnitz 5/6.3.45.
ME449 PM-T	FTR from mining sortie 12/13.3.45.
ME475 PM-L	
ME551 PM-V	
ME649	From 460 Squadron RAAF. FTR Essen 12/13.12.44.
ME665 PM-C	FTR Berlin 24/25.3.44.
ME671	To 300 Squadron.
ME673 PM-J/I	FTR Mailly-le-Camp 3/4.5.44.
ME674 PM-T	FTR Revigny 12/13.7.44.
ME698 PM-U	From 460 Squadron RAAF.
ME721 PM-M	FTR Nuremberg 30/31.3.44.
ME722 PM-E	FTR Duisburg 21/22.5.44.

ME736	From 622 Squadron. FTR Friedrichshafen 27/28.4.44.
ME738 PM-S	FTR Friedrichshafen 27/28.4.44.
ME741 PM-G	FTR Düsseldorf 22/23.4.44.
ME746	From 166 Squadron.
ME773 PM-U	FTR Revigny 14/15.7.44.
ME799 PM-K	FTR Stuttgart 28/29.7.44.
ME847 PM-R	From 15 Squadron. to 57 Squadron.
ME848 PM-E	From 15 Squadron. FTR Nuremberg 16/17.3.45.
ND329 PM-A	FTR Frankfurt 22/23.3.44.
ND334	Collided with JB530 (103 Squadron) in Elsham Wolds circuit on return from Leipzig 19/20.2.44.
ND362 PM-Q	From 576 Squadron. FTR Aachen 27/28.5.44.
ND363 PM-A	FTR Berlin 15/16.2.44.
ND381	To 1 Lancaster Finishing School.
ND397 PM-R	FTR Stettin 5/6.1.44.
ND402	From 576 Squadron. Crashed while landing at Elsham Wolds on return from Essen 27.3.44.
ND408 PM-T	FTR Leipzig 19/20.2.44.
ND411 PM-J	FTR Mailly-le-Camp 3/4.5.44.
ND417 PM-P	FTR Augsburg 25/26.2.44.
ND420 PM-G	FTR from mining sortie 9/10.4.44.
ND572	To 57 Squadron.
ND613 PM-R	From 625 Squadron. FTR Fontaine-le-Pin 14.8.44.
ND624 PM-F	FTR Aachen 24/25.5.44.
ND629 PM-G	FTR Dortmund 22/23.5.44.
ND632	Crashed while landing at Ford on return from Rüsselsheim 25/26.8.44.
ND638	Damaged beyond repair over Karlsruhe 24/25.4.44.
ND656	From 460 Squadron RAAF. To 1666 Conversion Unit.
ND700 PM-X	FTR Hasselt 11/12.5.44.
ND847 PM-R	FTR Essen 26/27.4.44.
ND861 PM-H	From 300 Squadron. Crashed in Humber Estuary while training 4.1.45.
ND903 PM-G	From 576 Squadron. FTR Stuttgart 25/26.7.44.
ND905 PM-B	FTR Mailly-le-Camp 3/4.5.44.
ND925 PM-C	FTR Aachen 27/28.5.44.
ND990	Abandoned over Carnaby on return from Revigny 12/13.7.44.
ND993 PM-I	FTR Revigny 12/13.7.44.
NE117 PM-J	FTR Stuttgart 28/29.7.44.
NE136 PM-L	FTR Revigny 14/15.7.44.
NE173 PM-F	FTR Vire 6/7.6.44.
NF909 PM-J	FTR Pforzheim 23/24.2.45.
NF913 PM-H	FTR Dessau 7/8.3.45.
NF999 PM-T	FTR Munich 7/8.1.45.
NG173	
NG276 PM-E	FTR Leuna 6/7.12.44.
NG360 PM-F	
NG391	To 166 Squadron.

NG420 PM-Q	FTR Cologne 24/25.12.44.
NG491 PM-R	FTR Hanau 18/19.3.45.
NG492 PM-D	FTR Nuremberg 16/17.3.45.
NN758 PM-S	FTR Nuremberg 16/17.3.45.
NN766 PM-R	FTR Munich 7/8.1.45.
PA217 PM-Z	
PA278	
PA303 PM-E	
PA319	
PA985	Crash-landed in Buckinghamshire on return from Stuttgart 28/29.7.44.
PA997	To 576 Squadron.
PA999 PM-S	FTR Revigny 12/13.7.44.
PB147 PM-C	FTR Stuttgart 28/29.7.44.
PB363 PM-F	FTR La Nieppe 18.8.44.
PB365 PM-B	FTR Stettin 29/30.8.44.
PB465 PM-F	FTR Dortmund 29.11.44.
PB528 PM-D	FTR Hanover 5/6.1.45.
PB563 PM-G	FTR Chemnitz 5/6.3.45.
PB637 PM-L	FTR from mining sortie 6/7.1.45.
PB673	To 626 Squadron.
PB786	To 153 Squadron.
PB898	To 1660 Conversion Unit.
PD198 PM-W	From 9 Squadron.
PD236 PM-X	To 57 Squadron.
PD272 PM-K	FTR Mannheim 1.3.45.
PD281 PM-B/S	
PD335	From 166 Squadron.
PD365	To 166 Squadron.
RA500 PM-B	FTR Dessau 7/8.3.45.
RA515 PM-N	FTR Pforzeim 23/24.2.45.
RA528	
RA566	
RA579	
RE121 PM-I	
RF186	
RF193 PM-G	To 57 Squadron.
RF229	

HEAVIEST SINGLE LOSS
28/29.07.44. Stuttgart 4 Lancasters FTR. 1 Crashed on return.

Printed in Great Britain
by Amazon